THE JUVENILE JUSTICE SYSTEM

DELINQUENCY, PROCESSING, AND THE LAW

SEVENTH EDITION

Dean John Champion
Texas A & M International University

Alida V. Merlo
Indiana University of Pennsylvania

Peter J. Benekos
Mercyhurst University

PEARSON

Boston   Columbus   Indianapolis   New York   San Francisco   Upper Saddle River
Amsterdam   Cape Town   Dubai   London   Madrid   Milan   Munich   Paris   Montreal   Toronto
Delhi   Mexico   City   Sao Paulo   Sydney   Hong Kong   Seoul   Singapore   Taipei   Tokyo

Vice President and Executive Publisher: *Vernon Anthony*
Senior Acquisitions Editor: *Eric Krassow*
Assistant Editor: *Tiffany Bitzel*
Editorial Assistant: *Lynda Cramer*
Director of Marketing: *David Gesell*
Senior Marketing Manager: *Mary Salzman*
Senior Marketing Coordinator: *Alicia Wozniak*
Marketing Assistant: *Les Roberts*
Media Project Manager: *Karen Bretz*
Project Manager: *Jessica Sykes*

Production Manager: *Susan Hannahs*
Creative Director: *Jayne Conte*
Cover Design: *Axell Design*
Cover Photo: *Fotolia*
Full-Service Project Manager: *Dhanya Ramesh, Jouve India*
Composition: *Jouve India*
Printer/Bindery: *Edwards Brothers Malloy*
Cover Printer: *Lehigh-Phoenix Color*
Text Font: *11/14 Adobe Garamond Pro*

Credits and acknowledgments borrowed from other sources and reproduced, with permission, in this textbook appear on the appropriate page within the text.

Library of Congress Cataloging-in-Publication Data
Champion, Dean J.
  The juvenile justice system : delinquency, processing, and the law / Dean John Champion, Alida V. Merlo, Peter J. Benekos. — 7th ed.
    p. cm.
  ISBN 978-0-13-276446-9
  1. Juvenile justice, Administration of–United States.   2. Juvenile courts–United States.   I. Merlo, Alida V.   II. Benekos, Peter J.   III. Title.

  KF9779.C425 2013
  345.73'08--dc23

                                                        2011052871

10 9 8 7 6 5 4

ISBN-13: 978-0-13-276446-9
ISBN-10:   0-13-276446-6

To Gerri
To Kevin and Alexandra
To Pat

Brief Contents

Contents

9

The Adjudicatory Process: Dispositional Alternatives

10

Nominal Sanctions: Warnings, Diversion, and Alternative Dispute Resolution

11

12

Preface

The Juvenile Justice System: Delinquency, Processing, and the Law, Seventh Edition, is a comprehensive study of the juvenile justice system. It examines how juvenile offenders are defined and classified, and it utilizes the current literature to illustrate the significant stages of juvenile processing and recent changes. One integral feature of this book is the distinction between status offenses and delinquent offenses. This difference has consequences for juveniles and can affect their processing in the system.

The U.S. Supreme Court cases that address youth exemplify the legal bases for decisions about juveniles. Historical landmark Supreme Court cases are included, along with decisions from various state courts that show juvenile justice trends. A legalistic perspective highlights the constitutional rights afforded juveniles and how various components of the juvenile justice system relate to them.

The history of juvenile courts is described, including significant events that have influenced the evolution of juvenile justice. The review of the juvenile court indicates that it has adopted a more punitive stance in the last 25 years. One indication of this trend is the expansion of waiver (certification or transfer) provisions that state legislatures enacted. These policies were intended to prevent serious juvenile offending and to authorize more severe (adult) punishment when compared with the sanctions that juvenile judges may impose. However, juvenile crime was declining before most of these laws were enacted. Nonetheless, the number of youth in adult prisons and jails increased in the 1990s, but it has decreased subsequently.

Juveniles who are transferred to criminal courts are not necessarily the most serious, dangerous, or violent offenders. Transferred youth include property offenders, drug offenders, or public order offenders. Once juveniles are waived to the jurisdiction of criminal courts, their age can be considered as a mitigating factor. However, juveniles in adult court can receive the same sanctions as adults. Currently, juveniles who are convicted of murder in the criminal court can be sentenced to life without parole. In 2005, the U.S. Supreme Court determined that the death penalty for youth under the age of 18 violates the Eighth Amendment ban on cruel and unusual punishment. In this edition, case law prohibiting the death penalty and the Supreme Court decision on life without parole sentences for youth are discussed.

Juveniles are classified not only according to the type of offense but also according to the nature of offenses committed. Delinquency is defined and measured according to several indices, such as the *Uniform Crime Reports,* the *National Crime Victimization Survey,* and the *National Youth Survey.* There is no single resource that discloses the true amount of crime and delinquency in the United States.

Organization of the Book

The major components of the juvenile justice system, including law enforcement, prosecution and the courts, and corrections, are featured. Police deal with youth informally every day, and they use discretion in deciding whether to initiate a referral to court or another agency or take the youth into custody. The roles of the prosecutor and defense attorney and their participation in the critical stages of the process are discussed. The juvenile correctional process is presented in a broad context. Correctional strategies ranging from probation to incarceration are featured, along with a discussion of the strengths and limitations of various policies and programs. Probation remains the dominant sanction for juvenile offenders. Thus, community-based correctional programs for juvenile offenders are assessed and innovative strategies are disscussed. Electronic monitoring and home confinement are described along with residential placements and aftercare. Particular attention is devoted to evidence-based practice and to Balanced and Restorative Justice initiatives.

Most chapters present career snapshots of professionals who work with juvenile offenders in different capacities. These include juvenile court judges, juvenile probation officers, researchers, students, detention center administrators, treatment specialists, and counselors. The profiles are intended to show why they have chosen their careers and what they find rewarding about working with youth. In addition, the professionals identify what they believe are the requirements, characteristics, and skills to be successful. To work with juvenile offenders effectively, special training, preparation, commitment, and education are required. The professionals describe on-the-job experiences with juveniles, and their narratives help students understand some of the situational difficulties they address in the course of their careers. In addition to seeing a client succeed, their work can be stimulating and inspiring in various ways. The career snapshots illustrate diverse aspects of juvenile justice system in which future criminal justice scholars and practitioners might pursue their goals.

Every effort has been made to include current references. At the time this book went into production, the most recent material available was the basis for tables, figures, and juvenile justice statistics. The most contemporary material is not always that current, however. For instance, government documents that include juvenile justice statistics are published a year or longer after the information is actually collected and analyzed. Therefore, it is not unusual for a government document published in 2011 to report "recent" juvenile delinquency statistics for 2008 or earlier. This situation is common, because governmental compilation and reporting of such information are complex processes. It is not possible, therefore, for the government to regularly report 2012 information in 2012. The historical factual information about juveniles and the juvenile justice system does not change, however. Also, there are few revisions in juvenile laws each year. However, new data are collected, analyzed, and interpreted regularly by researchers and government agencies. Therefore, those seeking the most current information about trends in juvenile delinquency and other statistical information can obtain some of these data from Internet sites identified in each chapter. We have endeavored to provide the reader with the most recent policies and data available at the time this manuscript was written.

Features

Several important features are incorporated in this book. First, there are learning objectives that outline what each chapter is designed to accomplish. Key terms that are fundamental to understanding the juvenile justice system, the criminal justice system, and various programs and processes are highlighted. A complete glossary of these terms is provided. Each chapter also contains a summary, highlighting the chapter's main points.

Questions for review are included at the end of the chapter. Students are encouraged to read and answer these questions based on the chapter information provided. These questions may also be used in preparation for examinations. At the end of each chapter, Internet sites are listed that will be useful in researching significant historical events or factual information relevant to juvenile justice and its many organizations and agencies. Every effort has been made to include relevant Internet sites that were functional and current at the time of this edition's publication.

New to this Edition

New materials in this edition include:

- Updated review of U.S. Supreme Court cases
- Review of recent research on adolescent brain development
- Developments in disproportionate minority contact in the juvenile justice system
- Review of evidence-based programs
- Examination of policy shifts in juvenile justice
- Expanded and updated Internet website information
- New Career Snapshots

For instructors, a Test Bank, My Test, and PowerPoint presentations are available to download. To access supplementary materials online, instructors need to request an instructor access code. Go to **http://www.pearsonhighered.com/irc**, to register for an instructor access code. Within 48 hours after registering, instructors will receive a confirming e-mail, including an instructor access code. Upon receipt of the code, go to the site and log in for full instructions on downloading materials.

For students, a MyCrimeKit website is available that offers book-specific learning objectives, chapter summaries, flashcards, practice tests, as well as video clips and media activities to aid student learning and comprehension. An access code is needed for this supplement as well. The access code can be packaged with the book for a discounted price, or students can purchase an access code separately from the MyCrimeKit site at **http://www.MyCrimeKit.com**.

Any questions about the text, presentation, or factual information, as well as any inadvertent inaccuracies, may be sent directly to the authors through the contact information below:

Alida V. Merlo
Department of Criminology
Indiana University of Pennsylvania
411 North Walk
Indiana, Pennsylvania 15705-1002
(724) 357-2720
E-mail: amerlo@iup.edu

Peter J. Benekos
Department of Criminal Justice
Mercyhurst College
501 East 38th Street
Erie, Pennsylvania 16546-0001
(814) 824-2328
E-mail: pbenekos@mercyhurst.edu

Reviewers

Wendie Johnna Albert, Keiser University; James J. Drylie, Kean University; Lorna E. Grant, North Carolina Central University; Randolph M. Grinc, Caldwell University; Vanessa Poyren, Fort Scott Community College.

Acknowledgments

Any textbook is the result of teamwork. We appreciate all those who contributed. First, we thank the reviewers who examined and critiqued the previous editions of this book and make helpful and insightful suggestions for revisions. We are indebted to Eric Krassow, our editor, who has been supportive of our projects. Eric's assistant editor, Tiffany Bitzel, provided valuable assistance and direction at critical points throughout the book's development. We recognize and thank Jessica Sykes and Dhanya Ramesh, the Project Managers, who were instrumental in making sure that the manuscript and the accompanying materials were closely monitored and completed. An additional thanks to Wesley Morrison who was the copyeditor. Thanks also to Alicia Wozniak, Senior Marketing Coordinator, who facilitated the publicity the new edition. We are happy to have been able to work with all of them. In fact, the entire editorial and production staff at Pearson helped to shape and improve this edition. We also thank Gerri Champion for her support and assistance with the Seventh Edition.

The Career Snapshots were generously contributed by former students, professionals in the field we have had the honor to work with, committed scholars, and researchers. We appreciate their willingness to share their knowledge and experience.

We also applaud and honor our undergraduate and graduate students who teach us new and diverse ways to understand and approach juvenile justice. Their interest in juvenile justice inspires us, and our experiences in the classroom helped to shape this book. Four of our students deserve special mention: Caitlin Ross from Mercyhurst College and Ashley Yungmeyer, Michael Campagna, and Louis Fisher from Indiana University of Pennsylvania. They assisted us in identifying and incorporating appropriate ancillary materials for this edition.

Most importantly, we thank our families, Kevin Ashley, Alexandra Ashley, and Pat Benekos, for their love and support. We appreciate all that you do.

About the Authors

Dean John Champion, before his death from leukemia in 2009, was Professor of Criminal Justice at Texas A&M International University in Laredo, Texas. Previously, Dr. Champion taught at the University of Tennessee–Knoxville, California State University–Long Beach, and Minot State University. He earned his Ph.D. from Purdue University and his B.S. and M.A. degrees from Brigham Young University. He also completed several years of law school at the Nashville School of Law.

Dr. Champion wrote and/or edited over 40 texts and other works. His published books for Prentice Hall include *The Juvenile Justice System: Delinquency, Processing, and the Law,* Sixth Edition (2010); *Leading U.S. Supreme Court Cases in Criminal Justice: Briefs and Key Terms* (2009); *Administration of Criminal Justice: Structure, Function, and Process* (2003); *Statistics for Criminal Justice and the Statistics for Criminal Justice and Criminology,* Third Edition (2010); *Research Methods for Criminal Justice and Criminology,* Third Edition (2006); *Corrections in the United States: A Contemporary Perspective,* Fourth Edition (2005); *Probation, Parole, and Community Corrections,* Fifth Edition (2008); and *Policing in the Community* (with George Rush) (1996). Works from other publishers include *The Sociology of Organizations* (McGraw-Hill, 1975); *Research Methods in Social Relations* (John Wiley & Sons, 1976); *Sociology* (Holt, Rinehart, and Winston, 1984); *The U.S. Sentencing Guidelines* (Praeger Publishers, 1989); *Juvenile Transfer Hearings* (with G. Larry Mays) (Praeger Publishers, 1991); *Measuring Offender Risk* (Greenwood Press, 1994); *The Roxbury Dictionary of Criminal Justice: Key Terms and Leading Supreme Court Cases,* Third Edition (Roxbury Press, 2005); and *Criminal Justice in the United States,* Second Edition (Wadsworth, 1998).

Alida V. Merlo is Professor of Criminology at Indiana University of Pennsylvania in Indiana, Pennsylvania. Previously, Dr. Merlo taught at Westfield State University in Westfield, Massachusetts. She earned her Ph.D. from Fordham University, her M.S. from Northeastern University, and her B.A. from Youngstown State University.

Dr. Merlo has conducted research and published in the areas of juvenile justice, criminal justice policy, and women and the law. She is the coauthor with Peter J. Benekos of *Crime Control, Politics & Policy,* Second Edition (LexisNexis/Anderson) and coeditor (with Peter J. Benekos) of *Controversies in Juvenile Justice and Delinquency,* Second Edition (LexisNexis/Anderson). She also coedited (with Joycelyn M. Pollock) *Women, Law & Social Control,* Second Edition (Allyn & Bacon). She is the Past President of the Academy of Criminal Justice Sciences.

Peter J. Benekos is Professor of Criminal Justice and Sociology at Mercyhurst College in Erie, Pennsylvania. Dr. Benekos was a Visiting Professor at Roger Williams University in Rhode Island. He earned his Ph.D. from the University of Akron, his M.A. from the University of Cincinnati, and his B.S. from Clarion University.

Dr. Benekos has conducted research and published in the areas of juvenile justice, corrections, and public policy. He is the coauthor (with Alida V. Merlo) of *Crime Control, Politics & Policy,* Second Edition (LexisNexis/Anderson) and coeditor (with Alida V. Merlo) of *Controversies in Juvenile Justice and Delinquency,* Second Edition (LexisNexis/Anderson).

1

An Overview of Juvenile Justice in the United States

Learning objectives

AFTER READING THIS CHAPTER, THE STUDENT WILL BE ABLE TO:

- Explain the concept of *parens patriae*.
- Differentiate between the types of juvenile offenders, including delinquents and status offenders.
- Explain the structure of the juvenile justice system and the roles and functions of various juvenile justice agencies.
- Summarize how juvenile offenders are processed through the criminal justice system.
- Understand the meaning of the deinstitutionalization of status offenders.

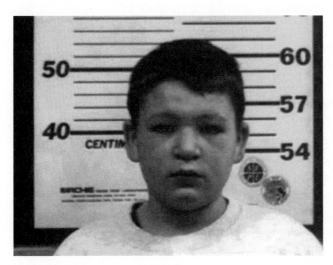

(HO/AFP/Getty Images/Newscom)

Introduction

The juvenile justice system is unique. This book explains the system and how it has evolved. The organization of this chapter is as follows: First, the juvenile justice system is described. Certain features of juvenile justice are similar in all states. Various professionals work with youth, and they represent both public and private agencies and organizations. From police officers to counselors, professionals endeavor to improve the lives of youth.

Every jurisdiction has its own criteria for determining who juveniles are and whether they are under the jurisdiction of the juvenile court. A majority of states classify juveniles as youth who range in age from 7 to 17 years, and juvenile courts in these states have jurisdiction over these youth. Some states have no minimum-age provisions and consider each case on its own merits, regardless of the age of the juvenile.

Because juveniles are not considered adults and, therefore, fully responsible for some of their actions, special laws have been established that pertain only to them. Thus, violations specific to juveniles are referred to as *status offenses*. Juveniles who commit such infractions are categorized as status offenders. Juveniles who engage in acts that are categorized as crimes are juvenile delinquents, and their actions are labeled juvenile delinquency. In brief, delinquent acts for youth would be crimes if committed by adults. By contrast, status offenses are not considered crimes if adults engage in them. Examples of status offenses include runaway behavior, truancy, unruly behavior, and curfew violation. The characteristics of youth involved in such behaviors will also be described.

In 1974, the U.S. Congress enacted the Juvenile Justice and Delinquency Prevention Act (JJDPA). This act, although not binding on the states, encouraged all states to remove their status offenders from secure institutions—namely secure juvenile residential or custodial facilities—where they were being held. States subsequently removed status offenders from institutions and placed these youth with community, social service, or welfare agencies. This process is called the deinstitutionalization of status offenses (DSO) and will be described in some detail.

Next, a general overview of the juvenile justice system is presented. While later chapters will focus upon each of these components in greater detail, the juvenile justice system consists of the processes involved whenever juveniles come in contact with law enforcement. Several parallels exist between the criminal and juvenile justice systems. For those juveniles who advance further into the system, prosecutors make decisions about which cases to pursue. The prosecutors' decisions are often preceded by petitions from different parties requesting a formal juvenile court proceeding. These youth have their cases adjudicated. Compared to criminal court judges, however, juvenile court judges have a more limited range of sanctions. Juvenile court judges may impose nominal, conditional, or custodial dispositions. These dispositions will be described more fully in the following sections.

The Juvenile Justice System

The **juvenile justice system**, similar to **criminal justice**, consists of a network of agencies, institutions, organizations, and personnel that process juvenile offenders. This network is made up of **law enforcement agencies**, also known as **law enforcement**; **prosecution and the courts**; corrections, probation, and parole services; and public and private programs that provide youth with diverse services.

The concept of juvenile justice has different meanings for individual states and for the federal government. No single, nationwide juvenile court system exists. Instead, there are 51 systems, including the District of Columbia, and most are divided into local systems delivered through either juvenile or family courts at the county level, local probation offices, state correctional agencies, and private service providers. Historically, however, these systems have a common set of core principles that distinguish them from criminal courts for adult offenders, including (1) limited jurisdiction (up to age 18 in most states); (2) informal proceedings; (3) focus on offenders, not their offenses; (4) indeterminate sentences; and (5) confidentiality (Feld, 2007).

When referring to juvenile justice, the terms *process* and *system* are used. The "system" connotation refers to a condition of homeostasis, equilibrium, or balance among the various components of the system. By contrast, "process" focuses on the different actions and contributions of each component in dealing with juvenile offenders at various stages of the processing through the juvenile justice system. A "system" also suggests coordination among elements in an efficient production process; however, communication and coordination among juvenile agencies, organizations, and personnel in the juvenile justice system may be inadequate or limited (Congressional Research Office, 2007).

In addition, different criteria are used to define juveniles in states and the federal jurisdiction. Within each of these jurisdictions, certain mechanisms exist for categorizing particular juveniles as adults so that they may be legally processed by the adult counterpart to juvenile justice, the criminal justice system. During the 1990s, a number of state legislatures enacted procedures to make it easier to transfer jurisdiction to the adult system (Snyder and Sickmund, 2006). These changes signaled a shift in the perception of youth, who were now being viewed as adults and subject to the same processes and most of the same sanctions.

Who Are Juvenile Offenders?

Juvenile Offenders Defined

Juvenile offenders are classified and defined according to several different criteria. According to the 1899 Illinois Act that created juvenile courts, the **jurisdiction** of such courts would extend to all juveniles under the age of 16 who were found in violation of any state or local law or ordinance (Ferzan, 2008). About one-fifth of all states place the upper age limit for juveniles at either 15 or 16 years. In most other states,

---

juvenile justice system

Stages through which juveniles are processed, sanctioned, and treated after arrests for juvenile delinquency.

criminal justice

An interdisciplinary field studying the nature and operations of organizations providing justice services to society; consists of lawmaking bodies, including state legislatures and Congress, as well as local, state and federal agencies that try to enforce the law.

law enforcement agencies, law enforcement

Any organization whose purpose is to enforce criminal laws; the activities of various public and private agencies at local, state, and federal levels that are designed to ensure compliance with formal rules of society that regulate social conduct.

prosecution and the courts

Organizations that pursue cases against juvenile offenders and determine whether they are guilty or innocent of offenses alleged.

juvenile offenders

Children or youth who have violated laws or engaged in behaviors that are known as statute offenses.

jurisdiction

Power of a court to hear and determine a particular type of case; also, the territory within which a court may exercise authority, such as a city, county, or state.

the upper age limit for juveniles is under 18 years; an exception is Wyoming, where the upper age limit is 19 years. Ordinarily, the jurisdiction of juvenile courts includes all juveniles between the ages of 7 and 18. Federal law defines juveniles as any persons who have not attained their 18th birthday (18 U.S.C., Sec. 5031, 2009).

The Age Jurisdiction of Juvenile Courts

The age jurisdiction of juvenile courts is determined through established legislative definitions among the states. The federal government has no juvenile court. Although upper and lower age limits are prescribed, these age requirements are not uniform among jurisdictions. Common law has been applied in many jurisdictions where the minimum age of accountability for juveniles is seven years. Youth under the age of seven are presumed to be incapable of formulating criminal intent and are thus not responsible under the law. While this presumption may be refuted, the issue is rarely raised. Thus, if a six-year-old child kills someone, deliberately or accidentally, he or she likely will be treated rather than punished. In some states, no lower age limits exist to restrict juvenile court jurisdiction. Table 1.1 shows the upper age limits for most U.S. jurisdictions.

The states with the lowest maximum age for juvenile court jurisdiction include New York and North Carolina. In these states, the lowest maximum age for juvenile court jurisdiction is 15. The states with the lowest maximum age of 16 for juvenile court jurisdiction are Connecticut, Georgia, Illinois, Louisiana, Massachusetts, Missouri, New Hampshire, South Carolina, Texas, and Wisconsin (Szymanski, 2007). All other states and the federal government use 18 years as the minimum age for

Table 1.1
AGE AT WHICH CRIMINAL COURTS GAIN JURISDICTION OVER YOUTHFUL OFFENDERS, 2008

Age (years)	States
16	New York and North Carolina
17	Connecticut, Georgia, Illinois, Louisiana, Massachusetts, Missouri, South Carolina, Wisconsin, and Texas
18	Alabama, Alaska, Arizona, Arkansas, California, Colorado, Delaware, District of Columbia, Florida, Hawaii, Idaho, Indiana, Iowa, Kansas, Kentucky, Maine, Maryland, Michigan, Minnesota, Mississippi, Montana, Nebraska, Nevada, New Hampshire, New Jersey, New Mexico, North Dakota, Ohio, Oklahoma, Oregon, Pennsylvania, Rhode Island, South Dakota, Tennessee, Utah, Vermont, Virginia, Washington, West Virginia, Wisconsin, and Federal Districts
19	Wyoming

Source: Jeffrey A. Butts, Howard N. Snyder, Terrence A. Finnegan, Anne L. Aughenbagh, and Rowen S. Poole (1996). *Juvenile Court Statistics 1993: Statistics Report.* Washington, DC: Office of Juvenile Justice and Delinquency Prevention. Updated 2011 by authors.

criminal court jurisdiction. Under the JJDPA, juveniles are individuals who have not reached their 18th birthday (18 U.S.C., Sec. 5031, 2009).

Juvenile offenders who are especially young (under age seven in most jurisdictions) are often placed in the care or custody of community agencies, such as departments of human services or social welfare. Instead of punishing children under the age of seven, various kinds of treatment, including psychological counseling, may be required. Some states have further age-accountability provisions. Tennessee, for instance, presumes that juveniles between the ages of 7 and 12 are accountable for their delinquent acts, although this presumption may be overcome by their attorneys through effective oral arguments and clear and convincing evidence.

Some states have no minimum age limit for juveniles. Technically, these states can decide matters involving children of any age. This control can result in the placement of children or infants in foster homes or under the supervision of community service or human welfare agencies. Neglected, unmanageable, abused, or other children in need of supervision are placed in the custody of these various agencies at the discretion of juvenile court judges. Thus, juvenile courts generally have broad discretionary power over most persons under the age of 18. Under certain circumstances that will be discussed in a later chapter, some juveniles, particularly 11- and 12-year-olds, may be treated as adults in order to prosecute them in criminal court for alleged serious crimes.

Parens Patriae

Parens patriae is a concept that originated with the King of England during the 12th century. It literally means "the father of the country." Applied to juvenile matters, *parens patriae* means that the king is in charge of, makes decisions about, and has the responsibility for all matters involving juveniles. Within the scope of early English common law, parents had primary responsibility in rearing children. However, as children advanced beyond the age of seven, they acquired some measure of responsibility for their own actions. Accountability to parents was shifted gradually to the state whenever youth seven years of age or older violated the law. In the name of the king, chancellors in various districts adjudicated matters involving juveniles and the offenses they committed. Juveniles had no legal rights or standing in any court; they were the sole responsibility of the king or his agents. Their future depended largely upon chancellor decisions. In effect, children were wards of the court, and the court was vested with the responsibility of safeguarding their welfare (McGhee and Waterhouse, 2007).

Chancery courts of 12th- and 13th-century England (and in later years) performed various tasks, including the management of children and their affairs as well as care for the mentally ill and incompetent. Therefore, an early division of labor was created, involving a three-way relationship among the child, the parent, and the state. The underlying thesis of *parens patriae* was that the parents were merely the agents of society in the area of childrearing, and that the state had the primary and legitimate interest in the upbringing of children. Thus, *parens patriae* established a type of

> **parens patriae**
> Literally "parent of the country"; doctrine where the state oversees the welfare of youth; originally established by the King of England and administered through chancellors.

fiduciary or trust-like parent–child relationship, with the state able to exercise the right of intervention to limit parental rights (Friday and Ren, 2006).

Since children could become wards of the court and subject to its control, the chancellors were concerned about the future welfare of these children. The welfare interests of chancellors and their actions led to numerous rehabilitative and/or treatment measures, including placement of children in foster homes or assigning them to perform various tasks or work for local merchants (Rockhill, Green, and Furrer, 2007). Parents had minimal influence on these child placement decisions.

In the context of *parens patriae,* it is easy to trace this early philosophy of child management and its influence on subsequent events in the United States, such as the child savers movement, houses of refuge, and reform schools. These latter developments were both private and public attempts to rescue children from their environments and meet some or all of their needs through various forms of institutionalization.

Modern Interpretations of *Parens Patriae*

Parens patriae continues in all juvenile court jurisdictions in the United States. The persistence of this doctrine is evidenced by the wide range of dispositional options available to juvenile court judges and others involved with the early stages of offender processing in the juvenile justice system. Typically, these dispositional options are either nominal or conditional, meaning that the confinement of any juvenile for most offenses is regarded as a last resort. Nominal or conditional options involve various sanctions (e.g., verbal warnings or reprimands, diversion, probation, making financial restitution to victims, performance of community service, participation in individual or group therapy, or involvement in educational programs), and they are intended to reflect the rehabilitative ideal that has been a major philosophical underpinning of *parens patriae.*

The Get-Tough Movement

The treatment or rehabilitative orientation reflected by *parens patriae,* however, is somewhat in conflict with the themes of accountability and due process. Contemporary juvenile court jurisprudence stresses individual accountability for one's actions. The **get-tough movement** emphasizes swifter, harsher, and more certain justice and punishment than the previously dominant, rehabilitative philosophy of American courts (Mears et al., 2007). Overall, youth are viewed as "mini-adults" who make rational choices that include the deliberate decision to engage in crime (Merlo and Benekos, 2000). In the last 20 years, states have modified their statutes to allow release of the names of juveniles to the media, to allow prosecutors to decide which youth should be transferred to adult court, and to open juvenile court proceedings to the public. These actions are consistent with a more punitive attitude toward youth (Merlo, 2000).

For juveniles, this includes the use of nonsecure and secure custody and sanctions that involve placement in group homes or juvenile facilities. For juveniles charged with violent offenses, this means transfer to the criminal courts, where more

get-tough movement

View toward criminals and delinquents favoring maximum penalties and punishments for crimes or delinquent acts.

severe punishments, such as long prison sentences or even life imprisonment, can be imposed. Although legislatures have enacted laws making it possible to transfer youth to adult court, it is not clear that these policies reflect the public's opinion regarding how best to address juvenile offending (Applegate, Davis, and Cullen, 2009). The public may favor a juvenile justice system separate from the adult criminal justice system, and evidence suggests a strong preference for a system that disposes most juveniles to treatment or counseling programs in lieu of incarceration, even for repeat offenders (Applegate, Davis, and Cullen, 2009; Piquero et al., 2010).

Parens patriae has been subject to the U.S. Supreme Court's interpretation of the constitutional rights of juveniles. Since the mid-1960s, the Supreme Court has afforded youth constitutional rights, and some of these are commensurate with the rights enjoyed by adults in criminal courts. The Court's decisions to apply constitutional rights to juvenile delinquency proceedings have resulted in a gradual transformation of the juvenile court toward greater criminalization. As juvenile cases become more like adult cases, they may be less susceptible to the influence of *parens patriae*.

Another factor is the gradual transformation of the role of prosecutors in juvenile courts. As more prosecutors actively pursue cases against juvenile defendants, the entire juvenile justice process may weaken the delinquency prevention role of juvenile courts (Sungi, 2008). Thus, more aggressive prosecution of juvenile cases is perceived as moving away from delinquency prevention for the purpose of deterring youth from future adult criminality. Fifteen states, according to Snyder and Sickmund (2006), now authorize prosecutors to decide whether to try a case in adult criminal court or juvenile court. The intentions of prosecutors are to ensure that youth are entitled to due process, but the social costs may be to label these youth in ways that will propel them toward, rather than away from, adult criminality (Mears et al., 2007).

Juvenile Delinquents and Delinquency

Juvenile Delinquents

Legally, a **juvenile delinquent** is any youth under a specified age who has violated a criminal law or engages in disobedient, indecent, or immoral conduct and is in need of treatment, rehabilitation, or supervision. A juvenile delinquent is a **delinquent child** (Champion, 2009). These definitions can be ambiguous. What is "indecent" or "immoral conduct?" Who needs treatment, rehabilitation, or supervision? And what sort of treatment, rehabilitation, or supervision is needed?

Juvenile Delinquency

Federal law says that **juvenile delinquency** is the violation of any law of the United States by a person before his or her 18th birthday that would be a crime if committed by an adult (18 U.S.C., Sec. 5031, 2009). A broader, legally applicable definition of juvenile delinquency is a violation of any state or local law or ordinance by anyone who has not yet achieved the age of majority. These definitions are qualitatively more precise than the previously cited ones.

juvenile delinquent, delinquent child

Anyone who, under the age of majority, has committed one or more acts that would be crimes if committed by an adult.

juvenile delinquency

Violation of the law by any person before his or her 18th birthday; punishable by juvenile courts; violation of any law or ordinance by anyone who has not achieved the age of majority.

Definitions of Delinquents and Delinquency

Juvenile courts often define juveniles and juvenile delinquency according to their own standards. In some jurisdictions, a delinquent act can be defined in various ways. To illustrate the implications of such a definition for any juvenile, consider the following scenarios:

Scenario 1 It is 10:15 P.M. on a Thursday night in Detroit. A curfew is in effect for youth under age 18 prohibiting them from being on city streets after 10:00 P.M.

CAREER SNAPSHOT

(Courtesy of Peter J. Benekos)

Name: Caitlin Ross
Position: Law Student

School attending:
University of Maine School of Law

Background

As an undergraduate at Mercyhurst College, I was a double major in Criminal Justice and Marriage and Family Studies. I graduated with a B.A. in each field. I worked hard in classes and maintained a high GPA, which was very important when it came time to apply to law schools. In my first two years at college, I took very broad classes so that I could explore many career options; and in my final two years, I began choosing classes that were tailored to my interests and the career path I wanted to pursue. I was able to take many prelaw and juvenile justice courses, which have greatly benefited me already. Through a constitutional law course, I was able to participate in a mock trial. I took on the role of the defense attorney, and it was an incredibly rewarding experience.

In a class of my sophomore year, I was asked to create a program that served people in some way. After doing extensive research and discovering how ineffective juvenile defense is in many areas of our country, I created a program meant to aid public defenders in educating their juvenile clients about the system and their rights. That spring, I applied for a summer internship at Pine Tree Legal Assistance in Maine, and I was offered the position because of the work I had done on my program. At Pine Tree, I obtained some experience in the legal field by handling a number of public interest cases. My summer at Pine Tree proved to me that my interest in the law was not fleeting. In the spring of my junior year, I began interning in the Juvenile Division of the Erie County Public Defender's Office. I showed one of the defense attorneys the program I had created, and she was excited to adapt and use it because she wanted to improve her client outreach. Every Friday, we went to the local detention centers and met with her clients to discuss their cases and their due process rights. Her relationship with her clients improved quickly and significantly, and I left the internship confident that I wanted to be a juvenile defense attorney.

I also worked for a professor on campus as a research assistant. For two years, I assisted him with a research project tracking juvenile offenders processed in the adult system. In addition to this work, I wrote papers on juvenile defense and potential policy changes, and I presented them at three conferences over two years. These experiences allowed me to gain some expertise in juvenile defense as well as make connections with professors and criminal justice professionals around the country.

I took the LSAT the summer before my senior year, and in the fall, I applied to a number of law schools. I chose Maine Law for a number of reasons, including their juvenile defender's clinic, their location, and their scholarship offer. I graduated feeling I had spent my time as an undergraduate well and was ready to take on the challenges of law school.

Advice to Students

My advice to undergraduate students is to make the most of the resources your school and community have to offer. Academic success is important, but it is not the only piece of the undergraduate experience that matters. There are many ways to explore careers and determine your strengths, such as through volunteer programs, school clubs, research opportunities with professors, and internships. Pick internships and activities related to the field in which you see yourself working: Not only will these activities "pad" your resume, they will also help you explore your interests. If you are interested in a particular office that does not do internships, ask if there is anything you can do to get involved with their work—my internship position at the public defender's office was created for me because I asked. Create opportunities for yourself, and make the most of your college experience: Not only will you get what you want, you will also show future employers and graduate schools that you are driven and resourceful.

A police officer in a cruiser notices four juveniles standing at a street corner, holding gym bags, and conversing. One youth walks toward a nearby jewelry store, looks in the window, and returns to the group. Shortly thereafter, another boy walks up to the same jewelry store window and looks in it. The officer pulls up beside the boys, exits the vehicle, and asks them for IDs. Each of the boys has a high school identity card. The boys are 16 and 17 years of age. When asked about their interest in the jewelry store, one boy says that he plans to get his girlfriend a necklace like one in the store window, and he wanted his friends to see it. The boys then explain that they are waiting for a ride, because they are members of a team and have just finished a basketball game at a local gymnasium. One boy says, "I don't see why you're hassling us. We're not doing anything wrong." "You just did," says the officer. He makes a call on his radio for assistance from other officers and makes all the boys sit on the curb with their hands behind their heads. Two other cruisers arrive shortly, and the boys are transported to the police station, where they are searched. The search turns up two small pocket knives and a bottle opener. The four boys are charged with "carrying concealed weapons" and "conspiracy to commit burglary." Juvenile authorities are notified.

Scenario 2 A highway patrol officer spots two young girls with backpacks attempting to hitch a ride on a major highway in Florida. He stops his vehicle and asks the girls for IDs. They do not have any but claim they are over 18 and are trying to get to Georgia to visit some friends. The officer takes both girls into custody and to a local jail, where a subsequent identification discloses that they are, respectively, 13- and 14-year-old runaways from a Miami suburb. Their parents are looking for them. The girls are detained at the jail until their parents can retrieve them. In the meantime, a nearby convenience store reports that two young girls from off the street came in an hour earlier and shoplifted several items. Jail deputies search the backpacks of the girls and find the shoplifted items. They are charged with "theft." Juvenile authorities are notified.

Are these scenarios the same? No. Can each of these scenarios result in a finding of delinquency by a juvenile court judge? Yes. Whether youth are "hanging out" on a street corner late at night or have shoplifted, it is possible in *a juvenile court in the United States* that they could be defined collectively as delinquents or delinquency cases.

Of course, some juvenile offending is more serious than other types. Breaking windows or violating curfew would certainly be less serious than armed robbery, rape, or murder. Many jurisdictions divert less serious cases away from juvenile courts and toward various community agencies, where the juveniles involved can receive assistance rather than the formal sanctions of the court.

Should one's age, socioeconomic status, ethnicity or race, attitude, and other situational circumstances influence the police response? The reality is that juveniles experience subjective appraisals and judgments from the police, prosecutors, and juvenile court judges on the basis of both legal and extralegal factors. Because of their status as juveniles, youth may also be charged with various noncriminal acts. Such acts are broadly categorized as status offenses.

Status Offenders

status offenses

Any act committed by a minor that would not be a crime if committed by an adult (e.g., truancy, runaway, or unruly behavior).

Status offenders are of interest to both the juvenile justice system and the criminal justice system. **Status offenses** are acts committed by juveniles that would bring the juveniles to the attention of juvenile courts but would not be crimes if committed by adults. Typical status offenses include running away from home, truancy, and curfew violations. Adults would not be arrested for running away from home, truancy, or walking the streets after some established curfew for juveniles. However, juveniles who engage in these behaviors in particular cities may be grouped together with more serious juvenile offenders who are charged with armed robbery, aggravated assault, burglary, larceny, auto theft, or illicit drug sales. Overall, there has been an increase in the number of youth being processed for status offenses. From 1985 to 2004, the number of status offense cases that were petitioned to the court doubled (ACT 4 Juvenile Justice, n.d.).

Runaways

runaways

Juveniles who leave their home for long-term periods without parental consent or supervision.

It is difficult to determine exactly how many youth are runaways in the United States. Some youth actually do run away from their parents or caretakers, while others are "thrown out." It was estimated that in 1999, more than 1.6 million youth were either runaway or thrownaway (Snyder and Sickmund, 2006). In terms of arrests for runaways, it was estimated that in 2008, there were over 100,000 arrests of runaways in the United States (Puzzanchera, 2009).

Runaways are those youth who leave their homes, without permission or their parents' knowledge, and who remain away from home for periods ranging from a

One type of status offense is underage drinking.
(Courtesy of Dean John Champion)

couple of days to several years. Many runaways are apprehended eventually by police in different jurisdictions and returned to their homes. Others return because they choose to go back. Some runaways remain permanently missing, although they likely are part of a growing number of homeless youth who roam city streets throughout the United States (Slesnick et al., 2007). Information about runaways and other types of status offenders is compiled annually through various statewide clearinghouses and the federally funded National Incidence Studies of Missing, Abducted, Runaway, and Throwaway Children (NISMART) (Sedlak, Finkelhor, and Hammer, 2005).

Runaway behavior is complex. Some research suggests that runaways can have serious mental health needs (Chen, Thrane, and Whitbeck, 2007). In addition, these youth may seek others like themselves for companionship and emotional support (Kempf-Leonard and Johansson, 2007). Runaways view similarly situated youth as role models and peers, and they may engage in delinquency with other youth. Studies of runaways indicate that boys and girls often have familial problems (e.g., neglect and parental drug use) and have been physically and sexually abused by their parents or caregivers (McNamara, 2008b). Evidence suggests that youth who run away may engage in theft or prostitution to finance their independence away from home. In addition, these youth may be exploited by peers or adults who befriend them (Armour and Haynie, 2007).

Some research confirms that runaways tend to have low self-esteem as well as an increased risk of being victimized on the streets (McNamara, 2008b). Although all runaways are not alike, there have been attempts to profile them. Depending upon how authorities and parents react to children who have been apprehended after running away, there may be either positive or negative consequences.

Youth who run away may hitchhike.
(Courtesy of Dean John Champion)

Various strategies have been used to address runaway youth. Congress first enacted the Runaway and Homeless Youth Act in 1974 (Runaway and Homeless Youth Act, 1974). In 2008, the 110th Congress amended the Act and continued to authorize funding for outreach programs, shelters, and transitional living (Reconnecting Homeless Youth Act, 2008). These services are available in many cities. On the streets, outreach workers share information about and make referrals for counseling services, medical care and treatment, and other kinds of community assistance programs. Runaway shelters have been established to offer runaways a nonthreatening residence and social support system in various jurisdictions. These shelters locate services that will help meet the runaways' needs. Shelters are a short-term option designed to stabilize youth and, if possible, reunite them with family. Finally, services are also available for older youth who cannot return home and require assistance in moving into independent living quarters (McNamara, 2008b).

Truants and Curfew Violators

Truants

truants

Juveniles who are habitually absent from school without excuse.

Status offenders also include truants as well as curfew and liquor law violators. **Truants** are those who absent themselves from school without school or parental permission. The national data on truancy rates are problematic for several reasons: One school district can define truancy differently than another district; sociodemographic characteristics of truants are not normally maintained, even by individual schools; and no consistent, central reporting mechanisms exist for data compilations about truants. For instance, one state may define a truant as a youth who absents himself or herself from school without excuse for five or more consecutive school days. In another state, a truant may be defined as someone who misses one day of school without a valid excuse.

Truancy is more likely to occur in urban schools than in suburban schools. Research suggests that truancy is a "gateway activity" (McNamara, 2008b, p. 47) for further problem behaviors ranging from gang behavior to substance abuse. For example, Chiang et al. (2007) found that about two-thirds of all male youth arrested while truant tested positive for drug use.

Truancy is not a crime. It is a status offense. Youth can be charged with truancy and brought into juvenile court for status offense adjudication. Truancy is taken quite seriously in many jurisdictions.

truancy courts

Special courts that convene to determine strategies to utilize for youth who absent themselves from school.

Several states have developed formal mechanisms to deal with the problem of truancy. The Family Court system of Rhode Island has established **truancy courts** to increase status offender accountability relating to truancy issues. Chronic truants are referred to the Truancy Court, where their cases are handled. The process involves the truant youth, the parents/guardians, a truant officer, and a Truancy Court magistrate. The purpose of the Truancy Court is to avoid formal juvenile court action. Youth can do this by obeying the behavioral requirements outlined, which include (1) attending school every day, (2) arriving to school on time, (3) behaving in school, and (4) completing classroom work and homework. Failure to comply with one or more of these requirements may result in a referral to Family Court or placement in a program administered by the Department of Children, Youth, and Families. The youth might be subject to increasingly punitive sanctions if the truancy persists following the Truancy Court hearing.

The Truancy Court also requires parents to sign a form that permits the release of confidential information about the truant. This information is necessary to devise a treatment program and provide any counseling or services the truant may require. Thus, the Family Court is vested with the power to evaluate, assess, and plan activities designed to prevent further truancy, and various interventions are initiated to enhance the youth's awareness of the seriousness of truancy and the importance of staying in school.

Delaware has a truancy prevention program that is available throughout the state. Five judges deal with truant youth and their families, and they utilize an approach similar to the drug court model. The same judge works with the youth and the family throughout the process. Parents are encouraged to be responsible for their children, and the court collaborates with a number of social service agencies to work with the family and offer services to family members. Research suggests that this approach has been effective in reducing truancy in the state, and in helping youth stay in school (McNamara, 2008b).

Curfew Violators

Curfew violators are those youth who remain on city streets after specified evening hours when they are prohibited from loitering or are not in the company of a parent or guardian. In 2010, more than 73,000 youth were arrested for violating curfew and loitering laws in the United States (U.S. Department of Justice, 2011).

curfew violators
Youth who violate laws and ordinances of communities prohibiting them from being on the streets after certain evening hours (e.g., 10:00 P.M.); curfew itself is a delinquency prevention strategy.

Shoplifting is a common delinquent offense.
(Courtesy of Dean John Champion)

stigmas, stigmatization

Social process whereby offenders are perceived as having undesirable characteristics as the result of incarceration or court appearances; criminal or delinquent labels are assigned to those who are processed through the criminal and juvenile justice systems.

Juvenile Justice and Delinquency Prevention Act (JJDPA) of 1974

Legislation recommending various alternatives to incarceration, including deinstitutionalization of status offending, removal from secure confinement, and other rehabilitative treatments.

Office of Juvenile Justice and Delinquency Prevention (OJJDP)

Agency established by Congress under the JJDPA of 1974; designed to remove status offenders from the jurisdiction of juvenile courts and dispose of their cases less formally.

In an effort to decrease the incidence of juvenile crime during the mid-1990s, many cities throughout the United States enacted curfew laws specifically applicable to youth. The theory is that if juveniles are obliged to observe curfews in their communities, they will have fewer opportunities to commit delinquent acts or status offenses (Urban, 2005). For example, in New Orleans, Louisiana, in June 1994, the most restrictive curfew law went into effect. Under this law, juveniles under age 17 were prohibited from being in public places, including the premises of business establishments, unless accompanied by a legal guardian or authorized adults. The curfew began at 8:00 P.M. on weeknights and 11:00 P.M. on weekends. Exceptions were made for youth who might be traveling to and from work or were attending school, religious, or civil events. A study on the impact of this strict curfew law, however, revealed that juvenile offending shifted to noncurfew hours (Urban, 2005). Furthermore, the enforcement of this curfew law by New Orleans police was difficult, because curfew violations often occurred outside of a police presence. If anything, the curfew law tended to induce rebelliousness among those youth affected by the law. The research indicates that curfew laws have not been an especially effective deterrent to status offending or delinquency generally (Adams, 2003; Urban, 2005). Nonetheless, in the summer of 2011, the Mayor of Philadelphia imposed a temporary 9:00 P.M. curfew on Friday and Saturday nights in specific geographical areas to prevent flash mobs, who had attacked some residents, from congregating in the city (CNN Wire Staff, 2011).

Juvenile and Criminal Court Interest in Status Offenders

Among status offenders, juvenile courts are most interested in chronic or persistent offenders, such as those who habitually appear before juvenile court judges (Hill et al., 2007). Some research suggests that greater contact with juvenile courts can result in youth acquiring labels or **stigmas** as either delinquents or deviants (Feiring, Miller-Johnson, and Cleland, 2007). Therefore, diversion of juvenile offenders from the juvenile justice system has been advocated and recommended to minimize **stigmatization**.

One increasingly popular strategy is to remove certain types of offenses from the jurisdiction of juvenile court judges (Trulson, Marquart, and Mullings, 2005). Because status offenses are less serious than juvenile delinquency cases, many state legislatures have pushed for the removal of status offenses from juvenile court jurisdiction. The removal of status offenders from the discretionary power of juvenile courts is, in part, an initiative based on the deinstitutionalization of status offenders (DSO).

The Deinstitutionalization of Status Offenses (DSO)

The JJPDA of 1974

Congress enacted the **Juvenile Justice and Delinquency Prevention Act (JJDPA) of 1974** in response to a national concern about growing juvenile delinquency and youth crime (Bjerk, 2007). This Act authorized establishment of the **Office of Juvenile Justice and Delinquency Prevention (OJJDP)**, which is extremely helpful and influential in funding research and disseminating data and information about juvenile offending and prevention. The Act had two main provisions: (1) to remove juveniles who were involved in status offenses from secure detention or juvenile correctional facilities within two years of the legislation and (2) to make certain that youth were not held in facilities where they would have contact with adults convicted of a crime (OJJDP, n.d.). This mandate became known as the **deinstitutionalization of status offenders (DSO)**. Although state participation was voluntary, funding for state initiatives was tied to state compliance with the legislation (Schwartz, 1989).

Changes and Modifications in the JJDPA

Throughout its history, the JJDPA has been reviewed and amended by Congress. In 1977, Congress increased and expanded its earlier initiatives in the deinstitutionalization of status offenders and its restrictions on sight and sound separation for juvenile offenders in adult institutions (OJJDP, n.d.). In 1980, Congress recommended that states refrain from detaining juveniles in jails or adult lockups. These requirements were enhanced in the 1984 amendments to the legislation.

In 1988, Congress also directed that states examine their secure confinement policies relating to minority juveniles and determine reasons—and justification—for the disproportionately high rate of minority confinement. The **disproportionate minority confinement (DMC)** requirement prompted states to investigate why minority youth were incarcerated at a higher rate and to develop strategies to address the imbalance. When Congress reauthorized the legislation in 1992, there was a focus on girls in the system, and states were required to examine existing programs for girls and make certain that the programs were specific to their needs. States also were to ascertain that each youth was treated equally (Chesney-Lind and Irwin, 2006).

The 2002 revisions to the Act expanded DMC to include all parts of the juvenile justice process. Today, DMC refers to **disproportionate minority contact** (Snyder and Sickmund, 2006). Subsequent amendments and authorizations of the JJDPA have occurred since it was enacted, and Congress is currently considering the proposed reauthorization of the legislation.

For approximately 20 years, Congress has directed that any participating state would have up to 25 percent of its formula grant money withheld to the extent that the state was not in compliance with each of the JJDPA mandates. Thus, state compliance with the provisions of the JJDPA was encouraged by providing grants-in-aid to jurisdictions wanting to improve their juvenile justice systems and facilities. Overall, states have endeavored to comply with the JJDPA mandate throughout their juvenile justice systems, and the Act has served as a significant catalyst for reform initiatives.

DSO Defined

The best definition of DSO is the removal of status offenders from juvenile secure institutions. Deinstitutionalization of youth from training schools, reform schools, and other secure juvenile facilities was first stipulated by Congress.

deinstitutionalization of status offenses (DSO)
Eliminating status offenses from the broad category of delinquent acts and removing juveniles from, or precluding their confinement in, juvenile correctional facilities; the process of removing status offenses from the jurisdiction of juvenile courts so that status offenders cannot be subject to secure confinement.

disproportionate minority confinement (DMC).
Refers to the number and percentage of minority youth in correctional custodial institutions (e.g., detention centers, residential facilities, and reform schools; the rate of confinement for youth in these correctional environments exceeds their representation in the general youth population; in amendments to the Juvenile Justice and Delinquency Prevention Act of 1974, Congress directed the states to gather data and attempt to address this disproportionality.

disproportionate minority contact

In 2002, Congress amended the Juvenile Justice and Delinquency Prevention Act to require states to gather data on minority youth who come to the attention of the juvenile justice system; and to determine if these contact data are commensurate with minority representation in the general youth population; rather than focusing only on youth in confinement, this reflects contacts with youth at all stages of juvenile justice processing.

deinstitutionali-zation.

Mandate that was part of the Juvenile Justice and Delinquency Prevention Act of 1974 requiring states to remove youth who had been placed in detention or other custodial institutions for their involvement in status offenses (e.g., running away, truancy, and curfew violations).

Deinstitutionalization

Deinstitutionalization refers to the removal of status offenders from secure juvenile institutions, such as state industrial or training schools. Before the JJDPA of 1974, states incarcerated both status and delinquent offenders together in reform schools or industrial schools (Champion, 2008a). Should truants, curfew violators, runaways, and difficult-to-control children be placed in secure facilities together with adjudicated juvenile burglars, thieves, robbers, arsonists, and other violent and property felony offenders? Clearly, substantial differences exist between status offenders and delinquent offenders.

Congress determined that requiring status offenders to live and interact with delinquents in secure confinement, especially for prolonged periods of time, is detrimental to status offenders and inconsistent with the mission of the juvenile court. The exposure of status offenders to the criminogenic influence of, and close association with, serious delinquents adversely affects the social and psychological well-being of status offenders. The damage to a status offender's self-concept and self-esteem, coupled with the further immersion into the system, was perceived as problematic (Champion, 2008a).

Subsequently, states have implemented deinstitutionalization policies for status offenders. To expedite the removal of status offenders from secure juvenile facilities, the federal government made available substantial sums of money for establishing alternative social services. Overwhelmingly, states have complied with the regulations and successfully accessed the federal money allocated.

Under certain conditions, however, states may incarcerate status offenders who are under some form of probationary supervision. For instance, a Texas juvenile, E.D., was on probation for a status offense (*In re E.D.*, 2004). During the term of E.D.'s probation, she violated one or more of the conditions of probation. The juvenile court elected to confine E.D. to an institution for a period of time as a sanction for the probation violation. E.D. appealed, contending that as a status offender, she should not be placed in a secure facility. The Court of Appeals in Texas disagreed and held that the juvenile court judge had broad discretionary powers to determine E.D.'s disposition, even including placement in a secure facility. The appellate court noted that secure placement of a status offender is warranted whenever the juvenile probation department has (1) reviewed the behavior of the youth and the circumstances under which the juvenile was brought before the court, (2) determined the reasons for the behavior that caused the youth to be brought before the court, and (3) determined that all dispositions, including treatment, other than placement in a secure detention facility or secure correctional facility have been exhausted or are clearly inappropriate.

The juvenile court judge set forth an order that (1) it is in the child's best interests to be placed outside of her home, (2) reasonable efforts were made to prevent or eliminate the need for the child's removal from her home, and (3) the child, in her home, could not be provided the quality of care and support that she needs to meet the conditions of probation. There was no suggestion in the record that the judge failed to comply with these three major requirements. Thus, this ruling suggests that despite the deinstitutionalization initiative, status offenders may be incarcerated if they violate court orders while on probation.

Diverting Dependent and Neglected Children to Social Services

A different application of DSO deals with **dependent and neglected children**. While the juvenile court continues to exercise jurisdiction over dependent and neglected youth, programs have been established to receive referrals of these children directly from law enforcement officers, schools, parents, or even the youth. These diversion programs provide crisis intervention services for youth, and their aim is to eventually return juveniles to their homes. However, more serious offenders may need services provided by shelter homes, group homes, or even foster homes (Sullivan, Veysey, et al., 2007). Collaborative community programs have been established to address this need.

Potential Outcomes of DSO

There are three potential outcomes of the DSO:

1. The number of status offenders in secure confinement, especially in local facilities, may be reduced. Greater numbers of jurisdictions are adopting deinstitutionalization policies, so the actual number of institutionalized status offenders should decrease.

2. **Net-widening**, or bringing youth into the juvenile justice system who would not have been involved in the system previously, may swell. Some state jurisdictions may have increased the number of status offenders in the juvenile justice system following DSO. Previously, status offenders in those states would have been handled informally. When specific community programs were established for status offenders, however, the net widened, and youthful offenders were eligible to be placed in programs that offered specialized social services. The result is that more youth can come into contact with the system.

3. **Relabeling**, or defining youth as delinquent or emotionally disturbed who in the past would have been defined and processed as status offenders, may occur in certain jurisdictions following DSO. For instance, police officers in some jurisdictions might label juvenile curfew violators or loiterers as larceny or burglary suspects and detain these youth. In brief, by attaching a new or different label to the behavior, youth can be brought into the juvenile justice system.

Based upon the last 38 years, DSO has clearly become not just widespread but also the prevailing juvenile justice policy. The DSO requirements stipulated that agencies and organizations contemplate new and innovative strategies to cope with youth with diverse needs, which has resulted in various programs to better serve status offenders. Greater cooperation and collaboration among the public, youth services, and community-based treatment programs facilitate developing the best program policies and practices. The implementation of DSO has helped foster these initiatives.

dependent and neglected children
Youth considered by social services or the juvenile court to be in need of some type of intervention, supervision, or placement due to circumstances in their homes or families that are beyond their control.

net-widening
Bringing juveniles into the juvenile justice system who would not otherwise be involved in delinquent activity; applies to many status offenders (also known as "widening the net").

relabeling
Action, usually taken by police officers, of redefining juvenile acts as delinquent when in fact such acts are harmless or status offenses; result is harsher treatment by police of arrested juveniles.

Some Important Distinctions between Juvenile and Criminal Courts

Some of the major differences between juvenile and criminal courts are indicated below. These general principles reflect most jurisdictions in the United States.

1. Juvenile courts are civil proceedings designed for juveniles, whereas criminal courts are proceedings designed to try adults charged with crimes. In criminal courts, adults are the focus of criminal court actions, although some juveniles may be tried as adults in these same courts. The civil–criminal distinction is important, because an adjudication of a juvenile court case does not result in a criminal record for the juvenile offender. In criminal courts, either a judge or a jury finds a defendant guilty or not guilty. In the case of guilty verdicts, offenders are convicted and acquire criminal records. These **convictions** follow offenders for the rest of their lives. However, when juveniles are found to be involved in delinquent behavior by juvenile courts, states can authorize procedures to seal or expunge juvenile court adjudications once the youth reaches adulthood or the age of majority.

2. Juvenile proceedings are more informal, and criminal proceedings are more formal. Attempts are made in many juvenile courts to avoid the prescribed aspects that characterize criminal proceedings. Juvenile court judges frequently address juveniles directly and casually, and proceedings are sometimes conducted in the judge's chambers rather than a courtroom. Despite attempts by juvenile courts to minimize formal proceedings, juvenile court procedures in recent years have become increasingly formalized. At least in some jurisdictions, it may even be difficult to distinguish criminal courts from juvenile courts in terms of their formality.

3. In 30 states (including the District of Columbia), juveniles are not entitled to a trial by jury; in 10 states, juveniles have a constitutional right to a jury trial; and in 11 states, youth can be granted a jury trial under specific circumstances (Szymanksi, 2002). In all criminal proceedings, defendants are entitled to a trial by jury if the crime or crimes they are accused of committing carry a possibility of incarceration for more than six months. Judicial approval is required to hold a jury trial for juveniles in some jurisdictions. This is one more manifestation of the legacy of the *parens patriae* doctrine in contemporary juvenile courts. Eleven states have legislatively mandated jury trials for juveniles in juvenile courts if they are charged with certain types of offenses, are above a specified age, may be sentenced to an adult facility, and request a jury trial (Szymanksi, 2002, p.1).

4. Juvenile court and criminal court are **adversarial proceedings**. Juveniles may or may not wish to retain or be represented by counsel (*In re Gault*, 1967). In a juvenile court case, prosecutors allege various infractions or law violations by the juveniles, and these charges can then be refuted by juveniles or their counsel. If juveniles are represented by counsel, defense attorneys are permitted to offer a defense to the allegations. Criminal courts are obligated to provide counsel for anyone charged with

convictions

Judgments of a court, based on a jury or judicial verdict or on the guilty pleas of defendants, that the defendants are guilty of the offenses alleged.

adversarial proceedings

Opponent-driven court litigation, where one side opposes the other; prosecution seeks to convict or find defendants guilty, while defense counsel seeks to defend their clients and seek their acquittal.

a crime if the defendant cannot afford to retain his or her own counsel and could be sentenced to a term of incarceration (*Argersinger v. Hamlin,* 1972). Every state has provisions for providing defense attorneys to indigent juveniles who are to be adjudicated in juvenile court. However, a recent review of state procedures suggests that not all youth receive the assistance of effective counsel (Ross, 2011).

5. Criminal courts are **courts of record**, whereas transcripts of juvenile proceedings are made only if the state law authorizes them. **Court reporters** record all testimony presented in most criminal courts. State criminal trial courts are courts of record, where either a tape-recorded transcript of the proceedings is maintained or a written record is kept. Thus, if trial court verdicts are appealed by the prosecution or defense, transcripts of these proceedings can be presented by either side as evidence of errors committed by the judge or other violations of due process rights. Juvenile courts, however, are not courts of record. Therefore, in any given juvenile proceeding, whether a juvenile court judge will ask for a court reporter to transcribe the adjudicatory proceedings depends on the specific jurisdiction. One factor that inhibits juvenile courts from being courts of record is the expense of hiring court reporters for this work. Furthermore, the U.S. Supreme Court has declared that juvenile courts are not obligated to be courts of record (*In re Gault,* 1967). Nonetheless, in some jurisdictions, juvenile court judges may have access to a court reporter to transcribe or record all court matters.

6. The **standard of proof** used for determining one's guilt in criminal proceedings is **beyond a reasonable doubt**. The less rigorous civil standard of **preponderance of the evidence** is used in some juvenile court cases. However, the U.S. Supreme Court has held that if any juvenile is in jeopardy of losing his or her liberty as the result of a delinquency adjudication by a juvenile court judge, then the evidentiary standard must be the criminal court standard of beyond a reasonable doubt (*In re Winship,* 1970). The Court's decision dealt with youth who could be incarcerated for any period of time, whether for one day, one month, one year, or longer. Thus, juveniles in juvenile court who confront the possible punishment of confinement in a juvenile facility are entitled to the evidentiary standard of beyond a reasonable doubt in determining their involvement in the act. Juvenile court judges apply this standard when adjudicating a juvenile's case and the loss of liberty is a possibility.

7. The range of penalties juvenile court judges may impose is limited, whereas in most criminal courts, the range of penalties may include life-without-parole sentences or even the death penalty. The jurisdiction of juvenile court judges also typically ends when the juvenile reaches adulthood. Some exceptions are that juvenile courts may retain jurisdiction over mentally ill youthful offenders indefinitely after they reach adulthood. In California, for instance, the Department of the Youth Authority supervises youthful offenders ranging in age from 11 to 25.

The purpose of this comparison is to illustrate that criminal court actions are more serious and have harsher long-term consequences for offenders compared with

courts of record
Any court where a written record is kept of court proceedings.

court reporters
Court officials who keep a written word-for-word and/or tape-recorded record of court proceedings.

standard of proof
The type of evidence required to sustain a petition of delinquency against a juvenile, depending on the seriousness of the offense; how guilt is measured or determined.

beyond a reasonable doubt
Evidentiary standard used in criminal courts to establish guilt or innocence of a criminal defendant and utilized in delinquency proceedings.

preponderance of the evidence
Standard used in civil courts to determine defendant or plaintiff liability and where the result does not involve incarceration.

juvenile court proceedings. Juvenile courts continue to be guided by a strong rehabilitative orientation in most jurisdictions, where the most frequently used sanction is probation. In 2007, probation was used in approximately 56 percent of the cases in which a juvenile was adjudicated delinquent (Livsey, 2010, p. 1). Criminal courts also use probation as a sanction in about 60 percent of all criminal cases, and in 2009, about 4.2 million adult offenders were on probation (Glaze, 2010). Although juvenile courts may be utilizing more punitive sanctions, many youth continue to receive treatment-oriented punishments rather than incarceration in secure juvenile facilities. Secure confinement is viewed by most juvenile court judges as a last resort, and this disposition is reserved for only the most serious youthful offenders (LaMade, 2008).

An Overview of the Juvenile Justice System

The Ambiguity of Adolescence and Adulthood

Police have broad discretionary powers in their encounters with the public and in dealing with street crime, and police handle a large number of youth informally. However, police arrests and detentions of juveniles in local facilities remain the primary way that a juvenile enters the juvenile justice system.

Some juveniles are clearly children. It is difficult to find youth under 13 who physically appear to be 18 or older. Yet, nearly 10 percent of all juveniles held for brief periods in adult jails each year are 13 or younger (OJJDP, 2007). For juveniles 14 to 17 years of age, visual determination of one's juvenile or nonjuvenile status is increasingly difficult. This might explain why police officers initially—and mistakenly—may take youthful offenders to jails for identification and questioning.

Other ways that juveniles can enter the juvenile justice system include referrals from or complaints by parents, neighbors, victims, and others (e.g., social work staff or probation officers) unrelated to law enforcement. Dependent or neglected children may be reported to police initially, and in investigating these complaints, police officers may take youth into custody until arrangements for their care can be made. Alternatively, police officers may apprehend youth for alleged crimes.

Being Taken into Custody

Being **taken into custody** is another term for arrest. Rarely are dependent or neglected youth taken into custody, but police might apprehend a runaway or missing youth and then hold him or her until the parent or guardian is notified (Armour and Haynie, 2007). Youth on the streets after curfew may also be taken into custody by police.

When youth are taken into police custody, it generally means that they are suspected of delinquent behavior. Formal charges may be filed against them once it is established which court has jurisdiction in their cases. Police may determine that the juvenile court has jurisdiction, depending on the age or youthfulness of the offender.

taken into custody

A decision made by a police officer that a youth should be held temporarily.

Similar to adults, teens are arrested, handcuffed, and taken into custody.
(Courtesy of Mark C. Ide)

Conversely, the prosecutor and/or judge may decide that the criminal court has jurisdiction and the youthful offender should be charged as an adult.

Juveniles in Jails

In 2009, approximately 7,200 juveniles under the age of 18 were being held in jails (Minton, 2010). About 80 percent of these juveniles were being held as adults. This represents roughly one percent of all inmates held in jails for 2009, and it does not reflect the total number of juveniles who are brought to jail annually after they have been arrested by police. Many youth are held for short periods of time (e.g., two or three hours) even though they have not been specifically charged with an offense. Legislators in Illinois have enacted a statute preventing police officers from detaining juveniles in adult jails for more than six hours (Arya, 2011). Such laws reflect the **jail removal initiative**, in which states are encouraged to avoid holding juveniles in adult jails, even for short periods.

The Illinois policy preventing the police from detaining juveniles in jails except for limited periods is consistent with a major provision of the JJDPA of 1974. Although the JJDPA is not binding on any state, it does advise law enforcement officials to treat juveniles differently from adult offenders if juveniles are taken to jails for brief periods. For instance, the JJDPA recommends that youth be separated in jails by sight and sound from adult offenders. Furthermore, they should be held in nonsecure areas of jails for periods not exceeding six hours and should not be restrained in any way with handcuffs or other devices while detained. Their detention should only be as long as is necessary to identify them and reunite them with their parents, guardians, or a responsible adult from a public youth agency or family services.

jail removal initiative
Action sponsored by the OJJDP and the JJDPA to dissuade law enforcement officers from taking juveniles to jail.

jails

City- or county-operated and -financed facilities designed to house misdemeanants serving sentences of less than one year, pretrial detainees, witnesses, juveniles, vagrants, and others.

lockups

Small rooms or cells designed for confining arrested adults and/or juveniles for short periods, such as 24 hours or less.

preventive detention

Authority to detain suspects before trial without bail where suspects are likely to flee from the jurisdiction or pose serious risks to others.

pretrial detention, preventive pretrial detention

Holding delinquent or criminal suspects in incarcerative facilities pending their forthcoming adjudicatory hearing or trial.

Even more serious delinquent offenders brought to jail to be detained should be processed according to JJDPA recommendations. Sight and sound separation from adult offenders is encouraged, although juveniles alleged to have committed delinquent offenses are subject to more restrictive detention provisions. The general intent of this aspect of the JJDPA is to minimize the adverse effects of labeling and victimization that might occur if juveniles are treated like adult offenders. Another factor is the recognition that most of these offenders' cases will eventually be handled by the juvenile justice system. Any attributions of criminality arising from how juveniles are treated while they are in adult jails are considered to be incompatible with the rehabilitative ideals of the juvenile justice system and the outcomes or consequences ultimately experienced by most juvenile offenders. Thus, some of the JJDPA goals are to prevent juveniles from being influenced, psychologically or physically, by adults through jail contact, to prevent their victimization, and to insulate them from defining themselves as criminals, which might occur through processing.

Despite new laws designed to minimize or eliminate holding juveniles in adult **jails** or **lockups**, even for short periods of time, juveniles continue to be held in jails. Their detention may be related to a number of factors. For example, juveniles can appear to be older to police officers than they really are. They may present false IDs or even no IDs, offer fictitious names when questioned, or refuse to provide police with any information about their true identities. It takes time to determine who the youth are and which responsible adult or guardian should be contacted. Some runaways who police apprehend are from different states, and planning may be required for their parents or guardians to reunite with them. Juveniles can also be aggressive, assaultive, and obviously dangerous. They are sometimes confined or restrained, if only to protect others. Some youth are even suicidal and need temporary protection.

The U.S. Supreme Court has held that **preventive detention** of juveniles for brief periods can be used without violating their constitutional rights, especially for those offenders who pose a danger to themselves or others (*Schall v. Martin,* 1984). In that particular case, a juvenile, Gregory Martin, was detained at the police department's request for serious charges. Gregory refused to give his name or other identification and was perceived to be dangerous, either to himself or to others. His preventive detention was upheld by the Supreme Court as not violating his constitutional right to due process. Before this ruling, however, many states had similar laws that permitted pretrial and preventive detention of both juvenile and adult suspects. Although **pretrial detention** presupposes a forthcoming trial of those detained and preventive detention does not, both terms are often used interchangeably—or even combined, as in the term **preventive pretrial detention** (Brookbanks, 2002).

Referrals

Figure 1.1 is a diagram of the juvenile justice system. Although each jurisdiction in the United States has its own methods for processing juvenile offenders, Figure 1.1 encompasses most of these stages. As shown on this diagram, a majority of juvenile encounters with the juvenile justice system are through referrals from police officers.

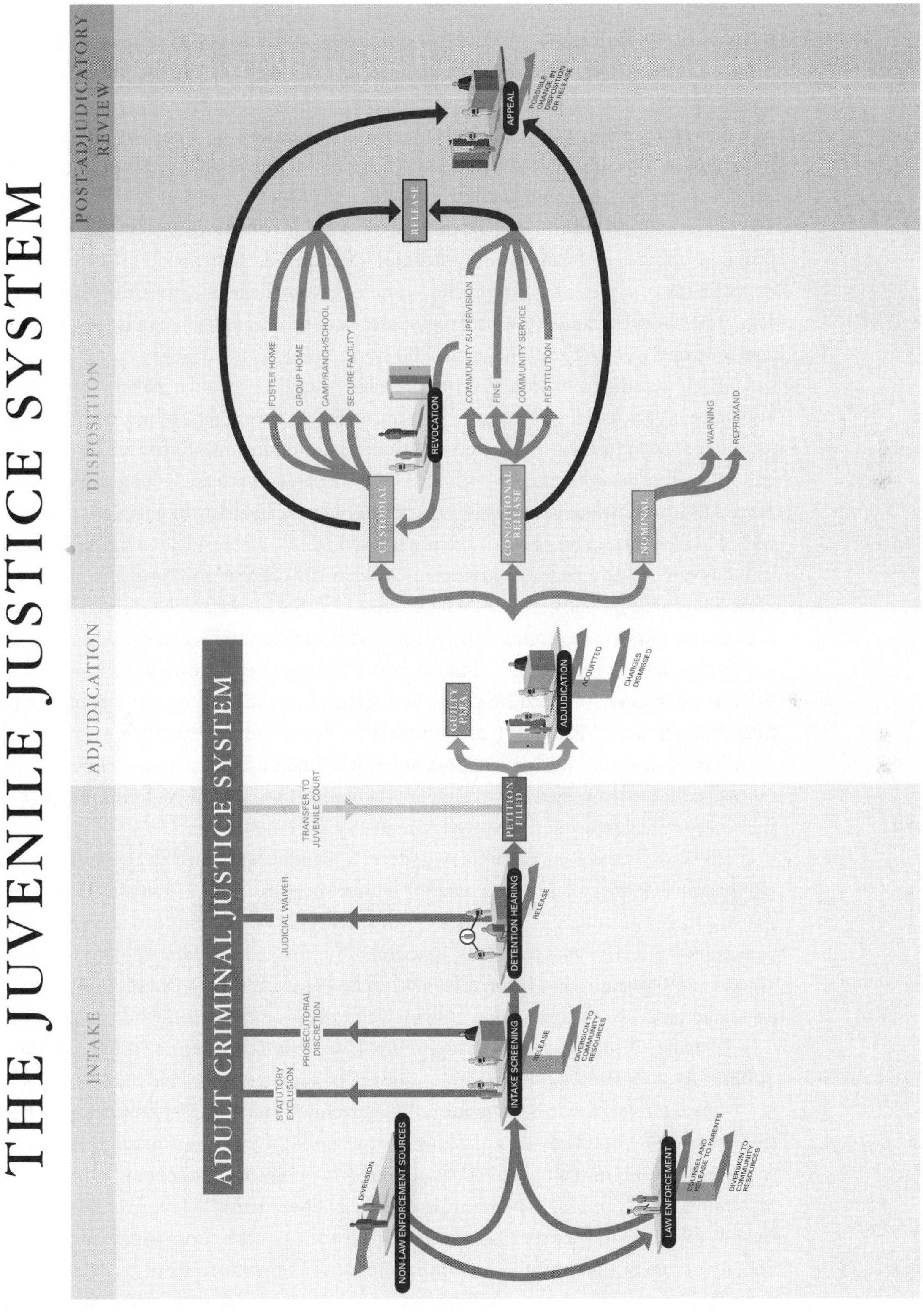

THE JUVENILE JUSTICE SYSTEM

Figure 1.1
Diagram of the Juvenile Justice System

referrals

Any action which
involves bringing a
youth to juvenile court
by a law enforcement
officer, interested
citizen, family member,
or school official;
usually based upon law
violations, delinquency,
or unruly conduct.

Referrals are notifications made to juvenile court authorities that a juvenile requires the court's attention. Referrals can be made by various individuals, including concerned parents, school principals, teachers, neighbors, truant officers, and social service providers. However, most referrals to juvenile courts are made by law enforcement officers. In 2007, police referrals accounted for approximately 83 percent of the delinquency cases, but some variation occurs in offense categories. For example, police referrals occurred in over 93 percent of cases involving drug law violations or property offenses (Puzzanchera, Adams, and Sickmund, 2010, p. 31). Referrals may be made for runaways; truants; curfew violators; unmanageable, unsupervised, or incorrigible children; children with drug or alcohol problems; or any youth suspected of committing a crime (Kuntsche et al., 2007).

Each jurisdiction throughout the United States has its own policies relating to how referrals are handled. In Figure 1.1, following an investigation by a police officer, juveniles are counseled and released to parents; referred to community resources; cited and referred to juvenile intake, followed by a subsequent release to parents; or transported to juvenile detention or shelter care to be held. Each of these actions is the result of police discretion. The discretionary action of police officers who take youth into custody for any reason is governed by what the officers observed. If a youth has been loitering, especially in cities with curfew laws for juveniles, the discretion of police officers might be to counsel the youth and release him or her to the parents without further action. If the youth violated liquor laws or committed some minor infraction, he or she may be cited by police and referred to a juvenile probation officer for further processing. Most youth are returned to the custody of their parents or guardians. However, some youth are apprehended while committing serious crimes. If that occurs, police officers typically transport the youth to a juvenile detention center or shelter to await further action by juvenile justice system personnel.

In New Mexico, for example, whenever a juvenile is referred to the juvenile justice system for any offense, the referral is first screened by the Juvenile Probation/Parole Office. Juvenile probation/parole officers (JPPOs) are assigned to initially review a police report and file. This function is performed, in part, to determine the accuracy of the report and if the information is correct. If the information is accurate, an intake process will commence, in which the youth undergoes further screening by a JJPO assigned to the case by a supervisor (New Mexico Juvenile Justice Division, 2002).

Once a referral has been made to the Juvenile Probation/Parole Office, a decision is made whether to file a petition or to handle the case informally. About 56 percent of all delinquency cases are handled formally (Puzzanchera, Adams, and Sickmund, 2010, p. 37). A **petition** is an official document filed in juvenile court on the juvenile's behalf that specifies the reasons for the youth's court appearance. These documents assert that juveniles fit within the jurisdictional categories of dependent or neglected, status offender, or delinquent, and the reasons for such assertions are usually provided. Filing a petition formally places the juvenile before the juvenile court judge. However, juveniles may come before juvenile court judges in less formal ways.

petition

A document whereby
an official or private
individual can bring
charges against a
juvenile and ask the
juvenile court to hear
the case.

About 44 percent of the cases brought before the juvenile court each year are nonpetitioned cases (Puzzanchera, Adams, and Sickmund, 2010, p. 37).

When individual cases are handled informally, JPPOs in jurisdictions in New Mexico have several options. Whenever youth are determined to require special care, are neglected or dependent, or are otherwise unsupervised by adults or guardians, JPPOs may refer them to a Juvenile Early Intervention Program (JEIP). The JEIP is a highly structured program for at-risk, nonadjudicated youth. Other states have similar programs designed to help youth who might need specific services.

Depending upon the jurisdiction, however, the majority of alleged juvenile delinquents will be advanced further into the juvenile justice system. Some status offenders, especially recidivists, will also progress through the system. Alternatively youth may be held in juvenile detention facilities temporarily to await further action. Other youth may be released to their parent's custody, but these juveniles may be required to reappear later for further court action. Most of these youth will subsequently be interviewed by an **intake officer** in a proceeding known as **intake**. Figure 1.2 shows an example of a juvenile court referral form used by an intake officer.

Intake

Intake varies among jurisdictions. Intake is a **screening** procedure usually conducted by a juvenile probation officer and during which several recommendations can be made. Some jurisdictions conduct **intake hearings** or **intake screenings**, where information and explanations are solicited from relevant individuals, such as police, parents, neighbors, or victims. In other jurisdictions, intake proceedings are quite informal, usually consisting of a dialogue between the juvenile and the intake officer. These are important proceedings, regardless of their degree of formality. Intake is a major screening stage in the juvenile justice process, where further action against juveniles may be contemplated or required. Intake officers can hear complaints against juveniles and informally resolve the less serious cases, or they can be juvenile probation officers who perform intake as a special assignment. Also, juvenile probation officers may perform diverse functions, including intake, enforcement of truancy statutes, and juvenile placements (Champion, 2008a).

Intake officers also consider the youth and his or her attitude, demeanor, age, seriousness of offense, and a host of other factors. Has the juvenile had frequent prior contact with the juvenile justice system? If the offenses alleged are serious, what evidence exists against the offender? Should the offender be referred to social service agencies or for psychological counseling, receive vocational counseling and guidance, acquire educational or technical training and skills, be issued a verbal reprimand, be placed on some type of diversionary status, or be returned to parental custody? Interviews with parents are conducted as a part of an intake officer's information gathering. Although intake is supposed to be an informal proceeding, it is nevertheless an important stage in juvenile processing. The intake officer often acts in an advisory capacity, because he or she is the first juvenile court contact children and their parents will have following an arrest or being taken into custody. The youth and the

---

intake officer

Juvenile probation officer or other court representative who conducts screenings and preliminary interviews with alleged juvenile offenders and their families.

intake

Critical phase in which a juvenile probation officer or other official determines whether to release juveniles to parental custody or recommend their detention for further juvenile court action.

screening

Procedure used by intake and prosecution to determine which cases have prosecutive merit and which ones do not. Decision to divert cases from the court to other agencies and organizations or to proceed with formal processing.

intake hearings, intake screenings

Proceedings in which a juvenile official, such as a juvenile probation officer, interviews a youth charged with a delinquent or status offense and his/her parents or guardian to determine the best strategy for dealing with the behavior that resulted in the referral to court.

Fourth Juvenile Court, Division 1, 1234 Main Street, Laredo, TX 78041

Date:_____

Juvenile Court Referral

Intake Case #   _____

Intake Officer: _____

Badge #:   _____

District: _____

_____

Name of Juvenile

_____

Address

_____

City, State

_____   _____

Name(s) of Parent(s)/Guardian(s)   Marital Status

_____

Address of Parent(s)/Guardian(s)

_____

Telephone Number of Parent/Guardian

Name and Relation to Juvenile of Referring Person: _____

Delinquency/Status Offense Allegation(s) _____
_____

Prior Record of Juvenile, if any: _____
_____

_____

Signed by:

_____

Child/juvenile   Date

_____

Parent/guardian   Date

_____

Parent/guardian   Date

Approved by:

_____

Court attorney   Date

_____

Judge Date

Figure 1.2

Juvenile Court Referral Form

Source: Prepared by authors.

parents have a right to know the charge(s). It is indicated to the youth and the parents that the intake hearing is a preliminary inquiry and not a fact-finding session to determine one's guilt, and the intake officer advises the youth that statements made by the child and/or parents may be used in court if such action is warranted.

In most jurisdictions, depending upon the discretion of intake officers, intake results in one of five actions: (1) dismiss the case, with or without a verbal or written reprimand; (2) remand the youth to the custody of the parents; (3) remand the youth to the custody of the parents, but with provisions for or referrals to counseling or special services; (4) place the youth on informal probation or supervision; or (5) refer the youth to the juvenile prosecutor for further action and possible filing of a delinquency petition (Champion and Mays, 1991). In 2007, more than half the cases referred to the juvenile court for delinquency resulted in a formal petition being filed (Knoll and Sickmund, 2010).

Theoretically, at least, only the most serious juveniles will be referred to detention to await a subsequent juvenile court appearance. For a youth to be detained while awaiting a juvenile court appearance, a detention hearing must be conducted. Juveniles considered for detention generally are determined to be a danger to the community, are believed likely to be harmed if released, or are perceived as likely to flee the jurisdiction to avoid prosecution in juvenile court. Other youth may be released to the custody of their parents, sometimes with a referral to community service organizations; usually, these community resources are intended to meet the specific needs of particular juvenile offenders. For serious cases, a petition is filed with the juvenile court. The juvenile court prosecutor further screens these petitions and

Police officers explain drugs, alcohol, and tobacco and their effects to classes of students in schools.
(Anne Vega/Merrill Education)

decides which ones merit an appearance before the juvenile court judge. In Alaska, for example, a petition for adjudication of delinquency is used to bring delinquency cases before the juvenile court.

Other petitions may allege status offending, such as truancy, runaway behavior, curfew violation, or violation of drug or liquor laws (McNamara, 2008b). Not all petitions result in formal action by a juvenile court prosecutor. Like prosecutors in criminal courts, juvenile court prosecutors prioritize which cases they will pursue. This case ranking depends upon a number of factors, including the seriousness of the alleged offense, the volume of petitions filed, the time estimated for the juvenile court judge to hear and act on these petitions, and the sufficiency of evidence supporting these petitions (Backstrom and Walker, 2006). As shown in Figure 1.3, however, there has been a more formal response to youthful offending in the last two decades, and more delinquency cases referred to the juvenile court result in a formal petition than those that are handled informally.

Alternative Prosecutorial Actions

Cases referred to juvenile prosecutors for further action tend to be more serious. Exceptions might include those youth who are chronic offenders or technical probation violators and nonviolent property offenders (e.g., status offenders, vandalism, petty theft, or public order offenders).

Juvenile court prosecutors have broad discretion. They may cease prosecutions against alleged offenders or reduce the charges in the petition from felonies to misdemeanors or from misdemeanors to status offenses. In some instances, prosecutors may

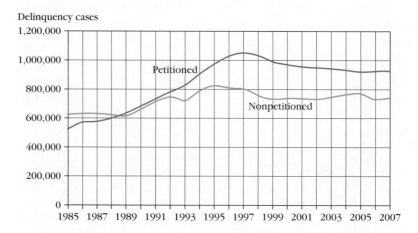

Since 1989, delinquency cases have been more likely to be handled formally, with the filing of a petition for adjudication, than informally

Figure 1.3
Number of Delinquency Cases Formally Processed: 1989–2007
Source: Charles Puzzanchera, Benjamin Adams, and Melissa Sickmund (2010).
Juvenile Court Statistics 2006–2007. Pittsburgh, PA: National Center for Juvenile Justice.

Police encounters with juveniles on city streets sometimes lead to arrests and juvenile processing.
(© A. Ramey / PhotoEdit)

divert some of the more serious juvenile cases for processing by criminal courts. The least serious cases are disposed of informally. Prosecutors either file petitions or act on petitions filed by others, such as intake officers, the police, school officials, or interested family and citizens (LaMade, 2008).

Adjudicatory Proceedings

Jurisdictions vary considerably concerning juvenile court proceedings. In some states, juvenile courts appear to be emulating criminal courts. The physical features of criminal courts are present, including the judge's bench, tables for the prosecution and defense, and a witness stand. Further, evidence suggests that courts are currently holding juveniles more accountable for their actions (LaMade, 2008).

Besides the more formal atmosphere of juvenile courts, the procedure is becoming increasingly adversarial. The prosecutor represents the state, and the youth is entitled to be represented by defense counsel. However, research shows that only about 50 percent of the juvenile offenders in delinquency proceedings have the assistance of counsel (Bishop, 2010; LaMade, 2008). Typically, juvenile court judges have discretion in determining how court proceedings are conducted. Juvenile defendants alleged to have committed various offenses may or may not be entitled to a jury. In 2007, only 11 states provided jury trials for juveniles in juvenile courts, and these jury trials were restricted to a narrow list of serious offenses.

After hearing the evidence presented by both sides in any juvenile proceeding, the judge decides or adjudicates the matter in an **adjudication hearing**, sometimes called an **adjudicatory hearing**. **Adjudication** is a judgment or action on the petition

adjudication hearing, adjudicatory hearing
Formal proceeding involving a prosecuting attorney and a defense attorney where evidence is presented and the juvenile's involvement is determined by the juvenile judge.

adjudication
Judgment or action on a petition filed with the juvenile court.

filed with the court. If the petition alleges that the youth is a delinquent, the judge determines whether this is so. If the petition alleges that the juvenile involved is dependent, neglected, or otherwise in need of care by agencies or others, the judge decides the matter. If the adjudicatory hearing fails to yield facts supporting the petition filed, the case is dismissed, and the youth exits the juvenile justice system. If, however, the adjudicatory hearing supports the allegations in the petition, the judge must **dispose** of the juvenile's case according to a range of sanctions (Champion and Mays, 1991).

Juvenile Dispositions

Disposing of a juvenile's case is the equivalent of sentencing adult offenders. When adult offenders are convicted of crimes, they are sentenced. When juveniles are adjudicated delinquent, the judge makes a disposition. At least 12 different **dispositions** or sanctions are available to juvenile court judges if the facts alleged in petitions are upheld (Jarjoura et al., 2008). These dispositions are (1) nominal, (2) conditional, or (3) custodial options.

Nominal Dispositions

Nominal dispositions are either verbal warnings or reprimands and are the least punitive dispositional options. The nature of such verbal warnings or reprimands is a matter of judicial discretion. The youth is released to the custody of the parents or legal guardians, and this completes the juvenile court action (Foley, 2008). Nominal dispositions are most often utilized for low-risk, first offenders who may be considered the least likely to recidivate and commit new offenses (Abbott-Chapman, Denholm, and Wyld, 2007). The emphasis of nominal dispositions is on rehabilitation and fostering

dispose

To decide the sanction to be imposed on a juvenile following an adjudication hearing.

dispositions

Sanctions resulting from a delinquency adjudication; may be nominal, conditional, or custodial.

nominal dispositions

Adjudicatory disposition resulting in minor sanctions, such as warnings and/or probation.

Juvenile offenders have the right to testify on court in their defense.
(© Design Pics Inc. / Alamy)

a continuing, positive, reintegrative relationship between the juvenile and his or her community (Ross, 2008).

Conditional Dispositions

Most **conditional dispositions** involve probation, which is the most frequently imposed sanction. Youth are placed on probation and required to comply with certain conditions for a specified period lasting from several months to a couple of years. The nature of the conditions to be fulfilled depends on the specific needs of the offender and the offense committed. If youth have alcohol or drug dependencies, they may be required to undergo individual or group counseling and some type of therapy to cope with substance abuse (McMorris et al., 2007). Juvenile court judges impose probation as a disposition more than any other sanction (Puzzanchera, Adams, and Sickmund, 2010).

Property offenders may be required to make restitution to victims or to compensate the court in some way for the damage they have caused (Jarjoura et al., 2008). In a growing number of jurisdictions, **restorative justice** is practiced, in which offenders and their victims are brought together for the purpose of mediation. Youth learn to accept responsibility for what they have done, and their accountability is heightened (Swanson, 2005). Many jurisdictions have gravitated toward a more balanced approach in sanctioning youth, where the emphasis is upon restorative and victim-centered justice. The aim of balanced and restorative justice is to (1) promote public safety and the protection of the community, (2) heighten accountability of youth toward victims and the community for offenses committed, and (3) increase competency and improve character development to assist youth in becoming responsible and productive members of society (Champion and Mays, 1991).

Offenders with behavioral disorders may require more intensive supervision while on probation (Abatiello, 2005). Those considered to be high risks for recidivism may be required to undergo electronic monitoring and house arrest as part of their supervision by juvenile probation officers. These and similar strategies are part of the growing area of community corrections and intermediate punishments, in which greater emphasis is placed upon community reintegration and rehabilitation (Rivers, 2005). During the 1990s, a gradual intensification of punishments for juveniles, including probation dispositions, occurred (Wilkerson, 2005). This emphasis on punishment is a reflection of state legislatures' tougher stance toward juveniles.

The terms and conditions of the disposition are outlined by the judge and probation staff. Obeying the law, attending school, maintaining employment, reporting to the probation officer, attending vocational training or education courses, appearing at subsequent court hearings, avoiding the use of drugs and alcohol, and refraining from possessing dangerous weapons are standard probation conditions. Furthermore, the judge may include other conditions, such as mandatory counseling or therapy, depending upon the particular needs exhibited by the offender.

In terms of formal dispositions for delinquent youth, judges use probation most often for property offenses. In 2007, 35 percent of youth who were adjudicated delinquent for a property offense were placed on probation. However, from 1985 to 2007,

conditional dispositions
Result of a delinquency adjudication obligating youth to comply with one or more conditions of probation or a similar program.

restorative justice
Mediation between victims and offenders whereby a suitable sanction is imposed and agreed to by offender and victim; may involve victim compensation and some offender service.

custodial dispositions

Either nonsecure or secure options resulting from a delinquency adjudication which involve placement in a group home, ranch, camp, or a juvenile custodial institution.

nonsecure custody, nonsecure confinement

Custodial disposition in which a juvenile is placed in a group home, foster care, or other non secure residential setting where he or she is permitted to leave with permission of parents, guardians, or supervisors.

secure custody, secure confinement

Incarceration of juvenile offender in facility that restricts movement in community; similar to an adult penal facility involving total incarceration.

the use of probation actually increased for the three other delinquent offense categories (person offenses, drug offenses, and public order offenses), and it decreased for property offenses (Puzzanchera, Adams, and Sickmund, 2010).

Custodial Dispositions

Custodial dispositions are classified according to **nonsecure custody** or **nonsecure confinement** and **secure custody** or **secure confinement**. Nonsecure custody consists of placing juveniles in shelter care, foster homes, group homes, camps, or ranches. These are short-term options, and they are often designed to lead to more permanent placement arrangements for juveniles. Juveniles have freedom of movement, and they can generally participate in school and other activities. It is assumed that if they are in the care of others in foster homes or shelters, curfews will be implicitly (if not explicitly) enforced (McNamara, 2008b).

Placement in a secure custodial environment is considered by most juvenile court judges as the last resort for serious offenders. Some of the reasons for this include the concern that youth will become more criminalized as a result of living with other delinquents, overcrowding in secure juvenile facilities, a general reluctance among judges to incarcerate youth because of adverse labeling effects, and the potential effectiveness of certain intermediate punishments through community-service agencies. Fewer than 10 percent of all juveniles processed by juvenile courts annually are subsequently placed in either nonsecure or secure facilities (LaMade, 2008).

Juvenile Corrections

Since 2000, the number of youth in residential facilities (both public and private) has been declining, and in 2008, as Figure 1.4 shows, fewer than 81,000 juveniles were in residential correctional programs (Sickmund, 2010). Juvenile residential facilities range from small, temporary facilities to large, long-term public facilities, and states vary in their use of residential placement. For example, Sickmund (2010) reported that six states account for 46 percent of the youth in residential facilities.

Juvenile Probation

Juveniles adjudicated delinquent may be placed on probation or in secure confinement, depending upon the seriousness of the misconduct, the juvenile court judge, and the recommendations of and evaluations by the probation staff. Depending upon juvenile probation officer caseloads in various jurisdictions, probation may in some cases be as intense as intensive supervised probation for adults and in other cases considerably less restrictive. Placement in different types of probationary programs is dependent upon how the youth is classified. However, juvenile court judges have not consistently applied legal variables in their decision making about juvenile secure placements. More rational legal criteria for secure confinement decision making have been recommended (Sullivan, Veysey, et al., 2007).

Between the 2000 peak and 2008, the number of juvenile
offenders in residential placement declined 26%

Number of juvenile offenders in residential placement

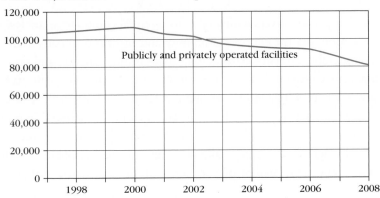

Figure 1.4
Number of Youth in Residential Placement: 1997–2008
Source: Melissa Sickmund (2010). Juveniles in Residential Placement,
1997–2008. Washington, DC: Office of Juvenile Justice and Delinquency
Prevention.

Intensive as well as regular probation may involve restitution to victims and/or
community service. In 2007, over 560,000 juveniles were placed on probation in
various state jurisdictions (Livsey, 2010). Juveniles may be placed in community-
based residential programs or participate in various therapies and treatments or training as part of their probation conditions (Champion and Mays, 2001).

Confinement in state industrial schools is the juvenile equivalent of incarceration in a state prison for adults. This type of confinement is considered to be **hard
time** for many juveniles. The California Youth Authority operates various facilities to
house juvenile offenders in secure confinement. Lengths of commitment vary for offenders, depending upon the seriousness of their adjudication offenses (OJJDP, 2007).
However, recent research suggests that long-term confinement in juvenile institutions
does not reduce recidivism (Mulvey, 2011).

Juvenile Aftercare

When juveniles have completed a specified period of time in a residential setting, they
usually are considered for release by a juvenile paroling authority. If selected, the
youth undergo a period of supervision under an appropriate state or community
agency. In the adult system, this is referred to as parole; in the juvenile system, it is
called **aftercare**. In 2006, there were 95,000 juveniles on aftercare in various state jurisdictions (American Correctional Association, 2007).

hard time
Also known as flat
time; actual amount of
secure confinement
juveniles must serve as
the result of a custodial
disposition from a
juvenile court judge.

aftercare
A wide variety of
programs and services
for juveniles, including
halfway houses,
counseling services,
employment
assistance, and medical
treatment designed to
assist youth after their
release from residential
placement.

SUMMARY

The juvenile justice system is an integrated network of agencies, institutions, and organizations that process juvenile offenders. Its essential components are law enforcement, prosecution and the courts, community and institutional corrections, and aftercare. Considerable diversity exists among states in the structure and operations of the juvenile justice system. State statutes stipulate the maximum age limits for youth used by juvenile courts. The most common maximum age for juvenile court jurisdiction is 17, although maximum age limits of 18, 16, and 15 are found in some states. Lower age limits also vary, with some juvenile courts having no lower age limits. Children under age seven are generally considered to be incapable of formulating criminal intent and are treated by one or more community agencies rather than juvenile courts.

Delinquency is any act committed by a juvenile that would be a crime if committed by an adult. Any criminal act committed by someone who has not reached the age of majority would also define delinquency. A status offense is any act committed by a juvenile that would not be a crime if committed by an adult. Common status offenses include runaway behavior, curfew violation, incorrigibility, and truancy. Several policies have been established to differentiate between status and delinquent offenders. The JJDPA of 1974 was designed to remove status offenders from secure institutions where more hard-core delinquent offenders might be housed. This was called the DSO. The general meaning of DSO is the deinstitutionalization of status offenders from institutions, diverting dependent and neglected children to social services, and divestiture of jurisdiction by juvenile courts over status offenders.

The traditional orientation of juvenile courts has been characterized by the philosophy of *parens patriae*. This perspective vests juvenile courts with individualized sanctioning powers intended to treat rather than punish youth. During the last 40 years, juvenile courts have become increasingly adversarial, resembling criminal courts. Presently, juvenile courts are due process bodies, influenced significantly by the get-tough movement that espouses more punishment-centered sanctions for juveniles. Despite this get-tough stance, juvenile court judges exhibit philosophical principles that guide their decision making about youth. Judges attempt to balance the aims of due process and justice with individualized treatments and therapies intended to rehabilitate and reintegrate youthful offenders.

The juvenile justice system and the criminal justice system parallel one another in several respects. Juveniles suspected of committing delinquent acts are taken into custody or arrested. Youth are referred to juvenile court by police, school authorities, social service agencies, or parents. These referrals are made whenever juveniles are believed to have violated one or more laws. More than half of all juvenile cases are petitioned; a petition is a formal document seeking a hearing for the juvenile in a juvenile court. An adjudicatory hearing is a formal court proceeding much like a criminal trial. Judges usually impose dispositions on juveniles who have been adjudicated. These include nominal dispositions or verbal warnings, conditional dispositions or probation, and custodial dispositions, which may involve incarceration.

Various dispositions are available to juvenile court judges that parallel some of the punishments available for criminal offenders, including probation. Community-based sanctions include probation, intensive supervised probation, home confinement, electronic monitoring, community service, restitution, fines, day reporting programs, and/or placement in a halfway house. Other dispositions may include placement in a secure facility. Once juveniles have served a portion of their disposition in these facilities, they may be released under supervision or aftercare. Juvenile aftercare is much like adult parole in that it is community-based and conditional.

KEY TERMS

QUESTIONS FOR REVIEW

1. What are the principal components of the juvenile justice system? Why do some view juvenile justice as a process rather than a system?

2. Why is there a general lack of uniformity among juvenile courts in the United States?

3. What is the age range for juvenile courts in the United States? Which factors make it difficult to provide a consistent definition of this age range among states? Explain.

4. What is the doctrine of *parens patriae*? What are its origins? Does *parens patriae* continue to influence juvenile courts today? Why, or why not?

5. What is the Juvenile Justice and Delinquency Prevention Act (JJDPA) of 1974? What are its implications for juveniles?

6. What is meant by DSO? What are some of its outcomes for juvenile offenders?

7. What is the current situation with youth in residential placement?

8. What are some major differences between juvenile and criminal courts?

9. What are dispositions? How do they resemble sentences for adult criminals? What are three types of dispositions? Define and give an example of each.

10. Distinguish between juvenile probation and aftercare. What is the difference between secure confinement and nonsecure confinement?

11. Are juvenile courts primarily treatment-centered or punishment-centered? What is the get-tough movement, and what are some reasons for its existence?

INTERNET CONNECTIONS

ABA Juvenile Justice Committee
http://www2.americanbar.org/sections/criminaljustice/CR200000/Pages/default.aspx

Administration for Children and Families
http://www.acf.hhs.gov/

Child Protect: Children's Advocacy Center
http://www.childprotect.org/

Children's Defense Fund
http://www.childrensdefense.org/

National Center for Juvenile Justice
http://www.ncjj.org

National Council of Juvenile and Family Court Judges
http://www.ncjfcj.org/

Office of Justice Programs

http://www.ojp.usdoj.gov/

http://www.ojp.usdoj.gov/programs/juvjustice.htm

Office of Juvenile Justice and Delinquency Prevention

http://www.ojjdp.gov/

The Future of Children

http://www.futureofchildren.org

Youth For Justice: Teaching Youth About the Law

http://www.youthforjustice.org/

2

The History of Juvenile Justice and Origins of the Juvenile Court

Learning Objectives

AFTER READING THIS CHAPTER, THE STUDENT WILL BE ABLE TO:

- Outline the history and development of juvenile justice and juvenile courts.
- Identify the different methods by which juvenile crime data are gathered, categorized, measured, and reported.
- Summarize juvenile crime rates and trends.
- Describe the limitations and problems of measuring juvenile crime.
- Describe the factors that lead to career escalation and/or a transition to adult crime.
- Summarize juvenile victimization, including school violence.

(Courtesy of Dean John Champion)

Introduction

In the early 1990s, the rising rate of juvenile violent crime produced a public panic that resulted in more punitive policies toward youthful offenders. The rate of arrest per 100,000 youth ages 10 to 17 in 1994 was 525, compared to a rate of 334 in 1980 (Figure 2.1). Media attention and get-tough legislative reactions raised serious doubts about the future of the juvenile justice system. With headlines such as "The Coming of the Super-Predators" (DiIulio, 1995) and "Old Enough to Do the Crime, Old Enough to Do the Time," some questioned the need for a separate system for younger offenders (Feld, 1998, 1999). Should rehabilitation still be the mission of the juvenile court, or should this be abandoned in favor of a punishment? Should a separate system even be maintained for youth?

Research on public opinion indicates Americans believe that rehabilitation should be the purpose of the juvenile justice system and that a separate system should be maintained (Cullen et al., 1998; Piquero et al., 2010). As juvenile violence (as well as adult criminal violence) declined in the late 1990s, a more rational review of public policy, by both the public and those working in the system itself, reinforced the original intent and mission of the juvenile justice system. By 2008, the juvenile arrest rate for violent crime had decreased to 288 per 100,000 youth ages 10 to 17 (Figure 2.1), and the outlook for the juvenile court was more optimistic (Piquero et al., 2010).

Why is there a separate system of justice for juvenile offenders? What are the origins and goals of this specialty court for children and youth? This chapter will review the history of the juvenile justice system in the United States and explain the development of a separate system of justice for youth. In 1999, the first centennial of the juvenile court was celebrated, but the characteristics of the court have been transformed from its original policies and procedures. The formality of juvenile courts today did not begin to emerge until the 1960s and 1970s.

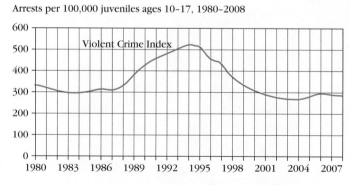

Figure 2.1

Juvenile Arrest Rate Trends
Source: Charles Puzzanchera (2009). Juvenile Arrests 2008.
Washington, DC: Office of Juvenile Justice and Delinquency
Prevention, p. 5.

The historical antecedents of the juvenile justice system are rooted in England during the 16th century, when youthful offenders were under the jurisdiction of the king. Justice for youth was dispensed through political appointees known as chancellors. These persons made decisions about juveniles according to what they believed to be in the child's best interests. When the American colonies were established, English influence over how youth were treated continued. Between the early 1600s and late 1800s, a gradual transformation occurred that influenced how youthful offenders were handled. Many of the events that shaped the contemporary system of juvenile justice and offender processing will be presented and described.

Two key cases, *Ex parte Crouse* (1839) and *People ex rel. O'Connell v. Turner* (1870), will be examined. These cases were influential in shaping policies about child welfare, guardianship, and punishments for various types of juvenile behaviors. During the 40-year interval following the Civil War, several philanthropists, religious groups, and political groups contributed to promoting important reforms. The child savers movement emerged, and houses of refuge were constructed and operated. Crucial legislation in different states was enacted, establishing both truancy laws and juvenile courts. Gradually, children gained greater recognition and were given special treatment, moving them well beyond their early conceptualization as chattel and their unfair and unilateral treatment in primitive children's tribunals. These and other critical events will be described. Early juvenile courts were noted particularly for their paternalistic views toward youth through the doctrine of *parens patriae* and individualized decision making based on a youth's best interests as determined by the courts.

How much delinquency and status offending are there in the United States? While there is a "dark figure" of delinquent offending (i.e., delinquency that is not known or not reported; also known as hidden delinquency), official and unofficial measures are used to identify the extent and frequency of youthful misbehaviors. Different data sources are used in tracking juvenile offending, including the *Uniform Crime Reports*, the *National Crime Victimization Survey*, the National Juvenile Court Data Archive, and *The Sourcebook of Criminal Justice Statistics*. These will be described and discussed. Additional sources include the *National Youth Survey* and the *Monitoring the Future Survey*. These national surveys will also be defined and described. An important source of unreported delinquency and status offense information is self-reports, or disclosures by juveniles to private researchers about the nature and extent of their offending. Some of the strengths and weaknesses of these different information sources, including self-reports, will be discussed as well.

As with adult crimes, juvenile crimes are classified as violent offenses and property offenses. Violent offenses include murder, rape, aggravated assault, and robbery. In recent years, several incidents of school violence have been reported by the media. Thus, school violence, patterns, and trends will also be reviewed. This chapter also describes youth who are considered to be at risk of becoming delinquent. Several risk factors, such as family instability, poor school adjustment, lower socioeconomic status, low self-control and self-esteem, and antisocial behavior will be described. In addition, some violent offending is gang related (George and Thomas, 2008). Juvenile gangs and gang activities often form along racial or ethnic lines, and some of their characteristics will be reviewed. While very few youth commit murder, this topic will be introduced as well.

One concern of criminologists is whether less-serious offenders, such as status offenders, progress to more serious offenses. This phenomenon is known as career escalation, and some authorities believe that less-serious juvenile offending, if not detected and corrected, will eventually lead to more serious offending. It is uncertain whether career escalation occurs for most juveniles who commit less-serious offenses. Career escalation and juvenile violence trends will be examined.

This chapter concludes with an examination of female juveniles and how their patterns of delinquency have changed in recent years. Female juvenile offenders will be profiled, and trends among female offending will be described. Female juveniles have increasingly become involved in gang activities, so juvenile female gang formation will be examined. Since more female juvenile offenders have come to the attention of police, myths and misconceptions about female juveniles have been perpetuated. These myths and misconceptions will be described.

The History of Juvenile Courts

Juvenile courts are a relatively recent American phenomenon. However, modern American juvenile courts have various, less-formal European antecedents. In biblical times, Roman law vested parents with almost exclusive responsibility for disciplining their offspring. Age was the crucial determinant of whether youth were subject to parental discipline or to the more severe penalties invoked for adult law violators. While the origin of this demarcation or cutting point is unknown, the age of seven was used in Roman times to separate infants from those older children who were accountable to the law for their actions (Congressional Research Service, 2007). During the Middle Ages, English **common law** established under the monarchy adhered to the same standard. In the United States, several state jurisdictions currently apply this distinction and consider that children below the age of seven are not accountable for criminal acts.

Under the laws of England during the 1500s, **shires** (counties) and other political subdivisions were organized to carry out the will of the king. Each shire had a **reeve**, or chief law enforcement officer. In later years, the term *shire* was combined with the term *reeve* (*shire-reeve*) to create the word *sheriff*, a term that is now applied to the chief law enforcement officer of most U.S. counties. While reeves enforced both criminal and civil laws and arrested law violators, other functionaries, called **chancellors**, acted on the king's behalf and dispensed justice according to his wishes. These chancellors held court and settled disputes that included simple property trespass, property boundary disagreements, and assorted personal and property offenses, including public drunkenness, thievery, and vagrancy. The courts conducted by chancellors

common law
Authority based on court decrees and judgments that recognize, affirm, and enforce certain usages and customs of the people; laws determined by judges in accordance with their rulings.

shires
Early English counties.

reeve
Chief law enforcement officer of English counties, known as shires.

chancellors
Civil servants who acted on behalf of the King of England during the Middle Ages; chancellors held court and settled property disputes, trespass cases, and minor property offenses as well as acts of thievery, vagrancy, and public drunkenness.

were known as **chancery courts** or **courts of equity**. Today, some jurisdictions in the United States, such as Tennessee, have chancery courts where property boundary disputes and contested wills may be adjudicated by chancellors. These courts have other jurisdiction as well, although they deal primarily with equity cases (e.g., breaches of contract, specific performance actions, and child custody cases).

No distinctions were made regarding age or gender when punishments were administered in England during the 1700s. Youthful offenders aged seven or older experienced the same harsh punishments imposed on adults. Stocks and pillories, whipping posts, branding, ducking stools, and other forms of corporal punishment were administered to juveniles as well as to adult offenders for many different types of crimes. In some instances, **banishment** was used as a way of punishing more serious offenders. Some of these offenders were transported to Pacific islands, which were owned by the British and converted into penal colonies. This was known as **transportation**. Many prisoners died in these colonies. The death penalty was also invoked frequently, often for petty crimes, and incarceration of offenders was particularly sordid. Women, men, and youth were confined together in jails for lengthy periods. No attempts were made to classify these offenders by gender or age, and all prisoners slept on hay loosely thrown on wooden floors.

Workhouses and Poor Laws

Eighteenth-century jails were patterned largely after **workhouses** that were common nearly two centuries earlier. In 1557, for example, **Bridewell Workhouse** was established in London. Although the manifest aim of such places was to punish offenders, Bridewell and other, similar facilities were created primarily to provide cheap labor to satisfy mercantile interests and demands. Interestingly, jailers and sheriffs profited greatly from leasing their inmates to various merchants to perform semiskilled and skilled labor. These same jailers claimed that the work performed by inmates for mercantile interests was largely therapeutic and rehabilitative, although in reality, the primary incentive for operating such houses was profit and personal gain. Exploitation of inmates for profit in these and other workhouses was perpetuated by jailers and sheriffs for many decades, and the general practice was accepted by an influential constituency of merchants and entrepreneurs.

At the time of the Bridewell Workhouse, English legislators had already established several statutes known as the **Poor Laws**. These laws targeted debtors who owed creditors, and for those unable to pay their debts, sanctions were imposed. Debtors' prisons were places where debtors were incarcerated until they could pay their debts. Because they needed to work to earn the money required to pay off their debts, and because opportunities for earning money for prison labor were almost nonexistent, imprisonment for debts was tantamount to a life sentence. Many offenders were incarcerated indefinitely, or until someone, perhaps a relative or an influential friend, could pay off their debts for them.

The Poor Laws were directed at the poor or socioeconomically disadvantaged. In 1601, additional statutes were established that provided constructive work for

chancery courts, courts of equity

Courts of equity rooted in early English Common Law where civil disputes and matters involving children may be resolved.

banishment

Sanction used to punish offenders by barring them for a specified number of miles from settlements or towns; often a capital punishment, since those banished could not obtain food or water to survive the isolation.

transportation

Early British practice of sending undesirables, misfits, and convicted offenders to remote territories and islands controlled by England.

workhouses

Early penal facilities designed to use prison labor for profit by private interests; operated in shires in mid-16th century and later.

Bridewell Workhouse

Sixteenth-century London jail (sometimes gaol) established in 1557; known for providing cheap labor to business and mercantile interests; jailers and sheriffs profited from prisoner exploitation.

Poor Laws

Regulations in England in the Middle Ages designed to punish debtors by imprisoning them until they could pay their debts; imprisonment was for life or until someone else could pay their debts.

indentured servant system, indentured servants

Voluntary slave pattern in which persons entered into a contract with merchants or businessmen, usually for seven years of service, wherein merchants would pay for their voyage to the American colonies.

Hospital of Saint Michael

Custodial institution established in Rome in 1704; provided for unruly youth and others; youth were assigned tasks, including semiskilled and skilled labor.

youth deemed by the courts to be vagrant, incorrigible, truant, or neglected. In general, education was not an option for these youth—it was an expensive commodity available almost exclusively to children from the upper social strata. For the masses of poor, education was usually beyond their reach; they spent most of their time earning money to pay for life's basic necessities. They had little or no time to consider education as a realistic option (Champion, 2008a).

Indentured Servants

During the 1700s, youth became apprentices, usually to master craftsmen, in a system of involuntary servitude. This servitude was patterned in part after the **indentured servant system. Indentured servants** entered voluntarily into contractual agreements with various merchants and businessmen to work for them for extended periods of up to seven years. This seven-year work agreement was considered by all parties to be a mutually beneficial way of paying for the indentured servant's passage from England to the colonies. In the case of youthful apprentices, however, their servitude, for the most part, was compulsory. Furthermore, it usually lasted until they reached adulthood, or age 21.

During the Colonial period, English influence on penal practices was apparent in most New England jurisdictions. Colonists relied on familiar traditions for administering laws and sanctioning offenders. It is no coincidence, therefore, that much of the criminal procedures in American courts today trace their origins to legal customs and precedents inherent in British jurisprudence during the 1600s and 1700s. However, relatively little attention was devoted to the legal status of juveniles during this period, or to how to manage them. In fact, more than a few juveniles were summarily executed for relatively petty offenses (Champion, 2008a).

Hospital of Saint Michael

In other parts of the world during this same era, certain religious groups were gradually devising institutions that catered primarily to youthful offenders. For example, in Italy, a corrective facility was established in 1704 to provide for unruly youth and other young people who violated criminal laws. This facility was the **Hospital of Saint Michael**, constructed in Rome at the request of Pope Clement XI (Sellin, 1930). This institution was misleadingly named, however, because the youth it housed were not ill. Rather, they were assigned various tasks and trained to perform semiskilled and skilled labor—useful tools that would enable them to find employment more easily after their release from Saint Michael. During rest periods and evening hours, youth were housed in individual cells.

The Child Savers and Houses of Refuge

As more American families gravitated toward large cities, such as New York, Philadelphia, Boston, and Chicago, during the early 1800s to find work, increasing numbers of children roamed the streets, most often unsupervised by working parents who could not afford child care services. Lacking familial controls, many of these youth committed acts of vandalism and theft. Others were simply idle, without visible means of support, and were designated as vagrants. Again, religious organizations intervened to protect unsupervised youth from the perils of life in the streets. Believing that these youth would subsequently turn to lives of crime as adults, many reformers and philanthropists sought to save them from their plight.

Thus, in different cities throughout the United States, various groups were formed to find and control these youth by offering them constructive work programs, healthful living conditions, and above all, adult supervision. Collectively, these efforts became widely known as the **child savers movement**. **Child savers** came largely from the middle and upper classes, and their assistance to youth took many forms (Platt, 1969). Food and shelter were provided to children who were in trouble with the law or who were simply idle. Private homes were converted into settlements where social, educational, and other important activities could be provided for needy youth. The child savers were not limited to the United States. In Scotland and England during the 1850s, child-saving institutions were abundant, with philosophies and interests similar to those of the child-saving organizations in the United States. In England particularly, middle-class values were imposed on the children of the working class through institutional education, training, and discipline, and eventually, several juvenile reformatories were established for the purpose of institutional control (Blevins, 2005).

In the United States, more than a few child-saving organizations sought to impose their class, ethnic, and racial biases on the poor, immigrants, and minority women. A middle-class gender ideology of maternal care was imposed upon working- and lower-class mothers. Many of these mothers were declared unfit and in need of state control, because they did not conform to the cultural ideal espoused by middle- and upper-class child savers. Thus, there was the general charge that child savers sought to control and resocialize the children of the so-called dangerous classes for the benefit of the capitalist entrepreneurs (Platt, 1969). However, not everyone today agrees that the child savers exploited children. In certain cities, such as Wilmington, Delaware, the child savers movement emphasized education rather than work. Furthermore, the ultimate aims of this movement in Delaware and several other states were largely altruistic and humanitarian. Even in contemporary youth corrections, the child saver orientation influences the care and treatment strategies of personnel (Blevins, 2005).

The **New York House of Refuge** was established in New York City in 1825 by the **Society for the Prevention of Pauperism** (Campbell and Gonzalez, 2007). Subsequently imitated in other communities, **houses of refuge** were institutions largely devoted to managing status offenders, such as runaways or incorrigible children. Compulsory education and other forms of training and assistance were provided to these children. However, the strict, prison-like regimen of this organization was not entirely therapeutic for its clientele. Many of the youthful offenders who were sent to such institutions, including the House of Reformation in Boston, were offspring of immigrants. Often, they rebelled when exposed to the discipline of these organizations,

child savers movement, child savers
Organized effort during early 1800s to provide assistance, including food and shelter, to wayward youth.

New York House of Refuge
Established in New York City in 1825 by the Society for the Prevention of Pauperism; managed largely status offenders, with compulsory education provided.

Society for the Prevention of Pauperism
Philanthropic society that established first reformatory in New York in 1825, the New York House of Refuge.

houses of refuge
Juvenile institutions, the first of which was established in 1825 as a means of separating juveniles from the adult correctional process.

and many of these youth eventually pursued criminal careers as a consequence. Thus, it would appear that at least some of these humanitarian and philanthropic efforts by child savers and others had adverse consequences for many affected juveniles.

Another facility with a notorious reputation for how it treated juveniles was the Western House of Refuge in Rochester, New York, which operated during the 1880s. Juvenile inmates of this facility were considered to be deviant and criminal. In reality, however, the youth institutionalized at the Western House of Refuge were primarily orphaned, abused, or neglected. Their treatment consisted of hard labor and rigid discipline. Fortunately, not all houses of refuge were like this one. In California, for instance, several houses of refuge were operated in ways that stressed vocational training, educational instruction, and some amount of aftercare when youth were ultimately released (Champion, 2008a).

Up until the late 1830s, there was little or no pattern to the division of labor between parental, religious, and state authority. As private interests continued to include larger numbers of juveniles within the scope of their supervision, various jurisdictions sought to regulate and institutionalize these assorted juvenile assistance, treatment, and/or intervention programs. In many communities, city councils sanctioned the establishment of facilities to accommodate youth who were delinquent, dependent, or neglected.

Ex Parte Crouse (1839)

In 1839, a decision in a state case gave juvenile authorities considerable power over parents in the management and control of their own children. *Ex parte Crouse* (1839) was a case involving a father who attempted to secure the release of his daughter, Mary Ann Crouse, from the Philadelphia House of Refuge. The girl had been committed to the Philadelphia facility by the court because she was considered to be unmanageable. She was not given a trial by jury, and her commitment was made arbitrarily by a presiding judge. A higher court rejected the father's claim that parental control of children is exclusive, natural, and proper, and it upheld the power of the state to exercise necessary reforms and restraints to protect children from themselves and their environments. While this decision was only applicable to Pennsylvania citizens and their children, other states took note of it and sought to invoke similar controls over errant children in their jurisdictions. Essentially, children in Pennsylvania were temporarily deprived of any legal standing to challenge decisions made by the state on their behalf.

Reform Schools and *People ex rel. O'Connell v. Turner* (1870)

Throughout the remainder of the 19th century, different types of institutions were established to supervise unruly juveniles. In roughly the mid-1800s, **reform schools** in several jurisdictions were created. One of the first state-operated reform schools was opened in Westboro, Massachusetts, in 1848, and by the end of that century, all states had reform schools of one sort or another. All of these institutions were characterized by strict discipline, absolute control over juvenile behavior, and compulsory work at

reform schools
Different types of vocational institutions designed to both punish and rehabilitate youthful offenders; operated much like prisons as total institutions.

various trades. Another common feature was that they were controversial (Coalition for Juvenile Justice, 2007).

The primary question raised by reform school critics was "Do reform schools reform?" Many juveniles continued to commit delinquent acts after being released from these schools and eventually became adult criminals, so the rehabilitative value of reform schools was seriously challenged. The Civil War exacerbated the problem of unruly youth, since many families were disrupted and children were left without fathers. Orphans of dead soldiers were commonplace in the post–Civil War period. Such children were often committed to reform schools, regardless of whether they had committed criminal offenses. Many status offenders were also sent to reform schools, simply because they were vagrants. Most of these children did not need to be reformed. Rather, they needed homes and noninstitutional care.

One state, Illinois, was particularly aggressive when it came to confining juveniles in reform schools. Many of these incarcerated juveniles were children of immigrant workers in and around Chicago, and they were often rounded up and imprisoned for simple loitering or playing in the city streets. The Chicago Reform School was especially notorious as a site where such youth were sent and confined. In 1870, however, the Illinois Supreme Court decided a case that ultimately prohibited such juvenile arrests by police and incarcerations. This was the case of *People ex rel. O'Connell v. Turner* (1870). Even so, few legal challenges to state authority were made by complaining parents, both because of the awesome power of the state and because of its control over juvenile matters. However, an Illinois case paved the way for special courts for juveniles and an early recognition of their rights.

In this case, a youth, Daniel O'Connell, was declared vagrant and in need of supervision and committed to the Chicago Reform School for an unspecified period. O'Connell's parents challenged this court action, claiming that his confinement for vagrancy was unjust and untenable. Existing Illinois law vested state authorities with the power to commit any juvenile to a state reform school as long as a "reasonable justification" could be provided. In this instance, vagrancy was a reasonable justification. The Illinois Supreme Court, however, distinguished between misfortune (vagrancy) and criminal acts in arriving at its decision to reverse Daniel O'Connell's commitment. In effect, the court nullified the law by declaring that reform school commitments of youth could not be made by the state if the "offense" was simple misfortune. The court reasoned that state interests would be better served if commitments of juveniles to reform schools were limited to those committing more serious criminal offenses rather than those who were victims of poverty. The Illinois Supreme Court further held that it was unconstitutional for youth who had not been convicted of criminal conduct or afforded legal due process to be confined in the Chicago Reform School. One result of this decision was the eventual closure of the Chicago Reform School two years later, and as one alternative to incarceration, Illinois youth without adult supervision were placed under the care of social service agencies and benevolent societies. Both individuals and groups established community residential facilities for displaced or wayward youth (Champion, 2008a).

Community-Based Private Agencies

Jane Addams
Established Hull House in Chicago in 1889; assisted wayward and homeless youth.

In 1889, **Jane Addams** established and operated Hull House in Chicago, Illinois (Addams, 1912). Hull House was a settlement home used largely by children from immigrant families in the Chicago area. In those days, adults worked long hours, and many youth were otherwise unsupervised and wandered about their neighborhoods looking for something to do. Using money from various charities and philanthropists, Addams supplied many children with creative activities to alleviate their boredom and monotony, and she integrated these activities with moral, ethical, and religious teachings in an effort to deter these youth from lives of crime.

Truancy Statutes

Truants were first created as a class of juvenile offenders in 1852 in Massachusetts, where the first compulsory school attendance statute was passed. Many other states adopted similar statutes, until all jurisdictions had compulsory school attendance provisions by 1918. Some historians have erroneously credited Colorado as having drafted the first juvenile court provisions. In fact, the Colorado legislature enacted the Compulsory School Act of 1899, the same year that the first juvenile court was established in Illinois (Reddington, 2005). The Colorado action was aimed at preventing truancy, and although Colorado legislators labeled such youth as "juvenile disorderly persons," this action did not lead to the creation of a Colorado juvenile court.

School-age youth may be truants and attract police interest.
(Courtesy of Dean John Champion)

The Illinois Juvenile Court Act

The Illinois legislature established the first juvenile court on July 1, 1899, by passing the **Act to Regulate the Treatment and Control of Dependent, Neglected, and Delinquent Children**, or the **Illinois Juvenile Court Act**. The Act provided for limited courts of record, where notes might be taken by judges or their assistants, to reflect judicial actions against juveniles. The jurisdiction of these courts, subsequently designated as **juvenile courts**, would include all juveniles under the age of 16 who were found in violation of any state or local law or ordinance. Also, provision was made for the care of dependent and/or neglected children who had been abandoned or otherwise lacked proper parental care, support, or guardianship. No minimum age was specified that would limit the jurisdiction of juvenile court judges. However, the Act provided that judges could impose secure confinement on juveniles 10 years of age or older by placing them in state-regulated juvenile facilities, such as the state reformatory or the State Home for Juvenile Female Offenders. Judges were expressly prohibited from confining any juvenile under 12 years of age in a jail or police station. Extremely young juveniles would be assigned probation officers who would look after their needs and placement on a temporary basis.

The Illinois Juvenile Court Act says much about the times and how the legal status of juveniles was interpreted and applied. The full title of the Act is revealing. According to the Act, it was applicable only to

> "...children under the age of sixteen (16) years not now or hereafter inmates of a State institution, or any training school for boys or industrial school for girls or some institution incorporated under the laws of this State, except as provided [in other sections]..." For purposes of this act the words dependent child and neglected child shall mean any child who for any reason is destitute or homeless or abandoned; or dependent upon the public for support; or has not proper parental care or guardianship; or who habitually begs or receives alms; or who is found living in any house of ill fame or with any vicious or disreputable person; or whose home, by reason of neglect, cruelty or depravity on the part of its parents, guardian or other person in whose care it may be, is an unfit place for such a child; and any child under the age of eight (8) years who is found peddling or selling any article or singing or playing any musical instrument upon the streets or giving any public entertainment. The words delinquent child shall include any child under the age of 16 years who violates any law of this State or any city or village ordinance. The word child or children may mean one or more children, and the word parent or parents may be held to mean one or both parents, when consistent with the intent of this act. The word association shall include any corporation which includes in its purposes the care or disposition of children coming within the meaning of this act.

Act to Regulate the Treatment and Control of Dependent, Neglected, and Delinquent Children, Illinois Juvenile Court Act

Passed by Illinois legislature in 1899; established the first juvenile court among the states; also known as the Illinois Juvenile Court Act.

juvenile courts

Formal proceeding with jurisdiction over juveniles, juvenile delinquents, status offenders, dependent or neglected children, children in need of supervision, or infants.

Even more insightful is what happened when such children were found. What were the limits of court sanctions? The Illinois law authorized juvenile court judges to take the following actions in their dealings with dependent and neglected children:

> When any child under the age of sixteen (16) years shall be found to be dependent or neglected within the meaning of this act, the court may make an order committing the child to the care of some suitable State institution, or to the care of some reputable citizen of good moral character, or to the care of some training school or an industrial school, as provided by law, or to the care of some association willing to receive it embracing in its objects the purpose of caring or obtaining homes for dependent or neglected children, which association shall have been accredited as hereinafter provided.

For juvenile delinquents, similar provisions were made. Judges were authorized to continue the hearing for any specific delinquent child from time to time and could commit the child to the care and guardianship of a probation officer. The child might be permitted to remain in *its* own home, subject to the visitation of the probation officer. Judges were also authorized to commit children to state training or industrial schools until such time as they reached the age of their majority or adulthood (Champion, 2008a).

Juveniles as Chattel

The choice of the word *it* shows how youth were viewed in those days. In early English times, children were considered to be chattel, lumped together with the cows, pigs, horses, and other farm property one might lawfully possess. The Illinois Juvenile Court Act itself was sufficiently ambiguous so as to allow judges and others considerable latitude or discretion about how to interpret juvenile behaviors. For example, what is meant by proper parental care or guardianship? What is habitual begging? Is occasional begging acceptable? Would children be subject to arrest and juvenile court sanctions for walking city streets playing a flute or other musical devices? Who decides what homes and establishments are unfit? Where are the criteria that describe a home's fitness? It has almost always been presumed that juvenile court judges know the answers to these questions, and their judgments, regardless of their foundation, rationality, or consistency with due process, have been and still are seldom questioned.

These statements reflect the traditionalism that juvenile court judges have manifested over the years (Campbell and Gonzalez, 2007). Taking dependent and neglected or abandoned children and placing them in training or industrial schools is the functional equivalent of adult incarceration in a prison or jail. And in 1899, the Illinois legislature gave juvenile court judges absolute control over the lives of all children under age 16 in the State of Illinois. During the next 10 years, 20 states passed similar acts to establish juvenile courts. By the end of World War II, all states had created juvenile court systems. However, considerable variation existed among these court systems, depending on the jurisdiction. Not all of these courts were vested with a consistent set of responsibilities and powers.

Children's Tribunals

Earlier versions of juvenile courts were created in Massachusetts in 1874. These included, for instance, **children's tribunals**, sometimes referred to as **civil tribunals**. These informal mechanisms were used to adjudicate and punish children charged with crimes, and they were entirely independent from the system of criminal courts for adults. Usually, judges would confer with the equivalent of a social worker and then decide how best to deal with a wayward youth. Under the tribunal system, youth were not entitled to representation by counsel, and the proceedings occurred in secret, away from public view. Furthermore, there were no formal presentations of evidence against the accused youth, no transcripts, no cross-examination of witnesses, and no right to appeal a judicial decision.

Some years later, Colorado implemented an education law in 1899 known as the **Compulsory School Act** (Shepherd, 1999). Although the Act was primarily targeted at truants, it also encompassed juveniles who wandered the streets during school hours without any obvious business or occupation. These youth were termed *juvenile disorderly persons*, and they were legislatively placed within the purview of truant officers and law enforcement officers who could detain and hold them for further action by other community agencies. While both Massachusetts and Colorado created these different mechanisms specifically for dealing with juvenile offenders, they were not juvenile courts in the same sense as those established by Illinois in 1899. Furthermore, these truancy-oriented courts are not an exclusively American creation. In England, for example, precourt tribunals have been established to decide whether families should be taken to court because of a child's nonattendance at school. The intent of such tribunals is to normalize families and destroy deviant identities juveniles might acquire because of their school absences. Both parents and children must reassure the judge that regular school attendance will be forthcoming.

Informal Welfare Agencies and Emerging Juvenile Courts

The juvenile court has evolved from an informal welfare agency into a scaled-down, second-class criminal court as the result of a series of reforms that have diverted less-serious offenders to social service agencies and moved more-serious offenders to criminal courts for processing (Feld, 2007). Several policy responses have been recommended as options. These include (1) restructuring the juvenile courts to fit their original therapeutic purposes; (2) accepting punishment as the purpose of delinquency proceedings, coupled with criminal procedural safeguards; and/or (3) abolishing juvenile courts altogether and trying young offenders in criminal courts, with certain substantive and procedural modifications.

From *Gemeinschaft* to *Gesellschaft* and Reconceptualizing Juveniles

Before the establishment of juvenile courts, how were juvenile offenders processed and punished? How were dependent and neglected children treated? Social scientists would probably describe village and community life in the 1700s and 1800s by citing the

children's tribunals, civil tribunals Informal court mechanisms originating in Massachusetts to deal with children charged with crimes apart from the system of criminal courts for adults.

Compulsory School Act An 1899 Colorado law targeting truant youth; erroneously regarded as first juvenile court act, which was actually passed in Illinois in 1899, and dealt with delinquent conduct.

gemeinschaft

Term created by Ferdinand Tonnies, a social theorist, to describe small, traditional communities where informal punishments were used to punish those who violated community laws.

dominant social and cultural values that existed then. The term *gemeinschaft* might be used here to describe the lifestyle one might find in such settings. It is a term utilized to characterize social relations which are being highly dependent upon verbal agreements and understandings and informality. Ferdinand Tonnies, a social theorist, used *gemeinschaft* to convey the richness of tradition that would typify small communities where everyone was known to all others. In these settings, formal punishments, such as incarceration in prisons or jails, were seldom used. More effective than incarceration were punishments that heightened public humiliation through stocks and pillars and other corporal measures. Sufficient social pressure was exerted so that most complied with the law. Thus, in *gemeinschaft* communities, people would probably fear social stigma, ostracism, and scorn more than loss of freedom through incarceration (Kidd, 2007).

In these communities, youth were considered to remain children through adolescence, eventually becoming adults as they began to perform trades or crafts and earned independent livings apart from their families. Children performed apprenticeships over lengthy periods under the tutorship of master craftsmen and others, and many of the terms we currently use to describe delinquent acts and status offenses were nonexistent then. As the nation grew, however, urbanization and the increasing population density of large cities changed social relationships gradually but extensively. Tonnies described the nature of this gradual shift in social relationships from a *gemeinschaft*-type of social network to a *gesellschaft*-type of society. In *gesellschaft* societies, social relationships are more formal, contractual, and impersonal, and there is greater reliance on codified compilations of appropriate and lawful conduct as a means of regulating social relations.

gesellschaft

Term created by Ferdinand Tonnies, a social theorist, to describe more formalized, larger communities and cities that relied on written documents and laws to regulate social conduct.

sweat shops

Exploitative businesses and industries that employed child labor and demanded long work hours for low pay.

As urbanization gradually occurred, the concept of children was reconceptualized. During the period of Reconstruction following the Civil War, there were no child labor laws, and children were increasingly exploited by industry and businesses. In their early years, children were put to work for low wages in factories, also known as **sweat shops**, where long hours were required and persons worked at repetitive jobs on assembly lines. By the end of the 19th century, in part because of these widespread nonunionized and unregulated sweat shop operations and compulsory school attendance for youth during their early years, loitering youth became increasingly visible and attracted the attention of the general public and law enforcement.

Specialized Juvenile Courts

Special courts were subsequently established to adjudicate juvenile matters, and the technical language describing inappropriate youthful conduct or misbehaviors was greatly expanded and refined. These new courts were also vested with the authority to appoint probation officers and other persons considered suitable to manage juvenile offenders and enforce the new juvenile codes that most cities created. Today, larger police departments have specialized juvenile units or divisions in which only juvenile law violations or suspicious activities are investigated.

In retrospect, the original aggregate of child savers had much to do with inventing delinquency and its numerous, specialized subcategories as we know them today.

At the very least, they contributed to the formality of the present juvenile justice system by defining a range of impermissible juvenile behaviors that would require an operational legal apparatus to address. Once a juvenile justice system was established and properly armed with the right conceptual tools, it was a relatively easy step to enforce a fairly rigid set of juvenile behavioral standards and regulate most aspects of youth conduct. This seems to be a part of a continuing pattern designed to criminalize the juvenile courts and hold juveniles accountable to the same standards as adult offenders (Blevins, 2005).

As juvenile court systems became more widespread, it was apparent that these proceedings were quite different from those of criminal courts in several respects. As noted above, different terms were used to distinguish delinquents from adult offenders and to recognize that this was not a criminal court (Table 2.1). Largely determined by the judge, these proceedings typically involved the juvenile charged with some offense, and a petitioner claiming the juvenile should be declared delinquent, a status offender, dependent, or neglected. The judge would weigh the evidence and decide the matter. Juveniles themselves were not provided with opportunities to solicit witnesses or even give testimony on their own behalf. Defense attorneys were largely unknown in juvenile courtrooms, since there were no significant issues to defend and the issue of guilt or innocence was not in question. The focus was on the best interests of the child.

Juvenile court proceedings were closed to the general public, primarily to protect the identities of the youth accused. However, a latent function of such secrecy was to obscure from public view the high-handed and discriminatory decision making that characterized many juvenile court judges. In short, they did not want the general public to know about the subjectivity and arbitrary nature of their decisions. On the

Table 2.1

TERMS USED WITH JUVENILE DELINQUENTS COMPARED TO ADULT OFFENDERS

Juvenile Term	Adult Term
Adjudication hearing	Trial
Adjudicated delinquent	Convicted offender
Aftercare	Parole
Commitment	Incarceration
Delinquent act	Crime
Detention	Jail
Disposition hearing	Sentencing
Petition	Indictment, charge
Take into custody	Arrest

basis of allegations alone, together with uncorroborated statements and pronouncements from probation officers and others, juvenile court judges were free to declare any particular juvenile either delinquent or nondelinquent. The penalties that could be imposed were wide-ranging, from verbal reprimands and warnings to full-fledged incarceration in a secure juvenile facility. Virtually everything depended upon the opinions and views of the presiding juvenile court judges, and their decisions were not appealable to higher courts.

Throughout much of the 20th century, juveniles had no legal standing in American courts. Their constitutional rights were not at issue, because they did not have any constitutional protections in the courtroom. No rules of evidence existed to govern the quality of evidence admitted or to challenge the reliability or integrity of testifying witnesses. In most jurisdictions, juveniles were not entitled to jury trials unless the juvenile court judge approved, and most juvenile court judges opted for bench trials rather than granting jury trials to juvenile defendants. Because these proceedings were exclusively civil in nature, the rules of criminal procedure governing criminal courts did not apply. Juveniles did not acquire criminal records; rather, they acquired civil adjudications of delinquency. Yet, the incarceration dimension of the juvenile justice system has almost always paralleled that of the criminal justice system. Industrial or training schools, reform schools, and other types of secure confinement for juveniles have generally been nothing more than juvenile prisons. Thus, for many adjudicated juvenile offenders sentenced to one of these industrial schools, these sentences were the equivalent of imprisonment.

Children and Due Process

Such unchecked discretion among juvenile court judges continued well into the 1960s. One explanation for the authority exercised by judges is mass complacency or apathy among the general public about juvenile affairs. Juvenile matters were considered to be relatively unimportant and trivial. Another explanation is the prevalent belief that juvenile court judges knew what was best for adjudicated offenders and usually prescribed appropriate punishments. Based on the ideas of *parens patriae* and judicial benevolence, juvenile court judges were trusted to act in the best interests of the child. This justified the informal juvenile court, which did not need due process rights or protections for youth.

In 1966, however, the U.S. Supreme Court raised concern about the abuse of discretion and signaled a different perspective when it determined that certain protections were necessary if a youth was transferred to criminal court. In *Kent v. United States* (1966), the Supreme Court decided that basic due process rights, including an investigation and a hearing, were essential before a youth could be transferred from juvenile court jurisdiction. While the due process only applied to waiver decisions, *Kent* was significant, because the Court acknowledged that youth needed some fundamental protection. A year later, the Court decided the case of *In re Gault* (1967) and applied more stringent standards to juvenile court judge decision making, thus making the court more accountable by ensuring due process rights.

Briefly, Gerald Gault was a 15-year-old Arizona youth who allegedly made an obscene telephone call to an adult female neighbor. The woman called police, suggested that the youth, Gault, was the guilty party, and Gault was summarily taken into custody and detained for nearly two days. The woman was never brought to court as a witness, and the only evidence she provided was her initial verbal accusation made to the police on the day of Gault's arrest. Gault himself allegedly admitted that he dialed the woman's number, but he claimed that a boyfriend of his actually spoke to the woman and made the remarks she found offensive. Partly because Gault had been involved in an earlier petty offense and had a "record," the judge, together with the probation officer, decided that Gault was dangerous enough to commit to the Arizona State Industrial School, Arizona's main juvenile penitentiary, until he reached 21 years of age or juvenile corrections authorities decided he was rehabilitated and could be safely released. According to Arizona law, the sentence was unappealable. Any adult convicted of the same offense might have been fined $50 and/or sentenced to a 30-day jail term, but in Gault's case, he received six years in a juvenile prison, complete with correctional officers carrying firearms, high walls, locked gates, and barbed wire.

Appropriately, the U.S. Supreme Court referred to the court of the judge who originally sentenced Gault as a kangaroo court. Gault's sentence was reversed, and several important constitutional rights were conferred upon all juveniles as a result. Specifically, all of Gault's due process rights had been denied. He had been denied counsel, had not been protected against self-incrimination, had not been permitted to cross-examine his accuser, and had not been provided with specific notice of the charges against him. Now, all juveniles enjoy these rights in every U.S. juvenile court.

It is important to note that Arizona was not alone in its harsh and one-sided treatment of juvenile offenders. What transpired in the *Gault* case was occurring in juvenile courts of most other jurisdictions at that time. The *Gault* case served to underscore the lack of legal standing of juveniles everywhere, and substantial juvenile justice reforms were established as a result (D'Angelo and Brown, 2005).

The Increasing Bureaucratization and Criminalization of Juvenile Justice

After the *Gault* case and other important Supreme Court decisions affecting juveniles, the nature of juvenile courts began to change. This transformation was not consistent, however, and began to reflect competing images of juvenile justice. The U.S. Supreme Court continued to view juvenile courts as basically rehabilitative and treatment-centered apparatuses, thus reinforcing the traditional doctrine within the context of various constitutional restraints. Nevertheless, episodic changes in juvenile court procedures and the juvenile justice system generally suggested that it was becoming increasingly similar to criminal courts. Furthermore, many juvenile courts moved away from traditional methods of conducting adjudicatory hearings for juveniles. Instead of individualized decision making and a rehabilitative orientation, many judges were more interested in mechanisms that streamline the processing of juvenile cases and offenders. In fact, some juvenile courts have used mathematical models to establish profiles of juvenile offenders to expedite the adjudicatory process. This has been termed **actuarial justice** by some authorities, and it means that the traditional orientation of juvenile justice and punishment has been supplanted by the goal of efficient offender processing (LaMade, 2008). In Minnesota, the development of new Rules of Procedure for Juvenile Court and the current administrative assumptions and operations of these courts, with limited exceptions, often render them indistinguishable from criminal courts and the procedures those courts follow.

Measuring Juvenile Delinquency: The *Uniform Crime Reports* and *National Crime Victimization Survey*

Two official sources of information for both adult and juvenile crime are the *Uniform Crime Reports* and the *National Crime Victimization Survey.*

Uniform Crime Reports

The *Uniform Crime Reports (UCR)* has been published annually since 1930 by the Federal Bureau of Investigation (FBI) in Washington, DC. The *UCR* is a compilation of arrests for different offenses according to several time intervals. Periodic reports of arrests are issued quarterly to interested law enforcement agencies. All rural and urban law enforcement agencies are requested, on a voluntary basis, to submit statistical information about 29 different offenses. Most of these agencies submit arrest information. Thus, the *UCR* represents over 15,000 law enforcement agencies throughout the United States.

Crime in the *UCR* is classified into two major categories, Part I offenses and Part II offenses. Part I offenses, also known as **index offenses**, are considered to be the most serious, and eight serious felonies are listed. These include murder and nonnegligent manslaughter, forcible rape, robbery, aggravated assault, burglary, larceny-theft, motor vehicle theft, and arson. Table 2.2 presents the eight major index offenses and their definitions.

These eight major offenses are classified as felonies. **Felonies** are violations of criminal laws that are punishable by terms of imprisonment of one year or longer in state or federal prisons or penitentiaries. These offenses are also known as index offenses, because they provide readers with a sample of key or **index crimes** that can be charted quarterly or annually, according to different jurisdictions and demographic and socioeconomic dimensions (e.g., city size, age, race, gender, and urban–rural). Thus, the crime categories listed are not intended to be an exhaustive compilation. However, it is possible to review these representative crime categories to obtain a general picture of trends across years or other desired time segments.

The *UCR* also lists a second group of offenses known as Part II offenses. These include misdemeanors and status offenses, such as embezzlement, stolen property, vandalism, carrying weapons, drug abuse violations, sex offenses, driving under the influence, liquor law violations, vagrancy, suspicion, curfew and loitering violations, runaway behavior, and disorderly conduct (Henry and Kobus, 2007). A **misdemeanor** is a

Table 2.2
UNIFORM CRIME REPORT, PART I: CRIMES AND THEIR DEFINITION

Crime	Definition
Murder and nonnegligent manslaughter	Willful (nonnegligent) killing of one human being by another
Forcible rape	Carnal knowledge of a female, forcibly and against her will; assaults or attempts to commit rape by force or threat of force are included
Robbery	Taking or attempting to take anything of value from the care, custody, or control of a person or persons by force or threat of force or violence and/or by putting the victim in fear
Aggravated assault	Unlawful attack by one person upon another for the purpose of inflicting severe or aggravated bodily injury
Burglary	Unlawful entry into a structure to commit a felony or theft
Larceny-theft	Unlawful taking, carrying, leading, or riding away of property from the possession or constructive possession of another, including shoplifting, pocket picking, purse snatching, and thefts of motor vehicle parts or accessories
Motor vehicle theft	Theft or attempted theft of a motor vehicle, including automobiles, trucks, buses, motor scooters, and snowmobiles
Arson	Any willful or malicious burning or attempt to burn, with or without intent to defraud, a dwelling house, public building, motor vehicle, or aircraft and the personal property of another

Source: U.S. Department of Justice, Federal Bureau of Investigation (2009). *Crime in the United States, 2008.* Washington, DC: U.S. Government Printing Office.

violation of criminal laws that is punishable by an incarcerative term of less than one year in city or county jails. Status offenses listed, including runaway behavior, truancy, and violation of curfew, are not considered to be crimes, although they are reported together with criminal offenses to give a more complete picture of arrest activity throughout the United States. The offenses listed are not an exhaustive compilation. Rather, a sample listing of crimes based on arrests is provided.

As Hagan (2011) explains, understanding crime trends is more useful for comparative purposes if the data are reported as rates rather than as number of offenses. The **crime rate** is a statistic that presents the total number of crimes per 100,000 population (Hagan, 2011, p. 31). The formula for calculating rates is

$$\text{crime/population} \times 100,000 = \text{crime rate}$$

Since the crime rate controls for population size, examining crime rates for different cities or states, or between different years when populations may increase or decrease, allows reasonable comparisons. For example, the number of arrests for aggravated assault in the United States in 2010 was 778,901; in Washington, DC, the number was 3,360.

misdemeanor

Crime punishable by confinement in city or county jail for a period of less than one year; a lesser offense.

crime rate

Statistic that presents the total number of crimes per 100,000 population.

National Crime Victimization Survey (NCVS)

Published in cooperation with the U.S. Bureau of the Census; a random survey of 60,000 households, including 127,000 persons 12 years of age or older; includes 50,000 businesses; measures crime committed against specific victims interviewed and not necessarily reported to law enforcement officers.

victimization

Basic measure of the occurrence of a crime; a specific criminal act affecting a specific victim.

incident

Specific criminal act involving one crime and one or more victims.

cleared by arrest

Term used by the Federal Bureau of Investigation in the *Uniform Crime Reports (UCR)* to indicate that someone has been arrested for a reported crime; does not necessarily mean that the crime has been solved or that the actual criminals who committed the crime have been apprehended or convicted.

Obviously, the population of the United States in 2010 (308,745,538) was larger than the population in Washington, DC (601,723). Using the arrest rates for aggravated assaults allows comparisons of one city to the United States. In this example for 2010, the rate of aggravated assault in the United States was 252.3 per 100,000 population, compared to 558.4 per 100,000 in Washington, DC (The Disaster Center, 2011). Similarly, in Massachusetts, with a 2010 population of 6,547,629, the aggravated assault crime rate was 331.8 per 100,000. In comparison, Massachusetts with a population more than 10 times that of Washington, DC, has a lower rate of aggravated assault.

National Crime Victimization Survey

Compared with the *UCR*, the ***National Crime Victimization Survey (NCVS)*** is conducted annually by the U.S. Bureau of the Census. It is a random survey of approximately 60,000 dwellings, about 127,000 youth aged 12 and over, and approximately 50,000 businesses. Subsamples of persons are questioned by interviewers who compile information about crime victims. Those interviewed are asked whether they have had different types of crime committed against them during the past six months to one year. Through statistical analysis, the amount of crime throughout the general population can be estimated (Champion, 2008a).

The *NCVS* provides information about criminal victimizations and incidents. **Victimization** is a basic measure of the occurrence of a crime and is a specific criminal act that affects a single victim. An **incident** is a specific criminal act that may involve one or more victims. Because the *NCVS* reflects an amount of crime allegedly perpetrated against a large sample of victims, it is believed to be more accurate as a national crime estimate than the *UCR*. Thus, whenever comparisons of crime from the *UCR* are made against the *NCVS*, the *NCVS* reports between two to four times the amount of crime as indicated by the official law enforcement agency arrest figures in the *UCR*.

Strengths of These Measures

One strength of these indicators of crime in the United States is the sheer numbers of offenses reported. Few alternative sources of information about crime in the United States exhibit such voluminous reporting. In addition, regional and seasonal reports of criminal activity are provided. The *UCR* also reports the proportion of different types of crime that are **cleared by arrest**, meaning that someone has been arrested and charged with a particular crime. Another favorable feature of both the *UCR* and the *NCVS* is that numbers of arrests and reported crimes can be compared across years. Therefore, the *UCR* reports percentage increases or decreases in the amount of different types of crime for many jurisdictions and over various time periods. And although the *NCVS* does not purport to survey all crime victims, the randomness inherent in the selection of the target respondents is such that generalizations about the U.S. population are considered to be reasonably valid.

A primary advantage of the *NCVS* over the *UCR* is that victims offer interviewers information about crimes committed against them. In many instances, these respondents disclose that they did not report these crimes to police. The reasons for not reporting crimes to police vary, although these victims often believe that the police cannot do much about their victimization anyway. Rape victims may be too embarrassed to report these incidents, or they may feel that they were partially to blame. Furthermore, in some of these cases, family members or close friends may be the perpetrators, and victims may be reluctant to press criminal charges.

Weaknesses of These Measures

Certain limitations of the *UCR* and *NCVS* are well documented. Focusing upon the *UCR* first, we may cite some of the more important weaknesses of these statistics. For instance, the *UCR* figures do not provide an annual per capita measure of crime frequency. Because law enforcement agencies are not compelled to submit annual information to the FBI, some agencies fail to report their arrest activity, and those that do may fail to report crime uniformly. Also, crimes of the same name vary in definition among jurisdictions. In North Dakota, for instance, "rape" is not listed as a crime; rather, it is called "gross sexual imposition." This conceptual variation in how identical offenses are labeled among the states frustrates efforts by the FBI and others to track different types of crimes accurately and consistently.

The *UCR* only reports arrests, not the actual amount of crime. In addition, when arrests are reported in the *UCR*, only the most serious offenses are often reported. Thus, if a robbery suspect is apprehended, he or she may possess burglary tools, a concealed weapon, and stolen property and may have caused physical injuries to victims. All of these events are crimes, but only the robbery—the most serious offense—will be reported to the FBI. Therefore, there is much basis for the belief that these official reports of crime are, at best, underestimates. Arrest activity in the *UCR* may then be attributable to fluctuations in police activity rather than actual fluctuations in criminal activity. Finally, although they only make up a fraction of national criminal activity, federal crimes are not reported in the *UCR*.

Both the *NCVS* and the *UCR* overemphasize street crimes and underemphasize corporate or white-collar crimes. Self-reported information contained in the *NCVS* is often unreliable. Sometimes, for example, victims interviewed may not be able to identify certain actions against them as crimes. For instance, date rapes may be reported as assaults. Also, persons may not be able to remember clearly certain criminal events. Fear of reprisals from criminals may compel some victims not to disclose their victimizations to interviewers, and some victimization data reported in the *NCVS* may be either exaggerated or more liberally reported. For various reasons, interviewees may lie to interviewers in disclosing details of crimes committed against them.

Despite these criticisms, the *UCR* and *NCVS* provide valuable data for interested professionals. The fact that virtually all law enforcement agencies rely to some extent on these annual figures as valid indicators of criminal activity in the United States suggests that their utility in this regard is invaluable. Supplementing this information are other, more detailed, reports of selected offense activity. The U.S. Department of Justice's Bureau of Justice Statistics publishes a tremendous amount of information annually about different dimensions of crime and offender characteristics and behavior.

This supplemental information, together with the data provided by the *UCR* and *NCVS*, may be combined to furnish a more complete picture of crime in the United States. Several alternative data sources are discussed in the following section.

Additional Sources

National Juvenile Court Data Archive
Compendium of national statistical information and databases about juvenile delinquency.

One of the best compendiums of data specifically about juveniles and juvenile court adjudications is the **National Juvenile Court Data Archive**. When the federal government began collecting data pertaining to juveniles in 1926, the data were dependent upon the voluntary completion of statistical forms by juvenile courts in a limited number of U.S. jurisdictions. Today, however, the National Juvenile Court Data Archive contains over 800,000 annual automated case records of juveniles in various states. Numerous data sets are currently available to researchers and may be accessed for investigative purposes. These data sets are nonuniform, although they ordinarily contain information such as age at referral, gender, race, county of residence, offense(s) charged, date of referral, processing characteristics of the case (e.g., incarceration and manner of handling), and the disposition of the case (Champion, 2009).

In 1975, however, the Office of Juvenile Justice and Delinquency Prevention (OJJDP) assumed responsibility for the National Juvenile Court Data Archive, which it now runs in addition to publishing periodic reports of juvenile offenses and adjudicatory outcomes. Today, the OJJDP publishes periodic compilations of current juvenile offender data in a statistical briefing book, summarizing important delinquency statistics and trends. Every few years, the OJJDP also publishes a comprehensive summary of juvenile justice information in a national report, *Juvenile Offenders and Victims* (OJJDP, 2007).

The Sourcebook of Criminal Justice Statistics
Compendium of statistical information about juvenile and adult offenders; court facts, statistics, and trends; probation and parole figures; and considerable additional information; published annually by the Hindelang Criminal Justice Research Center at the University of Albany, SUNY; funded by grants from the U.S. Department of Justice, Bureau of Justice Statistics.

Another compendium of offender characteristics of all ages is *The Sourcebook of Criminal Justice Statistics* published annually by the Hindelang Criminal Justice Research Center and supported by grants from the U.S. Department of Justice. This is perhaps the most comprehensive source currently available, since it accesses numerous governmental documents and reports annually to keep readers abreast of the latest crime figures. Among other things, it describes justice system employment and spending, jail and prison management and prisoner issues, judicial misconduct and complaints, correctional officer characteristics, crime victim characteristics and victimization patterns, delinquent behavior patterns and trends, and considerable survey information. Numerous tables of data are presented that summarize much of the information reported by various private and governmental agencies. Useful annotated information is also provided to supplement the tabular material.

Statistics pertaining to juvenile offenders include juvenile admissions and discharges from public and private incarcerative facilities, average length of stay by juveniles in these facilities, a profile of the juvenile custody facilities, demographic information about juveniles detained for lengthy terms, criminal history or prior records of juveniles, illegal drug and alcohol use among juveniles, waiver information, and offense patterns according to socioeconomic and demographic factors. Each annual sourcebook is somewhat different from those published in previous years, although much of the material in subsequent editions has been updated from previous years.

Self-Report Information

While these official sources of crime and delinquency are quite useful, a common criticism is that they tend to underestimate the amount of offense behaviors that actually occur in the United States. As a result, those interested in studying juvenile offense behaviors have frequently relied upon data derived from self-reports. The **self-report** is a data collection method involving an unofficial survey of youth or adults in which the intent is to obtain information about specific types of behavior not ordinarily disclosed through traditional data collection methods, including questionnaires, interviews, polls, official agency reports, or sociodemographic summaries. This information is called **self-report information**. Self-report surveys are believed to be more accurate and informative compared with official sources of crime and delinquency information.

The exact origin of the use of self-reports is unknown. However, in 1943, Austin L. Porterfield investigated **hidden delinquency**, or delinquency neither detected by nor reported to police. Surveying several hundred college students, he asked them to disclose whether they had ever engaged in delinquent acts. While all of the students reported that they had previously engaged in delinquent acts, most also reported that they had not been caught by police or brought to the attention of the juvenile court (Porterfield, 1943).

In 1958, James Short and Ivan Nye conducted the first self-report study of a delinquent population. They obtained self-report information from hundreds of delinquents in several Washington State training schools, then compared this information with self-report data from hundreds of students in three Washington State communities and three Midwestern towns. Their findings revealed that delinquency was widespread and not specific to any social class. Furthermore, both seriousness and frequency of juvenile offending were key determinants of juvenile court treatment of youthful offenders and public policy relating to delinquents (Short and Nye, 1958).

Generally, self-report studies accomplish two important research objectives: (1) describing and understanding behavior and (2) predicting behavior. Self-report information provides considerable enriching details about persons under a variety of circumstances and furnishes important descriptive information about what people think and do. Such descriptions include how persons were treated as children and the events that were most significant to them as they grew to adulthood. The more that is learned about the significant occurrences in a child's life, the better the predictive schemes to explain present—and to forecast future—behaviors. Self-reports, therefore, are an important source of information for descriptive and theoretical purposes, and from a theoretical standpoint, self-reports represent one important means of theory verification.

Some of the popular self-report surveys conducted annually are the *National Youth Survey* and the *Monitoring the Future Survey*. These are large-scale surveys of high-school students that focus upon particular behaviors. In addition, the Institute

self-report, self-report information

A survey of youth (or adults) based upon disclosures these persons might make about the types of offenses they have committed and how frequently they have committed them; considered to be more accurate than official estimates.

hidden delinquency

Infractions reported by surveys of high-school youth; considered to be "hidden" because it most often is undetected by police officers; disclosed delinquency through self-report surveys.

National Youth Survey

Study of large numbers of youth annually or at other intervals to assess extent of delinquency among high-school students.

Monitoring the Future Survey

Study of 3,000 high-school students annually by the Institute for Social Research at the University of Michigan; attempts to discover hidden delinquency not ordinarily disclosed by published public reports.

for Social Research at the University of Michigan annually solicits information from a national sample of 3,000 high-school students. These informative reports are frequently cited in the research literature, which attests to the integrity, reliability, and validity of this information among noted juvenile justice professionals.

These national surveys involve administering confidential questionnaires and checklists to high-school students. Students are asked to indicate which behaviors they have engaged in during the past six months or the previous year. Although considered to be unofficial sources of information about delinquency and delinquency patterns, these self-disclosures are thought by many professionals to be a more accurate reflection of delinquent behaviors than official sources, such as the *UCR*—assuming that their responses are truthful. Ordinarily, simple checklists are given to students, and they are asked to identify those behaviors they have done, not necessarily those for which they have been apprehended. An example of such a checklist is shown in Table 2.3.

Table 2.3
SAMPLE SELF-REPORT QUESTIONS FROM THE *NATIONAL YOUTH SURVEY*

On how many DAYS did you use any marijuana in the LAST MONTH (30 days)?

[ ] None

[ ] 1 or 2 days in the last month

[ ] 3 to 5 days in the last month

[ ] 6 to 9 days in the last month

[ ] 10 to 19 days in the last month

[ ] 20 to 31 days in the last month

On the days you use marijuana, how many times did you use it?

[ ] Once a day

[ ] Twice a day

[ ] 3 or more times a day

[ ] I don't use marijuana

Have you EVER TRIED marijuana?

[ ] Yes

[ ] No

Do you think your best friend uses marijuana sometimes?

[ ] Yes

[ ] No

Source: National Youth Survey, U.S. Department of Health and Human Services. OMB no. 0930. (Available at http://www.emt.org/userfiles/NYS_Baseline_12-18_Version.pdf.)

Self-reports also enable researchers to determine whether offending patterns among juveniles are changing over time. Substantial self-report information exists that characterizes violent juvenile offenders and catalogs the many potential causal factors that are associated with violence, such as gang involvement (Daigle, Cullen, and Wright, 2007). Self-reported data about juvenile offenses suggest that a sizeable gap exists between official reports of delinquent conduct and information disclosed through self-reports.

Self-reports reveal much more delinquency than is reported by either the *UCR* or the *NCVS*. However, since the *NCVS* information is also a form of self-disclosure, some investigators have found greater compatibility between delinquency self-reporting and the *NCVS* than between delinquency self-reporting and the *UCR,* which reports only arrest information. In any case, self-reports of delinquency or status offense conduct have caused researchers to refer to these undetected offending behaviors as hidden delinquency.

Some investigators question whether self-report information is reliable. Do youth tell the truth about their conduct, whatever the reported behavior? Some reported information is more easily refuted or confirmed by independent means. In the cases of illicit alcohol, tobacco, or drug use, independent tests may be conducted to determine the veracity of self-report information. In one school district, for instance, over 50 percent of all high-school students interviewed disclosed through self-reports that they smoked. Subsequent analyses of saliva specimens from the same students, however, revealed that less than 10 percent of them tested positive for tobacco use. For reasons unknown to the researchers, about half of the high school students reported that they used tobacco when most of them, in fact, did not. Were they bragging? Was this peer pressure in action? In view of the evidence, this is the strong implication.

The relationship between early childhood and the onset of status offending or delinquency has been heavily investigated using this method (Bowman, Prelow, and Weaver, 2007). Typically, parent–child association and attachment are linked with delinquent conduct (Beaver, Wright, and Delisi, 2007). Samples of delinquents and nondelinquents are asked to provide self-reports of their early upbringing, including their perceived closeness with parents and the disciplinary methods used to sanction misconduct. For instance, the etiology of delinquency as related to different family processes according to race/ethnicity has been studied. Does a sample of inner-city, high-risk youth reflect important differences in family processes according to race/ethnicity?

Information about runaways is almost exclusively determined from self-report studies. For example, it has been found that runaways, compared with other types of status offenders, have greater levels of family violence, rejection, and sexual abuse. Not unexpectedly, at least based upon self-report experiences, runaways were from families where there was less parental monitoring of juvenile behavior, warmth, and supportiveness (Chen, Thrane, and Whitbeck, 2007).

In a more general analysis of early childhood experiences involving adolescent maltreatment and its link with delinquency, self-reports have disclosed that some youth who are violent as adults have histories of maltreatment from family members

(Lemmon and Verrecchia, 2009; Mersky and Reynolds, 2007). Lemmon and Verrecchia (2009), for example, concluded that the effects of childhood maltreatment on subsequent delinquency and aggression were affected by the "duration, frequency, and severity of the maltreatment" (p. 141). Child maltreatment is generally classified into "physical abuse, sexual abuse, psychological abuse, and neglect" (Lemmon and Verrecchia, 2009, p. 134). While the research is not consistent, the maltreatment–delinquency relationship is indicative of the concept of risk factors, which are predictive, but not absolute, in explaining delinquency.

CAREER SNAPSHOT

(Courtesy of Peter J. Benekos)

Name: Amy C. Eisert
Position: Director, Mercyhurst Civic Institute

Colleges Attended: Bowling Green State University, Mercyhurst College, and Capella University

Degrees: B.S in Criminal Justice, M.S. in Administration of Justice, and A.B.D. in Human Services–Criminal Justice

Background

I knew that I always wanted to explore a career in the juvenile justice field, and my dislike toward math assisted in pushing me into a social science field. I never realized that I would later find the perfect career as a "data geek." I received my Bachelor's of Science from Bowling Green State University in Criminal Justice with a minor in Sociology and a Master's of Science in Administration of Justice from Mercyhurst College. I am currently a doctoral candidate at Capella University working toward a Ph.D. in Human Services, specializing in criminal justice.

When I graduated with my undergraduate degree, I knew I had an interest in working with youth but did not know where to begin. I had been offered opportunities to continue my education through graduate school; however, not knowing what exactly my specific interests were, I held off on pursing my higher education and decided to take a more colorful path entering the workforce. I started off as a residential counselor at a residential treatment facility. After two years of seeing youth revolving through the residential door, I felt I could have a greater impact working earlier on the continuum before home care, so I received training and started work as a family-based mental health therapist, working with youth and their families in their home settings. Through my work as a family therapist, I came to understand the struggles of some parents and families in seeking help from systems for their troubled youth. This led me to take on a position creating and implementing a new program for incorrigible youth. While working in the new incorrigible program, I recognized inefficiencies in programming, policies, and practices that I could neither prove nor disprove due to lack of data. It is at this time that I returned to school to pursue my master's degree, which led me to finding my niche as a research analyst.

As a research analyst, and now the director of a research institute, it is my job to promote data-driven decision making, support cost-effective strategies, develop and track program outcomes, and facilitate collaborative efforts within my community. Many times, I take an advisory role in the identification, implementation, and evaluation of new programming, policies, and practices as well as work to strengthen existing programming. With funding constraints on prevention and other youth programming, my role adds accountability to services, assuring that the programming dollars are being well spent. In addition, I often assume the role as facilitator, working not only with the juvenile justice system but with all interrelated fields, including the criminal justice system, drug and alcohol, child welfare, health, mental health, and education. It is my job to promote cross-system collaboration, because the most efficient systems work to build off of the strengths of others.

Advice to Students

My advice for current undergraduate students would be to recognize that learning is an ongoing and interactive process. Make a point to draw from every interaction that you have with every person you encounter, whether it be a youth, a parent, a professor, another student, your own family, or anyone else. Embrace your personality, and utilize it as a tool in working with others. Whether you are working at a desk or in the community, building relationships is instrumental. Accept that your reality and view of the world is based off of your own experiences that may not be the same as those of others. I would encourage students to take the colorful path. Take advantage of any opportunities through internships, service learning, and volunteering. Those experiences not only increase the length and quality of your resume, they enhance your human experience in working with others, which will be the key to your success regardless of your field of work.

School violence is an increasingly important topic of discussion among parents, school officials, and juvenile justice professionals (Choi, 2007; Lawrence, 2009). Although the media suggest that school violence is pervasive, the sensationalism attached to school shootings does not accurately represent the extent of this violence (Slater, Hayes, and Ford, 2007). In 1998, for example, 1,960 victims of murder in the United States were under the age of 18. Of these, 43 victims (2 percent) were school-associated deaths (Lawrence, 2009; Snyder and Sickmund, 1999). Of 1,748 total homicides in the 2006–2007 school year, 30 (1.7 percent) were recorded as school homicides (Dinkes, Kemp, and Baum, 2009).

In summary, self-reports of crime and delinquency are a valuable source of information to researchers. Research projects with exploratory, descriptive, and/or experimental study objectives benefit from the use of self-report data. Descriptions of different types of delinquents and the development of useful intervention strategies for delinquency prevention have been assisted greatly by the use of self-reports. The broad application of self-reports in virtually every facet of criminology and criminal justice suggests the long-term application of this data collection method.

Violence and Nonviolence: Career Escalation?

How much violent crime is committed by juveniles? Are juveniles likely to escalate to more serious offenses during their youthful years as they become more deeply involved in delinquent conduct? Are certain kinds of juvenile offenders more or less susceptible to intervention programs and treatments as means of reducing or eliminating their propensity to engage in delinquent conduct? Are schools new battle zones for gang warfare and other forms of violence? Certainly, the media have heightened our awareness about the presence—and violence—of youth gangs in various cities (Crooks et al., 2007). Startling information about extensive drug and alcohol use among juveniles is frequently broadcasted or reported (West, 2005). Is there currently an unstoppable juvenile crime wave throughout the United States?

School Violence

Violence among schoolchildren in the United States has received increased attention in recent years and is a serious problem in other countries as well. The media suggest that school violence is pervasive (Slater, Hayes, and Ford, 2007). In Miami, Florida, for example, high-school students have reported both serious and frequent victimization. In many of these reports, dangerous weapons, such as firearms, were used to effect the victimization (Schexnayder, 2008). There are many explanations for school violence, ranging from psychological explanations (attention-deficit/hyperactivity disorder, or ADHD) to sociological (peer group association or need for group recognition) to biological (glandular malfunction) (Bratina, 2008; Hinduja, Patchin, and Lippman, 2008).

Fortunately, school violence is seldom fatal. In 2007, students ranging in age from 12 to 18 were victims of about 235,000 incidents of nonfatal, serious, violent crimes in their schools. Outside of school, 720,000 similar incidents involved this age group. During the period from 2003 to 2007, more than half (56 percent) of all public schools reported either a serious violent crime (e.g., murder or rape), or a less-serious violent crimes (e.g., assault) to the police (OJJDP, 2007). In many instances, bullying behavior has also been reported as school violence, although psychological rather than physical harm is more often inflicted through bullying behavior compared with assaultive behavior that might result in student injuries (Brewer, 2008; Dussich and Maekoya, 2007; Estell, Farmer, and Cairns, 2007).

A general response to school violence throughout the United States has led to the development of several aggressive policy changes. School systems have trained teachers and students how to react in ways that will rapidly contain potentially serious school violence. Special response police forces are being trained to be more effective in providing ancillary support for school administrators and staff. Intensive prevention training for all involved parties, after-school academic enrichment programs, enforcement of and punishment for firearms possession and drug use/sales on campus, and developing a standardized system of early detection and assessment of at-risk students are being implemented on a national basis (Pires and Jenkins, 2007). Evidence of the success of these initiatives is the dramatic reduction in school violence between 1996

Focus on Delinquency

It happened on January 19, 2007. John Odgren, 16, a student at Lincoln–Sudbury Regional High School in Cambridge, Massachusetts, followed a fellow student, James Alenson, 15, into the school bathroom. Odgren was a special needs student who did not know Alenson, had never been teased by Alenson, had never been shunned by Alenson, and didn't even know his name. When inside the bathroom with Alenson, Odgren attacked Alenson with a sharp knife, slashing his throat and stabbing him through the heart and abdomen. Alenson stumbled into the hallway and collapsed. A third student in one of the bathroom stalls heard everything, including Alenson saying, "What are you doing? You are hurting me." The student followed Odgren into the hallway, where he saw Odgren stoop over Alenson and check his pulse. Odgren turned, saw the other student, and then exclaimed, "I did it. I just snapped. I don't know why." Following his arrest by police, Odgren appeared in a Middlesex Superior Court and pleaded not guilty to first-degree murder. Odgren was ordered to a state hospital for a 20-day evaluation. In the meantime, it was learned that Odgren was prone to explosive episodes, was verbally abusive, and at times became physically aggressive against his parents, teachers, and specialists. He had been formerly placed in an alternative

school, Caldwell Alternative School, in Fitchburg, Massachusetts, in 2002. At age 12, Odgren had been diagnosed as a highly intelligent but troubled preadolescent with poor social skills. He had a hyperactivity disorder and Asperger's disorder, a mild form of autism. Several specialists familiar with Asperger's disorder claim that those with such a condition are no more prone toward violence than others. While at the alternative school, Odgren was suspended three times for undisclosed explosive episodes including physical aggression. Officials refused to elaborate, citing student confidentiality. In the meantime, Odgren's parents told the media that their son needed training in social skills but never received such training. Prosecutors sought to try Odgren on first-degree murder charges as an adult. Should the juvenile court have jurisdiction over this case? Who is to blame for Alenson's death? Are Massachusetts authorities at fault for placing a disturbed youth such as Odgren in a normal high-school environment where he could pose a threat to others?

Source: Adapted from Jesse Harlan Alderman (2007, March 6), "Massachusetts Stabbing Victim Chosen Randomly," *Boston.com* (available at http://www.boston.com/news/nation/articles/2007/03/06/mass_stabbing_victim_chosen_randomly/).

and 2007. One of the contributing factors to this decline has been the establishment of a zero-tolerance policy in many school systems, which imposes more stringent penalties on youthful offenders who bring dangerous weapons to their schools (Schexnayder, 2008).

At-Risk Youth and the Pittsburgh Youth Study

Who are at-risk youth? **At-risk youth** are often those who suffer from one or more disadvantages, such as lower socioeconomic status, dysfunctional family conditions, poor school performance, learning or language disabilities, negative peer influences, and/or low self-esteem (Abbott-Chapman, Denholm, and Wyld, 2007; Owens-Sabir, 2007). It is difficult to forecast which youth will become delinquent and which will not. For many decades, researchers have attempted to profile so-called at-risk youth by assigning to them various characteristics that seem to be associated with hard-core delinquents (Busseri, Willoughby, and Chalmers, 2007). In 1986, investigators began a longitudinal study of 1,517 inner-city boys from Pittsburgh, Pennsylvania. The Pittsburgh Youth Study followed three samples of boys for over a decade to determine how and why boys became involved in delinquent and other problem behaviors (Browning and Loeber, 1999, p. 1). Boys were randomly selected from the first, fourth, and seventh grades and then tracked over time.

Eventually, three developmental pathways were defined that display progressively more serious problem behaviors. The first pathway, authority conflict, involves youth who exhibit stubbornness before age 12 and then they move on to defiance and avoidance of authority. The second pathway, covert, includes minor covert acts, such as lying, followed by property damage and moderately serious delinquency and then serious delinquency. The third pathway, overt, starts with minor aggression, followed by fighting and violence. Risk factors identified and associated with delinquency among the Pittsburgh youth include impulsivity; IQ; personality; forces in an individual's environment, including parents, siblings, and peers; and factors related to family, school, and neighborhood (Bowman, Prelow, and Weaver, 2007).

Specifically, at-risk youth in the Pittsburgh Youth Study tended to have greater impulsivity, lower IQ, and a lower threshold for experiencing negative emotions, such as fear, anxiety, and anger. These youth were also more inclined to be involved in thrill-seeking and acting without caution. Family risk factors included poor supervision by parents, family receipt of public assistance (welfare), and lower socioeconomic status. The greatest demographic variable associated with delinquency was having a broken family. Living in a bad neighborhood doubled the risk for delinquency.

These aggregate data are interesting, but they fail to enable researchers to forecast with accuracy which youth will become delinquent and which ones will not. Maybe this is too much to ask without more definitive criteria for identifying potential juvenile offenders. Nevertheless, a profile of at-risk youth has been generated to the extent that various intervention programs can be attempted in certain jurisdictions. The theory is that if at-risk youth can be identified according to proven prior characteristics derived from delinquency research, then perhaps one or more interventions

At-risk youth
Any juvenile considered to be more susceptible to the influence of gangs and delinquent peers; characterized as those who have learning disabilities, greater immaturity, lower socioeconomic status, and parental dysfunction and are otherwise disadvantaged by their socioeconomic and environmental circumstances.

can be attempted with some or all of those youth who are at risk. Many interventions attempted are flawed in different ways, however. Thus, much more research is needed to establish truly effective interventions that make a difference in affecting a youth's future behavior (Case, 2007).

Juvenile courts have utilized various types of interventions involving at-risk youth (Barnes, 2005). Since the mid-1970s, the National Council of Juvenile and Family Court Judges has sought to focus national attention on abused and neglected children. Youth placed in foster care and/or suffering from various forms of sexual or physical abuse in their families are considered to be at-risk and in need of special treatment from various social services. It has been found, for instance, that one strategy for assisting at-risk youth is to educate family and juvenile court judges in ways to improve their court practices (Adoption and Foster Care Analysis and Reporting System, 2008). The National Council of Juvenile and Family Court Judges has also established the Permanency Planning for Children Department, with 17 Model Courts in at least 16 states. These Model Courts have implemented a number of programs to deal with at-risk youth and their families. Such programs can easily be replicated in other jurisdictions. For instance, court calendars are generated to ensure that judicial decision makers are assigned to specific dependency cases and will remain on those cases until the children involved achieve permanence, either by being safely reunited with their families or by being placed in permanent adoptive homes. Family group conferencing and mediation programs are also incorporated into several of these Model Court jurisdictions. Proper handling of cases involving these types of at-risk youth tends to decrease the likelihood that placed youth will become delinquent in the future. Family group conferencing has been extended to many states, including Indiana (McGarrell and Kroovand-Hipple, 2007).

Gang Violence

gangs

Groups who form an allegiance for a common purpose and engage in unlawful or criminal activity; any group gathered together on a continuing basis to engage in or commit antisocial behavior.

Juvenile justice professionals are interested in the increased incidence of gang formation and membership behavior. **Gangs** and the gang phenomenon are widespread throughout the United States. Street gangs are evident in suburban and rural communities as well as in major urban centers. The National Gang Center reported that 32 percent of all communities experienced gang problems in 2008 (Egley, Howell, and Moore, 2010).

Generally, gangs tend to organize along racial or ethnic lines, often for mutual protection against other gangs. The gang problem in the United States is increasing, and despite many intervention and prevention efforts, youth gangs have proliferated since 1980 (Taylor et al., 2008). In 1980, for instance, there were 2,000 gangs in 286 jurisdictions, with over 100,000 gang members. By 2007, there were more than 34,500 gangs in 5,380 jurisdictions, with over 1.5 million gang members (OJJDP, 2007). While remaining both widespread and prevalent, the number of active gangs and gang members reportedly declined during the period from 2007 to 2008. In 2008, a total of 27,990 gangs and 774,000 gang members were estimated to be active. For the period from 2002 to 2008, however, these figures represent a 28 percent increase in the number of gangs and a six percent increase in gang members (Egley, Howell, and Moore, 2010).

While national trend data are not definitive concerning female gang members and the types of offenses they commit, independent investigations of selected jurisdictions suggest that the number of female gangs in the United States is also increasing (Graves, 2007). About eight percent of all gang members are female, and studies suggest that they join gangs for the same reasons males join gangs but generally leave gangs at an earlier age than males (Esbensen et al., 2008).

Kids Who Kill

Juveniles who commit homicide are relatively rare (Haynie, Steffensmeier, and Bell, 2007). Of the 17,000 homicide offenders reported by the *UCR* in 2007, only 1,200 (7 percent) of these involved juveniles under age 18 (OJJDP, 2007). Some juveniles begin their careers of gang violence, including murder and attempted murder, as early as age six. An increasing amount of youth violence, including homicide, is linked to gang membership (Marriott, 2007). Actually, according to the *National Youth Gang Survey Analysis* (National Gang Center, n.d.), two cities, Los Angeles and Chicago, are responsible for approximately one-third of the gang-related murders.

Apart from gang-related murders, many youth kill one or more of their family members, such as their mothers or fathers. Studies of youth who kill their parents show that these youth are often severely physically or sexually abused and that they are particularly sensitive to stressors in the home environment. Many juvenile murderers have chemical dependencies for which they require treatment. Juvenile murderers also exhibit greater psychotic and conduct disorder symptoms compared with other types of juvenile offenders (Titterington and Grundies, 2007).

Some murders committed by juveniles are sexually motivated and occur when victims threaten to tell others, but even something as specific as sexually motivated juvenile murder is misunderstood by the public (Hensley, Tallichet, and Singer, 2005). A wide variety of reasons is provided for explaining or rationalizing adolescent murders, although any excuse is rarely accepted as mitigating. One frequently cited reason for gang violence was that it was an expected part of gang initiation rites. Most often cited as mitigating factors in juvenile homicides are troubled family histories and social backgrounds; psychological disturbances; mental retardation; indigence; and substance abuse. Treatments often include psychotherapy, psychiatric hospitalization, institutional placement, and psychopharmacological agents (Johnson, 2005; Marriott, 2007).

Trends in Juvenile Violence

Violence committed by juveniles increased between the late 1980s and early 1990s (see Figure 2.1). Subsequently, juvenile violence has declined (Belshaw and Lanham, 2008). In 2008, "the juvenile murder arrest rate was 3.8 arrests per 100,000 youth between the ages of 10 and 17" (Puzzanchera, 2009, p. 1). This is 74 percent less than the 14.4 arrests per 100,000 in 1993. In part, this decline may be one indication that various youth crime intervention programs are working (Matrix Research and Consultancy, 2007).

One such initiative is Project Safe Neighborhoods, a collaborative effort between probation, parole, and other community-based agencies and law enforcement to provide training and technical assistance related to supervising juvenile offenders and preventing them from acquiring and using firearms (Bynum, 2005; Decker, 2005; Project Safe Neighborhoods, 2005). One concomitant of youth violence is access to firearms, and the impact of gun violence is especially strong for juveniles and young adults (Lewis et al., 2007). In 2004, there were 1,500 murder victims under the age of 18. This is nearly 50 percent lower than the peak year of 1993, when there were 2,900 juvenile deaths. About half of these deaths were from firearms. Various policies and laws have been implemented to intervene in gun-related violence (McDevitt, 2005). Sources of illegal guns are increasingly interrupted; penalties have been increased for illegal possession and carrying of guns; and persons who supply at-risk youth with firearms for violence (e.g., probationers, gang members, and drug traffickers) are being prosecuted more aggressively. Simultaneously, programs are in place to treat and deal with those youthful offenders who have mental disorders and/or substance abuse problems (Bowman, 2005).

Career Escalation

career escalation
Moving as a juvenile offender to committing progressively more serious offenses; committing new, violent offenses after adjudications for property offenses would be career escalation.

pathways
Developmental sequences over the course of adolescence that are associated with serious, chronic, and violent offenders.

Do status offenders progress to more serious offending, such as juvenile delinquency? Do juvenile delinquents become adult offenders? This phenomenon is known as **career escalation**. Presently, no one knows for sure whether status offenders or delinquents progress toward more serious offending as they get older. This generalization applies to both male and female offenders. One problem is that different **pathways**, or developmental sequences over the term of adolescence, are associated with serious, chronic, and violent offenders (Kuntsche et al., 2007). Thus, a single trajectory or pathway cannot be used as a general forecast of career escalation, whenever it occurs. Furthermore, career escalation among delinquent youth may suggest that situational factors, such as whether youth come from abusive families and where drug and/or alcohol dependencies are evident, are more significant predictors of future, more serious offending rather than pathways to the onset of delinquent offending.

With little more information than whether youth commit particular status or delinquent acts at particular ages, long-term predictions of future career escalation among these juveniles are simply unwarranted. Arrest rates for juvenile offenders change drastically within short-term cycles of three years. Also, there are different varieties of juvenile violence (McGarrell, 2005). About half of all juvenile violence is gang-related, for example, and this type of violence is quite different from the violence exhibited by youth who kill their parents or other youth out of anger or frustration. In fact, researchers have been aware of these different types of violence and their origins for several decades (Lansford et al., 2007).

Interest in career escalation among juveniles heightened during the 1970s and 1980s, when delinquency and crime increased appreciably. Statistical correlations between rising crime and delinquency rates and the amount of status and delinquent offending led to the tentative conclusion that career escalation was occurring. In retrospect, and after a closer examination of adult recidivists, a clear pattern of career escalation among juvenile offenders has not been revealed.

More than any other factor, domestic violence and an abusive family environment seem to be critical determinants of whether certain youth from such families will become chronic and persistent offenders. When recurrent maltreatment persists, Lemmon and Verrecchia (2009) found that there is a relationship between that maltreatment and chronic and violent delinquent behavior in a sample of youth at-risk. By contrast, child placement services seem to decrease violent and persistent offending (Lemmon and Verrecchia, 2009). These findings suggest that intervention and placement may reduce the likelihood of further violent offending among youth who are subjected to continued maltreatment.

Female Versus Male Delinquency: Cataloging the Differences

In 2007, girls were involved in 30 percent of all juvenile arrests. However, of the total number of juveniles held in either public or private juvenile secure facilities in that year, approximately 15 percent of these detainees were female (American Correctional Association, 2007). Also, about 15 percent of all youth in juvenile community correctional programs were female (American Correctional Association, 2007). These figures indicate that female juvenile arrestees are committed to secure facilities at a lower rate than male juveniles and that females are also returned to their communities more frequently after serving shorter secure confinement terms (OJJDP, 2007).

Profiling Female Juvenile Offenders

Are there significant differences between male and female juvenile offenders? Yes. Female juvenile offenders tend to be involved to a greater degree in less-serious types of offending, including runaway behavior, curfew violations, unruly behavior, larceny-theft, and drug abuse. In fact, juvenile female offenders of the 1990s and 2000s appeared to be similar in demographic characteristics compared to female juvenile offenders of the 1980s. Survey data show that many female juveniles have prior histories of being sexually or physically abused, come from a single-parent home, and lack appropriate social and work-related skills (Mellins et al., 2007).

Evidence indicates, however, that growing numbers of female juveniles are entering the juvenile justice system annually, at younger ages, and for more violent offending (Morris and Gibson, 2008). Over 60 percent of all female juveniles charged with juvenile delinquency in 2007 were under age 16. Additionally, increasing numbers of female juveniles are being transferred to criminal courts for prosecution as adult offenders. Approximately 40 percent of all transferred female juvenile cases involved a violent offense as the most serious charge. Several important risk factors have been identified and associated with higher incidences of female offending (Graves, 2007). These include:

1. Alcohol and/or drug abuse.
2. Various antisocial behaviors.

**Police officer escorts a girl who has been appre-
hended into a detention unit.**
(© Mikael Karlsson/Alamy)

3. African-American background.

4. Depression or history of depression.

5. History of parental violence.

6. Lower socioeconomic status.

7. Coming from a single-parent home.

8. Inability to engage in problem solving.

9. Poor interpersonal relations with others.

Trends in Female Juvenile Offending

In the past two decades, the pattern of female delinquent offending compared with male delinquent offending has been changing. Between 2000 and 2007, there was a substantial increase in the number of female juvenile arrestees compared with their male counterparts. In 2000, for instance, only about 15 percent of all juvenile arrestees were female. By 2007, however, this figure had risen to over 30 percent. Furthermore, arrests of female juveniles for violent offenses increased during the period from 2000 to 2007. About 25 percent of all female arrestees in 2007 were involved in violent crimes, compared with only 15 percent of all juvenile violent crime arrestees for 2000. One possible explanation is the increased involvement of female juveniles in gangs (Schaffner, 2006).

As the information in Figure 2.2 demonstrates, the number of female juveniles known to be homicide offenders increased from 120 in 1980 to 159 in 1992, and then dropped to 88 in 2006 (compared to 1,340, 2,296, and 1,165, respectively, for male juvenile offenders). Based on these data, females have not been as violent as males. Even as the juvenile arrest rates for violent crimes have decreased, however, the decrease in female arrests has been less than that of males (Table 2.4).

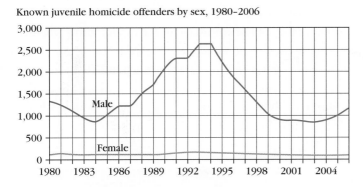

Known juvenile homicide offenders by sex, 1980-2006

Figure 2.2
Juvenile Homicide Offenders
Source: Adapted from Charles Puzzanchera and Wei Kang (2010).
Easy Access to the FBI's Supplementary Homicide Reports: 1980–
2008. *(Available at http://www.ojjdp.gov/ojstatbb/offenders/qa03102
.asp?qaDate=2008.)*

Table 2.4
PERCENTAGE CHANGE IN MALE AND FEMALE JUVENILE ARRESTS FOR VIOLENT CRIMES, 1996–2005.

Type	Girls	Boys
Aggravated assault	−5.4%	−23.4%
Simple assault	+24.0%	−4.1%
Violent Crime Index	−10.2%	−27.9%
All crimes	−14.3%	−28.7%

Source: Girls Study Group (2008). *Violence by Teenage Girls: Trends and Context.* Washington, DC: Office of Juvenile Justice and Delinquency Prevention, p. 4. (Available at http://www.ncjrs.gov/pdffiles1/ojjdp/218905.pdf.)

Like their male counterparts, female youth gangs most often form along racial and/or ethnic lines (Valdez, 2007). The most common reason for female juveniles to join gangs is for protection, often from abusive sexual or physical encounters with their fathers at home. Another important reason is simple rebellion against parents. For many female juvenile gang members, their membership gives them status among their peers and enables them to profit in illicit drug activities. It is difficult to estimate the number of girls who are gang members. Conservatively, about 10 percent of all juvenile gang members in the United States today, or about 150,000, are female, but estimates have ranged between 9 and 22 percent, depending upon the survey conducted. Although female gangs commit fewer violent crimes compared with male gangs, 38 percent of female youth gang-offending involves violent crimes, while 37 percent of their offending involves drug offenses. Therefore, female youth gangs should be taken seriously (Graves, 2007). Studies of youth gangs in various jurisdictions, such as Alabama, suggest similar findings (Martin et al., 2008).

Is there a new breed of violent juvenile female offender emerging? No. Is female delinquency skyrocketing out of control? No. We do not know whether female juveniles are becoming more violent, although some evidence suggests that they are. We *do* know that juvenile courts are processing larger numbers of female juveniles and that greater numbers of delinquency adjudications involve girls. As the information in Table 2.4 suggests, while juvenile arrests for both boys and girls decreased from

Female delinquency seems to be increasing, although experts disagree.
(Courtesy of Dean John Champion)

1996 to 2005, the decrease for girls was less than the decrease for males. In the past, some juvenile court judges acted in a paternalistic manner toward female juveniles, and their offenses were often downgraded or downplayed in seriousness. However, in more recent years, there has been more equitable treatment of female juveniles by the juvenile courts (Graves, 2007).

Myths and Misconceptions: Changing Views of Juvenile Female Offenders

Several variables differentiate males and females in the juvenile justice system. First, males are more likely than females to offend at some point during their adolescence, although self-reports from female juveniles in a nationwide survey in 2007 revealed that 94 percent of them disclosed that they had committed at least one delinquent act (OJJDP, 2007). Traditionally, females who offend during adolescence have been considered to violate sex-role norms. Second, much male offending is property-related, while it is assumed that female delinquency is predominantly sexual. Third, female delinquents seem to come from broken homes at a higher rate than their male counterparts. Therefore, their delinquency is often attributed to deficient family relationships. Fourth, female delinquents are characterized as having greater mental instability and nonrational behavior, whereas male juvenile offenders are characterized as rational, adventurous, and simply testing the bounds of their adolescence.

Two major events triggered the change from a liberal to a conservative approach in juvenile justice throughout the United States. First, states passed legislation in response to public perceptions of increased violent crime among juveniles. Second, status offenses were removed from the jurisdiction of juvenile courts in many states. Greater priority was given to getting tough with juvenile offenders. Regarding female juveniles, Schaffner (2006) has identified three major political–legal periods: (1) the paternalistic period (1960–1967), during which female delinquents were dealt with more severely than males by the juvenile courts "for their own good;" (2) a due process period (1968–1976), which reflected the impact of various legal decisions, such as *In re Gault* (1967); and (3) a law-and-order period (1977–1980), during which the court adjusted to the new conservatism of the late 1970s. Therefore, presumed changes in the rates in female juvenile offending during these years were more attributable to policy shifts in the treatment of female juveniles rather than actual increases in the rate of female criminality.

As we have seen, however, the nature of female juvenile offending is definitely changing and increasing (Schaffner, 2006). While policy revisions and juvenile court views toward female offenders have probably occurred during the early 2000s, increased female juvenile offending has been observed. At the very least, female delinquency is becoming increasingly similar to male delinquency in a number of respects, and court treatment of male and female juveniles is becoming more equalized (Schaffner, 2006).

SUMMARY

Before the juvenile court was established, child savers provided food, shelter, and other services to children who wandered the streets unsupervised. Houses of refuge were established, such as the Western House of Refuge in Rochester, New York. The power of the state in regulating juvenile affairs was established by court decisions such as *Ex parte Crouse* in 1839, which usurped parental control over unmanageable children.

In Illinois and other states, reform schools were established following the Civil War, when many children were orphaned. Simple vagrancy, begging, or wandering the streets aimlessly were sufficient grounds to commit youth to such facilities, which were notorious for their harsh conditions, strict discipline, and compulsory labor. In 1870, the case of *People v. ex rel. O'Connell v. Turner* was decided. This case resulted in the successful removal of a juvenile, whose only offense was that he was vagrant and in need of supervision, from an Illinois reform school. In the 1880s, growing numbers of social welfare agencies, such as Hull House, a settlement home operated by Jane Addams in Chicago, were established. During the 1890s, compulsory education was the rule rather than the exception for youth, and Colorado passed the first truancy statute in 1899, thus providing for the compulsory education of juveniles. Other states quickly followed suit and passed similar laws. One function of these laws was to keep children occupied during daytime hours and under the close supervision of school authorities.

The first juvenile court was established in Illinois in 1899. This new type of court was vested with a great deal of power over juvenile affairs, and for many decades, this and similar courts in other jurisdictions functioned like social welfare agencies. Decisions were almost always made on behalf of juveniles and in their best interests, a traditional philosophy rooted in early English jurisprudence called *parens patriae*. These courts established an assortment of punishments, and they most often imposed such punishments in closed proceedings. Children had no legal standing. Therefore, juvenile rights were never considered as an important issue.

Over the next 60 years, the similarities between juvenile and criminal courts increased. Juvenile courts evolved into due process courts that emulated criminal courts in many ways, and the traditional philosophy of juvenile courts waned. Status offenders and delinquent offenders, as well as children in need of supervision, were within the purview of juvenile courts. In time, the formality of juvenile courts intensified such that these courts became increasingly criminalized. Less-serious juveniles were gradually shifted to social welfare agencies for processing.

Several official and unofficial sources for measuring the nature and extent of delinquency and status offending include the *Uniform Crime Reports (UCR)* and the *National Crime Victimization Survey (NCVS)*. Both the *UCR* and *NCVS* are flawed in different respects. Other sources of crime and delinquency include the National Juvenile Court Data Archive, *The Sourcebook of Criminal Justice Statistics,* the *National Youth Survey,* and the *Monitoring the Future Survey*. Some information about delinquency and crime is available through self-reports. Self-reports are considered to be less reliable by authorities, although some experts contend that they disclose hidden delinquency, thus suggesting that more delinquency is committed annually than is officially reported. While delinquency trends and surveys of youth violence have been studied by authorities, the prevalence of career escalation is unclear, and most youth age out of delinquent behavior. School violence, which has captured public attention to a greater degree in recent years, continues, although recent evidence from official reports suggests that it is declining.

Since at-risk youth are more likely to engage in delinquent behavior, researchers attempt to identify characteristics of children who are at risk and to develop early intervention programs to reduce delinquency. Generally, at-risk youth have lower socioeconomic status, lower IQs, lower school achievement; exhibit more learning disabilities and ADHD; and demonstrate antisocial behaviors. Less fully developed cognitive abilities and poor social adjustment are also associated with at-risk youth. Studies of different pathways or developmental sequences leading to different types of offending have achieved some degree of success in recent years.

Gangs and gang violence have also been studied. Although gang interventions have been developed and implemented in recent years, these programs have had varied success in reducing the prevalence of gangs. There were approximately 27,900 gangs in the United States in 2008, with approximately 774,000 members. A small but growing proportion of gangs consists of female juveniles, and arrests of female juveniles have increased from 10 to 25 percent during the period from 2000 to 2007. Gangs offer protection, recognition, esteem, and ways of gaining status that are often unavailable to youth through their schools and other conventional organizations. Like their male counterparts, female gang members seek to meet similar needs by becoming violent and aggressive. While arrests of female youth have increased, the data do not suggest a crime wave of female delinquents. Official figures, however, point to a need for greater attention to girls to provide gender-specific interventions and programs as deterrents to delinquency.

KEY TERMS

common law, 42
shires, 42
reeve, 42
chancellors, 42
chancery courts, 43
banishment, 43
transportation, 43
workhouses, 43
Bridewell Workhouse, 43

Poor Laws, 44
indentured servant
  system, 44
indentured servants,
  44
Hospital of Saint Michael,
  44
child savers movement,
  45

child savers, 45
New York House of
  Refuge, 45
Society for the
  Prevention of
  Pauperism, 45
houses of refuge, 45
reform schools, 46
Jane Addams, 48

QUESTIONS FOR REVIEW

1. What were workhouses and their functions? How did the Poor Laws influence those confined to workhouses?

2. What were houses of refuge and reform schools? Were they successful in accomplishing their objectives? Why, or why not?

3. Who were child savers, and how did the child-saving philosophy influence the subsequent development of juvenile courts?

4. What were the cases of *Ex parte Crouse* and *People ex rel. O'Connell v. Turner*? What was their significance for juvenile justice?

5. What was the Illinois Juvenile Court Act, and what was its significance for juvenile courts?

6. What are some important differences between the *Uniform Crime Reports (UCR)* and the *National Crime Victimization Survey (NCVS)*? What are some strengths and weaknesses of the *UCR* and *NCVS*? What are some other sources of information about delinquency and crime? How reliable are these sources?

7. What is self-report information? Is it more or less accurate compared with data reported by the *Uniform Crime Reports (UCR)* or *National Crime Victimization Survey (NCVS)*? What are several problems that accompany self-report information?

8. Who are at-risk youth, and why do they interest criminal justice professionals? Why are such youth targeted for interventions? What are pathways, and why are they significant in relation to career escalation?

9. Why is there growing interest in female juvenile gangs? What are some general trends in female juvenile delinquency, and are these trends of interest to authorities?

10. What are some myths and misconceptions about female juveniles? How have these myths and misconceptions influenced social policies relevant to female delinquents? What are some general characteristics of female delinquents?

INTERNET CONNECTIONS

Children Now
http://www.childrennow.org/

Drug War Chronicle
http://www.stopthedrugwar.org/chronicle

Justice Policy Institute
http://www.justicepolicy.org/

Justice Project
http://www.thejusticeprojectkc.org/

Mercyhurst Civic Institute
http://www.civicinstitute.org/

National Center for Juvenile Justice
http://www.ncjj.org

National Council of Juvenile and Family Court Judges
http://www.ncjfcj.org/

National Council on Crime and Delinquency
http://www.nccd-crc.org/

National Gang Center
http://www.nationalgangcenter.gov/

Office for the Victims of Crime
http://www.ovc.gov/

Office of Juvenile Justice and Delinquency Prevention
http://www.ojjdp.gov

3

Theories of Delinquency and Intervention Programs

Learning Objectives

AFTER READING THIS CHAPTER, THE STUDENT WILL BE ABLE TO:

- Explain the role of theory and research pertaining to causes of juvenile crime.
- Summarize the principles and influence of the classical school of criminology.
- Describe biological theories of juvenile crime and delinquency.
- Describe psychological theories of juvenile crime and delinquency.
- Describe sociological theories of juvenile crime and delinquency.
- Summarize integrated theories of juvenile crime and delinquency.
- Summarize other explanations of delinquency.
- Describe various delinquency prevention and community intervention programs.

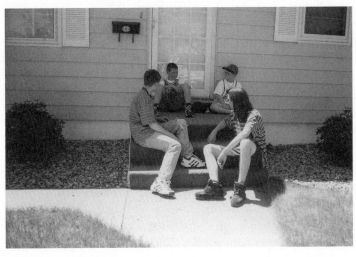

(Courtesy Dean John Champion)

Introduction

For many centuries, criminologists and others have sought to develop plausible and useful explanations for why people engage in deviant behavior and crime. Why do juveniles commit crimes? What are the different forces that cause them to rob, steal, assault, rape, and kill? This chapter will describe theories that explain juvenile delinquency in various forms.

Theories are tools that are useful in developing explanations of relationships between variables such as drugs and crime, peer pressure and gang violence, and family instability and antisocial behavior. Theories attempt to explain and predict how two or more variables are interrelated. There are many types of delinquent behavior to explain, and no single theory has been developed to account for this behavior adequately. As with most human behaviors, delinquency is not easily explained. For example, serious juvenile delinquency is associated with various vulnerabilities and social adversities. Therefore, it is difficult to predict which youth will develop serious offending patterns (McAra and McVie, 2010). Instead, numerous delinquency theories have been proposed, elaborated, and tested to explain individual delinquency as well as the delinquency phenomenon.

This chapter is divided into four parts. The first part presents a variety of theories grouped according to biological, psychological, and sociological themes. The biological theme explores delinquency as the result of internal or biological factors. Biological determinism is discussed, which posits that much of what juveniles do is rooted in genetics and predispositions to behave in given ways (Beaver et al., 2008). Heredity is examined as a possible reason for why youth might acquire delinquent propensities. Biological theories include sociobiology, the *XYY* theory, low IQ, and physical characteristics believed to be linked to delinquency.

Psychological and sociological explanations of delinquency are also presented. The importance of early childhood experiences on adolescent behavior and delinquency is explored through psychoanalytic theory developed by Sigmund Freud and others. Social learning theory posits that different maturational stages influence a youth's subsequent development and demeanor. Sociological theories, including the concentric zone hypothesis, are also discussed. This concentric zone hypothesis attempts to link rapid urban changes, familial disruptions, and social instability with delinquency. The anomie theory of delinquency suggests that delinquents are innovators, discontent with conformity. The labeling theory proposes that associations with other delinquents and identification or being "labeled" as a delinquent have adverse impacts on how youth define themselves. Bonding and strain theories are discussed, as are other theories with sociological roots, including containment theory, neutralization or drift theory, differential association, and cultural transmission.

The second part of the chapter examines the general question of which theory seems best. Different criteria are examined as bases for evaluating these theories and their usefulness for explaining various types of delinquent behavior. Various factors that identify children at risk are listed and described.

The third part of this chapter evaluates different models for dealing with juvenile offenders, such as the rehabilitation model, the treatment or medical model, the noninterventionist model, the due process model, the just deserts or justice model, the crime control model, and the Balanced and Restorative Justice model. These models typify how different actors in the juvenile justice system orient themselves toward delinquents and delinquency and assist in explaining their helping behaviors.

The chapter concludes with an examination of a few different interventions that have been, and are continuing to be, used in preventing or minimizing delinquency and of the factors or social and psychological conditions that are associated with its occurrence. Most interventions reflect one or more theories of delinquency and can easily be associated with different prevention programs. Thus, theories are not just an attempt to explain behavior. They are often used to structure experiences and situations that can be applied in useful ways that might deter youth from becoming delinquents. Recidivism rates for delinquents vary for different programs, and some intervention programs work with certain types of juvenile offenders but not with others. Not all intervention programs are effective in reducing delinquent behavior, but rigorous evaluations of some programs have identified strategies that are more successful in preventing and deterring delinquent behaviors. These evidence-based programs demonstrate best practices for working with youth, and some have been classified as Blueprints for Violence Prevention and Model Programs. A positive outlook persists among criminal justice professionals, and new and different interventions and strategies for combating delinquency are continually being developed.

Classical and Biological Theories

In this section, classical and biological theories of criminality and delinquency will be examined. These include (1) classical theory, (2) positivist theory or biological determinism, (3) sociobiology, and (4) the *XYY* theory.

Classical Theory

Classical theory is a criminological perspective indicating that people have free will to choose either criminal or conventional behavior. Thus, people choose to commit crime for reasons of greed or personal need. Crime can be controlled by criminal sanctions, which should be proportionate to the guilt of the perpetrator.

Philosophers have speculated about the causes of crime for centuries, and they have elaborated diverse explanations for criminal conduct. In the 1700s, criminologists devised explanations for criminal behavior that have persisted to this day. Deeply rooted in the general principles of Christianity, the classical school of criminology originated with **Cesare Beccaria (1738–1794)** and his book *On Crimes and Punishments* (1764). Subsequent scholars who adopted perspectives about crime different from those of Beccaria labeled his views as classical, since they included an inherent conflict between good and evil and provided a standard against which other views of crime could be contrasted.

classical theory
A criminological perspective emphasizing that people have free will to choose criminal or conventional behavior as a means of achieving their personal goals.

Cesare Beccaria (1738–1794)
Developed classical school of criminology; believed corporal punishment to be unjust and ineffective and that crime could be prevented by plain legal codes specifying prohibited behaviors and punishments; promoted "just deserts" philosophy.

classical school

Line of thought that assumes that people are rational beings who choose between good and evil.

The **classical school** assumes that people are rational beings who exercise free will in choosing between good actions and evil ones. Within the classical context, societal progress and perpetuation are paramount, and individuals must each sacrifice a degree of their freedoms so that all persons can pursue happiness and attain their respective goals. Evil actions operate adversely for societal progress and merit punishment. Because evil acts vary in their seriousness, however, the severity of punishments for those actions should be adjusted accordingly. Beccaria believed that punishments should be swift, certain, and just, where the penalties are appropriately adjusted to fit particular offenses. The primary purposes of punishment are deterrence and just deserts. In an ideal world, people will refrain from wrongdoing to avoid the pain of punishment. Furthermore, whatever punishment is imposed should be equivalent to, or proportional in severity with, the amount of social and physical damage caused by those found guilty of crimes. Thus, fines and/or imprisonment were common penalties for those found guilty of property crimes and violent offenses (Rhoades and Zambrano, 2005). In addition, the origins of different sentencing schemes in the United States today can be traced to Beccaria's classical theory. Most states have mandatory sentences for specific offenses, including use of a firearm during the commission of a felony. Also, most state statutes carry sentences of determinate lengths and/or fines that are roughly commensurate with the crime's severity.

Less than two decades after Beccaria outlined his philosophy of crime and punishment, Jeremy Bentham (1748–1832), an English philosopher, advanced a similar scheme in his book, *An Introduction to the Principles of Morals and Legislation* (1790). Bentham was known for his belief that **hedonism**, or the pursuit of pleasure, was a primary motivator underlying much social and personal action. Simply put, humans seek to acquire pleasure and avoid pain. Thus, in this pleasure–pain framework, Bentham formulated his views about the worth and intent of punishment. Like Beccaria, Bentham believed that the objectives of punishments were to deter crime and to impose sanctions sufficient to outweigh any pleasures criminals might derive from the crimes they commit. Therefore, many would-be offenders might desist from crime because the threat of punishment would more than offset the projected pleasure derived from their criminal actions. Those more persistent offenders would be subject to painful punishments adjusted according to the severity of their offenses.

hedonism

Jeremy Bentham's term indicating that people avoid pain and pursue pleasure.

Under the prevailing common law of that period, those under the age of seven were not held accountable for their actions or subject to the same kinds of punishments prescribed for adults. However, older youth eventually were vested with responsibilities for their own actions and were subject to punishments similar to those of adults. One contemporary view of juvenile delinquents is that juveniles must accept responsibility for their actions. If they choose to ignore societal values and persist in violating the law, they must be held accountable for these offenses and punished accordingly.

In reality, the classical school of criminology is not so much an explanation of why crime or delinquency exists but, rather, is a statement about how various offenses should be punished to frustrate criminal conduct. However, some elements of explanation are contained in classical thought. Bentham, for instance, would probably speculate that persistent criminal offenders are gamblers, in a sense, because they regard the calculated risk of being caught and punished for crimes as secondary to the pleasurable benefits derived from committing those crimes. The pleasure of crime outweighs the pain of punishment. Beccaria might argue that criminals are comprised of those who have failed to inculcate societal values or respect for the common good.

This perspective has received attention from contemporary theorists such as Kohlberg (1981), who constructed a theory of moral development to account for both deviant and conforming behaviors. This theory is properly classified in a social learning context, and it will be discussed briefly in the section on psychological theories. Although Kohlberg's theory of moral development has been both supported and rejected by adherents and critics, some experts believe that his views may have intuitive value for furnishing insight regarding more aberrant modes of criminality. Furthermore, the theory may improve our understanding of a wide range of delinquent acts if integrated into a perspective that is sensitive to how varying social contexts shape individual inclinations.

Biological Theories

At the other end of the continuum is **determinism**, the view that a specific factor, variable, or event is a determinant of individual actions or behaviors. Determinism rejects the notion of free will and choice, relying instead on properties that cause human beings to behave one way or another. Determinism is strongly evident in biological theories of criminal and delinquent behavior.

Generally, theories of determinism seek to associate criminal, delinquent, and deviant conduct with biological, biochemical, or genetic bases in a direct, causal relation. According to this view, juvenile delinquency is a selective phenomenon, in that it does not occur spontaneously. Delinquents are destined to become delinquent because of factors beyond their own control and/or because of the presence of certain internal factors. In turn, nondelinquents are destined to be nondelinquent because of the presence of different internal factors. The idea that known, predisposing factors cause delinquent behaviors conveniently shifts the responsibility for delinquent conduct from youth themselves to some internal or external source.

Although the attribution of criminality and delinquency to biological causes dates to prebiblical times, such determinism, known as **biological determinism**, was given a degree of academic dignity in the work of an Italian physician and criminologist, **Cesare Lombroso (1835–1909)**, during the 1860s. Considered by many professionals to be the father of criminology, Lombroso was influenced by the work of Charles Darwin (1809–1882). Darwin's major writing, *The Origin of the Species,* was both revolutionary and evolutionary, arguing in part that human beings evolved from lower animal forms over thousands of years. Natural selection and survival of the fittest were key principles of Darwin's evolutionary theory. Lombroso was intrigued by these principles and applied them in his explanation of criminal conduct.

determinism
Concept holding that persons do not have free will but, rather, are subject to the influence of various forces over which they have little or no control.

biological determinism
View in criminology holding that criminal behavior has a physiological basis; genes, foods and food additives, hormones, and inheritance are all believed to play a role in determining individual behavior; genetic makeup causes certain behaviors to become manifest, such as criminality.

Cesare Lombroso (1835–1909)
His school of thought linked criminal behavior with abnormal, unusual physical characteristics.

atavism

Positivist school of thought arguing that a biological condition renders a person incapable of living within the social constraints of a society; the idea that physical characteristics can distinguish criminals from the general population and are evolutionary throwbacks to animals or primitive people.

positivism

Branch of social science that uses the scientific method of the natural sciences and that suggests human behavior is a product of social, biological, psychological, or economic factors.

positive school of criminology

School of criminological thought emphasizing analysis of criminal behaviors through empirical indicators, such as physical features, compared with biochemical explanations; postulates that human behavior is a product of social, biological, psychological, or economic forces; also known as the "Italian School."

According to Lombroso, criminals were products of heredity. Successive generations of human beings inherited genetically not only physical features from their ancestors but also behavioral predispositions, such as propensities toward criminal conduct or antisocial proclivities. Since heredity is more or less binding on future generations, it made sense to Lombroso and many of his disciples that certain physical characteristics would also be inexorably related to criminal behavior. Therefore, physical appearance would be a telling factor in whether certain persons would be predisposed to criminality or other types of deviant behavior. This led Lombroso to conjecture extensively about criminal types and born criminals. Height, weight, hair and eye color, physiognomic features (e.g., jaw sizes and angles, earlobe shapes, finger lengths, and hand sizes), and assorted other anatomical characteristics were painstakingly measured and charted by Lombroso. Samples of both willing and unwilling volunteers, including populations of Italian prisoners and soldiers, were obtained for his analyses. Eventually, Lombroso concluded that many of the physiological characteristics shared by criminals were indicative of stunted evolutionary growth. Indeed, Lombroso considered criminals to be throwbacks typical of earlier evolutionary stages. This view of criminals is known as **atavism** and is strongly suggestive of subhuman qualities.

Lombroso's views became known popularly as **positivism**, and the **positive school of criminology** originated. This view rejected the free will and choice doctrines espoused by Beccaria and other classical theorists. Rather, it said that criminal conduct more likely emanated from biochemical and genetic factors peculiar to criminal types. Lombroso made further refinements by concluding that certain physical features (e.g., sloping foreheads, compressed jaws, large earlobes, long and slender fingers, and excessive facial and body hair) would tend to indicate the type of criminal behavior expected from those observed.

Although Lombroso limited his theoretical and empirical work primarily to adult criminals, his strong focus upon the heredity factor was easily generalizable to juveniles. Thus, he simultaneously provided explanations for both criminal and delinquent conduct that relied almost exclusively on genetic factors. In later years, however, Lombroso altered his opinion about the key role played by genetics in promoting criminal behavior. In part, this change resulted from extensive scientific studies of both juveniles and adults that disclosed little relation between physiological features and criminal behaviors. Also, the development of other social sciences, such as sociology and psychology, led him to assign a more prominent role to the social milieu as a prerequisite to criminal or delinquent conduct.

Despite the fact that specific biological features or characteristics could not be positively connected with specific types of criminal conduct, certain professionals in the early 1900s continued to regard biological determinism as a plausible explanation for criminality and delinquency. During the 1930s, Hooton (1939) and Kretschmer (1936) established physical typologies of criminals that were given some credence by the academic community. In the 1940s, Sheldon (1949) provided what later became both a popular and an elaborate description of genetic types that seemingly manifested certain kinds of criminal characteristics.

Sheldon defined three major categories of body types, including **mesomorphs**, or strong, athletic individuals; **ectomorphs**, or thin, submissive beings; and **endomorphs**, or fat persons. He assigned point valuations to each person observed and attempted to describe behaviors most typical of them. Mesomorphs were believed to typify those who manifested criminal or delinquent behaviors. Unfortunately, little consistency existed in his descriptions of those sharing these bodily characteristics. Particularly disturbing was the fact that many nondelinquents and noncriminals were classified as mesomorphs. His work was soundly criticized by other professionals who concluded that no relation between body type and criminality could be established (Sutherland, 1951).

Although Sheldon's work was subsequently discounted, some researchers continued to investigate the relation between biology and criminal propensities and regard such a connection as plausible. For instance, research conducted by Sheldon and Eleanor Glueck in 1950 targeted 1,000 white male youth, 500 of whom were delinquent and 500 of whom were nondelinquent (Glueck and Glueck, 1950). Mesomorphic characteristics similar to those described by Sheldon were found among 60 percent of the delinquents studied, while only 30 percent of the nondelinquents shared these characteristics. The Gluecks interpreted their findings conservatively and never said that delinquency is caused by mesomorphic characteristics; nevertheless, they described delinquents generally as more agitated and aggressive compared with nondelinquents. Over five decades later, we can look back at the Gluecks' study and argue, particularly in view of the increased incidence of juvenile gangs in many larger U.S. cities, that more-muscular youth probably are more likely to be gang members compared with less-muscular youth. Furthermore, the fact that the Gluecks confined their analysis to white male juveniles means that they excluded from consideration racial and ethnic groups that have become increasingly conspicuous in American society and associated with certain types of delinquency.

Sociobiology

In recent decades, criminologists have reaffirmed the significance of the biological contribution to criminality and delinquency (Turner, Hartman, and Bishop, 2007). Genetic researchers and biologists have promoted **sociobiology**, or the study of the "biological basis for social action" (Wilson, 1975, p. 16). While this new field is not necessarily biological determinism or positivism revisited, it nevertheless stimulates interest in and directs our attention toward the role of genetics in human behavior. Presently, it is believed that a connection exists, but we are unable to elaborate this connection (Wilson, 1975).

The XYY Theory

Closely associated in principle with the sociobiological explanation of criminality and delinquency is the *XYY* **theory**, which asserts that certain chromosomal abnormalities may precipitate violence and/or criminal conduct. *X* chromosomes designate female characteristics and are regarded as passive, while *Y* chromosomes designate male

---

mesomorphs
Body type described by Sheldon; persons are strong, muscular, aggressive, tough.

ectomorphs
Body type described by Sheldon; persons are thin, sensitive, delicate.

endomorphs
Body type described by Sheldon; persons are fat, soft, plump, jolly.

sociobiology
Scientific study of causal relation between genetic structure and social behavior.

XYY theory
Explanation of criminal behavior suggesting that some criminals are born with an extra Y chromosome, characterized as the "aggressive" chromosome compared with the passive X chromosome; an extra Y chromosome produces greater agitation, greater aggressiveness, and criminal propensities.

characteristics and are regarded as aggressive. Normally, an *XX* chromosomal combination produces a female, while the *XY* chromosomal combination yields a male. Sometimes, however, an extra *Y* chromosome insinuates itself into the *XY* formula to produce an *XYY* type. The input from this additional aggressive chromosome is believed to be responsible, at least in some instances, for criminal behaviors among those observed to possess it. Unfortunately, this chromosomal combination exists in less than 5 percent of the population. Thus, it lacks sufficient predictive utility when considered on its own merits.

Other Biologically Related Explanations

In addition to designating specific body types, physical features, and heredity as crucial manifestations or causes of delinquency and criminal behavior, other biological or physical causes have been advanced in previous years. Feeblemindedness, mental illness, low intelligence, physical deformity including assorted stigmas, and glandular malfunction or imbalance have been variously described as concomitants of delinquency and criminality (Xiaoying, 2005).

Much research exists regarding the relation of criminal and delinquent behavior to physical deformities and glandular malfunctions. While these ideas that glandular malfunctions and physical defects are somehow causally related to various forms of deviant behavior may be interesting, no consistent groundwork has been provided that empirically supports any of these notions. Regarding stigmas, for instance, Goffman (1961) has observed that unusual behaviors are often elicited from those possessing stigmata by defining audiences of others who regard such stigmata with repulsion. Thus, those with stigmas of one type or another, such as facial disfigurement, react to the reactions of others toward them, sometimes behaving as they believe others expect them to behave. It is not the stigma that causes deviant behavior but, rather, the reactions of stigmatized persons who respond to the reactions of others. No scientific continuity has been conclusively established between stigmata and criminality.

Some relatively recent investigations have attempted to correlate antisocial and delinquent behavior with early exposure to lead and other toxicants. These investigations have also included examinations of delinquent youth exposed to drug use by one or both parents and determined by prenatal and postnatal exposures to the drugs. Interestingly, a positive correlation has been drawn between prenatal exposure to certain drugs and toxicants like environmental contaminants from mothers and subsequent behavioral problems of children during their infant years through adolescence (Apel et al., 2007).

Another documented prenatal influence on children and adolescence is **fetal alcohol syndrome**, or **fetal alcohol spectrum disorders**. Pregnant women who drink heavily place the fetus at increased risk for developmental and behavior problems. The syndrome includes deficits in intellectual functioning, slower physical development, and problems with psychosocial skills (Lynch et al., 2003). Other impairments are impulsivity, hyperactivity, and learning disabilities (Fast and Conry, 2009). While

fetal alcohol syndrome
Consequences that alcohol has on the developing fetus.

fetal alcohol spectrum disorders
Refers to a range of effects in an individual whose mother drank alcohol during pregnancy; includes physical, learning, and mental effects, which can be long term.

these conditions raise the risk of subsequent delinquent behavior, environmental factors (e.g., family background, exposure to abuse or neglect, and peer influence) also need to be considered. Research does, however, suggest a relationship between Fetal Alcohol Syndrome and contact with the justice system (Fast and Conry, 2009).

It is also the case that ingestion of certain substances or drugs can interact with the biological system to elicit different types of behaviors, some of which are deviant and delinquent (Estell et al., 2007; Tubman, Gil, and Wagner, 2004). While it is impossible to tell for sure whether biological explanations of delinquent conduct have contributed to the establishment of such programs, it is clear that many individual and group activities involving youthful offenders are geared toward developing coping skills. And often, coping with physical and/or psychological inadequacies is an essential part of growing out of the delinquent mode of conduct (Lee and Hoaken, 2007).

Psychological Theories

Theories that attribute delinquent behaviors to personality maladjustment or some unusual cognitive condition are categorically known as **psychological theories**. These theories focus on the learning process, or the process whereby humans acquire language, self-definitions, definitions of others, and assorted behavioral proprieties (Chapple, 2005). Because the precise mechanisms involved in the learning process are elusive and cannot be inspected or investigated directly, each psychological theory is inherently subjective and may be debated endlessly regarding its relative merits and explanatory effectiveness. In addition, psychological theories do not address the social order; they focus instead on the human psyche to explain delinquency (Hagan, 2011). In this section, two psychological explanations for delinquent conduct will be examined: (1) psychoanalytic theory and (2) social learning theory.

Psychoanalytic Theory

Early pioneers of psychological theories were Sigmund Freud, Karen Horney, and Carl Jung. Studies concentrated on personality systems, how they are formed, and how personality and behavior are intertwined. The most popular psychologist of the period was Sigmund Freud (1856–1939), who was one of the first theorists to present a systematic explanatory scheme for personality emergence and development (Hagan, 2011). Freud's investigations and writings eventually became widely known as **psychoanalytic theory**.

According to Freud, at the core of psychoanalytic theory are three major personality components, known as the id, ego, and superego. The id is the uncontrolled, "I want" component prevalent among all newborn infants. The desire of the id is for immediate gratification. Thus, infants typically exhibit little or no concern for others as they seek to acquire things they like or admire. As infants mature to young children, the id is suppressed to a degree by the ego, another personality component. The ego is a recognition of others and a respect of their rights and interests. Eventually, higher-level moral development occurs through the superego, or conscience. When

psychological theories

Explanations linking criminal behavior with mental states or conditions, antisocial personality traits, and early psychological and moral development.

psychoanalytic theory

Sigmund Freud's theory of personality formation through the id, ego, and superego at various stages of childhood; maintains that early life experiences influence adult behavior.

children begin to feel guilty if they have deprived others of something wrongfully, this is a manifestation of the superego in action, according to Freud. Eventually, a libido, which is a basic drive for sexual stimulation and gratification, emerges as well. The onset of puberty is a common event signaling the importance of the libido. Again, the ego and superego function to keep the libido in check.

Deviant behavior generally, and criminal behavior and delinquency specifically, may be explained as the result of insufficient ego and superego development (Maruna, Matravers, and King, 2004). The id dominates and seeks activities that will fulfill the urges or needs it stimulates. Parent–child relations are often cited as primary in the normal development of the ego and the superego. Therefore, if some children lack control over their impulses and desires, the blame is often placed at the parents' feet for their failure to inculcate these important inhibitors into the youth's personality system (Lord, Jiang, and Hurley, 2005).

Psychoanalytic theory stresses early childhood experiences as crucial for normal adult functioning to occur. Traumatic experiences may prevent proper ego or superego development. Adults may develop neuroses or psychoses that may be traceable to bizarre childhood events or other traumatic experiences. Research on juvenile sex offenders, for example, has indicated that when compared to non–sex offenders, these youth tended to exhibit higher rates of social isolation, a history of maltreatment, prior violent victimization, and separation (physical or emotional) from one or both of their parents (*Juveniles Who Have Sexually Offended*, 2001). In fact, it may be useful to view juvenile rape as a violent, impulsive act committed by youth with a low level of ego integration.

Social Learning Theory

social learning theory

Applied to criminal behavior, theory stressing the importance of learning through modeling others who are criminal; criminal behavior is a function of copying or learning criminal conduct from others.

Social learning theory is somewhat different from psychoanalytic theory. In social learning theory, traumatic early childhood experiences may be important determinants of subsequent adult personality characteristics, but the primary factors influencing whether one conforms to or deviates from societal rules are those experiences youth have while learning from others, such as their parents (Moseley, 2005). Adults in any institutional context (e.g., schools, churches, and homes) provide role models for children to follow. Homes that are beset with violence and conflict between spouses are poor training grounds for children. Children often learn to cope with their problems at home in ways that are labeled antisocial or hostile (Apel et al., 2007). Even the punishments parents impose on children for disobeying them are translated into acceptable behaviors that children can direct toward their own peers (Bowman, Prelow, and Weaver, 2007).

In its most simplified form, social learning theory implies that children learn to do what they see significant others, such as their parents, do. Poor parental role models have been emphasized as a probable cause of poor adolescent adjustment and delinquent behavior. The importance of the family in the early social development of children has been cited as influential in contributing to youth delinquency. Children who use violence to resolve disputes with other children likely have learned such behaviors in homes where violence is exhibited regularly by parents (Ingram et al., 2005).

Youth can learn to use alcohol, drugs, and weapons through their peer group associations.
(Monkey Business Images/Shutterstock.com)

If delinquency is fostered through social learning, then certain social learning intervention models might be useful for assisting youth to learn different, more acceptable behaviors. In fact, if youth who exhibit learning or developmental disabilities in school can be identified accurately, teachers may modify classroom curricula in ways that increase opportunities, skills, and rewards for these children (Wallace, Minor, and Wells, 2005).

Some researchers have examined the relationship between delinquency and whether children are learning disabled (Lee and Hoaken, 2007). Learning-disabled children suffer a double disadvantage, in a sense, because their learning disabilities have likely contributed to poor school performance and social adjustments. Such learning disabilities may impair judgment regarding peer associations, and these children might have encounters with the law more frequently than other youth. When they are evaluated at intake or later in juvenile court, their school records are "evidence" against them. Some may erroneously conclude that learning disabilities produce delinquent conduct when, in fact, other factors are at work. Teachers themselves may become impatient with learning-disabled children, particularly if their conditions are unknown in advance. A lack of rewards from teachers may have deep emotional impacts for some learning-disabled children, thus creating a vicious cycle of failure for such youth.

These psychological theories stress the importance of early moral and cognitive development in later behaviors (Lee and Hoaken, 2007). Many delinquency prevention programs have been designed for early interventions with at-risk youth. Therefore, it is not unusual to see attempts by public agencies and professionals to intervene through early training or educational programs in schools.

Sociological Theories

It is worth noting that the theories advanced thus far have related deviant, criminal, and/or delinquent behaviors to factors almost exclusively within individuals (i.e., their minds, their bodies, or both). These theories have been described elsewhere as inside notions (e.g., the positivist view, glandular malfunction, *XYY* theory, sociobiology, and low IQ), primarily because they identify internal factors as causally important for explaining deviation of any kind. While these inside notions have persisted over the years to provide plausible explanations for why criminals and delinquents commit their various offenses, other explanations have also been advanced that shift certain causes of deviant conduct to factors outside of, or external to, individuals. Sociologists have encouraged a strong consideration of social factors as major variables that can account for the emergence and persistence of delinquent conduct (Swain, Henry, and Baez, 2004).

It is perhaps most realistic to regard these different perspectives as mutually overlapping rather than as mutually exclusive. Thus, we might view social learning theory as predominantly a psychological theory with certain sociological elements. The biological factor may figure significantly into the delinquency equation, particularly when considering the matter of developmental disabilities of a physical nature in the social learning process. A pragmatic view will be adopted here, and we will regard any explanation as useful, provided that it is accompanied by some predictive utility. The sociological theories of juvenile delinquency presented in this section include (1) the concentric zone hypothesis, (2) the subculture theory of delinquency, (3) the anomie theory of delinquency, (4) labeling theory, (5) bonding theory, and (6) Agnew's general strain theory.

The Concentric Zone Hypothesis and Delinquency

During the early 1900s, large cities such as Chicago, Illinois, were undergoing rapid expansion as one result of the great influx of laborers from farms and rural regions into city centers to find work. Urbanization emanated from the center of the city outward, and such expansion caused some of the older inner-city neighborhoods to undergo a dramatic transition. Sociologists at the University of Chicago and elsewhere studied the urban development of Chicago. Social scientists Ernest W. Burgess and Robert E. Park defined a series of concentric zones around Chicago, commencing with the core (or "loop") in downtown Chicago and progressing outward, away from the city center, in a series of concentric rings. The outward ring or zone immediately adjacent to the central core was labeled by Burgess and Park as an **interstitial area**, or **zone of transition**. This was the immediate periphery of downtown Chicago and was characterized by slums and urban renewal projects. This area was also typified by high delinquency and crime. These researchers believed that other cities might exhibit growth patterns and concentric zones similar to those identified in the Chicago area. Thus, the **concentric zone hypothesis** of urban growth originated, accompanied by descriptions of different social and demographic characteristics of those inhabiting

interstitial area
In concentric zone hypothesis, the area nearest the center of a city undergoing change, such as urban renewal; characterized by high rates of crime.

zone of transition
An area that is both nearest the city center and undergoing rapid social change; believed to contain high rates of crime and delinquency.

concentric zone hypothesis
Series of rings originating from a city center and emanating outward, forming various zones characterized by different socioeconomic conditions; believed to contain areas of high delinquency and crime.

each zone. Interest in such neighborhoods affecting a youth's behavior continues (Schaefer-McDaniel, 2007).

Concurrent with Burgess and Park's efforts was an investigation of delinquency patterns in Chicago conducted by Clifford Shaw and Henry McKay (1972). These researchers studied the characteristics of delinquent youth in the zone of transition and compared their backgrounds with those of other youth inhabiting more stabilized neighborhoods in the zones farther removed from the inner core of downtown Chicago. They based their subsequent findings and probable causes of delinquency on the records of nearly 25,000 delinquent youth in Cook County, Illinois, between 1900 and the early 1930s. Essentially, Shaw and McKay found that over this 30-year period, delinquency within the interstitial zone was widespread and tended to grow in a concomitant fashion with the growth of slums and deteriorating neighborhoods. For many of these youth, both of their parents worked in factories for long hours. Large numbers of juveniles roamed these Chicago streets with little or no adult supervision. Family stability was lacking, and many youth turned toward gang activities as a means of surviving, gaining recognition and status, and achieving certain material goals.

Compared with other zones, the zones in transition were typically overcrowded, replete with families of lower socioeconomic status (SES). No zones, however, were completely free of delinquency. In other zones, however, families were more affluent and stable, and accordingly, less delinquency was observed compared with delinquency within interstitial areas. Shaw and McKay explained delinquency in these transitional areas as likely attributable to a breakdown in family unity and pervasive social disorganization. Interstitial areas lacked recreational facilities, and schools and churches were run-down. As a result, youth literally played in the streets, with little or nothing to occupy their time other than to form gangs and commit delinquent acts. Because many of the same gangs formed at the turn of the century were still in existence in the early 1930s, Shaw and McKay believed that gang members perpetuated gang traditions and gang culture over time through cultural transmission.

One immediate effect of Shaw and McKay's work was to divert explanations of delinquency away from biological explanations, such as genetics and physical abnormalities, to more sociological explanations (Ingram et al., 2005). The long-range influence of the pioneering work by Shaw and McKay is evident in contemporary studies seeking to link neighborhood characteristics with delinquent conduct (Khalili, 2008; Liberman, Raudenbush, and Sampson, 2005). Generally, these studies have been supportive of Shaw and McKay's work, although other factors closely associated with those residing in slum areas have also been causally linked with delinquency. One of these factors is SES (Dahlgren, 2005).

Studies investigating the relation between SES and delinquency have generally found more frequent, and more violent, types of juvenile conduct among youth of lower SES (Wolfgang and Ferracuti, 1967), while less-frequent and less-violent conduct has been exhibited by youth from families of upper SES (Liberman, Raudenbush, and Sampson, 2005). Some of this research also suggests that juveniles who are identified with lower SES seem more likely to do poorly in school compared to juveniles with higher SES.

It may be that students from families of lower SES may reflect different values and achievement orientations compared with youth from families with higher SES. This factor may figure significantly in the rate of juvenile school successes or failures. School dropouts or underachievers may, in fact, turn toward other underachievers or dropouts for companionship, recognition, and prestige. Thus, a complex and vicious cycle is put into motion, with certain conditions and characteristics of lower SES leading to poor academic performance, growing antisocial behavior, and subsequent delinquent conduct. However, describing the concomitants of delinquents or their prominent characteristics does not necessarily pinpoint the true causal factors associated with their conduct in any predictive sense. After all, many lower-SES youth adjust well to their academic work and refrain from delinquent activities. Also, many seemingly well-adjusted and academically successful, higher-SES youth may engage in certain forms of delinquent conduct (Apel et al., 2007).

While the relationship between SES and delinquency is generally accepted, efforts to explain the dynamic effect of SES on delinquency suggest that "economic problems which are more characteristic of lower-SES youth are associated with delinquency" (Agnew et al., 2008, p. 159). Research indicates that the degree and the extent of economic problems that youth are exposed to (e.g., quality of housing, history of family poverty, quality of education, and exposure to environmental hazards) are important variables in the relationship. This suggests a cumulative effect of lower-SES conditions on delinquency (Agnew et al., 2008).

Youth gang growth in the United States and other countries has increased antisocial behavior.
(Monkey Business Images/Shutterstock.com)

Some research has associated having money, or possessing monetary resources, as being positively related to delinquent conduct. Thus, especially among higher-SES youth, having money becomes a risk factor for criminal conduct, in that it reduces family attachments, leads to increased dating, and increases illicit drug use (Ingram et al., 2005). It may be that efforts to facilitate adolescent entrance into the adult world of earning, spending, credit, and financial obligation may produce unintended consequences—namely increased use of drugs and greater misbehavior.

The attraction of having wanted luxury items, such as clothes, CDs, cell phones, and expensive cars, may be overwhelming when compared with the mere promise that delayed gratification somehow will improve life at some distant, uncertain point in the future. The proceeds from adolescent employment and parental allowance may facilitate values and behaviors that divorce youth from the responsibility accompanying entrance into the adult world of economic relationships. In a sense, then, parents and employers may be the economic agents responsible for subsidizing adolescents' delinquency and drug use (Pires and Jenkins, 2007).

The Subculture Theory of Delinquency

During the 1950s, sociologist Albert Cohen recognized and described a **subculture of delinquency**. Delinquent subcultures exist, according to Cohen (1955), within the greater societal culture. However, these subcultures contain value systems and modes of achievement, and of gaining status and recognition, apart from those of the mainstream culture. Thus, if we are to understand why many juveniles behave as they do, we must pay attention to the patterns of their particular subculture (Copes and Williams, 2007).

The notion of a delinquent subculture is fairly easy to understand, especially in view of the earlier work of Shaw and McKay (1972). While middle- and upper-class children learn and aspire to achieve lofty ambitions and educational goals and receive support for these aspirations from their parents as well as predominantly middle-class teachers, lower-class youth are at a distinct disadvantage from the outset. They are born into families where their primary familial role models have not attained these high aims themselves and where these aspirations and attainments may even be alien and rejected.

At school, these youth are often isolated socially from upper- and middle-class youth. Therefore, social attachments are formed with others who are similar to themselves. Perhaps these youth dress differently from other students, wear their hair in a certain style, or use coded language when talking to peers in front of other students. They acquire a culture unto themselves, one that is largely unknown to others. In a sense, much of this cultural isolation is self-imposed. However, it functions to give them a sense of fulfillment, reward, self-esteem and recognition apart from other reward systems. If these students cannot achieve one or more of the various standards set by middle-class society, then they create their own standards and prescribe the means to achieve them.

subculture of delinquency

A culture within a culture where the use of violence in certain social situations is commonplace and normative; Marvin Wolfgang and Franco Ferracuti devised this concept to depict a set of norms apart from mainstream conventional society, in which the theme of violence is pervasive and dominant; learned through socialization with others as an alternative lifestyle.

Cohen (1955) is quick to point out that delinquency is not a product of lower SES per se. Rather, children with lower SES are at greater risk than others of being susceptible to the rewards and opportunities a subculture of delinquency might offer in contrast with the middle-class reward structure. Experiments have subsequently been conducted with delinquents in which these subcultures have been targeted and described, and the norms of these subcultures have been used as intervening mechanisms to modify delinquent behaviors toward nondelinquent modes of action. The Provo Experiment, for example, was influenced by the work of Cohen (Empey and Rabow, 1961).

In the Provo Experiment, samples of delinquent youth in Provo, Utah, were identified in the late 1950s and given an opportunity to participate in group therapy sessions at Pine Hills, a large home in Provo that had been converted into an experimental laboratory. In cooperation with juvenile court judges and other authorities, Pine Hills investigators commenced their intervention strategies assuming that juvenile participants (1) had limited access to success goals, (2) performed many of their delinquent activities in groups rather than alone, and (3) committed their delinquent acts for nonutilitarian objectives rather than for money (Empey and Rabow, 1961). The investigators believed that since these youth had acquired their delinquent values and conduct through their subculture of delinquency, they could unlearn these values, and learn new values, by the same means. Thus, groups of delinquents participated extensively in therapy directed at changing their behaviors through group processes. The investigators believed that their intervention efforts were largely successful and that the subcultural approach to delinquency prevention and behavioral change was fruitful.

The subcultural theme was devised by Wolfgang and Ferracuti (1967). Later, Wolfgang, Figlio, and Sellin (1972) investigated large numbers of boys from Philadelphia, Pennsylvania, in a study of birth cohorts (see also Miller, 2007). In that study, approximately six percent of all boys accounted for more than 50 percent of all delinquent conduct from the entire cohort of over 9,000 boys (Wolfgang, Figlio, and Sellin, 1972). These were chronic recidivists who were also violent offenders. Wolfgang theorized that in some communities, subcultural norms of violence attract youth. These boys regard violence as a normal part of their environment, and they both use violence themselves and respect the use of violence by others.

On the basis of evidence amassed by Wolfgang and Ferracuti (1967) and by Wolfgang, Figlio, and Sellin (1972), it appeared that predominantly lower-class and less-educated males formed a disproportionately large part of this subculture of delinquency. Where violence is accepted and respected, its use is considered to be normal, and normative for the offenders. Remorse is an alien emotion to those using violence and who live with it constantly. Thus, it is socially ingrained as a subcultural value. This theme would suggest that violence and aggression are learned through socialization with others, even one's own siblings (Lee and Hoaken, 2007).

Another important contribution to explaining the dynamics of delinquent subculture is the idea of **Lower Class Focal Concerns** as proposed by Miller (1958). He identified that lower class youth develop their own norms and values (e.g., codes) in

lower class focal concerns

Walter Miller used this term to refer to those aspects of the subculture that are important; these aspects require attention by members of the subculture.

response to their frustration and inability to achieve middle-class goals. He recognized six concerns or values that characterize lower class youth: (1) trouble, (2) toughness, (3) smartness, (4) excitement, (5) fate, and (6) autonomy. Essentially, being street-wise, seeking excitement (e.g., by fighting, stealing, and using drugs), being independent, and being cool provided a way to establish identity and earn reputation for lower class youth.

In his 1999 book *Code of the Street,* Elijah Anderson documented the interpersonal violence of youth in the context of their public life and social organization in the inner-city ghetto. Anderson found that as rules of order and law weakened, they were replaced by informal rules on the street that proscribed violence as a means to earn respect. Youth who experienced alienation from mainstream society and lived in economic disadvantage could find status and credibility by following the **code of the street**. Similarly, in their research on youth violence, Stewart and Simons (2009) also identified street values that emerged to compensate for limited opportunities to achieve conventional success and respect.

The Anomie Theory of Delinquency

Anomie theory was used by the early French social scientist Emile Durkheim, who investigated many social and psychological phenomena, including suicide and its causes (Springer and Frei, 2008). One precipitating factor leading to certain suicides, according to Durkheim, was anomie or normlessness. What Durkheim intended by the term was to portray a condition in which people's lives, their values, and various social rules were disrupted and in which those people found it difficult to cope with their changed life conditions. Thus, they would experience **anomie**, a type of helplessness, and perhaps even hopelessness. Most persons usually adapt to drastic changes in their lifestyles or patterns, but a few may opt for suicide because they lack the social and psychological means to cope with the strain of change (Konty, 2005).

Merton (1957) was intrigued by Durkheim's notion of anomie and how persons adapt to the strain of changing conditions. He devised a goals-and-means scheme as a way of describing different social actions that persons might use for making behavioral choices. Merton contended that society generally prescribes approved cultural goals for its members to seek (e.g., new homes, jobs, and automobiles). Furthermore, appropriate, legitimate, or institutionalized means are prescribed for the purpose of attaining these goals. Not everyone is equally endowed with the desire to achieve societal goals, however, nor are they necessarily committed to using the prescribed means to achieve these goals.

Merton described five different **modes of adaptation** that people might exhibit (Choi and Lo, 2002). These modes included **conformity** (persons accept the goals of society and work toward their attainment using societally approved means), **innovation** (persons accept the goals of society but use means to achieve them other than those approved by society), **ritualism** (persons reject the goals of society but work toward other, less-lofty goals by institutionally approved means), **retreatism** (persons reject goals and the means to achieve goals, retreat or escape from mainstream society,

---

code of the street

Norms and values of lower-class youth that emphasize violence and respect.

anomie theory

Robert Merton's theory, influenced by Emile Durkheim, alleging that persons acquire desires for culturally approved goals to strive to achieve but adopt innovative, sometimes deviant, means to achieve these goals (e.g., someone may desire a nice home but lack or reject the institutionalized means to achieve this goal and instead using bank robbery, an innovative mean, to obtain money to realize the culturally approved goal); implies normlessness.

anomie

Condition of feelings of helplessness and normlessness.

modes of adaptation

A way that persons who occupy a particular social position adjust to cultural goals and the institutionalized means to reach those goals.

conformity

Robert Merton's mode of adaptation characterized by persons who accept institutionalized means to achieve culturally approved goals.

Focus on Delinquency

It happened in Georgia. T.J.S., 15, opened fire at his high school, wounding six classmates with a .22-caliber rifle. Subsequently, he was subdued by school teachers and other students when he ran out of ammunition for the rifle and then attempted to kill himself with a second gun in his possession. T.J.S. was handled by the criminal court, and he entered a plea of guilty but mentally ill. He received a sentence of 40 years in prison and 65 years on probation. In 2001, the sentence was reduced to 20 years in prison.

From the start, T.J.S.'s attorneys have never denied that T.J.S. was the shooter. He has acknowledged that he opened fire on other students with the rifle and that he wounded several of them during the shooting spree. One of his attorneys said, "We have never disputed that the shots were fired by T.J.S. The depths of his illness, the circumstances surrounding the case—these are the things that will be examined at the trial." T.J.S. eventually entered a plea of not guilty by reason of insanity to all of the shooting charges. If he was found not guilty by reason of insanity, he could be institutionalized in a mental hospital or freed. Should the insanity plea be accepted in cases such as this? How frequently is the insanity defense used in criminal cases? Does it excuse criminal conduct? Should T.J.S. be allowed to go free merely by alleging that he was insane at the time he shot other students? What do you think?

Source: Adapted from the AP Online (2000, April 1), "School Shooting Suspect Enters Plea" (available at http://www.highbeam.com/doc/1P1-25644281.html); CNN Justice (2001, August 16), "Sentence Reduced for Georgia High School Shooter" (available at http://articles.cnn.com/2001-08-16/justice/school.shooter_1_parole-board-parole-hearing-columbine-shootings?_s=PM:LAW).

innovation

Robert Merton's mode of adaptation in which persons reject institutionalized means to achieve culturally approved goals; instead, they engage in illegal acts, considered innovative, to achieve their goals.

ritualism

Mode of adaptation suggested by Robert Merton in which persons reject culturally approved goals but work toward lesser goals through institutionalized means.

and establish their own goals and means to achieve them, e.g., hermits, street people, or "bag ladies"), and **rebellion** (persons seek to replace culturally approved goals and institutionalized means with new goals and means for others to follow).

Of these, the innovation mode characterizes juvenile delinquents, according to Merton. Juvenile delinquency is innovative in that youth accept culturally desirable goals but reject the legitimate means to achieve these goals. Instead, they adopt illegitimate means, such as theft, burglary, or violence. Many youth may crave new clothes, automobiles, and other expensive material items. Since they may lack the money to pay for these items, one alternative is to steal them. This is regarded by Merton as one innovative response arising from a condition of anomie and the strain it emits.

Many intermediate punishment programs today are designed to assist youth in devising new strategies to cope with everyday life rather than to use crime or delinquent conduct to achieve their goals. VisionQuest, Homeward Bound, and various types of wilderness experiences incorporate adaptive experiences as integral features of these programs. Those youth with substantial energy are sometimes placed in camps or on ranches, where they can act out some of their feelings and frustrations. These programs deliberately cater to youth who are innovative but lack a clear sense of direction.

Labeling Theory

Another important sociological approach to explaining delinquent conduct is **labeling theory**. Labeling theory's primary proponent is Edwin Lemert (1951, 1967a,

1967b). However, other social scientists have also been credited with originating this concept (Becker, 1963; Kitsuse, 1962).

Labeling stresses the definitions people have of delinquent acts rather than delinquency itself. Applied to delinquent conduct, Lemert (1967b) was concerned with two primary questions:

1. What is the process whereby youth become labeled as delinquent?
2. What is the influence of such labeling on these youths' future behavior?

Lemert assumed that no act is inherently delinquent, that all persons at different points in time conform to or deviate from the law, that persons become delinquent through social labeling or definition, that being apprehended by police begins the labeling process, that youth defined as delinquent will acquire self-definitions as delinquents, and finally, that those defining themselves as delinquent will seek to establish associations with others also defined as delinquent (Hart, 2005).

Not every youth who violates the law, regardless of the seriousness of the offense, will become a hard-core delinquent. Some infractions are relatively minor offenses. For example, experimenting with alcohol and getting drunk, trying certain drugs, joyriding, and petty theft may be one-time events never to be repeated (Kuntsche et al., 2007). However, getting caught enhances the likelihood that any particular youth will be brought into the juvenile justice system for processing and labeling. Youth who have adopted delinquent subcultures are often those who have attracted the attention of others, including the police, by engaging in wrongful acts or causing trouble. Wearing the symbols of gang membership, such as jackets emblazoned with gang names, helps to solidify one's self-definition of being delinquent (Taylor et al., 2008).

Getting caught begins the cycle of delinquency for many youth.
(Laima Druskis/Pearson)

retreatism
Mode of adaptation suggested by Robert Merton in which persons reject culturally approved goals and institutionalized means and do little or nothing to achieve; homeless persons, "bag ladies," vagrants, and others sometimes fit the retreatist profile.

rebellion
Mode of adaptation suggested by Robert Merton in which persons reject institutional means to achieve culturally approved goals and create their own goals and means to use and seek.

labeling theory
Explanation of deviant conduct attributed to Edwin Lemert whereby persons acquire self-definitions that are deviant or criminal; persons perceive themselves as deviant or criminal through labels applied to them by others; the more people are involved in the criminal justice system, the more they acquire self-definitions consistent with the criminal label.

labeling
Process whereby persons acquire self-definitions that are deviant or criminal; process occurs through labels applied to them by others.

primary deviation

Part of the labeling process whenever youth engage in occasional pranks and not especially serious violations of the law.

secondary deviation

A stage in labeling theory that suggests delinquency and violations of the law become part of self-image and normal behavior rather than just occasional pranks.

Lemert (1967b) suggested that juvenile deviation may be primary deviation or secondary deviation. **Primary deviation** occurs when youth spontaneously violate the law by engaging in occasional pranks. Law enforcement authorities may conclude that these pranks are not particularly serious. However, if juveniles persist in repeating their deviant and delinquent conduct, they may exhibit secondary deviation. **Secondary deviation** occurs when delinquency becomes consistent with adolescent self-image and behavior patterns or lifestyle. Thus, delinquency is viewed as a social label applied by others to those youth who have relatively frequent contact with the juvenile justice system (Hart, 2005). The strength of this social labeling is such that juveniles themselves adopt these social labels and regard themselves as delinquent. This, too, is a vicious cycle of sorts, in that one phenomenon (social labeling by others of some youth as delinquent) reinforces the other (labeled youth acquiring self-definitions as delinquent and engaging in further delinquent conduct consistent with the delinquent label).

Lemert's labeling perspective has probably been the most influential theory relative to policy decisions by juvenile courts to divert youth away from the formal trappings of court proceedings (Hart, 2005). The sentiment is that if we can keep youth away from the juvenile justice system, they are less inclined to identify with it. Accordingly, they are also less likely to define themselves as delinquent and to engage in delinquent conduct. Although diversion programs are not always successful in deterring youth from further immersion in the juvenile justice system, they are intended to prevent the labeling associated with the process and to provide the youth with an alternative to further offending (Murrell, 2005).

Youth workers may testify in court about delinquency and its causes or why some youth act in certain ways.
(Richard Logan/Pearson)

Bonding Theory

Bonding theory, or **social control theory**, derives primarily from the work of Travis Hirschi (1969). This theory stresses processual aspects of youth becoming bonded or socially integrated into the norms of society (Mack et al., 2007). The greater the integration or bonding, particularly with parents and school teachers, the less the likelihood that youth will engage in delinquent activity. Different dimensions of bonding include **attachment** (emotional linkages with those we respect and admire), **commitment** (enthusiasm or energy expended in a specific relationship), **belief** (moral definition of the rightness or wrongness of certain conduct), and **involvement** (intensity of attachment with those who engage in conventional conduct or espouse conventional values) (Baron, 2007; Baron and Forde, 2007).

Based on Hirschi's model, delinquency is "inherently appealing" to adolescents who seek excitement and peer approval (Tontodonato and Hagan, 2009, p. 37). It is these bonds, and the strength of the bonds, that inhibit or minimize delinquent behavior. When the bonds are broken or weakened, youth are more at-risk for delinquency (Tontodonato and Hagan, 2009).

Hirschi investigated large numbers of high school students to test his bonding theory. More academically successful students seemed to be bonded to conventional values and significant others, such as teachers and school authorities, compared with less-successful students. Those students who apparently lack strong commitment to school and to education generally are more prone to become delinquent than are those students with opposite dispositions (McCartan and Gunnison, 2007). However, since Hirschi limited his research to students in high-school settings, he has been criticized for not applying his bonding theory to juvenile samples in other, nonschool settings.

Furthermore, Hirschi has failed to explain clearly the processual aspects of bonding. Also, because rejecting or accepting conventional values and significant others is a matter of degree, and because youth may have many attachments with both delinquent and nondelinquent juveniles, bonding theory has failed to predict accurately which youth will eventually become delinquent. This is regarded as a serious limitation (Beaver, Wright, and DeLisi, 2007). However, as Tontodonato and Hagan (2009) concluded in their critique of Hirschi's bond theory, "like other social process theories, bond theory assumes that any person (regardless of social class) has the potential to be delinquent; the key factor to consider is socialization into the values and beliefs of society and the strength of social ties" (p. 37).

Agnew's General Strain Theory

Strain theory was developed from the anomie theory described by Emile Durkheim and Robert Merton (Baron, 2007). Anomie theory stresses the breakdown of societal restraints on individual conduct. Merton elaborated on this breakdown by describing the emerging cultural imbalance between the goals and norms of individuals in society. The strain component is apparent, because although many lower-SES youth have

bonding theory
Emile Durkheim's notion that deviant behavior is controlled to the degree that group members feel morally bound to one another, are committed to common goals, and share a collective conscience.

social control theory
Explanation of criminal behavior that focuses on control mechanisms, techniques, and strategies for regulating human behavior, leading to conformity or obedience to society's rules posits that deviance results when social controls are weakened or break down so that individuals are not motivated to conform to them.

attachment
The most important element of social control theory; refers to identification with parents, teachers, and peers as well as attention to their opinions and a sensitivity to their priorities; fosters conformity.

commitment
One of the four elements of social control theory; refers to the individual's investment in conventional society as evidenced by efforts directed toward academic expectations and success, reputation, career, and society

belief
One element of social control theory; includes an understanding of respect for authority and the law; also refers to a recognition of the rights of others and adherence to a common value system.

involvement
One element of social control theory; refers to the work, sports, school, and recreational activities that necessitate large blocks of time and indicate that a person is engaged with these pursuits and the community.

strain theory
A criminological theory positing that a gap between culturally approved goals and legitimate means of achieving them causes frustration, which leads to criminal behavior.

adopted middle-class goals and aspirations, they may be unable to attain these goals as a result of their individual economic and cultural circumstances (Ellwanger, 2007). This is a frustrating experience for many of these youth, and such frustration is manifested by the strain to achieve difficult goals or objectives. While middle-class youth also experience strain in their attempts to achieve middle-class goals, it is particularly aggravating for many lower-class youth, who sometimes do not receive the necessary support from their families (Song and Royo, 2008).

Robert Agnew views strain theory as cutting across all social classes (Walls, Chapple, and Johnson, 2007). Agnew modified Merton's theory and elaborated on a general strain theory of crime and delinquency. General strain theory is differentiated from control theory in that control theory is based on the premise that the breakdown of society, or the weakening of social ties, frees individuals to commit delinquent acts. Control theory also suggests that the absence of significant relationships with nondeviant others means less social control from others over delinquent behavior. In addition, general strain theory is differentiated from social learning theory, which stresses forces in groups that lead persons to view crime in positive ways. Social learning theory suggests that youth eventually find themselves in relationships with others who are deviant and delinquent and that these relationships are viewed as positive and rewarding. In contrast, general strain theory focuses on the pressures that are placed on youth to commit delinquency. These pressures occur in the form of maltreatment by others, causing youth to become upset and to turn to crime as a negative reaction (Lee and Hoaken, 2007; Mack et al., 2007).

Agnew believes that strain can be measured in different ways. In the subjective method, investigators determine whether delinquents believe they dislike the way they have been treated by others. The objective method focuses upon identifying particular experiences in groups that delinquents say they would dislike if they were subjected to such experiences. Thus, different components of potential strain for juveniles can be predetermined and identified.

What are the major negative determinants of strain? One is the failure of youth to achieve positively valued stimuli. Youth seek money, status (especially masculine status), and respect. When youth are barred from attaining these goals, strain is created. Autonomy, the power over oneself, is also highly valued. In an effort to assert autonomy, youth may be thwarted from achieving this desired state and revert to delinquency to relieve strain and frustration. Thus, there are certain disjunctions in life, especially between aspirations and expectations. When someone achieves less than is expected, strain is experienced, and this frustration to achieve whatever is desired may be judged to be the result of unfairness. Thus, when a youth expects to achieve a desired result and does not achieve it, the failure experience is an unjust one.

Another way of measuring strain is to examine potential losses of positively valued stimuli. The loss of significant others, broken relationships with friends or romantic partners, or the theft of a valued possession may create strain. Some youth react to these losses by turning to delinquency to retrieve what was lost, to prevent further loss, or to seek revenge against those perceived as having caused the loss.

Yet another measure of strain consists of negative stimuli, such as child abuse, neglect, adverse relations with parents or teachers, negative school experiences, adverse relationships with peers, neighborhood problems, and homelessness (Bowman, Prelow, and Weaver, 2007). Even parental unemployment, family deaths, and illnesses can contribute to increasing delinquent behavior in adolescents. Also, the external environment itself can create many negative feelings among youth, including despair, defeatism, fear, and anger. Anger is especially significant as youth blame their negative circumstances and relationships on others. Those youth who experience repetitive incidents of stressful and frustrating experiences are more likely to engage in delinquent behaviors and in hostile and aggressive actions (LaTorre, 2008).

Coping with strain is complex, according to Agnew. Cognitive, emotional, and behavioral coping strategies might include rationalizing, placing less importance on goals originally sought, and/or accepting responsibility for failure to achieve goals. Positive stimuli rather than negative stimuli may be sought to counter the strain of one's experiences. Therefore, coping mechanisms may be either criminal or noncriminal. General strain theory includes constraints to nondelinquent behavior, as well as factors that may affect an individual's disposition to delinquent behavior. In this way, it is possible to predict the adaptations, delinquent or nondelinquent, that will be chosen.

One issue related to general strain theory that Agnew addresses is that male and female delinquents adapt differently to strain. While this differential reaction has not been explained fully, it has been suggested that female juveniles may lack the confidence and self-esteem that may be conducive to committing delinquency. Females may, in fact, devise strategies that include avoidance and escape in an effort to reduce or eliminate strain. Furthermore, females may have stronger relational ties compared with males. Thus, their strain-reduction efforts may be more successful. However, rising rates of female juvenile offending suggest that females may face strain in different forms than males do. For instance, females often face sexual, emotional, and physical abuse to a greater degree than their male counterparts (Owens-Sabir, 2007). These are negative stimuli. Thus, female juvenile response to such negative stimuli may include acting out in delinquent ways. More research is needed in the study of male–female juvenile differences relative to general strain theory and its gender-specific applications (Murrell, 2005).

In addition to studying differences in how males and females react to strain, researchers have also examined cross-cultural effects of strain. In a study using samples from Russia, Ukraine, and Greece, Botchkovar, Tittle, and Antonaccio (2009) found support for the effects of strain on criminal probability with Ukranian, but not with Russian and Greek, respondents. They suggest that "other factors, such as religiosity and self-control, may influence the effects of strain on criminal probability" (p. 160). They conclude that culture norms and social context also need to be considered when theorizing about the effects of strain on criminal behavior.

Additional Theoretical Explanations of Delinquency

containment theory

Explanation elaborated by Walter Reckless and others that positive self-image enables persons otherwise disposed toward criminal behavior to avoid criminal conduct and conform to societal values; every person is a part of an external structure and has an internal structure providing defense, protection, and/or insulation against peers, such as delinquents.

neutralization theory

Holds that delinquents experience guilt when involved in delinquent activities and that they respect leaders of the legitimate social order; their delinquency is episodic rather than chronic, and they adhere to conventional values while "drifting" into periods of illegal behavior; to drift, the delinquent must first neutralize legal and moral values.

drift theory

David Matza's term denoting a state of limbo in which youth move in and out of delinquency and in which their lifestyles embrace both conventional and deviant values.

Other explanations for delinquent conduct have also been advanced by various theorists. Those reviewed above for more in-depth coverage are intended to describe some of the thinking about why juveniles might engage in delinquent conduct. Some of the other approaches that have been advocated include containment theory, neutralization or drift theory, differential association theory, and differential reinforcement theory.

Containment theory is associated with the work of sociologist Walter Reckless (1967). Reckless outlined a theoretical model consisting of pushes and pulls in relation to delinquency. By pushes, he referred to internal, personal factors, including hostility, anxiety, and discontent. By pulls, he meant external, social forces, including delinquent subcultures and significant others. The containment dimension of his theoretical scheme consisted of both outer and inner containments.

Outer containments, according to Reckless, are social norms, folkways, mores, laws, and institutional arrangements that induce societal conformity. By inner containments, Reckless referred to individual or personal coping strategies to deal with stressful situations and conflict. These strategies might have a high tolerance for conflict or frustration and considerable ego strength. Thus, Reckless combined both psychological and social elements in referring to weak attachments of some youth to cultural norms, high anxiety levels, and low tolerance for personal stress. These persons are most inclined to delinquent conduct. A key factor in whether juveniles adopt delinquent behaviors, however, is their level of self-esteem (Taylor et al., 2008). Those with high levels of self-esteem seem most resistant to delinquent behaviors if they are exposed to such conduct while around their friends (Mueller and Hutchison-Wallace, 2005).

Neutralization theory, or **drift theory**, was outlined by David Matza (1964) and by Gresham Sykes and David Matza (1957). According to this theory, most juveniles spend their early years on a behavioral continuum ranging between unlimited freedom and total control or restraint. These persons drift toward one end of the continuum or the other, depending upon their social and psychological circumstances. If youth have strong attachments with those who are delinquent, then they drift toward the unlimited freedom end of the continuum and, perhaps, engage in delinquent activities. However, Matza indicated that the behavioral issue is not clear-cut. Juveniles most likely have associations with normative culture, such as their parents or religious leaders, as well as with the delinquent subculture, such as various delinquent youth. They may engage in delinquent conduct and regard their behavior as acceptable at the time they engage in it. Elaborate rationales for delinquent behavior may be invented by youth (e.g., society is unfair, victims deserve to be victims, or nobody is hurt by our particular acts). Thus, they effectively neutralize the normative constraints of society that impinge upon them. Specifically, these "techniques of neutralization" include **denial of responsibility, denial of injury, denial of victim, condemnation of the condemners**, and **appeal to higher loyalties** (Sykes and Matza, 1957). Therefore, at least some delinquency results from rationalizations created by youth that render delinquent acts acceptable under the circumstances (Wallace and Fisher, 2007). Appropriate preventative therapy for such delinquents might be to undermine their rationales for delinquent behaviors through empathic means. Also, activities that are geared toward strengthening family bonds are important, since greater attachments with parents tend to overwhelm the influence of associations with delinquent peers (Zimmermann and McGarrell, 2005).

Differential association theory was developed by Edwin Sutherland (1939) and is in some respects an outgrowth of the **cultural transmission theory** described by Shaw and McKay in their investigations of juvenile offenders in Chicago. Sutherland described a socialization process (learning through contact with others) whereby juveniles would acquire delinquent behaviors manifested by others among their close associates. It would certainly be an oversimplification of Sutherland's views to claim that associating with other delinquents would cause certain juveniles to adopt similar delinquent behaviors. Sutherland's scheme was more complex and multifaceted, and he suggested that some interpersonal dimensions characterize relations between law violators and others who behave similarly (Champion, 2008a). According to Sutherland, differential association consists of the following elements: (1) frequency, (2) priority, (3) duration, and (4) intensity. Thus, engaging in frequent associations and long-lasting interactions with others who are delinquent, giving them priority as significant others, and cultivating strong emotional attachments with them will contribute in a significant way to a youth's propensity to commit delinquent acts.

Explicit in Sutherland's scheme is the phenomenon of attachments with others who are delinquent. Thus, this is at least one similarity that differential association theory shares with containment theory and bonding. Sutherland sought to characterize relationships some juveniles have with delinquents as multidimensional relationships, and the association aspect was only one of these dimensions. Although Sutherland's work has been influential, widely quoted, and utilized by criminologists, some experts have been critical of his theory on various grounds. He never fully articulated the true meaning of intensity, for instance. How intense should a relation be between a delinquent and a nondelinquent before making a difference and causing the nondelinquent to adopt delinquent patterns of behavior? How frequently should nondelinquents be in the company of delinquents before such contact becomes crucial and changes nondelinquent behavior? These and other similar questions were never fully addressed by Sutherland. Nevertheless, differential association has influenced certain correctional policies and treatment programs for both juveniles and adults (Champion, 2008a).

Much like labeling theory, differential association theory has encouraged minimizing contact between hard-core criminal offenders and first-time offenders, also known as first-offenders. The use of prison is often the last resort in certain cases, since it is believed that more prolonged contact with other criminals will only intensify any criminal propensities first-offenders might exhibit. If they were diverted to some nonincarcerative option, however, they might not become recidivists and

denial of responsibility
One of the five forms of neutralization described by Gresham Sykes and David Matza; individuals suggest that their behavior or actions are the result of forces beyond their control.

denial of injury
One of the five forms of neutralization described by Gresham Sykes and David Matza; refers to offenders contending that their actions or behaviors did not really harm anyone and, therefore, they should not be blamed.

denial of victim
One of the five forms of neutralization described by Gresham Sykes and David Matza; refers to the offender suggesting that it is the victim's previous behavior that is really responsible for the current act; the offender suggests that the victim somehow "was asking for it."

condemnation of the condemners

One of the five techniques that Gresham Sykes and David Matza explained; the actions or motives of the individuals who do not approve of the act are questionable; they arbitrarily single out the offender; rather than focusing on the offender, the system should focus on the actors condemning the behavior.

appeal to higher loyalties

A technique of neutralization that suggests individuals have loyalties to groups or others; these loyalties are important and supercede any rules or laws that society imposes; offenders are engaging in acts to help their friends rather than to hurt someone else; their motives are altruistic.

differential association theory

Edwin Sutherland's theory of deviance and criminality through associations with others who are deviant or criminal; theory includes dimensions of frequency, duration, priority, and intensity; persons become criminal or delinquent because of a preponderance of learned definitions that are favorable to violating the law over learned definitions that are unfavorable to it.

commit new crimes. The same principle applies to delinquent first-offenders and accounts for the widespread use of noncustodial sanctions that seek to minimize a juvenile's contact with the juvenile justice system.

In 1966, Robert Burgess and Ronald Akers revised Sutherland's differential association theory and derived what they termed **differential reinforcement theory**. Differential reinforcement theory actually combines elements from labeling theory and a psychological phenomenon known as conditioning. Conditioning functions in the social learning process as persons are rewarded for engaging in certain desirable behaviors and for refraining from certain undesirable behaviors. Juveniles perceive how others respond to their behaviors (negative reactions) and may be disposed to behave in ways that will maximize their rewards from others.

In some respects, Burgess and Akers have also incorporated certain aspects of the **looking-glass self** concept originally devised by Charles Horton Cooley (1902). Cooley theorized that people learned ways of conforming by paying attention to the reactions of others in response to their own behavior. Therefore, Cooley would argue, we imagine how others see us. We look for other people's reactions to our behavior, and we interpret these reactions as either good or bad reactions. If we define others' reactions as good, we might feel a degree of pride and likely persist in the behaviors. As Cooley indicated, however, if we interpret their reactions to our behaviors as bad, we might experience mortification. Given this latter reaction, or at least our interpretation of it, we might change our behaviors to conform to what others might want and, thereby, elicit approval from them. While these ideas continue to interest us, they are difficult to conceptualize and investigate empirically. Akers and others have acknowledged such difficulties, although their work is insightful and underscores the reality of a multidimensional view of delinquent conduct.

An Evaluation of Explanations of Delinquent Conduct

Assessing the importance or significance of theories about delinquency is difficult. First, almost all causes of delinquent conduct outlined by theorists continue to interest contemporary investigators. The most frequently discounted and consistently criticized views are biological ones, although as we have seen, sociobiology and genetic concomitants of delinquent conduct continue to raise questions about the role of heredity as a significant factor in explaining delinquency. Some evidence suggests that television and movie violence triggers aggressive and violent behavior among different youth, yet blaming media violence for the actions of some youth fails to explain the absence of violence among other youth who are also exposed to it (Slater, Hayes, and Ford, 2007; Wallenius, Punamaki, and Rimpela, 2007). Still other explanations rely on attention-deficit/hyperactivity disorder (or ADHD) to explain why some youth become delinquent or behave in abnormal ways (Cary, 2005).

Psychological explanations seem more plausible than biological ones, although the precise relation between the psyche and biological factors remains unknown. Yet, if we focus on psychological explanations of delinquency as important in fostering delinquent conduct, then almost invariably, we involve certain elements of the social world in such explanations. Thus, mental processes are influenced in various ways by social experiences. Self-definitions, important to psychologists and learning theorists, are conceived largely in social contexts, in the presence of and through contact with others. It is not surprising, therefore, that the most fruitful explanations for delinquency are those seeking to blend the best parts of different theories that assess different dimensions of youth, such as their physique and intellectual abilities, personalities, and social experiences. Intellectual isolationism or complete reliance on biological, psychological, or sociological factors exclusively may simplify theory construction, but in the final analysis, such isolationism is unproductive. Certainly, each field has importance and contributes toward explaining why some youth exhibit delinquent conduct while others do not.

This perspective suggests explanations that integrate scientific evidence may be more useful in understanding and explaining delinquency both as a social phenomenon and as individual behavior. For example, the "diathesis-stress" model offers a biopsychosocial model that considers differences in individual vulnerabilities to delinquency (i.e., diathesis) but also recognizes the importance of external or environmental stresses to which individuals are exposed (Wicks-Nelson and Israel, 2005). In other words, whether adolescents with underlying vulnerabilities or risk factors (e.g., low IQ, low frustration tolerance, and poor self-concept) exhibit or manifest delinquent behaviors may depend upon environmental factors. Similarly, youth with low risk factors may become delinquent due to negative external stimulators and stresses (e.g., child abuse, exposure to violent subculture, and low SES). This perspective does not emphasize biological, psychological, or sociological theories of delinquency "but rather how successful will we be in describing how biological, psychological, and sociological factors interact to produce delinquent behavior" (Gamble and Eisert, 2009, p. 76).

Theories, Policies, and Intervention Strategies

From a purely pragmatic approach in assessing the predictive and/or explanatory utility of each of these theories, we may examine contemporary interventionist efforts that seek to curb delinquency or prevent its recurrence. As Hagan (2011) has explained, "crime policies, various programs and activities aimed at controlling crime, do not occur in a vacuum, but are guided by contemporary theory" (p. 110). One way of determining which theories influence policy and inform administrative decision making relative to juveniles is to identify the ways youthful offenders are treated by the juvenile justice system when they have been apprehended and adjudicated (Wallace, Minor, and Wells, 2005).

A preliminary screening of juvenile offenders may result in some being diverted from the juvenile justice system. One manifest purpose of such diversionary action is to reduce the potentially adverse influence of labeling on these youth. Thus, a long-term objective of diversion is to minimize recidivism among these youth. However,

cultural transmission theory

Explanation emphasizing transmission of criminal behavior through socialization; views delinquency as socially learned behavior transmitted from one generation to the next in disorganized urban areas.

differential reinforcement theory

Explanation that combines elements of labeling theory and a psychological phenomenon known as conditioning; persons are rewarded for engaging in desirable behavior and punished for deviant conduct.

looking-glass self

Concept originated by Charles Horton Cooley in which persons learn appropriate ways of behaving by paying attention to how others view and react to them.

while the intended effects of diversion are to reduce social stigma, such as a reduction in the degree of social stigmatization toward status offenders, the actual outcomes of diversion are presently unclear, inconsistent, and insufficiently documented (Kidd, 2007).

A promising idea in this area is that minimizing formal involvement with the juvenile justice system is favorable for reducing self-definitions as delinquent and avoiding the delinquent label. Thus, labeling theory seems to have been prominent in the promotion of diversionary programs. Furthermore, many divertees have been exposed to experiences that enhance or improve their self-reliance and independence. Many youth have learned to think out their problems rather than act them out unproductively or antisocially. When we examine the contents of these programs closely, it is fairly easy to detect aspects of bonding theory, containment theory, and differential reinforcement theory at work in the delinquency prevention process (Ousey and Wilcox, 2007).

Besides using diversion per se, with or without various programs, elements or overtones of other theoretical schemes can be present in the particular treatments or experiences juveniles receive as they continue to be processed throughout the juvenile justice system. At the time of adjudication, for example, juvenile court judges may, or may not, impose special conditions to accompany a sentence of probation. Special conditions may refer to obligating juveniles to make restitution to victims, performing public services, participating in group or individual therapy, or undergoing medical treatment in cases of drug addiction or alcohol abuse.

Learning to accept responsibility for actions, acquiring new coping skills to face crises and personal tragedy, improving educational attainment, and improving ego strength to resist the influence of delinquent peers are individually or collectively integral parts of various delinquency treatment programs, particularly where the psychological approach is strong (Bowman, Prelow, and Weaver, 2007).

Program outcomes are often used as gauges for the successfulness of their underlying theoretical schemes. Since no program is 100 percent effective at preventing delinquency, however, it follows that no theoretical scheme devised thus far is fully effective. Yet, the wide variety of programs that are applied today to deal with different kinds of juvenile offenders indicates that most psychological and sociological approaches have some merit and contribute differentially to delinquency reduction. Policy decisions are made throughout the juvenile justice system and are often contingent upon the theoretical views adopted by politicians, law enforcement personnel, prosecutors and judges, and correctional officials at every stage of the justice process. We may appreciate most theoretical views because of their varying intuitive value and selectively apply particular approaches to accommodate different types of juvenile offenders.

While there is no panacea for delinquency, scientific research has recognized strategies and programs that are more effective in dealing with delinquency. These studies rely on the outcomes of intervention and identify evidence-based approaches that work. The Office of Juvenile Justice and Delinquency Prevention maintains the

Model Programs Guide that offers a database of tested and proven programs for prevention and intervention. The easy-to-use portal (http://www.ojjdp.gov/mpg) guides users in matching juveniles who have specific risks with appropriate, evidence-based programs that reduce recidivism and enhance public safety. The categories of intervention include prevention, immediate sanctions, intermediate sanctions, residential, and reentry. The model assesses risk and protective factors in five domains— (1) community, (2) family, (3) school, (4) peers, and (5) individual—and identifies the type of programs best suited to the needs of the delinquent youth.

Similarly, **Blueprints for Violence Prevention** (http://www.colorado.edu/cspv/ blueprints/), developed by the Center for the Strategies and Prevention of Violence at the University of Colorado, identifies model and promising programs that use evidence-based approaches in preventing drug use and violence among youth. Over 800 programs have been evaluated to determine best practices that are effective in dealing with youth at risk for delinquency. The Center provides a matrix of criteria standards and a list of best programs.

Regarding theories of delinquency generally, their impact has been felt most strongly in the area of policy making rather than in behavioral change or modification. Virtually every theory is connected, in some respect, to various types of experimental programs in different jurisdictions. The intent of most programs has been to change behaviors of participants. However, high rates of recidivism characterize delinquency prevention innovations, regardless of their intensity or ingenuity. Policy decisions implemented at earlier points in time have long-range implications for present policies in correctional work. Probationers and parolees as well as inmates and divertees, adults and juveniles alike, are recipients or inheritors of previous policies laid in place by theorists who have attempted to convert their theories into practical experiences and action (Sungi, 2008).

Recent policy in juvenile justice favors the get-tough orientation, and programs are increasingly sponsored that heavily incorporate accountability and individual responsibility. At an earlier point in time, projects emphasizing rehabilitation and reintegration were rewarded more heavily through private grants and various types of government funding. No particular prevention, intervention, or supervision program works best, however. Numerous contrasting perspectives about how policy should be shaped continue to vie for recognition among professionals and politicians. The theories that have been described here are indicative of the many factors that have shaped present policies and practices, and the influence of these diverse theories is reflected in a variety of models that have been, and continue to be, used by juvenile justice practitioners. Some of these models are presented in the following section.

Models for Dealing with Juvenile Offenders

Policy models for dealing with juvenile offenders are presented and described here. Each model is driven by a particular view of juvenile delinquency and what might cause it. The causes of delinquency are many and diverse. Thus, not everyone agrees

Model Programs Guide
A database of evidence-based programs that provides a continuum of strategies for delinquency prevention and intervention.

Blueprints for Violence Prevention
Evidenced-based programs for delinquency prevention and intervention.

with any particular explanation, and not every expert dealing with juvenile offenders agrees that one particular model is most fruitful as a basis for delinquency intervention. Rather, these models serve as a guide to the different types of decisions that are made on behalf of or against specific juvenile offenders. Because each model includes aims or objectives that are related, to some degree, with the aims or objectives of other models, there is sometimes confusion about model identities. For example, some professionals may use a particular model label to refer to orientations that are more properly included in the context of other models. Other professionals say that they do not use any particular model but, rather, rely on their own intuition for exercising a particular juvenile intervention.

In addition, some recently developed interventionist activities have combined the favorable features of one model with those of others. These hybrid models are difficult to categorize, although they are believed to be helpful in diverting youth to more productive activities. One way of overcoming this confusion is to highlight those features of models that most directly reflect the aims of the hybrid models. The models discussed here include (1) the rehabilitation model, (2) the treatment or medical model, (3) the noninterventionist model, (4) the due process model, (5) the just deserts/justice model, (6) the crime control model, and (7) the Balanced and Restorative Justice model.

The Rehabilitation Model

rehabilitation model

Concept of youth management similar to medical model, in which juvenile delinquents are believed to be suffering from social and psychological handicaps; provides experiences to build self-concept; these experiences stress educational and social remedies.

Perhaps the most influential model that has benefited first-time juvenile offenders is the **rehabilitation model**. This model assumes that delinquency or delinquent conduct is the result of poor friendship or peer choices, poor social adjustments, the wrong educational priorities, and/or a general failure to envision realistic life goals and inculcate appropriate moral values (Haynie et al., 2005). In corrections, the rehabilitation model is associated with programs that change offender attitudes, personalities, or character (Salinas, 2008). These programs may be therapeutic, educational, or vocational. At the intake stage, however, there is little, if any, reliance on existing community-based programs or services that cater to certain juvenile needs. Intake officers who use the rehabilitation model in their decision-making activities will often attempt to impart different values and personal goals to juveniles through a type of informal teaching.

Intake officers who meet with nonviolent first-offenders usually do not want to see these youth move further into the juvenile justice system. Therefore, these officers may attempt to get juvenile offenders to empathize with their victims and to understand the harm they have caused by their actions. If a youth is being processed at the intake stage for theft, for example, the intake officer may emphasize the harmful effects of the theft for the owner from whom the merchandise was taken. Theft is a serious offense, but it is less serious than aggravated assault, rape, armed robbery, or murder. Thus, when a juvenile is very young and has committed this single theft offense, this is an ideal situation where intake officers can exercise strategic discretion and temper their decisions with some leniency.

In the context, however, of *parens patriae* and the rehabilitative framework guiding some of the intake officers, leniency does not mean there are no consequences. Doing nothing may send the wrong message to youth who have violated the law. The same may be said of police officers who encounter youth on streets and engage in police cautioning or stationhouse adjustments as alternative means of warning juveniles to refrain from future misconduct. Thus, it is believed the informal intake hearing itself is sufficiently traumatic for most youth that they will not be eager to reoffend. Advice, cautioning, and warnings given under such circumstances are likely to be remembered. It is also important to involve family members in these intake conferences. If a youth who has committed a delinquent act can see that his or her behavior has adversely affected family members, then the chances of recidivism may decline (Duran, 2005).

The Treatment or Medical Model

The **treatment model**, or **medical model**, assumes that delinquent conduct is like a disease, the causes of which can be isolated and attacked. Curative treatment may be effected by administering appropriate remedies. The treatment model is very similar to the rehabilitation model. Indeed, some persons consider the treatment or medical model to be a subcategory of the rehabilitation model (Boyd and Myers, 2005).

> **treatment model, medical model**
>
> This model considers criminal behavior as an illness to be treated; delinquency is also a disease subject to treatment.

The aim of the treatment model is to provide conditional punishments for juveniles that are closely related to treatment. Intake officers have the authority to refer certain youth to select community-based agencies and services, where they may receive the proper treatment. This treatment approach assumes that these intake officers have correctly diagnosed the illness and know best how to cure it (Davidson-Methot, 2004). Compliance with program requirements that are nonobligatory for juveniles is enhanced merely by the possibility that the intake officer may later file a delinquency petition with the juvenile court against uncooperative youth.

In a growing number of jurisdictions, social services are being utilized increasingly by juvenile courts and juvenile justice staff to treat various disorders exhibited by youthful offenders. Alcohol and drug dependencies characterize large numbers of arrested youth (Kuntsche et al., 2007). Therefore, treatment programs are provided for these youth so that they can learn about and deal with their alcohol or drug dependencies. Some youth need psychological counseling. Others require anger management training and courses to improve their interpersonal skills.

In Idaho, the juvenile justice system was overhauled along these lines by the legislature in 1995. Added services included two detention centers staffed by juvenile probation officers, an alternative school, psychological assessments of juveniles, treatment provisions by private agencies for juvenile sex offenders and drug/alcohol abusers, and mentoring provided by volunteers who also served on diversion boards and youth court programs (Spencer, 2007). Juvenile mentoring in both secure and nonsecure settings is receiving greater recognition (Bouhours and Daly, 2007). The 1992 reauthorization of the Juvenile Justice and Delinquency Prevention Act of 1974 recognized mentoring as significant for addressing problems of school attendance and

Juvenile Mentoring Program (JUMP)

Federally funded program administered by the Office of Juvenile Justice and Delinquency Prevention; promotes bonding between an adult and a juvenile relating on a one-to-one basis over time; designed to improve school performance and decrease gang participation and delinquency.

Big Brothers/Big Sisters of America (BBBSA)

Federation of over 500 agencies to serve children and adolescents; adults relate on a one-to-one basis with youth to promote their self-esteem and self-sufficiency; utilizes volunteers who attempt to instill responsibility, excellence, and leadership among assisted youth.

noninterventionist model

Philosophy of juvenile delinquent treatment meaning the absence of any direct intervention with certain juveniles who have been taken into custody.

delinquent activity, and a **Juvenile Mentoring Program (JUMP)** has been established in various jurisdictions.

One of the best-known mentoring programs is **Big Brothers/Big Sisters of America (BBBSA)**, which was started in 1904. The program matches one adult to one juvenile in a cost-effective intervention that reduces adolescent drug and alcohol use and improves youth–parent relationships. The BBBSA is a Blueprints for Violence Prevention Model Program (http://www.colorado.edu/cspv/blueprints/modelprograms/BBBS.html) that provides effective mentoring in the community and is consistent with social control theory. The volunteer provides a positive, prosocial model and involves youth in conventional activities that encourage a commitment to socially desirable goals.

One drawback to the treatment model generally is that great variations exist among community agencies regarding the availability of certain services as remedies for particular kinds of juvenile problems. Also, the intake officer may incorrectly diagnose the delinquent's behavior and prescribe inappropriate therapy. Certain types of deep-seated personality maladjustments cannot be detected through superficial informal intake proceedings (Boyd and Myers, 2005). In addition, simply participating in some community-based service or treatment program may be insufficient to relieve particular juveniles of the original or core causes of their delinquent behaviors. Some juveniles may have incarcerated parents, for example, and the effects of such circumstances have been unevenly studied (Champion and Mays, 1991). Nevertheless, intake screenings may lead to community-based agency referrals that may, or may not, be productive. In most jurisdictions, these are conditional sanctions that may be administered by intake officers without judicial approval or intervention.

The Noninterventionist Model

As the name implies, the **noninterventionist model** means the absence of any direct intervention with certain juveniles who have been taken into custody. The noninterventionist model is best understood when considered in the context of labeling theory (Lemert, 1967a). Labeling theory stresses that direct and frequent contact with the juvenile justice system will cause those having contact with it to eventually define themselves as delinquent. This definition will prompt self-definers to commit additional delinquent acts, because such behaviors are expected of those defined or stigmatized as such by others. Labeling theory advocates the removal of status offenders and other juveniles accused of nonserious offenses from the juvenile justice system, or at least from the criminalizing influence and trappings of the juvenile courtroom.

The noninterventionist model is strategically applied only to those juveniles who the intake officer believes are unlikely to reoffend if given a second chance or who are clearly status offenders without qualification (e.g., drug- or alcohol-dependent or chronic or persistent offenders) (Boyd and Myers, 2005). Intake officers who elect to act in a noninterventionist fashion with certain types of offenders may simply function as a possible resource person for juveniles and their parents. In cases involving runaways, truants, or curfew violators, it becomes a judgment call whether to refer youth and/or their parents to certain community services or counseling. The noninterventionist model would encourage no action by intake officers in nonserious or status offender cases except under the most compelling circumstances. Because not all runaways are alike, certain runaways may be more in need of intervention than others, for instance. Again, the aim of nonintervention is to assist youth in avoiding stigma and unfavorable labeling that might arise if they were to be involved more deeply within the juvenile justice system. Even minor referrals by intake officers could prompt adverse reactions from offenders so that future offending behavior would be regarded as a way of getting even with the system.

The noninterventionist model is consistent with the deinstitutionalization of status offenses (DSO) movement that has occurred in most jurisdictions. DSO was designed to divest juvenile courts of their jurisdiction over status offenders and remove these offenders from secure custodial institutions. Therefore, the primary intent of DSO was to minimize the potentially adverse influence of labeling that might occur through incarceration. Another intended function of DSO was to reduce the docket load for many juvenile court judges by transferring their jurisdiction over status offenders to community agencies and services. The noninterventionist strategy is significant here, because it advocates doing nothing about certain juvenile dispositions.

The works of Lemert (1967a) and Schur (1973) are relevant for the noninterventionist perspective. These authors have described **judicious nonintervention** and **radical nonintervention** as terms that might be applied to noninterventionist do-nothing policy. Judicious nonintervention allows some minimal level of intervention, but radical nonintervention counters traditional thinking about delinquency, which is to assume that the juvenile justice system merely needs to be improved.

Radical nonintervention argues that many of the current approaches to delinquency are not only fundamentally unsound but also harmful to youth whenever they are applied. Radical nonintervention assumes the following:

1. The delinquent is not basically different from the nondelinquent.
2. Most types of youthful misconduct are found within all socioeconomic strata.
3. The primary target for delinquency policy should be neither the individual nor the local community setting but, rather, the delinquency-defining processes themselves.

This view of nonintervention implies policies that accommodate society to the widest possible diversity of behaviors and attitudes, rather than policies that force as many individuals as possible to adjust to supposedly common societal standards. Subsidiary policies would favor collective action programs instead of those that single out specific individuals, and voluntary programs instead of compulsory ones. However, some critics suggest that such nonintervention is defeatist. Thus, rather than adopt a do-no-harm stance, juvenile justice system officials should be more concerned with doing good through their various approaches and programs.

judicious nonintervention
Use of minimal intervention in a youth's behavior and environment to effect changes in behavior.

radical nonintervention
Similar to a "do-nothing" policy of delinquency nonintervention.

The Due Process Model

The notion of due process is an integral feature of the criminal justice system. Due process is the basic constitutional right to a fair trial, to have an opportunity to be heard, to be aware of matters that are pending, to a presumption of innocence until guilt is established beyond a reasonable doubt, to make an informed choice whether to acquiesce or contest, and to provide the reasons for such a choice before a judicial official. An important aspect of due process is that police officers must have probable cause to justify their arrests of suspected criminals. Therefore, adolescent constitutional rights are given considerable weight in comparison with any incriminating evidence obtained by police or others (Abatiello, 2005).

Intake officers who rely heavily upon the **due process model** in their dealings with juveniles are concerned that the juveniles' rights are fully protected during every stage of juvenile justice processing. Therefore, these officers pay particular attention to how evidence was gathered by police against certain juveniles and whether the juveniles' constitutional rights were protected and police officers advised the juveniles of their right to counsel at the time of the arrest and/or subsequent interrogation. The higher priority given to due process in recent years is a significant juvenile justice reform. An intake officer's emphasis of due process requirements in juvenile offender processing stems, in part, from important U.S. Supreme Court decisions during the 1960s and 1970s, although professional associations and other interests have strongly advocated a concern for greater protection of juvenile rights.

Because of the interest some intake officers might take in due process rights, some intake hearings may be more formally conducted than others. Legal variables, such as present offense, number of charges, and prior petitions, would be given greater weight in the context of due process. Many offender dispositions seem to be affected by nonlegal variables as well, including the youth's attitude, grades in school, race/ethnicity, and school status.

Extralegal variables include race, ethnicity, gender, family solidarity, and SES. Studies of juvenile court dispositions in different jurisdictions reveal that minority offenders are dealt with more severely than white offenders. Minority youth, for example, may be more likely than white youth to be placed in custodial institutions or disposed to longer periods of probation. Besides being treated differently compared with white offenders, black juveniles have been subjected to greater detrimental labeling by the juvenile justice system over time. Differential treatment according to gender has also occurred in more than a few jurisdictions (Lemmon, Austin, and Feldberg, 2005). Ideally, juvenile justice decision making should be free from the influence of these and other extralegal variables, according to the due process model.

The Just Deserts/Justice Model

A strong rehabilitative orientation is prevalent throughout the juvenile justice system, in which the emphasis is upon serving the best interests of offending youth and the

due process model

Treatment model based on the constitutional right to a fair trial, to have an opportunity to be heard, to be aware of matters that are pending, to a presumption of innocence until guilt has been established beyond a reasonable doubt, to make an informed choice whether to acquiesce or contest, and to provide the reasons for such a choice before a judicial officer.

delivery of individualized services to them on the basis of their needs. *Parens patriae* explains much of the origin of this emphasis in the United States. However, the changing nature of juvenile offending during the last several decades and a gradual transformation of public sentiment toward more punitive measures have prompted certain juvenile justice reforms that are aimed at holding youth increasingly accountable for their actions and punishing them accordingly.

The **just deserts/justice model** is punishment-centered and seemingly revenge-oriented, where the state's interest is to ensure that juveniles are punished in relation to the seriousness of the offenses they have committed. Furthermore, those who commit identical offenses should be punished identically. This introduces the element of fairness into the punishment prescribed. The usefulness of this get-tough approach in disposing of various juvenile cases is controversial and has both proponents and opponents (Mears et al., 2007). It is significant in that such an approach represents a major shift of emphasis away from juvenile offenders and their individualized needs and toward the nature and seriousness of their actions.

Just deserts, as an orientation, has frequently been combined with the justice model or orientation. The justice orientation is the idea that punishments should be gauged to fit the seriousness of offenses committed. Therefore, juveniles who commit more serious acts should receive harsher punishments, treatments, or sentences than juveniles who commit less serious acts. Besides promoting punishment in proportion to offending behavior, the justice model includes certain victim considerations, such as provisions for restitution or victim compensation by offending juveniles.

The Crime Control Model

The **crime control model** theorizes that one of the best ways of controlling juvenile delinquency is to incapacitate juvenile offenders, either through some secure incarceration or through an intensive supervision program operated by a community-based agency or organization. Juvenile offenders may be incarcerated in secure facilities for short- or long-term periods, depending upon the seriousness of their offenses.

With the crime control perspective, intake officers identify chronic, persistent, and/or dangerous juvenile offenders for more formal and punitive handling in the juvenile justice system. If juveniles are believed to pose serious risks to others or are considered to be dangerous, intake officers can decide that the juveniles should be held in secure confinement pending a subsequent detention hearing. When juveniles who are chronic or persistent offenders are detained or incarcerated, they cannot reoffend. Treatment and rehabilitation are subordinate to simple control and incapacitation. Intake officers who favor the crime control view have few illusions that the system can change certain juvenile offenders. Rather, the best course of action in their minds is secure incarceration for lengthy periods, considering the availability of space in existing juvenile secure confinement facilities. In this way, youth are directly prevented from reoffending, because they are totally incapacitated. The cost-effectiveness of such incarceration of the most chronic and persistent juvenile

just deserts/justice model
Stresses offender accountability as a means to punish youthful offenders; uses victim compensation plans, restitution, and community services as ways of making offenders pay for their offenses; philosophy that emphasizes punishment as a primary objective of sentencing, fixed sentences, abolition of parole, and an abandonment of the rehabilitative ideal; rehabilitation is functional to the extent that offenders join rehabilitative programs voluntarily.

crime control model
Criminal justice approach that emphasizes containment of dangerous offenders and societal protection; a way of controlling delinquency by incapacitating juvenile offenders through some secure detention or intensive supervision programs operated by community-based agencies.

offenders in relation to the monies lost resulting from thefts, burglaries, robberies, and other property crimes is difficult to calculate. Incarceration is costly, however, and overcrowding in juvenile secure confinement facilities already plagues most jurisdictions.

In selected jurisdictions, **consent decrees** may include provisions for the electronic monitoring of certain juvenile offenders as an alternative to incarceration in a secure facility. These juveniles might be required to wear plastic bracelets or anklets that are devised to emit electronic signals and notify juvenile probation officers of an offender's whereabouts. Consent decrees are only for in-home placements and avoid the stigma of juvenile court appearances. They also contain conditions that must be fulfilled by the juvenile within a given time frame. Figure 3.1 shows a consent decree used by juvenile courts in various states. Consent decrees must be signed by the juvenile, the juvenile's parents, the juvenile court prosecutor, the juvenile's attorney (if one has been retained), and a social worker. A juvenile court judge also signs the consent decree. If the provisions are violated, the consent decree is revoked, and the case is reinstated. This reinstatement may require an appearance of the juvenile before the juvenile court.

Another alternative to incarceration for youth who are at risk for continued offending is **Multisystemic Therapy**. This is an intensive intervention that works with families in the community to address factors contributing to serious delinquent behavior. This is another evidence-based approach that helps parents develop skills to more effectively raise adolescents and to modify their delinquent prone behaviors. This Blueprints for Violence Prevention Model Program (http://www.colorado.edu/cspv/blueprints/modelprograms/MST.html) includes therapy and training to empower parents. The research demonstrates a reduction in both rearrest and out-of-home placements for at-risk youth. Unlike programs such as Scared Straight which have not been found to be effective, evidence-based programs like Multisystemic Therapy are supported by scientific research and have proven to be cost-effective and successful in keeping youth out of incarceration while providing interventions that promote nondelinquent behaviors.

The Balanced and Restorative Justice Model

In the 1990s, an alternative model for juvenile justice was initiated that incorporated the principles of restorative justice with the comprehensive mission of providing community safety and crime control along with offender accountability and competency development (Freivalds, 1996). The **Balanced and Restorative Justice Model (BARJ)** recognizes that crime harms the community, victims, and juvenile offenders. The approach holds the offender accountable to the victim while providing intervention to improve offender competencies and social skills and to promote nondelinquent behavior. This model transcends the punishment-versus-treatment models noted above and seeks to ensure public safety by balancing the needs and concerns of victims as well as offenders (Figure 3.2).

consent decrees
Formal agreements that involve children, their parents, and the juvenile court in which youth are placed under the court's supervision without an official finding of delinquency, with judicial approval.

Multisystemic Therapy
A Blueprints for Violence Prevention program that provides intensive family- and community-based treatment for managing delinquents with serious antisocial behavior.

Balanced and Restorative Justice (BARJ)
A juvenile justice system model that emphasizes accountability, public safety, and competency development.

Consent Decree

IN THE INTEREST OF: _____
                                    Name

_____

Address

_____

City, State

The parties stipulate and agree that the court may impose a consent decree, thereby placing said child under court supervision, consistent with the following conditions:

1. Court shall locate juvenile in out-of-home placement from _____ to _____
2. Placement shall be either in child/juvenile's home or out-of-home placement
3. Child/juvenile shall not commit any offense resulting in referrals to intake or other law violations, including local, state, or federal laws.
4. Child/juvenile shall pay restitution (where required) of $_____ payable to:

   _____

5. Child/juvenile shall perform community service at court discretion for _____ hours, under supervision by designated court officers.
6. Child/juvenile shall undergo counseling at court direction to appropriate facilities at the court's discretion.
7. Other _____

   _____

Signed by:

_____   _____
Child/juvenile   Date

_____   _____
Parent/guardian   Date

_____   _____
Parent/guardian   Date

Approved by:

_____   _____
Court attorney   Date

_____   _____
Judge   Date

Figure 3.1
A Consent Decree
Source: Authors.

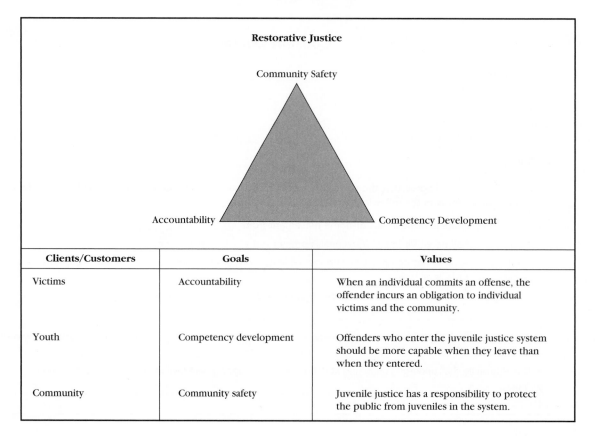

Figure 3.2

The Balanced Approach

Source: Office of Juvenile Justice and Delinquency Prevention (1998). Guide for Implementing the Balanced and Restorative Justice Model. Washington, DC: Office of Juvenile Justice and Delinquency Prevention, p. 6. (Available at http://www.ojjdp.gov/pubs/implementing/balanced.html#principles.)

In contrast to defining youth in negative and self-defeating terms, BARJ recognizes the potential to use evidence-based programs to prevent continued delinquency. By focusing on competency development, youth can learn the skills and knowledge to maintain lawful behavior. Five domains of competency development are (1) prosocial skills, (2) moral reasoning skills, (3) academic skills, (4) workforce skills, and (5) independent living skills (Torbet and Thomas, 2005).

As another goal or component of BARJ, youth are held accountable to the victim in ways that help them understand the impact their behavior has had on the victim and the community and to acknowledge their responsibility for the harm. In the context of the techniques of neutralization, BARJ confronts inaccurate beliefs that deny responsibility, victim, and injury (Sykes and Matza, 1957). Accountability can be achieved by (1) a victim impact statement, (2) victim community awareness classes, (3) an apology statement, (4) restitution and community service, and (5) restorative processes (Bender, King, and Torbet, 2006). In their assessment of the BARJ approach in juvenile justice, Lemmon and Verrecchia (2009) concluded: "As a means to holding offenders

Figure 3.3
Pennsylvania Balanced and Restorative Justice (BARJ)
Model
*Source: Juvenile Court Judges' Commission. Juvenile
Justice in Pennsylvania: Mission-Driven, Performance-
Based, Outcome-Focused.
Harrisburg, PA: Pennsylvania Juvenile Court Judges'
Commission, p. 4. (Available at http://www.portal.state
.pa.us/portal/server.pt/gateway/PTARGS_0_152425_
404126_0_0_18/monograph.pdf.)*

accountable while protecting the public, BARJ also promotes therapeutic interventions
to prevent cycles of delinquency and criminality" (p. 152). These multiple goals are
shown in Figure 3.3.

Delinquency Prevention Programs and Community Interventions

Since the 1980s, much has been done to establish delinquency prevention programs
in various communities that involve both citizens and police in joint efforts to combat
juvenile crime (Schaffner, 2005). Because of the diversity of offending among juveniles, it has been necessary to devise programs that target specific juvenile offender
populations. For instance, since youth violence also occurs in school settings, considerable resources have been allocated to address the problem of school violence and
reduce its incidence (Lawrence, 2006, 2009; Schexnayder, 2008).

At the same time that violence prevention programs are being used to reduce
school violence, some interventions seek to heighten the accountability of offenders
who are most prominently involved in school violence (Farrington and Ttofi, 2010;
Sampson, 2009). Placing police in schools to increase safety and security has become

more widespread, but also controversial, since zero-tolerance policies, which were intended to remove violent offenders, have resulted in more youth being sanctioned for less-serious behaviors (Stinchcomb, Bazemore, and Riestenberg, 2006; Sullivan et al., 2010). Programs that implement accountability principles often include school-based probation that provides skills training for at-risk youth (Schexnayder, 2008). In addition, school-wide and comprehensive, multifaceted programs to address bullying and violence have been effective in improving student safety and reducing violence (Sampson, 2009). Another promising alternative to suspension and expulsion is the use of "civil citations," which are a diversion policy that requires community service and holds youth accountable to the victims and school community (Sullivan et al., 2010). Lessons from school safety interventions indicate that programs should focus on "teaching and promoting effective social skills, relational aggression management, and peer interventions" (Benekos, 2010, p. 25).

Some programs target youthful sex offenders with services and counseling that are provided in community settings to assist juveniles with specific sex-related problems (Bouhours and Daly, 2007; van Wijk et al., 2007). Youth who engage in hate crimes are also targeted for intervention. Such programs educate youth about the risks of gang membership as well as some of the personal and social reasons why juveniles initially seek out gangs (Taylor et al., 2008). Even youth who are incarcerated in secure facilities are considered for intervention programs. Therefore, various forms of therapeutic intervention and skill-based programs are made available to youthful inmates in juvenile industrial schools for their rehabilitation and reintegration.

Effective intervention programs designed to prevent delinquent conduct can be started early in the developmental years (Crawley, Ritsema, and McKenzie, 2005). Families and school systems are logical settings for programs that can target a wide range of ages as well as at-risk behaviors and conditions with various intervention strategies. Some of these programs are described below.

The Nurse–Family Partnership

Nurse–Family Partnership (NFP)

A Blueprints for Violence Prevention program that provides intensive home visitation by trained nurses during prenatal and early childhood years.

One evidence-based delinquency prevention program that begins with at-risk pregnant mothers is the **Nurse–Family Partnership (NFP)**. During pregnancy and the first two years after birth, a specially trained nurse provides intensive and comprehensive home visits to improve prenatal care, early childhood parenting, and the mother's personal development. This is a Blueprints for Violence Prevention Model Program (http://www.colorado.edu/cspv/blueprints/modelprograms/NFP.html).

By promoting confidence and effective parenting skills, mothers are helped to bond with their children and to provide emotional and appropriate developmental care of infants. In addition, the NFP addresses plans for future pregnancies and the mother's educational and employment concerns. As a Model Program, the NFP acknowledges the importance of early intervention and the significance of the parent–child relationship. By focusing on prenatal behaviors (e.g., cigarette use and alcohol consumption), the NFP is able to improve the birth weight of babies and also reduce other risks of neurodevelopmental impairment.

Research has demonstrated that targeting at-risk mothers is an effective prevention program that reduces child abuse, subsequent births, and maternal problems due to alcohol and drug use. In addition, for adolescent children of mothers who had participated in the NFP (15-year follow-up), the number of arrests is also reduced. As a strategy for delinquency prevention, the NFP is cost-effective in reducing arrests and convictions of youth who are at risk for criminal and antisocial behavior.

The Support Our Students Program

The **Support Our Students (SOS) program** is loosely based on the crime control model and targets school-age children for after-school programs designed to provide them with extra learning opportunities. The SOS program is established to operate during the afternoon hours, when most of the juvenile delinquency in the community occurs. SOS is important for at least three reasons: (1) too many children have little or no adult supervision after school, (2) unsupervised children are more likely to become involved in criminal activities and other related behaviors, and (3) after-school programs have been shown to prevent many of the consequences of leaving children unsupervised.

This program has six important goals: (1) to reduce the number of students who are unsupervised after school, otherwise known as latch-key children; (2) to improve the academic performance of students participating in the program; (3) to meet the physical, intellectual, emotional, and social needs of students participating in the program and improve their attitudes and behavior; (4) to improve coordination of existing resources and enhance collaboration so as to provide services to school-age children effectively and efficiently; (5) to reduce juvenile crime in local communities served by the program; and (6) to recruit community volunteers to provide positive adult role models for school-age children and to help supervise their after-school activities (North Carolina Department of Juvenile Justice and Delinquency Prevention, 2008).

CASASTART Programs

CASASTART programs target high-risk youth, aged 11 to 13, who are exposed to drugs and criminal activity. These are neighborhood-based, school-centered programs that work with youth, their families, and their communities. Runaways and curfew violators may be referred to CASASTART by intake officers who believe this type of intervention will interrupt the cycle of social stigmatization that occurs if youth interact closely with delinquent peers at school and elsewhere. To some extent, at least, CASASTART is driven by the noninterventionist model.

Since their inception, CASASTART programs have been established in numerous communities throughout the United States. In McKeesport, Pennsylvania, for instance, a CASASTART program has been operating for several years. Its goals are to: (1) prevent and reduce drug and alcohol use; (2) promote good school attendance and academic performance, while lowering the incidence of disruptive behavior at school; (3) reduce drug-related crime and violence; and (4) reduce delinquent behavior. The McKeesport program achieves these goals on three levels: (1) building

Support Our Students (SOS) program
After-school intervention providing learning opportunities to children in high-crime areas.

CASASTART programs
Target high-risk youth exposed to drugs and delinquent activity; these programs decrease risk factors by greater community involvement.

resiliency in children, (2) strengthening families, and (3) making neighborhoods safer for children and their families (McKeesport CASASTART, 2008). By reaching children at the early ages of 11 to 13, it is believed that many youth can be diverted away from the negative influence of their delinquent peers.

The eight core components of CASASTART are: (1) community-enhanced policing/enhanced enforcement; (2) case management (13 to 18 families per case manager); (3) criminal/juvenile justice intervention; (4) family services, including parent programs, counseling, and organized parent–child activities; (5) after-school and summer activities for personal and social development, improving self-esteem, and studying cultural heritage; (6) education services, offering tutoring as well as work preparation opportunities; (7) mentoring through one-on-one relationships; and (8) incentives, both monetary and nonmonetary. CASASTART has reported lower rates of drug use among participants as well as more prosocial behavior (McKeesport CASASTART, 2008).

Project Safe Neighborhoods and Operation TIDE

Project Safe Neighborhoods

An initiative undertaken in many communities to reduce gun violence through banning possession of firearms by those with criminal records.

Project Safe Neighborhoods is a national initiative implemented to reduce violence attributable to firearms. It is also aimed at reducing gun violence among juveniles specifically by deterring youth from gaining access to or possessing firearms. Under this initiative, persons banned from possessing firearms include (1) convicted felons; (2) fugitives from justice; (3) illegal immigrants; (4) mental defectives or persons who have been committed at any time to a mental institution; (5) persons who have given up their U.S. citizenship; (6) persons dishonorably discharged from the armed forces; (7) anyone under court order to refrain from stalking, harassing, or threatening an intimate partner or other person; and (8) anyone convicted of a misdemeanor crime involving violence or a threat with a deadly weapon (Crawford, 2007).

Partnerships are established among various agencies of the federal government and local law enforcement agencies, schools, and other organizations. Intelligence gathering includes crime mapping, identifying hot spots (high-crime areas) in communities, and ballistics technology. Local and regional training relates to the proper use of firearms for interested persons. A deterrence message is delivered by different means to discourage local youth from possessing firearms. This initiative is aimed at gangs who most frequently use firearms in their illegal activities. Results thus far suggest that this initiative is having an impact on reducing the rate of firearm use among teens and particularly gangs. The rehabilitation model and its principal components have been used as inputs for driving such safe neighborhood initiatives (Khalili, 2008).

Operation TIDE

A composite of federal, state, and local law enforcement officers dedicated to reducing violence attributable to guns and gangs.

Flint, Michigan, is a part of the "Three Cities Initiative" sponsored by the U.S. Department of Justice's Project Safe Neighborhoods. The other two cities in Michigan targeted for this program are Saginaw and Jackson. One integral component of Project Safe Neighborhoods is a program called **Operation TIDE**. "TIDE" is an acronym for Tactical Intelligence Driven Enforcement. It is a task force comprised of federal, state, and local law enforcement agencies and officers devoted to reducing and/or eliminating gun and gang violence. Operation TIDE is effective because it prosecutes youthful offenders in accordance with stiff federal gun laws and sentences (Free Press, 2007).

Such interventions are only a few of many similar types of programs operating throughout the United States involving police and interested citizens in proactive and positive roles, where they are taking an active interest in preventing delinquent conduct through interacting closely with youth. These programs will not make juvenile offenders desist from delinquency, but many of them will heighten juvenile awareness of positive influences in their lives. Another positive effect of such programs is to assist police officers in understanding juveniles and their motives (Free Press, 2007). In addition, a National Institute of Justice funded evaluation of Project Safe Neighborhoods found that cities that implemented this violence prevention initiative had reduced rates of violent crime and also experienced a decline in gun-related violence (McGarrell et al., 2009). Using data from the Boston Ceasefire Program (i.e., the Boston Gun Project), researchers found that "youth violence was driven by a relatively small number of chronic offenders" (McGarrell et al., 2009, p. 8). After crackdowns on these youth, and collaborative efforts with youth service workers as well as probation and parole officers to target the known offenders, gun violence declined, and researchers identified that the police–probation partnership as well as community involvement were effective in reducing gun violence. Other cities implementing the Safe Neighborhoods Project have also experienced reductions in youth crime and gun violence (McGarrell et al., 2009).

SUMMARY

Theories about crime and delinquency have been classified into broad areas. These include classical and biological theories, psychological theories, and sociological theories. Classical theories assume that persons have free will to choose between good and evil and that they weigh the advantages and disadvantages of committing crime to achieve their various goals. Biological theories are rooted in the belief that a primary cause of delinquency is biological makeup and genetic structure. Determinism, which rejects free will and rational choice in explaining whether one conforms to or deviates from society's rules, is often used as an explanation for why delinquency and criminal acts are committed.

Biological theories include biological determinism, *XYY* theory, and sociobiology. Psychological theories stress the importance of cognitive development in acquiring criminal and delinquent characteristics. Psychoanalytic theory stresses early childhood experiences as crucial to determining adult behaviors. Another psychological theory is social learning theory, which proposes that different levels of learning occur at different stages of maturational development. Sociological theories stress social environmental factors as they impact behavior to produce criminal or delinquent conduct.

The subculture theory of delinquency suggests that a delinquent subculture, complete with its own norms and status structure, exists within the larger culture. Some manifestations of this theory are strain theory, anomie theory, and labeling theory. Labeling theory, which stresses the definitions people have of delinquent acts and how they come to define themselves as delinquent, is one of the more influential sociological theories to account for delinquent conduct. Bonding or social control theory is also prevalent and useful in explaining delinquency. It suggests that youth who bond successfully with school authorities and teachers, religious leaders, and family members will be less likely to engage in delinquent activities. The components of bonding theory are attachment, commitment, belief, and involvement. Other sociological theories include containment theory, neutralization theory, differential association theory, and cultural transmission theory. These theories focus on social forces that impact decision making, individual choices, and social interactions at critical points in adolescent development.

Evaluating theories of delinquency is often based on the predictive utility of particular theoretical schemes and the frequency with which any particular theory is used in prevention programs or delinquency intervention activities. However, each explanation of delinquency has variable importance according to how much recidivism is reduced by a theory's application. Many youth simply mature or grow out of their delinquency behavior. Thus, evaluations of theories are difficult to make.

Some models for dealing with juvenile offenders have been identified. These include the rehabilitation model, the treatment or medical model, the noninterventionist model, the due process model, the just deserts/justice model, the crime control model, and the Balance and Restorative Justice model. Each of these models reflects a professional orientation toward delinquents and suggests particular strategies that can be adopted for helping adolescents. The due process and just deserts/justice models emphasize legal rights and equal protection under the law, so there is a strong legal emphasis underlying such approaches. The crime control model stresses close supervision, or incarceration in a secure facility, of those offenders most likely to reoffend. This is not an especially popular strategy, because alternatives to incarceration are believed to be more conducive to rehabilitation and eventual societal reintegration.

Delinquency prevention programs are often community interventions intended to target and help at-risk youth. Generally, a particular theory or combination of theories is evident in the intervention programs. The implementation of evidence-based programs represents efforts in juvenile justice to use best practices in preventing and reducing delinquency.

KEY TERMS

classical theory, 83	classical school, 84	biological determinism, 85
Cesare Beccaria (1738–1794), 83	hedonism, 84	Cesare Lombroso (1835–1909), 85
	determinism, 85	

QUESTIONS FOR REVIEW

1. What is theory? What are some important components of theory? What are theories designed to do? Explain and discuss.

2. What is meant by biological determinism? How does biological determinism conflict with the classical school of criminology? Which theories are associated with determinism?

3. What are the major components of psychoanalytic theory? Describe the importance of the adolescent formative years to psychoanalytic theory. In what respect is childhood regarded as the "formative years?"

4. How does social learning theory differ from psychoanalytic theory?

5. How is cultural transmission theory related to the concentric zone hypothesis?

6. What is the role of socioeconomic status (SES) in juvenile delinquency? Who are at-risk youth? What are their characteristics?

7. What is meant by a delinquent subculture? How can we use information about a delinquent subculture to change delinquent behaviors in various communities?

8. What are some similarities and differences between Merton's theory of anomie and strain theory? In the theory of anomie, what mode of adaptation is most likely to be invoked by juvenile delinquents? What other modes of adaptation have been identified?

9. How are different theories of delinquent conduct evaluated? Which types of evaluation seem to be most useful?

10. What are four delinquency intervention programs? What is their relative successfulness in reducing delinquency?

INTERNET CONNECTIONS

Blueprints for Violence Prevention
http://www.colorado.edu/cspv/blueprints/

Center for the Study and Prevention of Violence
http://www.colorado.edu/cspv/index.html

National Center for Missing and Exploited Children
http://www.missingkids.com

National Center for Youth Law
http://www.youthlaw.org/

National Center on Education, Disability, and Juvenile Justice
http://www.edjj.org/

Office of Juvenile Justice and Delinquency Prevention Model Programs Guide
http://ojjdp.gov/mpg/

Open Society Foundations
http://www.soros.org/crime/

Youth Gangs in Schools
http://www.ncjrs.gov/pdffiles1/ojjdp/183015.pdf

4

The Legal Rights of Juveniles

Learning Objectives

AFTER READING THIS CHAPTER, THE STUDENT WILL BE ABLE TO:

- Identify the legal rights provided by the U.S. Constitution.
- Summarize how the legal rights of juveniles have changed over time.
- Summarize the impact of various landmark cases on juvenile justice.
- Describe the rights of juveniles at various locations and at various points within the juvenile justice system.
- Explain the issues and controversies surrounding the death penalty and life without parole for juveniles.
- Describe how the unification of criminal and adult courts affects juvenile cases.

(Irene Springer/Pearson)

Introduction

The intent of the juvenile court was to respond to children who were wayward and in need of intervention and supervision. While some youth may have committed crimes, the focus was not on guilt and punishment but, rather, on helping the youth. The court was designed to operate as a social welfare agency to focus on the best interests of the child. Juvenile court judges were given wide discretion to assess the needs of the delinquents and to decide the best ways to handle each case. Unlike criminal court, determining guilt or innocence was not necessary to intervene in the child's life. Therefore, youth did not require legal representation. Essentially, youth did not have legal rights and were at the mercy of the court.

The juvenile court was informal, and as noted in Chapter 2, new terminology was used to designate the nonadversarial nature of this special court for youth. Under the doctrine of *parens patriae*, judges had authority to act *in loco parentis* (the legal doctrine that permits the state to "act in place of the parents") and to consider individualized responses to meet specific needs of each youth. Because this special court for youth was not defined as a criminal court, the upper courts maintained a hands-off doctrine and deferred to judges to make decisions guided by the principles and mission of the juvenile court (Gomez and Ganuza, 2002).

From 1899 to the 1960s, the juvenile justice system was characterized as the "Traditional" model of treatment and rehabilitation. By the 1960s, however, concerns about excessive punitiveness and lack of legal protections for youth resulted in U.S. Supreme Court decisions that ended the hands-off approach and extended due process protections to youth. As a result, court procedures became more formal, juveniles were given the right to legal representation, and the court became more adversarial. This period of juvenile justice, from the 1960s to the 1980s, is recognized as the due process era, and it contributed to the transformation of juvenile justice.

What rights do delinquents have in court? What is the prevailing philosophy of the juvenile justice system? Which U.S. Supreme Court decisions transformed the handling of juvenile offenders? How should youth who commit serious crimes be handled? This chapter will explore these questions and the legal rights of juveniles.

The chapter opens with a brief examination of a historical account of the evolving rights of juveniles in the United States. From Colonial times until the mid-1960s, juveniles had no universally applicable legal entitlements. Subsequently, different states adopted a variety of policies for juveniles and how they should be treated. As reviewed earlier, Illinois established the first juvenile court in 1899, and for the next 67 years, most juvenile courts functioned much like social welfare agencies rather than legal systems.

The next section examines several landmark juvenile cases decided by the U.S. Supreme Court. The first three cases, *Kent v. United States* (1966), *In re Gault* (1967), and *In re Winship* (1970), are considered to be important legal decisions that opened the floodgates of juvenile litigation before the Supreme Court (known as the litigation explosion). Once the *Kent* case had been decided in 1966, it became much easier for the Court to impose precedent-setting decisions on juvenile courts in all jurisdictions. Other important cases soon followed, including *McKeiver v. Pennsylvania* (1971), *Breed v. Jones* (1975), and *Schall v. Martin* (1984), which granted various constitutional rights to juveniles. These cases will be presented and discussed.

In light of these decisions, juvenile courts in all jurisdictions have moved away from traditional approaches of treating juvenile offending toward due process rights similar to those provided to adult offenders. Today, the presence of attorneys in juvenile courts is more the rule rather than the exception. Although the U.S. Supreme Court refrained from granting jury trials to juveniles as a matter of right, under certain circumstances some states can grant jury trials to juvenile offenders. These and other issues, including the implications of granting juveniles greater constitutional rights and how the juvenile justice process has become increasingly legalistic and bureaucratized, will be examined.

A brief history of the death penalty for juveniles will also be presented. The death penalty is inherently controversial, and important cases in this area decided by the U.S. Supreme Court will be described. In 2005, the Supreme Court ruled that the application of the death penalty was unconstitutional for any youth who committed a capital offense under the age of 18 (*Roper v. Simmons*, 2005). The arguments both for and against the death penalty will be summarized.

Original Juvenile Court Jurisdiction: *Parens Patriae*

Until the mid-1960s, juvenile courts had considerable latitude in regulating the affairs of minors. This freedom to act in a child's behalf was rooted in the largely unchallenged doctrine of *parens patriae*. Whenever juveniles were apprehended by police officers for alleged crimes, they were turned over to juvenile authorities or taken to a juvenile hall for further processing. Youth were not advised of their rights to an attorney, to have an attorney present during any interrogation, or to remain silent. They could be questioned by police at length, without parental notification or legal contact. In short, they had little, if any, protection against constitutional rights violations and had no access to due process because of their status or standing as juveniles (Rehling, 2005).

When juveniles appeared before juvenile court judges in the early years of juvenile courts, youth almost never had the opportunity to give testimony on their own behalf and rebut evidence presented against them or to test the reliability of witnesses through cross-examination. This was rationalized at the time by asserting that juveniles did not understand the law and had to have it interpreted for them by others, principally juvenile court judges. (Subsequent investigations regarding the knowledge that youth have of their rights seems to confirm this assertion.) These early adjudicatory proceedings were also very informal, and they were conducted without defense counsel being present to advise their youthful clients. In this one-sided state of affairs, facts were alleged by various accusers, often persons such as probation officers or police officers.

litigation explosion
Rapid escalation of case filings before appellate courts, often based upon a landmark case extending rights to particular segments of the population (e.g., jail or prison inmates or juveniles).

Juvenile proceedings were largely nonadversarial, and juvenile court judges handled most cases informally and independently, depending upon the youth's needs and the seriousness of the offense. If judges decided that secure confinement would best serve the interests of justice and the welfare of the juvenile, then the youth would be placed in a secure confinement facility (juvenile prison) for an indeterminate period. These decisions were seldom questioned or challenged. When challenges did occur, however, higher courts would generally dismiss them as frivolous or without merit.

The Hands-Off Doctrine

A major reason for the silent acceptance of decisions by juvenile court judges was that the U.S. Supreme Court had repeatedly demonstrated its reluctance to intervene in juvenile matters or to question such decisions (known as the **hands-off doctrine**). In the case of *In re Gault* (1967), Justice Stewart typified the traditional orientation of former Supreme Courts by declaring

> [t]he Court today uses an obscure Arizona case as a vehicle to impose upon thousands of juvenile courts throughout the Nation restrictions that the Constitution made applicable to adversary criminal trials. I believe the Court's decision is *wholly unsound* [emphasis added] as a matter of constitutional law, and sadly unwise as a matter of judicial policy . . . The inflexible restrictions that the Constitution so wisely made applicable to adversary criminal trials have no inevitable place in the proceedings of those public social agencies known as juvenile or family courts. (387 U.S. at 78–79)

In many respects, juveniles were treated like adults without adult protections and rights. Youth had no legal standing and virtually no rights other than those extended by the courts. The right to a trial by jury, a basic right provided to a defendant who might be incarcerated for six months or more by a criminal court conviction, did not exist for juveniles unless juvenile court judges permitted such trials. Juvenile court judges generally did not favor jury trials for youth, however, because this was not consistent with the mission of the juvenile court. Even today, with only a few exceptions through state statutes, juveniles do not have an absolute right to a trial by jury. Thus, juveniles may be deprived of their freedom for many years on the basis of a personal judicial decision.

Because of the informality of juvenile proceedings in most jurisdictions, there were frequent and obvious abuses of judicial discretion. These abuses occurred because of the absence of consistent guidelines whereby cases could be adjudicated. Juvenile probation officers might casually recommend to judges that particular juveniles "ought to do a few months" in an industrial school or other secure confinement facility, and the judge might be persuaded to adjudicate these cases accordingly.

During the 1950s and 1960s, however, several forces were at work that would eventually have the conjoint consequence of making juvenile courts more accountable for specific adjudications of youthful offenders. One of these forces was increased

hands-off doctrine

Policy practiced by the federal courts in which official court policy was not to intervene in matters relating to juvenile issues; belief that juvenile justice administrators are in the best position to make decisions about welfare of juveniles.

parental and general public recognition of, and concern for, the liberal license taken by juvenile courts in administering the affairs of juveniles. The abuse of judicial discretion was becoming increasingly apparent. In addition, there was a growing disenchantment with, and apathy for, the rehabilitation ideal, although this disenchantment was not directed solely at juvenile courts (LaMade, 2008; Sungi, 2008).

The juvenile court as originally envisioned by the progressive movement was procedurally informal, characterized by individualized, offender-oriented dispositional practices. The contemporary juvenile court departs from this Progressive ideal. Today, juvenile courts are increasingly like criminal courts, featuring a more adversarial system and greater procedural formality.

The transformation of juvenile courts into more formal proceedings occurred as part of a national trend toward bureaucratization and as an institutional compromise between law and social welfare. Bureaucracy stresses a fixed hierarchy of authority, task specialization, individualized spheres of competence, impersonal social relationships between organizational actors, and impartial enforcement of abstract rules. Thus, in the context of bureaucracy, decision making is routinized rather than arbitrary. Personalities and social characteristics are irrelevant.

Applied to juvenile court proceedings, juvenile court decision making becomes a function of the nature and seriousness of the offenses committed and of the factual delinquent history of the juvenile defendant. Emotional considerations in bureaucratic structures are nonexistent. The bureaucratic approach is that juveniles should be held to a high standard of accountability for their actions. Furthermore, an individualized, treatment-oriented sanctioning system is inconsistent with bureaucracy and violates its general principles of impartiality. This type of system for juvenile justice seems to be consistent with the sentiments of some U.S. citizens and their belief that juvenile courts should get tough with juvenile offenders.

A major change from a *parens patriae*, state-based interests to a due process juvenile justice model means that decision making about youthful offenders is increasingly rationalized and that the principle of just deserts is fundamental. This also means that less discretionary authority will be manifested by juvenile court judges, as they decide each case more on the basis of offense seriousness rather than according to individual factors or circumstances and then prescribe punishments (LaMade, 2008).

Despite this due process and bureaucratic emphasis, juvenile courts have continued to retain many of their seemingly haphazard characteristics. Sound policies have been established, but their implementation has remained inconsistent and problematic for many juvenile courts (Whitehead, 2008). In addition, during the mid-1960s and through the 1980s, significant achievements were made in the area of juvenile rights. (Table 4.1 provides a general chronology of events relating to juvenile rights during the last 200 years.) Although the *parens patriae* philosophy continues to influence juvenile proceedings, the U.S. Supreme Court has vested youth with certain constitutional rights. These rights do not encompass all of the rights extended to adults who are charged with crimes. However, those rights conveyed to juveniles have thus far had far-reaching implications for how juveniles are processed. The general result of these Supreme Court decisions has been to bring the juvenile court system under constitutional control. Several of these landmark cases involving juvenile rights will be described in the following section.

Landmark Cases in Juvenile Justice

In recent decades, significant changes have occurred in the juvenile justice system and how youth are processed. In this section, we will examine rights that were extended to juveniles by the U.S. Supreme Court during the period from 1960 to 1990 (e.g., the due process era). Describing these rights will make clear which ones juveniles did not have until the landmark cases associated with them were decided. Then, a comparison will be made of juvenile rights and those rights enjoyed by adults charged with crimes in criminal courts. Despite sweeping juvenile reforms and major legal gains, important differences remain between the rights of juveniles and those of adults when both are charged with crimes (Wilkerson, 2005).

More recently, juvenile courts have become more punishment centered, with the justice/just deserts model influencing court decision making. Interests of youth are secondary, while community interests are seemingly served by juvenile court actions. Juveniles are being given greater responsibility for their actions, and they are increasingly expected to be held accountable for their wrongdoing (Feld, 2007). At the same time, some evidence suggests that youth have a poor understanding of their legal rights and, therefore, are disadvantaged by a more legalistic juvenile justice system (Billings et al., 2007).

Each of the cases presented here represents an attempt by juveniles to secure rights ordinarily extended to adults. Given these decisions, juveniles have fared well with the U.S. Supreme Court in past years. Juveniles still do not enjoy the full range of rights extended to adult offenders who are tried in criminal courts, but they have acquired due process privileges that were not available to them before the 1960s. *Kent v. United States* (1966), *In re Gault* (1967), and *In re Winship* (1970) comprise the "big three" of juvenile cases involving their legal rights. The remaining cases presented here address specific rights issues, such as the right against double jeopardy, jury trials as a matter of right in juvenile courts, preventive detention, and the standards that should govern searches of students and seizures of contraband on school property.

Kent v. United States (1966)

One of the first major juvenile rights cases that began to reform juvenile courts was *Kent v. United States* (1966). The decision established the universal precedents of requiring waiver hearings before juveniles could be transferred to the jurisdiction of a criminal court (except by legislative automatic waivers as discussed in this and other chapters, although reverse waiver hearings must be conducted at the juvenile's request) and of juveniles being entitled to consult with counsel before and during such hearings (Grisso, 1998).

The facts of the case are that in 1959, Morris A. Kent, Jr., a 14-year-old in the District of Columbia, was apprehended as the result of several housebreakings and

Table 4.1
CHRONOLOGICAL SUMMARY OF MAJOR EVENTS IN JUVENILE JUSTICE

Year	Event
1791	Bill of Rights passed by U.S. Congress
1825	New York House of Refuge established
1828	Boston House of Refuge founded
1839	*Ex parte Crouse* established right of juvenile court intervention in parent–child matters
1841	John Augustus initiates probation in Boston
1847	State institutions for juveniles opened in Boston and New York
1851	First adoption act in U.S. passed in Massachusetts
1853	New York Children's Aid Society established
1853	New York Juvenile Asylum created by Children's Aid Society
1855	Death penalty imposed on 10-year-old James Arcene in Arkansas for robbery and murder (earliest juvenile execution in the New England colonies was 16-year-old Thomas Graunger, for sodomizing a cow in 1642)
1866	Massachusetts statute passed giving juvenile court power to intervene and take custody of juveniles under age 16 whose parents are unfit
1868	Fourteenth Amendment adopted, establishing right to due process and equal protection under the law
1870	*People ex rel. O'Connell v. Turner* established that reform school commitments of youth could not be made on the basis of simple misfortune or vagrancy; limited institutionalization of youth to those who committed crimes; denied confinement of youth who were not afforded legal due process
1874–1875	Massachusetts established first Children's Tribunal to deal with youthful offenders
1881	Michigan commenced child protection with the Michigan Public Acts of 1881
1884	*Reynolds v. Howe* established state authority to place neglected children in institutions
1886	First child neglect case was heard in Massachusetts
1889	Indiana established children's guardians to have jurisdiction over neglected and dependent children
1890	Children's Aid Society of Pennsylvania, a foster home for juvenile delinquents used as an alternative to reform schools, was established
1891	Minnesota Supreme Court established doctrine of parental immunity
1897	*Ex parte Becknell* reversed disposition of juvenile who has not been given a fair trial
1899	Hull House established in Chicago by Jane Addams to assist unsupervised children of immigrant parents
1899	Compulsory School Act passed in Colorado established statutory regulation of truants
1899	Illinois Act to Regulate the Treatment and Control of Dependent, Neglected, and Delinquent Children passed; first juvenile court established in United States
1900	Case law began to deal with children's protective statutes

(Continued)

Table 4.1 CONTINUED

Year	Event
1901	Juvenile court established in Denver
1906	Massachusetts passed act providing for treatment of children not as criminals but as children in need of guidance and aid
1907	Separate juvenile court with original jurisdiction in juvenile matters established in Denver
1908	*Ex parte Sharpe* defined more clearly power of juvenile court to include *parens patriae*
1910	Compulsory school acts passed in different state jurisdictions
1912	Creation of U.S. Children's Bureau, charged with compiling statistical information about juvenile offenders; existed from 1912 to 1940
1918	Chicago slums studied by Shaw and McKay; found delinquency related to urban environment and transitional neighborhoods
1924	Federal Probation Act passed
1930	Children's Charter, White House Conference on Child Health and Protection, recognizing the rights of children
1938	Federal Juvenile Court Act passed
1954	*Brown v. Board of Education* established school desegregation
1959	Standard Family Court Act of National Council on Crime and Delinquency established that juvenile hearings are to be informally conducted
1966	*Kent v. United States* established juvenile's right to a hearing before transfer to criminal court, right to assistance of counsel during police interrogations, right to reports and records relating to transfer decision, and right to reasons given by the judge for the transfer
1967	*In re Gault* established juvenile's right to an attorney, right to notice of charges, right to confront and cross-examine witnesses, and right against self-incrimination
1968	*Ginsberg v. New York* established it is unlawful to sell pornography to a minor
1969	*Tinker v. Des Moines Independent Community School District* established the First Amendment applies to juveniles and protects their constitutional right to free speech
1970	*In re Winship* established juvenile's right to the criminal court standard of "beyond a reasonable doubt" when loss of freedom is a possible penalty
1971	*McKeiver v. Pennsylvania* established juvenile's right to a trial by jury is not absolute
1971	Twenty-Sixth Amendment ratified, granting the right to vote to 18-year-olds
1972	*Wisconsin v. Yoder* gave parents the right to impose their religion on their children
1972	Marvin Wolfgang published *Delinquency in a Birth Cohort*
1973	*In re Snyder* gave minors the right to bring legal proceedings against their parents
1973	*San Antonio Independent School District v. Rodriguez* established that differences in education based on wealth are not necessarily discriminatory
1974	Juvenile Justice and Delinquency Prevention Act (JJDPA), intended to deinstitutionalize status offenders, separate delinquents from status offenders generally, and divest juvenile court judges of their jurisdiction over status offenders, passed by U.S. Congress

Year	Event
1974	Office of Juvenile Justice and Delinquency Prevention (OJJDP), instrumental in promoting deinstitutional-ization of status offenders, established with passage of the JJDPA
1974	Federal Child Abuse Prevention Act passed by U.S. Congress
1974	Buckley Amendment (The Family Educational Rights and Privacy Act of 1974) to the Elementary and Secondary Education Act of 1965 gave students the right to see their own files with parental consent
1975	*Goss v. Lopez* established that a student facing school suspension has right to due process, prior notice, and an open hearing
1975	*Breed v. Jones* established that double jeopardy exists if a juvenile is adjudicated as delinquent in juvenile court on a given charge and tried for same offense later in criminal court; prohibits double jeopardy
1977	Report of the Senate Judiciary Committee, especially concerning the rights of the unborn and the right of 18-year-olds to vote, released.
1977	Juvenile Justice Amendment of 1977 passed by U.S. Congress
1977	*Ingraham v. Wright* established that corporal punishment is permissible in public schools and is not a violation of the Eighth Amendment
1977	American Bar Association adopted, Standards on Juvenile Justice
1977	Washington State amended its sentencing policies
1979	*Fare v. Michael C.* established totality of circumstances standard for evaluating propriety of custodial interrogations of juveniles by police without parents or attorneys present; defined *Miranda* rights of minors
1980	National concern increased over child abuse and neglect
1982	*Eddings v. Oklahoma* established the death penalty applied to juveniles is not cruel and unusual punishment per se
1982	Efforts to decarcerate status offenders escalated
1984	*Schall v. Martin* established the constitutionality of the preventive detention of juveniles
1985	*New Jersey v. T.L.O.* established lesser standard of search and seizure on school property; searches and seizures permissible without probable cause or warrant
1985	Wilson and Herrnstein published *Crime and Human Nature*, focusing attention on the biological causes of delinquency
1985	United Nations General Assembly adopts "Standard Minimum Rules for the Administration of Juvenile Justice"
1986	*Woods v. Clusen* established right of juveniles against aggressive police interrogation tactics by failing to observe juvenile's constitutional rights and provide for fundamental fairness
1986	Juvenile offenders waived to criminal court were executed, focusing attention on the death penalty administered to children
1987	Conservative trends resulted in 10,000 juvenile waivers to criminal courts
1988	Nationwide gang problem reemerged

(Continued)

Table 4.1 CONTINUED

Year	Event
1988	*Thompson v. Oklahoma* established the death penalty applied to juveniles convicted of murder who were under age 16 at the time of the murder is cruel and unusual punishment
1989	*Stanford v. Kentucky* and *Wilkins v. Missouri* established that the death penalty is not cruel and unusual punishment applied to juveniles convicted of murder who were age 16 or 17 at the time the murder was committed
1990	*Maryland v. Craig* allowed child abuse victims to testify on closed-circuit television in courts
1991	Juvenile violence rate hit all-time high of 430 acts per 100,000 adolescents
1995	Annual reported child abuse cases exceeded 3 million
1996	Michigan parents criminally convicted for failing to supervise delinquent son
1997	Juvenile crime rates began to stabilize in United States
1998	School shooting in Jonesboro, Arkansas, left five killed; raised questions about children and access to firearms
1999	School shootings increased; after mass murders of 15 persons by two students who commit suicide at a high school in Littleton, Colorado, public policies implemented to safeguard school systems from similar incidents in future
2000	*Santa Fe Independent School District v. Jane Doe* banned student-led prayer at sporting events, further defining separation of church and state in school settings
2002	U.S. Supreme Court strikes down federal law banning computer-generated images of minors engaging in sex, allowing virtual kiddie porn to be sold freely over the Internet
2004	40-year follow-up of Perry Preschool Project released; found fewer lifetime arrests and other social benefits accrued to participants
2005	*Roper v. Simmons* determined that execution of persons who were under age 18 at the time they commit capital crimes is prohibited by the 8th and 14th Amendments; overturned *Stanford v. Kentucky* and *Wilkins v. Missouri*, decided in 1989
2006	The Girls Study Group established by OJJDP to learn why an increasing number of girls were entering the juvenile justice system and to better understand how to prevent and intervene in girls' delinquency
2006	Illinois created a new Juvenile Justice Department in recognition that young people should be treated differently than adult offenders in the Department of Corrections
2007	The National Council on Crime and Delinquency and the Berkeley Center for Criminal Justice sponsored a national conference entitled "Juvenile Justice Reform: Forty Years After *Gault*"
2008	Colorado adopted a revised Children's Code that provides restorative justice options for most juvenile offenders
2008	OJJDP invested $71 million to develop and enhance mentoring services for at-risk youth and to support antigang strategies
2008	OJJDP awarded $267 million in discretionary grants to support delinquency prevention and child protection interventions
2009	*Safford Unified School District #1 v. Redding* granted Fourth Amendment protections to students from strip searches by school officials without reasonable suspicion

Year	Event
2009	Senator Jim Webb (D-VA) introduced legislation to create a national blue-ribbon commission to study criminal justice and make recommendations on system improvements
2010	*Graham v. Florida* banned life without parole for juveniles for nonhomicidal crimes
2010	The Bureau of Justice Statistics released its first *National Survey of Children in Custody* and reported that 1 in 10 youth confined in state juvenile facilities and large nonstate facilities reported being sexually victimized by staff in the previous 12 months
2010	U.S. Attorney General Eric Holder announced a $5.5 million initiative, *Defending Childhood,* to prevent exposure to violence to violence and to reduce the negative effects experienced by children exposed to violence

Source: Compiled by authors, 2008; revised 2011.

attempted purse snatchings. He was placed on probation in the custody of his mother. In 1961, an intruder entered the apartment of a woman, took her wallet, and raped her. Fingerprints at the crime scene were later identified as those of Morris Kent, who had been fingerprinted when apprehended for housebreaking in 1959. On September 5, 1961, Kent, now age 16, was taken into custody and interrogated for seven hours by the police. Kent admitted guilt and even volunteered information about other housebreakings, robberies, and rapes. Although the records are unclear about when Kent's mother became aware of his arrest, she obtained counsel for Kent shortly after 2:00 P.M. the following day. She and her attorney conferred with the Social Service Director of the Juvenile Court and learned there was a possibility Kent would be waived to criminal court. Kent's attorney advised the Director of his intention to oppose the waiver.

Kent was detained in a Receiving Home for one week. During that period, there was no arraignment and no determination by a judicial officer of the probable cause for Kent's arrest. His attorney filed the motion with the juvenile court opposing the waiver as well as a request to inspect records relating to Kent's previous offenses. Also, a psychiatric examination of Kent was arranged by his attorney, who argued that because his client was "a victim of severe psychopathology," it would be in Kent's best interests to remain within juvenile court jurisdiction, where he could receive adequate treatment in a hospital and would be a suitable subject for rehabilitation (*Kent v. United States*, 1966, p. 545).

Typical of juvenile court judges at the time, the judge in this case failed to rule on any of Kent's attorney's motions. He also failed to confer with Kent's attorney and/ or parents. In a somewhat arrogant manner, the juvenile court judge declared that "after full investigation, I do hereby waive" jurisdiction of Kent and directed that he be "held for trial for [the alleged] offenses under the regular procedure of the U.S. District Court for the District of Columbia" (*Kent v. United States*, 1966, p. 546). The judge offered no findings, nor did he recite any reason for the waiver or make mention of Kent's attorney's motions. Kent was later found guilty of six counts of

Focus on Delinquency

A vacant building in Baltimore, Maryland, was the scene of a fatal shooting that led to the death of a 14-year-old boy. Police were summoned to the vacant building by passersby who noticed a hole in a large fence and what appeared to be a fire in one of the upper floors of the building. When police arrived at the scene, they saw smoke coming out of a second-story window of the building and investigated. As they climbed the stairs of the building, they suddenly heard movement and yelling coming from above them. They entered the second story and came face to face with five persons who were wearing hooded sweatshirts. One person reached in his pocket and pulled out a shiny object that police believed to be a weapon. They drew their own pistols and fired several shots, wounding three of the persons. A third threw his hands over his head and lay on the floor. One suspect appeared to be bleeding profusely. As police approached, they observed that the bleeding person had been shot in the head and was dead. The other suspects were wounded in their chests and upper arms. Emergency vehicles were summoned, and the wounded persons were treated at a nearby hospital. The persons turned out to be five juveniles, aged 15 to 17. They were using the vacant building to do drugs. What was believed to be a firearm turned out to be a crack pipe. The surviving youth were charged with criminal trespass and possession of controlled substances, including crack cocaine and a firearm, which was in the pocket of the youth who surrendered and lay on the floor. The firearm was an unloaded .22 pistol. The youth were being held in juvenile detention pending a hearing. A background check of the youth revealed gang affiliations and lengthy juvenile records.

A trio of murders: (1) 18-year-old Justice Blackshere was found guilty of first-degree murder on August 22, 2007, for stabbing two former coworkers at a downtown restaurant in Detroit, Michigan. He murdered Chelios' Chili Bar manager Megan Soroka, 49, and chef Mark Barnard, 52. Blackshere had been fired in November 2006 from his busboy position and wanted to get his job back. Seven witnesses saw him kill the two victims. Mandatory life imprisonment was prescribed. (2) 16-year-old Jacob Brighton shot and killed his parents, 47-year-old Richard Brighton and 46-year-old Penny Brighton in Fort Pierce, Florida. In August 2007, Jacob was indicted by a grand jury on first-degree murder charges. Deputies who went to the Brighton home following reports of gunshots found Jacob, who flagged them down. "I've shot my parents. There's no point in rescue. They're dead," he said. No motive for the shootings was given. (3) 17-year-old Freddy Tellez, of Hailey, Idaho, was arrested by police following the murder of his 16-year-old girlfriend, Margarita Guardado. Guardado was struck in the head with a blunt object and then her body was set on fire. Tellez faces life in prison if convicted. No motive was given for the murder.

Sources: Associated Press (2008, 24 June), "Four Youths Arrested for Drugs; One Killed"; Yahoo Sports (2007, August 22), "Teen Found Guilty in Double-Murder at Chelios' Restaurant" (available at http://sports.yahoo.com/nhl/news?slug=txcheliosverdict); *West Palm Beach Florida News* (2007, September 12), "Boy Says He Shot Parents Because He 'Let Them Down'" (available at http://www.wpbf.com/news/14097569/detail.html); *Times-News* (2008, March 14), "Tellez Pleads Guilty to Murder of Teen" (available at http://magicvalley.com/news/local/article_355dfcca-41e2-5b73-a3fe-e444fab502f4.html).

housebreaking by a federal jury, although the jury found him "not guilty by reason of insanity" on the rape charge. Because of District of Columbia law, it was mandatory that Kent be transferred to a mental institution until such time as his sanity was restored. On each of the housebreaking counts, Kent's sentence was 5 to 15 years, or a total of 30 to 90 years in prison. His mental institution commitment would be counted as time served against the 30- to 90-year sentence.

Kent's conviction was later reversed by the U.S. Supreme Court on a vote of 5-4. This is significant, because it revealed a subtle shift in Supreme Court sentiment relating to juvenile rights. The majority held that Kent's rights to due process and to the effective assistance of counsel had been violated when he was denied a formal hearing on the waiver and his attorney's motions were ignored. It is also significant that the Court stressed the phrase "critically important" when referring to the waiver hearing. In adult cases, critical stages are those that relate to the defendant's potential loss of freedoms (i.e., incarceration), and because of the Kent decision, waiver hearings are now critical stages. Regarding the absence of effective assistance of counsel, this was also regarded by the Court as a "critically important" decision. The Court observed that

> the right to representation by counsel is not a formality. It is not a grudging gesture to a ritualistic requirement. It is of the essence of justice. . . . Appointment of counsel without affording an opportunity for a hearing on a 'critically important' decision is tantamount to a denial of counsel. (383 U.S. at 561)

In re Gault (1967)

In re Gault (1967) is perhaps the most noteworthy of all landmark juvenile rights cases. Certainly, it is considered to be the most ambitious. In a 7-2 vote, the U.S. Supreme Court articulated the following rights for all juveniles: (1) the right to a notice of charges, (2) the right to counsel, (3) the right to confront and cross-examine witnesses, and (4) the right to invoke the privilege against self-incrimination. The petitioner, Gault, also requested the Court to rule favorably on two additional rights:

Arrested youth had legal rights similar to those of adults.
(Courtesy of Dean John Champion)

(1) the right to a transcript of the proceedings and (2) the right to appellate review. The Court elected not to rule on either of these rights.

The facts of the case are that Gerald Francis Gault, a 15-year-old, and a friend, Ronald Lewis, were taken into custody by the Sheriff of Gila County, Arizona, on the morning of June 8, 1964. At the time, Gault was on probation as the result of "being in the company of another who had stolen a wallet from a lady's purse," a judgment entered on February 25, 1964 (*In re Gault*, 1967, p. 1). A verbal complaint had been filed by a neighbor of Gault, Mrs. Cook, alleging that Gault had called her and made lewd and indecent remarks. (With some levity, the U.S. Supreme Court said that "[i]t will suffice for purposes of this opinion to say that the remarks or questions put to her were of the irritatingly offensive, adolescent, sex variety" [387 U.S. at 4]).

When Gault was picked up, his mother and father were at work. Indeed, they did not learn where their son was until much later that evening. Gault was being held at the Children's Detention Home, and his parents proceeded to the Home. Officer Flagg, the deputy probation officer and superintendent of the Children's Detention Home where Gault was being detained, advised Gault's parents that a hearing would be held in juvenile court at 3:00 P.M. the following day. Flagg filed a petition with the court on the hearing day, June 9. This petition was entirely formal, stating only that "said minor is under the age of 18 years, and is in need of the protection of this Honorable Court; [and that] said minor is a delinquent minor." It prayed for a hearing and an order regarding the "care and custody of said minor." No factual basis was provided for the petition, and Gault's parents were not provided with a copy of it in advance of the hearing.

On June 9, the hearing was held, with only Gault, his mother and older brother, two probation officers (Flagg and Henderson), and the juvenile court judge (Judge McGhee) present. The original complainant, Mrs. Cook, was not there. No one was sworn at the hearing, no transcript was made of it, and no memorandum of the substance of the proceedings was prepared. The testimony consisted largely of allegations by Officer Flagg about Gault's behavior and prior juvenile record. A subsequent hearing was scheduled for and held on June 15. At the second hearing, all of the above were present, along with Ronald Lewis, his father, and Gault's father. What actually transpired is unknown, although there are conflicting recollections from all parties who were there. When Mrs. Gault asked why Mrs. Cook was not present, Judge McGhee said, "She didn't have to be present at that hearing." Furthermore, the judge did not speak to Mrs. Cook or communicate with her at any time. Flagg spoke with her once by telephone on June 9. Officially, the charge against Gault was "Lewd Telephone Calls." When the hearing was concluded, the judge committed Gault as a juvenile delinquent to the Arizona State Industrial School "for a period of his minority" (i.e., until age 21). (If an adult had made an obscene telephone call, he would have received a $50 fine and no more than 60 days in jail. In Gerald Gault's case, however, he was facing nearly six years in a juvenile prison for the same offense.)

A *habeas corpus* hearing was held on August 17, and Judge McGhee was cross-examined regarding his actions. After "hemming and hawing," the judge declared that

habeas corpus
Writ meaning "produce the body"; used by prisoners to challenge the nature and length of their confinement.

Gault had "disturbed the peace" and was "habitually involved in immoral matters." Regarding Gault's alleged "habitual immorality," the judge made vague references to an incident two years earlier, when Gault had been accused of stealing someone's baseball glove and had lied to police by denying that he had taken it. The judge also recalled, again vaguely, that Gault had testified some months earlier about making "silly calls, or funny calls, or something like that."

After exhausting their appeals in the Arizona state courts, the Gaults appealed to the U.S. Supreme Court. Needless to say, the Court was appalled that Gault's case had been handled in such a cavalier and unconstitutional manner. The Supreme Court reversed the Arizona court's decision, holding that Gault did, indeed, have the right to an attorney, the right to confront his accuser (Mrs. Cook) and to cross-examine her, the right against self-incrimination, and the right to have notice of the charges filed against him. Perhaps Justice Black best summarized the implications of this decision when he said, "This holding strikes a well-nigh fatal blow to much that is *unique* [emphasis added] about the juvenile courts in this Nation."

The right to an attorney, as well as the other rights conveyed to Gault, is now a pervasive feature of juvenile offender processing. The due process rights for juveniles that were established specifically in *In re Gault* (1967) are:

- Right to have notice of charges, including notification of parents and legal guardians.
- Right to counsel to represent interests.
- Right to confront accusers and to cross-examine witnesses and accusers.
- Right to protection against self-incrimination and the right to refuse to testify against oneself.
- Right to written record and transcript of court proceedings.
- Right to appellate review of finding of guilt.

Figure 4.1 shows an acknowledgment of one's rights when a juvenile is initially apprehended and his or her processing begins.

In re Winship (1970)

In re Winship (1970) was a less-complex case compared with *In re Gault* (1967). However, it established an important precedent in juvenile courts relating to the standard of proof used in establishing defendant guilt. The U.S. Supreme Court held that "beyond a reasonable doubt," a standard ordinarily used in adult criminal courts, was henceforth to be used by juvenile court judges and others in establishing a youth's delinquency. Formerly, the standard used was the civil application of "preponderance of the evidence."

The facts in the *Winship* case are that Samuel Winship was a 12-year-old charged with larceny in New York City. He purportedly entered a locker and stole $112 from a woman's pocketbook. Under Section 712 of the New York Family Court Act, a juvenile delinquent was defined as "a person over seven and less than 16 years of age

In the Juvenile Court for Glynn County State of Georgia

IN THE MATTER OF:

§ CASE NO.
§ SEX:
§ DOB:

A CHILD.

§ AGE:

ACKNOWLEDGMENT OF RIGHTS

The above-named child, along with the undersigned parent/guardian and/or attorney, state(s) as follows:

I understand that I have been charged with and that I am here today to answer to that charge(s). I have had explained and further understand the following:

1. I do not have to admit to the charge(s) against me or even say anything at all, and that if I choose not to say anything it will not be used against me.
2. I have the right to have the charge(s) against me served upon me in writing within a reasonable time.
3. I have the right to have a lawyer represent me, and if I cannot afford to hire a lawyer, the Court will provide one for me.
4. I understand that a lawyer is trained to understand court procedure and proceedings, knows how to conduct trials and how to properly introduce evidence and exclude improper evidence, knows how the law applies to the circumstances of my case, and knows how my rights and liberties may be affected by the court proceedings and how to protect my rights and liberties, and how to present my case and all matters favorable to me to the court, all of which I may not know.
5. I have had my right to be represented by a lawyer explained to me and I understand the danger of proceeding without a lawyer.
6. I have been told of the possible dispositions which the court can order if I admit to the charge(s) or if I am found to have committed a delinquent or unruly act(s) and those dispositions may include but are not limited to dismissal, informal adjustment, probation, commitment to the Department of Human Resources, Commitment to the Department of Juvenile Justice not to exceed six months, placement in the custody of the Division of Family and Children Services, community service, suspension of driving privileges, requiring school attendance, and restitution.
7. I have talked with my parents/guardian and/or lawyer about this case and have had all of the above explained to me and had the opportunity to ask questions and have had all my questions answered.
8. I have the right to have a trial before the judge. I can have witnesses there to testify for me, and I can question anyone who might testify against me. I have the right to an appeal from the trial if I disagree with the decision, and I have a right to receive a record and/or transcript of the proceedings in the event of an appeal.

After having been advised of the above, I do hereby:

( ) Elect to have a lawyer

(   ) Elect not to have a lawyer

This _____ day of _____, 20 _____.

_____
Signature of Child

_____
Signature of Parent

_____
Signature of Person Advising Rights

_____
Signature of Attorney/GAL

Figure 4.1

Acknowledgment of Rights (Glynn County, GA)
Source: Reprinted by permission of Glynn County, Georgia, Juvenile Court.

CAREER SNAPSHOT

(Courtesy of Peter J. Benekos)

Name: David Gianoni
Position: Supervisor, Juvenile Probation
Colleges Attended: Edinboro University of Pennsylvania and Mercyhurst College
Degrees: B.A. in Criminal Justice and M.S. in Administration of Justice

Background

I graduated from Edinboro University of Pennsylvania in May 1979 with a Bachelor of Arts degree in Criminal Justice. I was lucky, because I had a professor whom I admired that encouraged us to keep learning after we found employment in the field. He recommended reading journals related to the field to stay current with developing trends. This advice has stayed with me throughout my career.

In 1993, I enrolled at Mercyhurst College in the Master's program toward a degree in Administration of Justice through the Juvenile Court Judges' Commission. I received my Master's degree in May 1995. The Juvenile Court Judges' Commission paid for all expenses related to the degree, and the education was invaluable. The program came at a most opportune time for me as I had been in the field for about 14 years when I started the course work. That experience was very helpful when it came to writing research papers and understanding the research that was being done in the field.

I am currently a supervisor for Erie County Juvenile Probation in Erie, Pennsylvania. My job is to supervise seven probation officers to ensure that they prepare court reports in a timely manner and effectively supervise their clients. Each officer supervises from 35 to 50 individuals. Supervisors also read court orders and court reports to look for errors and for accuracy of information.

As a supervisor, it is imperative that you have a sound understanding of the court system and the processing of paperwork. I started my career as an Adult Probation Officer in 1979. I transferred to Juvenile Probation after eight years. Caseloads were very high in Adult, and I knew that I wanted to work more closely with individuals. The transfer was very difficult at first, because I discovered that the systems were completely different and I needed to relearn a new set of rules and paperwork. This process was a good thing, though, as I became very knowledgeable in two areas of the system.

Advice to Students

If you are interested in a job in probation, you will need a four-year degree in a related field, such as criminal justice, psychology, education, social work, or sociology. I often have students call me with two-year degrees looking for employment, and they are disappointed when I tell them they do not qualify. Also, I would stress that you need a well-rounded education. Learn how to gather information and make a good recommendation based on that data. Know how to write effectively so that you can then express that information in a clear, concise manner. We have had many good applicants lose out on a job due to poor writing and processing skills. Learn how to communicate with people, and become comfortable with talking in front of a roomful of people. At times, you need to be able to express yourself in very simple terms, but you also have to be able to effectively communicate your ideas to judges, attorneys, and other professionals.

Learn as much as you can about the people you will be supervising. Psychology classes are important to understand why people act the way they do. Also, if offered, take classes that help you understand the mental health field, including diagnoses and current medications. Today, most of the clients you will work with have some form of mental health diagnosis.

Once you have accomplished these things, make sure that you do an internship. Everyday experience in the field that interests you is the only way to know if that is the job for you. I was lucky in that my internship turned into a job when I graduated from college in 1979. When you arrive at your work site, make sure you are serious about the job. Be on time, and work hard every day. The people you impress in your internship may hire you or at least be a good reference in the future.

Finally, do not be afraid to continue learning and take on new responsibilities. You never know where these opportunities will lead you. When I was a new Probation Officer, I started teaching classes for Driving Under the Influence clients. I spent 20 years teaching these classes, and it not only gave me a great deal of education about the system but also helped me feel comfortable teaching and expressing my ideas. Later, I was asked to take part in a committee to develop a safety program for Probation Officers throughout the state of Pennsylvania. I became one of the first state-certified safety instructors in the field. These experiences prepared me to become a state-certified Control Tactics instructor for Probation Officers as well. All of these opportunities not only helped to further my career, they also kept me fresh with new ideas and interaction with other professionals.

who does any act, which, if done by an adult, would constitute a crime." Interestingly, the juvenile court judge in the case acknowledged that the proof to be presented by the prosecution might be insufficient to establish the guilt of Winship beyond a reasonable doubt, although he did indicate that the New York Family Court Act provided that "any determination at the conclusion of [an adjudicatory hearing] that a [juvenile] did an act or acts must be based on a preponderance of the evidence" standard (397 U.S. at 360). Winship was adjudicated as a delinquent and ordered to a training school for 18 months, subject to annual extensions of his commitment until his eighteenth birthday. Appeals to New York courts were unsuccessful.

The U.S. Supreme Court heard Winship's case and, in a 6-3 vote, reversed the New York Family Court ruling. A statement by Justice Brennan succinctly states the case for the beyond a reasonable doubt standard:

> In sum, the constitutional safeguard of proof beyond a reasonable doubt is as much required during the adjudicatory stage of a delinquency proceeding as are those constitutional safeguards applied in *Gault*—notice of charges, right to counsel, the rights of confrontation and examination, and the privilege of self-incrimination. We therefore hold, in agreement with Chief Justice Fuld in dissent in the Court of Appeals, that where a 12-year-old child is charged with an act of stealing which renders him liable to confinement for as long as six years, then, as a matter of due process, the case against him must be proved beyond a reasonable doubt. (397 U.S. at 368)

McKeiver v. Pennsylvania (1971)

The case of *McKeiver v. Pennsylvania* (1971) was important because in this decision, the U.S. Supreme Court held that juveniles are not entitled to a jury trial as a matter of right. It should be noted that as of 2007, nine states legislatively permitted jury trials for juveniles in juvenile courts if they so requested such trials, depending upon the seriousness of the alleged offense or offenses (Szymanski, 2008c).

The facts in the *McKeiver* case are that in May 1968, Joseph McKeiver, age 16, was charged with robbery, larceny, and receiving stolen goods. Although he was represented by counsel at his adjudicatory hearing and requested a trial by jury to ascertain his guilt or innocence, Judge Theodore S. Gutowicz of the Court of Common Pleas, Family Division, Juvenile Branch, of Philadelphia, Pennsylvania, denied the request. McKeiver was subsequently adjudicated delinquent, and on subsequent appeal to the U.S. Supreme Court, McKeiver's adjudication was upheld. Again, of interest to criminal justice analysts, the remarks of a Supreme Court Justice are insightful. Justice Blackmun indicated:

> If the formalities of the criminal adjudicative process are to be superimposed upon the juvenile court system, there is little need for its separate existence. Perhaps that ultimate disillusionment will come one day, but for the moment, we are disinclined to give impetus to it. (403 U.S. at 551)

Throughout the opinion delivered in the *McKeiver* case, it is apparent that the U.S. Supreme Court was sensitive to the problems associated with juvenile court procedure. Since criminal courts were already bogged down with formalities and lengthy protocol that frequently led to excessive court delays, it was not unreasonable for the Court to rule against perpetuating such formalities in juvenile courts. In this instance, however, we must recognize that the Court merely ruled it is not the constitutional right of juveniles to have a jury trial upon their request. This proclamation had no effect on individual states that wished to enact or preserve such a method of adjudicating juveniles as delinquent or nondelinquent. In 2007, a total of 11 states had legislative provisions for jury trial under special circumstances, and nine states provided the right to a jury trial (Szymanski, 2008c).

Breed v. Jones (1975)

The case of *Breed v. Jones* (1975) raised the significant constitutional issue of **double jeopardy**, which means being tried for the same crime twice. The Fifth Amendment provides protection against double jeopardy. Thus, if someone is charged with a crime and is then acquitted, they cannot be tried again for that same offense. This would violate their Fifth Amendment right against double jeopardy. In *Breed v. Jones*, the U.S. Supreme Court concluded that after a juvenile has been adjudicated delinquent for a particular offense, the youth cannot be tried again as an adult in criminal court for that same offense.

> **double jeopardy**
> Subjecting persons to prosecution more than once in the same jurisdiction for the same offense, usually without new or vital evidence; prohibited by the Fifth Amendment.

The facts of the case are that on February 8, 1971, in Los Angeles, California, Gary Steven Jones, age 17, was armed with a deadly weapon and allegedly committed robbery. Jones was subsequently apprehended, and an adjudicatory hearing was held on March 1. A petition was filed against Jones. After testimony was taken from Jones and witnesses, the juvenile court found that the allegations in the petition were true and sustained the petition. A dispositional hearing date was set for March 15. At that time, Jones was declared "not … amenable to the care, treatment and training program available through the facilities of the juvenile court" under a California statute (*Breed v. Jones*, 1975, p. 524). Jones was then transferred by judicial waiver to a California criminal court, where he could be tried as an adult. In a subsequent criminal trial, Jones was convicted of robbery and committed for an indeterminate period to the California Youth Authority. The California Supreme Court upheld the conviction.

When Jones appealed the decision in 1971, the U.S. Supreme Court reversed the robbery conviction. Chief Justice Warren Burger delivered the Court's opinion:

> We hold that the prosecution of [Jones] in Superior Court, after an adjudicatory proceeding in Juvenile Court, violated the Double Jeopardy Clause of the Fifth Amendment, as applied to the States through the 14th Amendment.

The Court ordered Jones's release outright or a remand to juvenile court for disposition. In a lengthy opinion, Justice Burger targeted double jeopardy as (1) being adjudicated as delinquent on specific charges in a juvenile court and (2) subsequently being tried and convicted on those same charges in criminal court. Within the context of fundamental fairness, such action could not be tolerated.

Schall v. Martin (1984)

In the case of *Schall v. Martin* (1984), the U.S. Supreme Court issued juveniles a minor setback regarding the state's right to hold them in preventive detention pending a subsequent adjudication. The Court said that the preventive detention of juveniles by states is constitutional if judges perceive these youth to pose a danger to the community or an otherwise serious risk if released short of an adjudicatory hearing. The *Schall v. Martin* decision was significant, in part, because many persons advocated the separation of juveniles and adults in jails, those facilities most often used for preventive detention. Also, the preventive detention of adults was not ordinarily practiced at that time. Since then, the preventive detention of adults who are deemed to pose societal risks has been upheld by the U.S. Supreme Court (*United States v. Salerno*, 1987).

The facts of the case are that 14-year-old Gregory Martin was arrested at 11:30 P.M. on December 13, 1977, in New York City. He was charged with first-degree robbery, second-degree assault, and criminal possession of a weapon. Martin lied to police at the time, giving a false name and address. Between the time of his arrest and December 29, when a fact-finding hearing was held, Martin was detained (a total of 15 days). His confinement was based largely on the false information he had supplied to police and the seriousness of the charges pending against him. Subsequently, he was adjudicated a delinquent and placed on two years probation. Later, his attorney filed an appeal, contesting his preventive detention as violative of the due process clause of the 14th Amendment. The U.S. Supreme Court eventually heard the case and upheld the detention as constitutional.

Juvenile Rights and the Transformation of the Juvenile Court

Since *In re Gault* (1967), U.S. Supreme Court decisions regarding the rights of juveniles have essentially transformed the juvenile court (Feld, 1999). A series of decisions, including those reviewed above, recognized that even youthful offenders require protections of due process and legal representation. With the end of the hands-off approach, the 1960s and 1980s were characterized as the due process era of juvenile justice. Table 4.2 summarizes some of the major rights available to juveniles and compares these rights with selected rights enjoyed by adults in criminal proceedings.

Some of the consequences of this model included (1) more formal court procedures that reduced discretion and individualized decisions, (2) a shift in emphasis from the best interests of the child to protecting youth from the abuses of the juvenile justice system, and (3) acknowledgement that youth have some degree of criminal culpability. The emphasis on procedural protections and the right to counsel also resulted in greater certainty, and severity, of punitive sanctions. Juveniles were provided rights that were more consistent with those followed in adult criminal court. For

Table 4.2

COMPARISON OF JUVENILE AND ADULT RIGHTS RELATING TO DELINQUENCY AND CRIME

Right	Adults	Juveniles
1. Beyond a reasonable doubt standard used in court	Yes	Yes
2. Right against double jeopardy	Yes	Yes
3. Right to assistance of counsel	Yes	Yes
4. Right to notice of charges	Yes	Yes
5. Right to a transcript of court proceedings	Yes	No
6. Right against self-incrimination	Yes	Yes
7. Right to trial by jury	Yes	No in most states
8. Right to defense counsel in court proceedings	Yes	Yes
9. Right to due process	Yes	Yes
10. Right to bail	Yes	No, with exceptions
11. Right to cross-examine witnesses	Yes	Yes
12. Right of confrontation	Yes	Yes
13. Standards relating to searches and seizures:		
a. "Probable cause" and warrants required for searches and seizures	Yes, with exceptions	Yes, with exceptions
b. "Reasonable suspicion" required for searches and seizures without warrant	No	Yes
14. Right to hearing before transfer to criminal court or to a reverse waiver hearing in states with automatic transfer provisions	Not applicable	Yes
15. Right to a speedy trial	Yes	No
16. Right to *habeas corpus* relief in correctional settings	Yes	Yes
17. Right to rehabilitation	No	Yes
18. Criminal evidentiary standards	Yes	Yes
19. Right to hearing for parole or probation revocation	Yes	Yes
20. Bifurcated trial, death penalty cases	Yes	Not Applicable
21. Right to discovery	Yes	Limited
22. Fingerprinting, photographing at booking	Yes	Yes, with exceptions
23. Right to appeal	Yes	Limited
24. Waivers of rights:	Knowingly, intelligently	Totality of circumstances
25. Equal protection clause of 14th Amendment applicable	Yes	Yes, with exceptions
26. Right to court-appointed attorney if indigent	Yes	Yes
27. Transcript of criminal/delinquency trial proceedings required	Yes	Limited

(Continued)

Table 4.2   **CONTINUED**

Right	Adults	Juveniles
28. Pretrial detention permitted	Yes	Yes
29. Plea bargaining	Yes, with exceptions	Limited
30. Burden of proof borne by prosecution	Yes	Yes
31. Public access to trials	Yes	Limited
32. Conviction/adjudication results in criminal record	Yes	Yes

Source: Compiled by authors, 2011.

example, *In re Gault* resulted in notice of charges, legal assistance, and protection from self incrimination.

The intent of reformers who established the juvenile court was to provide civil rather than criminal proceedings and to adhere to the doctrine of *parens patriae* (Feld and Schafer, 2010a). As noted earlier, this model was not adversarial and did not require determination of guilt. In addition, court records were confidential to protect youth from having a criminal record and to recognize rehabilitative expectations. After *Gault*, and the criticisms of arbitrary decisions and questionable rehabilitative interventions and outcomes, juvenile courts drifted from their original assumptions and practices and began to mirror criminal courts. Youth who were taken into custody for more serious offenses were also more likely to be transferred to adult jurisdiction.

During the 1980s and 1990s, as arrests of youth and adults for violent crimes began to increase, a get-tough mood further eroded the rationale of the juvenile court. With increased media coverage of the drug war, youth gangs, and gun violence, a moral panic about youth contributed to a fearful and frustrated public. In response, legislatures passed punitive policies that targeted youth with increased penalties that lowered the age of majority and reduced the number of offenses excluded from juvenile court jurisdiction (Benekos and Merlo, 2009).

Seventeen states in the 1990s revised the purpose clause of the juvenile court to reflect greater emphasis on public safety and more accountability for youth (Torbet and Szymanski, 1998). By 2008, only 14 states permitted or required delinquency hearings to be open to the public, and in another 21, these hearings were open depending on age and offense of the delinquent (Szymanski, 2008a). In 2009, a total of 41 states had no age restrictions on fingerprinting alleged or adjudicated youthful offenders. In North Carolina, for example, youth ages 10 and older can be fingerprinted (Szymanski, 2010a). With court records, 31 states do not permit juvenile records to be sealed, expunged, or deleted if the delinquent was convicted of a felony, misdemeanor, or adjudicated delinquent (Szymanski, 2010b).

As explained by Szymanski (2010b), "sealing means placing court records in a separate file not accessible to the general public," and expungement means court "records are deemed never to have existed or the actual destruction of court records" (p. 1). Regarding jurisdiction of juveniles, all states have provisions to prosecute and sentence juveniles as adults. A review by the National Center for Juvenile Justice determined that 46 states have provisions for judicial waiver, 15 states provide that waiver is decided by prosecutors, and 29 states have statutory exclusion, which means that original jurisdiction is in adult criminal court (Griffin, 2008).

These provisions demonstrate the difference in how juvenile offenders are treated by the courts. From informal, child-focused hearings to more formal, offense-focused proceedings, juvenile court has "converged with criminal court" to reflect "procedural, jurisdictional, and sentencing philosophy" similarities (Feld, 1999, p. 287). In his critique of these developments, Feld (1999) noted that "judicial decisions, legislative amendments, and administrative changes have transformed the juvenile court from a nominally rehabilitative welfare agency into a scaled-down second class criminal court for young people" (p. 287).

The consequences of receiving due process rights and expanding get-tough policies for juvenile offenders have raised questions about the need for a separate juvenile court. Feld (1993), for example, proposed that the juvenile court should be abolished and that all offenders, regardless of age, should receive equal guaranteed rights and safeguards in one criminal court. For convicted offenders, a "youth discount" would be provided to modify length of sentences to reflect diminished culpability of delinquents. For example, a 16-year-old offender would receive 66 percent of the adult sentence compared to a 14-year-old offender, who would receive 33 percent of the sentence.

While Feld's proposal is not without merit, the convergence of adult and juvenile courts has not eliminated acknowledgement that the prevalence of delinquency is an adolescent phenomenon and that most youth age out of their offending. The small percentage of youth who commit serious crimes and follow a persistent path of criminality can be transferred out of juvenile court and handled in criminal court jurisdiction. As juvenile crime rates have declined and evidence-based programs have been successful in preventing and reducing delinquency, the juvenile justice system has developed a more balanced approach, which recognizes the constitutional rights of youth but also has not abandoned the rehabilitative mission. As presented in Chapter 3, the Balanced and Restorative Justice model, preserves the juvenile court mission while holding youth accountable for their delinquent acts.

Juvenile Right to Waive Rights

With the number of the legal rights extended to juveniles since 1966, on some occasions juveniles may waive various rights, such as the right to counsel, at one or more critical stages of their juvenile justice system processing. In one case, *West v. United States* (1968), a juvenile had waived his right to counsel as well as several other important rights that had been extended to juveniles through the *Gault* decision. A nine-point standard for analysis was established by the Fifth Circuit Court of Appeals when the *West* disposition was imposed and an appeal followed. The nine-point standard was devised so that judges could determine whether *any* juvenile is capable of understanding and waiving one or more of his or her constitutional rights. These nine points are:

1. Age.
2. Education.
3. Knowledge of the substance of the charge and the nature of the right to remain silent and the right to an attorney.
4. Whether the accused is allowed contact with parents, guardian, attorney, or other interested adult.
5. Whether the interrogation occurred before or after indictment.
6. Methods used in interrogation.
7. Length of interrogation.
8. Whether the accused refused to voluntarily give statements on prior occasions.
9. Whether the accused had repudiated an extrajudicial statement at a later date.

While these nine points are interesting and relevant, the fact that they were articulated by the Fifth Circuit Court of Appeals meant they were not binding on federal district courts in other circuits. For that matter, because these were rights conveyed through a federal circuit, they were not binding on any particular state jurisdiction, even a state within the territory of the Fifth Circuit Court of Appeals.

Subsequently, a totality of circumstances test was established in the case of *Fare v. Michael C.* (1979), which involved a juvenile who was interrogated by police without parental consent or attorney presence. Michael C. was a youth on probation and charged with murder. When he asked to see his probation officer during a later police interrogation, the investigating detectives denied his request. They said that probation officers are not attorneys and, thus, are not permitted to participate in interrogations of suspects. Michael C. subsequently waived his right to an attorney, answered police questions, and gave incriminating evidence that led to his conviction for murder. He later appealed, contending that his right to counsel had been violated when the police refused to allow him to see his probation officer. However, the U.S. Supreme Court found that Michael C. had made an intelligent, understanding, and voluntary waiver of his rights when questioned by the police. The Court used the totality of circumstances standard, which was adopted from an earlier case involving an adult offender.

This U.S. Supreme Court case has resulted in several mixed decisions among appellate courts concerning interrogations of youthful suspects. For instance, in *Woods v. Clusen* (1986), the Seventh Circuit Court of Appeals ruled that a 16.5-year-old's confession was inadmissible, because the juvenile had been taken from his home at 7:30 A.M., handcuffed, stripped, forced to wear institutional clothing but no shoes or socks, shown pictures of the crime scene, and intimidated and interrogated for many hours. These police tactics were criticized by the Court, and the investigators were reprimanded for their failure to uphold and respect the offender's constitutional rights and provide fundamental fairness.

Research by Grisso (1998), for instance, shows that juveniles have little grasp of their constitutional rights. Grisso studied a large sample of juveniles and found that only 10 percent of them chose not to waive their rights when serious charges were alleged. Grisso found that these youth (1) demonstrated less comprehension than adults of their *Miranda* rights, (2) had less understanding of the wording of the **Miranda warning**, (3) misunderstood their right to counsel, and (4) did not understand their right to remain silent, believing that they could later be punished if they failed to tell about their criminal activities (*Miranda v. Arizona*, 1966).

State policies and practices are inconsistent when it comes to providing counsel for juveniles. Different circumstances on a state-by-state basis show significant variation. Research on state statutory provisions shows unequal distribution of legal rights for juveniles regarding appointment of defense counsel and waivers of the right to counsel (Caeti, Hemmens, and Burton, 1996). Only about half of all states have vested juvenile court judges with the discretion to appoint counsel for juveniles, while even fewer states provide strict rights waiver requirements and mandatory defense counsel appointments. In her report entitled *Access to Counsel*, Jones (2004) found that even though the right to counsel was established in 1967 in *In re Gault*, many juveniles do not have legal representation in the early stages of court proceedings, and when attorneys are provided, they often lack adequate time to prepare for effective representation. Studies of juvenile legal representation demonstrate that "youth often waive their right to counsel" even when it goes against their "best interests" (Jones, 2004, p. 7).

This is an important concern, because juvenile policies have become more punitive and the consequences of court dispositions can be more severe for youth. Scientific research on adolescent brain development presents evidence that youth, especially in their early teens, lack comprehension of legal concepts and consequences. As a result, youth are susceptible to coercion and intimidation by law enforcement and court personnel (Levick and Desai, 2007). The right to counsel for juveniles is fundamental, because developmentally, youth are not prepared to "understand, manage or navigate" the justice system (Levick and Desai, 2007, p. 182). In addition, legal counsel helps "ensure the rights of youth" and their access to services and programs that characterize the "rehabilitative mission of juvenile court" (Levick and Desai, 2007, p. 182).

In spite of the disparities among states, "all jurisdictions extend the right to counsel" for youth charged with delinquency (Szymanski, 2008b, p. 1). Juveniles, however, can waive this right if it is "knowing, intelligent, and voluntary." In their study of juveniles' rights to counsel in Minnesota, Feld and Schaefer (2010b) review the intent of *Gault* to provide youth with "fundamentally fair" procedures (p. 329). While the U.S. Supreme Court did not require that counsel be appointed, it did require judges to advise youth and their parents about the right to counsel.

After a 1995 Minnesota law mandated that counsel be appointed for youth charged with felonies or gross misdemeanors, Feld and Schaefer (2010b) found that

Miranda warning
Statement given to suspects by police officers advising them of their legal rights to counsel, to refuse to answer questions, to avoid self-incrimination, and others.

judges permitted nearly "one-third of youth who were convicted of felonies and serious misdemeanors to waive counsel" (p. 350). Those authors concluded that the law had limited impact on increasing the right of counsel for youth and, in some jurisdictions, that legal representation for youth was lower than that for adults (p. 344).

Research on adolescent development continues to recognize that youth lack the competence, understanding, and maturity to waive legal representation. As a result, Feld and Schaefer (2010b) discuss the importance for states to legislate policies that "prohibit waivers of counsel by juveniles charged with crimes" (p. 350). This becomes even more important as juveniles are receiving more punitive, adult-like consequences for their adjudications (Szymanski, 2008b).

Kids for Cash

On January 28, 2009, the Pennsylvania Supreme Court relieved Judge Mark A. Ciavarella of Luzerne County of all judicial duties and terminated the senior judge certificate for Judge Michael T. Conahan (Administrative Office of Pennsylvania Courts, 2009). After investigations by the Juvenile Law Center and the U.S. Attorney's Office in the Middle District of Pennsylvania, the judges were charged with federal crimes "relating to the alleged receipt of $2.8 million in illegal payments from the owners of two juvenile detention facilities" (Interbranch Commission on Juvenile Justice, 2010, p. 5).

Over a period of years, the two judges received payoffs to send hundreds of youth to detention, often after improperly denying the juvenile defendants their constitutional right to counsel. The judicial corruption and rights were so "extensive and egregious" that the Pennsylvania Supreme Court vacated (to make legally void) all of the adjudications from 2003 to 2008 that were handled by Judge Ciavarella (Interbranch Commission on Juvenile Justice, 2010, p. 6). In addition, all of the youth had their cases expunged (Interbranch Commission on Juvenile Justice, 2010). The Pennsylvania Supreme Court action was unprecedented and reflected the serious infringement of due process rights of vulnerable youth and the blatant disregard for juvenile court rules and procedure. Based on its investigation of how youth were treated and the disposition of cases, the Juvenile Law Center (n.d.) identified this as the worst juvenile justice scandal in U.S. history.

The investigation identified 1,866 cases handled by Judge Ciavarella that were improperly (and illegally) denied counsel. Without counsel present to represent juvenile defendants, Judge Ciavarella was unchallenged in placing youth in institutions, often for minor offenses that would usually result in an informal adjustment or consent decree. On September 9, 2009, a 48-count indictment was filed against the two judges charging them with using the court as a "criminal enterprise to enrich themselves" (Interbranch Commission on Juvenile Justice, 2010, p. 17). Witnesses reported that Judge Ciavarella used "fear and intimidation" as well as "reprisal and retribution" to maintain autocratic rule over the court (Interbranch Commission on Juvenile Justice, 2010, p. 23).

Former Judge Ciavarella pleaded guilty in February 2009, but after a federal judge did not accept the 87-month sentence that was part of the plea agreement,

Ciavarella withdrew his plea. On September 29, 2010, a grand jury returned a new, 39-count indictment, and Ciavarella was tried in February 2011. He was convicted on 12 counts, including racketeering and conspiracy, mail fraud, and filing false tax returns, and acquitted on the 27 others. Ciavarella was sentenced to 28 years in federal prison. Former judge Conahan pleaded guilty to racketeering conspiracy and was sentenced to 17.5 years (Janoski and Sisak, 2011; Sisak and Sweet, 2011).

The lesson from Luzerne County is not only that youth who appear in court require due process protections and legal counsel but also that those rights need to be insured. While Luzerne County was an exceptional scandal, it underscores the issue of juvenile rights and the potential for abuse. As the Interbranch Commission on Juvenile Justice (2010) concluded, the situation in Luzerne County "demonstrates what happens when judicial power is divorced from the constraints of law" (p. 62). While this chapter examines some legal developments and issues regarding juvenile rights and constitutional protections for youth, the kids for cash sandal underscores the importance of those rights.

Juveniles and Fourth Amendment Rights: Search and Seizure

Concerns about due process protection for juveniles who are taken into custody and petitioned to court were addressed by the U.S. Supreme Court in *In re Gault* (1967). Another concern that demonstrates the ambivalence toward juvenile and juvenile rights is the extent to which youth can be subject to search and seizure. Juveniles are still minors and do not enjoy the same rights as adults. Police have greater latitude in detaining youth (e.g., protective custody, curfew violations, and truancy), and they can exercise a lower level of suspicion in stopping youth and taking them into custody (e.g., reasonable suspicion).

In the context of school safety and increased surveillance of students, two cases illustrate concerns about the extent of Fourth Amendment protections that youth can expect in school. In the first, *New Jersey v. T.L.O.* (1985), the U.S. Supreme Court ruled that school officials did not violate the student's Fourth Amendment rights. In this case, a 14-year-old girl was caught violating school rules by smoking a cigarette in the school bathroom. When confronted by the principal, she denied that she had been smoking. The principal examined her purse and discovered a pack of cigarettes, some rolling papers, money, marijuana, and other drug materials. This information was turned over to police, who charged the girl with delinquency. She was convicted. The girl's attorney sought to exclude the seized evidence, because it was believed to be in violation of her Fourth Amendment right against unreasonable searches and seizures. The U.S. Supreme Court heard the case and ruled 6-3 in favor of school officials, declaring that they only need reasonable suspicion, not probable cause, to search students and their possessions while on school property. When students enter their schools, they are subject to a lower standard when suspected of wrongdoing or carrying illegal contraband in violation of school rules than that applied to adults. The Court determined that the rolling papers provided the reasonable suspicion needed to suspect that T.L.O. might also have drugs in her purse. Therefore, the Court deferred to school officials and the concerns of school safety.

In the second case, *Safford Unified School District #1 v. Redding* (2009), in 2003 in Arizona, 13-year-old Savana Redding was called from class to the principal's office to respond to allegations made by another student that Redding had provided her with ibuprofen pills. Possession of ibuprofen was a violation of school policy. Based on the tip, the Assistant Principal, Kerry Wilson, told the school nurse to conduct a strip search of Redding. Redding was ordered to remove her clothing down to her underwear and bra, then told to pull out and shake out her underclothing. No drugs were found.

Redding filed a suit against the Safford Unified School District alleging that her Fourth Amendment right to privacy had been violated by the search. In this 8-1 decision, the U.S. Supreme Court ruled that Redding's rights had been violated and that school officials did not have "sufficient suspicion" to conduct an intrusive search for over-the-counter drugs that did not present a danger to the school. The *Safford v. Redding* decision underscores that the extent of the search needs to be reasonably related to the purpose of the search. Essentially, the Court ruled that the strip search was not warranted by the age and sex of the student and the nature of the infraction of school policy. In *New Jersey v. T.L.O.* (1985), the Court recognized that the rolling papers justified reasonable suspicion to conduct further search of the student. However, in *Safford v. Redding* (2009), a case that took almost six years, the Court determined that that the degree of intrusion was not reasonably related to the facts of the case, and the Court restricted the authority of school officials while affirming the rights of the student.

Jury Trials for Juvenile Delinquents

Juveniles generally do not receive jury trials. Less than one-fourth of all states permit jury trials for juveniles by statute. In 11 states, jury trials are available to juveniles only if judges permit them. In most cases, therefore, the judgment of the juvenile court is final for all practical purposes, and while appeals of decisions by juvenile court judges can be initiated in certain circumstances, they are generally not filed.

The National Center for Juvenile Justice (n.d.) reviewed state jurisdictions to determine their status concerning jury trials and other formal procedures for juveniles. The categories created by this investigation included (1) states providing no right to a jury trial for juvenile delinquents under any circumstances, (2) states providing a right to a jury trial for juvenile delinquents under any circumstances, and (3) states providing a right to a jury trial for juvenile delinquents under limited special circumstances (Szymanski, 2008c). States fell into these three categories as follows:

1. *States providing no right to a jury trial for juvenile delinquents under any circumstances:* Alabama, Arizona, California, Delaware, District of Columbia, Florida, Georgia, Hawaii, Indiana, Iowa, Kentucky, Louisiana, Maine, Maryland, Mississippi, Missouri, Nebraska, Nevada, New Jersey, New York, North Carolina,

North Dakota, Oregon, Pennsylvania, South Carolina, South Dakota, Tennessee, Utah, Vermont, Washington, and Wisconsin.

2. *States providing a right to a jury trial for juvenile delinquents under any circumstances:* Alaska, Massachusetts, Michigan, Montana, New Mexico, Oklahoma, Texas, West Virginia, and Wyoming.

3. *States providing the right to a jury trial for juvenile delinquents under special circumstances:* Arkansas, Colorado, Connecticut, Idaho, Illinois, Kansas, Minnesota, New Hampshire, Ohio, Rhode Island, and Virginia.

Source: Szymanski, 2008c.

The Future of the Juvenile Court

Gelber (1990) has speculated what the juvenile court might be like during the first several decades of the 21st century. He envisions a court, conceivably renamed the Juvenile Services Consortium, with two tiers. The first tier will be devoted to adjudicating offenders under age 14. These offenders will always receive rehabilitative sanctions, such as probation or placement in conditional, community-based correctional programs. The second tier consists of those aged 14 to 18. For these juveniles, jury trials will be available, and these offenders will be subject to the same incarcerative sanctions that can be imposed by criminal courts.

Gelber's two-tiered juvenile court projection may not be far off the mark in relation to societal expectations for such courts in future years. The public mood seems to be in favor of just deserts-based sentencing and toward due process for juvenile offenders. The two-tiered nature of Gelber's projected court organization would seemingly achieve this get-tough result, although provisions would remain for treatment-centered rehabilitative sanctions for younger offenders. In a sense, this two-tiered court projection seems to be nothing more than lowering the age jurisdiction of criminal courts from 18 to 14. However, Gelber's intent is to preserve the jurisdictional integrity of the juvenile justice system in relation to the criminal justice system. In any case, this would be an effective compromise between those favoring the traditional rehabilitative posture of juvenile courts and those favoring a shift to more punitive court policies and practices.

The Death Penalty for Juveniles

The first documented execution of a juvenile in colonial New England occurred in 1642. Thomas Graunger, a 16-year-old was caught sodomizing a horse and a cow. Graunger was tried, convicted of bestiality, and executed. The youngest age at the death penalty was imposed, however, is 10. A poorly documented case of a 10-year-old convicted murderer in Louisiana occurred in 1855. A more celebrated case, that of James Arcene, occurred in Arkansas in 1885. Arcene was 10 years old when he robbed and murdered his victim. He was eventually arrested at age 23 before being executed (Streib, 1987).

Table 4.3
JUVENILE OFFENDERS EXECUTED, BY STATE, 1976–2005.

State	Number of Juveniles Executed
Texas	13
Alabama	0
Mississippi	0
Arizona	0
Louisiana	0
North Carolina	0
South Carolina	1
Florida	1
Georgia	1
Pennsylvania	0
Virginia	3
Nevada	0
Missouri	1
Oklahoma	2

Source: Death Penalty Information Center (2010). *Juvenile Offenders Executed, by State, 1976–2005.* (Available at http://www.deathpenaltyinfo.org/juvenile-offenders-executed-state-1976-2005.)

Since 1976, when the U.S. Supreme Court decided that the death penalty was not cruel and unusual punishment (*Gregg v. Georgia*, 1976), 22 juvenile offenders have been executed (Table 4.3). Texas has had the highest number of juvenile executions (13 juvenile, or 59 percent of total), followed by Virginia (three juveniles, or 14 percent) and Oklahoma (two juveniles, or nine percent) (Death Penalty Information Center, 2010). The last offender to be executed who was a juvenile at the time of the crime was Scott Allen Hain. At age 32, he was executed in Oklahoma on April 3, 2003. At age 17, Hain and a codefendant, Robert Lambert, carjacked and robbed Laura Lee Sanders and Michael Houghton in Tulsa on October 6, 1987. After the robbery, they locked the victims in the trunk of their car, cut the gas line, and ignited the vehicle (Edmondson, 2003).

On December 31, 2004, a total of 71 offenders on death row had committed their crimes when they were under the age of 18. At the time, this represented about two percent of the 3,487 condemned offenders in the United States (Death Penalty Information Center, 2010). This gives a good picture of the situation when on March 1, 2005, in the case of *Roper v. Simmons* (to be discussed later in this section), the Supreme Court ruled that the minimum age at which a juvenile could be executed was 18. Before the *Roper* decision, the minimum age of execution was 16. Immediately after *Roper*, in 2006, about 11 percent of the offenders on death row were under the age of 20 (Death Penalty Information Center, 2010).

Before *Roper v. Simmons*, the U.S. Supreme Court had ruled on select capital punishment cases involving juvenile offenders. A frequently cited case in these appeals was *Eddings v. Oklahoma* (1982). This case raised the question of whether the death penalty as applied to juveniles was cruel and unusual punishment under the Eighth Amendment. In its ruling, the Court avoided the issue and did not say that the penalty was cruel and unusual punishment, but the Court also did not say that it was not cruel and unusual. What the Justices decided was that the youthfulness of the offender is a mitigating factor of great weight that may be considered. Therefore, all jurisdictions where death penalties could be imposed were left to draw their own conclusions and interpretations of the Court's remarks about juvenile death penalty cases.

Even after the *Roper* decision, however, the issue of juveniles and the death penalty has not been completely removed from discussion. While a very small number of youth commit murder, some of the cases are brutal and provoke emotional and angry responses. In 2008, a total of 2,111,200 juvenile offenders were arrested. Of these, 1,280 (less than one percent) were charged with murder and nonnegligent homicide (Puzzanchera, 2009). The nature of juvenile justice, however, is that a strong belief persists that substantial efforts are necessary by juvenile courts and correctional facilities to rehabilitate juveniles rather than incarcerate or execute them.

Rationale For and Against the Death Penalty

The primary reasons for supporting the death penalty in certain capital cases are threefold: (1) retribution, (2) deterrence, and (3) just deserts. Some of the reasons to oppose the death penalty are (1) it is barbaric, (2) it may be applied in error to someone who is not actually guilty of a capital offense, (3) it is nothing more than revenge, (4) it is more costly than life imprisonment, (5) it is applied arbitrarily, (6) it does not deter others from committing murder, and (7) most persons in the United States are opposed to the death penalty (Death Penalty Information Center, 2010; Ingram, 2008). A summary of these arguments is presented in Table 4.4.

Arguments for and against the death penalty pertain to juveniles as well. The media have assisted in sensationalizing capital crimes by juveniles, and to some extent, this has contributed to support for imposing the death penalty on juveniles who commit murder. Those favoring the death penalty say it is "just" punishment and a societal revenge for the life taken and the harm inflicted by the offender. It is an economical way of dealing with those who will never be released from confinement. It is usually administered more "humanely" through lethal injection. It functions as a deterrent to others to refrain from committing capital crimes. Opponents say it is cruel and unusual punishment. They claim the death penalty does not deter those who intend to take another's life. It is barbaric and uncivilized (Buckler, Swatt, and Salinas, 2008). Other countries do not impose it for any type of offense, regardless of its seriousness. It makes no sense to kill as a means of sending messages to others not to kill (Dario and Holleran, 2008).

For juveniles, the argument is supplemented by the fact that age functions as a mitigating factor. In any capital conviction, the convicted offender is entitled to a bifurcated trial where guilt is established first and then punishment is imposed in view of any prevailing mitigating or aggravating circumstances. Was the crime especially

Table 4.4
RATIONALE FOR AND AGAINST THE DEATH PENALTY

Yes	No
1. Financial costs to taxpayers of capital punishment is several times that of keeping someone in prison for life.	1. The death penalty gives closure to the victim's families who have suffered so much.
2. It is barbaric and violates the "cruel and unusual" clause in the Bill of Rights.	2. It creates another form of crime deterrent.
3. The endless appeals and required additional procedures clog our court system.	3. Justice is better served.
4. We as a society have to move away from the "eye for an eye" revenge mentality if civilization is to advance.	4. Our justice system shows more sympathy for criminals than it does victims.
5. It sends the wrong message: why kill people who kill people to show killing is wrong.	5. It provides a deterrent for prisoners already serving a life sentence.
6. Life in prison is a worse punishment and a more effective deterrent.	6. DNA testing and other methods of modern crime scene science can now effectively eliminate almost all uncertainty as to a person's guilt or innocence.
7. Other countries (especially in Europe) would have a more favorable image of America.	7. Prisoner parole or escapes can give criminals another chance to kill.
8. Some jury members are reluctant to convict if it means putting someone to death.	8. It contributes to the problem of overpopulation in the prison system.
9. The prisoner's family must suffer from seeing their loved one put to death by the state, as well as going through the emotionally-draining appeals process.	9. It gives prosecutors another bargaining chip in the plea bargain process, which is essential in cutting costs in an overcrowded court system.
10. The possibility exists that innocent men and women may be put to death.	
11. Mentally ill patients may be put to death.	
12. It creates sympathy for the monstrous perpetrators of the crimes.	
13. It is useless in that it doesn't bring the victim back to life.	

Source: Joe Messerli (2009). Should the Death Penalty Be Banned as a Form of Punishment?

brutal? Did the victim suffer? Was the murderer senile or mentally ill? Was the murderer a juvenile? Because age acts as a mitigating factor in cases where the death penalty is considered for adults, there are those who say the death penalty should not be applied to juveniles under any condition. Early English precedents and common law assumed that those under age seven were incapable of formulating criminal intent. Thus, they were absolved from any wrongdoing. Between ages 7 and 12, however, a presumption exists that the child is capable of formulating criminal intent, and in every jurisdiction, the burden is borne by the prosecution for establishing beyond a reasonable doubt that the youth was capable of formulating criminal intent.

While each case is judged on its own merits, there are different views on this issue involving the murderer. The survivors of the victim demand justice, and the justice they usually seek is the death of the one who brought about the death of their own. This is a

Defense counsels represent youth charged with crimes.
(Scott Cunningham/Pearson)

Focus on Delinquency

In 1977, in Fort Jackson, South Carolina, a 17-year-old mentally retarded youth and a 16-year-old companion were living with a 22-year-old soldier in a rented, run-down house. Alcohol, THC, PCP, marijuana, and other drugs were readily available. On a warm Saturday, October 29, after heavy drinking and consuming drugs, the three decided to look for a girl to rape. They drove to a baseball park in nearby Columbia. They parked next to a young couple, a 17-year-old boy and his 14-year-old girlfriend. On orders from the soldier, they shot the boy three times with a high-powered rifle, killing him instantly. Then, they drove off with the girl to a secluded area, where each of the three raped her repeatedly. Finally, they killed her by shooting her and mutilating her body.

The three were soon arrested by police. The youngest youth agreed to testify against the soldier and the 17-year-old in exchange for a lighter punishment. Both the soldier and the 17-year-old

eventually entered guilty pleas and were sentenced to death. After lengthy appeals, the soldier was executed by South Carolina authorities on January 11, 1985. Finally, on January 10, 1986, James Terry Roach, the 17-year-old who had killed the boy and girl and mutilated the girl's body, was executed in the South Carolina electric chair. Justice was served. Or was it? A crowd cheered outside the prison walls as the execution of Roach occurred. Roach wrote his last letter, and as he was strapped into the electric chair, he read it with shaky hands: "To the families of the victims, my heart is still with you in your sorrow. May you forgive me just as I know that my Lord has done." Two one-minute surges of electricity hit him, and he was pronounced dead at 5:16 A.M.

Source: Adapted from Victor L. Streib (1987). *The Death Penalty for Juveniles.* Bloomington, IN: Indiana University Press, pp. 125–127.

manifestation of the eye-for-an-eye philosophy (e.g., revenge and retaliation). In many respects, it is an accurate portrayal of why the death penalty is imposed on both juveniles and adults. It is supposed to be a penalty that fits the crime committed. However, attorneys and family members of those convicted of capital crimes cannot help but feel compassion for their doomed relatives. Someone they love is about to lose his or her life. Yet, had not the murderer taken someone's life in the process? Does taking another life bring back the dead victim? Does taking the life of the murderer fulfill some higher societal purpose? The arguments and views on the death penalty are continuous.

U.S. Supreme Court Death Penalty Cases for Juveniles

evolving stand-ards of decency

Used to assess the progress of a maturing society in determining what is usual and cruel punishment in context of the Eighth Amendment.

Since the early 1980s, the U.S. Supreme Court has ruled on questions regarding executions of juveniles. The cases have been significant in providing a legal foundation for such executions and in demonstrating **evolving standards of decency**. These cases include *Eddings v. Oklahoma* (1982), *Thompson v. Oklahoma* (1988), *Stanford v. Kentucky* (1989), *Wilkins v. Missouri* (1989), and *Roper v. Simmons* (2005). The case of *Graham v. Florida* (2010), which involved the related issue of a life sentence without parole, will also be discussed.

As a prelude to discussing these cases, it should be noted that until 1988, a total of 16 states had minimum-age provisions for juvenile executions (executions of those under age 18), with the minimum age ranging from 10 (Indiana) to 17 (Georgia, New Hampshire, and Texas). When *Thompson v. Oklahoma* was decided in 1988, the minimum age for juvenile executions in all states was raised to 16. The following year, the Supreme Court upheld the death sentences of a 16-year-old and a 17-year-old. In 2005, however, in *Roper v Simmons*, the Court finally ruled that the death penalty for offenders under the age of 18 was cruel and unusual punishment.

Eddings v. Oklahoma (1982)

On April 4, 1977, Monty Lee Eddings and several other companions ran away from their Missouri homes. In a car owned by Eddings's older brother, they drove without direction or purpose, eventually reaching the Oklahoma Turnpike. Eddings had several firearms in the car, including rifles that he had stolen from his father. At one point, Eddings lost control of the car and was stopped by an Oklahoma State Highway Patrol officer. When the officer approached the car, Eddings stuck a shotgun out of the window and killed the officer outright. When Eddings was subsequently apprehended, he was waived to criminal court on a prosecutorial motion. Efforts by Eddings and his attorney to oppose the waiver failed.

In a subsequent bifurcated trial, several aggravating circumstances were introduced and alleged, while several mitigating circumstances, including Eddings's youthfulness, mental state, and potential for treatment, were considered by the trial judge. However, the judge did not consider Eddings's "unhappy upbringing" and "emotional disturbance" as significant mitigating factors to offset the aggravating ones (*Eddings v.*

Oklahoma, 1982, pp. 188–189). Eddings's attorney filed an appeal, and although the Oklahoma Court of Criminal Appeals reversed the trial judge's ruling, the U.S. Supreme Court reversed the Oklahoma Court of Criminal Appeals. The reversal pivoted on whether the trial judge had erred by refusing to consider the "unhappy upbringing and emotionally disturbed state" of Eddings. The trial judge had previously acknowledged the youthfulness of Eddings as a mitigating factor, but the *fact* of Eddings's age, 16, was significant in this case precisely because the majority of justices did not consider it to be significant. Rather, they focused upon the issue of introduction of mitigating circumstances specifically outlined in Eddings's appeal. Oklahoma was now in the position of lawfully imposing the death penalty on a juvenile who was 16 years old at the time he committed murder.

Thompson v. Oklahoma (1988)

William Wayne Thompson was convicted of murdering his former brother-in-law, Charles Keene, who had been suspected of abusing Thompson's sister. In the evening hours of January 22/23, 1983, Thompson and three older companions left his mother's house, saying "We're going to kill Charles" (*Thompson v. Oklahoma*, 1988). Early the next morning, Charles was beaten to death by Thompson and his associates with fists and handheld weapons, including a length of pipe. Thompson later told others, "We killed him. I shot him in the head and cut his throat in the river." Thompson's accomplices told police shortly after their arrest that Thompson had shot Keene twice in the head, and then cut his body in several places (e.g., throat, chest, and abdomen) so that, according to Thompson, "the fish could eat his body." When Keene's body was recovered on February 18, 1983, the medical examiner indicated that Keene had been shot twice in the head, had been beaten, and that his throat, chest, and abdomen had been cut.

Because Thompson was 15 years old at the time of the murder, juvenile officials transferred his case to criminal court. This transfer was supported, in part, by an Oklahoma statutory provision indicating that there was "prosecutive merit" in pursuing the case against Thompson. Again, the subject of the defendant's youthfulness was introduced as a mitigating factor (among other factors), together with aggravating factors such as the "especially heinous, atrocious, and cruel" manner in which Keene had been murdered. Thompson was convicted of first-degree murder and sentenced to death.

Thompson filed an appeal that eventually reached the U.S. Supreme Court. The Court examined Thompson's case at length, and in a vigorously debated opinion, it overturned his death sentence and indicated in its conclusory dicta that

> petitioner's counsel and various *amici curiae* [brief filed as a friend of the court] have asked us to "draw the line" that would prohibit the execution of any person who was under the age of 18 at the time of the offense. Our task, today, however, is to decide the case before us; we do so by concluding that the 8th and 14th Amendments prohibit the execution of a person who was under 16 years of age at the time of his or her offense. (108 S.Ct. at 2700)

Accordingly, Thompson's death penalty was reversed.

Officially, this Supreme Court action effectively drew a temporary line of 16 years of age as a minimum for exacting the death penalty in capital cases. This "line" awaited subsequent challenges, however.

Stanford v. Kentucky (1989)

Kevin Stanford was 17 years old when, on January 17, 1981, he and an accomplice repeatedly raped, sodomized, and eventually shot to death 20-year-old Baerbel Poore in Jefferson County, Kentucky. This *occurred* during a robbery of a gas station where Poore worked as an attendant. Stanford later told police, "I had to shoot her [since] she lived next door to me and she would recognize me . . . I guess we could have tied her up or something or beat [her up] . . . and tell her if she tells, we would kill her" (*Stanford v. Kentucky*, 1989, p. 366). A corrections officer who interviewed Stanford said that after Stanford made that disclosure, "he (Stanford) started laughing."

The jury in Stanford's case found him guilty of first-degree murder, and the judge sentenced him to death. The U.S. Supreme Court eventually heard his appeal (simultaneously with that of Heath Wilkins, discussed in the next section), and in an opinion that addressed the "minimum age for the death penalty" issue, upheld Stanford's sentence. In December 2003, however, the governor of Kentucky commuted Stanford's death sentence to life imprisonment without parole, with the proclamation that "we ought not to be executing people who, legally, were children" (*Lexington Herald Leader*, 2003, p. B3).

Wilkins v. Missouri (1989)

Heath Wilkins was 16 years old when he stabbed to death Nancy Allen Moore, a 26-year-old mother of two who was working behind the counter of a convenience store in Avondale, Missouri. Wilkins and his accomplice, Patrick Stevens, agreed with Wilkins's plan that they would kill "whoever was behind the counter" because "a dead person can't talk," and on July 27, 1985, the two entered the convenience store to rob it. Once inside, they stabbed Moore, who fell to the floor. When Stevens had difficulty opening the cash register, Moore, mortally wounded, offered to help him. Wilkins stabbed her three more times in the chest, two of the knife wounds penetrating Moore's heart. Moore began to beg for her life, whereupon Wilkins stabbed her four more times in the neck, opening up her carotid artery. She died shortly thereafter. Stevens and Wilkins netted $450 in cash and checks, some liquor, cigarettes, and rolling papers from the robbery/murder site. Wilkins was convicted of first-degree murder and the judge sentenced him to death.

The U.S. Supreme Court heard this case simultaneously with that of *Stanford v. Kentucky*, because the singular issue was whether the death penalty was considered to be cruel and inhumane as it pertained to 16- and 17-year-olds. At that time, not all states had achieved consensus about applying the death penalty to persons under the age of 18 as a punishment for capital crimes. Although several justices dissented from the majority view, the Court upheld the death sentences of Stanford and Wilkins, concluding that we discern neither a historical nor a modern societal consensus forbidding the imposition of capital punishment on any person who murders at 16 or 17 years of age. Accordingly, we conclude that such punishment does not offend the Eighth Amendment's prohibition against cruel and unusual punishment. (109 S.Ct. at 2980)

Thus, this crucial opinion underscored age 16 as the minimum age at which the death penalty could be administered. However, this age standard would be changed 16 years later in the case of *Roper v. Simmons* (2005).

Roper v. Simmons (2005)

In March 2005, the U.S. Supreme Court revisited the issue of administering the death penalty to juveniles under the age of 18. Despite their decisions in the cases of *Wilkins v. Missouri* (1989) and *Stanford v. Kentucky* (1989), evolving community standards between 1989 and 2005, public opinion surveys concerning the death penalty for juveniles, as well as United Nations sentiment and pressure, had created a sociopolitical climate that placed the United States almost alone in its stance toward application of the death penalty to persons under the age of 18. In *Roper v. Simmons* (2005), the Court weighed the arguments and ruled against the death penalty for juveniles.

The facts of the case are that in Fenton, Missouri, in 1993, Christopher Simmons, age 17, told two other youth, Charles Benjamin, age 15, and John Tessmer, age 16, that he wanted to commit burglary by breaking and entering and then commit murder, tying up a victim, and then throwing the victim from a bridge. Simmons assured Benjamin and Tessmer that they could "get away with it because they were minors" (*Roper v. Simmons*, 2005, p. 2). At 2:00 A.M. one morning, Simmons, Benjamin, and Tessmer met to carry out a burglary and murder, but Tessmer left before they started out to do their deeds. Simmons and Benjamin went to the home of Shirley Crook, a woman who had previously been involved in an auto accident with Simmons. They entered her home through an open window, and she awakened. Crook recognized Simmons, who bound her with duct tape, including tape placed over her eyes and mouth. Simmons and Benjamin then took her to a railroad trestle spanning the Meramec River, tied her hands and feet with wire, and covered her entire face with duct tape. Next, they threw her from the trestle into the river, where she drowned. Simmons later bragged to others that he had killed a woman because "the bitch had seen my face." Fishermen in the river found Crook's body, and investigating detectives linked her death with Simmons, who was taken into custody for questioning. Simmons gave a videotaped confession describing his heinous actions to police and was subsequently convicted of first-degree murder and sentenced to death. Aggravating factors included the especially heinous nature of the murder; committing the murder for money; and attempting to conceal the crime by disposing of Crook's body in the river. His acts were described as wantonly vile, horrible, and inhuman. Mitigation included that Simmons had no prior juvenile record.

Simmons appealed his conviction to the Missouri Supreme Court, alleging incompetence of counsel. He also alleged an altered mental state, because he had a difficult home environment, had poor school attendance and performance, had abused alcohol and drugs, and had exhibited dramatic changes in behavior. The Missouri Supreme Court affirmed his conviction and death sentence. A second appeal was subsequently filed, alleging that it was a violation of his 8th and 14th Amendment rights for the state to execute him, since he was under 18 and a juvenile when he had committed the crime. The Missouri Supreme Court set aside his death sentence and resentenced him to life imprisonment without the possibility of parole or release except by act of the governor.

Prosecutors appealed, and in a precedent-setting action, the U.S. Supreme Court voted 5-4 to affirm the Missouri Supreme Court, effectively overturning their earlier decisions in the cases of *Stanford v. Kentucky* (1989) and *Wilkins v. Missouri* (1989), in which the ages of 16 and 17, respectively, were approved for lawful executions. The Court declared that it is unconstitutional to execute juveniles under the age of 18 at the time they committed a capital offense. In its lengthy opinion, the Court noted United Nations provisions against executing persons under the age of 18, the fact that the United States was among a very limited number of countries that continued to execute juveniles under age 18, and evolving community standards that increasingly opposed executing juveniles. The Court also alluded to a "national consensus" against the death penalty for juveniles, although evidence presented to support such a view of national sentiment was sketchy.

This U.S. Supreme Court decision likely was influenced, to some extent, by international sentiment and an emerging sociopolitical climate that opposed executing juveniles under the age of 18 for any reason. The decision brought the United States into line with most other world nations. The Court supported its decision with alternative rationales other than political ones, however. It observed that juveniles are not fully formed adults; that they have an underdeveloped sense of responsibility; that they lack maturity; that they are more vulnerable or susceptible to negative influences and outside pressures, including peer pressure; and that they have less control over their own environment. Further, the Court said that the character of juveniles is not as well formed as that of adults and that their personality traits are more transitory and less fixed. Thus, the Court recognized the diminished culpability of juveniles in capital cases. It also observed that retribution and deterrence fail to justify imposing the death penalty on juvenile offenders.

Recognizing that some might take issue with their decision to raise the legal age at which youthful offenders could be executed, the U.S. Supreme Court noted that drawing the line at 18 years of age is subject to the objections always raised against categorical rules. The qualities that distinguish juveniles from adults do not disappear when an individual turns 18. By the same token, some under 18 years already have attained a level of maturity that some adults will never reach. However, for the reasons the Court noted, a line must be drawn, and the age of 18 is the point where society draws the line for many purposes between childhood and adulthood. Therefore, the Court concluded that 18 is the age at which eligibility for the death penalty ought to rest.

Because of this U.S. Supreme Court decision, juveniles who were convicted of capital crimes and sentenced to death when they were under 18 at the time their crimes were committed had their death sentences set aside. Much Supreme Court decision making is not retroactively applicable to previous decisions by other courts. However, this decision profoundly affected the status of all persons on death row in the United States who were under age 18 at the time of their crimes, effectively eliminating the death penalty for these juveniles as a prosecutorial option. No doubt most, if not all, states with capital murder statutes for juveniles under the age of 18 will commute these sentences either to life imprisonment or to life without the possibility of parole. (In almost every state, the governor exercises the power to grant clemency, pardons, and other more lenient actions relative to juveniles convicted of capital crimes. E.g., in Texas, Governor Rick Perry commuted death sentences for 28 juvenile offenders to life in prison.)

Because of the declining frequency with which juveniles had been executed in the years leading up to the *Roper* decision, the death penalty issue as it applies to juveniles is not as prevalent as it once was. There will be continuing support and opposition in society for the death penalty for the reasons presented earlier (Dario and Holleran, 2008). However, it is doubtful that future major changes will be made concerning death penalty policy toward youthful offenders aged 18 or under now that the United States is aligned with United Nations policy.

Graham v. Florida (2010)

In *Roper*, the U.S. Supreme Court ruled that the death sentence for juveniles was cruel and unusual and in contrast to evolving standards of decency. A life sentence without parole, however, is in effect a death sentence to prison. And on May 17, 2010, using the *Roper* rationale, the Court ruled that a life sentence without the chance for parole for a nonhomicidal crime is not permitted under the Eighth Amendment's cruel and unusual punishments clause (*Graham v. Florida*, 2010).

Two cases from Florida were appealed to the U.S. Supreme Court challenging the constitutionality of life imprisonment without the possibility of parole for juveniles. In the first, Terrance Jamar Graham was 22 years old and serving a life sentence for a July 2003 burglary of a restaurant that he committed when he was 16 years old. In December 2003, Graham pled guilty to the charges of armed burglary with assault and attempted armed robbery. He was sentenced to serve 12 months in a pretrial facility and three years of probation. In June 2004, he was released from confinement. Six months later, in December 2004, he was charged for an armed home invasion robbery that also resulted in a violation of probation for possession of a firearm and commission of a crime. Graham denied the charges, but in January 2006, he was found in violation of probation and sentenced for the initial burglary to the maximum penalty, life in prison. Because Florida has no parole, Graham did not have an opportunity for release (other than by executive clemency) and was sentenced to life without the possibility of parole.

For the 2004 armed robbery, he was sentenced to 15 years to be served concurrently with the life sentence (Farina-Henry and Vaughan, 2010; *Graham v. Florida*, 2010).

In the second case, Joe Harris Sullivan was 13 years old when in 1989 he and two juvenile accomplices, ages 15 and 17, burglarized an empty home and stole money and jewelry. Sullivan and an accomplice returned to the house when the occupant, a 72-year-old woman, was home and assaulted and raped her. Because of the serious nature of the offense, Sullivan was tried as an adult, convicted of rape and sexual assault, and sentenced to life without parole (*Sullivan v. Florida,* 2010).

Oral arguments for both cases were heard by the U.S. Supreme Court on November 9, 2009. On May 17, 2010, the Court dismissed the *Sullivan* appeal (writ of certiorari) "as improvidently granted" (e.g., procedural problems) and ruled in *Graham* that life without a chance of parole for a juvenile in a nonhomicidal offense was unconstitutional (*Graham* v. *Florida*, 2010, p. 26). The Court referenced the *Roper* decision and reaffirmed that juvenile offenders are less culpable and should be treated differently from adults. In addition, the Court considered world views and concluded that life sentences for nonhomicidal crimes are rejected throughout the world (*Graham v. Florida*, 2010).

In the 6-3 ruling, Justice Anthony M. Kennedy said that states must provide a "meaningful" chance for juveniles to demonstrate that they should be released. He noted that in 11 states, 129 juveniles were serving life without parole for nonhomicidal crimes, and 77 of these juveniles (60 percent) were in Florida. The Court's ruling did not forbid states from sentencing an offender who is younger than 18 to life in prison, but the Court clarified: "A State need not guarantee the offender eventual release, but if it imposes a sentence of life it must provide him or her with some realistic opportunity to obtain release before the end of that term" (*Graham v. Florida*, 2010, pp. 31–32.)

Public Sentiment About the Death Penalty for Juveniles

As noted above, before *Roper* in 2005, support for and use of the death penalty for juvenile offenders was waning. As Fagan and West (2005) reported, sentiments were mitigating for its continued use. In 1989, the federal government (civilian and military) and 38 states had statutes that permitted the death penalty. Of those, 21 had a minimum age of 18 years, 5 had a minimum age of 17 years, and 14 mandated a minimum age of 16 years. Actual executions of juveniles, however, were sparingly conducted. As reviewed by Streib (2003), the application of the death penalty was essentially embraced by only Texas, Oklahoma, and Virginia.

In addition, public sentiment was also opposed to the juvenile death penalty. In 2001, the Princeton Survey Research Associates found that while 72 percent of respondents supported the death penalty, only 38 percent supported it for offenders under the age of 18 (Death Penalty Information Center, 2010). Similarly, a Gallup poll in 2002 identified that 72 percent of respondents supported the death penalty, but that support dropped to 26 percent for juvenile offenders (Death Penalty Information Center, 2010).

Another significant mitigating development in the issue of juvenile capital punishment was the use of neuroscience to demonstrate the difference in adolescent brain development. While it is generally recognized that youth are different, scientific research using functional Magnetic Resonance Imaging (fMRI) to map brain activity revealed that the areas of the brain dealing with cognitive control and decision making, such as the prefrontal cortex, are underdeveloped in youth. The prefrontal cortex is responsible for executive functions, such as making choices, evaluating alternatives, and exercising judgments about right and wrong (McGuire and Botvinick, 2010). Based on his research concerning adolescent neuroscience, psychologist Laurence Steinberg (2009) has found that adolescents respond more favorably to reward, are prone to risk preference and sensation seeking, and are impulsive. Adolescents are between the immaturity of childhood and the responsibility of adulthood.

In summary, in reviewing state laws and practices on the juvenile death penalty (e.g., consensus), considering the scientific evidence on adolescent development, and taking into account foreign laws and practices on the execution of minors, the U.S. Supreme Court concluded that the diminished culpability of youth and the evolving standards of decency mitigated against the death penalty (Benekos and Merlo, 2005). As Burillo (2010) concluded, the Court recognized the developmental differences between adults and juveniles and ruled that capital punishment for juvenile offenders was cruel and unusual punishment and a violation of the Eighth Amendment.

Unification of Criminal and Juvenile Courts

There are different types of courts in every U.S. jurisdiction. Usually, these courts have general, original, and concurrent jurisdiction, meaning that some courts share adjudicatory responsibilities involving the same subject matter. In Arkansas, for example, chancery courts have jurisdiction over juvenile delinquency cases, although separate county courts may also hear cases involving juveniles. Tennessee county courts, circuit courts, and juvenile courts have concurrent jurisdiction over delinquency and other types of juvenile cases (e.g., children in need of supervision and child custody cases). In Colorado, district courts have general jurisdiction over criminal and civil matters, probate matters, and juvenile cases. However, specific juvenile courts in Colorado hear juvenile cases as well.

Court unification is a general proposal that seeks to centralize and integrate the diverse functions of all courts of general, concurrent, and exclusive jurisdiction into a more simplified and uncomplicated scheme. One way of viewing court unification is that it is ultimately intended to abolish concurrent jurisdiction wherever it is currently shared among various courts in a common jurisdiction, although no presently advocated court unification model has been shown to be superior to others proposed. Thus, there are different ways of achieving unification, and not everyone agrees about which method is best. One example of court unification is Pennsylvania.

Before 1969, Pennsylvania had two appellate courts and numerous local courts that functioned independently of one another (Yeager, Herb, and Lemmon, 1989). Even the Pennsylvania Supreme Court lacked full and explicit administrative and

court unification
Proposal to centralize and integrate the diverse functions of all courts of general, concurrent, and exclusive jurisdiction into a more simplified and uncomplicated scheme.

supervisory authority over the entire judicial system. As the result of the Pennsylvania Constitutional Convention of 1967 to 1968, a new judiciary article, Article V of the Pennsylvania Constitution, was framed. Vast changes were made in court organization and operations, and a family division was established to deal exclusively with all juvenile matters. A 10-year follow-up evaluation of Pennsylvania's court unification concluded that the present court organization is vastly superior to the pre-1969 court organization. Efficiency and economy were two objectives sought by these court changes, and both aims were achieved.

Earlier studies of jurisdictions representing various degrees of unification have been conducted to assess whether greater economy, coordination, and speed are necessarily associated with maintaining records and processing cases (Hill et al., 2007). Georgia, Iowa, Colorado, New Jersey, and Connecticut were examined. Data were collected from records maintained by state administrative officials and local trial courts, and interviews were conducted with key court personnel. A total of 105 courts were selected for analysis, including courts of general and limited jurisdiction as well as juvenile courts. More centralized organizational schemes only partially fulfilled the expectations of these researchers. In addition, Henderson et al. (1984) reported that under centralization, poorer areas were likely to do better financially, although courts in well-off areas faced tighter budget restrictions. Greater uniformity of operations was observed in most jurisdictions. Further, centralization of court organization tended to highlight problems in previously neglected areas, including family and juvenile services. Their findings relating to differences in the effectiveness and efficiency of case processing in trial courts in both decentralized and centralized systems, however, were inconclusive.

Implications of Court Unification for Juveniles

For juveniles, court unification poses potentially threatening consequences. For example, in those jurisdictions where considerable fragmentation exists in the processing of juvenile cases or where concurrent jurisdiction distributes juvenile matters among several different courts, juveniles, especially habitual offenders, may be able to benefit because of a general lack of centralization in record keeping. Thus, juveniles may be adjudicated delinquent in one juvenile court jurisdiction, but this record of adjudication may not be communicated to other courts in adjacent jurisdictions. In time, a national record-keeping network will be functional, in which all juvenile courts may access information from other jurisdictions. Currently, however, the confidentiality of record keeping is a structural constraint that inhibits the development of such extensive record sharing. As has been reported in earlier chapters, however, one major change in juvenile justice record keeping, has been the creation of various state repositories of juvenile information that can be shared among interested agencies. This is considered to be a part of the get-tough movement and is intended to hold juveniles more accountable for their offending by giving authorities in different jurisdictions greater access to their prior offense records (Mears et al., 2007).

A separate and distinct juvenile justice system apart from the criminal justice system has the primary goal of individualized treatment, with therapy and rehabilitation as dominant factors. However, a separate juvenile justice system is also designed to hold juveniles strictly accountable for their actions. Thus, less use may be made of secure confinement and greater use made of probation and parole, with the primary objectives of offering restitution to victims, compensating communities and courts for the time taken to process cases, and performing community services to learn valuable lessons.

Politicizing Juvenile Justice

The political approach to juvenile justice is to rely on legislatures to enact laws that reform the juvenile justice system. As explained earlier, the increase in juvenile arrests during the 1980s and 1990s prompted legislators to enact get-tough policies that transformed how youth were handled by the courts. With the continuing decrease in juvenile crime and the stressful economic conditions facing most states, legislators are reevaluating crime control policies, and several organizations are in strategic positions to offer their guidance and assistance in formulating new juvenile policies. The American Bar Association, the American Legislative Exchange Council, and the Institute of Judicial Administration have provided legislators with model penal codes and proposed juvenile court revisions to introduce consistency throughout an inconsistent juvenile justice system. Two model juvenile justice acts have evolved—the Model Delinquency Act and the Model Disobedient Children's Act. Among other things, these acts, respectively, distinguish between delinquent and status offenders and make provisions for their alternative care, treatment, and punishment. Both acts are designed to hold juveniles responsible for their acts—and to hold the system accountable for its treatment of these youth as well.

There are concerns, however, whether these model penal codes are functional and in the best interests of youth. Some codes may weaken the current protection extended to dependent children or children in need of supervision. Further, a serious erosion of judicial discretion may occur, accompanied by increased use of pretrial detention for juveniles when serious crimes are alleged. In addition, status offenders may be jailed for violating court orders. It is difficult to devise a code of accountability founded on the principle of just deserts that nevertheless performs certain traditional treatment functions in the old context of *parens patriae*, and codes of any kind promote a degree of blind conformity or compliance with rules for the sake of compliance. With greater codification of juvenile procedures, less latitude exists for judges and others to make concessions and to impose individualized dispositions when appropriate. The very idea of individualized dispositions, while appealing to just deserts interests, invites abuse through discriminatory treatment on racial, ethnic, gender, and socioeconomic grounds.

In addition to codes for juvenile justice reform, the Office of Juvenile Justice and Delinquency Prevention (OJJDP) is an important government agency for developing, funding, and evaluating juvenile justice policy and programs. The OJJDP works to establish priorities and initiatives that improve the juvenile justice system and provide effective and evidence-based programs for families and youth. The OJJDP was enacted in 1974 and has been instrumental in funding research and evaluation, in disseminating information and legislative developments, and in supporting efforts such as the Girls Study Group, mentoring programs, youth courts, activities to reduce disproportionate minority contact, targeting missing and exploited children, and antigang initiatives. As the Mission Statement of the OJJDP states:

> The Office of Juvenile Justice and Delinquency Prevention (OJJDP) provides national leadership, coordination, and resources to prevent and respond to juvenile delinquency and victimization. OJJDP supports states and communities in their efforts to develop and implement effective and coordinated prevention and intervention programs and to improve the juvenile justice system so that it protects public safety, holds offenders accountable, and provides treatment and rehabilitative services tailored to the needs of juveniles and their families. (http://www.ojjdp.gov/about/missionstatement.html)

SUMMARY

For over 150 years since the United States was formed, juveniles had little or no legal standing. Matters were decided on their behalf according to their best interests by judges in accordance with the *parens patriae* doctrine. Although this doctrine is inherently discriminatory in its individualization of decision making relative to juveniles, it persists today among juvenile courts.

The U.S. Supreme Court was reluctant to become involved in juvenile matters for many decades, because it believed that a youth's interests were the province of juvenile courts. However, discriminatory treatment of juveniles became too substantial for the Court to ignore. In 1966, a precedent-setting case, *Kent v. United States*, was decided. This ruling declared that juveniles have a right to a hearing before being transferred to criminal court for prosecution as an adult. The cases of *In re Gault* (1967) and *In re Winship* (1970) immediately followed. These cases gave youth the right to a notice of charges against them, the right to confront and cross-examine their accusers, the right against self-incrimination and to give testimony in their own behalf, and the right to an attorney. In addition, the civil standard of proof necessary to confine youth in secure facilities—namely, the preponderance of the evidence—was changed to the criminal standard of beyond a reasonable doubt. A pattern of gradually accruing rights for juveniles was established, and today, juveniles enjoy almost the full range of rights that adults do.

Several implications of greater rights for juveniles include more equitable treatment for juveniles through less juvenile court disparity, greater certainty of punishment through greater emphasis upon due process and justice, greater likelihood of juveniles acquiring juvenile records, and a greater likelihood of having one's case moved from the jurisdiction of juvenile courts to criminal courts.

A controversial issue relating to juveniles is the age at which they can be executed for committing capital crimes. Until 2005, juveniles aged 16 or older could be executed for capital offenses in most of the jurisdictions with death penalties. The landmark death penalty cases as the bases for this decision were *Wilkins v. Missouri* (1989) and *Stanford v. Kentucky* (1989). However, in March 2005, the U.S. Supreme Court decided the case of *Roper v. Simmons*. In this ruling, the Court declared that executions of juveniles under the age of 18 were unconstitutional. All juveniles on death row at the time of this decision had their sentences commuted to life, either with or without the possibility of parole. This newer standard comports with most other United Nations members where juveniles are defined as those under age 18 and executions of such persons are prohibited. Both proponents and opponents of the death penalty have advanced arguments favoring their respective positions, and these arguments were discussed. In 2010, in *Graham v. Florida*, the Supreme Court also ruled that a life sentence without the chance for parole for a nonhomicidal crime is not permitted under the Eight Amendment's cruel and unusual punishments clause.

Because juveniles have acquired greater rights, commensurate with those of adult criminal offenders, court unification has been proposed. Arguments for and against court unification were examined. Presently, public policy favors maintaining separate court systems for adults and juveniles. This situation is unlikely to change in the near future.

KEY TERMS

litigation explosion, 129	*habeas corpus*, 140	evolving standards of
hands-off doctrine, 130	double jeopardy, 145	decency, 160
	Miranda warning, 151	court unification, 167

QUESTIONS FOR REVIEW

1. How has the get-tough movement influenced juvenile rights?

2. What is the hands-off doctrine? What is the significance of the hands-off doctrine for juvenile cases appealed to the U.S. Supreme Court? What juvenile case set a precedent by eliminating the hands-off doctrine?

3. What was the significance of *Kent v. United States* (1966) and *In re Gault* (1967)?

4. What is the standard of proof currently used in juvenile courts when a juvenile's liberty is in jeopardy? What case was significant in evolving this standard of proof?

5. What is the case of *Breed v. Jones* (1975) and its significance for juvenile rights?

6. What are some distinctions between the cases of *Wilkins v. Missouri* (1989) and *Stanford v. Kentucky* (1989) on the one hand and *Roper v. Simmons* (2005) on the other?

7. What are three arguments for and three arguments against the death penalty?

8. What was the significance of the case of *Thompson v. Oklahoma* (1988) and whether juveniles could be executed for committing capital crimes?

9. What was the decision in *Graham v. Florida* (2010)? What rationale was used by the U.S. Supreme Court in deciding this case?

10. What are some problems with establishing court unification in the United States?

INTERNET CONNECTIONS

Building Blocks for Youth
http://www.cclp.org/building_blocks.php

Children and Family Justice Center
http://www.law.northwestern.edu/cfjc/

Criminal Justice Policy Foundation
http://www.cjpf.org/

Death Penalty Information Center
http://www.deathpenaltyinfo.org/

Equal Rights for All
http://www.equalrights4all.org/

Juvenile Justice Committee
http://www2.americanbar.org/sections/criminaljustice/CR200000/Pages/default.aspx

Juvenile Justice Information Center
http://198.170.117.218/jjic/index.php

National Juvenile Defender Center
http://www.njdc.info/

Office of Juvenile Justice and Delinquency Prevention
http://www.ojjdp.gov/

5

Juveniles and the Police

Learning Objectives

AFTER READING THIS CHAPTER, THE STUDENT WILL BE ABLE TO:

- Summarize the history of police–juvenile relationships.
- Summarize juveniles' attitudes toward the police.
- Describe police discretion and the factors that influence discretion.
- Summarize how police process juveniles.
- Describe how police agencies are structured to deal with juvenile crime.
- Summarize developing trends in how police deal with juveniles.
- Outline the development of gangs in the United States.
- Describe the types and activities of gangs.
- Summarize efforts to prevent and control gangs.

(Courtesy of Dean John Champion)

Introduction

In Alameda, California, in 2007, police arrested six juveniles between the ages of 13 and 16 in connection with the shooting death of Ichinkhorloo Bayarsaikhan on Halloween night. Bayarsaikhan, age 15, was shot about 10:30 P.M. at Washington Park while she and a group of 10 friends were being robbed. The victim's family was thankful that the six suspects were arrested. In an unrelated incident in Pemberton Township, New Jersey, police observed a suspicious young driver behind the wheel of a dark vehicle at 5:15 A.M. A brief investigation of the car and its occupants showed that six teens were in the car. The driver had no license, liquor bottles were discovered, and an automatic handgun was recovered from the floor of the rear seat. One round appeared to be jammed in the gun barrel. The youth were charged with possession of a handgun, possession of alcoholic beverages, and curfew violations.

Sources: Adapted from Eric Turowski (2007, November 9), "Three Suspects Arrested in Alameda Teen's Slaying—One Suspect Released Pending Further Investigation," *Alameda Examiner* (available at http://www.alamedasun.com/index .php?option=com_content&task=view&id=2281&Itemid=10); Tony J. Hagan (2007, September 24), "Police Arrest Six Juveniles," *Times of Trenton* (available at http://blog.nj.com/timesupdates/2007/09/police_arrest_six_juveniles.html).

When police officers encounter youth on the streets, they never know how serious the situation is or the potential dangers those youth pose. In the incidents described above, cold-blooded murderers were apprehended in one case, and in the other, innocent-appearing youth were prevented from using a dangerous weapon to harm officers or others. Police officers can relate to these different and unpredictable kinds of encounters with youth, which can range from harmless to lethal.

This chapter will describe the role of police in various interactions with juveniles. An examination of police discretionary powers and how discretion is both used and abused will be presented. Police departments are increasingly sensitive to the issue of how juveniles should be treated. Larger police agencies have established juvenile units, the exclusive function of which is to investigate issues involving children and youth. These units have developed policies that will be reviewed.

The prevalence and growth of juvenile gangs will be examined along with the efforts of police to respond to gangs and gang problems. As juvenile gangs have become more visible because of media reports, misconceptions about gangs and their crime activities have developed. As a result of gang studies, researchers have classified and categorized various types of gangs according to their structure, organization, and operation. Some of these classification schemes will be described and discussed. Females have also formed gangs, and this phenomenon will be described.

This chapter considers responses to juveniles in their contacts with the police. Some important factors that affect the nature of police–youth contact and outcomes will be presented. Socioeconomic status (SES), race/ethnicity, and gender all play important roles in how different juvenile–police encounters occur and in the resulting outcomes of these encounters.

The nature of decision making in juvenile arrests is described next. Juvenile arrests are complicated by the fact that it is not always easy for police officers to know the ages of youth they encounter. Some juveniles possess false identification or no information, thus making it difficult for police officers to know with certainty who they have arrested and how such persons should best be handled. Juveniles can be booked, photographed, fingerprinted, and otherwise subjected to many of the procedures associated with adult offenders. These procedures will be described.

In a majority of U.S. jurisdictions, juvenile courts have divested themselves of jurisdiction over status offenders. Despite divestiture, some police officers have continued to respond to status offenders as though they were delinquents. Status offending may be relabeled by police as delinquent acts, and police officers may respond to the behaviors as if they are criminal acts. Both status and delinquent offenders can be held by police, and the influence of race, ethnicity, SES, and gender on such police behaviors toward juvenile status offenders is an issue in policing and juvenile justice. The implications of divestiture of jurisdiction over status offenders as all the detention process itself will be discussed.

Police also have opportunities to provide delinquency prevention and early intervention services to youth and to partner with other community agencies in responding to youth. Some police strategies and initiatives including school-based programs will be reviewed.

Police Discretion: Use and Abuse

Police officers are the frontline or first responders in the prevention as well as control of street crime committed by juveniles (Myers, 2004). Depending on the circumstances, police officers are vested with considerable **discretionary powers**, ranging from verbal warnings in interactions with youth to the application of deadly force (*Tennessee v. Garner*, 1985). Police discretion is the range of behavioral choices police officers have within the limits of their power. Beyond the formal training police officers receive from law enforcement agency training academies, police discretion is influenced by many other factors, including the situation as well as the race, ethnicity, gender, SES, and age of those confronted. This indicates that both legal and extralegal factors are considered when police exercise their authority to selectively enforce the law.

> **discretionary powers**
> Relating to the police role, police discretion is the ability of police officers to choose among a range of alternatives in dealing with a particular situation in a manner consistent with departmental policies and procedures; police have authority to use force to enforce the law if, in the officer's opinion, the situation demands it.

Roles and Expectations of Police Officers

The public tends to define the role of police officers in various ways. The police are expected to address a number of social problems, and the nature of this involvement is that police intervene in various situations to ensure that matters do not get worse. As a result, police training is geared to reflect this broad public expectation (Shafer, Carter, and Katz-Bannister, 2004). Training manuals for police officers include numerous examples of field situations, including how to deal with domestic disturbances, traffic violations, narcotics, civil disorders, vice, drunkenness, federal offenses, and juveniles (Myers, 2004).

Much of the **situationally based discretion** in confronting crime in the streets and the public is covert. Most of what transpires in the interaction between police officers and suspects is known only to these actors. Thus, it is difficult to consistently enforce high standards of accountability for police in their diverse public encounters. In short, police officers make on-the-spot decisions about whether to move beyond simple verbal warnings or reprimands to more formal actions against those stopped and questioned on suspicion. Considering the circumstances or the situation, law enforcement officers may be more or less aggressive. This is an example of the "street level bureaucracy" described by Lipsky (2010). This phenomenon refers to public service workers who have wide discretion when working with the citizens, and police work clearly demonstrates this type of public–citizen interaction.

situationally based discretion

Confronting suspicious behavior or, crime in the streets on the basis of immediate situational factors, time of night, presence of weapons, numbers of offenders; requires extensive personal judgments by police officers.

Gangs of teens on the streets in front of stores can draw the attention of police. (© Leila Cutler/Alamy)

Contributing to the various roles of police officers is **community policing**, which is a major reform that broadens the police mission from a narrow focus on crime to a mandate that encourages officers to explore creative solutions for a host of community concerns, including crime, fear of crime, disorder, and neighborhood decay. Community policing rests on the belief that only by working together will people and the police be able to improve the quality of life in the community, with the police acting not only as enforcers but also as advisors, facilitators, and supporters of new community-based, police-supervised initiatives (Bayley and Nixon, 2010).

One immediate effect of community policing in many neighborhoods is to place greater discretionary power in the hands of police officers, whether they are on foot or in cruisers. An implicit effect of community policing is to create better relations between the police department and the community, causing community residents to place greater trust in the police rather than to fear them (Geller and Belsky, 2009). In such communities, police officers may be expected by supervisors to take a greater interest in youth, even where petty infractions are involved. Police officers can even be held accountable for failing to respond to minor infractions and for not intervening when necessary.

As Lipsky (2010) observed, however, there can be a dilemma about whether or not to get involved in the activities of minor offenders. In more sensitive settings, where race and ethnicity may play an important role, law enforcement officers may be criticized unfairly by citizens for simply doing their jobs. Further, stopping and detaining juveniles are not particularly popular activities for police officers. One reason is that juvenile court judges are inclined to be more lenient with juvenile first-time offenders or minor offenders. Generally, juvenile courts consider youth to be chronic offenders only after they have received a few adjudications. Consequently, the effort police officers spend taking youth into custody and completing paperwork can seem like an inefficient use of time when youth may be released with only verbal warnings or informal adjustments from judges. There are also additional regulations governing how juveniles should be processed and detained when brought to detention centers and jails following encounters with police officers. These procedures for juvenile offender processing discourage police–juvenile interactions except under the most serious circumstances and where serious crimes have been committed.

Nevertheless, police officers regularly encounter juvenile offenders during their patrols, or **beats**. During 2007, in fact, 83 percent of the delinquency cases that were handled by juvenile courts were referred by law enforcement agencies (Puzzanchera, Adams, and Sickmund, 2010). Because of the informal nature of many police–juvenile encounters, the *Uniform Crime Reports* and other official sources for arrest information fail to disclose the complete incidence of all juvenile contacts with police. In 2008, there were approximately 2.11 million juvenile arrests, about half of which were petitioned to juvenile courts for further action (Puzzanchera, 2009). In addition, self-reports from juveniles in elementary schools and high schools suggest more delinquent activity as well as contacts with police that do not necessarily result in arrests or being taken into custody for brief periods (Office of Juvenile Justice and Delinquency Prevention, 2007).

community policing
Activities conducted by law enforcement officers to enhance public relations between police and the community; foot patrols and other "back-to-the-people" patrol strategies are considered to be integral elements of community policing.

beats
Patrol areas assigned to police officers in neighborhoods.

Juvenile Gang Units in Police Departments

In the early years of police–juvenile encounters, police departments operated under a type of siege mentality. In Los Angeles, for example, the Zoot Suit Riots of 1943 involved a 10-day attack by military servicemen on alleged Mexican-American youth gang members. Extraordinarily repressive police policies were implemented at that time, and police–juvenile relations were strained for many decades (Mauro, 2005). Subsequently, police departments throughout the nation, particularly larger municipal police departments with 200 or more officers, established specialized juvenile units as a part of their organizational structure to deal with different types of offenders. Not all of the police activities in these juvenile units have been directed at gang violence or violent offenses committed by juveniles, however. Those targeted for active police intervention and assistance have included truants, runaways and missing children, property offenders and those who commit vehicular theft, curfew violations, and school-related offenses (Thurman and Zhao, 2004). Even relatively small departments in remote geographical areas now have at least one juvenile officer who deals exclusively with juvenile affairs. However, every police officer who encounters juveniles while policing becomes a juvenile officer temporarily.

The activities of juvenile units, or **youth squads**, are largely directed toward delinquency prevention (Santana, 2005). These units tend to be **reactive units**, in that they respond to public requests for intervention and assistance whenever offenses committed by juveniles are reported. That is, these officers react to calls from others about crimes that have already been committed or are in progress. Gang fights or break-ins involving youth would activate these juvenile units. In contrast, police officers who patrol city streets are most often **proactive units** involved in contacts with juveniles who may or may not be offenders and/or law violators. These officers are

youth squads

Teams of police officers in police departments whose responsibility is to focus on prevention as well as particular delinquency problems.

reactive units

Police youth squad units that respond to calls for service when suspicious youth activities or delinquency are reported.

proactive units

Police units assigned to monitor and patrol high-delinquency areas in an effort to deter youth from engaging in illegal conduct.

Focus on Delinquency

It happened in Jacksonville, Florida. Fourteen-year-old Latosha Marks was charged with first-degree murder in the stabbing death of her 15-year-old foster brother, DeShawn Hutchinson. Subsequently convicted of murder, Marks was sentenced to seven years in prison and 10 years of probation. Hutchinson's biological mother said, "I still can't sleep and it's bothering me badly. That was my child. She's a child still, but just like they give adults time, they should give her time. Murder's a murder." Marks was also ordered to undergo psychiatric counseling.

Source: Adapted from Shannon Houghton (2005, June 30), "Dead Teen was Suspect's Foster Brother," *The Florida Times-Union* (available at http://jacksonville.com/tu-online/stories/063005/met_19126587.shtml).

It happened in Honolulu, Hawaii. A 15-year-old boy was arrested on May 25, 2007, on charges that he raped and murdered 51-year-old Karen Ertell. The unnamed boy was also charged with additional counts of murder and rape of another woman. Other charges against the boy included burglary, possession of confidential personal information, theft of credit cards, and fraudulent use of credit cards. Authorities are seeking to try the youth as an adult.

Source: Adapted from Rod Ohira (2007, July 31), "Hawaii Teen Charged with Rape, Murder," *Honolulu Advertiser* (available at http://the.honoluluadvertiser.com/article/2007/Jul/31/ln/hawaii707310345.html).

almost constantly on the lookout for suspicious activities. They monitor the streets and investigate potentially troublesome situations.

As reported by the National Gang Center (2010), police efforts at gang suppression or control involve community policing as well as gang enforcement and tactical units. The collaboration and information sharing that police and police units have are important to their efforts in targeting youth and gang members. The increased visibility of delinquent gangs organized along ethnic and racial lines in many cities and the violence such gangs manifest have caused police departments to establish task forces of special police officers who monitor and investigate gang activities (National Gang Center, 2010; Santana, 2005). Gang intelligence provides information for the development of programs, social interventions, and community mobilization (National Gang Center, 2010).

Police interest in gangs is most often focused upon prevention rather than retaliation (Mauro, 2005). Prevention measures by police include profiling gang members, methods used by gangs to recruit new members, neighborhood conditions that spawn and perpetuate gang activity, and the influence and presence of gang members in prison settings; providing materials and strategies for parents and school authorities to use for coping with gang activities; and examining gang structure (Katz, Webb, and Decker, 2005).

By 1997, all 51 jurisdictions in the United States had made extensive changes in their laws concerning juveniles who commit violent or serious crimes (Torbet and Szymanski, 1998). In turn, these legislative changes caused numerous police departments to implement programs to achieve certain delinquency prevention objectives contemplated by these changes (West, 2005). Many of these programs involve the establishment of formal gang units.

Proactive Restorative Policing

In Bethlehem, Pennsylvania, a Police Family Group Conference (FGC) Project was established in the mid-1990s and coordinated by the Bethlehem Police Department (McCold and Wachtel, 1998). First-time, moderately serious juvenile offenders were randomly assigned either to formal adjudication in juvenile court or to a diversionary **restorative policing** process involving FGCs. Police-based FGCs use trained police officers to facilitate meetings, which are attended by juvenile offenders, their victims, and their families and/or friends to discuss the harm caused by the offender's action and to create an agreement to repair the harm. Data were obtained and analyzed for 80 participants, 180 victims, and 169 parents within the Bethlehem FGC. These data were compared with control groups having similar characteristics. The FGC participation rate was 42 percent, 100 percent of the conferences produced an agreement on restorative actions, and 94 percent of all offenders were in full compliance with the agreements. The FGC also seemed to produce lower rearrest rates among participants, and perceptions of fairness were as high as 96 percent for all participants. Researchers concluded that the Bethlehem Police Department was able to reduce recidivism substantially among FGC participants while avoiding net-widening. The analysis also demonstrated that police officers were able to conduct FGCs successfully and without

restorative policing

Police-based family group conferencing with participants including police, victims, youth, and their families to discuss the harm caused by the youth and to create an agreement to repair the harm; similar to restorative justice.

special training. Thus, with this restorative intervention, police can have a salient role in working with youth and families to reduce delinquency and to develop a productive partnership with youth.

Youth Gangs and Minority Status

Types and Numbers of Gangs

There are various classifications of gangs. For example, gangs have been classified as scavenger gangs, territorial gangs, and corporate gangs. **Scavenger gangs** form primarily as a means of socializing and for mutual protection. **Territorial gangs** are organized for the purpose of preserving a fixed amount of territory, such as several city blocks (Crawford, 2007). They maintain control over these geographical areas and repel efforts by other gangs to invade their territory or turf. The most violent gangs are **corporate gangs**. These types of gangs emulate organized crime syndicates. They are more profit motivated and rely on illicit activities, such as drug trafficking, to further their profit interests (Katz, Webb, and Decker, 2005). Corporate gangs use excessive violence, including murder, to carry out their goals. Often, innocent bystanders are gunned down as victims of gang retaliation against rival gangs and gang members (Martin et al., 2008). Thus, while all types of gangs pose dangers to the public, corporate gangs are more dangerous than scavenger or territorial gangs.

Less-conventional gangs, such as the Skinheads and taggers, have also been targeted by some youth gang bureaus and other police agencies within departments. The Skinheads claimed at least 100,000 members worldwide in 2004, and they have a cumulative record of gang violence involving weapons. Taggers and tagging crews generally have less structure and are more localized, and they are not characterized as having economic motivations. Taggers may band together and create property damage with graffiti and vandalism. As a result, they present challenges to law enforcement and threaten communities. Membership in tagging crews is less stable compared to other types of gangs, and taggers see themselves more as artists than as gangsters and seek "notoriety and recognition" and "attach status to having their work seen" (Weisel, 2004, Updated 2009, p. 8). Taggers, however, do engage in fighting between crews and can also "graduate to more sophisticated or harmful crimes" (Weisel, 2004, Updated 2009, p. 11).

It is not always cities with large populations where police gang units are deployed. In Alabama, for instance, law enforcement agencies in 46 cities with populations of 10,000 or more have reported substantial gang activities in their jurisdictions (Martin et al., 2008). Alabama officials report that their gang visibility is comparable to that reported by larger cities, especially concerning the amount of female involvement or participation in gangs, the trappings of gang culture, and other critical gang elements. Officials in other jurisdictions have reported similar gang presence and activity as well (Grant, 2008).

In 1995, the National Youth Gang Center, which merged with the National Gang Center in October 2009, conducted an extensive survey that became known as the **National Youth Gang Survey (NYGS)** (Wilson, 2001). Subsequently, the NYGS has been conducted annually to track gang activities and describe critical gang

---

scavenger gangs
Groups formed primarily as a means of socializing and for mutual protection.

territorial gangs
Groups of youth organized to defend a fixed amount of territory (e.g., several city blocks).

corporate gangs
Juvenile gangs emulating organized crime; profit-motivated gangs that rely on illicit activities (e.g., drug trafficking) and violence to further their profits.

National Youth Gang Survey (NYGS)
Conducted annually since 1995; purpose of survey is to identify and describe critical gang components and characteristics and to track gang activites.

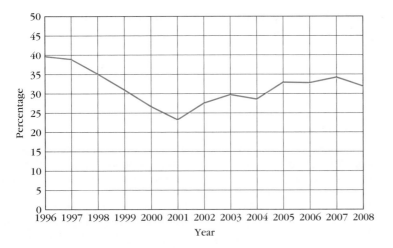

Figure 5.1
Trend in the Prevalence of Gang Problems, 1996–2008
Source: Arlen Egley, Jr., James C. Howell, and John P. Moore (2010).
Highlights of the 2008 National Youth Gang Survey. *Washington, DC:*
Office of Juvenile Justice and Delinquency Prevention, p. 1. (Available at
http://www.ncjrs.gov/pdffiles1/ojjdp/229249.pdf.)

components and characteristics. As shown in Figure 5.1, based on data from the 2008 NYGS, gang activity was prevalent in about 32 percent of all communities (Egley, Howell, and Moore, 2010). More than 27,900 gangs were estimated to exist in 2008, up from 27,000 gangs in 2007. In 2008, gang membership was estimated to be 774,000 members, down from 788,000 members in 2007 (Egley, Howell, and Moore, 2010; Office of Juvenile Justice and Delinquency Prevention, 2007). From 2002 to 2008, gang membership increased six percent, and the number of gangs increased 28 percent (Egley, Howell, and Moore, 2010, p. 1). As shown in Figure 5.2, however, in

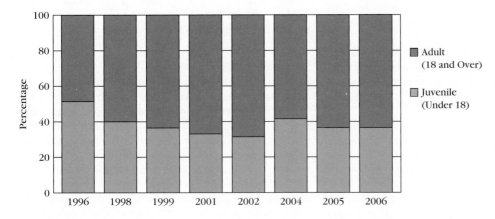

Figure 5.2
Age of Gang Members
Source: National Youth Gang Center (2009). National Youth Gang Survey Analysis. *(Available at*
http://www.nationalgangcenter.gov/Survey-Analysis.)

almost each year of the NYGS, the data indicate that adult gang members (age 18 and older) exceeded the number of juvenile gang members (under 18).

At least nine types of gangs were identified in the original NYGS: (1) juvenile gangs, (2) street gangs, (3) taggers, (4) drug gangs, (5) satanic groups, (6) posses (friends

CAREER SNAPSHOT

Name: David Sanner
Position: Director of Support Services, Erie County Prison, Erie, Pennsylvania

Colleges Attended: Edinboro University of Pennsylvania and Mercyhurst College

Degrees: B.A. in Psychology, M.S in Psychology, and M.S in Administration of Justice

Background

During undergraduate coursework I wanted to begin working in the field and decided to "volunteer" at an adolescent facility. I was hired full-time and assigned to third shift so that I could finish my degree and begin graduate school. I ended up staying for three years, serving as "housing parent," life-skills instructor, counselor, and academic proctor. It was during these years that I discovered the rigors of the field and that the demands of the individuals were to be taken seriously. Success requires formal education and working experience. Juveniles are emotional, impulsive individuals, seeking guidance and knowledge. Their abilities and inabilities collide with needs for rewards and pleasures. Peers and internal drives rather than parents set the tone for which direction they choose.

Subsequent to working in juvenile justice, I held various professional and management positions in state corrections and private nonprofit treatment. Throughout this work, I have found that providers often do not know how to succeed or are not supplied the tools necessary for success.

Beginning in 2006, I have worked as Director of Support Services for the Erie County Prison in Erie, PA. The facility, a local county jail with a capacity of 902, was accredited by the American Correctional Association (ACA) in 2010. Primary duties include serving as director of treatment and accreditation manager. Directing treatment means being responsible for the creation of new programming and for the supervision of staff involved in education, institutional and community counseling, drug and alcohol, mental health, cognitive programming, electronic monitoring, and volunteer and religious services. Accreditation manager responsibility includes managing the entire accreditation process, which encompasses legal requirements, policy and procedure, outcome measures, and internal auditing of standard compliance.

Related to the incarceration of adolescents, I am responsible for the development of a comprehensive Youthful Offender policy and program and for supervising the program to ensure it meets established standards for the security and care of juveniles. Youthful offenders make up less than one-half of a single percent of admissions to the facility. From 2008 through 2010, only 66 of nearly 14,000 admissions were under age 18. Despite this low number, all staff must be trained in the unique developmental needs and the specific security precautions that must be taken whenever a juvenile is present. Unique needs mandate separation from adults to the greatest extent possible. Juveniles have physical, emotional, social, and educational needs that differentiate them from others they are incarcerated with. Because of their needs and susceptibility, special screening considerations (medical, educational, and security/housing) must be taken immediately. Safety and security dictates a more formal structure be placed on juveniles and the staff who works with them. Structure includes otherwise routine activities such as gym and recreation, shower times, daily meals that meet higher caloric needs, and visitation. Additionally, age-appropriate group and case management services, medical services, and education must be provided. Juveniles demand considerable staff resources and a team approach that can be quite burdensome. Even though adolescents may be legally incarcerated in an adult jail, they are still individuals with special developmental issues.

Advice to Students

Education is a key to success for incarcerated juveniles, and it is crucial to undergraduate students who hope to work in the field. For too long, the adult system has been required to deal with juveniles in ways that might have made operational sense but were uncertain or unproven. Systems need to be smarter with the limited resources provided by the public. In addition, working experience is essential. Education without experience fosters approaches to change that cannot possibly last. Anyone who wants to achieve must prioritize education and experience equally. Education and the willingness to work, often starting at the bottom, with consistency and integrity are recommended. By doing so, you develop the reputation needed to be given an opportunity to implement change deserving the justice system.

who hang out and commit crimes as a group), (7) crews, (8) stoners, and (9) terrorist groups. Traditionally, gangs were formed by racial, ethnic, or religious groups. Today, gangs are based on needs to identify with a group (Martin et al., 2008). Other gang researchers have used different categories or classifications. For example, in an early study, Huff (1989) identified three major gang types: (1) hedonistic gangs (use of drugs and party activities), (2) instrumental gangs (property offenders and some drug use), and (3) predatory gangs (violent offenders). Maxson and Klein (1995) categorized five types of gangs: (1) traditional (large number of members with specific territory), (2) neotraditional (smaller and newer than traditional gangs), (3) compressed (small number without territorial claims), (4) collective (ill-defined with short history), and (5) specialty (more serious gang involved in drug activity).

Minority Status

The fact of racial and ethnic disproportionality in the juvenile justice system is underscored by a study undertaken by Darlene Conley (1994), who investigated the juvenile justice system of a western state. Juvenile courts in six counties were selected as the target for her research. A representative sample of 1,777 juvenile cases was drawn, together with 170 in-depth interviews involving court personnel, community leaders, defense attorneys, prosecutors, law enforcement officers, parents, youth, and others. The study also included 65 hours of participant observation covering court proceedings and plea bargaining that involved adjudicated juveniles. Focus group interviews with juveniles were conducted as well. Conley found that compared to

Suspected gang members may be searched and/ or taken into custody by police on suspicion.
(Courtesy of Dean John Champion)

whites, blacks were 2 times more likely to be arrested, 5 times more likely to be referred to juvenile court, 5 times more likely to be detained, 3 times more likely to be charged, 2.5 times more likely to be adjudicated delinquent, and 11 times more likely to be placed in secure confinement for a lengthy period. Hispanics were also overrepresented in the same counties, although these youth were not processed as extensively as blacks. Similar findings relative to dissimilar treatment of minority juveniles have been reported elsewhere (Proctor and Mullings, 2008; Taylor et al., 2008).

Female Gangs

How prevalent are female gangs in the United States? Do female gangs commit similar types of offenses compared with male gangs? In 2007, it was estimated that there were over 150,000 female gang members in the United States, accounting for about 10 percent of all gang membership (Office of Juvenile Justice and Delinquency Prevention, 2007).

Contemporary descriptions of female gang members suggest that they typically lack a formal education, have violent experiences at their schools, have seriously dysfunctional family lives, and have experienced various social problems, including poverty, substance abuse, and gang violence. Interviews with a sample of female gang members from Texas indicated that they often join gangs to achieve power and protection, engendering respect from others based upon fear; and that they often resort to more-serious criminal conduct. Membership in female gangs also often is contingent upon one's ethnic or racial status. Many times, family disintegration and community deterioration lead female gang members to create their own subculture in which recognition can more easily be attained. Another factor is the lack of appropriate intervention,

Rising proportional female gang membership has been associated with rising female juvenile violence.
(REUTERS/Lucy Nicholson)

diversion, and treatment alternatives available to female juveniles compared with their male counterparts. With the presence of such gender inequities, young female involvement in delinquent behavior is more easily explained (Valdez, 2007).

Profiling of female gang members has been limited, in part because of their inaccessibility by researchers. It is too early to make sweeping generalizations about female delinquents and whether they are becoming more violent (Kelly, 2005). More attention needs to be directed toward understanding their interpersonal behaviors as well as certain institutionalized patterns of a patriarchal society. According to the National Gang Intelligence Center (2009), however, while the number of females in male gangs is increasing, female gangs continue to be a "rare phenomenon" (p. 12). For neighborhoods with high crime rates and social disorganization, about 32 percent of males and 29 percent of females claim gang membership. In these high-risk areas, girls are increasingly involved in gang activities and affiliations. Because female youth are at higher risk for victimization in areas characterized by poverty and lack of legitimate opportunities, gang membership and violent behaviors may be ways to prevent or reduce their victimization.

While data indicate an increase in female arrests for simple assaults, the level of violent offending by female youth has been fairly consistent over the last 20 years (Zahn et al., 2008) (Figures 5.3 and 5.4). Girls who join gangs, however, especially those who join male gangs, are more likely to engage in violent behaviors and to participate in delinquent activities. Although estimates vary, some evidence indicates that "gang involvement for girls is for a shorter duration" than for boys and peaks around 14 to 15 years of age (Zahn et al., 2008, p. 14). Partly due to their smaller numbers, female gangs are less likely to be the focus of law enforcement efforts. As reported by

Police officers at the scene of accidents attempt to ensure that youth are safe.
(© Image Source/Alamy)

Arrests per 100,000 juveniles ages 10–17

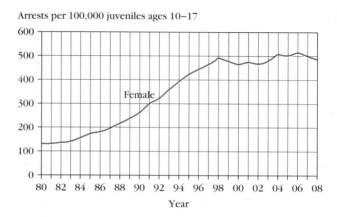

Figure 5.3
Arrests of Females Ages 10–17 for Simple Assaults, 1980–2008
Source: Charles M. Puzzanchera (2009). Juvenile Arrests 2008.
Washington, DC: Office of Juvenile Justice and Delinquency
Prevention. (Available at http://www.ncjrs.gov/pdffiles1/
ojjdp/228479.pdf.)

Arrests per 100,000 juveniles ages 10–17

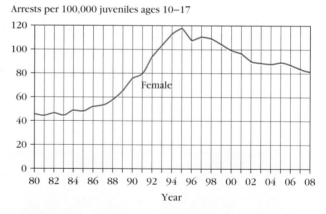

Figure 5.4
Arrests of Females Ages 10–17 for Aggravated Assault,
1980–2008
Source: Charles M. Puzzanchera (2009). Juvenile Arrests 2008.
Washington, DC: Office of Juvenile Justice and Delinquency
Prevention. (Available at http://www.ncjrs.gov/pdffiles1/
ojjdp/228479.pdf.)

the National Gang Intelligence Center (2009), police have more difficulty identifying female gang members, and when they are identified, police attempt to find alternative intervention programs for the girls (p. 12).

Juvenile Response to Police Officer Contacts

Police officers who observe juveniles in pairs or larger groupings, particularly in areas known to be gang dominated, may assume that these youth are gang members, and this observation may heighten police officer interest in and activity against them. The nature of this heightened interest and activity may be more frequent stopping and questioning of juveniles on the basis of their appearance and geographical location and whether they are minority youth. The precise impact of police–gang interactions is unclear, although in some jurisdictions, proactive policing against gang members has created sufficient conflict necessary to unify and perpetuate some gangs.

While it is unknown whether police officers discriminate against certain youth or single them out for stopping and questioning on the basis of racial or ethnic factors, there may be patterns of police behavior that appear to be discriminatory on racial or ethnic grounds. In some jurisdictions, minority youth stops, arrest rates, and detentions are at least three times as high as those for white youth.

Much police officer activity, however, is centered in high-crime areas that tend to be inhabited by large numbers of persons in lower SES, and those areas with large numbers of persons of lower SES are also those that contain larger concentrations of minorities (Greenleaf, 2005). Thus, some selectivity regulates where police officers concentrate their patrol efforts as well as which youth they target for questioning and who they choose to ignore. Some observers believe that this opens the door to allegations of police officer harassment against juvenile offenders on the basis of subjectively determined stereotypical features, such as a youth's appearance (Crawford, 2007).

Police interest in youth on city streets may be aroused by loitering, acting too polite, or acting too impolite.
(S. M. Wakefield/Pearson)

Interestingly, how youth behave toward police officers whenever they are stopped and questioned seems to make an important difference in what the officers will eventually do. The appearance and demeanor of youth stopped by police officers and their subsequent actions seems to indicate that youth who are poorly dressed and/or behave defiantly and belligerently toward police are more likely to be harassed and, possibly, arrested. Related research is consistent with these early findings and suggests that cooperative, neatly dressed youth stand a better chance of avoiding being stopped, questioned, or arrested by police (Crawford, 2007).

Some police officers indicate that a youth's demeanor when responding to police questioning on the street is crucial to whether the youth will be taken into custody, even if temporarily. Therefore, if youth do not display the proper amount of deference toward police officers whenever they are stopped and questioned, the youth stand a good chance of being taken to the police station for further questioning (Grant, 2008). Interestingly, youth also may be too polite and arouse the suspicions of police officers. Thus, there is an elusive range of politeness that minimizes a youth's chances of being taken into custody. It is possible to be too polite or not polite enough so that police officers are sufficiently aggravated or motivated to act.

Despite statutory safeguards about detaining youth in adult jails for long periods and the division of labor relating to youthful offender processing in any jurisdiction, police officers do exercise discretion with juveniles they question who are either acting suspiciously or belligerently. If any pretext exists for assuming that certain youth have been or are engaging in delinquent acts, they can be subject to temporary detention by police officers. In many instances, these detention decisions by police are purely arbitrary.

The following is a review of discretionary actions that may be taken by police officers when encountering youth on the street:

1. In the absence of citizen complaints, police officers may ignore the behaviors of youth they observe. The most frequent types of encounters police officers have with juveniles do not stem from complaints filed by others. Rather, police officers observe youth under a wide variety of circumstances. The situation and the circumstances are important. Youth walking down a street in pairs during daylight hours, for example, will not attract the same kind of attention as pairs of youth walking the streets late at night. It depends upon what the officers regard as serious behaviors: If youth are on skateboards on the sidewalks of the main street of a local community, they may or may not be posing risks to other pedestrians; if youth are playing ball on a vacant lot near other homes in a neighborhood, they may or may not be disturbing others. Police action in each case is probably unwarranted.

2. Police officers may act passively on some complaints about juvenile behaviors. If a store owner complains that youth are jeopardizing the safety of store customers by riding their skateboards down crowded city streets, police officers may respond by directing youth to other streets for their skateboarding. If neighbors complain that youth are making too much noise playing in a nearby vacant lot,

officers may appear and advise youth to play elsewhere. The intent of police officers in these situations is twofold. First, they want citizens to know they are there doing something. Second, they want citizens to know action has been taken and the problem no longer exists. Police officers may continue to determine that the behaviors they observe are not especially serious, and in these instances, police warnings are ordinarily sufficient to satisfy complainants. Because complaints were made, dispositions of those complaints are usually logged officially. Police officers may or may not choose to name the youth who are warned. Rather, they may file a generalized report briefly describing the actions taken.

3. Police officers may take youth into custody and release them to parents or guardians without incident. Youth who may be acting suspiciously or who are in places where their presence might indicate an intent to do something unlawful (e.g., youth crashing in an uninhabited house after their party) are likely to be taken into custody for more extensive questioning. In many instances, these **stationhouse adjustments** may result in their release to parents with warnings by police to refrain from suspicious conduct in the future. While these actions are official in the sense that police officers actually took youth into custody for a brief period and made records of these temporary detentions, they do not result in official action or intervention by intake officers or juvenile courts.

4. Police officers may take youth into custody and refer them officially to community service agencies for assistance or treatment. Sometimes, youth appear to police to be under the influence of drugs or alcohol when they are stopped and questioned. Other youth may not have parents or guardians responsible for their conduct. They may be classified by police officers as runaways. In these cases, police officers arrange for various community services to take custody of these juveniles for treatment or assistance. These youth will be under agency care until arrangements can be made for their placement with relatives or in foster homes. Youth with chemical dependencies may undergo medical treatment and therapy. In either case, juvenile courts are avoided. In many jurisdictions, drug courts are being established to deal with juveniles who are dependent on alcohol or chemicals (Armstrong, 2008; Miller, Miller, and Barnes, 2007).

5. Police officers may take youth into custody, file specific charges against them, and refer them to juvenile intake, where they may or may not be detained. Only a small percentage of all juveniles detained by police will subsequently be charged with offenses. Conservatively, probably less than 10 percent of all juveniles who have contact with police officers annually engage in serious violent or property offenses. Therefore, many youth are taken into custody for minor infractions, and their referrals to juvenile intake may or may not result in short- or long-term confinement. Once a referral is made, the discretion of whether to process certain juveniles further into the juvenile justice system shifts from police officers to intake officers. Juveniles who are deemed to be dangerous, violent, or nonviolent but persistent offenders are most likely to be subject to detention

stationhouse adjustments
Decisions made by police officers about certain juveniles taken into custody and brought to police stations for processing and investigation; adjustments often result in verbal reprimands and release to custody of parents.

pending adjudication by a juvenile court. Police officers may respond to citizen complaints or actually observe juveniles engaging in illegal conduct. The likelihood of taking these youth into custody for such wrongdoings alleged or observed is increased accordingly.

6. Police officers may take youth into custody, file criminal charges against them, and statutorily place them in jails pending their initial appearance, a preliminary hearing, and a subsequent trial. Some juveniles may be classified as adults for the purpose of transferring them to criminal courts, where they might receive harsher punishments. Jurisdictions such as Illinois; Washington, DC; New York; and California are a few of the locations where **automatic transfer laws** exist and where some juveniles are automatically under the authority of criminal courts rather than the juvenile courts. Therefore, police officers *must* act in accordance with certain statutory provisions when handling juvenile offenders whenever they effect arrests of suspects. They often have no choice in the matter. Thus, an increase in get-tough policies toward violent or serious juvenile offenders has restricted some of the discretion that police have when confronting juveniles on city streets.

automatic transfer laws
Jurisdictional laws that provide for automatic waivers of juveniles to criminal court for processing; legislatively prescribed directive to transfer juveniles of specified ages to jurisdiction of criminal courts.

In a study of police officer discretion in Canada, Carrington and Schulenberg (2004) found that factors such as the community and the situation of the offense provided a context for police dispositions. Recognizing the importance of the type of offense, level of injury, prevalence of a weapon, age and sex of the offender, and number of previous contacts with the police, the researchers concluded that youth with more prior contacts were more likely to be charged. Their research underscores the numerous variables that influence police discretion and whether formal or informal action is taken with youth.

In summary, police discretion is exercised the most during the normal course of police patrols. Youth who stand the best chance of being targeted for special police attention include minorities who are acting suspiciously and live in high-crime neighborhoods known as gang territories (Khalili, 2008). Also increasing the likelihood of being taken into custody is the demeanor or behaviors exhibited by youth, whether they are polite or impolite to police officers. Apart from any illicit conduct actually observed by or reported to police officers, a youth's appearance and behaviors are key considerations in whether they will be harassed and/or detained temporarily by police. However, comparatively few youth are arrested in relation to the actual number of police–juvenile encounters on city streets.

Arrests of Juveniles

As noted previously, police have become less inclined to deal with youth informally (Burfeind and Bartusch, 2011). Arrests of juveniles are, by degree, more serious than acts of bringing youth into custody. Since youth may be taken into custody for suspicious behavior or any other pretext, all types of juveniles may be detained temporarily at police headquarters or at a sheriff's station, department, or jail. Suspected runaways, truants, or curfew violators may be taken into custody for their own welfare or protection, not necessarily for the purpose of facing subsequent offenses. It is standard policy in most jurisdictions, considering the sophistication of available social services, for police officers and correctional administrators to turn over juveniles to the appropriate agencies as soon as possible after these youth have been apprehended or taken into custody (Burek et al., 2008).

Before police officers refer juveniles to intake officials or juvenile probation officers for further processing, they ordinarily complete an arrest report, noting the youth's name, address, parent's or guardian's name and address, offenses alleged, circumstances, whether other juveniles were involved and apprehended, the juvenile's prior record, if any, height, weight, age, and other classificatory information. If immediate action against the juvenile is warranted, the police officer may complete and file an application for filing a juvenile court petition.

Except in unusual circumstances and where youth are especially violent and pose a danger to others or themselves, they will be released to the custody of their parents or guardians following a brief detention and booking. In some instances, juveniles fail to appear later at their scheduled appointments with either the juvenile court or intake officers. When such persons fail to appear for scheduled proceedings against them, juvenile court judges issue orders for their immediate apprehension and detention. Parents may become involved as well, because it is their responsibility to ensure that their children appear at any scheduled proceedings.

In reviewing the issue of "reasonable discretion" when confronting youth, the Iowa City Police Department (2011) allows the following policy options, with the choice left to the discretion of the officer:

1. Release without further action.
2. Informal counseling to inform the youth of the consequences of his actions.
3. Informal referrals to community services.
4. Referral to parents or responsible adult.
5. Informal counseling of parents or responsible adult.
6. Limited nonsecure custody and warning at the police department.
7. Issuance of summons or complaint.
8. Arrest under nonsecure custody.
9. Arrest under secure custody.

Juvenile–Adult Distinctions

According to the Juvenile Justice and Delinquency Prevention Act (JJPDA) of 1974 and its subsequent amendments, juveniles must be separated from adults, both by sight and by sound, and treated as juveniles as soon as possible following their apprehension. Many juveniles who are brought into custody and charged with offenses that might be either felonies or misdemeanors if committed by adults may be clearly distinguishable as juveniles. It would be difficult to argue that a 10-year-old child could pass for 18 or older. However, other juveniles who are taken into custody may or may not appear to be under 18, and if they deliberately intend to conceal information about their identity or age from officers, it is relatively easy for them to do so. This is a common occurrence because many juveniles are afraid that police will notify their parents. Fear of parental reaction may sometimes be more compelling than fear of police officers and possible confinement in a jail.

Because juveniles generally have less understanding of the law compared with adults, especially those adults who make careers out of crime, they may believe that they will be better off if officers believe that they are adults and not juvenile offenders. If they are identified positively as juveniles, then parents will invariably be notified of their arrest. If they are thought to be adults, however, then perhaps there is a chance they might be released after spending a few hours or even a day or two confined in a jail cell. These youth often underestimate the resources police have at their disposal to verify information received from those booked after arrests. With proper identification, adults are ordinarily entitled to make bail and obtain early temporary release from jail. If fake IDs are used by these juveniles, however, this information is easily detected and arouses suspicions and interest in these youth. They will likely be detained as long as it takes to establish their true identities and ages. Furnishing police officers with false information can result in a youth being placed in preventive detention, and police officers are entitled to use preventive detention lawfully in such cases (*Schall v. Martin,* 1984).

The Ambiguity of Juvenile Arrests

An arrest is formally defined as the legal detention of a person to answer for criminal charges or (infrequently at present) civil demands. In addition to "age ambiguity," however, little uniformity exists among jurisdictions about how an arrest is defined in practice. Even greater ambiguity exists regarding what constitutes a juvenile arrest (Burek et al., 2008). It is suggested that increasing numbers of police departments are proactively changing their police–juvenile policies so that decision making regarding juvenile processing will be more rational and effective. In responding to citizen calls for police service, it is not always clear to police which laws apply to youth and their behaviors. As Cox et al. (2008) conclude, there is "obvious ambiguity" as to whether "any formal rule of law applies" in some instances of youthful misbehaviors (p. 171).

Early research by Klein, Rosenzweig, and Bates (1975) focused on juvenile arrest procedures followed by 49 suburban and urban police departments in a large metropolitan county. Over 250 police chiefs and juvenile officers and their supervisors were surveyed, some of whom participated in follow-up, in-depth interviews about juvenile arrests and processing. Among police chiefs, fewer than 50 percent were in agreement that booking juvenile suspects was the equivalent of arresting them. Further, respondents variously believed that arrests involved simple police contact with juveniles and cautioning behavior. Others believed that taking youth into custody and releasing them to parents constituted an arrest. Less than half of those surveyed appeared to be thoroughly familiar with juvenile rights under the law and with the different restrictions applicable to their processing by police officers. Record keeping and other activities related to juvenile processing by police have not changed much in subsequent years (Bureau of Justice Statistics, 2008).

Booking, Fingerprinting, and Photographing Juvenile Suspects

Under the JJDPA of 1974, its subsequent revisions, and recommendations from the National Advisory Committee on Criminal Justice Standards and Goals (1976), significant restrictions were placed on law enforcement agencies concerning how juveniles should be processed and regarding the nature and types of records that may be maintained relating to such processing. Under the JJPDA of 1974, for instance, status offenders were separated from delinquent offenders through deinstitutionalization of status offenses (DSO). According to the JJPDA, status offenders should not be taken to jails for temporary detention. Rather, they should be taken to social service agencies for less-formal dispositions. One intent of the JJPDA was to minimize the adverse impact and labeling influence associated with jails (Decker, 2005). While DSO is fairly common in most jurisdictions, police discretion causes a proportion of status offenders to be processed as delinquent. Thus, some status offenders mistakenly are thought to be involved in criminal or delinquent behavior and continue to be placed in U.S. jails annually, even though such housing is only for a few hours.

Because most juveniles are under the jurisdiction of juvenile courts, which are extensions of civil authority, procedural safeguards for juveniles prescribe conduct for both police and jail officers in their dealings with juveniles. For example, it is common practice for jail officers to photograph and fingerprint adult offenders. This is the basic booking procedure. However, juveniles are often processed differently at the point of booking. Most jurisdictions have traditionally restricted photographing and fingerprinting juveniles to purposes related solely to their identification and eventual placement with parents or guardians. Fingerprinting is also useful if property crimes have been committed and fingerprints have been left at crime scenes. In response to the increases in juvenile crime during the 1980s and 1990s, states did enact legislation mandating that juvenile offenders be photographed and fingerprinted (Szymanski, 2010a).

The statutes and restrictions on fingerprinting juvenile delinquents vary, but 41 states do not specify any age restrictions. Ten states have set a minimum age for law enforcement officers to fingerprint delinquents: North Carolina and Wisconsin, age 10; New York, age 11; Hawaii, age 12; New Mexico, age 13; and Indiana, Nebraska, New Jersey, North Dakota, and Utah, age 14 (Szymanski, 2010a). In her review of statutory age restrictions on fingerprinting delinquents, Szymanski (2010a) found appellate courts have generally ruled that juveniles "do not have a constitutional right" to have their "fingerprint records destroyed" (p. 1). She concludes that in statutes and case law, juvenile fingerprinting remains a debated, unsettled issue.

Interrogations of Juvenile Suspects

Until 1966, custodial interrogations of criminal suspects by police were largely un-regulated. Many of these custodial interrogations involved police brutality against particular suspects who were believed to be guilty of certain crimes. Suspects were denied access to defense counsel, and they were interrogated for many hours at a time, often without food, water, or rest. More than a few suspects confessed to crimes they did not commit simply to end these brutal interrogations. In 1966, however, the U.S. Supreme Court heard the case of *Miranda v. Arizona*.

Miranda was arrested on suspicion of rape and kidnapping. He was not permitted to talk to an attorney, nor was he advised of his right to one. He was interrogated by police for several hours, eventually confessing and signing a written confession, and was later convicted. Miranda appealed, contending that his right to due process had been violated because he had not first been advised of his rights to remain silent and to have an attorney present during a custodial interrogation. The U.S. Supreme Court agreed and set forth what later became known as the *Miranda* warning. This monumental decision provided that confessions made by suspects who were not notified of their due process rights cannot be admitted as evidence. Suspects must be advised of certain rights before they are questioned by police; these rights include the right to remain silent, the right to counsel, the right to free counsel if a suspect cannot afford one, and the right to terminate questioning at any time.

When the *Miranda* warning became official policy for police officers during arrests of criminal suspects, the warning and its accompanying constitutional safeguards were not believed by police to be applicable to juveniles. Thus, law enforcement officers continued to question youth about crimes during several post-*Miranda* years. Therefore, because it is generally accepted that a juvenile's understanding of the law is poor, it might be further assumed that juveniles could be more easily manipulated by law enforcement authorities (Rehling, 2005).

A decision to protect juveniles from making incriminating Fifth Amendment–type statements was handed down by the U.S. Supreme Court in 1979 in the case of *Fare v. Michael C.* Michael C. was a juvenile charged with murder. During a preliminary interrogation, Michael C. was alone with police officers and detectives. Neither an attorney nor his parents were present. Michael C. asked to see his probation officer. However, the interrogating detectives denied this request, because a probation officer is not an attorney and cannot be permitted to function as a defense counsel under these circumstances. Subsequently, Michael C. waived his right to counsel and answered police questions. He was convicted of murder and then appealed, alleging that his right to counsel had been violated when he asked to see his probation officer and his request had been denied by the investigating officers. The Court considered Michael C.'s case and determined that Michael C. had, indeed, made an intelligent, understanding, and voluntary waiver of his rights. The standard devised by the U.S. Supreme Court was the **totality of circumstances** test, which was essentially a standard they had adopted earlier in a criminal case involving an adult offender. Thus, the Court said that juvenile

totality of circumstances

Sometimes used as the standard whereby offender guilt is determined or where search-and-seizure warrants may be obtained; officers consider entire set of circumstances in their decision to proceed with questioning a youth and allowing him/her to waive the right to counsel.

rights waivers should not be based on one sole characteristic or procedure but, rather, on all of the relevant circumstances of the case. Undoubtedly, this decision had led many states to enact statutes that specifically render inadmissible any statements juveniles might make to police in the absence of parental guidance or consent.

In another Fifth Amendment case, however, the U.S. Supreme Court clarified its view in *Miranda* that when conducting an interrogation, police do not have to take individual characteristics such as age into consideration (*Yarborough v. Alvarado*, 2004). In this case, 17-year-old Michael Alvarado was interviewed without his parents by Los Angeles County Sheriff's Detective Cheryl Comstock. Alvarado was not arrested before the interview, but some doubt exists as to whether he was "in custody" during the interview itself. Based on his statements, he was convicted of second-degree murder and robbery. The Court ruled 5-4 that in *Miranda*, the suspect's age was not mentioned, nor was it a mandated consideration. Thus, in the Court's rationale, the police followed reasonable consideration when interviewing Alvarado, and the conviction was upheld (*Yarborough v. Alvarado*, 2004).

Expungement and Sealing Policies

Historically, once photographs and fingerprints had been taken, they were destroyed as soon as possible following their use by police (Torbet et al., 1996). If such records still exist in police department files after juveniles have reached the age of their majority, these juveniles may seek a court order to have their records expunged or sealed through **expungement orders**. Expungement orders are usually issued from judges to police departments and juvenile agencies to destroy any file material relating to one's juvenile offense history. Policies relating to records expungements vary among jurisdictions. Expunging one's juvenile record, sometimes known as **sealing records of juveniles**, is a means of preserving and ensuring confidentiality of information that might otherwise be harmful to adults if disclosed to others, such as employers.

Theoretically, sealing of records is intended as a rehabilitative device, although not all juvenile justice professionals believe that sealing one's records and enforcing the confidentiality about one's juvenile past through expungement is always beneficial to the general public. State policies about police fingerprinting of juvenile suspects are diverse and inconsistent among jurisdictions. Further, considerable disagreement continues to exist about how fingerprint and related information should be used by either juvenile or criminal courts in their subsequent processing of youthful offenders. Forty-seven states permitted fingerprinting of juveniles in 2007, while 46 states allowed photographing of them for law enforcement purposes (Office of Juvenile Justice and Delinquency Prevention, 2007). In 2009, all states had statutes specifying circumstances for fingerprinting juveniles, and 41 states had no age restrictions on fingerprinting (Szymanski, 2010a).

Most states have increased the number of years that a youth must wait before his/her juvenile record can be sealed or expunged. Thus, one's juvenile record may not be expunged for several years after the person has become an adult. Even when juvenile

> **expungement orders, sealing records of juveniles**
>
> Deletion of one's arrest or court record from official sources; in most jurisdictions, juvenile delinquency records are expunged when one reaches the age of majority or adulthood or according to the legislative requirements stipulated in the particular jurisdiction.

Juvenile appears before a juvenile court judge for status offender behavior.
(Courtesy of Mark C. Ide)

records are sealed, however, this may not be permanent. In 31 states, courts can order the unsealing of juvenile records (Szymanski, 2010c, p. 1). Figure 5.5 shows an order to seal a juvenile's records used by the juvenile court in Glynn County, Georgia.

In 2008, a total of 25 states specified that if any juvenile has committed a violent or other serious felony, his or her juvenile record cannot be sealed or expunged. "As of the end of 2009, all states but Rhode Island had established procedures for sealing or expunging" juvenile records (Szymanski, 2010c, p. 1). With an erosion of privacy rights for juvenile delinquents, most states specify that juvenile court records can be unsealed. This applies primarily to violent and serious offenders (Szymanski, 2010c).

By 2007, 34 states had mandated open proceedings and the release of juvenile records to the public, particularly where serious offenses are involved. Further, many states now expose juvenile court records to school officials or require that schools be notified whenever a juvenile is taken into custody for a violent crime or a deadly weapon is used. Another widely adopted policy change is that 44 states have lowered the age at which juvenile court records may be made available to the public. Also, these states have established statewide repositories of information about violent and serious juveniles (Office of Juvenile Justice and Delinquency Prevention, 2007).

Status Offenders and Juvenile Delinquents

A controversial issue in juvenile justice is how status offenders should be classified and managed. Because this category of offenders is labeled as "status offenders," the implication is that all status offenders are somehow alike and should be treated similarly in all jurisdictions (Ross, 2008). This implication, however, is as incorrect as assuming that all juvenile delinquents are alike and should be treated similarly. After all, if we think about the etiology of runaway behavior compared with the respective etiologies

IN THE JUVENILE COURT OF GLYNN COUNTY
STATE OF GEORGIA

IN THE INTEREST OF:

ORDER SEALING RECORDS

The above-named Petitioner having come before this Court with his/her application to seal his/her records, and it having been shown to the satisfaction of the Court that the Petitioner has been rehabilitated and that he/she has not been charged with any crime during the period of time between his/her termination of probation and the filing of this application and it being further found that the **District Attorney's Office, Glynn County Police Department, Glynn County Sheriff's Office and the Brunswick City Police Department** were apprised of the Application for Sealing Records and they agree to a waiver of Hearing on the same as evidenced by Exhibit "A".

It is **ORDERED** that the records of   are sealed and all index references to the Petitioner shall be deleted. The Court, the Petitioner, law enforcement officers and all departments shall reply that no record exists with respect to the Petitioner upon inquiry in any matter.

IT IS FURTHER ORDERED that a copy of this **ORDER** shall be transmitted forthwith to the **District Attorney's Office, Glynn County Police Department, Glynn County Sheriff's Office and the Brunswick City Police Department**.

Inspection of the Petitioner's sealed files and records may hereafter be permitted only upon **Order of this Court**.

This the

Figure 5.5
Order Sealing Records (Glynn County, GA)
Source: Reprinted by permission of Glynn County, Georgia Juvenile Court.

of curfew violation, truancy, incorrigibility, liquor law violation, and sex offenses, different sets of explanatory factors are likely to account for each type of deviant conduct. Thus, different treatments, remedies, or solutions would be required for dealing with each effectively.

In 1974, the JJDPA acknowledged some major differences between status offenders and delinquents by mandating that status offenders should not be institutionalized and treated as though they had committed crimes. Rather, they should be diverted from the processing of juvenile courts that seemingly criminalize their behaviors. The DSO initiative was designed to destigmatize status offenders and intervene to help youth avoid further misbehavior. By managing status offenders less formally and dealing with their behaviors largely by counseling and assistance provided through community-based services, it was reasoned that not only would the youth be less likely to define themselves as delinquent, others would be less likely to define them as delinquent. The long-range implication of such differential treatment is that status offenders will not be inclined to progress or escalate to more serious types of offenses compared with those more-serious delinquent offenders who are exposed to the **criminogenic environment** of the juvenile courtroom (Austin, 2003). Some of the risk taking and impulsive behaviors labeled as status offenses are considered to be typical adolescent adjustments that teens will outgrow (Scott and Steinberg, 2008). Thus, this developmental model of adolescence supports the rationale of the DSO initiative.

Five major categories of status offenses are (1) truancy, (2) running away, (3) ungovernability/incorrigibility, (4) violating curfew laws, and (5) violating underage liquor laws. In 2007, about 36 percent of the status offense arrests were for violating underage liquor laws (n = 141,000), 36 percent were for violating curfew laws (n = 143,000), and 28 percent were for running away (n = 108,900) (Office of Juvenile Justice and Delinquency Prevention Deinstitutionalization of Status Offenders Best Practices Database, n.d.). In his report on juvenile arrests, Puzzanchera (2009) found similar patterns in arrests for these status offenses: 35 percent were for liquor law violations (n = 131,800), 36 percent were for curfew violations (n = 133,100), and 29 percent were for running away (n = 109,200). The data in Figure 5.6 illustrate the trend in arrest rates for liquor law violations from 1980 to 2008. In 2008, the arrest rate was 395 youth per 100,000. In comparison, in 2008, there were 407 arrests per 100,000 for curfew and loitering violations (Figure 5.7) and 327 arrests per 100,000 for running away (Figure 5.8). Between 1997 and 2008, the rate for curfew and loitering declined 41 percent, and between 1980 and 2008, the arrest rate for running away declined 35 percent. For curfew and liquor law violations, trend data indicate decreases in the number of arrests. From 2006 to 2010, arrests for curfew law violations decreased 37 percent to 47,537, and arrests for liquor law violations decreased 33 percent to 42,649 (U.S. Department of Justice, Federal Bureau of Investigation, 2011, Table 35).

After the JJDPA was implemented and individual states adopted DSO policies, a 95 percent reduction occurred in the number of status offenders who were placed in some type of secure confinement (Office of Juvenile Justice and Delinquency

criminogenic environment

Setting where juveniles may feel like criminals or may acquire the characteristics or labels of criminals; settings include courtrooms, juvenile institutions, and adult institutions.

Arrests per 100,000 juveniles ages 10–17, 1980–2008

Figure 5.6
Juvenile Arrest Rates for Liquor Law Violations, 1980–2008
Source: OJJDP Statistical Briefing Book *(2009). "Juvenile Arrest Rate Trends."*
(Available at http://www.ojjdp.gov/ojstatbb/crime/JAR_Display.asp?ID=qa05216.)

Arrests per 100,000 juveniles ages 10–17, 1980–2008

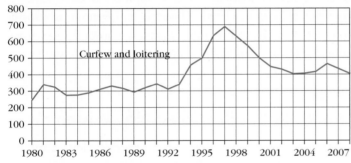

Figure 5.7
Juvenile Arrest Rates for Curfew and Loitering, 1980–2008
Source: OJJDP Statistical Briefing Book *(2009). "Juvenile Arrest Trends."*
(Available at http://www.ojjdp.gov/ojstatbb/crime/JAR_Display.asp?ID=qa05219.)

Arrests per 100,000 juveniles ages 10–17, 1980–2008

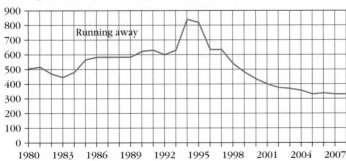

Figure 5.8
Juvenile Arrest Rates for Running Away, 1980–2008
Source: OJJDP Statistical Briefing Book *(2009). "Juvenile Arrest Trends."*
(Available at http://www.ojjdp.gov/ojstatbb/crime/JAR_Display.asp?ID=qa05220.)

Prevention, 2007). However, some of those detained consisted of status offenders who violated court orders or one or more conditions imposed by juvenile court judges at the time of their adjudications.

Status offenders tend to exhibit less recidivism compared with those referred to juvenile court for delinquent acts. Further, the earlier juveniles are referred to juvenile court, for whatever reason, the more likely they will be to reoffend and reappear in juvenile courts. Therefore, diversionary procedures employed by police officers at their discretion when confronting extremely youthful offenders or those who are not doing anything particularly unlawful would seem to be justified on the basis of existing research evidence (Champion, 2008a).

The DSO initiative is perceived by some individuals, however, as tantamount to relinquishing juvenile court control over misbehaving youth, and not all support this particular policy. A strong undercurrent of *parens patriae* persists, especially pertaining to those status offenders who need supervision and guidance from caring adults. Retaining control over status offenders is one means whereby the juvenile court can compel them to receive needed assistance and/or appropriate treatment. However, disagreement exists about the most effective forms of intervention to provide status offenders. One problem experienced by more than a few juvenile justice systems is inadequate resources for status offenders, and others require less-drastic interventions as alternatives to incarceration.

Divestiture and Its Implications: Net-Widening

Divestiture means that juvenile courts relinquish their jurisdiction or authority over certain types of offenders, such as status offenders. Various community agencies and social service organizations take over the responsibility for ensuring that status offenders will receive proper assistance and treatment. Referrals to juvenile court, with possible imposition of formal sanctions and punishments, are no longer warranted. Thus, if a juvenile court in Kansas or Colorado were to divest itself of authority over status offenders or **children in need of supervision (CHINS)**, then officials processing status offenders, such as police officers, would probably take such offenders to social service agencies or other community organizations designed to deal with these youth.

children in need of supervision (CHINS)

Any children determined by the juvenile court and other agencies to be in need of care or supervision.

Relabeling Status Offenses as Delinquent Offenses

Because of police discretion, hanging out or common loitering may be defined by police as behaviors associated with casing homes, businesses, and automobiles as future targets for burglary and theft. Curfew violation, runaway behavior, and truancy can easily be reinterpreted or relabeled as attempted burglary or attempted larceny. And these acts are sufficiently serious and provocative to bring more juveniles into the juvenile justice system, thereby widening the net.

Net-widening occurs whenever juveniles who would ordinarily have been dealt with by police differently before divestiture are brought into the juvenile justice system (Norris, Twill, and Kim, 2008). Before divestiture, many status offenders would have received verbal warnings by police or informal sanctions instead of being taken into custody. However, when police officers relabel status offenses as criminal actions, more juveniles will be netted into the juvenile justice system in the postdivestiture period than was the case in the predivestiture period.

Protecting Status Offenders from Themselves

Many runaways and truants may have certain mental health or educational needs that can only be met through mandatory participation in a mental health therapy program or educational intervention (Salinas, 2008). Court intervention may be necessary to ensure that juveniles take advantage of these services, and informal dispositions of status offense cases may not have the legal coercion of a juvenile court order. Thus, participation in various assistance programs is either voluntary or strongly recommended.

Agency response in accommodating youth with various problems, however, seems to be selective and discriminatory. Often, youth most in need of certain agency services are turned away as unqualified. Thus, status offender referrals to specific agencies may be unproductive, particularly if the status offenders are psychotic, violent, or drug/alcohol dependent (Kuntsche et al., 2007). As a result, some propose that status offenders should remain in the jurisdiction of the juvenile court (Siegel and Welsh, 2009, p. 27). Some status offending is similar to delinquent behavior and can be a gateway to more serious problems and behaviors, so intervention by the court could be an effective delinquency prevention strategy as well as an important public safety policy. This issue also affects how police respond to status offenders and contributes to the ambiguity police face in dealing with juvenile offenders. Are youth demonstrating typical adolescent behavior, or is the behavior a precursor to a criminal trajectory?

Redefining the Role of Police with Youth

Police officers can take a more proactive role as interventionists in the lives of youth and juvenile offenders. For instance, Trojanowicz and Bucqueroux (1990, p. 238) observe that

> young people do not launch long-term criminal careers with a daring bank robbery, an elaborate kidnapping scheme, or a million-dollar dope deal. Yet the traditional police delivery system does not want officers "wasting" much time tracking down the kid who may have thrown rocks through a few windows at school. Narcotics officers on their way to bust Mr. Big at the dope house cruise right by those fleet-footed 10-year-old lookouts. And a call about a botched attempt by a youngster to hotwire a car would not be much of a priority, especially where far more serious crimes occur every day.

These criminologists indicate that officers should be encouraged to intervene and take minor offenses and juvenile infractions seriously. It is possible for police officers to identify at-risk youngsters in particular neighborhoods or situations and to assist them in desisting from future delinquency (Khalili, 2008). Operation SHIELD provides a good example of this role for police (Benekos and Merlo, 2007).

Operation SHIELD, which was developed in 1996 by the Westminster Police Department in Orange County, California, is an example of proactive policing (Wyrick, 2000). The objective of this program is "to identify at-risk youth" and then refer them to appropriate community programs and resources for intervention services (Wyrick, 2000, p. 1). As police respond to routine calls (e.g., domestic violence), they encounter youth in home situations that expose them to negative influences of crime, drugs, and violence. Officers use these contacts to identify potential SHIELD youth, who are then referred to the SHIELD Resource Officer (SRO), who conducts a risk assessment and determines whether referral is indicated and, if so, which agencies or resources are appropriate (Merlo and Sozer, 2009). The case management aspect of SHIELD ensures follow-through and reassessment of the referral. In critiquing this police initiative, Wyrick (2010, p. 6) concluded that

> [t]he critical supporting factor for Operation SHIELD is not funding—it is the commitment and support of law enforcement administrators and personnel who are dedicated to preventing delinquency.

School Resource Officers

Schools are also an arena where police presence and roles have "changed and become more prevalent in recent years" (Lawrence, 2007, p. 207). In expanding the role of police in delinquency prevention, officers assigned to schools are characterized as a "new species of public servant: a hybrid of educational, correctional, and law enforcement official" (Brown, 2006, p. 593). In the data from the Law Enforcement Management and Administration Statistics (LEMAS), "more than a third of all sheriff's offices and almost half of all local police departments have assigned sworn officers to serve in schools" (Brown, 2006, p. 591). In addition to maintaining order and enhancing security, police have a variety of duties, which include delinquency prevention through such programs as D.A.R.E. (Drug Abuse Resistance Education) and G.R.E.A.T. (Gang Resistance Education and Training). While evaluations of these programs are mixed, these police initiatives are well known, widely reported, and extensively implemented throughout schools in the United States (Lawrence, 2007, p. 207).

While the educational role of these programs is emphasized, police also counsel students, present crime prevention information, advise officials on school security, investigate critical incidents, and serve as a liaison between schools and the juvenile justice system (Brown, 2006; Merlo and Sozer, 2009; Lawrence, 2007). In England, Brown (2006) notes that the school police officers are designated as School Liaison Officers and are charged with "school safety" as well as "with enhancing community–school relationships" that focus on social services (p. 592). In South Korea, the school police initiative that was facilitated in Pusan by the Korean National Police Agency is known as "school guardians" or "school protectors" (Brown, 2006, p. 593). In this model, former police officers as well as educators volunteer to provide safety,

---

Operation SHIELD

Police program in Orange County, California, to identify at-risk children and youth and refer them to appropriate social service agencies for early intervention services delinquency prevention, and positive presence, all of which demonstrate civic responsibility (Brown, 2006).

An alternative model of the police role in school initiatives is "school-based partnerships" (SBPs), as reported by Uchida et al. (2006). These programs are funded by the Office of Community Oriented Policing Services (COPS Office) and incorporated the **SARA** model (Scanning, Analysis, Response, and Assessment) to identify problems, develop responses, and evaluate results. Uchida et al. reported that 275 law enforcement agencies were funded to partner with schools. In addition to reducing assaults, violence, school-related problems, and truancy, evaluations of some of the partnerships identified increased student, teacher, and parent involvement in prevention efforts, such as "peer mediation, teen court, and Crime Watch" (Uchida et al., 2006, p. 22). In discussing one partnership, between Miami Police Department and Booker T. Washington Senior High School, Uchida et al. (2006) underscored the positive effect the program had on the "attitudes and lives of some officers" (p. 23). While not all partnerships achieved the levels of success anticipated, "the most successful partnerships had clear roles among participants with strategic goals and shared priorities" (Uchida et al., 2006, p. 31). School-based police initiatives offer the potential to control school crime, improve school safety, and develop effective partnerships.

In spite of some successful school police initiatives, concern exists that programs emphasizing zero-tolerance approaches are less effective and counterproductive (Bazemore, Stinchcomb, and Leip, 2004). Similarly, Lawrence (2007) questions whether the presence of school resource officers "criminalizes" school discipline. He notes that school policies have, in effect, "criminalized some student misconducts" that are "not a salient safety threat" (p. 209). Brown (2006) also notes the potential for this effect, "because the officers are the new authoritative agents in the school environment" (p. 591). The concern is that as police exert more formal social controls, school officials acquiesce their role in disciplinary functions. This is not, however, the case in all schools.

In Baltimore County, Maryland (2010), for example, the school resource officer program clearly distinguishes that police officers are not responsible for school disciplinary problems but, rather, focus on investigating crimes and patrolling school neighborhoods. Police officers receive special training that prepares them to be teachers, counselors, and law enforcers. This is identified as the **TRIAD model** for school resource officers, a policing model used in schools that includes enforcement, teaching, and counseling roles for officers.

In summary, police–school partnerships provide opportunities for police, teachers, parents, and administrators to collaborate in improving school safety. Initiatives that encompass more than security and control are also capable of facilitating a safer learning environment, reducing delinquency, and improving community relations. Police officers also report job satisfaction in their expanded roles.

Police Probation Partnerships

The **Boston Gun Project** was initiated in the 1990s as a partnership between law enforcement and juvenile probation (as well as with local and federal prosecutors and

SARA
Proactive policing approach that uses Scanning, Analyzing, Responding, and Assessing to guide problem solving.

TRIAD model
A policing model used in schools that includes enforcement, teaching, and counseling roles for officers.

Boston Gun Project
Police and probation officer partnership to target juveniles on probation for special supervision to reduce gun violence.

other community agencies) to suppress youth violence by targeting gangs and guns (Kennedy et al., 2001). The project, also known as Operation Night Light, paired police and probation officers to conduct curfew checks and home visits for juvenile probationers. This strategy proved to be effective, and other communities adopted the "Boston Strategy" model (Mertens, 2006). For example, in 1997, the Office of Juvenile Justice and Delinquency Prevention funded "Partnerships to Reduce Juvenile Gun Violence" in Baton Rouge, Louisiana; Oakland, California; and Syracuse, New York (Mertens, 2006). These collaborations included ride-along programs that facilitated information exchange and shared enforcement of probation conditions.

Modeling their program after one in San Diego, California, the Anchorage Police Department and the Anchorage Office of Juvenile Probation joined forces for a program called the Anchorage Coordinated Agency Network (CAN) in 1999 (Giblin, 2002). The program had two goals: (1) enhance the surveillance of juveniles on probation and (2) provide youth with a positive role model (Giblin, 2002, pp. 117–118). The first goal was easily quantifiable. Research indicated that youth in the CAN program had more technical violations than the control group who received traditional probation services (Giblin, 2002, p. 134). By contrast, successful police officer–youth contacts and the quality of those meetings were not as easily discerned. Although these qualitative data are important to those who strive to establish partnerships, they are not typically considered in assessing a program's success.

In their evaluation of the San Bernardino, California, IMPACT/Operation Nightlight program, Worrall and Gaines (2006) identified that in addition to enhanced supervision, information sharing and record keeping are also benefits of this approach to supervising and monitoring juvenile probationers. The IMPACT/Nightlight initiative was aimed at reducing juvenile crime, and data indicated evidence of crime reductions and "a possible general deterrent effect" (Worrall and Gaines, 2006, p. 588). In discussing this type of "intergovernmental partnership," Worrall and Gaines (2006) recognized that "collaboration is the current buzzword in criminal justice" and that projects pairing police and juvenile probation officers have demonstrated problem-solving partnerships and the potential to reduce crime (pp. 579–580). They caution, however, that not all "partnerships are created equal," and some issues, such as Fourth Amendment requirements and distortion of the probation service mission, can be usurped because of "heightened supervision" of probationers (Worrall and Gaines, 2006, p. 586).

Rather than rely on police and probation officers exclusively, a team approach that involves probation officers, mental health workers, police, alcohol and drug treatment staff, and restorative justice workers has also been utilized. In Ventura County, California, a four-year probation project, the South Oxnard Challenge Project (SOCP) was established to deal with youthful offenders (Lane et al., 2005). Youth between 12 and 18 years of age in Ventura County participated by random assignment to either traditional probation or the SOCP program. The youth in the traditional probation group received the same services as all youth on regular probation receive through the local court. By contrast, the "SOCP youth experienced more contacts and services," and the community center where the counselors and staff worked was located in their neighborhood (Lane et al., 2005, p. 43).

Although the results of the SOCP program demonstrated few differences in terms of recidivism between the two groups, there were some important outcomes. First, the program demonstrated that representatives from a variety of agencies, from law enforcement to recreation and mental health, could work collaboratively in the community where the youth lived. Without this concentrated effort, it is unlikely that the youth would have received this level of services (Lane et al., 2005, p. 46). Second, the approach illustrated that dealing with youth in a less-harsh and less-punitive way does not exacerbate their delinquent involvement. Third, although this research focused on recidivism outcomes, other outcomes that may not be quantified are also important, such as improved staff morale and enhanced community relations. As Lane et al. (2005) suggest, these kinds of "successes" can improve the quality of life for offenders and residents (p. 47). In short, collaborative endeavors may offer unparalleled opportunities for justice professionals and the community to work together to deal with youth in programs that focus not only on reducing recidivism but also on improving school performance, community relations, and family interactions.

Another collaboration strategy that partners police with social service agencies has focused on the problem of juvenile runaways (Dedel, 2006). Essentially, this is a problem-solving approach to help juveniles in dealing with conditions at home that precipitate running away. In addition to the traditional police role of locating missing and runaway youth, police become involved in identifying parent–child conflicts and working with service providers to ensure that conflict resolution and/or counseling are provided. While police play a secondary role, their engagement in this approach is consistent with the principles of community-oriented policing reflecting elements of Operation SHIELD, such as risk assessment, referral, and collaboration with community agencies.

The Truancy Recovery Program in Richmond, California, is similar to the juvenile runaway programs in that police first encounter truant youth and are the gatekeepers to the program (White et al., 2001). This police–school partnership is promoted as a delinquency prevention program, because truancy is recognized as a risk factor. In their evaluation, White et al. (2001) found that youth who completed the program had better subsequent attendance, reduced disciplinary incidents, and reduced delinquent activities.

In their review of delinquency prevention interventions that target "child delinquents" (i.e., offenders that are younger than age 13), Loeber, Farrington, and Petechuk (2003) identified programs that are "well organized, integrated," and "involve coordinated efforts" of police, court officials, and mental health services (p. 11). As with the other police collaborations cited above, a problem-oriented policing model is applied to identifying young children who are at risk for delinquency. The responses demonstrate comprehensive strategies in which police are integral to prevention and intervention with child delinquents. Considering that there has been a 33 percent increase in the number of child delinquents handled by juvenile courts through the 1990s (Snyder, 2001), these efforts are considered to be important in reducing the number of youth who become serious offenders (Loeber, Farrington, and Petechuk, 2003).

These police programs and strategies demonstrate the role of police in prevention, intervention, and suppression of youth crime (Benekos and Merlo, 2007). As Lawrence (2007) has explained, police are not only the most "visible" officials in responding to youth, they are also instrumental in influencing youth perspectives and attitudes (p. 204). Police roles include both child protection and delinquency prevention and suggest the salience of police service in complementing juvenile justice policy.

Because of these initiatives, some observers have recommended that police departments have separate units to deal with juveniles. While this has already been accomplished in larger city police departments throughout the United States, many smaller police departments and sheriff's offices lack the staff or facilities to accommodate such special units. Smaller departments rely on individual officers to assume responsibilities for managing juvenile offenders and performing related tasks. Most initial contact with juveniles on the streets is usually made by patrolling, uniformed police officers (Greenleaf, 2005).

Police officers will continue to be the primary responders to juveniles who violate criminal laws. Offense seriousness and the totality of circumstances are important variables affecting how police deal with youth (Duran, 2005). Youth who have contact with police, however, often have not committed crimes and may be status offenders or children reported to police as children in need of supervision, also known as CHINS (Lee, 2008). The use of discretion by police officers is especially crucial in dealing with status offenders. One police response for status offenders and less-serious delinquents is to divert the youth to alternative and informal services, where cases can be handled with minimal visibility and less intrusiveness.

SUMMARY

The relationship between police and juveniles is considered to be diffuse, because police officers are able to exercise situationally based discretion. Police officers have generally regarded contact with juveniles on the streets unfavorably, since the juvenile justice system handles a majority of juvenile cases with leniency. Most juvenile offending involves minor delinquent conduct. Therefore, many police officers regard "real" police work as catching criminals rather than processing juveniles.

Some large police departments in the United States have gang units, which are largely reactive. These youth squads are oriented toward delinquency prevention, and they respond to reports of delinquent activity, especially if it appears to be gang related. Several studies of youth gangs have been conduced, and various types of youth gangs have been identified. Gang members also include girls, but the number of female gang members is difficult to accurately identify.

Responses by juveniles to police officer contacts vary. Police officers need less justification to intervene in juvenile activities and have discretionary powers in responding to the juveniles they confront. Officers can ignore youth, may act passively on citizen complaints about juveniles, may take youth into custody for a few hours and release them later through stationhouse adjustments, may take youth into custody and refer them to social service agencies or to juvenile court authorities, or may arrest youth and charge them with criminal offenses.

Even when juveniles are arrested, their behavior may not be clear evidence of criminality. Arrested juveniles sometimes have no identification or use false identification. In recent years, youth who are believed to have committed more serious offenses are usually photographed, fingerprinted, and booked in a manner similar to that used with adult criminal offenders. While the characteristics and behaviors of status offenders may not differ significantly from juvenile delinquents, efforts are made in most jurisdictions to separate status offenders from delinquent offenders. In some cases, however, in an effort to provide youth with services that available by the juvenile justice system and social services networks, relabeling and net-widening may occur.

Some demographic variables have been linked with how juveniles are treated by the police and the juvenile justice system. Gender, SES, race, and ethnicity continue to be extralegal factors that are used by officials in the juvenile justice system to make decisions and determine appropriate sanctions. There are different opinions about whether the juvenile justice system discriminates against juveniles based on ethnicity, race, gender, or SES.

While police have a reactive, enforcement role when dealing with youthful offenders, they also have opportunities to engage in preventive and early intervention programs that identify and target at-risk youth to receive social services. This proactive role and partnership capacity of police are important components of policing youth.

KEY TERMS

discretionary
  powers, 175
situationally based
  discretion, 176
community policing, 177
beats, 177
youth squads, 178
reactive units, 178
proactive units, 178
restorative policing, 179
scavenger gangs, 180

territorial gangs, 180
corporate gangs, 180
National Youth Gang
  Survey (NYGS), 180
stationhouse
  adjustments, 189
automatic transfer
  laws, 190
totality of
  circumstances, 194
expungement orders, 195

sealing records of
  juveniles, 195
criminogenic
  environment, 198
children in need of
  supervision
  (CHINS), 200
Operation SHIELD, 202
SARA, 203
TRIAD model, 203
Boston Gun Project, 203

QUESTIONS FOR REVIEW

1. What is situationally based police discretion? How is this discretion used and abused?

2. How are police officer roles considered to be diffuse regarding interactions with juveniles?

3. What are youth squads and gang units? What are their functions?

4. What is proactive, restorative policing? What are some of its characteristics?

5. What proportion of gangs in the United States are female gangs? What are some general characteristics of female gang members?

6. What are the four different discretionary actions police officers may take in relation to juveniles they encounter?

7. Why are juvenile arrests sometimes considered to be ambiguous?

8. Under what circumstances can police officers book, fingerprint, and photograph juvenile suspects?

9. How does divestiture of jurisdiction lead to net-widening?

10. What is the role of police in Operation SHIELD?

INTERNET CONNECTIONS

Community Oriented Policing Services (COPS)
http://www.cops.usdoj.gov/

Federal Gang Violence Act
http://www.gpo.gov/fdsys/pkg/BILLS-105s54is/pdf/BILLS-105s54is.pdf

Fight Crime: Invest in Kids
http://www.fightcrime.org/

Girls Study Group
http://girlsstudygroup.rti.org/

Juvenile Justice Initiative
http://www.jjustice.org/

Juvenile Law Center
http://www.jlc.org/

Justice Policy Institute
http://www.justicepolicy.org/

National Center for Juvenile Justice
http://www.ncjj.org

National Gang Center

http://www.nationalgangcenter.gov

PreventViolence.org: Strategies to Keep Youth Safe

http://www.preventviolence.org/

STRYVE: Striving to Reduce Youth Violence Everywhere

http://www.safeyouth.gov/Pages/Home.aspx

6

Intake and Preadjudicatory Processing

Learning Objectives

<small>AFTER READING THIS CHAPTER, THE STUDENT WILL BE ABLE TO:</small>

- Describe the movement toward the deinstitutionalization of status offenses.
- Describe pretrial procedures and decisions of the juvenile court.
- Describe the intake process and the role of the intake officer.
- Summarize the legal and extralegal factors that affect the intake process.
- Explain plea bargaining.

(*Laima Druskis/Pearson*)

Introduction

Intake is usually considered to be the first screening of youth where important decisions are made about their further involvement in the system. Intake officers, who may be juvenile probation officers assigned to juvenile courts for the purpose of screening juveniles, deal with many types of juvenile cases and make decisions about which cases should be referred to juvenile prosecutors. Referred cases are those in which a delinquency petition will be filed or the youth may be considered for adult prosecution. In other cases, intake officers may recommend diversion. Each jurisdiction differs in handling juveniles who commit similar offenses. Should juveniles who wave toy guns at passing motorists be treated similar to youth who commit armed robbery or attempted rape? Which criteria should intake officers consider in trying to act in the best interests of the youth?

Approximately 2.1 million juveniles (under the age of 18) were taken into custody by police in 2008 (Puzzanchera, 2009). After arrest, these juveniles were screened before moving further into the juvenile justice system. In 2007, more than 1.6 million cases were referred, and of these, 44 percent were "handled informally in the juvenile justice system" through intake (Puzzanchera, Adams, and Sickmund, 2010, p. 37). This chapter will describe the intake process. In addition to the intake process, the intake process and the intake officers who engage in these screening processes will also be examined.

The U.S. Supreme Court has determined that juveniles have a number of the same constitutional rights as adult offenders charged with crimes. These Court decisions have affected the intake process in various ways. Due process has become an increasingly important theme governing juvenile offender processing, for example, and the intake process reflects those changes. In this chapter, the formalization of the intake process will be described.

This chapter also examines legal and extralegal factors that influence how juvenile offenders are treated. These factors include offense seriousness, the type of crime committed, the nature of evidence, the prior record of the juvenile, age, gender, race and ethnicity, family stability, and socioeconomic status (SES). Extralegal factors, such as race and ethnicity, SES, gender, age, and demeanor, contribute to decision making at different processing stages (Burke, 2008). Both legal and extralegal factors affect how professionals proceed while acting in the best interests of the youth. Both types of factors will be explored in some detail, and research will be presented to indicate the presence of such factors in judicial decision making as well as at other points in juvenile offender processing and treatment.

Police use their discretion to make judgments about which juveniles are arrested and which ones are released with verbal warnings or reprimands. Even with the increasing formalization of the intake process, intake officers also exercise discretion in handling cases. Intake officers may make decisions based on the youth's prior contact with the juvenile court, appearance, the attorney representing a juvenile, and the demeanor of the parents or the youth. The nature of one's offending is a determining factor as well. Different dimensions of the decision-making process about juvenile offenders will be explored, and parallels between the intake process and plea bargaining will be discussed.

What Is Intake?

Intake, or an intake screening, is the second major step in the juvenile justice process. Intake is a filtering procedure whereby intake probation officers or other juvenile court professionals decide whether detained juveniles should be (1) unconditionally released from the juvenile justice system, (2) released to parents or guardians subject to a subsequent juvenile court appearance, (3) released or referred to one or more community-based services or resources, (4) placed in secure confinement subject to a subsequent juvenile court appearance, (5) placed on informal probation or supervision, or (6) waived or transferred to the jurisdiction of criminal courts (Toth, 2005).

Police refer the largest number of delinquency cases to the juvenile court (Figure 6.1). In fact, in 2007, over 80 percent of delinquency cases were referred by police officers (Puzzanchera, Adams, and Sickmund, 2010). When the data from 1985 to 2007 are compared, law enforcement officers referred fewer public order offenses in 2007 but more person, property, and drug offenses (Puzzanchera, Adams, and Sickmund, 2010). Puzzanchera, Adams, and Sickmund (2010) posit that this may be due to the fact that the public order offense category includes probation violations and contempt-of-court cases and that probation officers are most likely to be involved in these referrals.

Intake

Critical phase in which a determination is made by a juvenile probation officer or other official whether to release juveniles to their parent's custody, detain juveniles in formal detention facilities for a later court appearance, or release them to parents pending a later court appearance.

Processing serious youthful offenders begins with an arrest and detention.
(Rhoda Sidney/Pearson)

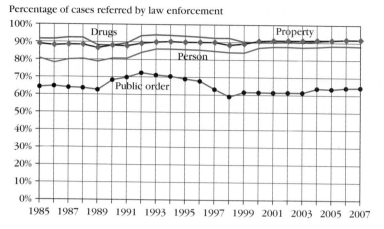

Figure 6.1

Police Make Most Delinquency Referrals to Juvenile Court
Source: Charles Puzzanchera, Benjamin Adams, and Melissa Sickmund
(2010). Juvenile Court Statistics, 2006–2007. Pittsburgh, PA: National
Center for Juvenile Justice.

Intake usually occurs in the office of an intake officer, who may also be a juvenile probation officer. However, in some jurisdictions, intake can occur in an agency or organization that is outside of the juvenile court (Puzzanchera, Adams, and Sickmund, 2010). The juvenile intake officer schedules an appointment with the juvenile and the juvenile's parents to consider the allegations made against the youth. The attorney representing the juvenile's interests may attend as well, although the primary purpose of the intake hearing is to screen juveniles and determine whether the youth would benefit from further services or immersion in the juvenile justice system. The meeting itself is generally conducted informally, without court reporters and other personnel who are normally associated with the formal juvenile court. The intake officer gathers information about the juvenile and the family and prepares a social history report (Figure 6.2). Typically, victims do not attend, but this depends upon the jurisdiction. (Victims sometimes receive a notice regarding intake hearings and adjudications similar to that shown in Figure 6.3.)

The U.S. Supreme Court has not extended the full range of **due process** guarantees for juveniles to intake proceedings, largely because of their informal nature. Thus, numerous interjurisdictional variations exist concerning the intake process and the extent to which one's constitutional rights are safeguarded or protected.

The Discretionary Powers of Intake Officers

The role of intake officers cannot be underestimated. While police officers are guided by rules and regulations that require specific actions, such as taking juveniles into custody, when certain events are observed or reported, the guidelines governing intake actions and decision making are less obvious. In most jurisdictions, intake proceedings are not open to the public, involve few participants, and do not guarantee a juvenile's constitutional rights like an adjudicatory hearing would. Although juveniles

due process

Basic constitutional right to a fair trial, presumption of innocence until guilt is proven beyond a reasonable doubt, the opportunity to be heard, and to be aware of a matter that is pending.

Social History Report

Routing Information

TO: _____

FROM: _____ DATE: _____

AREA: _____ OFFICE: _____

REPORT REQUESTED BY: _____

Case Identification

CASE NAME: _____

SERIAL: _____ STATUS: _____

BIRTH DATE: _____ SEX: ___ RACE: _____

JPC ASSIGNED CASE: _____

1. IDENTIFYING DATA
   a. Youth's birthplace:
   b. Youth's birth status:
   c. Other names used:
   d. Youth's address at time of commitment:
   e. With whom living at time of commitment:
   f. Family's relationship to youth:
   g. Legal guardian:
   h. Social security number: Youth: Father: Mother:

2. PERSONS AND AGENCIES INTERVIEWED

3. AGENCIES THAT HAVE WORKED WITH YOUTH AND FAMILY

4. DELINQUENCY HISTORY (USE ONLY AS SUPPLEMENTAL TO COURT REPORT. IDENTIFY ANY PARTICULAR CHRONIC AND/OR PECULIAR PROBLEMS.)

5. DEVELOPMENTAL HISTORY
   a. Early history (Use only when obvious value in detailing youth's problems.)
   b. Medical history (Detail only if pertinent.)
   c. Description of youth (How parents perceive youth, attitudes, and behavior patterns.)

6. FAMILY HISTORY—REVISED
   a. Marital history and youth's previous living situations
   b. Father
   c. Mother
   d. Siblings
   e. Family income
   f. Parents' perception of problem
   g. Impression of family functioning
      (1) How parents relate to youth
      (2) Parents' concept of discipline
      (3) Evaluation of parent role (how they should/do perform as parents)
      (4) JPC's impression of performance and evaluation (identify strengths and weaknesses)
      (5) Family's financial resources, including benefits, veterans, Social Security, welfare, etc., medical/hospital insurance
          (Note: Income is reported elsewhere—preadmission history.)

7. COMMUNITY INFORMATION
   a. Placement possibilities, including own home. (Note attitudes, family structural compatibility, and other placement considerations.)
   b. Community attitudes toward placement
      (1) Neighbors
      (2) School officials

(Continued)

Figure 6.2
Social History Report
Source: Authors.

8. SCHOOL AND VOCATIONAL HISTORY
   a. School performance
      (1) Last school attended and grade completed
      (2) Level of scholastic performance
   b. Vocational history
      (1) Part-time or full-time jobs held
      (2) Performance evaluation
9. IMPRESSIONS AND RECOMMENDATIONS
   a. Overall evaluation by JPC
   b. Family's willingness to become involved and cooperate
   c. Problem list (JPC's perception of specific problems)
   d. Strengths and assets of family and youth which can be used in dealing with problems.

Figure 6.2 *Continued*

may exercise one or more of their constitutional rights during an intake hearing or proceeding, the informal nature of many intake proceedings is such that constitutional rights are not usually the primary focus. Primarily, these proceedings consist of intake officers compiling information during their interviews with juveniles who have been referred. The long-term effects of intake decision making can be serious and have profound implications for juvenile offenders (Toth, 2005).

Intake officers may utilize their own powers of observation, feelings, and past experiences rather than a list of specific decision-making criteria to determine what they believe is best for each juvenile. Each case is different from others, despite the fact that several types of offenses occur with great frequency (e.g., shoplifting and theft, burglary, and other property crimes). Some juveniles may have lengthy records of predelinquent or delinquent behavior, whereas others are first-offenders. Many jurisdictions have standard forms that intake officers complete during the interview.

On occasion, intake officers will have access to several alternative indicators of a juvenile's behavior, both past and future, through screening instruments that help to measure one's risk or likelihood of reoffending. The probation departments in California, for example, use standardized questionnaires "to identify risks, needs, strengths, and abilities of individual youth" (Administrative Office of the Courts, 2011, p. 1). The assessment includes screening for mental health and substance abuse disorders and helps determine the overall risk the juvenile presents to the community. Screening instruments need to be developmentally appropriate, and courts need to recognize that the instruments are primarily diagnostic, not predictive. Utilizing this information, intake officers attempt to decide what should be done for juveniles who are referred to juvenile court.

The Massachusetts Youth Screening Instrument (MAYSI-2) developed by Grisso and Barnum (2000) is used to identify youths with potential mental health issues. The instrument measures mental, emotional, and behavioral problems and

State of Michigan

Circuit Court _____

Juvenile Court Intake

Date: _____

Notice to Victims

Under Paragraph §3406.9221 of the Michigan Juvenile Code, the following information is being provided on your behalf because you were a victim of a crime committed by the following juvenile:

_____

Name of Juvenile

❑ The juvenile's case was adjudicated on: _____

❑ The disposition for the juvenile was: _____

❑ The juvenile's case was closed in _____ County and referred to _____ County where the juvenile resides.

❑ The juvenile was placed under a deferred prosecution agreement with court-ordered obligations.

❑ Restitution in the amount of $ _____ has been ordered paid to you as victims by _____

_____

❑ Repairs or services to victims are required and must be performed by _____

❑ The juvenile has been placed in ❑ secure ❑ nonsecure confinement at _____

_____

and will be released from confinement on or about: _____

An agreement was reached between the juvenile court and juvenile/juvenile's attorney to restitution orders and/or repairs or services to restore any victim damages and the fair value of losses.

If the obligations of this agreement are not fulfilled in their entirety, then the juvenile's program may be revoked. At such time, a hearing will be conducted to determine further disposition of the juvenile. You will be notified in writing and by mail of the time and place of such a hearing, if one is needed and scheduled. You are permitted to present information, verbal and/or written, unfavorable or favorable to the juvenile involved at any future hearing.

Any questions relating to the above actions we have taken may be directed to the _____ County Court, 1224 S. 4th Place, Grand Rapids, MI, 55667. You may also telephone this court at 555-236-4298 to determine the status of the juvenile's disposition at any time.

Please refer to Case # _____ as required by law under §3406.2668 of the Michigan Juvenile Code for any future inquiries.

All decisions by this court are reviewed by the juvenile court prosecutor and judge.

_____   _____   _____
Signature of Victim   Date   Telephone Number

Figure 6.3
Notice to Victims
Source: Authors.

helps intake officers in their decisions regarding how to handle the youth. The instrument can be administered in 15 minutes and quickly interpreted to identity problems that may need immediate attention.

Juvenile probation officers are vested with limited powers; they do not have the full adjudicatory authority of juvenile court judges. However, because intake officers review cases where youth are involved in minor offending and more serious delinquency, these officers do have a number of options available to them. They can divert a case to social services, recommend a full-fledged juvenile prosecution, or request deferred prosecution. The juvenile court prosecutor must consent to deferring prosecution of the juvenile. The intake officer oversees any special conditions or orders set forth in the deferred prosecution order (Figure 6.4), and the juvenile, the juvenile's parents, and the intake officer sign an agreement for deferred prosecution in which a beginning and an ending date are stipulated. The agreement may be terminated for a variety of reasons, such as the juvenile or the juvenile's parent(s) failing to observe one or more conditions. If a youth successfully fulfills the obligations of the deferred prosecution agreement, the youth will not have to appear in a juvenile court. Even though the agreement is "formal," the process is quite informal compared with conventional juvenile court proceedings.

Few studies of intake officers have been conducted to determine the success of their actions in influencing the lives of those they screen. For instance, 81 juvenile male offenders were court-referred to Lakeside Center, a residential treatment center in St. Louis, Missouri, during the period from 1986 to 1987. Previously, these juveniles had been rated and evaluated by intake officers. The officers reviewed social and referral history information, and they conducted an admission interview with each youth. The intake officers rated these juveniles as "good," "fair," or "poor" in terms of their likelihood for reoffending. After the juveniles had attended the Lakeside Center for a period of time, a majority successfully completed the program. However, 27 percent failed to complete it. Those who completed the program were far less likely to reoffend later when follow-up studies were conducted. Specific juveniles who had been rated earlier by intake officers as having a "fair" or "poor" prognosis reoffended at a much higher rate compared with those rated by these officers as having a "good" prognosis. Researchers concluded that intake officer assessments of the future conduct of juveniles they screened were highly reliable, especially when accompanied by an independent risk assessment device to measure their propensity to reoffend (Sawicki, Schaeffer, and Thies, 1999).

As noted, the process of intake is far from uniform in juvenile courts. In some instances, intake officers do not believe that a comprehensive assessment of all juveniles is necessary at the point of intake (Toth, 2005). Juvenile court policies also may not be clearly articulated, which may lead to some confusion among intake officers about how intake screenings should be conducted and which variables should be considered as critical in intake decision making. In addition, the wide variety of early interventions suggests a lack of consistency among jurisdictions and in how effectively intake officers perform their jobs.

Evidence also indicates that intake officers may be referring more cases for formal processing than in previous years. For example, Puzzanchera, Adams, and Sickmund

State of Michigan, Circuit Court
_____ County

IN THE INTEREST OF:

Deferred Prosecution Agreement

_____

Name

_____

Date of Birth

Case # _____

The prosecutor for the County of _____ comes before the court and requests deferred prosecution for the above titled juvenile. Neither the interests of the state nor the juvenile will be served at this time by formal adjudicatory proceedings, and it is the intake officer's belief that a delinquency petition not be filed presently. Rather, the juvenile, parents/guardians, and/or counselors appointed by the county will carry out the following conditions and terms, between the dates of _____ and _____. Upon the termination of this time period, a re-evaluation will be conducted by the court and prosecutor to determine the nature of future action against the juvenile. Satisfactory fulfillment of all terms and conditions contained in this agreement may lead to an expungement recommendation and such an order shall be entered by the court. If it is deemed that one or more court-ordered obligations have not been fulfilled as outlined below, the court at it's discretion will reinstitute proceedings against the juvenile and move forward with an adjudicatory hearing.

Court-Ordered Obligations:

❏ Restitution in the amount of $_____
❏ Obedience of all local, state, and federal ordinances
❏ Attendance at school and satisfactory academic performance
❏ Submission to recommended psychological testing and assessment
❏ Obedience to lawful legal guardians and/or parents or guardians ad litem
❏ Participation in teen court program or other suitable rehabilitative intervention
❏ Parental participation in parenting skills courses as designated by the court
❏ Avoidance of association with others involved in delinquent acts or who are truant
❏ Other: _____

It is so ordered on this date: _____

❏ The deferred prosecution is granted
❏ The deferred prosecution is denied

_____

Signature of Judge

_____

Signature(s) of parents, guardians, guardians ad litem

_____

Figure 6.4
Deferred Prosecution Agreement
Source: Authors.

Arrested youth often appear before juvenile court judges for a preliminary review of their cases.
(Courtesy of Dean John Champion)

(2010) reported that juvenile court data from 2007 indicate there is less likelihood of a case being handled informally than in 1985. In fact, the number of petitioned cases increased 75 percent between 1985 and 2007 (Puzzanchera, Adams, and Sickmund, 2010). Overall, more youth are being processed through the juvenile justice system, and a more formal approach to youth has evolved.

The kinds of cases for which formal petitions were filed in 2007 were not entirely predictable (Figure 6.5). For example, homicide, rape, robbery, and aggravated assault are person offenses; one might assume that they are more likely to result in a formal petition being filed. However, public order offenses and drug law violations, along with larceny/theft, burglary, and auto theft cases, also were included in the formal delinquency petitions being filed in 2007 (Puzzanchera, Adams, and Sickmund, 2010). In brief, the type of offense does not appear to mandate what will happen with cases.

Decisions to refer youth to the juvenile justice system might seem like a benevolent approach. However, there is little empirical evidence to support that position. Recent research by Petrosino, Turpin-Petrosino, and Guckenberg (2010) examined 29 experimental studies conducted on juveniles over a 35-year period and found that "system processing results in more subsequent delinquency" (p. 38).

The Increasing Formalization of Intake

Intake is an important stage of a juvenile's processing and it is essential that intake officers provide fair and equitable treatment of juveniles. Both legal and extralegal factors influence intake decision making in various jurisdictions. For instance, a study of the intake process in Iowa provides information about intake proceedings that

In 2007, juvenile courts petitioned 56% of all delinquency cases

Most serious offense	Petitioned cases	Percentage of total delinquency cases	Percentage of all petitioned cases, 2007		
			Younger than 16	Female	White
Total delinquency	**926,000**	**56%**	**51%**	**23%**	**61%**
Total person	**238,400**	**58**	**59**	**26**	**54**
Violent Crime Index*	67,800	79	55	17	43
Criminal homicide	1,200	83	35	13	53
Forcible rape	3,300	77	62	4	68
Robbery	26,700	86	53	10	29
Aggravated assault	36,600	74	57	24	50
Simple assault	140,200	51	59	32	57
Other violent sexual offenses	11,800	75	72	6	66
Other person offenses	18,600	58	56	25	61
Total property	**314,200**	**53**	**54**	**20**	**65**
Property Crime Index**	211,000	53	54	23	63
Burglary	79,500	76	56	10	66
Larceny-theft	106,300	42	53	33	62
Motor vehicle theft	20,300	76	50	20	55
Arson	4,800	59	72	14	73
Vandalism	56,900	52	61	13	76
Trespassing	23,200	43	53	17	55
Stolen property offenses	12,800	72	47	14	54
Other property offenses	10,300	57	37	32	67
Drug law violations	**108,300**	**57**	**37**	**16**	**67**
Public order offenses	**265,000**	**56**	**47**	**26**	**61**
Obstruction of justice	153,100	71	42	26	60
Disorderly conduct	47,800	38	62	31	53
Weapons offenses	24,600	60	54	10	59
Liquor law violations	10,200	28	29	27	88
Nonviolent sex offenses	6,100	53	63	17	70
Other public order offenses	23,300	53	47	29	72

*Includes criminal homicide, forcible rape, robbery, and aggravated assault.

** Includes burglary, larceny-theft, motor vehicle theft, and arson.

Note: Detail may not add to totals because of rounding.

Figure 6.5
Type, Number, and Percentage of Juvenile Court Cases Resulting in a Formal Petition for Delinquency, 2007
Source: Charles Puzzanchera, Benjamin Adams, and Melissa Sickmund (2010). Juvenile Court Statistics, 2006–2007. *Pittsburgh, PA: National Center for Juvenile Justice.*

suggests extralegal factors can work to influence intake officer decision making. Leiber (1995) investigated a random sample of referrals to juvenile courts in Iowa during the period from 1980 to 1991. Included in his study were 3,437 white juveniles, 2,784 black juveniles, and 350 Hispanic juveniles. Agency records provided detailed information about how the cases were disposed of and processed at different stages, commencing with intake. Leiber found that the ultimate case outcome was influenced mostly by legal factors, such as offense seriousness, prior record of offending, and age. However, he also found compelling evidence of discrimination in offender processing at the intake stage. Black juveniles tended to receive a larger proportion of recommendations from intake officers for further proceedings in the juvenile justice system. Black juveniles were also less likely than white and Hispanic juveniles to receive diversion or other lenient outcomes from the intake proceeding.

Often, these disparities in processing juveniles at the intake stage are attributable to the subjective views of intake officers. While most intake officers are well intentioned in their individualization of juvenile treatment, some general bias is inherent in such individualization. This unconscious bias most likely occurs as the result of gender, race and ethnicity, and socioeconomic factors (Baron, 2007).

Regardless of whether any particular jurisdiction exhibits differential, preferential, or discriminatory treatment toward juvenile offenders at *any* stage of their processing, there are those who believe that increased defense attorney involvement for at least the most serious cases is a necessity (Burke, 2008). The primary reason for defense attorney involvement in the early stages of a juvenile's processing is to ensure that the juvenile's due process rights are observed. If extralegal factors somehow influence an intake officer's view of a particular case, then the impact of these extralegal factors can be diffused or at least minimized by the presence of a defense attorney. In a 10-year examination of juvenile attorney use trends, data from five states (California, Montana, Nebraska, North Dakota, and Pennsylvania) suggested that the presence of an attorney in juvenile proceedings increased substantially during the 1980s (Champion, 2008a).

The increased presence of counsel in juvenile proceedings at virtually any stage may have both positive and negative effects (Feld, 2007). On the positive side, an attorney's presence can preserve due process. Intake officers and other juvenile court actors, including judges, are inclined to apply juvenile law more precisely under circumstances where defense counsel are present and represent youthful offenders. Where the youth is not represented by counsel, however, the law might be relaxed to the point where some juveniles' rights are minimized. On the negative side, a defense attorney in juvenile proceedings also can make the proceedings more "criminal." When an attorney defends a youth in juvenile court, the proceedings resemble criminal proceedings, and there may be greater emphasis on due process. In circumstances where defense counsel and prosecutors argue the facts of the case, youth cannot help but be influenced by this adversarial event. While due process protections for juveniles have been upheld by the U.S. Supreme Court, one consequence has been the transformation to a more formal juvenile court.

This experience can be viewed as traumatic, and juveniles may identify with criminals who go through essentially the same process. Labeling theorists believe that youth who identify with criminals will eventually label themselves as criminal or delinquent and, thus, will be harmed from the experience (Lemert, 1967a). The assumption that labeling can adversely influence youth who are first-offenders or have been referred for status offenses provides support for informality in intake proceedings and greater utilization of diversion programs. Nevertheless, it is important to recognize that youth are held accountable at various stages of juvenile justice processing (Ross, 2008).

The Emphasis on Greater Accountability

Recent legislation and policies in juvenile justice emphasize greater accountability from youth and from those who work with juvenile offenders from intake through adjudication and disposition (Feld, 2007). As previously discussed, there is significant variation among juvenile justice systems throughout the United States. Increasingly, juvenile courts are seeking new methods and techniques, such as expanded intake functions and nonadversarial resolution of disputes, not only to create smoother case processing for juvenile courts but also to provide more efficient, just, and enforceable solutions to youth problems. Accountability for the judiciary requires that the court act comprehensively in providing social services either directly or through referral. This accountability involves not only the enforcement of dispositional orders requiring the parties and families to respond but also the effective functioning of the agencies and service providers. The court is required to hold itself responsible for its case processing and management systems. This is a significant shift from the traditional treatment of juveniles by courts under the doctrine of *parens patriae*.

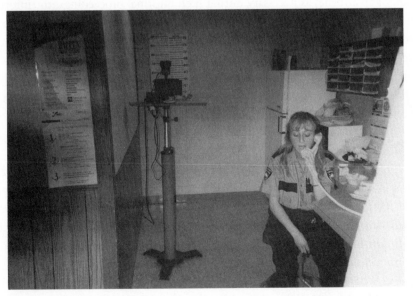

Youth taken into custody may be booked, including being photographed and fingerprinted.
(Courtesy of Dean John Champion)

Intake Proceedings: Where Do We Go from Here?

Intake officers make assumptions about the future conduct of each juvenile and try to determine how best to proceed. In some jurisdictions, personality tests are administered to youth to determine their degree of social or psychological adjustment or aptitude. Those considered to be dangerous, either to themselves or to others, may be held in detention centers or other juvenile custodial facilities until a detention hearing is conducted. Florida Juvenile Assessment Centers administer a battery of tests to juveniles during intake, including clinical screenings by psychiatric professionals (Dembo et al., 2000b). For sex offenders in some jurisdictions, other psychological assessments are made and inventories administered, such as the Tennessee Self-Concept Scale, Beck Depression Inventory, the Rape-Myth Acceptance Scale, the Adversarial Sexual Attitudes Scale, the Assessing Environments Scale, the Buss-Durkee Hostility Inventory, and the Youth Self-Report (Worling, 1995). On the basis of these and other criteria, intake officers decide whether additional steps are necessary in juvenile offender processing.

Intake officers can refer juveniles to community-based services or agencies where they will receive treatment, such as for alcohol or drug dependency. Intake officers also may recommend that certain juveniles be detained in secure facilities to await a subsequent adjudication of their cases by juvenile court judges. Therefore, any action they take, other than outright dismissal of charges, that requires juveniles to fulfill certain conditions (e.g., attend special classes or receive therapy from some community agency or mental health facility) is based on their presumption that the juvenile is guilty of the acts alleged by complainants.

When parents or guardians or the juveniles themselves contend that the intervention of an attorney is necessary during such informal proceedings, the informality of the proceedings is reduced. In addition, the presence of counsel may place more constraints on intake officers. Intake officers have the authority to require youth to participate in therapy, make restitution, or comply with other conditions to avoid further involvement in the juvenile justice process. Ultimately, failure to comply with the intake officer's decision can result in the filing of a formal petition against juveniles and an appearance before a juvenile court judge.

Intake Compared with Plea Bargaining

There are parallels between juvenile intake hearings and criminal plea bargaining (Champion, 2008a). In **plea bargaining**, prosecutors and defense attorneys negotiate a guilty plea and a sanction that are acceptable to both parties. Ordinarily, plea bargaining occurs before any formal disposition or trial. Thus, the accused waives certain constitutional rights, including the right to a trial by jury, the right to confront and cross-examine witnesses, and the right against self-incrimination.

A plea bargain is an admission of guilt to one or more criminal charges, and it is anticipated by defendants entering guilty pleas that leniency will be extended to them in exchange for their pleas. For many cases, this exchange is a reasonable one. In adult

plea bargaining
Preconviction agreement between the defendant and the state whereby the defendant pleads guilty with the expectation of a reduction in the charges, a promise of sentencing leniency, or some other government concession short of the maximum penalties that could be imposed under the law.

cases, other factors being equal, convicted offenders who plea bargain typically do receive more lenient sanctions than those who subject the state to the time and expense of jury trials (Champion, 2008a).

Plea bargaining also is favored by those who believe that it expedites the criminal justice process and saves the state considerable time and expense otherwise allocated to trials as well as to the important prosecutorial burden of proving the defendant's guilt beyond a reasonable doubt. Although some jurisdictions prohibit plea bargaining (e.g., Alaska and selected counties throughout the United States), the U.S. Supreme Court has determined that plea bargaining is constitutional in any jurisdiction that opts to utilize it (*Brady v. United States,* 1970).

During intake hearings, intake officers have tremendous discretion regarding specific outcomes for youth, especially those for whom minor offending is alleged. Apart from certain state-mandated hearings that must precede formal adjudicatory proceedings by juvenile court judges, no constitutional provisions require states to conduct such hearings. Intake officers usually do not hear legal arguments or evaluate the sufficiency of evidence on youth who appear before them. These proceedings usually result in adjustments, where intake officers adjust disputes or allegations informally. Thus, it may not be in the child's best interests for parents to retain counsel to represent their children at this early and critical screening stage. When counsel is retained, however, the informal negotiations that occur between defense counsel and intake officers resemble plea bargaining.

As noted previously, the role of the intake officer is to review the allegations, assess the juvenile, and make a recommendation on how the case should be handled.

Increasing numbers of juvenile cases are plea bargained.
(*Eugene Gordon/Pearson*)

The presence of defense counsel during this and related hearings, however, may limit choices and result in more formal negotiations. While defense counsel is concerned with the client's best interests, the intake officer considers community safety, amenability to treatment and supervision, agency resources, and referral options. As the intake officer and defense counsel negotiate the case, outcomes may become more restricted.

Parens Patriae Persists

There is evidence that intake officers in many jurisdictions fully support the *parens patriae* philosophy. For example, a study of intake probation officers in a southwestern U.S. metropolitan jurisdiction revealed that probation officers believed they were the primary source of their juvenile clients' understanding of their legal rights, although these same probation officers did not themselves appear to have a sound grasp or understanding of these same juvenile rights (Lawrence, 1984). In the same study, juveniles believed that they clearly understood their legal rights. However, interview data from them suggested that, in general, they actually tended to have a very limited understanding of their rights. Based on these results, Lawrence (1984) recommended that probation officers who perform intake functions should receive more training and preparation for these important roles.

Juvenile court judges have been criticized for ineffective decision making about the conditions of probation and the social and community services youth should receive. Judges' options may be limited primarily due to the lack of social services in their communities. Thus, even if judges wanted to maximize their effectiveness in placing youth in treatment programs or referring them to agency programs that could help, their intentions can be hampered by an absence of such programs.

Studies of intake dispositions in several jurisdictions have found that intake dispositions can be influenced by extralegal factors, such as family, school, and employment. The intake officer's emphasis on social adjustment factors rather than legal factors reflects a strong paternalistic orientation in dispositional decision making. In some instances, intake officers determine cases according to what they perceive to be in the best interests of the children involved rather than according to legalistic criteria, such as witness credibility, tangible evidence, and prior offending record (Holsinger and Latessa, 1999).

Typically, intake officers are not dealing with cases that require expert legal judgment. In some incidences, youth appearing before intake officers are alleged to be involved in serious offending behaviors, and they may be recidivists. In addition, evidentiary information presented by arresting officers is overwhelming in some cases, and these cases tend to be rather serious. Therefore, intake officers will send these juveniles to juvenile court and/or arrange for a detention hearing so that the offender may be confined for his or her own safety as well as for the safety of others. Increasingly, serious juvenile offenders are referred to juvenile prosecutors with recommendations that these juveniles be considered for transfer to the criminal courts. The assumption is that juveniles transferred to criminal courts will be eligible for more severe sanctions similar to those normally reserved for adult offenders. However, the kind of case referred for criminal court influences the sanctions that will be imposed. For example, a youth tried and convicted in adult court for burglary as a first-offender typically will not be sent to prison, but a youth tried and convicted in adult court for murder can still be sentenced to life without possibility of parole (Champion, 2008a; *Graham v. Florida*, 2010). By contrast, if a youth is adjudicated delinquent in the juvenile court as a result of his or her involvement in a burglary, the juvenile court judge might send him or her to a secure residential facility. In brief, one cannot state that all juveniles sent to adult court will be treated more harshly for all types of offenses than those retained in juvenile court.

Legal Factors

A distinction is made between legal and extralegal factors that relate to intake decision making as well as other stages of the juvenile justice process. **Extralegal factors** include, but are not limited to, juvenile offender attitudes, school grades and standing, gender, race or ethnicity, parental involvement, SES, and age. **Legal factors** are factual information about the offense alleged, such as offense seriousness, the type of crime committed, any inculpatory (incriminating) or exculpatory (exonerating) evidence against offending juveniles, and the existence or absence of prior juvenile records or delinquency adjudications. Age also functions as a legal factor for certain types of offenses. Four specific legal variables are examined: (1) offense seriousness, (2) type of crime committed, (3) inculpatory or exculpatory evidence, and (4) prior record.

Offense Seriousness

Offense seriousness pertains to whether bodily harm was inflicted or death resulted from the juvenile's actions. Offenses considered to be serious include forcible rape, aggravated assault, robbery, and homicide. These are crimes against persons or violent crimes. By degree, they are more serious than property offenses, including vehicular theft, larceny, and burglary.

In recent years, there has been an increasing emphasis on drug use among youth, and it has been suggested that this is one of the more serious crime problems (Pires and Jenkins, 2007). Large cities in the United States have youth gangs, some of which are involved in drug trafficking (Frisher et al., 2007). However, Williams and McShane (2009) contend that it is difficult to determine which behavior, drugs or gang membership, occurred first. In 2007, 57 percent of the total delinquency cases that resulted in a formal petition being filed were classified as drug law violations (Puzzanchera, Adams, and Sickmund, 2010). One result of arrest and adjudication for drug trafficking among youth is the provision, in some juvenile courts, for more stringent penalties to be imposed on drug sales and possession. Thus, crimes do not always have to be violent to be considered serious.

extralegal factors
Characteristics influencing intake decisions, such as juvenile offender attitudes, school grades and standing, gender, race, ethnicity, socioeconomic status, and age.

legal factors
Variables influencing the intake decision relating to the factual information about delinquent acts; offense seriousness, type of crime committed, prior record of delinquency adjudications, and evidence of inculpatory or exculpatory nature.

As noted, intake is a screening mechanism designed to separate the more serious cases from the less serious ones as juveniles are processed by the system. Intake officers perform classification functions, where they attempt informally to categorize juveniles according to legal and extralegal criteria. Clearly, intake is not an infallible process. Much depends upon the particular experience and training of individual intake officers, juvenile court caseloads, and the nature of cases subject to intake decision making.

The discretionary powers of intake probation officers are in some ways equivalent to prosecutors in criminal courts. Intake officers may direct cases further into the system, may defer cases pending fulfillment of conditions, or may dismiss cases from additional court processing. In response to juvenile justice reforms, juvenile courts have advocated for more objective criteria in evaluating youthful offenders during the early stages of their processing, particularly at intake.

Type of Crime Committed

Another factor in screening cases for subsequent processing by the juvenile justice system is the type of offense committed (Holsinger and Latessa, 1999). Is the offense property-related or violent? Was the act a felony or a misdemeanor? Were there victims who were injured? Did the youth act alone or in concert with others, and what was the nature of the juvenile offender's role? Was the youth an initiator or leader, and did he or she encourage or incite others to offend? Intake officers are more likely to refer cases to juvenile prosecutors when juveniles are older (i.e., 16 years of age and over) and where the alleged offenses are especially serious compared to younger, first-time property offenders.

Inculpatory or Exculpatory Evidence

Offense seriousness and type of crime are influential at intake hearings, but intake officers also consider the inculpatory evidence police officers and others have to demonstrate the offender's involvement. Direct evidence (e.g., eyewitness accounts of the juvenile's behavior), tangible objects (e.g., weapons), and the totality of circumstances provide the intake officer with reasonable information about where the case would eventually end if it reached the adjudicatory stage in a juvenile court.

Intake officers can also consider exculpatory evidence or materials and testimony from others informally that provide alibis for juveniles or mitigate the seriousness of their offenses. Evidentiary factors are important in establishing one's guilt or innocence, but police referrals of juveniles to intake usually indicate that the officers acted based on the situation they confronted. It is unusual for officers to refer juvenile cases to the intake stage without a valid reason, although some officers might do so because of the limited resources available without court involvement.

Prior Record

Intake officers review prior records of delinquency adjudications and referrals to the juvenile court and factor these data into their decisions. In various jurisdictions, and even in other countries like Canada, prior records strongly suggest that earlier treatments and/or punishments may have been ineffective at preventing offender recidivism (Peterson, Ruck, and Koegl, 2001). Therefore, the current behavior and the prior record merit consideration.

It might be logical to assume that intake officers would deal more harshly with youth who have prior records of delinquency adjudications. A prior record could suggest persistence and chronicity, perhaps even a rejection of and resistance to prior attempts at intervention and treatment. In fact, harsher punishments and dispositions have been observed in some of these cases. In others, however, youth might have been improperly diagnosed or placed in a setting that did not meet their needs. In addition, some offense categories, like robbery or assault, might have greater priority than curfew violation or running away for intake officers.

The previous disposition of a particular juvenile's case also seems to be a good predictor of subsequent case dispositions for that same offender. For instance, dispositions for prior offenses may be related to new dispositions for these very same offenses. Thus, if a juvenile formerly had been adjudicated delinquent on a burglary charge and was placed on probation for six months, a new burglary charge against that same juvenile may result in a similar probation sanction with some modifications.

Extralegal Factors

Intake officers consider carefully the decisions they make during screening hearings. They want to be fair to all juveniles, but at the same time, they are interested in individualizing their decisions according to each case. This means that they must balance their interests and objectives to achieve multiple goals, some of which may be in conflict. Further, in recent years, greater pressure has been exerted on all juvenile justice components to implement those policies and procedures that will increase offender accountability at all stages of processing. Thus, a balanced approach may be recommended. Three major goals of the balanced approach for probation officers serving in various capacities in relation to their clients include (1) protecting the community, (2) imposing accountability for offenses, and (3) equipping juvenile offenders with competencies to live productively and responsibly in the community.

In the context of attempting to achieve these three objectives, several extralegal characteristics of juvenile offenders have emerged that influence the equality of treatment youth may receive at intake. These extralegal factors are (1) age, (2) gender, (3) race and ethnicity, and (4) SES.

Age

Age is both a legal and an extralegal factor in the juvenile justice system. Age is legally relevant in decisions about waiver to criminal court jurisdiction. Waiver or transfer of juveniles under the age of 16 to criminal courts does not occur frequently. In the extralegal sense, older youth may be assumed to be more responsible for their actions compared with younger youth, and are often treated accordingly. Arrest data also show that the peak ages of criminality occur between the 16th and 20th birthdays

(Courtesy of Alida V. Merlo)

Name: Alison S. Burke
Position: Assistant Professor, Department of Criminology and Criminal Justice, Southern Oregon University, Ashland, Oregon

Colleges Attended: University of New Mexico, University of Colorado at Denver, and Indiana University of Pennsylvania

Degrees: B.A. in Psychology, Master's of Criminal Justice (M.C.J.), and Ph.D. in Criminology

Background

After I received my bachelor's degree in Psychology from the University of New Mexico, I worked for several years before returning to school and earning a Master's of Criminal Justice (M.C.J.) from the University of Colorado at Denver. I waited another year after graduating with my master's degree before beginning my doctoral education.

When I graduated with my B.A., I wanted to use my psychology degree to help people. That led me to apply for a position with the Division of Youth Corrections Amnesty Unit. I had never worked with adjudicated youth. The youth were referred from the Division of Child Care, Division of Youth Corrections (DYC), and the Division of Mental Health. I worked with adolescent boys between the ages of 13 and 18 in a locked, medium-security youth residential facility. The boys had a history of abuse and/or neglect, drug use, gang ties, metal health issues, and broken families. My job was to provide a safe and stable environment where the youth could work on their behavior modification treatment goals. Unfortunately, this job also had a lot of staff turnover, so it was difficult to provide a stable environment when we were constantly short staffed and/or training new staff.

After several years of working behind locked doors, I decided to work at a youth group home. My main responsibility was to help teens transition from secure facilities to independent living. I counseled the residents on independent living skills, education goals (either graduating from high school or earning their GED), employment, self-sufficiency, and money management. It was rewarding to see formerly incarcerated youth join sports teams in high school, go to school dances, get jobs at movie theaters or restaurants, and plan for their lives as adults. It was also extremely difficult when youth would use drugs or get arrested and start their cycle again.

After working with adjudicated youth, I realized that the system was broken. Many youth were released only to be incarcerated again. Most of the kids returned to dysfunctional family lives or to the same situations that initially got them into trouble. I did not like this system, and I decided to return to school to learn how to change it.

Now I am on the faculty at a university, and I teach undergraduate criminology and criminal justice classes. Most of the classes I teach are theory-based courses, which draw on criminological theories, research, and policies. I frequently talk to my students about the DYC kids I worked with and the situations I observed in youth corrections. Many of the theories we discuss in class are directly applicable to the lives of youth, such as gang involvement and differential association or poverty and social disorganization. Applying the theory to real life helps bridge the gap from academia to the real world.

Advice to Students

I recommend that students take two steps. First, take classes that interest you. Enroll in classes that you find challenging and interesting, and apply what you learn in the classroom to the real world. You can do this through service learning classes, community-based learning classes, or volunteer work. Get the most out of your education, and think of your education as gaining new knowledge, not as job training. Your major will not get you a job; the critical thinking skills and writing skills you learn along the way will. You never know where your life might take you.

Second, I urge students who want to work with youth to understand that youth are an extremely vulnerable population. They need stability and encouragement. Unfortunately, I saw many people who worked in youth corrections use their job as a stepping stone to something else or burn out and quit in a relatively short period of time. The work is not glamorous or high paying; it is stressful and sometimes depressing. But it is also very rewarding. It is important to remember that incarcerated juveniles are still kids, and they still goof off, push limits, and act like kids. They need caring individuals who are invested in their success. You can make a difference.

(Office of Juvenile Justice and Delinquency Prevention, 2007). Perhaps some intake officers believe that their decision making should be more punitive against older juveniles than against younger ones.

When young children are involved in predelinquent or delinquent behavior, however, the system tends to view it as serious. Thus, younger offenders are often treated with greater interest and attention compared with older offenders. This perception is supported by risk assessment instruments used by both juvenile and adult corrections departments throughout the United States. These instruments use age as an important component in arriving at one's degree of risk or dangerousness. The younger the offender, the greater the weight assigned. This means that if youth become involved with delinquent acts at earlier ages, then greater weight is noted, and one's dangerousness score increases (Champion, 1994). This evidence demonstrates the seriousness with which age is regarded as a predictor of chronic and persistent recidivism, whether property or violent offending is involved.

For intake officers, the offender's age appears to influence their decision making in a way similar to prosecutors when they assess the seriousness of identical offenses committed by both youth and adults. For example, armed robbery is not as serious for some prosecutors when committed by a 12-year-old as it is when the offender is a 21-year-old. Applied to intake decision making, officers may regard certain offenses as less serious when the youth is 13 years and under, while those 14 years and older may have those same offenses viewed as more serious. There are no precise age divisions that separate younger from older youthful offenders when one's age is functioning as an extralegal factor (Toth, 2005).

Gender

Generally, traditional patterns of female delinquency have persisted. Because there are so few female juvenile offenders compared with their male counterparts, the influence of gender on intake decision making and at other stages of the juvenile justice process has not been investigated extensively. In terms of formal petitions for delinquency being filed in 2007, girls accounted for 23 percent (Puzzanchera, Adams, and Sickmund, 2010). Historically, explanations for gender differences in girls' and boys' comparative rates of offending have ranged from different socialization experiences to impulsivity, self-control differentials, and victimization and abuse (Chapple and Johnson, 2007).

Differential treatment of male and female offenders in both the juvenile and criminal justice systems is well documented. According to Chesney-Lind and Shelden (2004), girls who are having problems at home are at a disadvantage during the intake process. However, some of the traditional reasons provided for such differential treatment, especially about female juveniles and their delinquency patterns, appear to be misconceived or have little basis in fact (Beaver et al., 2008).

Within the just deserts, justice, or crime control frameworks, attention in the juvenile justice system is focused on the act more than on the juveniles committing the act or their physical or social characteristics. Thus, gender differences leading to differential treatment of offenders who behave similarly would not be acceptable. However, the differential treatment of male and female juveniles in the United States and other countries persists (Chapple and Johnson, 2007).

A contributing historical factor may be the paternalistic view of juvenile court judges and others in the juvenile justice system. Differences between the arrest rates of

Focus on Delinquency

On June 17, 2011, a North Carolina teenager, Rebecca Blackmore, gave birth and then stabbed her infant daughter to death. She went to a medical center and told authorities that she had given birth but that the baby had died. Blackmore was 16 years old, and the Currituck County Sheriff charged her as an adult with first-degree murder. While North Carolina is considering changing the age to 18, suspects 16 and older are charged as adults, regardless of the crime. Originally denied bail, Rebecca Blackmore was later released from the Currituck County Detention Center on $250,000 bond. The autopsy revealed that the baby girl was stabbed multiple times and was left in a closet at Blackmore's home. If Blackmore is convicted, she could be sentenced to life without parole.

Incidents of teen neonaticide (killing of newborn babies within 24 hours of life) such as this are not unusual, and they raise questions about how to handle this type of teen killer. As in many states,

North Carolina has a Safe Haven law that allows mothers to bring their newborn babies to a hospital within seven days and avoid criminal charges. In her report on mothers who kill their young, Slater (2004) found that "pregnancy denial" is typical of young, first-time mothers who are abandoned by the father and fear reprisals from parents, peers, and teachers. While they may have low self-esteem and emotional immaturity, they do not suffer from mental illness, but they do fear abandonment. Statistics highly underestimate the prevalence of neonaticide, but between 150 and 300 women reportedly kill their infant babies each year (Slater, 2004). How do you think the case of Rebecca Blackmore should be handled?

Source: Adapted from Jeff Hampton (2011, September 21), "N.C. Teen Charged with Killing Newborn is Out on Bond," *The Virginian-Pilot* (available at http://hamptonroads.com/2011/09/nc-teen-charged-killing-newborn-out-bond).

female and male juveniles and in the proportion of female versus male offenders who subsequently are formally charged as delinquent suggest girls are involved in substantially fewer behaviors that result in formal court processing. This finding is supported by the national data, which indicate that girls in 2007 were less likely to be referred for formal adjudication and less likely to be found delinquent than their male counterparts (Puzzanchera, Adams, and Sickmund, 2010).

Race and Ethnicity

More important as predictors of decision making at virtually every stage of the juvenile justice process are race and ethnicity. Race and ethnicity appear to be significant predictor variables in arrest and detention discretion as well as in the decision to file a formal petition.

Bishop (2009) contends that minority youth are disadvantaged with respect to intake interviews and meetings that help to establish whether the youth is suitable for referral to a diversion program. Minority youth and their parents are less likely to have access to transportation and child care, and they may not have the ability to take time from work for appointments or interviews related to consideration for diversion from the court. In addition, research suggests that black youth are at a disadvantage because their parents are viewed as uncooperative or unable to provide appropriate supervision (Bishop, 2009).

Another factor that can influence intake, the school record, includes academic performance as well as disciplinary infractions, and both academic performance and

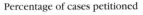

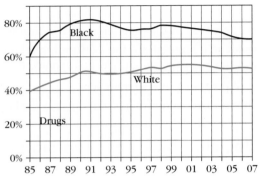

Figure 6.6
Formal Processing of Black and White Youth for Drug Offences, 1985–2007
Source: Charles Puzzanchera, Benjamin Adams, and Melissa Sickmund (2010). Juvenile
Court Statistics, 2006–2007. Pittsburgh, PA: National Center for Juvenile Justice.

school suspensions affect minority youth adversely. In particular, black and Hispanic youth are more likely to be in inner-city schools, which employ suspensions more often than suburban schools (Bishop, 2009).

National data from 2007 indicate that black youth are more likely to have formal delinquency petitions filed against them for drug offenses compared with white youth, and black youth also are more likely to be subject to formal processing than white youth for other delinquent offenses, as shown in Figure 6.6 (Puzzanchera, Adams, and Sickmund, 2010). Minority overrepresentation throughout the juvenile justice process has been reported in various jurisdictions (Burek et al., 2008).

Socioeconomic Status

Closely related to racial and ethnic factors as extralegal considerations in intake decision making is the **socioeconomic status (SES)** of juvenile offenders. It has been found that the poor as well as racial and ethnic minorities are disenfranchised in general by the juvenile justice system at various stages. This is true not only of juvenile courts in the United States, but also of those in other countries. One explanation for this alleged disenfranchisement is more limited access to economic resources among the poor and minorities. If the juvenile is from a middle-class family, his or her parents can afford services like counseling and alcohol and drug treatment that will preclude the youth from being formally processed. By contrast, lower-class juveniles can only participate in these kinds of services after they have been adjudicated delinquent (Bishop, 2009). This kind of differential treatment is widely recognized, but most professionals would suggest that the positive outcome of getting the youth the necessary services exceeds the concern that the poor are being treated differently (Bishop, 2009).

More restricted economic resources also reduce the quality of legal defenses that may be accessed by the socioeconomically disadvantaged. Greater reliance on public defenders is observed among the poor compared with those who are financially advantaged. A greater proportion of the socioeconomically disadvantaged may tend to

socioeconomic status (SES)

Station or level of economic attainment one enjoys through work; acquisition of wealth; the divisions between various levels of society according to material goods acquired.

acquiesce and quietly accept systemic sanctions that accompany allegations of wrong-doing rather than acquire counsel and contest the charges formally in court.

Black youth live primarily in the inner cities of the United States, and poverty, family disruption, residential segregation, low-performing schools, and social disorganization characterize these neighborhoods (Bishop, 2009). Poverty affects access to health care, recreational programs, and support services. Many of these factors appear to be related to disproportionate minority representation in the juvenile justice system.

Preliminary Decision Making: Diversion and Other Options

Diverting Certain Juveniles from the System

recidivism

Repeat offending, convictions, or adjudications for new offenses after prior convictions or adjudications, or any type of new offense following prior offense history.

Intake officers aspire to make decisions that will help youth and minimize the recidivism of those youth diverted from the system. **Recidivism** is a commonly used measure of program effectiveness in both adult and juvenile offender treatment and sanctioning strategies. Because of the fragmented nature of juvenile justice systems throughout the United States, it is extremely difficult to compile reliable, accurate information about the extent of juvenile recidivism. However, criminal justice practitioners estimate that the rate of recidivism among juveniles is similar to that for adult criminal offenders (Office of Juvenile Justice and Delinquency Prevention, 2007).

An intake officer's interest in the type of offense the youth allegedly committed focuses not only on the seriousness of the act itself and what should be done about it, but also on evidence that suggests recidivism rates vary substantially for different types of juvenile offenders. For example, studies of violent and nonviolent and of chronic and nonchronic juvenile recidivists suggest that greater proportions of chronic offenders repeat violent offenses compared with nonchronic offenders (Belshaw and Lanham, 2008). However, chronic offenders also commit subsequent nonviolent acts as well as violent ones. Despite the decrease in juvenile violence reported in Federal Bureau of Investigation arrest statistics, it remains the case that only a small proportion of youth may account for a majority of the violent crimes committed (Lansford et al., 2007).

Regarding juvenile justice policy, greater leniency with many offenders, particularly first-offenders, is often accompanied by less recidivism. Shay Bilchik (1996) reported that greater intrusion into the juvenile justice system characterizes more serious offenders, probably more chronic, persistent, dangerous, or habitual offenders—the category of youthful offenders who may be more likely to reoffend.

How Should We Deal with Chronic Violent Offenders?

Closely associated with recidivism among chronic violent offenders are predictor variables, such as whether the youth has delinquent siblings and/or significant others as associates, whether the juvenile has school problems, and whether the acts committed were misdemeanors or felonies. In a number of jurisdictions, chronic violent or serious offenders and other aggressive youth have been targeted for priority processing at intake and other stages. Harsher measures, including rapid identification of youth, expedited hearings, close monitoring of their cases, and segregation from other, less-serious offenders, have been employed by different Hawaiian juvenile justice units as a means of crime control.

The Search for Effective Treatment and Community Services

States may have programs with secure and nonsecure residential areas, close coordination and cooperation between the community and the criminal justice system, paraprofessional staff, alcohol and drug counseling, evidence-based practice, and provisions for remedial education and job training. However, limited budgets and other priorities in jurisdictions can prevent the development of such interventions. Some jurisdictions are unable to provide adequate treatment facilities and interventions that have been proven to be effective.

Getting Tough with Persistent Offenders

For persistent offenders and violent recidivists, and even for some violent first-offenders, the strategy employed at intake may be a waiver of jurisdiction to criminal courts (Champion, 2008a). Some jurisdictions, such as New York, Washington State, and Illinois, have automatic transfer laws that compel juvenile authorities to send certain types of juvenile offenders in a particular age range (normally age 16 or 17) directly to criminal court to be processed as adults. The intent of such waivers to criminal court is for harsher sanctions to be imposed on youthful offenders beyond those that can ordinarily be administered by juvenile court judges (Kuanliang, 2008).

The get-tough movement clearly authorizes incarceration for youth who have been adjudicated delinquent for violent offenses (Vivian, Grimes, and Vasquez, 2007). Anything less than secure confinement of youth adjudicated for aggravated assault, rape, robbery, or homicide may be considered as lenient. However, some

Juveniles can be detained pending court appearances.
(*Courtesy of Mark C. Ide*)

juvenile justice observers argue that there is presently too much incarceration, that incarceration is overdone, and that many youth can remain in their communities under close supervision, participating in productive self-improvement and rehabilitative programs (Mears et al., 2007).

Is There Too Much Juvenile Incarceration?

Several alternatives to confinement have been investigated (Trulson and Haerle, 2008). In 1987, the Delaware Plan was instituted whereby certain community programs were established as alternatives to incarcerating certain types of delinquent offenders. Brandau (1992) studied a sample of 363 youth adjudicated for various serious delinquency offenses assigned randomly to reform school, placed on probation, or sent to the Delaware Bay Marine Institute (DBMI), a community-based program designed to equip certain youth with coping skills and other useful experiences. Legal, social, and demographic variables were controlled, and youth were evaluated according to whether they were more likely to be assigned to the reform school following their delinquency adjudications. Subsequently, recidivism information was compiled for all youth to determine the influence of the different experiences on them. Youth in the DBMI program had recidivism rates similar to those placed on straight probation and those placed in reform schools. This finding is significant, because it shows that atleast in this instance, the DBMI program was about as effective as incarceration or probation for decreasing one's likelihood of recidivating. Since incarcerating juveniles is more expensive than placing them on probation or in the DBMI program, it is suggested that nonincarcerative, community-based alternatives should be used more frequently, even for serious offenders.

Some criminologists argue that secure confinement is overused in many instances when juveniles have been adjudicated (Champion, 2008a). Surveys of incarcerated youth suggest that over one-third of all youth in state training schools probably belong in less-secure settings. In more than a few jurisdictions, juvenile court judges may be using more punitive sanctions when disposing of cases through secure custody rather than imposing alternative, community-based punishments (Xiaoying, 2005). Increasingly emphasized, particularly as a cost-cutting measure, is focusing attention on methods or interventions that will reduce the recidivism rates of previously committed youth (Champion, 2008a).

Assessment of Guardianship

While most cases that are referred to the intake stage of the juvenile justice process involve some type of juvenile offending, criminal or otherwise, intake officers are often confronted with cases that require assessments of a youth's parents or guardians and the general sociocultural environment (Souhami, 2007). Ordinarily, children in need of supervision (CHINS), including unruly or incorrigible youth, dependent and/or neglected youth, and abused children, are channeled by police officers to certain community agencies for special services and placement. Departments of Health and Human Services, social welfare agencies, and family crisis or intervention centers are frequently contacted and receive youth for further processing. However, if CHINS are eventually subject to intake screenings, probation officers must evaluate the nature of the child's needs and the seriousness of the situation before a disposition of the case is made. Beyond the broad classification of CHINS, some youth may have chemical dependencies that precipitated their delinquent conduct and require medical attention rather than punishment.

These cases include youthful male and female prostitutes who originally may have been runaways and/or incorrigible, alcohol- or drug-dependent youth who have turned to burglary and petty theft to support their dependencies, psychologically disturbed or mentally retarded juveniles, and sexually exploited children (Kuntsche et al., 2007). If the facts disclosed at intake enable probation officers to make the strong presumption that certain youth should be diverted to human services shelters or community welfare agencies for treatment or temporary management, then this conditional disposition can be made. This decision is often predicated on the belief that a correlation exists between a child's predelinquent or delinquent behavior and physical, psychological, or sexual victimization from adults or significant others. Thus, it is imperative that early interventions be attempted with those considered to be at the greatest risk of chronic offending (Feiring, Miller-Johnson, and Cleland, 2007).

SUMMARY

Intake is a preliminary screening stage for deciding which juveniles should be processed further into the juvenile justice system. It is performed by professionals at social service agencies or by juvenile court staff who work closely with juvenile courts. Intake officers have broad discretionary powers, and their decisions about juveniles are based on both legal and extralegal factors.

Little uniformity exists among jurisdictions relating to the intake process. Defense counsel has an increased role in juvenile matters, and one consequence has been greater formalization of the intake process. With the greater involvement of defense attorneys, intake officers have been increasingly concerned about a youth's right to due process. This emphasis has been examined. Increasingly, informal negotiations occur between defense counsel and intake officers that resemble plea bargaining.

Both legal and extralegal factors are considered in determining outcomes for youth appearing at different stages of offender processing. Several legal variables are offense seriousness, type of crime committed, the presence or absence of inculpatory or exculpatory factors, prior record, and age. Extralegal factors include age, gender, race and ethnicity, and SES. The way that these factors are involved in offender processing was examined.

Preliminary decision making about youthful offenders may involve diversion, where a juvenile's case is temporarily removed from the juvenile justice system. Some juveniles are persistent offenders who may be either serious or nonserious. How should less-serious offenders who chronically offend be treated? There are no easy answers to this question. More-serious offenders may be incarcerated in secure facilities, although there is research indicating that too much juvenile incarceration already occurs and that it does not reduce recidivism (Mulvey, 2011). The tension between rehabilitation and greater leniency and the get-tough movement persists.

KEY TERMS

intake, 213	extralegal	socioeconomic status
due process, 214	factors, 227	(SES), 233
plea bargaining, 224	legal factors, 227	recidivism, 234

QUESTIONS FOR REVIEW

1. What is the intake process? Who performs the intake role? What are the duties of intake officers?

2. How much discretion does an intake officer have? In what respects can intake be compared with plea bargaining?

3. How are minority youth disadvantaged at the intake stage?

4. How has intake become increasingly formalized? How does the growing presence of defense counsels in juvenile matters increase intake formality?

5. How has the doctrine of *parens patriae* influenced the intake process?

6. What are several legal factors that influence intake decision making? How do these factors influence intake decision making?

7. What are several extralegal factors that influence decision making about juvenile offenders? Should extralegal factors be considered in any particular juvenile case? Why, or why not?

8. What types of juvenile offenders should be diverted from the juvenile justice system? Why?

9. Who are chronic and violent juvenile offenders? How should they be treated by the juvenile justice system?

10. Do we use incarceration too much for punishing juvenile offenders? Under what circumstances should incarceration be used? Which factors should determine whether a particular juvenile should be confined to an industrial school?

INTERNET CONNECTIONS

Aspen Education Group
http://www.aspeneducation.com

Believing in Girls
http://www.pacecenter.org

Center for the Prevention of School Violence
http://www.juvjus.state.nc.us/cpsv/

Girls' Justice Initiative
http://www.girlsjusticeinitiative.org/

Global Youth Justice
http://www.globalyouthjustice.org/

Human Rights and the Drug War
http://www.hr95.org/

Safe and Responsive Schools
http://www.indiana.edu/~safeschl/

Urban Institute
http://www.urban.org/

Vera Institute of Justice
http://www.vera.org/

Youth Law Center
http://www.ylc.org/

7

Prosecutorial Decision Making in Juvenile Justice

Learning Objectives

AFTER READING THIS CHAPTER, THE STUDENT WILL BE ABLE TO:

- Summarize the structure and key players of the juvenile court.
- Explain the role of the juvenile court prosecutor and how it is changing.
- Explain the role of public defenders and defense attorneys.
- Summarize adjudicatory hearings.
- Identify the factors that influence juvenile offender dispositions.
- Describe dispositional alternatives.

(Stan Wakefield/Pearson)

Introduction

Should prosecutorial charging decisions be influenced by a juvenile's age? What criteria should be used to determine whether youth are charged as adults? Should a 16-year-old youth who engages in robbery and is carrying a knife be tried as an adult or a juvenile? Should a 15-year-old who sells drugs be tried as an adult or a juvenile? These are difficult decisions for a prosecutor to make, and prosecutorial discretion varies among jurisdictions. The same behaviors committed by a juvenile may lead to a criminal trial in one jurisdiction but adjudication by a juvenile court judge in another.

This chapter will examine the role of juvenile court prosecutors. Juvenile court prosecutors exercise considerable discretion in deciding whether to pursue particular charges against juvenile offenders. The chapter begins with an examination of the transformation of the prosecutorial role, especially the changes resulting from the greater rights extended to juveniles by the U.S. Supreme Court. The evidentiary standard of beyond a reasonable doubt has altered what prosecutors must prove to make their cases against juveniles charged with serious offenses in juvenile court.

Next, the chapter will examine the general advocacy role of public defenders and defense attorneys who represent youthful clients in juvenile courts. Typically, speedy trials are not really an issue for juvenile offenders, because juvenile court adjudicatory proceedings and other stages of juvenile defendant processing are scheduled soon after the youth has been referred. However, there are occasions when delays occur due to competency examinations, maltreatment investigations, waiver hearings, and appeals. There are several reasons for accelerating the juvenile justice process, however, and these reasons will be examined and explained.

Defense counsel is available to any juvenile offender who is charged with a delinquent offense and could be subject to incarceration. Defense attorneys are advocates for juveniles and seek outcomes most favorable to their clients. The nature of the defense counsel role in plea bargaining will be described.

Working closely with the defense are *guardians ad litem,* or special guardians appointed by the juvenile court to assist in ensuring that a juvenile's rights are observed. Parents are also involved to varying degrees in making sure that their children are represented. The roles of *guardians ad litem* and parents respective to youthful defendants will be examined.

The Changing Prosecutorial Role in Juvenile Matters

The role of the prosecutor has been enhanced in the last 20 years. For example, in a number of states, prosecutors are authorized to file cases that involve youth directly in the criminal court. Typically, state statutes identify the kinds of cases that a prosecutor can transfer to adult court jurisdiction. As a result, prosecutors have more discretion in determining who is retained under the juvenile court jurisdiction and who will be moved to the adult criminal court. The consequences of adult prosecution and the attendant criminal record that accompany a conviction are not inconsequential.

Therefore, these changes illustrate the importance of the right to counsel for youth. Prosecutors recognize this right and take steps to protect youth in the juvenile court.

Juvenile court prosecutors have adjusted their orientation toward the treatment of juvenile defendants during the last several decades. As juveniles have acquired more legal rights, prosecutors have demonstrated that they are sensitive to these rights and constitutional safeguards and endeavored to ensure that they are protected. Constitutional rights violations can be challenged in the event of unfavorable juvenile court adjudications and/or sentences (White, 2008).

For example, the standard of proof in juvenile proceedings and the introduction of evidence have changed compared with the years before *In re Gault* (1967). Defense counsel may now aggressively challenge the quality of evidence against youth and how it was obtained, the accuracy of confessions or other incriminating utterances made by youth while in custody and under interrogation, the veracity of witnesses, and whether juveniles understand the rights they are asked to waive by law enforcement officers and others. Competency hearings may be required before certain juveniles are subjected to an adjudicatory hearing (LaSean, 2008). As indicated in Figure 7.1, more cases, in all categories of offenses, have been referred to prosecutors for formal processing in recent years.

Modifying Prosecutorial Roles by Changing the Standard of Proof in Juvenile Proceedings

Regarding the standard of proof in juvenile courts before 1970, it was customary to use the preponderance of the evidence standard in determining whether a juvenile was delinquent. This is a less-stringent standard compared with criminal court proceedings, in which the standard of proof used to determine a defendant's guilt is beyond a reasonable

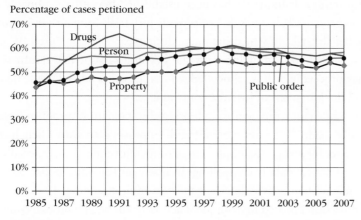

Figure 7.1

*More Cases Were Referred for Formal Processing in 2007 than in 1985
in All Four Offense Categories*
Source: Charles M. Puzzanchera, Benjamin Adams, and Melissa
Sickmund (2010). Juvenile Court Statistics 2006–2007. Pittsburgh, PA:
National Center for Juvenile Justice.

doubt. On the basis of using the preponderance of the evidence standard, juvenile court judges could find juveniles delinquent and incarcerate them in reform schools for months or even years. Thus, the loss of a juvenile's liberty rested on a finding by the juvenile court judge based on a relatively weak civil evidentiary standard. However, in the case of *In re Winship* (1970), the U.S. Supreme Court determined that the beyond a reasonable doubt standard should be applied during all juvenile court cases in which the juvenile was in danger of losing his or her liberty. Although a number of juvenile court jurisdictions continue to use the preponderance of the evidence standard for status offender or other kinds of cases, these jurisdictions now follow the Court ruling and use the standard of beyond a reasonable doubt whenever an adjudication of delinquency can result in confinement or loss of liberty.

Juveniles have benefited as a result of these new rights and evidentiary standards. The U.S. Supreme Court's decisions have sensitized law enforcement officers and prosecutors to be more careful and discriminating when charging juveniles with certain offenses. However, altering the evidentiary rules for proceedings against juveniles has not resulted in a reduction of police officer discretion, prosecutorial discretion, or judicial discretion. Juveniles continue to experience street-level justice by police officers. Nevertheless, juveniles are entitled to many constitutional protections. This includes determining their competency to be adjudicated if this issue arises (Sungi, 2008).

Despite the increased bureaucratization and emphasis on due process, juvenile courts continue to exhibit some of the traditionalism of the pre-*Gault* era. This means that only minor changes have occurred in the nature of juvenile adjudications. With the exception of those jurisdictions that provide jury trials for serious cases, juvenile court judges continue to make adjudicatory decisions as they did before *In re Winship* (1970). Thus, while adhering to the new evidentiary standards and proof-of-guilt requirements, juvenile court judges still exercise considerable discretion and decide whether a juvenile's delinquency has been established beyond a reasonable doubt. In addition, 80 percent of all states do not provide jury trials for youth in juvenile courts. Therefore, bench trials, in which the judge decides each case, are used. While it is assumed that judges are complying with the beyond a reasonable doubt standard in delinquency proceedings, it is acknowledged that its use is related to the quality of the defense and the judgment of juvenile court judges.

For juvenile court prosecutors, adopting the standard of proof of beyond a reasonable doubt made their cases more difficult to prove, even with a bench trial. Thus, the stage was set for greater use of plea bargaining in juvenile cases, especially when the evidence was not particularly compelling. In many jurisdictions, police officers do not regard juvenile offending as seriously as they do adult offending. Therefore, evidence-gathering procedures related to delinquent acts may not be as thorough compared with the investigation of adult crimes. Because of the traditional view that police and courts were acting in the best interests of the child, less attention was devoted to building a strong case against a youth. Historically, officers brought the youth to the juvenile court and let the professionals there determine how best to proceed.

For the most part, juvenile court prosecutors have adapted to their changing roles as the juvenile court has gradually transformed. The due process emphasis prompted prosecutors to prioritize their prosecutorial discretion according to a juvenile's offense history and offense seriousness. Nevertheless, this shift has not resulted in prosecutors ignoring potentially mitigating factors, such as undue exposure to violence and domestic abuse, in individual juvenile cases.

Eliminating the Confidentiality of Juvenile Court Proceedings and Record Keeping

Currently, there is greater access to juvenile court hearings. This also applies to inter-jurisdictional requests for juvenile information among the states. During the 1990s, considerable changes occurred regarding the confidentiality of juvenile court matters as well as juvenile records. Table 7.1 shows a summary of confidentiality provisions of the various states for 2008.

In 2008, for instance, 30 states had provisions for open hearings in juvenile or family court proceedings. Only eight states did not provide for the release of the names of those juveniles charged with serious offenses. All states, however, permit the release of court records to interested parties. These statutes identify prosecutors, law enforcement agencies and organizations, and the public as part of that designation. In fact, all states currently make available at least partial access to juvenile court records to any party showing a legitimate interest. This includes the youth, his or her parents, and the defense attorney. In such cases, information "may require a court order" (Snyder and Sickmund, 2006, p. 109). Legislation in most states also now authorizes schools to be notified when a youth has engaged in delinquent activity, and most states presently have state repositories of juvenile records and other relevant information about juvenile offending. Youth who are apprehended for alleged involvement in offenses like burglary, assault, or auto theft can be subjected to these procedures. Some states may decide to forward this information to a state repository designed for juvenile offender records, while others place that information in an adult offender database.

Although almost every state has policies regarding the sealing, expunging, or destruction of juvenile court records after certain dates, recent legislative changes have restricted the conditions under which these privileges can be invoked (Szymanski, 2010b). Therefore, juveniles today are considerably more likely to be excluded from applying to have their records sealed or expunged than in previous years. Open-records policies are increasingly favored by the public and juvenile justice professionals.

Kansas is an example of a state that has made substantial changes in its confidentiality provisions governing juvenile offenders. When the juvenile crime rate rose nationwide during the early to mid-1990s, juvenile crime in Kansas escalated accordingly. In an effort to hold juveniles more accountable for their actions, the Kansas State Legislature demanded a more open juvenile justice system. Several measures to enhance accountability were established:

1. Parents of offenders younger than 18 may be assessed the cost of certain services, such as probation and out-of-home placement services; juvenile offenders 18 and older can be assessed the costs.

Table 7.1

SUMMARY OF CONFIDENTIALITY PROVISIONS RELATING TO SERIOUS AND VIOLENT JUVENILE OFFENDERS, 2008

State	Open Hearing	Release of Name	Release of Court Record[a]	Statewide Repository[b]	Finger-printing	Photo-graphing	Offender Registration	Sealing/ Expunging of Records Prohibited
Totals	30	42	48	44	47	46	39	25
Alabama			•	•	•	•	•	
Alaska	•	•	•	•	•	•	•	•
Arizona	•	•	•	•	•	•	•	•
Arkansas		•	•	•	•	•	•	
California	•	•	•	•	•	•	•	•
Colorado	•	•	•	•	•	•	•	•
Connecticut			•			•		
Delaware	•	•	•		•		•	•
District of Columbia			•			•		
Florida	•	•	•	•	•	•	•	•
Georgia	•	•	•	•	•	•		•
Hawaii	•	•	•	•	•	•	•	
Idaho	•		•	•	•	•	•	
Illinois		•	•	•	•	•	•	
Indiana	•	•	•	•	•	•	•	
Iowa	•	•	•	•	•	•	•	•
Kansas	•	•	•	•	•	•	•	•
Kentucky		•	•	•	•	•		•
Louisiana	•	•	•	•	•	•	•	•
Maine	•	•					•	
Maryland	•		•	•	•	•		
Massachusetts	•	•		•	•	•	•	
Michigan	•		•	•	•	•	•	
Minnesota	•	•	•	•	•	•	•	•
Mississippi		•	•		•		•	
Missouri	•	•	•	•	•	•		
Montana	•	•	•	•	•	•		•
Nebraska		•	•	•			•	
Nevada	•	•	•	•	•	•	•	•

Table 7.1 CONTINUED

State	Open Hearing	Release of Name	Release of Court Record[a]	Statewide Repository[b]	Finger-printing	Photo-graphing	Offender Registration	Sealing/ Expunging of Records Prohibited
New Hampshire		•	•			•	•	
New Jersey		•	•	•	•	•	•	
New Mexico	•			•	•	•	•	
New York			•	•	•	•		
North Carolina			•	•	•	•	•	
North Dakota		•		•	•	•		
Ohio			•	•	•	•	•	
Oklahoma	•	•	•	•	•	•		•
Oregon		•	•					•
Pennsylvania	•	•	•	•	•	•		
Rhode Island		•	•	•			•	
South Carolina		•	•	•	•	•		•
South Dakota	•	•	•	•	•	•	•	•
Tennessee		•	•	•	•	•	•	
Texas	•	•	•	•	•	•	•	
Utah	•	•		•	•	•	•	•
Vermont					•	•		
Virginia	•	•	•	•	•	•	•	•
Washington	•	•	•	•	•	•	•	•
West Virginia		•	•	•				•
Wisconsin	•	•	•	•			•	
Wyoming		•	•	•	•	•	•	•

[a]All states allow records to be released to any party who can show a legitimate interest, typically by court order. In this category, • indicates a provision for juvenile court records to be specifically released to at least one of the following parties: the public, the victims(s), the school(s), the prosecutor, law enforcement, or social agency.

[b]In this category, • indicates a provision for fingerprints to be part of a separate juvenile or adult criminal history repository.

Source: Patricia Torbet and Linda Szymanski (1998). *State Legislative Responses to Violent Juvenile Crime: 1996–1997 Update*. Washington, DC: U.S. Department of Justice, p. 10. Updated 2008 by authors.

2. Courts may order families to attend counseling together.

3. Parents' health insurance policies may be accessed to pay for their child's care while in state custody. (Previously, Kansas paid for drug treatment and medical care expenses for juvenile offenders, because most insurance policies did not cover these costs while a juvenile offender was in state custody).

4. Hearings for juvenile offenders 16 and older are open to the public.
5. Official file records for juvenile offenders are open to the public. (Musser, 2001, pp. 112–113)

The Kansas law states that the official file for any juvenile at the time any act is alleged to have been committed shall be open for public inspection unless the judge determines that opening the official file is not in the best interest of the juvenile who is less than 14 years of age at the time of the offense. However, although the official file is open, not all records are. Personal history files, including reports and information the court receives, are privileged and may only be seen by the attorneys and juvenile intake and assessment staff or by order of a district court judge. Between 1995 and 2001, the Office of Juvenile Justice and Delinquency Prevention noted that more states had made substantial changes with juvenile records, such as greater identification of juveniles, while others were considering making juvenile records available to the public (Musser, 2001, p. 113). As Szymanski (2010b) noted, there is a trend toward more open proceedings and fewer restrictions on confidentiality today than in the early 1990s. This means that the **confidentiality privilege** juvenile offenders had for many decades has eroded.

Open Juvenile Court Proceedings

The greater formality of juvenile proceedings as well as their accessibility to the general public may affect the discretion of juvenile court judges. On occasion, juvenile court judges have made decisions that only incidentally relate to a juvenile's alleged offense. More formal and open proceedings and the presence of defense counsel representing a juvenile's interests and promoting due process might deter judges from such conduct. These kinds of safeguards might preclude the consideration of extralegal factors from the adjudicatory hearing.

The Prosecution Decision

State juvenile justice systems vary in their ability to process juvenile offenders quickly. In some jurisdictions, there are delays in filing charges against juveniles and in the scheduling of adjudicatory hearings. Juveniles arrested may have to wait months before their cases are heard by juvenile court judges.

Prosecutors in the juvenile court may delay filing charges against particular juveniles for a variety of reasons. One reason may be the need for further testing and diagnosis of the youth. Competency decisions must be made in certain cases where a youth's mental state is an issue. However, the most obvious reasons for delays—court caseload backlogs, crowded court dockets, insufficient prosecutorial staff, and excessive paperwork—are complex and not easily verifiable. It is possible that the professionals themselves can play a role in the process and the accompanying delay. In some jurisdictions where prosecutors and judges have aggressively addressed their caseload problems and forced the courtroom professionals to work more quickly, juvenile caseload processing has been accelerated. Thus, the time between a juvenile's arrest

confidentiality privilege
Right between the defendant and his or her attorney in which certain information cannot be disclosed to prosecutors or others because of the attorney–client relationship; for juveniles, records have been maintained under secure circumstances with access limited only to those in the criminal justice system who are involved in the case.

and disposition has been reduced significantly because of individual decision making and not because of resolutions to any organizational constraints or overwork (Jarjoura et al., 2008).

Even so, the increase in juvenile court caseloads is clearly a factor contributing to juvenile court delays. Cases take time to resolve, and they may involve difficult issues like maltreatment and abuse. Overall, juvenile courts have had insufficient resources to address the increased number of cases referred over the last few decades. In 2007, juvenile courts were handling about 4,600 cases per day (Puzzanchera, Adams, and Sickmund, 2010). These cases involve person offenses, drug offenses, property offenses, and public order offenses. For instance, drug offense cases accounted for 11 percent of all delinquency cases in 2007, compared with only seven percent of all cases in 1985. Although the number of person offenses and public order offenses increased between 1985 and 2007, the number of property offenses declined substantially, accounting for 61 percent of cases in 1985 but only 36 percent in 2007. Male offenders predominate, comprising 73 percent of the delinquency cases handled by juvenile courts in 2007. Similar to the pattern observed for male offenders, female juvenile involvement in person offenses, drug offenses, and public order offenses increased; and the female delinquency caseload increased about three percent each year from 1985 to 2007 (Puzzanchera, Adams, and Sickmund, 2010).

In a number of cases, youth are being diverted to victim–offender mediation, where various nonprofit, private organizations receive referrals from juvenile courts. The intent of such victim–offender mediation is to reach a resolution between victims and offenders without subjecting offenders to juvenile court and its adverse labeling impact. In communities with mediation programs, there is support from community residents. Financial support in the form of grants is provided from local, state, and federal agencies. Mediators may be interested citizens, retired judges, community leaders, or even intake officers who undertake these tasks during nonworking hours (Aisenberg et al., 2007).

Community prosecution is based on the premise that prosecutors' responsibilities extend beyond prosecuting cases. Specifically, they are expected to deal with public safety issues, deter criminal activity, and enhance the public's belief in the system (Wolf, 2010). When community prosecution is established, there are three principles that apply: "recognizing the community's role in public safety, engaging in problem solving, and establishing and maintaining partnerships" (Wolf, 2010, p. 45). To work effectively, prosecutors have to forge alliances and "partnerships with justice agencies, including police, probation, and aftercare, and with institutions outside the justice system, such as schools, social welfare agencies, and faith-based organizations" (Wolf, 2010, p. 45). These collaborations can prevent youth from entering or becoming further involved with the system and lead to the development of programs in the community.

Despite these alternatives to juvenile court action, juvenile court proceedings have become increasingly formalized. Furthermore, public access to these proceedings in most jurisdictions is increasing (Champion, 2008a). Thus, the presence of defense counsel, an adversarial setting—a trial-like atmosphere where witnesses testify for and

community prosecution
Prosecutor's role extends beyond prosecuting criminal and delinquent cases; prosecutor forms partnerships with professionals in criminal justice and schools, faith-based groups, and other members of the community to prevent delinquency and crime, solve problems, and ensure public safety.

against juvenile defendants—and adherence to Rules of Procedure for Juvenile Courts are clear indicators of greater formalization, bureaucratization, and criminalization, as Feld (2007) has suggested.

The Speedy Trial Rights of Juveniles

Juveniles have no federal constitutional right to a speedy trial. The U.S. Supreme Court has not decided any juvenile case that would entitle a juvenile to a speedy trial commensurate with adults in criminal courts. Adult criminal defendants are assured a speedy trial through the Sixth Amendment and the case of *Barker v. Wingo* (1972). This case led to the establishment of the **Barker balancing test**. Each state has established speedy trial procedures that establish time standards between different events, such as between the time of arrest and initial appearance, between an offender's initial appearance and arraignment, and between arraignment and trial. Even though juvenile courts are not included in the *Barker* decision, states attempt to conduct the adjudicatory hearing as quickly as possible.

> **Barker balancing test**
>
> Speedy trial standard, where delays are considered in terms of the reason or length and in accordance with time standards that have been established through an interpretation of the Sixth Amendment; from the case of *Barker v. Wingo* (1972).

For juveniles, standards vary among jurisdictions between comparable stages of juvenile justice processing, such as between arrest and intake, between intake and prosecutorial decision making and case filing, between case filing and adjudication, and between adjudication and disposition. However, some state legislatures have provided time standards that proscribe different maximum time limits between each of these events. Recent research suggests that the longer juveniles remain within the juvenile justice system, the more adverse the consequences for their subsequent recidivism and offending (Hill et al., 2007).

One reason juvenile case processing is different than adult court processing relates to the doctrine of *parens patriae*. Rather than focus on punishment and crime control, the emphasis is on rehabilitation and reform of the youth. Historically, juvenile courts attempted to provide services for all youth referred to the system. It was assumed that sufficient time had to be allocated for rehabilitation and that individualized justice was essential. However, the U.S. Supreme Court in *In re Gault* (1967) noted that juveniles, because of their status as juvenile offenders, do not have to waive their due process rights under the 14th Amendment to derive the benefits of the juvenile justice system, such as the greater concern for their well-being inherent in juvenile court proceedings. Instead, the Court suggested that the due process principles of fairness, impartiality, and orderliness are of paramount importance, despite the *parens patriae* philosophy. Essentially, the Court acted to formalize the juvenile court system and to protect the constitutional rights of youth, which had previously been disregarded or minimized when juvenile courts were acting informally but presumably in the best interests of the child.

Little research has been conducted on juvenile court prosecutors. One early study of juvenile court prosecutor attitudes investigated their perceptions about the effectiveness of juvenile court processing. The prosecutors who participated indicated that in at least some jurisdictions, their perceptions were that juvenile courts were relatively ineffective at rehabilitating juveniles (Ellsworth, Kinsella, and Massin, 1992).

These prosecutors contended that probation services are most vital to a youth's rehabilitation and that community programs and services intended to prevent delinquency tended to be inadequate, nonexistent, or ineffective. They believed that their rehabilitative impact in specific juvenile cases became less effective as the professionals' involvement in these cases increased. This study suggests support for strategies to move youth through the system more quickly to minimize their exposure to the process and facilitate treatment efforts.

Time Standards in Juvenile Court for Prosecutors and Other Professionals

State requirements that establish time limits for accomplishing various procedures within the juvenile justice process are not new. As early as 1971, various organizations endeavored to encourage the juvenile justice system to process cases more quickly. It was assumed that only legislatively created time standards would cause police, intake officers, prosecutors, and judges to process juvenile offenders more efficiently.

For instance, Butts (1996a) notes that the "Joint Commission on Juvenile Justice Standards led the way in 1971 with early time standards for juvenile processing. A product of the Institute of Judicial Administration (IJA) and the American Bar Association (ABA), the Joint Commission convened periodically over the next several years and issued 27 different volumes during the years 1977 through 1980" (pp. 544–547). The standards promulgated were intended as guidelines for juvenile courts and the juvenile justice system generally. The Joint Commission was guided by the principle that juvenile court cases should always be processed without unnecessary delay.

The IJA/ABA standards relating to processing juveniles were as follows:

Time	Action
2 hours	Between police referral and the decision to detain
24 hours	Between detention and a petition justifying further detention
15 days	Between police referral and adjudication if youth is detained
30 days	Between police referral and adjudication if youth is not detained
15 days	Between adjudication and final disposition if youth is detained

Note that in these time guidelines, law enforcement officers have a relatively short time to detain youth once they have been taken into custody. Once police officers have referred a youth to juvenile court, only two hours are recommended for a decision to be made about detaining the youth. If a youth is detained, then only 24 hours are allowed between the start of a youth's detention and the filing of a petition to justify further detention, and depending upon whether a youth is detained or released, the time limit recommended is either 15 or 30 days, respectively, between detention and adjudication. These guidelines are designed to facilitate efficient juvenile offender processing. Tables 7.2(a) and 7.2(b) show that only a handful of states thus far have adopted these or more rigorous standards for filing charges against juveniles.

CAREER SNAPSHOT

(Courtesy of Charles M. Puzzanchera)

Name: Charles M. Puzzanchera

Position: Senior Research Associate, National Center for Juvenile Justice, Pittsburgh, Pennsylvania

Statistics:

Colleges Attended: University of Florida and Indiana University of Pennsylvania

Degrees: B.A. in Criminology and M.A. in Criminology

Background

It is nearly 20 years since I graduated from the University of Florida, where I received a B.A. degree in Criminology. I distinctly remember not being entirely certain what to do following graduation: Law school, graduate school, and entering the workforce were viable options. After much deliberation, I decided to enroll in graduate school at Indiana University of Pennsylvania (IUP) to further my studies in Criminology. The generous assistantship offered by IUP made my decision a no-brainer. Looking back, I am still pleased with this choice.

During my undergraduate years, I had few professional development opportunities. This changed considerably once I arrived at IUP. Perhaps the most important opportunity offered to me—and the one that best prepared me for my profession—was serving as a graduate assistant for Dr. John "Jake" Gibbs. This experience did as much or more for my development than some classes. Jake was a fantastic mentor, and that experience cultivated my passion for research methods and statistics.

My last assignment at IUP was as a teaching associate, an experience I also enjoyed a great deal. Through teaching, I realized just how much I love the field of criminology. More importantly, I was able to develop a variety of skills that I still use— specifically, the ability to organize material and present it appropriately to various audiences. I continue to teach part-time, and I utilize my education and my professional experiences in the classroom.

At present, I am a Senior Research Associate at the National Center for Juvenile Justice (NCJJ), the research division of the National Council of Juvenile and Family Court Judges. The NCJJ has been my professional home for the last 13 years. During that time, I have been actively involved in the NCJJ's various research and dissemination efforts. While I am involved in many projects, one of my primary tasks is management of the *Statistical Briefing Book*, a website that contains comprehensive information about juvenile crime and victimization and about youth involved in the juvenile justice system. Additionally, I support the data analysis and data restructuring needs of the National Juvenile Court Data Archive project. Through these activities, I have become familiar with numerous national, state, and local data sets, including administrative data sets and data stemming from federal data collection efforts. Understanding how to use existing data to help answer questions or fill information gaps plays a central role in my professional life. I am also the lead author on two widely referenced juvenile justice reports, *Juvenile Court Statistics* and *Juvenile Arrests*.

My work at the NCJJ provides many unique opportunities, such as access to various data sets and the ability to pursue independent research. While the NCJJ does have a national focus, I am actively involved with numerous state and local justice agencies. Additionally, I am able to present to and interact with diverse audiences, and I have developed relationships with countless others who work in the juvenile justice arena, including judges, policymakers, practitioners, and researchers. To be sure, the work I do at the NCJJ speaks to my passion for research and allows me to contribute to the field of juvenile justice. I am lucky to work with talented colleagues who share this enthusiasm. I have learned a great deal over the years, and I still am very excited and inspired by my work.

Advice to Students

Reflecting on my past, I would like to think I have learned a few things worth sharing. First, do not discount the importance of your role in your own education. Your effort and commitment do matter. Second, if you are considering a future involving research, courses in research methods and statistics are essential. Typically, these courses inspire love or hate, and little else. Make peace with these topics; you will need them later. I use these skills daily, and I am thankful for the excellent training I received. Third, learn how to write about and present data; these are important skills.

Table 7.2(a)
ADJUDICATION AND DISPOSITION TIME STANDARDS AS REFLECTED IN COURT RULES AND STATE STATUTES

State	Mandatory	Adjudication	Disposition
Alabama	√		80% in 120 days[a]
			100% in 270 days[a]
Alaska	√		75% in 75 days[a]
			90% in 120 days[a]
			98% in 180 days[a]
Arizona		46 days (detained)[a]	30 days (detained)[c]
		90 days (not detained)[a]	45 days (not detained)[c]
Arkansas	√	100% in 14 days (detained)[a]	100% in 14 days (detained)[c]
California		15 days (detained)[a]	100% in 10 days (detained)[c]
		30 days (not detained)[a]	100% in 45 days (not detained)[c]
Colorado		100% in 90 days[a]	100% in 45 days[c]
Delaware	√	90% in 45 days[a]	
		100% in 90 days[a]	
District of Columbia	√		100% in 45–60 days (detained)[a]
			70% in 120 days (not detained)[a]
			90% in 180 days (not detained)[a]
			98% in 270 days (not detained)[a]
Florida		100% in 21 days (detained)[a]	
		100% in 90 days (not detained)[a]	
Georgia		10 days (detained)[a]	
		60 days (not detained)[a]	
Hawaii			100% in 90 days[a]
Idaho		45 days (detained)[b]	
		90 days (not detained)[e]	
Illinois	√	10 days (detained)[b]	
		120 days (not detained)[a]	
Indiana		20 days (detained)[a]	
		60 days (not detained)[a]	
Iowa		100% in 15 days (detained)[a]	100% in 30 days (detained)[c]
		100% in 30 days (not detained)[a]	100% in 40 days (not detained)[c]

(continued)

Table 7.2(a) CONTINUED

State	Mandatory	Adjudication	Disposition
Kansas		30 days (not detained)[a]	
Louisiana			30 days[c]
Maine			14 days[c]
Maryland		60 days[a]	30 days[c]
Massachusetts	√	100% in 21 days (detained)[a]	100% in 180 days (non-jury cases)[b]
		100% in 30 days (not detained)[a]	100% in 240 days (jury cases)[b]
		100% in 60 days (jury cases)[a]	
Michigan	√	90% in 84 days (detained)[a]	75% in 119 days (not detained)[a]
		100% in 98 days (detained)[a]	
		75% in 119 days (not detained)[a]	
		90% in 180 days (not detained)[a]	
		100% in 210 days (note detained)[a]	
Minnesota	√	90% in 90 days[a]	15 days (detained)[c]
		97% in 150 days[a]	45 days (not detained)[c]
		99% in 365 days[a]	
Mississippi		100% in 21 days (detained)[c]	100% in 14 days[c]
		100% in 90 days (not detained)[c]	
Missouri		60 days (protective custody)[d]	60 days (informal adjustment)[a]
			90 days (protective custody)[d]
Nebraska		100% in 180 days[a]	100% in 60 days[c]
Nevada			60 days[a]
New Hampshire	√	21 days (detained)[a]	21 days (detained)[c]
		30 days (not detained)[a]	30 days (not detained)[c]
New Jersey	√	30 days (detained)[a]	100% in 90 days[c]
New Mexico	√	30 days (detained)[a]	
		90 days (not detained)[a]	
New York	√		100% in 180 days[a]
North Carolina		30 days[a]	95% in 60 days (misdemeanor)[c]
			95% in 90 days (felony)[c]
			100% in 90 days (misdemeanor)[c]
			100% in 120 days (felony)[c]

Table 7.2(a) CONTINUED

State	Mandatory	Adjudication	Disposition
North Dakota			120 days (detained)[d]
			120 days (not detained)[a]
Ohio	√		100% in 90 to 365 days[a]
Oregon		100% in 15 days (detained)[a]	
		100% in 30 days (not detained)[a]	
Pennsylvania	√	15 days (detained)[a]	20 days (detained)[c]
		90 days (not detained)[a]	60 days (not detained)[c]
Rhode Island			100% in 180 days[a]
South Carolina			100% in 270 days[a]
Tennessee	√	30 days (detained)[a]	15 days (detained)[c]
		90 days (not detained)[a]	90 days (not detained)[c]
Texas		100% in 10 days (detained)[a]	100% in 15 days[c]
		100% in 30 days (not detained)[a]	
Utah	√	60 days[a]	30 days[c]
Vermont		15 days (detained)[a]	15 to 30 days[c]
Virginia	√	21 days (detained)[a]	30 days (detained)[c]
		120 days (not detained)[a]	
Washington			14 days (detained)[c]
			21 days (not detained)[c]
West Virginia	√	100% in 30 days[b]	100% in 45 days[c]
Wisconsin		20 days (detained)[a]	10 days (detained)[c]
		30 days (not detained)[a]	30 days (not detained)[c]
Wyoming	√	60 to 90 days[a]	60 days[c]

[a]Triggering event is filing of a petition/complaint.

[b]Triggering event is detention hearing.

[c]Triggering event is adjudication.

[d]Triggering event is detention.

[e]Triggering event is admit/deny hearing.

Source: Jeffrey A. Butts, Gretchen Ruth Cusick, and Benjamin Adams (2009). *Delays in Youth Justice.* Chicago, IL: Chapin Hall at the University of Chicago. (pp. 43–44). Printed with permission of the authors; Chapin Hall at the University of Chicago. Search of published statutes and administrative rules as applied to delinquency matters. Rules and statutes are those applying at the state level only; local provisions are not included.

Table 7.2(b)
TIME LIMITATIONS IN JUVENILE PROCEEDINGS AS SUGGESTED BY PROFESSIONAL STANDARDS

Detained Juveniles	Maximum days from referral to adjudication	Maximum days from adjudication to disposition	Total days from referral to Disposition
IJA/ABA (1977–80)	15	15	30
NAC/OJJDP (1980)	18	15	33
ABA Std. 252 (1984)	15[a]	15	30[a]
NDAA Std. 19.2 (1989)	30	30	60
NCJFCJ/OJJDP (2005)	10[c]	10	20
Released Juveniles			
IJA/ABA (1977–80)	30	30	60
NAC/OJJDP (1980)	65	15	80
ABA Std. 252 (1984)	30[b]	15	45[b]
NDAA Std. 19.2 (1989)	60	30	90
NCJFCJ/OJJDP (2005)	20[c]	20	40

[a]Deadline triggered by detention admission.
[b]Deadline triggered by filing of delinquency petition.
[c]Deadline triggered by initial hearing.
Source: Jeffrey A. Butts, Gretchen Ruth Cusick, and Benjamin Adams (2009). *Delays in Youth Justice.* Chicago, IL: Chapin Hall at the University of Chicago. (pp. 43–44). Printed with permission of the authors.

In addition, Butts (1996b) reports that similar time limits for juvenile processing were recommended contemporaneously by the National Advisory Committee for Juvenile Justice and Delinquency Prevention in 1980. These limits (Butts, 1996b, pp. 546–547) were:

Time	Action
24 hours	Between police referral and the report of intake decision if youth is detained
30 days	Between police referral and the report of intake decision if youth is not detained
24 hours	Between detention and detention hearing
2 days	Between intake report and the filing of a petition by the prosecutor if youth is detained
5 days	Between intake report and the filing of a petition by the prosecutor if youth is not detained
5 days	Between filing of the petition and the initial arraignment hearing

Time	Action
15 days	Between filing of the petition and adjudication if youth is detained
30 days	Between filing of the petition and adjudication if youth is detained
15 days	Between adjudication and final disposition

Again, the National Advisory Committee provided little latitude to juvenile court prosecutors in dispatching juvenile cases. In these particular scenarios, however, the intake stage was addressed. Not only were prosecutors obligated to file petitions against specified juveniles more quickly following intake, but the intake officers were required to make their assessments of juveniles and file reports of these assessments within a two-day period. One major difference in the National Advisory Committee recommendations and guidelines was the fact that if professionals in the juvenile justice system did not comply with these time standards, then cases against certain juveniles could be dismissed, but **without prejudice**, meaning that juvenile court prosecutors could revisit the original charges and refile them with the juvenile court at a later date. However, neither the IJA/ABA time guidelines nor the National Advisory Committee guidelines are binding on state jurisdictions. They are set forth as strongly recommended guidelines for juvenile court officials to follow.

> **without prejudice**
> To dismiss charges, but those same charges can be brought again later against the defendant.

In 34 states in 2007, juvenile court prosecutors were authorized to file charges against juvenile offenders whenever they decided to pursue this option (Office of Juvenile Justice and Delinquency Prevention, 2007). However, no binding legislative provisions were applicable to require them to act promptly and bring a youth's case before the juvenile court. In the meantime, 20 states established time limits that cannot be exceeded between the time of a juvenile's court referral and the filing of charges

Youth may feel isolated and alone when they are awaiting court appearances.
(© Peter Herman/Alamy)

by prosecutors. Tables 7.2(a) and 7.2(b) show various time limits imposed by states for juvenile court adjudication and disposition of cases. In New Hampshire, for instance, juvenile court prosecutors must file charges against juveniles within 21 days of their referral to juvenile court by police if such juveniles are placed in secure confinement. These same prosecutors must file charges against undetained juveniles within 30 days following the juvenile's referral to juvenile court by police. In Maryland, prosecutors have 60 days to file charges against either detained or undetained juveniles following their court referrals, while in Georgia, prosecutors must file charges within 10 days if juveniles are being detained. A failure to file charges against juveniles in these jurisdictions within the time periods specified results in a dismissal of their cases **with prejudice**, meaning that the prosecutors cannot refile charges against the same offenders.

with prejudice

To dismiss charges, but those same charges cannot be brought again later against the defendant.

Why Should the Juvenile Justice Process Be Accelerated?

Several compelling arguments can be made for applying juvenile justice processes quickly. One reason is that adolescence is a critical period during which youth undergo many changes. Maturational factors seem to be especially accelerated, while a juvenile's personality and response to peer pressures are modified in a variety of ways. A month may seem like a year to most adolescents. Secure confinement of 24 hours is a serious deprivation of a juvenile's freedom. Thus, when some juvenile cases undergo protracted delays of a year or longer, it may be difficult for the offender to accept the subsequent sanction for behavior that he or she engaged in months ago. Many juveniles, in fact, have ceased their involvement in delinquent behavior by the time their cases come before the juvenile court and ask why they are being sanctioned for an act that they engaged in when they were younger.

Studies of juvenile justice system delays suggest that the size of a jurisdiction plays an important part in how quickly juvenile cases are processed. In 2007, juvenile courts handled in excess of 1.6 million delinquency cases (Puzzanchera, Adams, and Sickmund, 2010). The sheer volume of cases affects how readily court professionals can process them. "In 1985, for example, the median processing time for juvenile cases in a large sample of U.S. county jurisdictions was about 44 days. By 1994, the median processing time in these same counties was 92 days" (Butts and Halemba, 1996, p. 131). For smaller jurisdictions, with fewer and presumably less-serious cases to process, case-processing time ranged from 34 to 83 days in 1994, while larger counties required from 59 to 110 days.

Delays in juvenile justice processing parallel those in criminal court processing of adult defendants. This would suggest that the juvenile justice cases were sufficiently serious to warrant more court time. For example, in 2007, although property offenses made up the bulk of cases in which youth were adjudicated delinquent by the juvenile court judge (34 percent), almost one-fourth (24 percent) of the cases in which youth were adjudicated delinquent were person offenses, and 12 percent were drug offenses (Puzzanchera, Adams, and Sickmund, 2010). One of the biggest increases in official court processing for delinquency occurred with public order offenses. In 2007, "they accounted for approximately 30 percent of the cases in which youth were found to be delinquent" (Puzzanchera, Adams, and Sickmund, 2010, p. 46).

Therefore, it has been recommended that juvenile justice case-processing time be decreased in an effort to move the disposition closer to the time when the offense was committed. In some instances, juveniles awaiting trial on one charge have had subsequent opportunities to reoffend. "When they are arrested for new offenses before being adjudicated for earlier offenses, their cognitive development may inhibit their understanding of the process and their disposition" (Butts, 1996b, p. 525).

Shine and Price (1992) provide two important reasons why juvenile cases should be processed quickly:

1. To maximize the impact on the juvenile that he or she has been caught in a criminal act, that the juvenile will be held accountable for what he or she has done, and that there will be consequences for this action, it is important that the case be resolved quickly. If the case continues for too long, the impact of the message is diluted, either because the juvenile has been subsequently arrested for other offenses and loses track of just what he or she is being prosecuted for or because the juvenile has not engaged in any further delinquent acts and feels that any consequences for the past offense are unfair.

2. If there are victims, unwarranted delays in juvenile case processing are unfair and damaging to victims. Many victims suffer some type of financial loss or

Focus on Delinquency

Two similar rape cases in a midwestern state had very different outcomes. The first rape case involved M.J., age 16. M.J. was accused of breaking into his neighbor's apartment and raping her 13-year-old daughter, R.P. He was arrested shortly after the incident when the girl's mother called police, reported the rape, and gave an accurate description of the rapist. R.P. said that she was glad M.J. was apprehended. M.J. was transferred to adult court to stand trial for rape. He decided to plead guilty in a plea bargain agreement, where he would be sentenced to 20 years, with 12 years served in the state prison and the rest served on probation. In addition, M.J. would be required to register as a sexual offender with the state and serve a concurrent, 10-year sentence for the burglary.

The second rape case involved S.V., a 16-year-old female. S.V. had a sexual relationship with one of her male neighbors, U.A., who was 13 years old. She believed that U.A. was in love with her and that this feeling somehow excused the sexual assault. The incidents were admittedly consensual between S.V. and U.A. However, between the arrest of S.V. and her trial, U.A. changed his mind. After S.V. had been transferred to adult court for a trial, U.A. told the jury, "I just feel like I've lost a lot of years being young. I want S.V. to go to jail because I don't want her doing it to anyone else." The prosecutor asked the judge to sentence S.V. to between 20 and 35 years, with 15 years suspended. However, the defense attorney asked for a three-year sentence of probation, because he said S.V. and U.A. were in love with each other. S.V. received five years of probation. The prosecutor was disappointed with the sentence and said it was inappropriate.

These two cases of rape occurred in the same state. Yet, there were very different outcomes. Should 16-year-old male rapists be treated differently from 16-year-old female rapists? Which factors do you think account for the great disparity in sentencing in the two cases?

Sources: Adapted from the Associated Press, "Boy Pleads Guilty to Rape, Gets 20 years," June 4, 2008; adapted from the Associated Press, "S.V., 16-Year-Old Female Rapist, Given Probation," June 26, 2008.

physical injury. Expenses are incurred. Faster resolutions of juvenile court cases can lead to more rapid compensation and victim restitution plans imposed by the court. Such compensation and victim restitution can alleviate any continued suffering victims may endure.

The Advocacy Role of Defense Attorneys and Public Defenders for Juveniles

Greater procedural formality in the juvenile justice system is reflected in the role of defense attorneys and public defenders for juveniles. Formerly, defense attorneys for juveniles were the juvenile probation officer or social case worker involved in the case. Without the requisite legal training and background, these professionals were disadvantaged in their attempts to defend youth in delinquency proceedings. Today, however, every juvenile court jurisdiction provides defense counsel for juveniles and their families who cannot afford to retain private counsel, especially for more-serious cases in which incarceration is a strong possibility. Typically, states provide counsel to indigent youth in three ways: "assigned counsel, contract [or] public defender models (Majd and Puritz, 2009, p. 546, cited by Ross, 2011). The public defender model is the most common in the United States for indigent youth.

It has been found that the presence of attorneys, who represent juvenile's interests and attempt to ensure that their constitutional rights are observed at each stage of the juvenile justice process, may affect the informal nature of intake. With defense counsel present, intake officers transform these proceedings into quasi-official hearings, and recommendations for subsequent dispositions might be more formal and harsh than if defense attorneys were not present. In fact, some intake officers have discouraged juveniles and their parents from availing themselves of an attorney's services at this stage, since their presence hampers informal adjustments of cases and limits youth compliance with informal probationary conditions. In some cases, intake officers consider themselves able to protect the youth and his/her understanding of legal rights, thereby eliminating the need for an attorney.

Two problems have been highlighted relating to the use of public defenders in juvenile courts. These problems include the limited resources and increasing caseloads of public defenders for juveniles in many jurisdictions. A study by the U.S. General Accounting Office (1995b) examined access to counsel in selected states and local juvenile delinquency proceedings. Data sources were relevant state statutes, state administrative procedures, and case law in 15 states; National Council on Juvenile Justice statistics for three states; national surveys of county prosecutors and public defenders; telephone interviews with selected state and local judges in eight states; and site visits to juvenile justice officials in four states. Statutes guaranteeing a juvenile's right to counsel existed in all 15 states examined. Overall, the rate of defense counsel representation for juveniles varied from 65 percent in Nebraska to 97 percent in California. Representation by offense category also varied, as did the overall impact of representation on case outcomes. In most cases where juveniles were not represented by counsel, juveniles were less likely to receive out-of-home placements, such as a disposition to an industrial school. However, this should not be interpreted to mean that defense counsel led to more juveniles receiving out-of-home placements. Rather, a better explanation is that defense attorneys were not used in the least-serious cases—namely, those that normally would not result in placement in an institution. Prosecutors and juvenile justice officials generally were pleased with the quality of counsel provided to juveniles, apart from their concerns about scarce resources and growing caseloads (U.S. General Accounting Office, 1995b).

For especially serious cases, defense attorneys are useful and necessary to safeguard juvenile rights and hold the juvenile justice system more accountable regarding its treatment of juvenile offenders. For instance, it is important for defense counsel to advise clients about the **statute of limitations** associated with various offenses, under which the government can bring charges only within specified time periods following the crime's occurrence. Some crimes, like murder, have no statute of limitations. Thus, there is an indefinite period of time when the state can formalize charges against a potential defendant for these crimes. The inclusion of defense attorneys in the juvenile justice process, under a new due process framework, is anticipated as a logical consequence of the rights juveniles now have based on various U.S. Supreme Court cases.

> **statute of limitations**
>
> Maximum time period within which a prosecution can be brought against a defendant for a particular offense; many criminal statutes have three- or six-year statute of limitations periods; there is no statute of limitations on homicide charges.

It should also be noted that defense attorneys are essential for protecting youth in delinquency proceedings that can be characterized as punitive (Kempf-Leonard, 2010). As Bishop (2010) noted, "delinquent adjudications can be used to enhance adult sentences" (p. 322). In addition, other penalties are associated with delinquency adjudication. For instance, the family and the youth "may be disqualified from welfare or other housing benefits" (Bishop, 2010, p. 322; see also Ross, 2011). In brief, effective defense counsel would appear to be necessary in safeguarding youth.

Attorneys for Juveniles as a Matter of Right

Juveniles are entitled to the services of attorneys at all stages of juvenile proceedings, and the presence of defense counsel in juvenile proceedings has escalated dramatically since the *Gault* decision. Although there continues to be regional variations in the proportionate representation of juveniles by defense counsel, especially when contrasting rural with urban areas, the overall trend has been toward attorney representation. Even so, research has shown that about half of all youth processed in the juvenile justice system are not represented by counsel (Feld, 2007; Ross, 2011).

Analyzing adjudication data from an earlier period in six jurisdictions, Feld (2007) discovered similar figures. Roughly half of all juveniles adjudicated delinquent in these state juvenile courts had legal representation at the time of their adjudications. It is unclear whether the juveniles who did not have defense counsel did not request an attorney. It would have been inconsistent with *Gault*—as well as unconstitutional—if these juveniles had requested defense counsel and been denied it in those jurisdictions. Feld, however, may have provided at least two plausible explanations for this finding. First, juveniles who were represented by attorneys in each of these jurisdictions, and who were also adjudicated as delinquent, tended to receive harsher sentences and dispositions from juvenile court judges compared with those juveniles who did not have defense counsel to represent them. Thus, it would seem that the presence of defense counsel in juvenile courts, at least in those jurisdictions examined by Feld, may have aggravated the dispositional outcome rather than mitigated it. Second, the more-serious offenders in those jurisdictions were more likely to retain or be assigned counsel. Thus, they would logically receive harsher sentences compared with less-serious offenders if they were ultimately adjudicated as delinquents. With the presence of defense counsel in juvenile proceedings becoming increasingly common, it is also likely that any adverse impact of defense attorneys on the outcomes of these proceedings will be reduced accordingly.

Defense Counsel and Ensuring Due Process Rights for Juveniles

The goal of defense attorneys in juvenile courts is to ensure that due process is fulfilled by all participants. Defense attorneys are the primary advocates of fairness for juveniles who are alleged to be involved in delinquent acts or other types of offenses. Minors, particularly very young youth, are more susceptible to the persuasiveness of adults. Law enforcement officers, intake officers, and prosecutors might solicit incriminating evidence from juveniles in much the same way as police officers and prosecutors might extract inculpatory information from suspects in criminal cases when certain constitutional safeguards were not in place. For adults, a major constitutional safeguard is the *Miranda* warning, which, among other things, advises those arrested for crimes of their right to an attorney, their right to terminate police interrogations whenever they wish and remain silent, and the right to have an attorney appointed for them if they cannot afford one (LaSean, 2008).

The U.S. Supreme Court's decisions about juvenile constitutional guarantees have provided procedural protections. Nevertheless, the possibilities of incarceration in secure juvenile facilities and/or transfer to criminal court jurisdiction where harsher penalties may be administered are sufficient to warrant the intervention of defense counsel in many juvenile cases. At the very least, defense counsel may protect youth from unnecessary conditional interventions from intake officers or juvenile court judges.

It is not the intention of defense attorneys to aggravate matters and cause their clients to receive harsher punishments than they would normally receive from the same judges if defense counsel were absent. In some respects, this potential outcome—or possibly not so potential outcome (Feld 2007)—is similar to the disparity in sentencing among adults who have similar criminal histories and are convicted for the same offenses but receive widely disparate sentences, depending upon whether their convictions are obtained through plea bargaining or a jury verdict in a criminal trial. There is no obvious reason for judges to impose differential punishments based on a request for a trial. One explanation, an extralegal and nonlegal one, is that the punishment is the penalty for obligating the state to expend resources and prove the case against the defendant in open court. Being aware of this type of sentencing disparity, defense attorneys counsel their adult clients, especially when there is strong inculpatory evidence, to plead guilty to fewer or reduced charges and accept a lesser penalty to avoid the more severe punishments that judges can impose upon conviction through a trial.

Are Attorneys Being Used More Frequently by Juvenile Defendants?

One survey of five states (California, Montana, Nebraska, North Dakota, and Pennsylvania) during the period from 1995 to 2005 found that attorney use by juvenile offenders increased systematically across these years (Champion, 2008b). Attorney presence and participation vary by jurisdiction, however. In the early 2000s, over 90 percent of all California juvenile cases involved either private or publicly appointed defense counsel. However, in states such as Nebraska and North Dakota, attorney use by juveniles occurred in about 65 percent of the cases.

The fact that youth are authorized to be represented by counsel does not necessarily result in assigning them attorneys. Recently, two judges in Luzerne County, Pennsylvania, were convicted for their involvement in a kids for cash scheme (see Chapter 4). These judges routinely pressured youth to waive their right to counsel, then adjudicated the youth without the presence of counsel and ordered them placed in specific private institutions. The judges received monetary payments from these institutions. Although these judges' behavior was particularly egregious, it does demonstrate that the mere presence of a statute authorizing counsel for youth does not guarantee that juveniles will be afforded their right to counsel (Ross, 2011).

It may seem that whenever youth invoke their right to an attorney, it would be under circumstances where the offenses alleged are serious or violent. While attorney use was more prevalent in states where serious and violent offenses were involved, it

Judges must determine offense seriousness to decide how a case proceeds.
(© Bill Burlington)

was also found that attorneys were used increasingly during the 10-year period for status offenders and those charged with public order, property, and drug offenses as well (Champion, 2008b). The primary implication of this research is that juvenile courts are experiencing greater defense attorney presence each year. If these states are representative of most U.S. jurisdictions, then the formalization of juvenile courtrooms is occurring with defense counsel representing youth in juvenile cases.

Does Defense Counsel for Juveniles Make a Difference in Their Case Dispositions?

Defense counsel in juvenile cases has resulted in various outcomes. In some instances, because of the greater formality of the proceedings when youth are represented by counsel, outcomes occur that may be unfavorable to juvenile defendants. For example, if an intake officer were inclined to divert a particular case from the juvenile justice system because in his or her judgment the youth will probably not reoffend, this decision may be modified if an attorney is present to represent the juvenile's interests. The intake officer may feel that a higher authority should decide the case. The mere presence of defense counsel may be intimidating. In an informal environment, the intake officer might act differently. Thus, actions by various professionals in the system may occur, depending upon the youth being represented or not represented by counsel.

In cases adjudicated before juvenile court judges, a defense counsel's presence can benefit the youth. Judicial discretion is affected to the extent that there is stricter or less-strict adherence to juvenile laws. Juvenile court judges might be more lenient with juveniles who are represented by defense counsel compared with those juvenile defendants who are not. This leniency manifests itself in various ways. For instance, juvenile court judges may impose probation more often than incarceration when juveniles are represented by counsel. Represented juveniles who are placed in a secure residential facility for a period of months may be in the facility for less time compared with those who were not. In brief, a defense attorney who is familiar with the court processes and the dispositional alternatives can be better equipped to offer the juvenile court judge alternatives on behalf of his or her client than a youth who appears without counsel.

Defense Counsel as *Guardians Ad Litem*

In some juvenile cases, child abuse has been alleged. Thus, defense counsel perform additional responsibilities as they attempt to ensure that the best interests of their clients are served in ways that will protect children from parents who abuse them (Salzinger, Rosario, and Feldman, 2007). *Guardians ad litem* are special guardians appointed by the court in which a particular litigation is pending. The *guardian ad litem* represents a youth in that specific litigation (Champion, 2009).

Most juvenile court jurisdictions have *guardian ad litem* programs where interested persons serve in this capacity. In some cases, a defense attorney can serve in dual roles as defense counsel and *guardian ad litem*. The *guardians ad litem* strive to benefit those they represent, and they provide legal protection from others. Defense counsel working as *guardians ad litem* may even act to further the child's best interests despite

guardians ad litem

Special authorities or guardians appointed by the court in which particular litigation is pending to represent a child or youth in court.

a child's contrary requests or demands. Thus, it is a different type of nonadversarial role performed by defense counsel.

Juvenile Offender Plea Bargaining and the Role of Defense Counsel

Often, it is thought that plea bargaining occurs only within the criminal justice system. However, juveniles can enter into plea agreements with juvenile court prosecutors. Plea bargaining is an invaluable tool to eliminate case backlogs that might occur in some of the larger juvenile courts.

Prosecutors are interested in concluding adjudications with sanctions, while defense counsel are interested in protecting their clients from more-serious charges that could influence their future lives and the possible sanctions that can be imposed. Defense counsel entering into plea agreements with juvenile court prosecutors usually negotiate for the least-restrictive option imposed on their juvenile clients. Most frequently, defense attorneys seek reductions in the charges against their clients by prosecutors. They are interested in reducing the stigma of a serious, negative juvenile court profile of their clients, and they ask for reduced charges from prosecutors (Kidd, 2007). Prosecutors benefit in that plea agreements speed up case processing and save them time from having to prove critical elements of the delinquent act against juvenile offenders.

The degree to which *parens patriae* is evidenced depends on whether a particular court has accepted and furthered the due process requirements created by *Gault*. If fairness is to be realized in the adjudicatory hearing of juveniles, judges and defense attorneys should know the rules of criminal procedure and evidence, and they must be aware that adjudications are serious for youth. Defense lawyers should realize that appellate review is both a necessary and a valuable weapon, although few juvenile court decisions are appealed. However, one problematic aspect of plea bargaining in the juvenile justice system is that admissions of guilt are elicited from juveniles without benefit of a trial.

SUMMARY

Juvenile court prosecutors have considerable discretion, including the ability to decide whether to prosecute juvenile cases in adult criminal court in some states. As greater rights have been extended to juveniles, prosecutors have been held to a higher standard in determining whether to prosecute youth. If prosecuting youth for delinquency with a chance that a disposition will entail confinement, prosecutors must prove beyond a reasonable doubt that juveniles are involved in the alleged offense. The changing nature of the prosecutorial role was described.

The time frames governing the processing of juveniles are greatly abbreviated compared with those governing adult offenders. The acceleration of the juvenile justice process is due, in large part, to the belief that juveniles will experience greater accountability and associate their illegal actions with the punishments they will eventually receive.

The appointment of public defenders and defense counsel to safeguard constitutional rights for youth is an integral part of the juvenile justice system. Defense counsel also is essential to assist in plea bargaining juvenile cases, to ensure that youth are protected, and increasingly, to explain the complexities of the process, the ramifications of adjudication or transfer, and the long-term effects of court involvement to the youth. The use of an attorney by juveniles has increased steadily in the United States during the last 40 years, and indications suggest that more youth will be represented in the next few years. However, defense counsel participation varies by state.

KEY TERMS

confidentiality
   privilege, 248
community
   prosecution, 249

Barker balancing
   test, 250
without prejudice, 257
with prejudice, 258

statute of
   limitations, 261
guardians ad litem, 264

QUESTIONS FOR REVIEW

1. How are juvenile courts becoming increasingly adversarial proceedings? How has the prosecutorial role in juvenile courts changed in recent years?

2. How has the beyond a reasonable doubt standard of proof modified the prosecutorial role?

3. Should confidentiality of juvenile records be maintained? Why, or why not?

4. What are some reasons for removing confidentiality surrounding juvenile records and opening juvenile courts to the general public?

5. What kinds of time standards govern prosecutorial decision making in the juvenile justice system? Are these time standards uniform across all jurisdictions?

6. What are some reasons for accelerating juvenile case processing?

7. Under what circumstances are public defenders appointed for juveniles? Do different types of defense counsel, public or private, make a difference in juvenile proceedings? Why?

8. Do juvenile offenders have the right to a speedy trial? In what ways do more accelerated time lines for concluding juvenile cases parallel the speedy trial provisions of criminal courts?

9. What is the significance of *Barker v. Wingo* (1972)? Does the *Barker* case have any influence on juvenile matters? Why, or why not?

10. How does the presence of defense counsel ensure that a juvenile's due process rights are preserved? What are *guardians ad litem*, and what are their functions?

INTERNET CONNECTIONS

ABA Center on Children and the Law
http://www.americanbar.org/groups/child_law.html

Campaign for Youth Justice
http://www.campaignforyouthjustice.org/

Coordinating Council on Juvenile Justice and Delinquency Prevention
http://www.juvenilecouncil.gov/

Federal Youth Court Program
http://www.ojjdp.gov/programs/ProgSummary.asp?pi=23

Fortune Society
http://www.fortunesociety.org/

National Association of Youth Courts
http://www.youthcourt.net/

Network for Good
http://www.networkforgood.org/

Office of Juvenile Justice and Delinquency Prevention
http://www.ojjdp.gov

Youth Court Websites by State
http://www.youthcourt.net/?page_id=40

8

Classification and Preliminary Treatment

Waivers and Other Alternatives

Learning Objectives

AFTER READING THIS CHAPTER, THE STUDENT WILL BE ABLE TO:

- Summarize the factors and offender characteristics that lead to juveniles being transferred to adult court.
- Explain the different ways that transfers to adult court take place.
- Differentiate between the different types of waivers.
- Explain how transfer or waiver hearings are conducted.
- Summarize adjudicatory hearings.
- Describe the advantages and disadvantages resulting from juvenile court adjudications.
- Describe additional considerations relating to transfers to criminal court.
- Summarize blended sentencing and the different blended sentencing models.

(Courtesy of Dean John Champion)

Introduction

When juvenile offenders commit serious crimes, such as rape, robbery, and aggravated assault, the juvenile court is challenged to determine the best way to handle the cases. One of the first considerations is jurisdiction: Should the case remain under the jurisdiction of the juvenile court, or should it be transferred to criminal court? Important factors, such as seriousness of the offense, age of the offender, prior record, and amenability to treatment, are taken into consideration.

From the beginning of juvenile courts in 1899, juvenile court judges have had the ability to transfer juveniles to criminal court. In 1966, in *Kent v. United States*, the U.S. Supreme Court established the criteria that juvenile judges should follow in assessing the appropriateness of removing youth from the juvenile court. The issue of transferring a juvenile case to adult court became more visible during the 1980s and 1990s, when there was an increase in serious crimes committed by juveniles. In response to the get-tough movement, states expanded eligibility for waiver and, under certain conditions, mandated that youth be excluded from juvenile court (Redding, 2010).

This chapter is about how juveniles are classified and handled by the courts. The considerations and mechanisms that are used in waiving or transferring juveniles to criminal court will be reviewed. The decision-making criteria used by judges will also be examined.

The terms *waiver* and *transfer* are used interchangeably. Waiver proceedings involve hearings to determine suitability for transfer. Also known as certification, these mechanisms establish that youth can be treated as adults for the purpose of criminal prosecution. The nature and rationale of waivers or transfers will be discussed. A description of transferred juveniles will be provided and explanations for why youth are processed by criminal courts reviewed.

Types of waivers, including judicial waivers, direct file, statutory exclusion, and demand waivers, will be distinguished. Judicial waivers, which are initiated by judges, may be discretionary, mandatory, or presumptive. Other types of waivers, such as direct file, are initiated by prosecutors. State legislatures have adopted statutory exclusion, in which the juvenile court is barred from hearing particular kinds of cases. In addition, juveniles may demand to have their cases heard and decided in criminal courts instead of juvenile courts.

The implications of waiver actions for juveniles will be described. Two favorable outcomes resulting from transfers to criminal court are that transferred or waived youth are entitled to a jury trial as a matter of right and that the full range of rights enjoyed by adult offenders are extended to transferred juveniles. The advantages and disadvantages of transfers for juveniles will be discussed, as will the different requirements for the amount of time permitted to process juvenile and adult cases.

The chapter will conclude by examining blended sentencing. In some jurisdictions, juvenile and criminal courts are using sentencing mechanisms that can be effective in sanctioning youth rather than using the transfer process. Blended sentencing statutes enable juvenile and criminal court judges to impose both juvenile and adult punishments simultaneously on selected juvenile offenders, depending upon the jurisdiction and its sentencing statutes. Variations of blended sentencing statutes will be described, and examples will be provided concerning how these proceedings may be applied.

Seriousness of the Offense and Waiver Decision Making

Seriousness of Juvenile Offending

Juveniles commit a small portion of all the violent crimes in the United States (Figure 8.1). In 2008, only 16 percent of all the arrests for violent crimes were offenders under the age of 18. The largest proportion of violent crime arrests of juveniles was for robbery (27 percent), followed by forcible rape (15 percent), aggravated assault (13 percent), and murder (10 percent) (Puzzanchera, 2009).

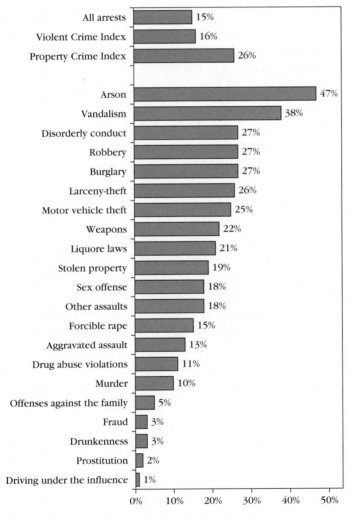

Figure 8.1

Percentage of Arrests Involving Persons Under Age 18, 2008
Source: OJJDP Statistics Briefing Book. *(Available at http://www .ojjdp.gov/ojstatbb/crime/qa05102.asp?qaDate=2008)*

In addition, very few youth in the overall adolescent population are arrested for violent crime. In 2008, the number of juvenile arrests for violent crimes was 96,000, which represents less than one percent of the total population of persons under the age of 18 (Puzzanchera, Adams, and Sickmund, 2010).

Investigations of the nature and seriousness of violent juvenile offending have been conducted by several researchers (Spano, Rivera, and Bolland, 2006). Some of the major causes of juvenile violence may be poor family relations, socioeconomically disadvantaged neighborhoods, poor school adjustments, peer pressure, greater availability of firearms, and greater dependence on alcohol or drugs (Mack et al., 2007).

Separating Status Offenders from Delinquent Offenders

One of the first steps taken to separate juveniles into different offending categories was the deinstitutionalization of status offenses (DSO). Also including divestiture, this major juvenile justice system reform was designed to remove the least-serious and noncriminal offenders from the juvenile courts in every jurisdiction.

Presumably and ideally, after DSO occurred, only juveniles who are charged with felonies and/or misdemeanors (i.e., delinquents) would be brought into the juvenile justice process and formally adjudicated in juvenile courts. These courts would also retain supervisory control over children in need of supervision, abused children, or neglected children. In reality, however, events have not turned out as legislators had originally anticipated or intended. Many status offenders continue to filter into the juvenile justice system in most jurisdictions (Feld, 2007).

When DSO occurred on a large scale throughout the United States during the late 1970s, several jurisdictions, including West Virginia, made policy decisions about how both nonserious and serious offenders would henceforth be treated by their juvenile justice systems. In West Virginia, for instance, the Supreme Court of Appeals ruled in 1977 that an adjudicated delinquent was constitutionally entitled to receive the least-restrictive alternative treatment consistent with his or her rehabilitative needs (*State ex rel. Harris v. Calendine,* 1977). While this decision did not eliminate institutionalizing more-serious or violent juveniles, it did encourage juvenile court judges to consider various alternatives to incarceration as punishments for youthful offenders. Related to DSO, the court also prohibited the commingling of adjudicated status offenders and adjudicated delinquent offenders in secure, prison-like facilities. Again, despite encouragement by the court for juvenile court judges first to attempt to apply nonincarcerative sanctions before imposing incarcerative penalties, the court did not necessarily rule out the secure confinement, long-term or otherwise, of status offenders as a possible sanction.

These mixed messages sent by the Supreme Court of Appeals of West Virginia did little, if anything, to restrict the discretionary powers of juvenile court judges. The court's emphasis on rehabilitation and alternative treatments to be considered by juvenile court judges reinforced the traditional concept of juvenile courts as rehabilitative rather than punitive sanctioning bodies. However, the court's ruling did lead to a substantial overhaul of the West Virginia juvenile code as well as a substantial drop in the incarcerated juvenile offender population in state-operated correctional facilities.

Juvenile Court Adjudications for Status Offenders

In many jurisdictions, DSO has reduced the volume of juvenile court cases over the years, but it has not prevented juvenile courts from continuing to adjudicate large numbers of status offenders annually. In 1995, an estimated 116,300 status offender cases were formally processed by juvenile courts. By 2008, the juvenile courts formally handled approximately 156,300 status offense cases. These recent data indicate an overall increase of 34 percent between 1995 and 2008. In terms of the rate of status offenders, in 2008, for every 1,000 youth in the population who were aged 10 or older and under the authority of a juvenile court, 5.1 status offense cases were formally processed (Puzzanchera, Adams, and Sickmund, 2011).

Proportionately, status offense cases processed formally by juvenile courts in 2006 comprised only 15 percent of the entire delinquency and status offense court caseload. In that year, juvenile courts formally processed approximately 27,000 runaway cases, 48,000 truancy cases, 26,500 ungovernability cases, 44,900 status liquor law violation cases, and 38,000 other miscellaneous status offense cases. Thus, truancy and liquor law violations were most often referred to juvenile courts for some type of action. About half of these referrals were made by police officers, and about 52 percent of all of these cases were adjudicated as status offenders (Office of Juvenile Justice and Delinquency Prevention, 2007). Among those status offense cases that were not adjudicated, 68 percent were dismissed, 22 percent resulted in informal sanctions other than probation or out-of-home placement (e.g., fines, community service, restitution, or referrals to other community agencies for services), 9 percent resulted in informal probation, and less than 1 percent resulted in placement. **Placement** refers to out-of-home placement, such as in a group home or foster care, and only rarely means secure confinement for status offenders in a state industrial school or reform school. Thus, juveniles who are subjected to these dispositional options are considered to be **placed**.

Formal adjudications become an official part of a juvenile's record. For offenders who are nonadjudicated, a formal decision is not rendered. Instead, an informal declaration is made by the judge to dispose of these cases with minimal intrusion into the families and lives of those affected by the court decision.

The Use of Contempt Power to Incarcerate Nondelinquent Youth

While most adjudicated status offenders are not sent to industrial schools or directed to alternative out-of-home placements, juvenile court judges wield considerable power to make status offenders comply with routine court directives. Truants may be ordered by the judge to attend school. Incorrigible youth may be ordered to obey their parents and remain law-abiding (Lee, 2008). Runaways may be ordered to

placement
One of several dispositions available to juvenile court judges following formal or informal proceedings involving juveniles in which either delinquent or status offenses have been alleged; adjudication proceedings yield a court decision about whether facts alleged in petition are true; if so, a disposition is imposed that may be placement in a foster or group home, wilderness experience, camp, ranch, or secure institution.

placed
Judicial disposition in which a juvenile is placed in the care and custody of a group or foster home or other type of out-of-home facility or program; also includes secure confinement in an industrial school or comparable facility.

participate in group counseling. Youth with alcohol or drug dependencies may be ordered to attend individual counseling and alcohol/drug education sessions on a regular basis. If certain status offenders fail to obey these judicial directives in any way, they are at risk of being cited for **contempt of court**. A contempt-of-court citation is a misdemeanor, and juvenile court judges can use their contempt power to incarcerate any status offenders who do not comply with their orders.

This judicial contempt power is unlimited, leading some observers to contend that the use of contempt power by juvenile court judges is an abuse of judicial discretion. This is because some juvenile court judges hold juveniles accountable for their actions and consider them like adults in terms of their understanding of the law. Contempt power also allows judges to circumvent and suspend procedural protections provided under state juvenile court acts. Furthermore, incarcerating status offenders as a punishment for contempt of court is inconsistent with legislative priorities. Thus, citing and incarcerating status offenders for contempt has created a dual system in which judges are free to uphold protective provisions of the Juvenile Justice and Delinquency Prevention Act or ignore them in favor of punishment by invoking contempt power. Therefore, status offenders are not fully insulated from incarceration as a punishment, despite the prevalence of DSO throughout the United States.

Delinquent Offenders and Juvenile Court Dispositions

Juvenile courts have made efforts to remove the majority of nonserious, nondelinquent cases and to target the resources of the juvenile justice system for youth charged with delinquent offenses or acts that would be criminal if adults committed them. In 2007, there were approximately 70.3 million youth in the United States under the age of 18. As illustrated in Figure 8.2, in that same year, juvenile courts in the United States processed about 1.7 million delinquency cases, representing about 2.4 percent of all youth (Puzzanchera, Adams, and Sickmund, 2010). Between 1960 and 1997,

contempt of court

A citation by a judge against anyone in court who disrupts the proceedings or does anything to interfere with judicial decrees or pronouncements.

Figure 8.2

Delinquency Cases Handled by Juvenile Courts, 1960–2007
Source: Charles Puzzanchera, Benjamin Adams, and Melissa Sickmund (2010). Juvenile Court Statistics 2006–2007. Pittsburgh, PA: National Center for Juvenile Justice. (Available at http://www.ncjj.org/PDF/jcsreports/jcs2007.pdf)

the number of cases increased by 360 percent, peaking at 1.86 million. From 1997 to 2007, the number of cases decreased by 11 percent (Figure 8.2).

About 56 percent of all cases processed in 2007 were handled formally, where a petition was filed requesting an adjudicatory hearing (Figure 8.3). Furthermore, about 63 percent of the formally processed cases resulted in delinquency adjudications. About half (56 percent) of all adjudicated cases received probation, and 19 percent received other sanctions. The remaining 25 percent of adjudicated delinquent cases received some form of placement. In 2007, juvenile courts waived jurisdiction to criminal courts in less than one percent of all formally handled cases (Puzzanchera, Adams, and Sickmund, 2010).

Between 1972 and 2006, interesting trends have occurred with respect to juveniles who have been arrested or taken into police custody. In 1972, for instance, about half of all juveniles taken into police custody (50.8 percent) were referred to juvenile courts, whereas 48 percent of these juveniles were handled by police and subsequently released. However, during the next 32 years, the percentage of referrals to juvenile court increased. By 2004, 65 percent of all juveniles taken into custody by police were referred to juvenile court, and only 18 percent were handled within police departments and released through stationhouse adjustments (Office of Juvenile Justice and Delinquency Prevention, 2007). The rest of the youth in police custody, including some status offenders, were referred to social service agencies for further processing.

Transfers, Waivers, and Certifications

In 2007, only 8,500 cases (less than one percent of all juvenile cases) were transferred from the jurisdiction of juvenile courts to the jurisdiction of criminal courts. By 2004,

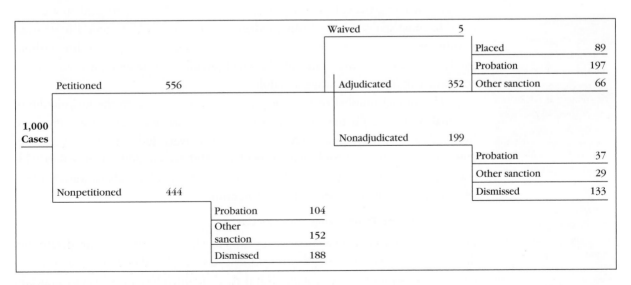

Figure 8.3
Juvenile Court Processing for Typical 1,000 Delinquency Cases, 2007
Source: OJJDP Statistical Briefing Book. (Available at http://ojjdp.gov/ojstatbb/court/JCSCF_Display.asp?ID=qa06601&year=2007&group=1&estimate=1)

48 state jurisdictions and the District of Columbia had statutes for juvenile court judges to waive jurisdiction over certain juveniles so that they could be transferred to criminal court. However, in 2007, all states had some type of mechanism in place so that specific juvenile offenders could be treated as adults for the purpose of a prosecution in criminal courts (Office of Juvenile Justice and Delinquency Prevention, 2007).

What Are Transfers?

Transfers refer to changing the jurisdiction of certain juvenile offenders to another jurisdiction, usually from juvenile court jurisdiction to criminal court jurisdiction. Transfers are also known as waivers, referring to a waiver or change of jurisdiction from the authority of juvenile court judges to criminal court judges (Haraway, 2008). Prosecutors or juvenile court judges decide that in some cases, juveniles should be waived or transferred to the jurisdiction of criminal courts. Presumably, those cases that are waived or transferred are the most-serious cases, involving violent or serious offenses, such as homicide, aggravated assault, rape, robbery, or drug dealing. These jurisdictions conduct transfer hearings (Kwak and Jeong, 2008).

In some jurisdictions, such as Texas and Utah, juveniles are waived or transferred to criminal courts through a process known as certification (Texas Youth Commission, 2005). A certification is a formal procedure whereby the state declares the juvenile to be an adult for the purpose of a criminal prosecution in a criminal court (McSherry, 2008). The results of certifications are the same as those for waivers or transfers. Thus, certifications, waivers, and transfers result in juvenile offenders being subject to the jurisdiction of criminal courts, where they are prosecuted as adult offenders. As a result, a 14-year-old armed robber, for instance, could be transferred to criminal court for a criminal prosecution on the charge. In criminal court, the juvenile, now being treated as an adult, can be convicted and sentenced to a prison term. In some states, criminal court judges have the option to impose **life without parole** sentences for certain convicted juvenile offenders. Imposing life without parole sentences is not within the jurisdiction of juvenile court judges. Their jurisdiction ends when an offender becomes an adult.

The annual number of juvenile cases which are waived to the jurisdiction of criminal courts has fluctuated. From 1985 to 1994, the number of cases increased from 7,200 to 13,100, an 81 percent increase in waivers. Judicial waivers peaked in 1994, with 13,100 cases, and then declined to 8,500 cases in 2007 (Figure 8.4). This is a 35 percent decrease in cases and illustrates that the trend in judicial waivers paralleled the trend in juvenile arrests for violent crime.

The Rationale for Transferring Juvenile Cases

Jurisdictional transfer is an alternative for cases in which the juvenile court determines that the offender is not amenable to treatment services, that the seriousness of the offense warrants more severe sanctions, and that the offender's prior record indicates that the court's resources have been exhausted. The basic rationale and expectation underlying the use of waivers is that the most serious juvenile offenders will be transferred to the jurisdiction of criminal courts, where harsher punishments are available

---

transfers, waivers

Proceedings where juveniles are remanded to the jurisdiction of criminal courts; also known as certifications and waivers.

transfer hearings

Proceedings to determine whether juveniles should be certified as adults for purposes of being subjected to jurisdiction of adult criminal courts, where more severe penalties may be imposed.

certification

Similar to waivers or transfers; in some jurisdictions, juveniles are certified or designated as adults for the purpose of pursuing a criminal prosecution against them.

life without parole

Penalty imposed as maximum punishment for youth convicted as adults in states; provides for permanent incarceration of offenders in prisons, typically without parole eligibility.

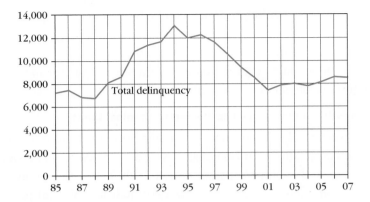

Figure 8.4
Number of Cases Judicially Waived to Criminal Court, 1985–2007
Source: Benjamin Adams and Sean Addie (2010). Delinquency Cases Waived to
Criminal Court, 2007. Washington, DC: Office of Juvenile Justice and Delinquency
Prevention. *(Available at http://www.ncjrs.gov/pdffiles1/ojjdp/230167.pdf.)*

and may be imposed (Brown, 2005). Because juvenile courts lack the judicial authority to impose sentences that continue into adulthood, the court may exercise this
authority to certify a juvenile as an adult for purposes of prosecution and let the adult
criminal court have jurisdiction to handle the case (Watts-Farmer, 2008). Some of the
reasons for waiver include:

1. To make it possible for harsher punishments to be imposed.

2. To provide just deserts and proportionately severe punishments for serious
   juvenile offenders who deserve such punishments.

3. To foster fairness and proportionality in administering punishments according
   to the seriousness of the offense.

4. To hold serious or violent offenders more accountable for what they have done.

5. To promote as a general deterrent to other juveniles that the system works and
   harsh punishments can be expected.

6. To provide a specific deterrent to decrease repeat juvenile offending.

7. To help youth realize the seriousness of their offending and to induce remorse
   and **acceptance of responsibility**.

Expected Characteristics of Offenders Transferred to Criminal Courts

Juvenile offenders designated for transfer or waiver generally demonstrate certain characteristics (McSherry, 2008). Age, offense seriousness, amenability to treatment, and
prior record (including previous referrals to juvenile court, intake proceedings and dispositions, or juvenile court delinquency adjudications) are important considerations.

Juvenile offenders who are classified as chronic, persistent, and violent are generally candidates for waiver review (Haraway, 2008). Youth who commit person offenses, such as rape, murder, robbery, and aggravated assault, can be reviewed for
prosecution in criminal court. Because of the therapeutic goals of the juvenile court

**acceptance of
responsibility**
Genuine admission or
acknowledgment of
wrongdoing; in federal
presentence
investigation reports,
for example, convicted
offenders may write an
explanation and
apology for the
crime(s) committed; a
provision that may be
considered in deciding
whether leniency
should be extended to
offenders during the
sentencing phase of
their processing.

and the emphasis on rehabilitation, treatment, and reform, less-serious property and drug offenders, a largely nonviolent class, are considered to be candidates for juvenile court processing. Based on this perspective, one would expect that most cases transferred to criminal court would be for person or violent offenses and the most serious and dangerous juvenile offenders (Brown, 2005).

Actual Characteristics of Offenders Transferred to Criminal Courts

Are the most serious juvenile cases the ones transferred to criminal courts for processing? In spite of this expectation, this has not always been the outcome. In 1985, property offense cases were the most frequently waived, with 3,800 cases, compared to 2,400 cases of person offenses (Figure 8.5). By 1994, judicial waiver of person offenses had peaked at 5,500 cases (42 percent of all waived cases), while 4,800 property offense cases were waived (37 percent of all judicially waived cases). Between 1994 and 2007, the number of waived person offense cases declined by 25 percent to 4,100 cases, which represented 48 percent of all the cases judicially waived to criminal court in that year (compared to 33 percent in 1985). In 2007, property offense cases represented 27 percent of the judicially waived cases (compared to 53 percent in 1985), and drug offenses represented 13 percent (compared to 5 percent in 1985). It should be noted that the increase in transfers of various drug crime cases in the early 1990s most likely corresponds to federal and state initiatives to prosecute drug offenders more aggressively and to impose more severe punishments.

Since the mid-1990s, when juvenile violent crime offending peaked, the trend in judicial waivers demonstrates that person offenses have become the most likely cases to be transferred by the juvenile court, but the data also indicate that about half of the judicial waiver cases are nonperson offense cases (e.g., property, drug, and public order). This suggests that juvenile court judges consider other variables in addition to the nature of the offense. The data in Figure 8.5, for example, do not reflect the prior record or amenability

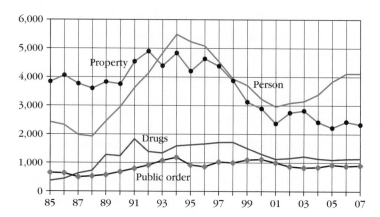

Figure 8.5
Delinquency Cases Judicially Waived to Criminal Court, 1985–2007
Source: Benjamin Adams and Sean Addie (2010). Delinquency Cases Waived to Criminal Court, 2007. Washington, DC: Office of Juvenile Justice and Delinquency Prevention. (Available at http://www.ncjrs.gov/pdffiles1/ojjdp/230167.pdf.)

to treatment. In the case of age, seven percent of the cases judicially waived to criminal court in 1985 were youth who were 15 years old or younger at the time of referral to juvenile court. This contrasts to 12 percent in 2007, which is a 71 percent increase in the number of cases waived for offenders aged 15 or younger. Nonetheless, the vast majority of juvenile waivers in 2007 (88 percent) included youth aged 16 or older. In their review of the data, Adams and Addie (2010) noted that "the offense profile and characteristics of cases judicially waived to criminal court have changed considerably" (p. 2).

In 2007, about 10 percent of all the cases judicially waived to criminal court represented female delinquents. This is still a small percent of cases, but it is also considerably more than the 5 percent in both 1985 and 1994. While person offense cases were more likely to be waived for male juvenile offenders, female delinquent cases were more likely to be waived for person and drug offenses. In 2007, cases involving "males were four times as likely to be judicially waived for person offenses as those involving females" (Adams and Addie, 2010, p. 3).

The comparison of black and white juvenile offender cases shows that judicial waivers increased between 1985 and 1994 for both races (Figure 8.6). After peaking in 1994 at 6,900 cases, the number of cases for white juveniles declined to 5,000 in 2007. For black juveniles, the number declined from 5,700 in 1994 to 3,200 in 2007. "For black juveniles waived to criminal court in 2007, person offense cases accounted for 63 percent of the waivers. In comparison, person offenses represented 40 percent of the waivers for white juveniles" (Puzzancherra, Adams, and Sickmund, 2010, p. 44).

In summary, trends in judicial waiver indicate:

■ The number of waived cases peaked in 1994 at 13,100 cases.

■ Between 1995 and 2007, the number of waived cases declined 43 percent, to 8,400.

■ Judicial waiver is most likely for person offense cases.

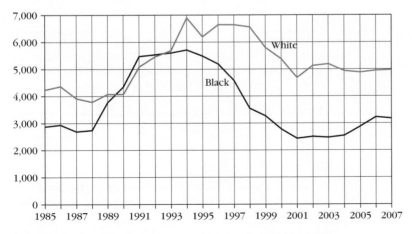

Figure 8.6
Number of Delinquency Cases Judicially Waived, by Race, 1985–2007
Source: Charles Puzzanchera, Benjamin Adams, and Melissa Sickmund (2010).
Juvenile Court Statistics 2006-2007. Pittsburgh, PA: National Center for Juvenile
Justice. (Available at http://www.ncjj.org/PDF/jcsreports/jcs2007.pdf.)

- Male juveniles are more likely to be waived than female juveniles.
- Older juveniles are more likely to be waived than younger juveniles.
- Black offenders are more likely to be waived for person offenses than white offenders.

It should be noted that the decline in the juvenile cases that are judicially waived may be a reflection of the increase in legislation passed by states to exclude certain juvenile offenders and juvenile offenses from juvenile court jurisdiction. This type of jurisdiction transfer is reviewed below.

Youngest Ages at Which Juveniles Can Be Transferred to Criminal Court

Table 8.1 shows the minimum age at which juveniles were eligible to be transferred or waived to criminal courts in 2008. In that year, 22 states had no specified age for transferring juveniles to criminal courts for processing. Two states, Kansas and Vermont, specified age 10 as the minimum age for transfer. Colorado, Missouri, and Montana established age 12 as the earliest age for juvenile waiver. Six states used age 13 and 16 states used age 14 as the minimum transfer age. The District of Columbia and New Mexico set the minimum transfer age at 15.

An indication of the get-tough response to juvenile crime in the 1990s is suggested by the information in Table 8.2, which shows how states have modified or enacted new transfer legislation provisions for juveniles. Under judicial waiver modifications, four states lowered the age for juveniles to be transferred to criminal court. One example of a significant age modification is Missouri, where the minimum age for juvenile transfers was lowered from 14 to 12 for any felony. Virginia lowered the

---

Table 8.1
MINIMUM AGE FOR TRANSFERRING JUVENILES TO ADULT COURT, 2008

Minimum Age	States
None	Alaska, Arizona, Delaware, Florida, Georgia, Hawaii, Idaho, Indiana, Maine, Maryland, Nebraska, Nevada, Oklahoma, Oregon, Pennsylvania, Rhode Island, South Carolina, South Dakota, Tennessee, Washington, West Virginia, and Wisconsin
10	Kansas and Vermont
12	Colorado, Missouri, and Montana
13	Illinois, Mississippi, New Hampshire, New York, North Carolina, and Wyoming
14	Alabama, Arkansas, California, Connecticut, Iowa, Kentucky, Louisiana, Massachusetts, Michigan, Minnesota, New Jersey, North Dakota, Ohio, Texas, Utah, and Virginia
15	District of Columbia and New Mexico

Source: Patrick Giffin (2008). *National Overviews. State Juvenile Justice Profiles.* Pittsburgh, PA: National Center for Juvenile Justice. (Available at http://www.ncjj.org/Research_Resources/State_Profiles.aspx.)

transfer age from 15 to 14. In addition, 10 states specified certain crimes that qualify youth for transfer to criminal courts. In six states, the age of criminal accountability was lowered, while 24 states authorized additional crimes to be included for automatic or direct file to criminal court jurisdiction.

Table 8.2

STATES MODIFYING OR ENACTING TRANSFER PROVISIONS, 2008

Type of Transfer Provision	Action Taken (Number of States)	States Making Changes	Examples
Discretionary waiver	Added crimes (7 states)	DE, KY, LA, MT, NV, RI, WA	Kentucky: 1996 provision permits the juvenile court to transfer a juvenile to crime court if 14 years old and charged with a felony with firearm.
	Lowered age limit (4 states)	CO, DE, HI, VA	Hawaii: 1997 provision adds language that allows waiver of a minor at any age (previously 16) if charged with first- or second-degree murder (or attempts) and there is no evidence that the person is committable to an institute for the mentally defective/mentally ill.
	Added or modified prior record provisions (4 states)	FL, HI, IN, KY	Florida: 1997 legislation requires that if the juvenile is 14 at the time of a fourth felony and certain conditions apply, the state's attorney must ask the court to transfer him or her and certify the child as an adult or must provide written reasons for not making such a request.
Presumptive waiver	Enacted provisions (2 states)	KS, UT	Kansas: 1996 legislation shifts the burden of proof to the child to rebut the presumption that the child is an adult.
Direct file	Enacted or modified (8 states)	AR, AZ, CO, FL, GA, MA, MT, OK	Colorado: 1996 legislation adds vehicular homicide, vehicular assault, and felonious arson to direct file statute.
Statutory exclusion	Enacted provision (2 states)	AZ, MA	Arizona: 1997 legislation establishes exclusion for 15- to 17-year-olds charged with certain violent felonies.
	Added crimes (12 states)	AL, AK, DE, GA, IL, IN, OK, OR, SC, SD, UT, WA	Georgia: 1997 legislation adds crime of battery if the victim is a teacher or other school personnel to list of designated felonies.
	Lowered age limit (1 state)	DE	Delaware: 1996 legislation lowers from 16 to 15 the age for which the offense of possession of a firearm during the commission of a felony is automatically prosecuted in criminal court.
	Added lesser-included offense (1 state)	IN	Indiana: 1997 legislation lists exclusion offenses, including any offense that may be joined with the listed offenses.

Source: Patricia Torbet and Linda Szymanski. (1998). *State Legislative Responses to Violent Juvenile Crime: 1996–1997 Update.* Washington, DC: U.S. Department of Justice, p. 5. Updated 2008 by authors.

Waiver Decision Making

Organizational and political factors can influence the use of transfers. In response to the increase in juvenile crime in the 1980s and 1990s, as noted above (see Figure 8.4), the use of judicial waivers also increased. In addition, legislatures took a get-tough approach to youthful offenders by enacting laws with more punitive sanctions that also made it easier to exclude youth from juvenile court by including more categories of crime. In spite of the political rhetoric regarding get-tough legislation, the use of judicial waivers has decreased since the mid-1990s, and the number of waivers has remained fairly constant in the 2000s (Adams and Addie, 2010).

In addition to judicial waiver, however, different types of waivers can be used to transfer jurisdiction of juveniles from juvenile to criminal courts (Zhang, 2008). One of these is automatic transfer or automatic waiver, which means that based on the age of the offender and the type of offense, the juvenile offender is automatically excluded and transferred to criminal courts. For example, offenders aged 15 or 16 who commit serious crimes, such as robbery, rape, and aggravated assault, or who use weapons to commit their crimes may qualify for exclusion or automatic transfer. This type of waiver, also known as legislative waiver, because it is mandated by legislative bodies, has statutory authority and essentially does not require discretionary action by prosecutors or judges. For other types of waivers, the decision-making process is more discretionary (Champion, 2008a).

The primary targets of waivers are intended to be the most-serious, violent, and dangerous juveniles who also may deserve more-serious sanctions that criminal courts can impose. As previously discussed, however, there may be differences between the types of juveniles who are actually transferred each year and those who are expected to be transferred. Because of the discretionary nature of some types of waiver, nonviolent

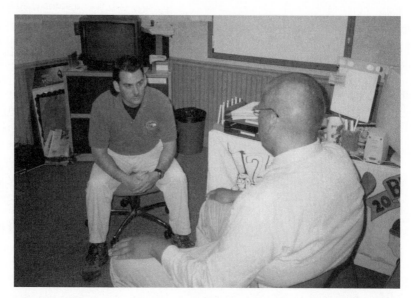

Informal conferences with youth often precede further juvenile court action.
(Courtesy of Dean John Champion)

juvenile offenders may be transferred to criminal courts. As noted above (see Figure 8.5), offenders who commit public order offenses (sometimes considered to be "victimless") or nonviolent drug offenses are transferred every year. In 1994, for instance, nearly half (45 percent) of all youth transferred to criminal court were charged with property or public order offenses. These offenses include theft, burglary, petty larceny, and disturbing the peace. Only 42 percent of those judicially transferred in 1994 were charged with person offenses or violent crimes. In 2007, about 25 percent of the judicially waived cases were drug or public order offenses. For some critics of juvenile justice policy, if transfers, waivers, or certifications were applied as they were designed, only serious, violent offenders would be transferred, and juvenile courts would handle the remaining cases (Haraway, 2008).

Why Do Property and Public Order Offenders Get Transferred to Criminal Court?

Why do juvenile courts send property offenders or public order offenders to criminal courts for processing? These are less-serious offenders compared with those committing aggravated assault, attempted murder, homicide, rape, and armed robbery. Studies of juvenile court judges disclose that persistent, nonserious offenders are transferred from juvenile courts because juvenile court judges determine that the court has exhausted its resources, as well as its patience, in working with these same offenders. They believe that if persistent offenders are sent to criminal court, this will be a better deterrent against future offending (McNeill and Batchelor, 2004).

Specific factors cited by juvenile court judges that result in the transfer of nonserious property, public order, or drug offenders to criminal court include:

1. Although property offenders are not especially serious or violent, their persistence in offending causes juvenile court judges to tire of their frequent appearances; transfers of these offenders to criminal court will "teach them a lesson."

2. Some jurisdictions mandate transfers to criminal court of those offenders who exceed some previously determined maximum of juvenile court adjudications; these may include property or public order offenders.

3. Individual differences among juvenile court judges dictate which juveniles are transferred, despite the seriousness of their offense; the offender's attitude, demeanor, and degree of remorse can influence judicial decisions.

4. Any kind of drug offense should be dealt with by criminal courts; thus, a simple "possession of a controlled substance" charge (e.g., prescription medicine) may be sufficient to qualify a juvenile for a criminal court transfer.

5. What is considered to be a serious or violent offense in one juvenile court jurisdiction may not be considered serious or violent in another jurisdiction; thus, different standards are applied to the same types of juveniles in different jurisdictions, sometimes referred to as justice by geography.

What sometimes happens, however, is that the criminal court prosecutors and judges tend to downplay the significance of these less-serious offenders. In some studies, at least half of the nonserious property offenders have their cases dismissed, diverted, or downgraded (Champion, 2005). Another 40 percent enter plea bargains and receive probation from criminal court judges. Criminal court judges do not necessarily want to put 14-year-old property offenders or public order offenders in adult institutions, where chronic overcrowding and the potential for sexual exploitation are pervasive. As a result, only a small number of nonserious offenders who are transferred annually are actually sentenced to confinement.

Thus, it is questionable whether waivers have functioned as effective deterrents to future juvenile offending (Haraway, 2008). Researchers have found that juveniles who are transferred to adult court generally return to crime more quickly, commit more offenses, and commit more-serious offenses than comparable youth who are handled in the juvenile court. In an early study in Florida, Bishop et al. (1996) found that reoffending was more prevalent among youth who were transferred to adult court. Flesch (2005) also found that adult court was inappropriate for youthful offenders, because it did not provide the level of rehabilitation services available in juvenile court. In his review of six major studies concerning the effects of transfer on crime and juveniles, Redding (2010) concluded that the evidence indicated transfer "substantially increases recidivism" compared with youth who are retained in the juvenile justice system (p. 6). These findings do not support the argument that transfer policies are an effective deterrent for juvenile offending.

Types of Waivers

There are four main categories of waiver actions: (1) judicial waivers, (2) direct file, (3) statutory exclusion or legislative waivers, and (4) demand waivers.

Judicial Waivers

The most recognized method of waiver from juvenile to criminal court is the result of direct judicial action. **Judicial waivers** give the juvenile court judge the authority to waive jurisdiction and transfer the case to criminal court. There are three kinds of judicial waivers: (1) discretionary, (2) mandatory, and (3) presumptive.

Discretionary waivers

Discretionary waivers empower a judge to waive jurisdiction over the juvenile offender and transfer the case to criminal court at their discretion. Thus, the judge may or may not decide to waive the youth to criminal court for processing (Champion, 2008a; Congressional Research Service, 2007). After assessing transfer criteria established in *Kent v. United States* (1966) and conducting a waiver hearing, the judge has the authority to determine whether to retain jurisdiction or waive the case.

In the *Kent* decision, the U.S. Supreme Court ruled that youth needed basic protections and due process, including representation by counsel. The Court also identified the criteria listed below to guide the court in evaluating appropriateness of waiver:

judicial waivers

Decision by juvenile judge to waive a juvenile to criminal court jurisdiction.

discretionary waivers

Transfer of juveniles to criminal courts by judges, at their discretion or in their judgment; also known as judicial waivers.

1. The seriousness of the alleged offense to the community and whether the protection of the community requires waiver.

2. Whether the alleged offense was committed in an aggressive, violent, premeditated, or willful manner.

3. Whether the alleged offense was against persons or against property, greater weight being given to offenses against persons, especially if personal injury resulted.

4. The prosecutive merit of the complaint, i.e., whether there is evidence upon which a Grand Jury may be expected to return an indictment (to be determined by consultation with the [prosecuting attorney]).

5. The desirability of trial and disposition of the entire offense in one court when the juvenile's associates in the alleged offense are adults who will be charged with a crime in [criminal court].

6. The sophistication and maturity of the juvenile as determined by consideration of his home, environmental situation, emotional attitude, and pattern of living.

7. The record and previous history of the juvenile, including previous contacts with [social service agencies], other law enforcement agencies, juvenile courts and other jurisdictions, prior periods of probation to [the court], or prior commitments to juvenile institutions.

8. The prospects for adequate protection of the public and the likelihood of reasonable rehabilitation of the juvenile (if he is found to have committed the alleged offense) by the use of procedures, services, and facilities currently available to the Juvenile Court (Snyder, Sickmund, and Poe-Yamagata, 2000, p. 3).

Mandatory waivers

In the case of **mandatory waiver**, the juvenile court judge *must* waive jurisdiction over the juvenile to criminal court if probable cause exists that the juvenile committed the alleged offense. Based on the evidence at arrest and the nature of the offense, if the judge determines that there is enough evidence to substantiate the charges, then the judge transfers the case to criminal court.

Presumptive waivers

Under the **presumptive waiver** scenario, judges still decide to transfer youth to criminal courts. However, the burden of proof concerning a transfer decision is shifted from the state to the juvenile. It requires that certain juveniles shall be waived to criminal court unless they can prove that they are suited for juvenile rehabilitation. In this respect, at least, they are similar to mandatory waivers. Defense counsel who wish to keep juvenile clients within the jurisdiction of the juvenile court have to convince the court that their clients deserve a juvenile court adjudicatory hearing rather than prosecution in criminal court.

Judicial waivers are often criticized because of their subjectivity, and the influence of extralegal factors in this important decision can generate a degree of unfairness and inequality. Appearance, demeanor, and attitude about the offense can emerge as significant factors that affect the judge's deliberation. These socioeconomic and

mandatory waiver
Automatic transfer of certain juveniles to criminal court usually on the basis of (1) their age and (2) the seriousness of their offense; e.g., a 17-year-old in Illinois who allegedly committed homicide would be subject to mandatory transfer to criminal court for the purpose of a criminal prosecution.

presumptive waiver
Requirement that shifts the burden to juveniles for defending against their transfer to criminal court by showing that they are capable of being rehabilitated.

behavioral criteria often overshadow the nature and seriousness of the alleged offenses. For example, two youth charged with identical offenses may appear at different times before the same judge. Yet, on the basis of impressions formed about the youth, the judge may decide to transfer one case to criminal court and adjudicate the other in juvenile court. Thus, in the context of this type of transfer, it is understandable how some persistent, nonviolent offenders may be waived to criminal court.

Direct File

When offenders are screened at intake and referred to the juvenile court for possible prosecution, prosecutors will conduct further screenings to determine which cases merit further action and formal adjudication by the court. Not all cases sent to prosecutors by intake officers automatically result in subsequent formal juvenile court action. Prosecutors may decline to prosecute certain cases, particularly if there are problems with witnesses (e.g., those who are missing or who refuse to testify), if there are evidentiary issues, or if the case can be handled without formal disposition. As noted, relatively few cases warrant waiver to criminal courts (Toth, 2005). Table 8.3 shows the states that had direct file or concurrent jurisdiction provisions in 2008.

With **direct file**, the prosecutor has the sole authority to decide whether a juvenile case will be heard in criminal court or juvenile court. Essentially, the prosecutor decides which court should have jurisdiction over the juvenile (Feld, 2007). Prosecutors in states with direct file power are said to have **concurrent jurisdiction**. This is another name for direct file. In Florida, for example, prosecutors have concurrent jurisdiction. They may file serious charges (e.g., murder, rape, aggravated assault, and robbery) against youth in criminal courts and present cases to grand juries for indictment, or they may elect to file the same cases in the juvenile court (D'Angelo and Brown, 2005). Prosecutor discretion is restricted by the age of the offender and the nature of the offense (Snyder, Sickmund, and Poe-Yamagata, 2000).

Statutory Exclusion

Statutory exclusion means that certain offenses are automatically excluded from the jurisdiction of juvenile courts by legislative enactment. In addition to seriousness of the offense, age of the offender is also part of the legislative exclusion. Thus, for example if a 17-year-old juvenile in Illinois is charged with murder, rape, or aggravated assault, the case is automatically excluded from the jurisdiction of the juvenile court and is mandated to criminal court. Minimum age criteria for 28 states with statutory exclusion provisions in the year 2008 are shown in Table 8.4.

Because state legislatures created statutory exclusion provisions, this waiver action is sometimes known as **legislative waiver**. And because these provisions mandate the waiver of juveniles to criminal court, it is also known as automatic waiver.

Demand Waivers

Under certain conditions and in some jurisdictions, juveniles may submit motions for demand waiver actions. **Demand waiver** actions are requests or motions filed by

Table 8.3

MINIMUM AGE CRITERIA IN STATES WITH CONCURRENT JURISDICTION AND DIRECT FILE PROVISIONS, BY OFFENSE, 2008

States	Minimum Age for Concurrent Jurisdiction[a]	Any Criminal Offense	Certain Felonies	Capital Crimes	Murder	Certain Offenses			
						Person Offenses	Property Offenses	Drug Offenses	Weapon Offenses
Arizona[b]	14		14						
Arkansas	14		14	14	14	14			14
Colorado	14		14		14	14	14		14
District of Columbia	16				16	16	16		
Florida[c]	NS[d]	16[e]	16	NS[f]	14	14	14		14
Georgia	NS			NS					
Louisiana	15				15	15	15	15	
Massachusetts	14		14			14			14
Michigan	14		14		14	14	14	14	
Montana	12				12	12	16	16	16
Nebraska	NS	16[g]	NS						
Oklahoma	15				15	15	15	16	16
Vermont	16	16							
Virginia	14				14	14			
Wyoming	14	17	14						

[a]Ages in the minimum age column may not apply to all offense restrictions but represent the youngest possible age at which a juvenile's case may be filed directly in criminal court.

[b]In Arizona, prosecutors have discretion to file directly in criminal court those cases involving juveniles aged 14 or older charged with certain felonies (defined in state statutes).

[c]In Florida, prosecutors may "direct file" cases involving juveniles aged 16 or older charged with a misdemeanor (if they have a prior adjudication) or a felony offense and those aged 14 or older charged with murder or certain person, property, or weapon offenses; no minimum age is specified for cases in which a grand jury indicts a juvenile for a capital offense.

[d]NS indicates that in at least one of the offense restrictions indicated, no minimum age is specified.

[e]Applies to misdemeanors and requires prior adjudication(s), which may be required to have been for the same or a more-serious offense type.

[f]Requires grand jury indictment.

[g]Applies to misdemeanors.

Source: Adapted from Howard N. Snyder and Melissa Sickmund. (1999). *Juvenile Offenders and Victims: 1999 National Report.* Pittsburgh, PA: National Center for Juvenile Justice. Updated 2008 by authors.

juveniles and their attorneys to have their cases transferred from juvenile courts to criminal courts.

Why would juveniles want to have their cases transferred to criminal courts? One reason is that most U.S. jurisdictions do not provide jury trials in juvenile courts as a matter of right (*McKeiver v. Pennsylvania,* 1971). Only about one-fifth of the states have established provisions for jury trials for juveniles at their request and

Table 8.4
MINIMUM AGE CRITERIA IN STATES WITH STATUTORY EXCLUSION, BY OFFENSE, 2008

States	Minimum Age for Concurrent Jurisdiction[a]	Any Criminal Offense	Certain Felonies	Capital Crimes	Murder	Person Offenses	Property Offenses	Drug Offenses	Weapon Offenses
Alabama	16		16	16				16	
Alaska	16					16	16		
Arizona[b]	15		15[c]		15	15			
Delaware[d]	15		15						
Florida	NS[e]	NS[f]				NS			
Georgia	13				13	13			
Idaho	14				14	14	14	14	
Illinois	13		15[g]		13	15		15	15
Indiana	16		16		16	16		16	16
Iowa	16		16					16	16
Louisiana	15				15	15			
Maryland	14			14	16	16			16
Massachusetts	14				14				
Minnesota	16				16				
Mississippi	13		13	13					
Montana	17				17	17	17	17	17
Nevada	NS	NS[c]			NS	16[c]			
New Mexico	15				15[g]				
New York	13				13	14	14		
Oklahoma	13				13				
Oregon	15				15	15			
Pennsylvania	NS				NS	15			
South Carolina	16		16						

Table 8.4 CONTINUED

States	Minimum Age for Concurrent Jurisdiction[a]	Any Criminal Offense	Certain Felonies	Capital Crimes	Murder	Certain Offenses			
						Person Offenses	Property Offenses	Drug Offenses	Weapon Offenses
South Dakota	16		16						
Utah	16		16[h]	16					
Vermont	14				14	14	14		
Washington	16				16	16	16		
Wisconsin	NS				10	NS[i]			

[a]Ages in the minimum age column may not apply to all offense restrictions but represent the youngest possible age at which a juvenile's case may be excluded from juvenile court.

[b]In Arizona, juveniles aged 15 or older must be tried in criminal court if they are charged with murder or certain person offenses or if they have prior felony adjudications and are charged with a felony.

[c]Requires prior adjudication(s), or conviction(s), which may be required to have been for the same or a more serious offense type.

[d]In Delaware, juveniles aged 15 or older charged with certain felonies must be tried in criminal court.

[e]NS indicates that in at least one of the offense restrictions indicated, no minimum age is specified.

[f]Only if escape or bail violation while subject to prosecution in criminal court.

[g]Requires grand jury indictment.

[h]Requires prior commitment in a secure facility.

[i]Only if charged while confined or on probation or parole.

Source: Adapted from Howard N. Snyder and Melissa Sickmund. (1999). *Juvenile Offenders and Victims: 1999 National Report.* Pittsburgh, PA: National Center for Juvenile Justice. Updated 2008 by authors.

depending upon the nature of the charges against them. In the remaining states, jury trials for juveniles are granted only at the discretion of the juvenile court judge, and most juvenile court judges are not inclined to grant jury trials to juveniles. Thus, if juveniles are (1) in a jurisdiction where they are not entitled to a jury trial even if they request one from the juvenile court judge, (2) face serious charges, and (3) believe that their cases would receive greater impartiality from a jury in a criminal courtroom, they may seek a demand waiver to have their cases transferred to criminal court.

Other Types of Waivers

Other types of waivers are (1) reverse waivers and (2) the once an adult/always an adult provision.

Reverse Waivers

A **reverse waiver** is an action by the criminal court to transfer a direct file or statutory exclusion case from criminal court back to juvenile court, usually at the recommendation of the prosecutor. Typically, juvenile offenders involved in reverse waiver hearings

reverse waiver

Motion to transfer a juvenile's case from criminal court to juvenile court following a legislative or automatic waiver action.

would be those who were automatically sent to criminal court because of statutory exclusion. After review of the case, criminal court judges can determine that criminal court is not appropriate and change the jurisdiction to juvenile court. Reverse waiver may also be initiated by defense counsel on behalf of juvenile clients.

Once an Adult/Always an Adult

The **once an adult/always an adult provision** is a serious and long-lasting consequence for juvenile offenders who are waived to criminal court. This provision requires that once juveniles have been convicted in criminal court, they are henceforth considered to be adults for the purpose of criminal prosecutions. Even if an offender is under the age of majority (e.g., 16), the youth, for purposes of the court, is an adult, and the case will be excluded from juvenile court. For example, a 12-year-old offender

Focus on Delinquency

It happened in Leonardtown, Maryland. Corey Ryder, a 17-year-old youth accused of attempting to murder his parents, stood before a criminal court judge at a hearing. Ryder had been arrested following his attempt to hire an undercover police officer to kill his parents. The undercover officer asked Ryder how he (Ryder) wanted the killing to be done. Ryder said in the tape-recorded conversation, "Two bullets is all it takes." Given Ryder's age, and under Maryland's statutory exclusion rules for juvenile offenders, Ryder was arrested, charged as an adult, and sent to criminal court. Ryder's defense counsel, public defender John Getz, asked the criminal court judge, Karen Abrams, to allow Ryder to be tried as a juvenile in juvenile court. A hearing followed to determine whether Ryder ought to be tried in juvenile court rather than in a criminal court.

Several state witnesses were called to testify that Ryder would benefit from state treatment for juveniles, which he would be denied if convicted of the crime in criminal court. Other witnesses testified about alleged abuse suffered by Ryder at the hands of his parents that led to his anger against them. Ryder had earlier moved out of his parent's home and had issues with parental authority. Another witness was Tara Klysz, Ryder's probation officer. Klysz said that Ryder had a long history of juvenile offending, including property destruction, drug abuse, and poor school behavior.

Countering the defense was Ryder's mother, who testified that her son had threatened to cut her throat and that she had discovered a large knife hidden in his room. She told the court she feared for her life. Another contrary testimony revealed that Ryder had been in several previous treatment programs and had failed to make visible progress in any of them. One electronic monitoring program appeared to have been successful when Ryder was obligated to attend school and conform to school rules. However, as soon as he was free of the electronic monitoring program, his bad behavior returned.

Judge Abrams considered the juvenile court option, eventually opting to send Ryder's case to juvenile court for processing. She justified her action by saying that there was something obviously wrong with Ryder and that prison was not the answer. She said that the juvenile court had the power to order psychiatric evaluations and furnish Ryder with needed services not otherwise provided for adult offenders. She advised Ryder in open court to take advantage of the treatment opportunities from the state and to learn to deal with the anger issues that caused him to commit the alleged offense in the first place. Probation Officer Klysz agreed with Judge Abrams that treatment would benefit Ryder more than imprisonment. Ryder's mother, however, was visibly shaken by Judge Abrams' decision. She was upset over the prospect that in the juvenile justice system, Ryder would be released on his 21st birthday, only four short years away. She asked, "How do I live? How does my family live?" The mother continued to fear for her life at the hands of her son, and she had no faith that any juvenile treatment program would improve him.

Should Ryder's case have been returned to juvenile court? Or should Ryder have been tried as an adult, considering his past failure record with so many interventions? What do you think?

Source: Adapted from Guy Leonard (2007, September 21), "Teen's Attempted Murder Trial Will Move to Juvenile Court," *Southern Maryland Online* (available at http://somd.com/news/headlines/2007/6441.shtml.)

is transferred to criminal court in Vermont and subsequently convicted of a crime. At age 15, if the same juvenile commits another crime, such as vehicular theft, he or she would be subject to prosecution in criminal court. Thus, a criminal court conviction means that the juvenile permanently loses access to the juvenile court. In a state without this provision, such as North Carolina in 2008, a juvenile was referred to family court until age 17, even if the youth had a criminal conviction. In 2008, 31 states had once an adult/always an adult provisions (Table 8.5).

State Variations in Waiver Use

Judicial waiver is the most popular type of waiver, and 46 states and the District of Columbia had this provision in 2008. Over half of all states (28) had statutory exclusion provisions in 2008. Reverse waivers, which are a response to automatic or legislative waivers, were used in 23 states in 2008. In addition, 31 states had enacted the once an adult/always an adult provision. Fifteen states had concurrent jurisdiction or direct file provisions in 2008. States have access to combinations of waiver provisions, and the most common is judicial waiver and statutory exclusion, used by 18 states in 2008. A summary of the juvenile transfer provisions for all states for 2008 is shown in Table 8.5.

Waiver and Reverse Waiver Hearings

Although judges have discretionary power in most jurisdictions, youth are still entitled to a hearing where they can present their case against waiver. While it is true that conviction in criminal court poses risks to juveniles in terms of potentially harsher penalties, it is also true that being tried as an adult entitles youth to the adult constitutional safeguards, including the right to a trial by jury. As a result, some juveniles may prefer waiver or transfer because they would be eligible for bail and may be treated more leniently by criminal courts.

Waiver Hearings

Juveniles who are waived to criminal court for processing are entitled to a hearing on the waiver if they request one (Massachusetts Statistical Analysis Center, 2001). A **waiver hearing** is a formal proceeding designed to determine whether the waiver action taken by the judge or prosecutor is the correct action and the juvenile should be transferred to criminal court. Many waiver hearings are preceded by a petition for a waiver of jurisdiction. The petition form used in Maine is illustrated in Figure 8.7. Waiver hearings are normally conducted before the juvenile court judge. These hearings are initiated through a **waiver motion**, in which the prosecutor usually requests the judge to send the case to criminal court. Following a petition for a waiver of jurisdiction, a notice of a hearing on such a waiver petition is issued.

Such hearings are to some extent evidentiary, because a case must be made for why criminal courts should have jurisdiction in any specific instance. As previously discussed, if waivers are to be used effectively, the most-serious offenders should

once an adult/always an adult provision
Legislation stipulating that once a juvenile has been transferred to criminal court to be prosecuted as an adult, that juvenile, regardless of the criminal court outcome, can never be subject to the jurisdiction of juvenile courts in the future; in short, the juvenile, once transferred, will always be treated as an adult if future crimes are committed, even though the youth is still not of adult age.

waiver hearing
Formal juvenile court processes usually requested by prosecutor to transfer juveniles charged with various offenses to a criminal or adult court for prosecution.

waiver motion
Formal request by prosecutor to juvenile court judge asking to transfer a juvenile's case from juvenile court to criminal court.

Table 8.5
JUVENILE TRANSFER PROVISIONS FOR ALL STATES, 2008

| State | Judicial Waiver | | | Concurrent Jurisdiction | Statutory Exclusion | Reverse Waiver | Once an Adult/Always an Adult |
	Discretionary	Presumptive	Mandatory				
Total Number of States	45	15	14	15	28	23	31
Alabama	•				•		•
Alaska	•	•			•		
Arizona	•			•	•	•	•
Arkansas	•			•		•	
California	•	•					•
Colorado	•	•		•		•	
Connecticut			•			•	
Delaware	•		•		•	•	•
District of Columbia	•	•		•			•
Florida	•			•	•		•
Georgia	•		•	•	•	•	
Hawaii	•						•
Idaho	•				•		•
Illinois	•	•	•		•		
Indiana	•		•		•		•
Iowa	•				•	•	•
Kansas	•	•					•
Kentucky	•		•			•	
Louisiana	•		•	•	•		
Maine	•						•
Maryland	•				•	•	
Massachusetts				•	•		
Michigan	•			•			•
Minnesota	•	•			•		•
Mississippi	•				•	•	•
Missouri	•						•
Montana				•	•		
Nebraska		•		•		•	

Table 8.5 CONTINUED

State	Judicial Waiver			Concurrent Jurisdiction	Statutory Exclusion	Reverse Waiver	Once an Adult/Always an Adult
	Discretionary	Presumptive	Mandatory				
Nevada	•	•			•	•	•
New Hampshire	•	•					•
New Jersey	•	•					
New Mexico					•		
New York					•	•	
North Carolina	•			•			
North Dakota	•	•		•			•
Ohio	•			•			•
Oklahoma	•			•	•	•	•
Oregon	•				•	•	•
Pennsylvania	•	•			•	•	•
Rhode Island	•	•		•			•
South Carolina	•			•	•	•	
South Dakota	•				•	•	•
Tennessee	•					•	•
Texas	•						•
Utah	•	•			•		•
Vermont	•			•	•	•	
Virginia	•			•	•	•	•
Washington	•				•		•
West Virginia	•			•			
Wisconsin	•				•	•	•
Wyoming	•			•		•	

[a]In states with a combination of transfer mechanisms, the exclusion, mandatory waiver, or concurrent jurisdiction provisions generally target the oldest juveniles and/or those charged with the most-serious offenses, while those charged with relatively less-serious offenses and/or younger juveniles may be eligible for discretionary waiver.

Source: Adapted from Howard N. Snyder and Melissa Sickmund. (1999). *Juvenile Offenders and Victims: 1999 National Report.* Pittsburgh, PA: National Center for Juvenile Justice. Updated 2008 by authors.

generally be targeted for transfer. Transferring less-serious and petty offenders accomplishes little in the way of enhanced punishments. Following a transfer or waiver hearing, the juvenile court judge either grants or denies the order to waive juvenile court jurisdiction over the juvenile. An order waiving juvenile court jurisdiction is shown in

STATE OF MAINE, CIRCUIT COURT _____ COUNTY

In the interest of: PETITION FOR WAIVER OF
                                                             JURISDICTION

_____
Name

                                                             Case #_____
_____
Date of Birth

1. It is requested that the court waive the juvenile to adult court.
2. I am the: ☐ prosecuting attorney   ☐ juvenile   ☐ judge
3. This petition is filed:

before the plea hearing
before adjudication, juvenile is 16 years of age or older, and denies charges

4. This request is based on the following allegation(s):

☐ Aggravated assault
☐ Felony murder
☐ Rape/forcible/statutory
☐ Armed robbery/robbery
☐ Distribution/possession of controlled substances
☐ Other: Describe_____

5. On or before the juvenile's 15th birthday, it is alleged the juvenile committed the following crime(s):
Crime   **Definition**   **Statute**

6. The facts supporting this waiver include the following:

_____
_____
_____

_____
Signature of petitioner

_____
Name (typed or printed)

_____
Date

Figure 8.7
Petition for Waiver of Jurisdiction
Source: Authors.

Figure 8.8. Once such an order has been issued, the juvenile is transferred to the jurisdiction of the criminal court. The order may be contested or appealed, but this matter must be taken up with a criminal court judge, who now has jurisdiction over the case and makes a determination if an appeal opposing the waiver has been filed.

In comparison to adult offenders, some juvenile cases that are waived to criminal courts appear minor, and it is not uncommon to see the use of probation or

---

STATE OF MICHIGAN, CIRCUIT COURT _____ COUNTY

IN THE INTEREST OF: Order Waiving Juvenile
                                                     Court Jurisdiction

_____

Name

_____

Date of Birth   Case # _____

The waiver was held on: _____which is the effective date of this order.

The court holds:

1. Petition alleging delinquency and waiver petition were filed.
2. Case has prosecutive merit.
3. Waiver petition is uncontested.
4. Juvenile was represented by an attorney, if required.
5. The court has reviewed the record of all factors indicated below in determining its action and why the juvenile was waived:

Prior Record and Personality Factors
☐ Was the juvenile developmentally or mentally disabled?
☐ Was the juvenile found delinquent on prior occasions?
☒ Did the juvenile inflict serious bodily injury to one or more victims?
☐ What were the juvenile's motives, attitude, and living pattern?
☐ What is the physical and mental maturity of the juvenile?
☐ What is the juvenile's prior treatment history, medical or otherwise?
☐ What were the juvenile's living conditions prior to the delinquent act?
☐ What is the juvenile's potential for responding to future treatment?
☐ Other: _____

Seriousness of offense
☐ Crime against persons/property
☐ Crime was violent in nature, aggravated, willful, premeditated

Adequacy of Juvenile System Facilities
☐ Nature of services available, including medical and psychiatric staff
☐ Suitability of placement of juvenile among others which will minimize risk
☐ Suitability of juvenile for placement in treatment/counseling program

It is so ordered:
☐ **The waiver petition is granted**
☐ **The waiver petition is denied**

_____

Signature of Judge   Date

Figure 8.8
Order Waiving Juvenile Court Jurisdiction
Source: Authors

diversion. Criminal court prosecutors may ***nolle prosequi*** cases before they reach the trial stage. These are cases in which the prosecutor may not have sufficient evidence or decides that the case would be better handled through some agency other than the criminal court.

nolle prosequi
Decision by prosecutor to decline to pursue criminal case against defendant.

reverse waiver hearings, reverse waiver actions

Formal proceedings to contest automatic transfer of juveniles to jurisdiction of criminal courts; used in jurisdictions with direct file or automatic transfer laws.

Reverse Waiver Hearings

In those jurisdictions with direct file or statutory exclusion provisions, juveniles and their attorneys may contest the waiver actions through **reverse waiver hearings** or **reverse waiver actions**, which are conducted before criminal court judges to determine whether to send the case back to juvenile court. As with waiver hearings, defense counsel and the prosecution attempt to make a case for their desired action. In many respects, both types of these hearings are similar to preliminary hearings or preliminary examinations conducted within the criminal justice framework. Some evidence and testimony are permitted, and arguments for both sides are heard. Once all arguments have been presented and each side has had a chance to rebut the opponents' arguments, the judge decides the matter.

Time Standards Governing Waiver Decisions

"[A]s of 1993 only a few states had time limits governing transfer provisions for juveniles" (Butts, 1996b, p. 559). In Michigan, for example, a motion for traditional waiver is required within 14 days after a petition has been filed (Michigan Judicial Institute, 2010). The motion must be personally served to the juvenile and/or his or her parents or guardians. Unless there is good reason for a delay, the juvenile is not subject to waiver if the transfer motion has not been filed in the required time. After the transfer motion is filed, the court has 28 days to begin the waiver hearing. If the motion to transfer is denied, the court has 28 days to begin the trial, or the juvenile will be released (unless other charges are pending). The purpose of the time requirements is to keep the proceedings moving so the juvenile is not detained indefinitely.

Implications of Waiver Hearings for Juveniles

Juveniles who contest their transfers to criminal court or attempt to obtain a reverse waiver are requesting to be treated as juveniles and be adjudicated in juvenile court. Not all juveniles who are the subject of transfer, however, seek to contest the transfer. There are implications for youth, depending upon the nature of their offenses, their prior records, and the potential penalties that the respective courts could impose. Under some circumstances, having a case transferred to criminal court may offer juvenile defendants advantages not routinely available if their cases were to remain in the juvenile court. In the following discussion, some of the advantages and disadvantages of being transferred will be examined.

Benefits of Juvenile Court Adjudications

Some considered benefits of having a case heard in juvenile court include:

1. Juvenile court proceedings are civil, not criminal. Thus, juveniles do not acquire criminal records.

2. Juveniles are less likely to be incarcerated.

3. Compared with criminal court judges, juvenile court judges have considerably more discretion in how to respond to youthful offenders.

4. Juvenile courts are traditionally more lenient than criminal courts.

5. Public understanding and greater tolerance is extended to offenders, especially nonviolent offenders, who are processed in the juvenile justice system.

6. Historically juvenile courts, unlike criminal courts, have not maintained an information exchange with other jurisdictions.

7. Life imprisonment is generally beyond the jurisdiction of juvenile judges, and dispositions are restricted by statutory age limits (except in cases of blended sentences, which will be discussed below).

Because juvenile courts are civil bodies, records of juvenile adjudications can be suppressed or expunged when adjudicated juveniles reach adulthood. Juvenile court judges also often act compassionately, such as by sentencing youthful offenders to probation, by issuing verbal warnings or reprimands, or by imposing nonincarcerative, nonfine alternatives as sanctions.

Another advantage is that juvenile courts are traditionally noted for their lenient treatment of juveniles. This may reflect the focus on the individual juvenile offender rather than on the type offense, which may result in imposition of prevailing punishments and penalties. For example, a national conference of juvenile justice researchers in New Orleans, Louisiana, recommended that juvenile courts should emphasize three general goals in their adjudication decisions: (1) protection of the community, (2) imposing accountability, and (3) helping juveniles and equipping them to live productively and responsibly in the community (Maloney, Romig, and Armstrong, 1988). This balanced approach to juvenile offenders is more constructive, because it recognizes the rehabilitative potential of youthful offenders. Surveys reveal that the public supports rehabilitation programs for youth and recognizes that prevention and treatment are effective with many juvenile offenders (Cullen, 2006; Nagin et al., 2006). Residential placement facilities are more likely to be used, especially in cases for juveniles who have relatively lower risk for failure compared with offenders with more extensive histories of delinquent conduct (Trulson and Haerle, 2008).

Tolerance or understanding of youth who commit offenses is more likely in juvenile court, which considers that juveniles often get into trouble because of social and economic circumstances. Individualized treatment may be preferable and include appropriate community-based facilities. In addition to holding youth accountable with less punitive dispositions, this also has the potential to promote greater respect for the law and to provide social services. Mandatory diversion policies have received some public support in various jurisdictions, especially where less-serious youthful offenders are involved. Not all juveniles require intensive supervision or incarceration but, rather, benefit from responsible supervision to guide them toward and assist them in various services and treatments (Dembo, Turner, and Jainchill, 2007).

Juvenile courts do not ordinarily exchange information with other juvenile courts in a coordinated national communication network. Local control over youthful

CAREER SNAPSHOT

(Courtesy of Dean John Champion)

Name: Michael D. Downey
Position: District Supervisor, Community Services Division, Minnesota Department of Corrections; past President, Minnesota Corrections Association

Colleges Attended: St. Cloud State University

Degrees: B.A. in Criminal Justice studies, graduate work in psychology

Background

Looking back at the past 36 years I have been in this field, corrections was actually my second career. While in my early years of college, I had a serious motorcycle accident. During this time, I came into contact with many medical and human services professionals. I admired their caring and warm spirit. Those experiences caused me to rethink my career plans. Eventually, I read an ad seeking college-trained individuals who would dedicate at least one to two years to be trained and serve as volunteer juvenile probation officers for Hennepin County, Minnesota. I was interviewed, accepted, and underwent extensive training to prepare predispositional investigations and make sentencing recommendations to the juvenile court. This was the beginning of what I have found to be a very interesting and fulfilling career path.

Work Experience

My first position in corrections was as a Volunteer Probation Officer for Hennepin County. I was assigned to a unit of staff covering the southern region of Minneapolis. Offense severity varied greatly with the youth, from possession of marijuana by a first-time offender to a 15-year-old young man awaiting sentencing for his fifth felony-level burglary who was known to every police officer in his south Minneapolis precinct. With this experience, I applied for a job as correctional counselor trainee with the Minnesota Department of Corrections at their prison in St. Cloud. That job was a truly interesting experience and involved very extensive training, including college classes and on-the-job training in every aspect of prison operations. While there, I worked in the prison reception unit. The prison held male offenders ages 18–25 but also juveniles who were certified to stand trial as adults. The youngest juvenile in the unit got a .45-caliber pistol as a present from his girlfriend for his 15th birthday, then shot and killed a grocery clerk after robbing the store. It was while working at the prison that I changed my college major and entered criminal justice, working the midnight shift and then attending college classes during the day. Being involved in academics by day and working nights

in the prison were amazing learning experiences. I was able to work briefly, out of class, as a case manager, then called a corrections agent. I met corrections agents in our field services unit who worked in the communities and cites throughout Minnesota, and I tried to get a job in that area.

My first experience was as a probation officer in a small, two-county department in central Minnesota. My caseload consisted of adult offenders and those juvenile offenders who were certified as adults. I started with a caseload of 35 in two counties. I worked in that county-managed department for 10 years, eventually leaving with a caseload of over 125 felony-level offenders. After 10 years of service, an opportunity developed, again with the Minnesota Department of Corrections.

I started as a corrections agent supervising an adult felony caseload, covering six counties, out of an office in Morris in late 1986. In the summer of 1988, I took what would be my last field agent job in Alexandria, supervising a caseload in only one county. This experience was an excellent one in that the county criminal justice system was one of the best networks I have ever worked in. I worked closely and partnered with juvenile probation officers on a regular basis. All partners in the county criminal justice systems worked very well together in providing excellent service to the community and making everyone safer. In the fall of 1993, a District Supervisor vacancy occurred in southeast Minnesota, and I was encouraged to apply.

In December 1993, I was promoted as District Supervisor of the Albert District for the state department of corrections. The district included offices throughout the region bordering Wisconsin to the east and Iowa to the south. It currently consists of eight offices in six counties, with 32 staff members under my supervision. They are comprised of adult and juvenile corrections agents, Sentencing-to-Service Crew Leaders, and professional support staff. Currently 1,760 adults and 140 juveniles are under my supervision in that region. Supervising our Sentencing-to-Service Crew Leaders is a very unique part of my job. This program is an opportunity for juvenile and adult offenders to be under close supervision while working on projects for the public good and meeting the conditions of their supervision.

Experiences

I have had the good fortune of working with some of the best professionals in the Minnesota corrections field over the past 36 years. Statewide associations have been many in the areas of planning, training, and career development. I have had the privilege of serving as the President of the Minnesota Correction Association and continue to serve on a program committee that sets the topics and training for our Annual Training Institute that has attracted over 1,000 colleagues in past years. My current affiliations enable me to utilize restorative justice practices in corrections throughout the state. I also represent our department on the Department of Human Services Problem Gambling Advisory

Committee that works on the awareness and prevention of problem gambling. I continue to encourage staff members to get involved in similar projects that take them out of day-to-day probation work in the hopes these activities enhance their careers and take them into larger realms of our business.

Working in the field of corrections can be very rewarding at times and also frustrating, but it is always interesting. With each new offender/client, we have the opportunity to make their lives richer and rewarding by working with case plans that meet their individual needs. Working with juveniles and their families is especially rewarding because of the opportunities we provide. With those many opportunities come many accounts of challenging and rewarding experiences. In one of my first cases, I was directed to do a predispositional investigation on a 15-year-old boy adjudicated for his fifth burglary conviction. When I first met with him, he disclosed that he had a stomach ulcer. He was truly conflicted by the young criminal life he was living. I worked with him closely through sentencing, and then the case was transferred to a field supervision officer. I lost track of him. While attending a wedding reception many months later, I met the boy's mother, who was working as a waitress, and she remembered me. She thanked me for all of my time spent with her son and the concern I had for him. She said he had turned his life around in many areas.

Although rewarding, our positions can be, at times, physically and emotionally challenging. I had a young adult under supervision for making threats of violence to family members, generally while intoxicated. The first months of supervision did not go well as he challenged my authority at every meeting. I had concerns that he may be still abusing alcohol. On a very cold February Sunday evening, I received a call from the local sheriff's department that the offender was again making threats of violence to neighboring family members and may be intoxicated. Assistance was requested, and two deputies accompanied me to the offender's residence. After knocking on the door, we announced our presence and that we were coming in. The offender was just inside the door and passed out in a reclining chair. As we looked behind us, there was a shotgun hanging above the door we had just entered. I asked one of the deputies to see if it was loaded. It was. We were three very lucky people that cold winter evening. The good ending to that story is that after his arrest, detention, and a court violation hearing, the offender entered in-patient alcohol rehabilitation and remained sober until his eventual discharge from supervision several years later.

Advice to Students

The most successful probation officers have some common qualities. They approach the job realizing their daily challenges will have them responding to job duties along a continuum of a police officer on one end and a social worker on the other. In the same day, maybe with the same offender, they will act accordingly to situations presented to them. They realize the job demands the enforcement of rules and conditions that provide for the public safety, but that is not their only responsibility. Along the continuum, they will also foster a relationship with the offender that provides for positive growth and change by effective counseling, case planning, and brokering of rehabilitative services. At the end of the day, they are more proud of the offenders they have helped along a positive path rather than the ones they have had to lock up.

I have been fortunate to work with many student interns and have attended student job fairs representing our agency. My advice to students is generally the same:

1. Don't be too impatient in getting hired right away in your chosen job.
2. Take advantage of entry-level positions in related fields, such as residential treatment centers, prisons, or county jails. Two of the last probation officers I hired had experience working with inmates in county jails. This is very transferable experience.
3. Keep up your network contacts. Keep in touch with those in the business, like supervisors of internships and local criminal justice partners.
4. If you are in an entry-level position, volunteer in an office like the one you want to eventually work in. This has the added benefit of learning and practicing the skills you will need for that job.
5. Update your resume frequently with new experiences and skill development, paid or unpaid.
6. Learn what is expected of the position you ultimately want. The Minnesota Correction Association is guided by evidence-based practices, as is much of the national scene. Learn risk assessment tools, presentence investigation practices, cognitive skill development of offenders, and case planning techniques.
7. Don't rely on just a related degree. Take advantage of continuing education opportunities, because this business keeps changing.

offenders has been traditional, but as youth have become more mobile, information exchange with computerized records has facilitated tracking of juvenile offenders. However, the probability that delinquent acts in one jurisdiction would come to the attention of juvenile officials in another may be less likely than with adult offenders. As a result, juveniles may seek to avoid processing in criminal court in hopes of minimizing their criminal record.

Any possibility of juvenile confinement triggers the need for legal assistance, including public defenders.
(Courtesy of Dean John Champion)

In addition, the small number of juveniles who reappear before the same juvenile court judge may find that the judge has better information about the circumstances and conditions in the juvenile's life. Repeat adjudications for juvenile offenders do not necessarily mean that youth will be placed or transferred to criminal court (Feld, 2007). Juvenile court judges may give juveniles the benefit of the doubt and impose nonincarcerative alternatives. Overcrowding in juvenile facilities may also influence the disposition (King, Melvin, and Biederman, 2008).

Finally, it is beyond the authority of juvenile court judges to impose extremely long sentences or life imprisonment. Offenders in juvenile court who have committed especially aggravated violent offenses face more limited sanctions than in the adult system. Incarceration in a juvenile facility, within statutory age limits, is the most punitive sanction available to juvenile court judges. If the case is waived, however, more severe sanctions are possible.

Unfavorable Implications of Juvenile Court Adjudications

Juvenile court adjudication may not always be favorable toward juveniles. The major drawbacks of having a case heard by juvenile court judges include:

1. Juvenile court judges have the authority to administer lengthy sentences of incarceration, not only for serious offenders but for status offenders as well.

2. In most states, juvenile courts do not provide juveniles with a trial by jury.

3. Using discretion in handling juveniles, judges may mitigate sanctions for various charges.

4. Juveniles do not enjoy the same range of constitutional rights in juvenile courts as adults do in criminal courts.

Adverse to juveniles, juvenile court judges may impose short- or long-term secure confinement, regardless of the seriousness of offenses. The case of *In re Gault* (1967) (discussed in Chapter 4) is an example of how juvenile court judges can impose lengthy custodial dispositions for youth who are adjudicated delinquent even for relatively minor offending. Officially, the charge against Gault was "Lewd Telephone Calls." For committing the same offense, an adult would have been fined $50 and might have served up to 30 days in a local jail. Gault, however, received a disposition of nearly six years of confinement, which the U.S. Supreme Court found to be excessive and overturned on several important constitutional grounds. Juvenile court judges, however, continue to have broad discretionary powers and may impose seemingly inappropriate long or short sentences, provided that they are consistent with the constitutional guarantees assured by *Gault*.

The case of *Gault* is not an isolated instance of sentencing youth who have committed petty offenses with long periods of secure confinement. Juvenile court judges can impose longer incarcerative sentences on property offenders compared with the criminal court sentences for adult property offenders. The policies governing the type of dispositions imposed on adjudicated juvenile offenders vary among jurisdictions.

Another disadvantage of juvenile courts is that a jury trial is generally determined by the discretion of prosecutors and juvenile court judges. As the U.S. Court determined in *McKeiver v. Pennsylvania* (1971), juveniles do not have the Sixth Amendment right to a jury trial, because the process in juvenile court is not a "criminal trial." This practice typifies juvenile courts in 30 states where juveniles do not have a right to jury trial. Juveniles may request and receive trials under certain circumstances in 21 states. The state legislatures of 10 states have made it possible for juveniles to receive jury trials upon request, and 11 states permit jury trials under more restrictive circumstances, which parallel the jury trial requests of defendants in criminal courts (Szymanski, 2002). Again, we must consider the civil–criminal distinction between juvenile and criminal court proceedings. Jury trials in juvenile courts retain the civil connotation, without juveniles acquiring criminal records. Jury trial convictions in adult criminal courts result in a criminal record.

A third concern with juvenile proceedings is the wide discretion available to juvenile court judges. While abuses are minimal, the potential exists for excessive leniency as well as excessive punishment, and either may occur at various stages of juvenile processing. Because of discretionary authority, juvenile courts have received criticisms from both the public and juvenile justice professionals. One continuing criticism is that juvenile courts avoid the accountability issue through the use of probation or diversion.

One significant drawback for juveniles is that they do not receive the same range of constitutional rights as adults do in criminal courts (Feld and Schaefer, 2010a, 2010b). In some jurisdictions, transcripts of proceedings are not made or retained for juveniles unless special arrangements are made beforehand. In addition, even though the U.S. Supreme Court has required that juvenile delinquents have access to counsel, juveniles are not always represented. In Minnesota, Feld and Schaefer (2010b) found inconsistent compliance on the part of judges in appointing counsel for youthful offenders (including status offenders), and they noted that the rate of representation for youth charged with felonies was less than that for adults charged with felonies.

Defense and Prosecutorial Considerations Relating to Waivers

Jury Trials

There is a great deal of variation among jurisdictions relating to trying and disposing of juvenile offenders. For example, juveniles are only infrequently given a jury trial if their cases are adjudicated in juvenile court. In nearly 80 percent of all state juvenile courts, jury trials for juveniles are denied. Table 8.6 shows the interstate variation in jury trials for juveniles in juvenile courts in 2008.

Implications of Criminal Court Processing

When juveniles are waived to criminal court, a full range of constitutional guarantees is available to them (Champion, 2008a). We have already examined the advantages of permitting or petitioning the juvenile court to retain jurisdiction in certain cases. An absence of a criminal record, limited punishments, greater leniency, and more discretionary options on the part of juvenile court judge make juvenile courts an attractive adjudicatory setting for youth. Even if the alleged crimes are serious, charges may be reduced, or youth may receive diversion, be referred to community services, or be given other nonadjudicatory penalties.

Table 8.6
INTERSTATE VARIATION IN JURY TRIALS FOR JUVENILES, 2008

Provision	States
Jury trial granted upon request by juvenile	Alaska, Kansas, Massachusetts, Michigan, Minnesota, Montana, New Mexico, Oklahoma, South Dakota, Texas, West Virginia, Wisconsin, and Wyoming
Juvenile denied right to trial by jury	Alabama, California, Florida, Georgia, Hawaii, Indiana, Iowa, Louisiana, Maine, Maryland, Mississippi, Nebraska, Nevada, New Jersey, North Carolina, North Dakota, Ohio, Oregon, Pennsylvania, South Carolina, Tennessee, Utah, Vermont, and Washington
No mention	Arizona, Connecticut, Colorado, Idaho, Illinois, Missouri, New Hampshire, New York, and Virginia

Source: Patricia Torbet and Linda Szymanski (1998). *State Legislative Responses to Violent Juvenile Crime: 1996–1997 Update.* Washington, DC: U.S. Department of Justice, Office of Juvenile Justice and Delinquency Prevention. Updated 2008 by authors.

Some of the implications for juveniles being processed through the criminal justice system were noted previously. First, depending upon the seriousness of the alleged offenses, a jury trial may be a matter of right. Second, lengthy incarceration in minimum-, medium-, and maximum-security facilities with adults becomes a real possibility (Champion, 2008a). Third, even though the U.S. Court determined that it is cruel and unusual punishment to sentence youth to life without parole for a nonhomicidal offense, the sanction is still possible for youth convicted of homicide (*Graham v Florida*, 2010).

Jury Trials as a Matter of Right for Serious Offenses

A primary benefit of transfer to criminal court is the right to a jury trial. This is conditional, however, and depends on the minimum incarcerative period associated with one or more criminal charges filed against the defendants. In only 12 state jurisdictions, juveniles have a jury trial right granted through legislative action (Office of Juvenile Justice and Delinquency Prevention, 2007). However, when juveniles reach criminal courts, certain constitutional provisions apply to them as well as to adults. With exceptions, defendants charged with a crime for which the possible sentence is six months of incarceration or more are entitled to a jury trial (*Baldwin v. New York*, 1970). Therefore, jury trials are not discretionary matters for judges to decide.

Juveniles who are charged with particularly serious crimes where several aggravating circumstances are apparent may receive unfavorable treatment from juries. Aggravating circumstances include a victim's death or the infliction of serious bodily injuries, committing an offense while on bail for another offense or while on probation or parole, use of extreme cruelty in the commission of the crime, use of a dangerous weapon in the commission of a crime, a prior record, and leadership in the commission of the offenses alleged. Mitigating circumstances (those factors that tend to lessen the severity of sentencing) include duress or extreme provocation, mental incapacitation, motivation to provide necessities, youthfulness or old age, and no previous criminal record.

Among the aggravating and mitigating circumstances noted, having a prior record or being a first-time offender is an important consideration. Youth who are transferred to criminal courts sometimes do not have previous criminal records. This does not mean that they have not committed crimes but, rather, that their records are **juvenile court records**. Juveniles may have **sustained petitions**, in which the facts alleged against them have been determined to be true by the juvenile court judge. However, this adjudication hearing is a civil proceeding. As such, these youth do not technically bring prior criminal records into the criminal courtroom. This is a favorable factor for juveniles to consider when deciding whether to challenge transfers or have their automatic waivers reversed. However, changes in state laws regarding the confidentiality of juvenile court records have been made so that greater access to such records is available. Thus, juvenile records may increasingly affect criminal court sentencing.

Another important factor relative to having access to a jury trial is that prosecutors often try to avoid them, preferring a plea bargain agreement instead. Plea bargaining, or plea negotiating, is a preconviction arrangement between the state and the

juvenile court records

Formal or informal statements concerning an adjudication hearing or court referral or actions involving a juvenile; a written document of a juvenile's prior delinquency or status offending.

sustained petitions

A finding that the facts alleged in a petition are true; a finding that the juvenile committed the offenses alleged, which resulted in an adjudication.

defendant where the defendant enters a guilty plea in exchange for leniency in the form of reduced charges or less-harsh sentencing. However, plea bargaining also involves an admission of guilt without benefit of a trial. For this reason, plea bargaining is often criticized. Plea bargaining in the United States accounts for approximately 90 percent of all criminal convictions (Anleu, 2010).

Jury trials are costly, and jury deliberations are unpredictable. If prosecutors can obtain guilty pleas from transferred juveniles, they assist the state and themselves in terms of the expense of prosecution and the time of jury trials. In addition, plea bargaining in transferred juvenile cases often results in convictions on lesser charges that would not have initially prompted the transfer or waiver from juvenile courts. However, this suggests that the criminal justice system is inadvertently circumventing the primary purpose of juvenile transfers through plea bargaining arrangements that are frequent procedures in adult criminal cases. Furthermore, when prosecutors file charges, the presumption is that sufficient evidence exists for successful prosecution. In cases where juveniles without serious charges are transferred, the evidence may be inadequate to warrant prosecution, and the cases are dismissed by prosecutors.

Similarly, reluctance to prosecute transferred juveniles may result from property crimes not being seen as serious in criminal court. Although national data are not recorded, it is estimated that 200,000 youth under the age of 18 are prosecuted in criminal court each year (Young and Gainsborough, 2000). While these cases may stand out from other cases coming before juvenile court judges, prosecutors and criminal court judges might regard them as relatively minor. Thus, juveniles enter the adult system from juvenile courts, where their offenses set them apart from most other juvenile offenders. In comparison to adults in criminal courts, however, the nature of their offense and their youthful age can improve the chances of having their cases dismissed or of being acquitted by juries. Most prosecutors wish to reserve jury trials for only the most serious offenders. Therefore, a general inclination is to treat youthful property offenders with greater leniency, unless they elect to *nolle prosequi* or dismiss the case.

As noted, one of the issues regarding juveniles who are transferred to adult court is whether they receive more severe sentencing in adult court as compared to juvenile court. The prevailing view is that juveniles receive more leniency in adult court. While some earlier research supported this view, this assumption of leniency may not be accurate. Kurlychek and Johnson (2010) found convincing evidence that juveniles who are transferred to criminal court receive more severe sentences in comparison to young adult offenders with similar cases. They observed this to be especially evident when the jurisdictional transfer was through judicial waiver. This may be attributed to the assumption that if waiver hearings in juvenile court determine the youth is not amendable to treatment or supervision, the case must be deserving of more punitive sanctions. Using data from the Maryland State Commission on Criminal Sentencing Policy, Kurlychek and Johnson (2010) found that "juveniles transferred to adult court for drug offenses received sentences that were six times longer when compared to young adults" (p. 747).

Blended Sentencing Statutes

In recent years, many states have legislatively redefined the juvenile court's purpose and goals by diminishing the role of rehabilitation and heightening the importance of public safety, punishment, and accountability in the juvenile justice system (Champion, 2008a). One of the most dramatic changes in the dispositional/sentencing options available to juvenile court judges is **blended sentencing**, which refers to the imposition of juvenile and/or adult correctional sanctions on serious and violent juvenile offenders who have been adjudicated in juvenile court or convicted in criminal court.

Blended sentencing statutes are intended to provide both juvenile and criminal court judges with a greater range of dispositional and/or sentencing options. In the 1980s and earlier, juvenile courts were more lenient with juvenile offenders. Dispositional decisions of juvenile court judges were more likely to be nominal or conditional, which usually meant verbal warnings and/or probation. While probation continues to be the juvenile court sanction of choice for adjudicated juveniles today, some states have enacted legislation that provides juvenile and criminal court judges with greater sanctioning powers. Thus, in states such as Colorado, Arkansas, and Missouri, juvenile court judges can impose sanctions that extend beyond the original jurisdictional authority. Juvenile court judges in New Mexico can place certain juveniles in either adult or juvenile correctional facilities. Criminal court judges in Florida, Idaho, Michigan, or Missouri can place those convicted of crimes in either juvenile or adult correctional facilities, depending upon the jurisdiction. These are more punitive dispositional and sentencing options that hold youthful offenders more accountable for serious offenses.

One of the consequences of blended sentencing statutes is that the use of transfers or waivers and subsequent waiver hearings are not necessary. By statute, juveniles in a state with blended sentencing statutes are either in juvenile or criminal court where the court can exercise one or both types of juvenile and adult sanctions.

Some judges have not embraced blended sentences in their courts even when they have statutory authority to impose them. In Michigan, for example, Eugene Arthur Moore, a juvenile court judge, criticized the Michigan legislature for enacting a blended sentencing statute. In sentencing a 13-year-old juvenile offender who had been convicted by the jury of second-degree murder, the judge imposed incarceration in a juvenile facility with release when the offender reached age 21. Judge Moore was critical of the national trend of trying and sentencing young offenders as adults and rejected the prosecutor's recommendation for a blended sentence (Bradsher, 2000).

One implication for juveniles sentenced under blended sentencing statutes is that it provides an incentive to demonstrate positive adjustment and to participate in counseling, training, or other developmental activities that will improve skills and psychological and social development. If poor institutional adjustment can jeopardize chances of release upon reaching adulthood, youth have a motivation to use confinement as an

blended sentencing
Any type of sentencing procedure in which either a criminal or a juvenile court judge can impose both juvenile and/or adult penalties.

opportunity for positive change. Juvenile court judges who recognize the motivational value of blended sentencing statutes are more inclined to support their use as juvenile justice reform.

Blended sentencing options are usually based on age or a combination of age and offense. There are five blended sentencing models, which are presented in Figure 8.9. These are (1) juvenile-exclusive blend, (2) juvenile-inclusive blend, (3) juvenile-contiguous blend, (4) criminal-exclusive blend, and (5) criminal-inclusive blend.

The Juvenile-Exclusive Blend

juvenile-exclusive blend
Type of sentence in which a juvenile court judge can impose either adult or juvenile incarceration as a disposition and sentence, but not both.

The **juvenile-exclusive blend** is a disposition by the juvenile court judge either to the juvenile correctional system or to the adult correctional system, but not both. Thus, a judge might order a juvenile adjudicated delinquent for aggravated assault to serve three years in a juvenile industrial school, or the judge may order the adjudicated delinquent to serve three years in a prison for adults. The judge cannot impose *both* types of punishment under this model. In 2008, only one state, New Mexico, provided such a sentencing option for juvenile court judges.

The Juvenile-Inclusive Blend

juvenile-inclusive blend
Form of sentencing in which a juvenile court judge can impose both adult and juvenile incarceration simultaneously.

The **juvenile-inclusive blend** involves a disposition by the juvenile court judge that is both a juvenile correctional sanction and an adult correctional sanction. For example, if a judge adjudicated a 15-year-old juvenile delinquent on a charge of vehicular theft, the judge might impose a disposition of two years in a juvenile industrial school or reform school. Furthermore, the judge might impose a sentence of three additional years in an adult penitentiary. Typically, however, the second sentence to the adult prison would be suspended, unless the juvenile violated one or more conditions of the original disposition and any conditions accompanying the disposition. Usually, this suspension period would run until the youth reaches age 18 or 21. If the offender were to commit a new offense or violate one or more program conditions, he or she would be placed in the adult prison to serve the second sentence originally imposed.

The Juvenile-Contiguous Blend

juvenile-contiguous blend
Sentence by a juvenile court judge in which the judge can impose a disposition beyond the normal jurisdictional range for juvenile offenders; for example, a judge may impose a 30-year term on a 14-year-old offender, but the juvenile is entitled to a hearing when he or she reaches the age of majority to determine whether the remainder of the sentence shall be served.

The **juvenile-contiguous blend** is a disposition by a juvenile court judge that may extend beyond the jurisdictional age limit of the offender. When the age limit of the juvenile court jurisdiction is reached, various procedures may be invoked to transfer the case to the jurisdiction of adult corrections. States with this juvenile-contiguous blend include Colorado, Massachusetts, Rhode Island, South Carolina, and Texas.

In 1987, the Texas legislature enacted a determinate sentencing law that is an example of the juvenile-contiguous blended sentencing model, whereby for certain offenses, the juvenile court may impose a sentence that may remain in effect beyond its extended jurisdiction. Under this law, a 15-year-old youth in Texas who has been adjudicated delinquent on a murder charge can be given a determinate sentence of from 1 to 30 years. At the time of the disposition in juvenile court, the youth is sent

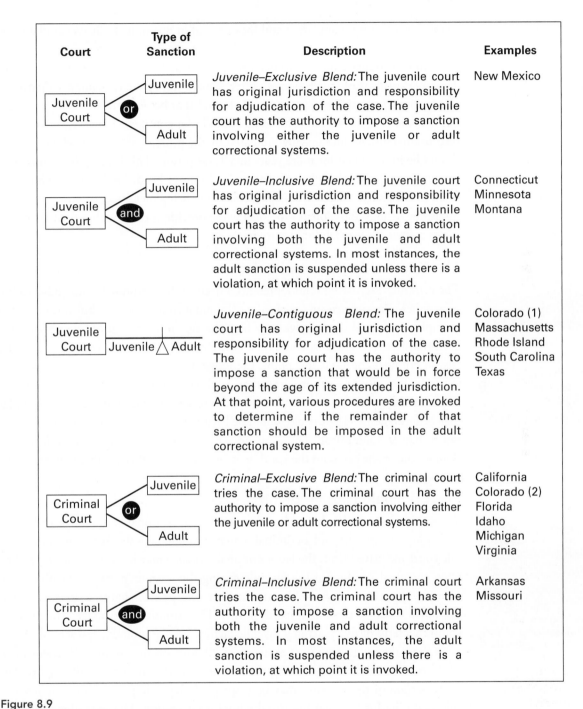

Court	Type of Sanction	Description	Examples
Juvenile Court (or)	Juvenile / Adult	*Juvenile–Exclusive Blend:* The juvenile court has original jurisdiction and responsibility for adjudication of the case. The juvenile court has the authority to impose a sanction involving either the juvenile or adult correctional systems.	New Mexico
Juvenile Court (and)	Juvenile / Adult	*Juvenile–Inclusive Blend:* The juvenile court has original jurisdiction and responsibility for adjudication of the case. The juvenile court has the authority to impose a sanction involving both the juvenile and adult correctional systems. In most instances, the adult sanction is suspended unless there is a violation, at which point it is invoked.	Connecticut Minnesota Montana
Juvenile Court	Juvenile △ Adult	*Juvenile–Contiguous Blend:* The juvenile court has original jurisdiction and responsibility for adjudication of the case. The juvenile court has the authority to impose a sanction that would be in force beyond the age of its extended jurisdiction. At that point, various procedures are invoked to determine if the remainder of that sanction should be imposed in the adult correctional system.	Colorado (1) Massachusetts Rhode Island South Carolina Texas
Criminal Court (or)	Juvenile / Adult	*Criminal–Exclusive Blend:* The criminal court tries the case. The criminal court has the authority to impose a sanction involving either the juvenile or adult correctional systems.	California Colorado (2) Florida Idaho Michigan Virginia
Criminal Court (and)	Juvenile / Adult	*Criminal–Inclusive Blend:* The criminal court tries the case. The criminal court has the authority to impose a sanction involving both the juvenile and adult correctional systems. In most instances, the adult sanction is suspended unless there is a violation, at which point it is invoked.	Arkansas Missouri

Figure 8.9

Models of Blended Sentencing Statutes

Sources: Shay Bilchik (1996). State Responses to Serious and Violent Juvenile Crime. Pittsburgh, PA: National Center for Juvenile Justice, p. 13; Patricia Torbet, Richard Gable, Hunter Hurst, and Imogene Montgomery (1996). State Responses to Serious and Violent Juvenile Crime. Washington, DC: Office of Juvenile Justice and Delinquency Prevention to the Texas Youth Commission and incarcerated in one of its facilities (similar to reform or industrial schools). By the time the youth reaches age 17.5 years, the juvenile court must conduct a hearing to determine whether the youth should be sent to the Texas Department of Corrections to serve some or all of the remaining sentence. At this hearing, the youth may present evidence in his or her favor to show why he or she has become rehabilitated and no longer should be confined. However, evidence of institutional misconduct may be presented by the prosecutor to show why the youth should be incarcerated for more years in a Texas prison. This hearing functions as an incentive for the youth to behave and try to improve his or her behavior while confined in the juvenile facility. This particular sentencing blend seems most effective at punishing serious and violent offenders while providing them with a final chance to access certain Texas rehabilitative programs.

The Criminal-Exclusive Blend

The **criminal-exclusive blend** represents a decision by a criminal court judge to impose either a juvenile court sanction or a criminal court sanction, but not both. For example, a criminal court judge may hear the case of a 15-year-old youth who has been transferred to criminal court on a rape charge. The youth is convicted in a jury trial in criminal court. At this point, the judge has two options: The judge can sentence the offender to a prison term in an adult correctional facility, or the judge can impose an incarcerative sentence for the youth to serve in a juvenile facility. The judge may believe that the 15-year-old would be better served in a juvenile industrial school rather than an adult prison. Thus, the judge may impose a sentence of adult incarceration, but he or she can send the youth to a facility where other youth are incarcerated.

criminal-exclusive blend

Form of sentencing by a criminal court judge in which either juvenile or adult sentences of incarceration can be imposed, but not both.

The Criminal-Inclusive Blend

The **criminal-inclusive blend** is a decision by the criminal court judge to impose both a juvenile penalty and a criminal sentence simultaneously. Again, as in the juvenile court-inclusive blend, the latter criminal sentence may be suspended, depending upon the good conduct of the juvenile during the juvenile punishment phase. For example, consider a 13-year-old gang member who participated in a drive-by shooting and was convicted of attempted murder. The criminal court judge sentences the youth to a term of five years in a juvenile facility, such as an industrial school. At the same time, the judge imposes a sentence of 20 years on the youth to be spent in an adult correctional facility following the five-year sentence in the juvenile facility. The adult portion of the sentence may be suspended, depending upon how the juvenile adjusts during his five-year industrial school incarceration. However, there is an additional component to this blend. If the juvenile violates one or more conditions of his confinement in the juvenile facility, the judge has the power to revoke that sentence and invoke the sentence of incarceration in an adult facility. Thus, a powerful incentive is provided for the youth to maintain positive adjustment and to engage in rehabilitation programs. Furthermore, with good behavior, the youth can be released

criminal-inclusive blend

Form of sentencing by a criminal court judge in which both juvenile and adult sentences can be imposed simultaneously.

following the period of juvenile confinement. The adult portion of the sentence is suspended if the court determines that the youth has benefited from the confinement and is not a risk to the community. One state with the authority of revocation and the ability to place youth in adult correctional facilities is Arkansas, although this alternative is rarely used by criminal court judges.

Jury Trials as a Matter of Right in All Juvenile Court Blended Sentencing Proceedings

When juveniles are tried as adults in criminal court, they are entitled to the full range of constitutional rights extended to criminal defendants, including the right to a jury trial. This same provision exists whenever juveniles are tried in juvenile courts and subject to the application of blended sentencing statutes. All states with the juvenile-inclusive blend, the juvenile-exclusive blend, or the juvenile-contiguous blend must grant juvenile defendants the right to a jury trial in juvenile court upon request.

If the jury verdict is guilty, the juvenile court judge has the option under one of these blended sentencing statutes, depending upon the state jurisdiction, to impose both a juvenile penalty and a criminal penalty, or either a juvenile penalty or a criminal penalty, but not both. Thus, juvenile court judges may exercise considerable discretion relating to dispositions and sentencing. If the juvenile court judge is in a state where both juvenile and criminal penalties may be imposed, such as Michigan, the judge may impose both types of penalties on a convicted juvenile, or the judge may impose the juvenile penalty but not the criminal penalty. This aspect of blended sentencing is totally discretionary with the judge.

SUMMARY

Distinguishing between different types of offenders is an integral part of juvenile offender processing. Status offenders are most frequently given lenient treatment, while delinquents usually receive harsher punishments. For the most-serious offenders, jurisdictions use waivers, transfers, or certifications for treating juveniles as adults for the purpose of criminal prosecutions. The rationale for using waivers is to provide harsher penalties for more-serious offenses, to hold offenders more accountable because of the more-serious offenses they commit, to promote greater fairness and just deserts in punishments according to offense seriousness, to provide a broader range of penalties that fit these crimes in terms of proportionality of the seriousness of them, to overcome the traditional leniency of juvenile courts, to promote general deterrence for other juveniles who might contemplate committing serious offenses, and to encourage youthful offenders to accept responsibility for their actions.

While only the most-serious juvenile offenders ideally should be designated for transfer to criminal courts, only about 40 percent of all transferred persons each year are violent offenders. Most other transferred juveniles are property offenders or drug users/abusers. Less-serious offenders are sometimes repeat offenders, and juvenile court judges may transfer these youth to avoid their continued juvenile court appearances. This is one justification for waiver.

Types of waivers include judicial waivers, discretionary waivers, mandatory waivers, presumptive waivers, direct file, and statutory exclusion. Another type of waiver is a demand waiver, in which a juvenile asks the juvenile court to waive him or her to the jurisdiction of the criminal court. Other types of actions include once an adult/always an adult provisions, in which juveniles who have been transferred to criminal court once are subsequently considered to be adults for criminal prosecutions if they continue to reoffend as juveniles and until they reach the age of their majority. Waiver hearings are conducted, and judges decide whether waivers should be granted. Stringent time standards exist governing the use of waiver actions. Hearings are proceedings where the relative merits of the transfer are discussed by the prosecutor and defense counsel. The presiding judge makes the final determination.

Both positive and negative implications of waivers for juveniles were described. Juvenile court adjudications can result in criminal records for adjudicated delinquents, but under some circumstances, these records can be expunged when youth become adults. Some juvenile court judges may impose secure confinement. However, juvenile courts do not have the same range of punishments that exist for adults who are processed by criminal courts. Life without parole dispositions are not available in juvenile court. If the case is serious enough to warrant this type of sentence, the court or the prosecutor can proceed to transfer jurisdiction to criminal court.

During the past 20 years, significant modifications have occurred in how juveniles are processed. Blended sentencing statutes have been created, making it possible for either juvenile or criminal courts to impose either juvenile court punishments, criminal court punishments, or both. Various blended sentencing statutes were described.

KEY TERMS

placement, 273
placed, 273
contempt of court, 274
transfers, 276
waivers, 276
transfer hearings, 276
certification, 276
life without parole, 276
acceptance of responsibility, 277
judicial waivers, 284

discretionary waivers, 284
mandatory waiver, 285
presumptive waiver, 285
direct file, 286
concurrent jurisdiction, 286
statutory exclusion, 286
legislative waiver, 286
demand waiver, 286
reverse waiver, 289

once an adult/always an adult provision, 291
waiver hearing, 291
waiver motion, 291
nolle prosequi, 295
reverse waiver hearings, 296
reverse waiver actions, 296
juvenile court records, 303

QUESTIONS FOR REVIEW

1. What are the implications of offense seriousness for the use of waivers in the juvenile justice system?

2. What is the rationale for distinguishing between status offenders and delinquent offenders in juvenile justice system processing?

3. What is contempt power as used by juvenile court judges? How does the use of contempt power by juvenile court judges influence status offenders?

4. What are several types of judicial waivers? What is the rationale for using transfers?

5. What are some of the ideal characteristics of youth targeted for transfers to criminal courts? What are the actual characteristics of youth who are transferred to criminal courts?

6. What is meant by the once an adult/always an adult provision? What implications does this policy have for affected youth?

7. What are some contrasts in direct file, legislative waivers, and demand waivers?

8. Under what circumstances are juveniles entitled to hearings on transfer decisions?

9. What are some favorable and unfavorable implications for juveniles if their cases are heard in juvenile courts instead of criminal courts? What are some positive and negative implications for juveniles if they have their cases heard in criminal courts?

10. What are five different types of blended sentencing statutes? What are some positive benefits of blended sentencing statutes for serious and violent juvenile offenders?

INTERNET CONNECTIONS

American Bar Association
http://www.americanbar.org/aba.html

Criminal Justice Policy Foundation
http://www.cjpf.org/

The Future of Children
http://www.princeton.edu/futureofchildren/index.xml

National Criminal Justice Reference Service
http://www.ncjrs.gov/

National Juvenile Defender Center

http://www.njdc.info/

Open Society Foundations
http://www.soros.org/crime/

The Sentencing Project
http://www.sentencingproject.org/template/index.cfm

Unusual Suspects Theatre Company
http://www.theunusualsuspects.org

9

The Adjudicatory Process

Dispositional Alternatives

Learning Objectives

<small>AFTER READING THIS CHAPTER, THE STUDENT WILL BE ABLE TO:</small>

- Identify the factors that influence juvenile offender dispositions and the various means of risk assessment.
- Describe disposition hearings and the use of predisposition reports.
- Recognize the role of classification in making decisions about how to handle juvenile offenders.
- Distinguish between legal and extralegal factors in decision-making
- Identify aggravating and mitigating circumstances and their role in assessing risk.
- Understand how victim-impact statements are used in determining dispositions.

(Eugene Gordon/Pearson)

Introduction

How do we know if arrested youth are dangerous? Should all dangerous youth be detained pending trial? Youth who rob stores at gunpoint and threaten the lives of others are most likely dangerous, and releasing them pending court proceedings may put a community in jeopardy. However, what about juvenile offenders possessing large amounts of drugs? If they are released pending legal review, they may not reoffend or be a threat to the community but they may flee the jurisdiction to avoid prosecution. Often, these are the two primary criteria used by authorities for making detention decisions.

This chapter will examine the adjudicatory process, focusing on factors that influence youthful offender dispositions. The first part of the chapter describes the nature of offenses and whether youth are first-offenders (first-time offenders) or repeat offenders. Offense seriousness is a primary consideration, along with age, association with others when the offense was committed, extent of participation in the offense, and other legal and extralegal factors. Juveniles are assessed and cases disposed by evaluating both aggravating factors (factors that intensify culpability in the offense) and mitigating factors (factors that lessen culpability in the offense). Aggravating and mitigating factors will be described, and their role in determining seriousness of the offender and how to handle the offender will be considered.

In the 1980s, more juvenile courts devised measures of risk or dangerousness as well as assessments of youthful client needs. By 2009, almost every juvenile court had devised such instrumentation. The next part of this chapter examines the concepts of dangerousness, risk, and needs assessment as these terms apply to evaluations of juveniles. While these instruments are not used exclusively to determine dispositions in the juvenile justice system, they do provide information to determine the nature and extent of services required to meet individual needs as well as the degree and type of supervision required for each offender. Risk and needs assessments are conducted by both juvenile probation and parole personnel. Several elements of risk assessment instruments will be described.

Some risk predictions, including actuarial, anamnestic, and clinical prediction, will be presented and defined. No prediction method is foolproof, however, and errors in prediction occur. Some offenders are predicted to be dangerous and turn out not to be dangerous. These are known as false positives. Other offenders are predicted not to be dangerous but turn out to be dangerous. These are known as false negatives. Efforts to predict dangerousness will result in both false positives and false negatives in the juvenile justice system, despite the fact that the instrumentation is constantly being revised and improved. Because of prediction errors, some youth are confined in secure facilities longer than other youth, and these incarceration differences maybe unwarranted. The issue of selective incapacitation will be examined.

In spite of prediction errors, instruments continue to be used to assess risk and needs. Examples will be provided and some hypothetical calculations will also be presented to illustrate how assessments of juveniles are performed. The contents of these instruments will be listed and explained. Also described will be the individual weighting criteria for items included on these instruments and how they are used to measure potential for recidivism.

One of the most critical documents in juvenile offender processing is the predisposition report. The chapter concludes with a detailed presentation and analysis of such reports and how they are used in the juvenile justice process. Similar to the presentence investigation (PSI) report prepared by probation officers for criminal offenders, the predisposition report furnishes information about youth. Plans are often devised for aftercare based on the contents of these reports. Examples of predispositional reports will be provided.

The Nature of the Offense

As Figure 9.1 shows, from 2000 through 2007, the number of cases handled in juvenile courts remained fairly constant (Knoll and Sickmund, 2010). In 2007, about half of the 1.7 million juvenile cases were processed formally. Of these "926,000 petitioned cases, 586,200 juveniles were adjudicated, and about 148,600 received some form of residential placement" (Knoll and Sickmund, 2010, p. 3). About 8,500 cases were recommended for transfer to criminal courts. In 2008, there were an estimated 2.1 million arrests of youth under age 18, and about 1.7 million of the cases were sent to the juvenile justice system for processing (Puzzanchera, 2009).

During the period from 1986 to 1996, violent crime by juveniles increased by nearly 70 percent nationally. This dramatic increase in juvenile violence resulted in greater public attention to juvenile offenders and how juvenile courts were handling them. As noted in previous chapters, however, more recent trends indicate that juvenile violence is decreasing in most jurisdictions. The incidence of violence among younger juveniles leveled off during the late 1990s and through 2007, declining slightly for offense-specific categories. In addition, from 1999 and 2008, juvenile

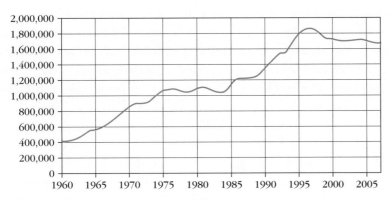

Figure 9.1

Juvenile Court Delinquency Caseload, 1960–2007

Source: Crystal Knoll and Melissa Sickmund (2010). Delinquency Cases in Juvenile Court, 2007. Washington, DC: U.S. Department of Justice, Office of Juvenile Justice and Delinquency Prevention. (Available at https://www.ncjrs.gov/pdffiles1/ojjdp/230168.pdf.)

arrests for aggravated assault decreased 22 percent for males. Of all arrests of youth under age 18 in 2008, approximately 96,000 were for violent or person offenses, such as aggravated assault, rape, and murder, and juvenile arrests accounted for 16 percent of all violent crime arrests and about 26 percent of all property crime arrests (Puzzanchera, 2009). While violent crime receives greater attention and concern, the majority of juvenile offenders are arrested and adjudicated for nonviolent crimes.

Adjudicated juveniles are subject to a range of juvenile court penalties, from verbal warnings and reprimands to secure confinement in private facilities or state industrial schools. Delinquent acts involving physical harm to others or the threat of physical harm are considered to be more serious and result in stronger sanctions. As presented in Chapter 6, intake officers perform the initial screening function and determine which cases can be handled informally and which require formal court processing.

Juvenile court prosecutors further screen those cases deciding which cases require prosecution. Prosecutors are influenced by numerous factors, including age of the offender, seriousness of the offense, and prior record. As a result of this review, prosecutors may proceed with selected cases and divert less-serious cases to informal case disposition, including alternative dispute resolution (Dembo, Wareham, and Poythress, 2006).

One consideration in this process is the ability and willingness of juveniles to compensate victims for their monetary losses through a program of restitution. The intake officer, teen courts, or peer juries may impose restitution as a condition of diversion. Satisfactory completion of such a diversion program means the juvenile will likely avoid formal delinquency adjudication. Because juvenile courts continue to view rehabilitation as an important goal, juvenile court judges seek to assist youth in avoiding negative consequences of more severe sanctions or secure confinement (Bowman, Prelow, and Weaver, 2007). When it is appropriate for the juvenile and for public safety, interventions in lieu of formal adjudication are considered.

While diversion is a consideration for less-serious offenders, residential placement and secure confinement are dispositions for more-serious juvenile offenders. Juvenile court's reluctance to incarcerate juveniles, however, has prompted some criticism that these courts are soft on crime, and several states, such as New York, have established juvenile offender laws designed to transfer the most serious offenders from juvenile court to criminal court. These kinds of sanctions are not effective in deterring juvenile violence. However, they are popular, and public officials may view them as a way to address juvenile crime (Buffington-Vollum, Edens, and Keilen, 2008).

Nevertheless, increasing rates of violence among juveniles during the early 1990s, especially for offenses such as aggravated assault, robbery, and homicide, and the increasing influence of the get-tough movement in juvenile courts, prompted legislatures to impose harsher sentences for juveniles who committed more-serious offenses. In this context, the nature of the offenses weighed heavily in deciding to formally handle serious offenders with adjudication. Even though juvenile violence has decreased in recent years, the get-tough initiatives established in the 1990s continue. As a result of youth gangs, violence, and involvement in illicit drugs, youth are more carefully evaluated for formal handling and consideration for possible placement in secure facilities (Taylor et al., 2008). In 2007, 56 percent of the delinquency cases which were referred to juvenile court were petitioned for formal handling, compared to 46 percent in 1985. In 2007, 6 percent of these petitioned cases were adjudicated delinquent (Knoll and Sickmund, 2010, p. 3).

First-Offender or Repeat Offender?

Is a juvenile a **first-offender** or a **repeat offender**? First-offenders have no prior record of delinquency, and their current offense is presumed to be their first offense. Repeat offenders have prior delinquency or criminal records, either delinquency adjudications or criminal convictions, or both.

> **first-offender**
> Criminals who have no previous criminal records; these persons may have committed crimes, but they have only been caught for the instant offense.

When examining the case file to determine whether to prosecute a youth, the question of whether the juvenile is a first-offender or a repeat offender is key. The tendency among prosecutors is either to divert petty first-offenders to conditional programs or to dismiss the cases outright. Diversionary programs often involve restitution or some form of victim compensation. Contracts are arranged between youth and their victims, whereby youth reimburse victims for their financial losses. These programs often involve mediators who are responsible for securing agreements between juvenile offenders and their victims. Known as alternative dispute resolution, these mediation programs are believed to be fairly widespread and effective (Champion, 2008a).

> **repeat offender**
> Any juvenile or adult with a prior record of delinquency or criminality.

Whether they are violent or property offenders, youth with prior records who are adjudicated delinquent may be more likely to receive some nonincarcerative sanction. Compared with first-offenders, however, chronic juvenile offenders have a greater chance of pursuing criminal careers as adults. Currently, no uniform policies exist among jurisdictions about how chronic offenders should be identified. During the 1990s, the compilation and centralization of state delinquency figures increased, as well as the openness and availability of this information to the public sector. However, because of poor record keeping and the lack of interjurisdictional record sharing, youthful offenders may be diverted from formal juvenile court processing despite their chronic recidivism (Trulson and Haerle, 2008). Some jurisdictions measure whether formal action should be taken against juveniles on the basis of the number of times they have been arrested. After four arrests, youth in some jurisdictions may be considered serious enough to have petitions filed against them as delinquents.

In 2007, based on data reported by the National Center for Juvenile Justice (NCJJ), 926,000 delinquency cases were petitioned to juvenile court for processing. Of these, 314,200, or 34 percent, were classified as property offenses. In comparison, 238,400 cases, or 26 percent, were for person offenses (NCJJ, 2010). Despite the relatively greater seriousness of violent offenses compared with property offenses, person offenders account for one-fourth of all petitioned cases (Champion, 2005). Status offenders continue to be processed by the juvenile justice system as well. Thus, it is unclear who is being targeted by get-tough policies nationwide, though ideally, only those most serious chronic and violent juveniles should be targeted for the harshest juvenile court penalties. Of the 238,400 cases for person offenses, 60 percent resulted in an adjudication of the youth, compared to 63 percent adjudication of the 314,200 property offenses (NCJJ, 2010).

Violent Juvenile Offender Programs

The strong rehabilitative and reintegrative principles characteristic of juvenile courts continue to influence how violent juvenile offenders are treated. This influence can be seen in various reintegrative programs designed especially for violent juvenile offenders, called **Violent Juvenile Offender Programs (VJOPs)**. These programs provide several positive interventions and treatments (Fagan, 1990). For instance, instead of long-term incarceration in secure confinement, many violent juvenile offenders are placed in community-based secure facilities, where they remain for short periods before being reintegrated into their communities. Transitional residential programs include sustained intensive supervision as youth are gradually given freedoms and responsibilities.

The VJOPs are based on a theoretical model integrating strain, control, and learning theories. Four program dimensions include:

1. *Social networking:* the strengthening of personal bonds (attitudes, commitment, and beliefs) through positive experiences with family members, schools, the workplace, or nondelinquent peers.

2. *Provision of opportunities for youth:* the strengthening of social bonds (attachment and involvement) through achievement and successful participation in school, workplace, and family activities.

3. *Social learning:* the process by which personal and social bonds are strengthened and reinforced; strategies include rewards and sanctions for the attainment of goals or for contingent behaviors.

4. *Goal-oriented behaviors:* the linking of specific behaviors to each client's needs and abilities, including problem behaviors and special intervention needs (e.g., substance-abuse treatment or psychotherapy) (Fagan, 1990, p. 240).

Violent juvenile offenders who have participated in these programs seem to be less inclined to recidivate. Fagan (1990) believes that "carefully implemented and well-managed intervention programs," or those that involve "early reintegration activities preceding release from secure care and intensive supervision in the community, with emphasis on gradual reentry and development of social skills to avoid criminal behavior," do much to "avert the abrupt return to criminality after release from the program" of these youth (p. 243). Those "youth exposed to more conventional and longer, secure confinement and treatment appear to recidivate at greater rates and to persist in their delinquent behaviors" (Fagan, 1990, p. 258). Therefore, it is difficult to formulate specific guidelines about how violent juvenile offenders ought to be handled in their juvenile court processing. Currently, competing philosophies of rehabilitation and just deserts recommend polarities in treatments, ranging from total diversion to total secure confinement (Kubena, 2008).

Violent Juvenile Offender Programs (VJOPs)

Procedures designed to provide positive interventions and treatments; reintegrative programs, including transitional residential programs for those youth who have been subject to long-term detention; provides for social networking, provision of educational opportunities for youth, social learning, and goal-oriented behavioral skills.

Is the First-Offender/Repeat Offender Distinction Relevant? Race, Ethnicity, and Socioeconomic Status Revisited

Juvenile courts aspire to be objective in conducting adjudicatory hearings and in imposing sanctions. As already discussed, legal variables, such as prior record and the seriousness of the current offense, are criteria used in determining appropriate sanctions, including graduated sanctions. Investigations of selected juvenile courts reveal that current offense seriousness and prior record are the most important variables in determining the dispositions of delinquents. However, juvenile courts have drawn criticism that adjudications and dispositions sometimes reflect extralegal factors, such as race, ethnicity, and socioeconomic status, rather than offense seriousness and prior record (Champion, 2008a). This is because of the disproportionately high representation of minorities in juvenile arrests, adjudications, and incarcerative dispositions (Eitle, Stolzenberg, and D'Alessio, 2005).

The issue of race and ethnicity is acknowledged as disproportionate minority contact (DMC), which reflects the phenomenon that minority youth are overrepresented in all stages of processing. For example, as explained by Puzzanchera (2009), black youth account for 16 percent of the population but represent 52 percent of all juvenile arrests for violent crimes. As presented in Figure 9.2, blacks are overrepresented in each category of processing except diversion, probation, and adjudication. The data indicate that black youth are more likely to be detained and formally processed, and these two decisions may facilitate petitions being filed on youth when there is insufficient evidence to support a delinquency adjudication.

Decision Points	All	White	Minority	Black	AIAN*	AHPI**
Population at risk (ages 10–17)	33,328,000	25,833,300	7,494,700	5,505,200	461,700	1,527,800
Juvenile arrests	1,928,200	1,294,500	633,700	591,600	23,700	18,400
Cases referred to juvenile court	1,666,100	1,060,900	605,200	558,100	24,200	22,900
Cases diverted	426,900	300,200	126,700	115,400	5,700	5,600
Cases detained	364,600	204,600	159,900	149,000	5,600	5,400
Cases petitioned	926,000	565,500	360,400	332,600	14,400	13,400
Cases adjudicated	586,200	367,900	218,300	199,600	10,200	8,600
Adjudicated cases resulting in probation	327,400	216,100	111,400	100,700	5,600	5,100
Adjudicated cases resulting in placement	148,600	85,000	63,600	58,600	2,900	2,000
Cases judicially waived	8,500	5,000	3,500	3,200	200	100

*AIAN: American Indian or Alaskan Native.
**AHPI: Asian, Hawaiian, or Pacific Islander.

Figure 9.2

Case Processing Summary Counts for Delinquency Offenses, 2007
Source: Charles M. Puzzanchera and Benjamin Adams (2010). National Disproportionate Minority Contact Databook. Developed by the National Center for Juvenile Justice for the Office of Juvenile Justice and Delinquency Prevention. Online. (Available at http://ojjdp.ncjrs.gov/ojstatbb/dmcdb/.)

The data indicate that white youth have a better chance than blacks or Hispanics of avoiding detention following arraignment. White juveniles also have a better chance of avoiding incarceration compared with blacks and Hispanics if they are adjudicated delinquent (Bradley, 2005). This charge against juvenile justice systems in the United States has led to a federal mandate to document the existence and nature of minority overrepresentation and to devise strategies to reduce such overrepresentation. One strategy designed to overcome the prejudicial effects of race, ethnicity, and social class is to establish objective criteria for juvenile justice decision making (Eitle, Stolzenberg, and D'Alessio, 2005).

Objective criteria can be applied to decision making at various points throughout the juvenile justice system. These criteria are found in most state criminal codes and describe various conditions or circumstances regarding juvenile offender dispositions, regardless of their seriousness. Some of these objective criteria include aggravating and mitigating circumstances.

Aggravating and Mitigating Circumstances

Important factors in determining how far any particular juvenile moves into the juvenile justice system are various aggravating and mitigating circumstances that accompany their acts. In the early stages of intake and prosecutorial decision making, aggravating and mitigating circumstances are often informally considered, and much depends on the amount of detail furnished by police officers about the delinquent events.

Aggravating circumstances are usually those actions by juveniles that tend to intensify the seriousness of their acts. Accordingly, when aggravating circumstances exist, subsequent punishment might be intensified. At the other end of the spectrum, mitigating circumstances are those factors that might weigh in the juvenile's favor. These circumstances might lessen the seriousness of the act as well as the severity of punishment imposed by juvenile court judges.

Aggravating Circumstances

aggravating circumstances

Factors that may enhance the severity of one's sentence; these include brutality of the act, whether serious bodily injury or death occurred to a victim during crime commission, and whether the offender was on probation or parole when crime was committed.

Aggravating circumstances applicable to both juveniles and adults can include:

1. *Death or serious bodily injury to one or more victims:* The most serious juvenile offenders are those who cause death or serious bodily injury to their victims. Homicide and aggravated assault are offenses that most directly involve death or serious physical harm to others, although it is possible to inflict serious bodily injury or deep emotional scars through armed robbery and even some property crimes, including burglary (Champion, 2008a). The harshest option available to juvenile court judges is commitment to secure confinement, such as an industrial school or reform school.

2. *An offense committed while the offender is awaiting other delinquency charges:* Are juveniles awaiting an intake hearing after being arrested for previous offenses? Some juveniles may commit new delinquent acts between the time they are

taken into custody for other offenses and the date of their intake hearing. These offenders are probably good candidates for temporary confinement in secure holding facilities until their cases can be heard by intake officers and delinquency petitions can be filed.

3. *An offense committed while the offender is on probation, parole, or other community release:* Offenders with prior adjudications who are serving current sentences may reoffend while on conditional release. One of the general conditions of diversion or probation is that youth refrain from further delinquent activity. Therefore, committing an offense is a violation of probation and considered to be a separate offense that may result in additional penalties. In effect, these incidents are a contempt of court, since they involve violations of direct court-ordered conditional activities. Conditional release programs have usually been granted to certain offenders because they were considered to be trustworthy by court officials. Violations of the court's trust are taken seriously, and it becomes less likely that violators will be considered for such privileges in the future.

4. *Previous offenses for which the offender has been punished:* A prior record is a strong indicator of chronicity and potential for future offending. Juvenile court judges may be less inclined toward leniency in sentencing youth with prior records, especially when serious delinquent acts have been committed. Repeat sex offenders, for example, are often treated more harshly by juvenile court judges because of potential risk to the community. Thus, regardless of whether the belief that a high rate of relapse among sex offenders is justified, the fact of being adjudicated a sex offender becomes an aggravating factor for many juvenile court judges (Bouhours and Daly, 2007).

5. *Leadership role in the commission of delinquency involving two or more offenders:* Especially in gang-related activities, a leadership role is an aggravating circumstance, and the court considers whether certain youth are gang leaders. Do they incite others to commit delinquent acts? Gang leaders are often targeted for the harshest punishments, because they are most visible to their peers and serve as examples of how the system deals with juvenile offenders. Those playing minor roles in gang-related activity might be treated more leniently by judges.

6. *A violent offense involving more than one victim:* As the number of victims increases, the potential for physical harm or death also increases. Robberies of convenience stores and other businesses involve settings where several customers might become victims. The number of victims or potential victims aggravates the delinquent conduct.

7. *Extreme cruelty during the commission of the offense:* Maiming or torturing victims during the commission of delinquent acts is considered to be extreme cruelty and deserving of enhanced punishments by juvenile court judges.

8. *Use of a dangerous weapon in the commission of the offense, with high risk to human life:* The second- and third-leading causes of death among juveniles under age 21

are homicides and suicides, respectively, and most of these events include the use of firearms (Metts, 2005). Using firearms to commit delinquent acts increases the potential harm to victim. Many states currently have mandatory **flat time**, or hard time, sentences associated with using firearms during the commission of felonies. This means that if someone uses a dangerous weapon during the commission of a crime, a mandatory sentence enhancement is included, which may be from two to five years in addition to the initial punishment.

Mitigating Circumstances

Mitigating circumstances can include:

1. *No serious bodily injury resulting from the offense:* Petty property offenders who do not endanger lives or injure others may have their sentences mitigated. Interestingly, however, property offenders account for the majority of long-term juvenile detainees in industrial schools or secure juvenile facilities.

2. *No attempt to inflict serious bodily injury on anyone:* Those juveniles who commit theft or burglary usually wish to avoid confrontations with their victims. While some juveniles prepare for such contingencies and, therefore, pose bodily threats to others, most youthful offenders committing such acts run away from the crime scene if discovered. This is evidence of their desire to avoid inflicting serious bodily harm on their victims.

3. *Duress or extreme provocation:* A compelling defense used in criminal court cases is that offenders were under duress at the time they committed their crimes. They may have been forced to act by others. Under such circumstances, youth may plead that they were coerced, or were acting under duress, when committing delinquent acts in concert with others. Gang membership and gang violence may be precipitated, to a degree, because of duress. For example, youth may join gangs for self-protection and to avoid being assaulted by other gang members.

4. *Circumstances that justify the conduct:* Circumstances that might justify one's conduct are mitigating factors. If youth act to protect themselves or others from physical harm, judges may find these circumstances sufficient to justify the conduct exhibited.

5. *Mental incapacitation or a physical condition that significantly reduces the offender's culpability in the offense:* This factor specifies conditions that relate to drug or alcohol dependencies or to mental retardation or mental illness. If youth are suffering from some form of mental illness or retardation or are alcohol or drug dependent, their condition may limit their capacity to understand and comply with the law.

6. *Cooperation with authorities in apprehending other participants in the act or making restitution to the victims for losses they suffered:* As with adults, youth who assist police in apprehending others involved in the crimes are credited with

---

flat time

Frequently known as hard time, meaning the actual amount of time one must serve while incarcerated.

mitigating circumstances

Factors that lessen the severity of the crime and/or sentence; these include young age, cooperation with police in apprehending other offenders, and lack of intent to inflict injury.

these positive deeds. In addition, juveniles who make restitution to victims or compensate them in part or in whole for their financial losses may have their cases mitigated through such restitution and good works.

7. *No prior record of delinquency:* First-offender juveniles, particularly those under age 16, are more likely to be considered eligible for more lenient treatment compared with recidivists.

8. *Age and youthfulness:* Generally, the younger the juvenile, the greater the mitigation. Under common law, for instance, persons who commit crimes and are under the age of seven are presumed to be incapable of formulating criminal intent. However, youth who are 8 to 12 years of age may be considered for some mitigation as well. Not being a fully formed adult renders a juvenile less mature and less capable of sound decision making. For example, it is more difficult for juveniles to comprehend the law and comply with it. Thus, youthfulness can be weighed against aggravating circumstances.

Juvenile Risk Assessments and Predictions of Dangerousness

In addition to aggravating and mitigating circumstances, other factors may affect the judicial decision. At each stage of the juvenile justice process, court officials want to know whether offenders are at risk to recidivate if they receive leniency. Prediction is uncertain, however. No one knows which offenders are more likely to recidivate, although certain factors correlate highly with recidivism (Trulson and Haerle, 2008). Therefore, ways of assessing juvenile dangerousness or risk to the community can be useful in influencing prosecutorial and judicial decision making.

Specifically, risk assessment is an element of a classification system and traditionally means the process of determining the probability that an individual will repeat unlawful or destructive behavior (Miller and Lin, 2007). **Risk prediction** takes several forms, including the prediction of violent behavior, of new offenses (recidivism), and of technical program violations associated with probation and parole.

Most states have some semblance of risk assessment of juvenile offenders, but only about half of the states have formal risk assessment instruments (Case, 2007). Some states, such as North Carolina and Arizona, use management information systems for data to track offenders. Risk assessment information is used with evidence-based programs to provide better matching of offender needs with the available services. This includes targeting high-risk offenders and providing a continuum of programs (Mattingly, 2011).

Dangerousness and Risk

The concepts of **dangerousness** and **risk** are often used interchangeably. Both dangerousness and risk convey propensities to cause harm to others or oneself. What is the likelihood that any particular offender will be violent toward others?

risk prediction
Assessment of some expected future behavior of a person, including criminal acts, arrests, or convictions.

dangerousness
Defined differently in various jurisdictions; prior record of violent offenses; potential to commit future violent crimes if released; propensity to inflict injury; predicted risk of convicted offender or of prison or jail inmate; likelihood of inflicting harm upon others.

risk
Potential likelihood for someone to engage in further delinquency or criminality.

Who are dangerous youth, and how do judges decide?
(Scott Cunningham/Pearson)

Does an offender pose any risk to public safety? What is the likelihood that any particular offender will commit suicide, or at least attempt it?

Risk (or dangerousness) instruments are screening devices intended to distinguish among different types of offenders for the purposes of determining initial institutional classification, security placement and inmate management, early release eligibility, and level of supervision required under conditions of probation or parole. These instruments contain information believed to be useful in forecasting future delinquent conduct or criminality (Case, 2007). This information is collectively referred to as **predictors of dangerousness and risk**. Most state jurisdictions and the federal government, however, regard these measures that forecast future criminality or delinquency as **risk/needs assessment instruments** rather than as dangerousness instruments per se (Case, 2007). There is considerable variability among states regarding the format and content of such measures as well.

Needs Assessment and Its Measurement

Besides measuring a juvenile's potential risk or dangerousness, it is important for juvenile justice practitioners to know what types of problems afflict particular youth. Many youth who enter the juvenile justice system are drug or alcohol dependent, have psychological problems, suffer from maladjustments in their homes or schools, or are impaired physically in some respect. Therefore, to determine the needs of juveniles, practitioners must assess juveniles who are processed.

Needs assessment instruments measure an offender's personal/social skills; health, well-being, and emotional stability; educational level and vocational strengths and weaknesses; alcohol/drug dependencies; mental ability; and other relevant life

---

predictors of dangerousness and risk

Assessment devices that attempt to forecast one's potential for violence or risk to others; any factors that are used in such instruments.

risk/needs assessment instruments

Predictive device intended to forecast offender propensity to commit new offenses or recidivate.

needs assessment

Instruments to identify social, psychological, and mental health needs of youth.

factors and highlight those areas for which services are available and could or should be provided (Salinas, 2008). As implied above, sometimes scales are combined to obtain information about both risks and needs, enabling those conducting such assessments to obtain both types of information from youth in one test administration. Not all juveniles need the same community services. There are diverse community resources available to meet a wide variety of needs exhibited by the youth who enter the juvenile justice system. Some juveniles require minimal intervention, while others need extensive treatments and services. Whether youth are confined in secure facilities or allowed to attend their schools and remain with their families in their communities, different provisions often must be made to individualize their needs. Needs assessment instruments are used to determine which specific services and treatments ought to be provided to each youth.

Attempts to forecast juvenile dangerousness/risk and needs are important, because many actors in the juvenile justice system use these predictions or forecasts as the basis for their decision making (Case, 2007). Intake officers who initially screen youthful offenders try to decide which offenders are most deserving of leniency and which should be referred for more formal processing. Prosecutors want to know which juveniles are most receptive to diversion and amenable to change. In this way, they can ensure that only the most serious and chronic offenders will be processed, while the remaining youth will have another chance to remain in their communities without juvenile justice system supervision. Judges also want to know which youth will likely reoffend if returned to their communities through probation or some other nonincarcerative option.

Selective Incapacitation

Some juvenile offenders may be penalized purely on the basis of their likelihood of future offending. Others may receive leniency, because they are considered to be good probation risks and unlikely to reoffend. Thus, some juveniles are selectively incapacitated.

Selective incapacitation refers to confining offenders who are predicted to pose a risk to others, usually on the basis of their prior record and/or risk score on some risk instrument. For adult criminals, attempts to forecast criminal behaviors have led to recommendations for selective incapacitation in many jurisdictions. Selective incapacitation involves incarcerating or detaining those persons believed to be likely recidivists on the basis of various behavioral and attitudinal criteria. The theory behind selective incapacitation is that if high-risk offenders can be targeted and controlled through long-term confinement, then their criminality will be limited.

Basically, incapacitation is a strategy for crime control involving the physical isolation of offenders from their communities, usually through incarceration, to prevent them from committing future crimes. The major harm is penalizing youth for acts they have not yet committed. Can the court legitimately punish anyone in the United States for suspected future criminality or delinquency? Whatever one's personal

selective incapacitation
Incarcerating individuals who show a high likelihood of repeating their previous offenses; based on forecasts of potential for recidivism; includes but not limited to dangerousness.

feelings in this regard, the answer is that such punishments are imposed each time probation recommendations are rejected in favor of incarceration.

Two types of incapacitation are (1) collective and (2) selective. Under collective incapacitation, crime reduction is accomplished through traditional, offense-based sentencing and incarcerative policies, such as mandatory minimum sentences. Under selective incapacitation, however, those offenders predicted to pose the greatest risk of future crimes become prime candidates for incarceration and for longer prison sentences. A problem in both the criminal justice system and the juvenile justice system, however, is that no universally acceptable implementation policies have been adopted in jurisdictions supporting the use of such incapacitation strategies. Furthermore, many of these instruments cannot distinguish adequately between risks posed by male juvenile offenders and those posed by female juvenile offenders (Case, 2007).

False Positives and False Negatives

At least two major dangers are inherent in risk or dangerousness predictions. First, youth who are identified as likely recidivists may receive harsher treatment compared with those who are considered to be unlikely to reoffend. Youth considered as good risks for probation or diversion, however, may eventually turn out to be dangerous, although predictions of their future conduct gave assurances to the contrary. Second, those youth who receive harsher punishment and longer confinement because they are believed to be dangerous may not, in fact, be dangerous. Therefore, we risk over-penalizing those who will not be dangerous in the future, although our forecasts suggest they will be dangerous. We also risk underpenalizing those believed by our forecasts not to be dangerous, because a portion will eventually turn out to be dangerous and seriously injure or even kill others (Case, 2007).

These two scenarios depict false positives and false negatives (Table 9.1). **False positives** are those persons predicted to be delinquent or dangerous in the future but who turn out not to be delinquent or dangerous. **False negatives** are those persons predicted not to be delinquent or dangerous in the future but who turn out to be delinquent or dangerous anyway. False positives are unduly punished because of our predictions, while false negatives do not receive sanctions, punishment, or future supervision (Champion, 2008a).

false positives
Offenders predicted to be dangerous who turn out not to be dangerous.

false negatives
Offenders predicted not to be dangerous who turn out to be dangerous.

Table 9.1
DELINQUENCY PREDICTIONS AND ERRORS

Outcome	Prediction	
	Risk (Delinquent Behavior)	No Risk (No Delinquent Behavior)
Delinquent Behavior	True positive	False negative
No Delinquent Behavior	False positive	True negative

Source: Prepared by the authors.

At present, the quality of risk assessment devices is such that practitioners cannot depend upon them as absolutely perfect indicators of future conduct (Champion, 1994; Miller and Lin, 2007). One problem is that many risk assessment instruments are tested on adult offenders rather than juvenile offenders. Also, follow-up periods for the assessments of predictive effectiveness are often relatively short, thus preventing researchers from validating the predictive utility of these scales over time. Still another issue in using risk assessments is gender bias. Research suggests the need to develop "gendered assessment instruments" for female delinquents (Emeka and Sorensen, 2009). Despite the continuing controversy surrounding the application of risk prediction measures and the criticisms by some researchers that such predictions are either impossible or inappropriate, predictions continue to be made.

Categories of Risk Predictions

Generally, risk assessment measures are one of the three following categories: (1) anamnestic prediction; (2) actuarial prediction; and (3) clinical prediction.

Anamnestic Prediction

Anamnestic prediction uses past sets of circumstances to predict future behaviors. If the current circumstances are similar to past circumstances in which previous offense behaviors were observed, then that youth will likely exhibit future offending.

Actuarial Prediction

Actuarial prediction is an aggregate predictive tool. Those youthful offenders who are being considered for diversion, probation, or aftercare are compared with former offenders who have similar characteristics. Performances and records of previous conduct in view of diversion, probation, or parole decisions serve as the basis for profiling the high-risk recidivist. Certain youth may exhibit characteristics similar to those of previous juveniles who became recidivists. The expectation is that these youth will likely recidivate as well.

Clinical Prediction

Clinical prediction involves professional assessments of diagnostic examinations and test results. The professional training of probation officers, prosecutors, and judges, as they experience working with youthful offenders which enables them to forecast probable behaviors of their present clients.

Clinical prediction involves the administration of psychological tests and personality assessment instruments. Certain background and behavioral characteristics are assessed as well. Some consider clinical prediction to be superior to actuarial and anamnestic prediction, although there is little support for this claim. Evidence does suggest, however, that actuarial prediction, the simplest prediction form, is equal to or more accurate than clinical prediction (Marchese, 1992).

anamnestic prediction
Projection of future behavior according to past circumstances.

actuarial prediction
Projection of future behavior based on a class of offenders similar to those considered for parole.

clinical prediction
Forecast of future behavior based on professional and expert training and working directly with offenders.

Common Elements of Risk Assessment Instruments

Risk assessment has evolved into the use of more precise and informative instruments. In his review of juvenile risk assessments, Schwalbe (2008) described three phases of assessment, beginning with "impressionistic" assessments, prediction and classification instruments, and treatment planning assessments (p. 1368).

Risk assessment measures for juvenile offenders contain several common elements (Case, 2007). Adapting these common elements to youthful offender scenarios, the following elements seem to be prevalent:

1. Age at first adjudication.
2. Prior delinquent behavior (a combined measure of the number and severity of priors).
3. Number of prior commitments to juvenile facilities.
4. Drug/chemical abuse.
5. Alcohol abuse.
6. Family relationships (parental control).
7. School problems.
8. Peer relationships.

For each of these elements, some evidence has been found to establish a definite association between these and recidivism potential. These associations are not always strong, but in an actuarial prediction sense, they provide a basis for assuming that each of these elements has some causal value. Therefore, the earlier the age of first adjudication and/or contact with the juvenile justice system, the greater the risk of recidivism (Loeber, Farrington, and Petechuk, 2003). Poor school performance, family problems and a lack of parental control, drug and/or alcohol dependencies, prior commitments to juvenile facilities, and a history of juvenile offending are individually and collectively linked with recidivism.

As an example of a risk assessment instrument currently in use, the California Youth Authority (2008) includes the following variables and response weights as a means of assessing one's risk level:

1. Age at first police contact:

   9 = score 6 points

   10 = score 5 points

   11 = score 4 points

   12 = score 3 points

   13 = score 2 points

   14 = score 1 point

   15 = score 0 points

2. Number of prior police contacts (number):

   Score actual number

3. Aggression and/or purse snatching:

   Yes = score 1

   No = score 0

4. Petty theft:

   Yes = score 1

   No = score 0

5. Use of alcohol or glue:

   Yes = score 1

   No = score 0

6. Usually three or more others involved in delinquent act:

   Yes = score 1

   No = score 0

7. Family on welfare:

   Yes = score 1

   No = score 0

8. Father main support in family:

   No = score 1

   Yes = score 0

9. Intact family:

   No = score 1

   Yes = score 0

10. Number of siblings:

    3 = score 1 point

    4 = score 2 points

    5+ = score 3 points

11. Father has criminal record:

    Yes = score 1

    No = score 0

12. Mother has criminal record:

    Yes = score 1

    No = score 0

13. Low family supervision:

   Yes = score 1

   No = score 0

14. Mother rejects:

   Yes = score 1

   No = score 0

15. Father rejects:

   Yes = score 1

   No = score 0

16. Parents wanted youth committed:

   No = score 1

   Yes = score 0

17. Verbal IQ:

   ≤69 = score 4

   70–79 = score 3

   80–89 = score 2

   90–99 = score 1

   100+ = score 0

18. Grade level:

   At grade level = score 1

   1 year retarded = score 2

   2 years retarded = score 3

   3 years retarded = score 4

   4+ years retarded = score 5

19. Negative school attitude:

   Score 0–3

20. School disciplinary problems:

   Yes = score 1

   No = score 0

On the basis of the score obtained, youth might be assigned the following risk levels:

Risk Level Score	Degree of Risk
0–22	Low
21–31	Medium
32+	High

Youth who receive scores of 0 to 22 are considered to be low risks, while those with scores of 32 or higher are considered to be high risks. California Youth Authority officials believe that while these scores do not necessarily indicate all youth with higher scores will be recidivists and all with lower scores will be nonrecidivists, there does appear to be some indication that these categorizations are generally valid. Thus, these classifications might be used to segregate more-serious offenders from less-serious ones in secure confinement facilities. Such scores also might be useful in the forecasts of future performance in diversion or probationary programs.

The Functions of Classification

When risk assessment measures or indices are examined critically, it is interesting to note how such important, life-influencing decisions are often reduced to six or seven predictive criteria. In addition to the instrumentation devised by the California Youth Authority discussed above, decisions about youth made by this organization are supplemented with several other important **classification** criteria, such as personality assessment tools, youth interviews, and professional impressions.

Classification systems perform several important functions:

1. Classification systems enable authorities to make decisions about appropriate offender program placements.

2. Classification systems help to identify needs and the provision of effective services in specialized treatment programs.

3. Classification assists in determining custody level if confined in either residential or institutional settings.

4. Classification systems help to adjust custody level during confinement by considering behavioral improvement and evidence of rehabilitation.

5. Classification systems may be used to target youth for particular services and/or programs to meet their needs while confined.

6. Classification systems may be used for offender management and deterrence relative to program or institutional rules and requirements.

7. Classification systems are useful for policy decision making and administrative planning relevant for institutional construction, the nature and number of facilities required, and the types of services to be made available within such facilities.

8. Classification systems enable courts to make better early release decisions about eligible offenders.

9. Classification systems can be used by community corrections agencies to determine youth who qualify for participation and those who do not.

10. Classification systems enable general assessments of risk and dangerousness to be made in anticipation of the type of supervision best suited for particular offenders.

classification
Means used by institutions and probation/parole agencies to separate offenders according to offense seriousness, type of offense, and other criteria.

11. Classification systems assist in decision making relevant for community crime control, the nature of penalties to be imposed, and the determination of punishment.

12. Classification systems enable authorities to determine whether selective incapacitation is desirable for particular offenders or offender groups.

For most states, the following general applications are made of risk assessment instruments at different client-processing stages:

1. To promote better program planning through optimum budgeting and deployment of resources.

2. To target high-risk and high-need offenders for particular custody levels, programs, and services without endangering the safety of others.

3. To apply fair and appropriate sanctions to particular classes of offenders and raise their level of accountability.

4. To provide mechanisms for evaluating services and programs as well as service and program improvements over time.

5. To maximize public safety as well as public understanding about the diverse functions of corrections by making decision making more open and comprehensible to both citizens and offender-clients.

Sound predictive models should exhibit validity and reality, be dynamic rather than fixed, serve practical purposes, reflect responsible judgment, and have both qualitative and quantitative components. To offer programs that are sensitive to the youth and the community's needs, more jurisdictions are relying on a risk assessment instrument to guide the courts in making the appropriate disposition. Juvenile justice professionals utilize these screening instruments to help them achieve their rehabilitative ideal. These assessments are intended to occur throughout the process rather than at just one stage.

Risk Prediction from Arizona and Florida

Two different risk prediction instruments have been devised by Arizona and Florida. As an exercise, read the following scenarios involving several hypothetical delinquents. Next, read through the particular risk prediction instruments, paying attention to their instructions for score determinations. Then, complete each instrument, and determine the total score for each juvenile.

It will be apparent that this task is easier for some instruments than for others. You will need to do several things when you compute scores for each of these juvenile offenders. You will need to keep track of their ages, how many formal and informal delinquency or status offender adjudications they have received, and whether they have escaped or attempted escape from a secure juvenile facility. In some of the instruments, you will also need to determine whether they are drug or alcohol dependent. A brief solution will be provided at the end of the two scenarios.

Scenario 1: Arizona and Ronald M.

Background. Ronald M. lives in Phoenix, Arizona. He is 14 years old. Ronald M. has been a member of the Scorpions, a Phoenix juvenile gang, for three years and has participated in several drive-by shootings, none of which has resulted in fatalities to the intended victims. Ronald M. is known to the police. When Ronald M. was 11, he was taken into custody for assaulting another student in his school. This was the result of a referral by the school principal. An intake officer adjusted the case and returned Ronald M. to the custody of his parents. Two months later, Ronald M. was taken into custody again, this time for beating another student with a lead pipe and causing serious bodily injuries. Again, the school principal referred Ronald M. to juvenile authorities for processing, and a delinquency petition was filed. This time, however, the juvenile court judge heard Ronald M.'s case and adjudicated him delinquent on the assault charge. Ronald M. was disposed to probation for one year.

While on probation, Ronald M. joined the Scorpions and was involved in at least three convenience store thefts and five crack cocaine sales. During the last such sale, an undercover police officer posing as a customer arrested Ronald M. and two of his gang companions and took them to the police station for processing. Ronald M. appeared again before the same juvenile court judge after a police referral. This time, the judge adjudicated Ronald M. delinquent on the drug charge and disposed him to an 18-month probationary term. In the meantime, during a routine drug screen at the local jail where Ronald M. was in preventive detention, he tested positive for cocaine and alcohol use. Under questioning, Ronald M. admitted to using drugs occasionally as well as to consuming alcohol at gang meetings.

When Ronald M. was 12 and still on probation, he was taken into custody by police following a burglary report at a local drug store. When officers apprehended Ronald M., he was crawling out of a back window of the drug store with several bottles of Percodan, a prescription pain reliever. Officers confiscated a loaded .22-caliber pistol, which Ronald M. was carrying in his jacket pocket. Officers filed a delinquency petition with the juvenile court, alleging several law violations, including burglary, theft, and carrying a concealed firearm. Ronald M.'s probation officer also referred Ronald M. to the juvenile court and recommended that his probation program be revoked, because he was in clear violation of his probation program requirements. The juvenile court judge adjudicated Ronald M. delinquent on the firearms charge as well as on the burglary and theft charges. He also revoked Ronald M.'s probation after a two-stage hearing during which substantial evidence was presented of Ronald M.'s guilt. Ronald M. was disposed to six months of intensive supervised probation with electronic monitoring.

Subsequently, Ronald M. has been adjudicated delinquent three more times. Police officers filed petitions with the juvenile court on all three occasions. Two of these delinquency adjudications were for felonies (aggravated assault and selling one kilogram of cocaine). For the aggravated assault offense, the juvenile court judge disposed Ronald M. to the Arizona State Industrial School, a secure-custody facility, for a term of six months. The judge also revoked Ronald M.'s probation program.

A predispositional report filed by the juvenile probation officer disclosed that Ronald M. has frequently been truant from school and has had serious behavioral problems when in school. He has had difficulty relating with other youth.

Two weeks ago, Ronald M. was taken into custody and charged with arson, a felony. He and two Scorpion gang members were observed by three eyewitnesses setting fire to the occupied home of a rival gang member. Fortunately, no one was injured in the resulting fire. The juvenile court judge has just adjudicated Ronald M. delinquent on the arson charge and has committed him to the Arizona State Industrial School for two years.

Using the Arizona Department of Juvenile Corrections (ADJC) Risk Assessment form illustrated in Figure 9.3, what is Ronald M.'s total risk score? What is Ronald M.'s risk category? What is Ronald M.'s most serious commitment offense? What is Ronald M.'s most serious prior adjudicated offense?

Calculating the ADJC Risk Score for Ronald M.   Before determining Ronald M.'s score on the ADJC Risk Assessment instrument, familiarize yourself with the instrument's contents. There are eight categories: (1) number of referrals, (2) number of adjudications, (3) age at first juvenile referral, (4) petition offense history, (5) petitions for felony offenses, (6) affiliation with a delinquent gang, (7) enrolled in school with no serious truancy or behavioral problems, and (8) known use of alcohol or drugs.

First, count the number of times Ronald M. has been referred to juvenile court on various charges. Count both referrals and delinquency petitions filed against Ronald M., because both actions are intended to bring juveniles before the juvenile court. In Ronald M.'s case, he was referred by the school principal on two occasions, with a delinquency petition filed on the second occasion. Ronald M. was referred again to juvenile court by police officers for selling crack cocaine. Later, he was referred to the juvenile court for burglary, theft, and carrying a concealed weapon. Ronald M.'s probation officer also referred him to the juvenile court because of a probation violation. Subsequently, Ronald M. was referred to juvenile court three more times, all resulting in delinquency adjudications. Two of these offenses were felonies: aggravated assault and selling cocaine. Finally, Ronald M. was most recently referred to the juvenile court for arson and adjudicated delinquent on that charge. Therefore, there are at least nine referrals of Ronald M. to juvenile court. Since this is "5 or More," give Ronald M. a +1 for R1, as shown in Figure 9.3.

Next, determine the number of Ronald M.'s adjudications. He was adjudicated delinquent on the school assault charge, the drug charge, and on the firearms, burglary, and theft charges. He has three additional adjudications for offenses including aggravated assault and selling cocaine, as well as one for arson. This adds up to seven delinquency adjudications. For R2, this is "5 or More," and therefore, we score R2 with a +1.

Ronald M.'s age at his first juvenile court referral was 11. For R3, this is "12 Yrs, 5 mos or Younger." Therefore, score R3 with a +1.

ADJC RISK ASSESSMENT

YOUTH NAME _____ K# _____ DATE OF ASSESSMENT _____

COMMITTING COUNTY _____ DATE OF ADMISSION _____ DOB _____

SCORE

R1   **Number of Referrals**   (_)
1 to 4 0
5 or More ....+1
_____

R2   **Number of Adjudications**   (_)
1 or 2 ....-1
3 or 4 0
5 or More ....+1
_____

R3   **Age at First Juvenile Referral**   (_)
12 yrs 5 mos. or Younger................................+1
12 yrs 6 mos. or Older....................................0
_____

R4   **Petition Offense History (check applicable below and add for score)**
A.(_) 2 or More Assaultive Offenses.................+1
B.(_) 2 or More Drug Offenses..........................+2
C.(_) 3 or More Property Offenses....................+1
D.(_) Weapons Offense or use in above.............+1

         R 4 Sub Total   _____
_____

R5   **Petitions for Felony Offenses**   (_)
0 to 2.. 0
3 or More..+1
_____

R6   **Affiliation with a Delinquent Gang**
No..0
Yes..+1
_____

R7   **Enrolled in School with no Serious Truancy or Behavioral Problems**
No.. 0
Yes..-1
_____

R8   **Known Use of Alcohol or Drugs**
No..-1
Yes.. 0
_____

                TOTAL RISK SCORE   _____

RISK CATEGORY (CHECK ONE)		
[ ] LOW(1 or Less)	[ ] MEDIUM (2-4)	[ ] HIGH (5+)

_____
Signature of Staff Completing Assessment Instrument

CURRENT COMMITMENT TYPE (CHECK ONE):   [ ] NEW COMMIT   [ ]ADJC REVOCATION

MOST SERIOUS COMMITMENT OFFENSE:

OFFENSE DESCRIPTION	ARS CODE	F/M CLASS	SUBCLASS	DATE

MOST SERIOUS PRIOR ADJUDICATED OFFENSE:

OFFENSE DESCRIPTION	ARS CODE	F/M CLASS	SUBCLASS	DATE

CLASS: 1,2,3,4,5,6 OR 9 = NOT APPLICABLE
F=FELONY   M=MISDEMEANOR   V=VIOLATION PROB. OR PAROLE   O=OTHER

Figure 9.3
Arizona Department of Juvenile Corrections Risk Assessment Instrument
Source: Reprinted with the permission of Arizona Department of Juvenile Corrections.

Ronald M.'s petition offense history includes "2 or More Assaultive Offenses." Score this portion of the risk instrument, R4A, with a +1. Ronald M. also has "2 or More Drug Offenses." Therefore, assign him a +2 in R4B. Although Ronald M. has participated in several thefts, as mentioned in the scenario, count only what police and other authorities actually know about Ronald M. and which types of offenses resulted in petitions filed with the juvenile court. He has a burglary and a theft charge for which petitions have been filed. Because this is not "3 or More Property Offenses," do not assign Ronald M. a score in R4C. However, give Ronald M. a +1 for "Weapons Offense or use in above." Thus, in the R4 Petition Offense History section, Ronald M. should receive a total score of 4.

The R5 section is "Petitions for Felony Offenses." Ronald M. has at least three or more of these. Therefore, assign him a score +1 for R5.

The R6 section is easy to score. Is Ronald M. a gang member? Yes. Therefore, he receives a score of +1 for R6.

The R7 section is also easy to score. Ronald M. has been enrolled in school in the past, but he has serious truancy problems. Therefore, assign him a score of 0 for R7.

Finally, for the R8 section, Ronald M. is known for his use of alcohol and drugs. Therefore, he must receive a score of 0 for R8.

Summing R1 through R8 results in: $1 + 1 + 1 + 4 + 1 + 1 + 0 + 0 = 9$. Therefore, Ronald M.'s total risk assessment score is 9. According to the ADJC Risk Assessment instrument, the risk category would place Ronald M. is "High" (5+ points).

Notice that there are other items to fill in on this form. One space is for "Most Serious Commitment Offense." We are not in a position to know how Arizona rates the seriousness of aggravated assault in relation to arson. However, these are the two offenses resulting in Ronald M.'s commitment to the Arizona State Industrial School. If arson were the more-serious offense, then this would be listed in the space for "Most Serious Commitment Offense," with an appropriate code and date. This would be a felony. For the "Most Serious Prior Adjudicated Offense," list aggravated assault, which is a felony as well. In addition, enter a code for this offense as well as the date of the adjudication.

Without the accompanying ADJC instruction manual for this instrument, you do not know how Ronald M.'s score of 9 will be used. In all likelihood, it will relate to his placement in the secure facility and the intensity of supervision he will receive while confined. Ronald M. is definitely a risk to others and must be monitored carefully. However, this score is only one of many criteria that are used in placement and level-of-custody decision making.

Figure 9.4 is a reassessment form, and it serves to give an impression of how much Ronald M. has improved his behavior since being admitted into the community-based program. In this form, attention is focused on peer relationships within a 30- to 90-day period; whether there have been problems with school or work adjustment during a similar time interval; and whether the client has had problems adjusting to

---

ADJC RISK REASSESSMENT

FOR YOUTH IN COMMUNITY PROGRAMS

YOUTH NAME _____ K# _____ DOB _____ DATE OF REASSESSMENT _____

For items 1 - 4 use initial Risk Assessment information

				SCORE

RE 1.   **Age At First Referral**   (_____)
            12 Years or Less ....+1
            13 Years or Older 0

RE 2.   **Number of Prior Referrals**   (_____)
            4 or Less 0
            5 or More ....+1

RE 3.   **Prior Petition Offense History**
            A (_____)   3 or More Property ....+1
            B (_____)   2 or More Assaultive Offenses ....+1
            C (_____)   2 or More Drug Offenses ....+2
            D (_____)   Weapons Offense...+1

                                    RE 3 SUBTOTAL   _____

RE 4.   **Prior Petitions For Felony Offenses**   (_____)
            2 or Less 0
            3 or More ....+1

Score All Following Items for Last 30/90 Days.

RE 5.   **Referrals To Court or For Revocation Hearing (Last 30/90 days)**
            None ....-1
            One ....+1
            Two or More...+2

RE 6.   **Use of Alcohol or Other Drugs (Last 30/90 Days)**
            No.. 0
            Yes...+1
            Check type (if any)   _____Alcohol   _____ Marijuana   _____ Other Drug

RE 7.   **Peer Relationships (Last 30/90 Days)**
            No Problems 0
            Associates with Delinquent Peers ....+1
            Associates with Gang Members   ....+2

RE 8.   **School or Work Adjustment (Last 30/90 Days)** _____ Where
            No Problems or Minor Problems...0
            Some Attendance /Behavior Problems ....+1
            Serious Work or School Attendance/Behavior Problems................+2

RE 9.   **Adjustment to Supervision/Compliance with Plan (Last 30/90 Days)**
            No Problems ....-1
            Minor Problems...0
            Serious Compliance Problems with Plan ....+1

                                    TOTAL SCORE   _____

RISK CATEGORY (CIRCLE ONE)
LOW (5 or Less) = LEVEL III   MEDIUM (6 - 10) = LEVEL II   HIGH (11 or HIGHER) = LEVEL I

Assigned Supervision Level_____   Override Y/N   Reason _____
                                                                     _____
                                                                     _____
                                                                     _____

Parole Officer's Signature _____   Date _____

Supervisor's Signature _____   Date _____

Figure 9.4
Arizona Department of Juvenile Corrections Risk Reassessment for Youth in Community Programs
Source: Reprinted with the permission of Arizona Department of Juvenile Corrections.

supervision or compliance with program requirements within the most recent 30- to 90-day period. In Ronald M.'s case, if he were placed in a community program instead of being incarcerated, he would be evaluated within a 30- to 90-day period following his community program placement. If he improved his behavior, there is a good possibility that his risk level (or risk category) could be reduced. This possible risk category reduction may have implications for how closely Ronald M. is supervised in his community-based program. It is also indicative of whether he is becoming rehabilitated and reintegrated.

Scenario 2: Florida and Susan R.

Background. Susan R. is 15 years old. She lives in Tampa, Florida, and is a sophomore in high school. Recently, a juvenile court judge adjudicated Susan R. delinquent for stealing a neighbor's car and joyriding. She drove the car into another state, where she wrecked it. Susan R. was accompanied by two other girls, who were subsequently identified as members of a female gang from Tampa. Susan R. has admitted that she, too, is a member of that same gang.

The auto theft charge is a third-degree felony. The judge has disposed her to two years of probation, together with mandatory psychological and substance-abuse counseling, because she had been using marijuana at the time of her arrest. She is currently receiving both psychological counseling and treatment for her substance abuse. The marijuana possession was a second-degree misdemeanor, although this charge was subsequently dropped pursuant to a plea bargain with the juvenile court prosecutor.

A predispositional report prepared by a juvenile probation officer for the juvenile court disclosed the following background factors for Susan R. She began her career of delinquency when she was 12 years of age. At that time, she shoplifted some cosmetics from a local department store. When she was confronted by a store security officer, Susan R. assaulted the officer by pushing her into a display counter. The glass broke, and the officer sustained severe lacerations. Susan R. was charged with theft and aggravated assault. The theft was related to a gang initiation. The juvenile court judge adjudicated her delinquent on both charges and ordered her committed to the Florida Industrial School, a secure facility, for a term of six months. Susan R. and another inmate escaped from this facility one evening, although they were apprehended three days later and returned to custody. Over the next few months, Susan R. tried to escape again on at least four different occasions. The juvenile court judge adjudicated her delinquent on an escape charge, and the term of her confinement in the Florida Industrial School was extended to one year. Susan R. was subsequently released from secure confinement at age 13 and returned to school. Over the next two years, she was involved in several minor incidents, involving low-level misdemeanors. In one instance, she was placed on diversion by the prosecutor, with judicial approval. A part of her diversion was performing 200 hours of community service as well as observance of a curfew. Her juvenile probation officer caught her violating curfew on at least three occasions and filed an affidavit with the juvenile court. Following the affidavit, the juvenile court judge verbally reprimanded Susan R. but he did not impose other sanctions.

An interview with Susan R.'s parents revealed that she is incorrigible. The parents say that they have no control over Susan R.'s actions. However, Susan R.'s siblings, a younger brother and a younger sister, report that their parents, who have frequent physical altercations in front of them and use drugs themselves, are seldom home to monitor them and their sister, Susan R. A counselor has concluded independently that the family has a history of domestic violence and that the home is quite unstable. Susan R.'s mother has been committed to a psychiatric institution in previous years for depression as well as schizophrenia. The mother is currently on medication for managing her depression. Susan R.'s father has a previous conviction for receiving stolen property, a second-degree misdemeanor. He has also been previously convicted of sexual battery and served six months in the county jail for this crime. In fact, at the present time, the Florida Department of Human Services is conducting an investigation of Susan R.'s family on charges of alleged child neglect.

Susan R. herself has no obvious developmental disabilities or prior mental illnesses, and she appears to be in good physical health. However, because of the history of her family, it has been recommended that she have a psychological assessment to determine her present mental state. Susan R. is currently unemployed and has no marketable skills. Thus, she would be unable to obtain and/or sustain employment if she were expected to work. It has been recommended that she take several vocational/technical courses to improve her skill level. Her peer relations are poor, and she is socially immature and withdrawn. She is easily led by others, as evidenced by the ease with which she was recruited into her gang. Most of Susan R.'s close peers are other gang members, and it has been determined that she has used marijuana frequently with her gang friends. She has poor school attendance, though when she has attended, she has been compliant and not disruptive. According to her teachers, Susan R. reads well and has no obvious learning disabilities. Susan R.'s home situation has been cited by the juvenile probation officer as a substantial mitigating circumstance, and she recommends a 5-point reduction in Susan R.'s risk score. The probation supervisor, who oversees risk assessment instrument preparation and administration, concurs with this recommendation and has chosen not to override it.

Figure 9.5 shows the Florida Department of Juvenile Justice Supervision Risk Classification Instrument. Notice that it consists of two parts. The first is a risk assessment scale, and the second is a needs assessment scale. Figure 9.5 also illustrates the Florida Department of Juvenile Justice Classification Matrix. This matrix is used to determine the level of a youth's placement in the Florida Department of Juvenile Justice based on a combination of the needs assessment score and the risk assessment score. For Susan R., and using the information in the above scenario, what is Susan R.'s risk assessment score? What is Susan R.'s needs assessment scores? According to the scores you have calculated, where should Susan R. be placed in the classification matrix?

Calculating the Florida Risk Assessment Score for Susan R. Again, when determining the score for any juvenile, you must first familiarize yourselves with the instrument's contents before computing a risk score. The Florida Department of Juvenile Justice Supervision Risk Classification Instrument (Figure 9.5) is divided into two parts: (1) risk assessment and (2) needs assessment. The first part also contains several

FLORIDA DEPARTMENT OF JUVENILE JUSTICE
SUPERVISION RISK CLASSIFICATION INSTRUMENT

Youth's Name: Sharon H Test   Court Docket #: _____

Juvenile Probation Officer: _____   Unit: _____

Date Completed: _____   DJJID: 532950   Referral ID: 1507938

RISK ASSESSMENT

A. INSTANT OFFENSE (most serious) ....

- Capital or life felony — 32 points
- 1st degree felony (violent) — 20 points
- 1st degree felony/2nd degree felony (violent) — 18 points
- 2nd degree felony/3rd degree felony (violent) — 15 points
- 3rd degree felony — 7 points
- 1st degree misdemeanor (violent) — 5 points
- 1st degree misdemeanor — 3 points
- 2nd degree misdemeanor — 1 point

B. PRIOR HISTORY (highest applicable score)

- Meets the criteria for Level 10 placement — 7 points
- Has met the definition of a SHO/IRT with this offense — 6 points
- Two or more prior non-related felonies resulting in adjudication or withheld adjudication — 3 points
- One felony or two or more non-related misdemeanors resulting in adjudication or withheld adjudication — 2 points
- One prior misdemeanor resulting in adj. or withheld adj. — 1 point

C. OTHER SCORING FACTORS (combined score) ....

- Current legal status CC/F (2 pts) - committed (4 pts)
- Previous completed CC/F (2 pts) committed (4pts)
- Previous technical violation (1 point per affidavit)
- Youth 12 years old/under at time of 1st charge (1pt)
- Substance use/abuse involved (1 pt.)
- History of escape or absconding (1pt.)
- Current or previous JASP/community arb. (2 pts each)
- Other previous or current diversion (1 pt. each)
- Domestic violence involved (youth as perpetrator) (2 pts each)
- Gang related offense (2 pt.)

D. A+B+C = SUBTOTAL   0

Mitigating (maximum 5 pts.)..................................(-)

Justification _____

Aggravating-consider pending offenses (max 5) ......(+)

Justification _____

TOTAL: A+B+C – mitigation + aggravating =   0

TOTAL RISK SCORE   0   TOTAL NEEDS SCORE   0

CLASSIFICATION DECISION (see matrix on page 3):

☐ Diversion   ☐ Minimum   ☐ General   ☐ Intensive

☐ Level 2   ☐ Level 4   ☐ Level 6   ☐ Level 8/10

OVERRIDE CLASSIFICATION DECISION (if applicable):

☐ Diversion   ☐ Minimum   ☐ General   ☐ Intensive

☐ Level 2   ☐ Level 4   ☐ Level 6   ☐ Level 8/10

OVERRIDE JUSTIFICATION: _____

JPO Initials _____ Date: _____

Supervisor Initials _____ Date: _____

NEEDS ASSESSMENT

FAMILY RELATIONSHIPS (score total points)   0

A. ....

- Parents unable/unwilling to control youth — 3 pts.
- Parent cooperative, some control — 1 pt.
- Youth in unstable independent living situation — 2 pts.
- Family history of domestic violence — 2 pts.
- Family history of abuse/neglect — 2 pts.
- Parent or sibling with criminal history — 1 pt.
- Parent with mental illness — 2 pts.
- Parent with substance abuse — 2 pts.
- Out of home dependency placement — 2 pts.
- Current abuse/neglect investigation — 3 pts.
- Youth is a parent — 3 pts.

B. PEER RELATIONSHIPS (score total pts)   0

- Socially immature — 1 pt.
- Socially withdrawn — 1 pt.
- Easily led by others — 1 pt.
- Exploits or aggressive to others — 1 pt.
- Peers have delinquent history or gang involvement — 3 pts.

C. SIGNIFICANT ADULT RELATIONS (score highest)   0

- Authority figure relationships are inconsistent — 1 pt.
- Youth unavailable/unwilling to positively relate to adult authority figures — 2 pts

D. EDUCATIONAL (score total pts.)   0

- Poor attendance/not enrolled (under 16) — 3 pts.
- Disruptive school behavior — 2 pts.
- Literacy problems — 2 pts.
- Learning disability — 2 pts.
- Withdrawn/expelled/suspended — 3 pts.
- Enrolled and failing — 2 pts.

E. YOUTH'S EMPLOYMENT (score total pts)   0

(youth over 16, not in school or youth with monetary needs)

- Currently developing marketable skills/no school — 1 pt.
- Needs to develop marketable skills — 2 pts.
- Currently unemployed — 2 pts.

F. DEVELOPMENTAL DISABILITY (score highest)   0

- Known dev. disability/no current services — 3 pts.
- Known dev. disability/with current services — 2 pts.
- Disability suspected/no diagnosis — 2 pts.

G. PHYSICAL HEALTH & HYGIENE (score total pts.)   0

- Medical or dental referral needed — 1 pt.
- Health or hygiene education needed — 1 pt.
- Handicap or illness limits functioning — 3 pts.

H. MENTAL HEALTH (score total pts.)   0

- Assessment needed — 2 pts.
- Prior history of mental health problems — 2 pts.
- Currently in treatment — 2 pts.
- Assessment indicates treatment needs/no current services — 3 pts.

I. SUBSTANCE ABUSE (score total pts.)   0

- Assessment needed — 2 pts.
- Occasional user — 1 pt.
- Frequent user — 3 pts.
- Assessment indicates treatment needs/no services — 3 pts.
- Receiving treatment services — 2 pts.

TOTAL NEEDS SCORE   0

April, 1998   Case Management: Intake   DJJ/IS Form 4

Page 1 of 3

Figure 9.5

Florida Department of Juvenile Justice Supervision Risk Classification Instrument
Source: Reprinted with permission of the Florida Department of Juvenile Justice.

FLORIDA DEPARTMENT OF JUVENILE JUSTICE
CLASSIFICATION MATRIX

NEEDS	RISK			
	LOW 0 10	MODERATE 11 17	HIGH 18 24	VERY HIGH 25 32
LOW 0 : : : 15	Diversion	Minimum Supervision General Supervision	Minimum Supervision General Intensive Supervision	Level 4 Level 6 Level 8/10
MODERATE 16 : : 30	Diversion	Minimum Supervision General Supervision	Intensive Level 2	Level 4 Level 6 Level 8/10
HIGH 31 : : : 45	Diversion Minimum Supervision	General Supervision	Intensive Level 2 Level 4	Level 6 Level 8/10
VERY HIGH 46+ : : :	Diversion Minimum Supervision	General Supervision Intensive Supervision	Level 2 Level 4 Level 6	Level 8/10

Figure 9.5 (*Continued*)

categories, including (1) instant offense (current offense), (2) prior history, and (3) other scoring factors.

For category A, "Instant Offense," Susan R. has recently been adjudicated delinquent on an auto theft charge, which is a third-degree felony. According to this risk assessment scale, a third-degree felony rates a score of 7 points.

For category B, "Prior History," assign Susan R. the "highest applicable score." This means that you are not supposed to add or sum the scores for all categories that fit Susan R. Given her delinquency history since age 12, including her escape from a secure facility, assault on a store security officer, and gang membership, she probably meets the criteria for "Level 10 placement." According to Florida officials, the risk score derived from this instrument at the time of a youth's arrest is used to make an appropriate recommendation to the state attorney's office (Champion, 2008a). Assume that Susan R. qualifies for Level 10 placement. Therefore assign her a score of 7 points.

Category C, "Other Scoring Factors," is additive, in that you are to consider a number of factors, each associated with specific points. These factors include current legal status (presently committed to a secure facility), previous completed commitment (to a secure facility), previous technical violation (in connection with a probation or parole program or diversion), age at time of first charge, substance use/abuse involvement, history of escape or absconding, current or previous community arbitration (alternative dispute resolution), other previous or current diversion, and gang-related offense. For each category that applies to Susan R., assign a score. Subsequently, sum the individual scores to determine the combined score for this category.

Currently, Susan R. is on probation. However, she has had a previous commitment to the Florida Industrial School. Therefore, assign her 4 points for this category. She also has a technical violation (violating curfew while on probation), and an affidavit has been filed in connection with this violation. Therefore, Susan R. receives another point.

In addition, Susan R. began her career of delinquency at age 12. Therefore, she receives 1 point. She is a substance abuser and so receives 1 point. She has a history of escape from the secure facility where she was placed, and this entitles her to 1 point. She has never participated in alternative dispute resolution, so she receives no points for this. However, she has been placed on diversion once in the past. Therefore, she receives 1 point. Although there is domestic violence in Susan R.'s home, she has never been the perpetrator. Therefore, she receives no points for this. Finally, she has had at least one gang-related offense, shoplifting, and receives 2 points for this. There are 10 factors as components of category C, and you add the various factor scores as follows: $0 + 4 + 1 + 1 + 1 + 1 + 0 + 1 + 0 + 2 = 11$ points. Susan R.'s total score for category C is 11.

Summing her scores for categories A, B, and C, you have $7 + 7 + 11 = 25$ points. Notice that for category D, "Subtotal," adjustments may be made for the presence of aggravating or mitigating circumstances. Anyone completing this risk assessment might choose to focus upon Susan R.'s violent acts, such as pushing the store security officer. They might also focus upon Susan R.'s escape from the Florida Industrial School and subsequent attempts to escape again. These factors might be considered as aggravating. However, substantial evidence exists that might constitute mitigating circumstances. Susan R.'s home life is a disaster. She has a dysfunctional family in which frequent physical altercations and drug use are evident. Background information about Susan R. from school officials suggests that but for her gang affiliation, she is a compliant and reasonably intelligent student. In the present scenario, the juvenile probation officer has recommended a 5-point reduction for Susan R., given her home circumstances. The probation supervisor has concurred with this recommendation. Therefore, there will probably be a 5-point reduction in Susan R.'s final score. This would be 25 − 5 = 20 points. Thus, Susan R.'s final risk assessment score would be 20.

One final word about the Florida risk reassessment device is in order. At the very bottom of the risk reassessment instrument shown in Figure 9.5, a classification decision is illustrated. However, immediately below this classification decision is an override classification decision. **Overrides** are decisions by someone in authority and with pertinent expertise to change whatever classification is yielded from the original risk score that has been computed. For instance, Susan R.'s score of 25 can be overridden for one or more reasons. The nature of the override is either to increase or to decrease the resulting score or classification decision. No risk assessment instrument captures every facet of the offender's case or circumstances. Therefore, if there are circumstances or facts that are relevant to cases such as Susan R.'s, then the original classification decision may be overridden. For instance, Susan R. may have been coerced into committing burglaries and thefts by her other gang members. Or, she may be emotionally immature for her age. Factors such as these may be detected through interviews with juvenile clients. Perhaps information is yielded through other means, such as reports from school or church officials. In any case, the particular score assigned to a juvenile client may be raised or lowered, provided that a reasonable justification is articulated to account for the override.

Computing Susan R.'s Florida Needs Assessment Score. The Florida Risk Classification Instrument shown in Figure 9.5 contains both a "Needs Assessment" component and a "Risk Assessment" component. You have already calculated the risk assessment component. Now compute Susan R.'s needs assessment score based on the scenario information provided earlier.

Again, familiarize yourself with the needs assessment instrument, the second part of the Florida Risk Classification Instrument. Nine areas are covered: (1) family relationships, (2) peer relationships, (3) significant adult relations, (4) educational factors, (5) youth's employment, (6) developmental disability (if any), (7) physical health and hygiene, (8) mental health, and (9) substance abuse. Some of these areas contain additive components, meaning that you must assign points to juveniles such as Susan R. if certain subparts of these areas pertain to youth's circumstances.

For category A, "Family Relationships," you know from the above scenario about Susan R. that her parents cannot control her. You also know that she lives in an unstable family environment, with a family history of domestic violence and abuse and/or neglect. In addition, one parent has a criminal history. You also know that the parents use drugs or abuse various substances. Furthermore, there is an ongoing investigation of this allegedly abusive environment by the Florida Department of Human

overrides
Actions by an authority in an institution or agency that overrule a score for or an assessment made of a client or inmate; raw scores or assessments or recommendations can be overruled; the function of override is to upgrade or downgrade the seriousness of offense status, thus changing the level of custody at which one is maintained in secure confinement; may also affect the type and nature of community programming for particular offenders.

344 CHAPTER NINE ■ THE ADJUDICATORY PROCESS

Services. Susan R. herself is not a parent. Therefore, you would score the 11 item in category A as follows:

Parents unable/unwilling to control youth	Yes	3 points
Parent cooperative, some control	No	0 points
Youth in unstable independent living situation	Yes	2 points
Family history of domestic violence	Yes	2 points
Family history of abuse/neglect	Yes	2 points
Parent or sibling with criminal history	Yes	1 point
Parent with mental illness	Yes	2 points
Parent with substance abuse	Yes	2 points
Out-of-home dependency placement	No	0 points
Current abuse/neglect investigation	Yes	3 points
Youth is a parent	No	0 points
Total		**17 points**

Category B, "Peer Relationships," has five components. Score these as follows:

Socially immature	Yes	1 point
Socially withdrawn	Yes	1 point
Easily led by others	Yes	1 point
Exploits or aggressive to others	No	0 points
Peers have delinquent history or gang involvement	Yes	3 points
Total		**6 points**

In category C, "Significant Adult Relations," you can assign Susan R. 1 point for "Authority figure relationships are inconsistent," however, you have no data to suggest that Susan R. is unavailable/unwilling to positively relate to adult authority figures. Thus, Susan R.'s total score for this category would be 1 point.

Category D, "Educational," has six components: (1) poor attendance/not enrolled (under 16), (2) disruptive school behavior, (3) literacy problems, (4) learning disability, (5) withdrawn/expelled/suspended, and (6) enrolled and failing. Susan R. has poor attendance at school, although she is not disruptive and has no literacy or learning disability problems. She has not withdrawn from school, nor has she been expelled or suspended. She is not failing her classes, despite her truancy. Therefore, give her 3 points for poor attendance, but 0 points for the other components. Her total score for category D is 3 points.

For category E, "Youth's Employment," Susan R. is not "over 16." Therefore, these subparts are not relevant for her, and she receives a score of 0 points for this category.

For category F, "Developmental Disability," Susan R. has no known developmental disabilities. Therefore, she receives a score of 0 points for this category.

For category G, "Physical Health and Hygiene," Susan R. is in good physical health. She needs no health or hygiene education, and no obvious handicaps or illnesses limit her functioning. Therefore, she receives a score of 0 points for this category.

Category H, "Mental Health," has four components: (1) assessment needed, (2) prior history of mental health problems, (3) currently in treatment, and (4) assessment indicates treatment needs/no current services. Susan R. receives 3 points because of the recommended mental health assessment. Furthermore, she is currently receiving psychological counseling for her substance-abuse problems and receives 2 points for this component. Otherwise, no other points apply to Susan R. Therefore, her total score is 5 points for this category.

Lastly, for category I, "Substance Abuse," an assessment of her substance-abuse problem is needed, as she is a frequent user of marijuana. Although a substance-abuse assessment is recommended and will likely be conducted, Susan R. is currently receiving mandatory substance-abuse counseling/treatment. Therefore, you would score category I as follows:

Assessment needed	Yes	2 points
Occasional user	No	0 points
Frequent user	Yes	3 points
Assessment indicates treatment needs/ no services	No (not yet, anyway)	0 points
Receiving treatment services	Yes	2 points
Total		**7 points**

If you sum the various categories, you will have the following cumulative score:

Category	Points
A	17
B	6
C	1
D	3
E	0
F	0
G	0
H	5
I	7
Total	**39**

Placing Susan R. on the Classification Matrix. With this needs assessment score of 39, we can use Susan R.'s risk score of 20 and determine where she should be placed in the Florida Department of Juvenile Justice Classification Matrix illustrated in Figure 9.5. This matrix cross-tabulates one's risk assessment and needs assessments scores, with one's risk assessment score across the top and one's needs assessment score down the left-hand side. Where these scores intersect in the body of the table defines the suggested nature of supervision Susan R. should receive by Florida juvenile corrections officials. Where a needs assessment score of 39 (High) intersects with a risk assessment score of 20 (High), a square is indicated with "Intensive," "Level 2," and "Level 4." Because you do not have an interpretive booklet from the Florida Department of Juvenile Justice, you do not know what these different levels mean, although you can determine that the levels range from 2 to 10, with 2 being the lowest level and 10 being the highest. "Intensive" would suggest that Susan R. should receive intensive supervision, regardless of the program, community or institutional, where she is ultimately placed. You know from Susan R.'s scenario that the juvenile court judge disposed Susan R. to two years of probation, with mandatory psychological and substance-abuse counseling. No doubt there were other conditions, such as community service and/or restitution. Because she stole a neighbor's car and wrecked it, Susan R. will be expected to make some restitution to the neighbor for the loss of the car.

Predisposition Reports

It should be emphasized that juvenile justice officials do not depend entirely on risk/needs instruments for their information about youth needs. Interviews with youth and their families are often conducted. Intake officers acquire extensive information about a youth's background. If certain youth are recidivists and have extensive juvenile records, some indication of their needs will already be on file. Thus, we will know what interventions have been applied in the past and whether these interventions have helped in any way. Further, the needs of male juvenile offenders often differ from those of female juvenile offenders. These gender differences are important and should be taken into consideration whenever assessment instruments are devised. Another source of information about youth and their needs comes from juvenile probation officers. These court officials compile information about a youth's background and furnish this material to juvenile court judges. Subsequently, dispositions are individualized according to the probation officer's report. This is known as a predisposition report.

Predisposition reports are used by juvenile court judges in their decision about sentencing juvenile offenders during the disposition hearings. The reports are often filed by juvenile probation officers, especially in serious cases (Foley, 2008). Reports contain background information about juveniles, facts relating to their delinquent acts, and recommendations from the probation officer for particular dispositions. They serve the function of assisting judges in making more informed disposition decisions and also as needs assessment devices in which probation officers and other juvenile authorities can determine program needs for youth. The information included in the

predisposition reports
Documents prepared by juvenile probation officer for juvenile judge; purpose of report is to furnish the judge with background about juveniles to make a more informed sentencing decision; similar to the presentence investigation (PSI) report.

CAREER SNAPSHOT

(Courtesy of Dean John Champion)

Name: Kristie M. Stake
Position: Probation Officer, Elko County Juvenile Probation, Elko, Nevada

Colleges Attended: University of Nevada

Degrees: B.S. in Social Work, POST Certified Instructor Training Coordinator

Background

As far back as I can remember, I envisioned a career in some form of law enforcement. When I was in college, I went on a few ride-alongs with the Reno Police Department, where my desire to enter into the field grew. I decided early on in my college education that I wanted to work with children and geared my curriculum toward social work in the event that a career in law enforcement did not pan out.

During the last year as an undergraduate, I had the opportunity of interning at the Carson City Juvenile Probation Department. I realized then that I had found my career preference and could not fathom finding something I would enjoy more. The department hired me as a probation officer aide, which pretty much meant I was a probation officer without the power of arrest and I had to run all my decisions by an official probation officer. I remained a probation officer aide for approximately one year, when a probation officer position came open within the department. I applied for the position and was extremely thrilled when I was hired.

After working with the Carson City Juvenile Probation Department, my husband was offered a law enforcement position in Elko, Nevada. We relocated there, and I was eventually hired as a probation officer for the Elko County Juvenile Probation Department.

When I first entered the field as an intern, I had a difficult time separating my personal feelings and the job. I believed every excuse and story I was told, and at times, I went home depressed because of the home lives of families I worked with. Unfortunately, one consequence of this job is developing a jaded view of the world. Constantly, I have to remind myself that not all juveniles are lying or scheming. There are those cases that pull at your heartstrings, but you have to have the ability to ask yourself if what you are doing is in their best interests or if it is because it will make you feel better.

A misconception some people have when dealing with juveniles is that they are "just kids," and at times, you may let your guard down. You must keep in mind if choosing this career path that juveniles are very impulsive and rarely think before they act. Once, I was in a meeting with one of my girls who was just kicked out of a counseling group. I told her she was going to jail, and as I was walking down the hall with her to the detention facility, she took off running. I was pregnant at the time and couldn't chase her. I had to call for police assistance, and they eventually apprehended her. What I should have done was called another probation officer into my office to escort her to detention.

Advice to Students

First and foremost, I would have to say that if you want to choose the field *parole* or *probation,* a degree is preferred, if not mandatory, in many departments. Although this does not necessarily make you better at your job, it will open doors for advancement and will also give you the "edge" when you are writing reports or testifying in court. When working on this degree, learning a second language, preferably one that is prevalent in your community, is something I would recommend and personally wish I would have done.

You should involve yourself as much as you can with the occupation you are exploring. If you want to be a police officer, go on ride-alongs or volunteer at the jail. If you want to be a probation officer, volunteer in the local detention center or any other juvenile facility. If internships are available in your field, take full advantage of these opportunities. If you are volunteering your time or are an intern, never think that you are too good to do something. If you are diligent and do what is asked of you without complaining, the department is more likely to hire you if a position becomes available. If you are lazy and pick and choose what you want to do because you are waiting for more exciting things to happen, you may pass up your dream job. Law enforcement is not all glitz and glory. Much of the time, you are dealing with people who are having the worst day of their lives and hate you. However, if you stick it out, you will likely help somebody more than you will ever know.

report is used to match youth to specific community-based organizations and agencies for treatments and programs designed to meet the offenders' needs.

The Predisposition Report and Its Preparation

A predisposition report is the functional equivalent of a **presentence investigation (PSI)** for adults. Trester (1981, pp. 89–90) summarized four important reasons why predisposition reports should be prepared:

presentence investigation (PSI)

Inquiry conducted about a convicted defendant at the request of the judge; purpose of inquiry is to determine worthiness of defendant for probation or sentencing leniency.

1. These reports provide juvenile court judges with a more complete picture of juvenile offenders and their offenses, including the existence of any aggravating or mitigating circumstances.

2. These reports can assist the court in tailoring the disposition of the case to an offender's needs.

3. These reports may lead to the identification of positive factors that indicate the likelihood of rehabilitation.

4. These reports provide judges with the offender's treatment history, which might indicate the effectiveness or ineffectiveness of previous dispositions and suggest the need for alternative dispositions.

It is important to recognize that predisposition reports are not required by judges in all jurisdictions. Similarly, legislative mandates obligate officials in others to prepare reports for all adjudicated juveniles. An example of a predisposition report from New Mexico is shown in Box 9.1. However, no specific format is universally acceptable for these reports.

Box 9.1

A Sample Predispositional Report from New Mexico
Children, Youth, and Families Department Juvenile Justice Division

Identifying Information*

Name: Mary Gleaves
DOB: October 15, 1993
SSN: Not applicable
Address: 301 1st St.
Las Cruces, NM
Phone Number: (444) 555-1212
P/G/C: Parents
Religious Preference: Unknown
Primary Language Spoken: English
Final Disposition: No contest plea
Final Disposition Date: Pending
AKA: Not applicable

Court Information

Completed By: Ann Jordan
Date Completed: October 10, 2007
Case Number: 123456
Cause Number: 7890
Judge: Hon. Mark Van Meter
County: McNabb
Defense Attorney: Charles Heffler
CCA: Unknown

I. Referral Information

Current Offense: On January 2, 2007, at 3:40 A.M., Mary Gleaves was taken (by her parents) to the hospital after she was bleeding profusely. Doctors there notified Mary Gleaves' parents that it was apparent she had just given birth to a baby. The location of the baby was unknown at the time, and doctors suspected that Mary Gleaves had possibly killed the baby. Police were notified and searched Mary Gleaves bedroom, where they found a full-term baby (deceased) in a trash can. Mary Gleaves allegedly told police that she did not know she was pregnant but gave birth to the

baby, by herself, on December 30, 2006. An autopsy report indicates that the baby girl, who was found with the umbilical cord still attached and wrapped around her neck, was alive at birth and died of asphyxiation. Mary Gleaves was arrested on January 11, 2007, and booked into McNabb County Jail, Juvenile Unit, at approximately 6:00 p.m.

On January 13, 2007, a petition was filed charging Mary Gleaves with: Count 1: Child Abuse (Intentionally Caused) (Death); or in the alternative, Child Abuse (Negligently Caused) (Death); or in the alternative, Child Abuse (Negligently Permitted) (Death); and Count 2:

Tampering with Evidence. Mary Gleaves' parents were able to post the 10 percent cash deposit of $10,000 bond, and Mary Gleaves was released home on January 14, 2007. A forensic evaluation was ordered at this time.

On September 22, 2007, Mary Gleaves entered into a plea agreement with the Children's Court Attorney. Mary Gleaves pleaded No Contest to Alternative Count 1: Child Abuse (Negligently Permitted) (Death). In exchange for the plea, the remaining counts in the petition were dismissed, and the state agreed to handle the case in a juvenile setting. There was no agreement as to the disposition in the matter, and a predispositional report was ordered.

Number of Co-offenders: 0

Victim Impact Mailed: ☐ Yes ☐ No ☐ Not applicable Response: ☐ Yes ☐ No

Victim Requests Restoration: ☐ Yes ☐ No

Victim-Impact Summary: A victim-impact statement is not applicable in this case. It should be noted, however, that Mary Gleaves has given two names for the father of her child. Initially, Mary Gleaves told investigators that she had sexual intercourse with Walter Brooks and that the condom broke. She said she had taken a pregnancy test at Planned Parenthood with negative results. During this officer's conversation with Mary Gleaves, however, she indicated that the father is John Johnson. She said that Johnson denied he is the father and that they do not have any contact with each other.

Chronological Report Attached: ☐ Yes ☐ No

Currently on Probation/Parole: ☐ Yes ☐ No

Location:

Prior Supervision

Cause Number	Begin Date	Type	Length	Expiration	Release Date	Release Type
Not applicable	October 13, 2005	Informal supervision	3 months	January 12, 2006	January 12, 2006	Now supervising under conditional release

Comments: Mary Gleaves was placed on informal supervision after her first referral to the probation department in October 2005. Mary Gleaves was referred to juvenile probation for a citation she had received for criminal trespass. Mary Gleaves and her two sisters, who were cited as a group of teens, were caught loitering at Grady's, a restaurant and popular hangout for youth. Mary Gleaves came to see this officer at least one time every week, without fail. Mary Gleaves turned in weekly grade checks from school, and attendance was verified.

Prior Commitment to Correctional Facility

Cause Number	Commit Date	Type	Length	Expiration	Dispatch Date	Dispatch Type
Not applicable	Not applicable	Not applicable	Not applicable	Not applicable	Not applicable	Not applicable

Comments: Mary Gleaves has had no prior commitments to correctional facilities.

Prior Youthful Offender: ☐ Yes ☐ No

Outstanding Restitution: ☐ Yes ☐ No ☐ Amount: $0.00

Outstanding Community Service: ☐ Yes ☐No ☐ Hours: 0

II. Social, Educational, and Substance-Abuse History

(Please include information on siblings, dependents, employment, parents' marital status, primary language spoken in home, current school status, special expectations, truancy, behavior problems, gang activity, weapons, extracurricular activities, alcohol, marijuana, and other drug use.)

A. Social

Mary Gleaves is the youngest of three daughters born to Martin and Jane Gleaves. Jean Gleaves is 19 years old, married, and living with her husband, William Smith, 21, and their infant son, Frederick. Olivia Gleaves, 18, lives in the family home along with Mary Gleaves. The family lives in a rented house in the Northeast Heights of Las Cruces and has for the past four years. The home is a three-bedroom home, which appears cluttered but clean. The front- and backyards seem moderately maintained, and the inside is well furnished. The ashes of Mary Gleaves' deceased baby sit on the fireplace mantel in an urn the shape of an angel. Baby Gleaves was cremated on January 28, 2007, after the Office of Medical Investigators released the body. For weeks after the incident, the mailbox outside the house and the cars belonging to the family and friends were decorated with tiny pink ribbons in remembrance of the baby. Mary Gleaves has moved out of the bedroom that she resided in at the time of the incident. Mary Gleaves' parents have moved into that room and report that Mary Gleaves is unable (emotionally) to go in there. As of May 1, 2007, Mary Gleaves was working at Best Industries. Mary Gleaves previously worked at McDonald's but lost her job shortly after the events of this case came to light. Mary Gleaves had to take four months off of work after the incident. She was an emotional wreck, making her "dysfunctional" and therefore unable to complete her job as expected. Taking this time off paid its toll on the family as well, and Martin Gleaves was forced to work even more at his job of 11 years. Martin Gleaves said that he had to "keep the family going" in a time when it seemed everything was falling apart. Mary Gleaves is currently working with her father at Best Industries, where she is working in the mail room. Mary Gleaves is currently considered a part-time employee, although she works 7.5 hours a day. Mary Gleaves has been there for three months and currently makes $6.50/hour. The remainder of her day is spent on her home schooling. Mary Gleaves spends much of her weekends babysitting her five-month-old nephew, Frederick.

Mary Gleaves attended Las Cruces Elementary School, where her mother was the President of the PTA. Both Mrs. Gleaves and her father report that Mary Gleaves was a good student and did fine in elementary school. Once in middle school, Mary Gleaves attended Craig Middle School. She and her family lived in the south valley, and Mary Gleaves said she was one of the very few blonde-haired, blue-eyed girls there. Mary Gleaves reported that she did fine in school but had problems with peers because of her race. The family eventually moved, and Mary Gleaves began attending Burgess Middle School. Mary Gleaves reported no problems at Burgess. Once in high school, Mary Gleaves began attending informal student parties, and she was very much into marijuana in her ninth-grade year. Mary Gleaves became involved with a boyfriend, who proved to be a bad influence on her. After her ditching classes became a habit, Mary Gleaves was referred to a truancy officer and ordered to complete community service. Mary Gleaves reportedly got back on track after her parents placed her on more structure and restriction. By the time this incident took place, Mary Gleaves was seemingly doing much better. Mary Gleaves was in the midterm of her sophomore year when this incident occurred and did not return following her arrest in January 2007. Mary Gleaves plans to continue with her home schooling until graduation. Incidentally, Mary Gleaves has done very well in this program and is now classified as a Junior, ahead of her schedule in mainstream educational setting. Mary Gleaves' sister, Olivia, also left her school after the incident when the publicity brought adverse reactions from her peers. Olivia, however, has since returned to the school and reportedly is not having any problems there. Jean Gleaves graduated from school before any of these circumstances arose.

As mentioned earlier, Mary Gleaves was referred to the probation department on one other occasion. In July 2005, police officers working a tac-plan in the northeast heights cited Mary Gleaves and her sisters for trespassing at a local restaurant. Officers were working in an effort to reduce the number of young people loitering in the various parking lots. Mary Gleaves and her sisters were at Grady's when the three of them were cited. Mary Gleaves came in to see this officer for her preliminary inquiry on October 13, 2005, and was placed on informal supervision. Mary Gleaves made weekly visits with this officer, called in regularly, and turned in school reports as requested. There does not appear to be any other legal history with the family.

It has been reported that there is tension and that marital conflict is present. According to the forensic evaluation, dated January 20, 2006, there were frequent fights about issues relating to the three daughters, money, and dad's drinking. Martin Gleaves has been said to have a "long-standing alcohol abuse Hell." Counseling was offered initially to help cope with the surrounding offense and any issues exacerbated by it; however, Martin Gleaves advised that he does not need any more counseling. Martin Gleaves reports that he will support Mary Gleaves throughout her counseling, but that he has no intention of continuing himself. Martin Gleaves reported that he does not believe the incident should be "dwelled on" and that "you have to go on, or it will tear you up." It was unclear whether Martin Gleaves would participate in further counseling or not.

Initially, Martin Gleaves sought counseling services for his family through the Employee Assistance Program that his employer provides. This program only allowed for five visits, and the family quickly exhausted that service. Dr. Martha Jordan, a private psychologist, was recommended, and Mary Gleaves has been seeing her for some time now. Mary Gleaves sees Dr. Jordan every two weeks, but no other family member attends. Mary Gleaves' sessions are on average one hour at a time. Mary Gleaves reports that she likes Dr. Jordan and feels comfortable working with her.

Mary Gleaves has admitted to using substances in the past, such as marijuana and acid. It is this officer's understanding that Mary Gleaves used acid on an experimental basis only and that marijuana was her drug of choice while in the ninth grade. It is also this officer's understanding that Mary Gleaves has not used any marijuana since June 2006. It is a concern, however, that Mary Gleaves admits to using alcohol on New Year's Eve 2005. This ap-parently took place at the house with her parents present along with other friends drinking as well. It is concerning that Mary Gleaves' parents would allow minors to drink in their home. This was not typical, however, according to Mary Gleaves but, rather, something of a celebration of the upcoming new year. Mary Gleaves advised her parents allow drinking on special occasions only.

B. Education/Employment

Diploma

☐ HS Diploma

Graduation Date: Pending

☐ GED Certificate

GED Date: Not applicable

Special Education

☐ Eligible for special education

☐ Ineligible for special education

☐ May require special education

Qualifications for Special Education: Not applicable

Level: Not applicable

Effective Date: Not applicable

C. School History

School Name	Type	Program	Program Type	Grade/Special Education	Start Date
Harcourt Learning Direct	Home school	Mail/correspondence school	Regular education	10	March 1, 2007

Comments: As mentioned earlier, Mary Gleaves is doing well in school and is now classified as a Junior in high school. Mary Gleaves mails in her school work and completes the assignments that she is provided through the Harcourt Learning Direct Program. Mary Gleaves has goals of completing her high school education and eventually obtaining a degree in automobile mechanics.

D. Mental Health/Substance Use History

Treatment

☐ Prior treatment inpatient

☐ Prior treatment outpatient

Date of Last Psychological Evaluation: April 17, 2006

Substance Use

☐ Alcohol

Frequency: Special occasions

☐ Marijuana

Frequency: Daily in the past

☐ Drugs

Frequency: Experimental

☐ Solvents

Frequency:

☐ Date Updated: November 7, 2006

Comments: Please refer to Section II above for details.

III. Juvenile Probation and Parole (JPPO) Overview Recommendation

(Include core services, P/G/C and client's view of needs, issues and strengths, treatment/residential placement, JPPO areas of concern and community-based service required if removal of client from home is recommended.)

Mary Gleaves appeared to be very nervous about the outcome of this case. Mary Gleaves acknowledged that she would like to continue working and complete her education. Mary Gleaves described herself as a very caring person who is "good minded" and prides herself in her good grades and employment history. Mary Gleaves' father was equally complimentary in his description of Mary Gleaves. Martin Gleaves described Mary Gleaves as a hard worker, energetic, focused, and good with chores at home, never having to be reminded to do them. The only negative issue that Mary Gleaves and her father could pinpoint was her need to stay on track with school. Nothing was mentioned in regard to counseling or the deep issues associated with the death of her child.

It is difficult to ascertain what Mary Gleaves' thoughts are about the incident itself. It is unfortunate that she was able to plead No Contest in that she now can keep her side of the story to herself. It has been very difficult to assess the situation given that much of the very important information will never have to be given by Mary Gleaves. It impedes treatment as well by not having to talk about the incident or specific actions in the matter as long as that is the case. Mary Gleaves' own state of mind is at risk. As Dr. Jordan described it, "Mary Gleaves has been greatly limited in her ability to work with other students, as she has not been permitted to talk about the offense." Dr. Jordan has been hampered in her ability to investigate with Mary Gleaves and her family the causes of the offense and to directly address them. When weighing the distinction between retribution, safety of the public, and the best interest of the child, it is difficult to suggest that incarceration is the most appropriate outcome. Mary Gleaves has been afforded the opportunity to show that she can comply with the structure and rules that the probation department can provide, and she has done that. Incarcerating her at this point would serve no purpose other than punishment, and this could impede the treatment process even further. Dr. Jordan feels that Mary Gleaves does not lack the capacity for empathy and concern for others. Furthermore, it is this officer's understanding that Mary Gleaves does not pose a threat to anyone. The amount of denial in this case is insurmountable, and the plea agreement encourages it. It is imperative that Mary Gleaves be allowed to engage in therapy to the point that she can talk about the incident and work, with her parents, to move past this and begin the lengthy process of intensive therapy. It is equally important that Mary Gleaves' family engage in therapy. According to the forensic evaluation, a likely factor in Mary Gleaves' situation is the stress in the family, characterized by parental alcohol abuse, depression, and chronic marital conflict. The results of these family problems affected the whole family. Mary Gleaves, it has been reported, is deficient in coping skills, judgment, problem solving, and decision making. Mary Gleaves, according to the forensic evaluation, appears to be "overwhelmed by especially stressful circumstances, and prone to ill-judged behavior at such times." Mary Gleaves, it reports, "does not seem to be a girl with antisocial or prominent aggressive tendencies, or characteristic tendencies toward remorseless use of others." Given these findings, it would seem appropriate to think that with support and supervision, and with intense therapy to recognize these contributing factors, Mary Gleaves is a low risk for repeat offenses and for presenting a danger to others.

It is this officer's recommendation that Mary Gleaves be given a term of probation for an extended period of time to be determined by the court but that addresses these crucial elements. It is highly recommended that Mary Gleaves be monitored closely to determine her progress and participation. It is also recommended that Mary Gleaves' parents be made party to the petition and monitored for their compliance in therapy as well. A referral to the Juvenile Intensive Probation Supervision (JIPS) program could also be made to address what could be a rocky transition from the intense publicity of this case back to more routine circumstances. It is also recommended that Mary Gleaves continue with intense psychotherapy and address specifics of the incident. The probation department would ideally work with the therapist in maintaining compliance and progress. Incarceration at this point would serve no other purpose than to address punishment and retribution. These issues could be served in the context of probation supervision just as well, while allowing Mary Gleaves to obtain the therapy that she desperately needs. Periodic judicial reviews could be used to further monitor compliance and progress. Community service is advised, and possible options with meaningful results could be explored through the context of therapy.

IV. Clinical Social Worker Comments

(Must be completed for mandatory referrals and court order.)
   Please refer to forensic evaluation dated January 20, 2007.

_____

Clinical Social Worker

Respectfully Submitted,   Approved:

_____   _____

Jane Brown, JPPO   Chief JPPO/Supervisor

---

*Fictitious names used because of New Mexico confidentiality provisions.

Some juvenile justice experts have reviewed the use of predisposition reports, including various approaches to developing the report. The reviews confirm these reports contain enriching and important information about youth that can be helpful to juvenile court judges in determining appropriate dispositions (Barfeind, 2008; Foley, 2008). Several aspects of an offender are crucial for investigations, analysis, and treatment. These include (1) personal health, both physical and emotional; (2) family and home situation; (3) recreational activities and use of leisure time; (4) peer group relationships (types of companions); (5) education; and (6) work experience. Predisposition reports are frequently recommended in all cases where the offenders are minors. However, the amount of time required to prepare predisposition reports and the restricted resources of juvenile courts sometimes limit reports to all but the most serious cases.

Various characteristics are included in most predisposition reports. These include (1) gender; (2) ethnic status; (3) age at first juvenile court appearance; (4) source of first referral to juvenile court; (5) reason(s) for referral; (6) formal court disposition; (7) youth's initial placement by court; (8) miscellaneous court orders and conditions; (9) type of counsel retained; (10) initial plea; (11) number of prior offenses; (12) age and time of initial offense; (13) number of offenses after first hearing; (14) youth's total offense number; (15) number of companions; (16) number of detentions; (17) no-contact recommendations, if ordered by the court; and (18) number of out-of-home placements (Barfeind, 2008). An example of a no-contact recommendation is shown in Figure 9.6.

Victim-Impact Statements in Predisposition Reports

Predisposition reports increasingly include a **victim-impact statement**. These statements are often prepared by victims themselves and appended to the report. They are intended to provide judges with information about the impact and consequences of the crime on the victim and the victim's family (NationalCenter for Victims of Crime, 2011). They describe the physical harm and monetary damage victims have sustained and can be used in the disposition to determine aggravating factors as well as to assign restitution as part of the disposition.

Since 1992, there has been a trend in state legislatures to increase the rights of victims of juvenile crime (Herman and Wasserman, 2001). By 1996, 22 state legislatures had enacted legislation addressing the victims of juvenile crime (Erez and Laster, 1999). This state legislation addresses the role of victims in various ways, such as:

1. Including victims of juvenile crime in that state's victim's bill of rights.
2. Notifying the victim upon release of the offender from custody.
3. Increasing opportunities for victims to be heard in juvenile court proceedings.
4. Expanding victim services to victims of juvenile crime.
5. Establishing the authority for victims to be notified of significant hearings (e.g., bail disposition).
6. Providing for release of the name and address of the offender and the offender's parents to the victim upon request.

> **victim-impact statement**
>
> Appendage to a predisposition report or presentence investigation (PSI) that addresses the effect of the defendant's actions against victims or anyone harmed by the crime or delinquent act; usually compiled by the victim.

COMMUNICATION: Communication in any form is contact. This includes verbal communication such as talking, and/or written communication such as letters, notes, messages, etc.

DIRECT CONTACT: One-on-one contact. This includes in person visits, touching, talking on the phone, letters, written notes, E-Mail, and/or making proximity contact.

PROXIMITY CONTACT: Being in the proximity (visual or physical presence) of a person (such as in the same house, yard, store, restaurant, vehicle, room, church, movie theater, etc.) where communication could be established. This includes driving by, following and/or waiting outside the home, property, place of employment, school, church and/or daycare of the victim/prohibited party.

INDIRECT CONTACT: Making contact through another person (such as friends or family) to send messages, pictures, and deliver or receive packages, gifts, notes, money, etc.

NON-VERBAL CONTACT: This includes waving, smiling, sign language, mouthing words, facial or body language, and obscene gestures.

SUPERVISED CONTACT: When an offender is allowed to have contact with the victim/prohibited party under prearranged conditions and times. These conditions and times must be approved **in writing prior to the contact.** Contact can only be approved by the supervising P.O. Your counselor or attorney cannot give approval.

I understand I am **not to contact or associate** (as defined above) with the victim/prohibited party until I receive written permission by the Court/Parole Board/Supervisory Authority and/or my Parole & Probation Officer. I understand that because of the nature of my offense, I have lost my privilege to have contact with the victim/prohibited party at this time. I understand it is **MY RESPONSIBILITY** to make every attempt to avoid contact with the victim/prohibited party. I also understand that if the victim/prohibited party attempts contact with me I am not to respond to or acknowledge them.

_____   _____

Parolee/Probationer Signature   Date

_____   _____

Parole & Probation Officer Signature   Date

Figure 9.6
No Contact Agreement/Association Defined

7. Enhancing sentences if the victim is elderly or handicapped (Torbet et al., 1996, p. 48).

States enacting such legislation include Alabama, Alaska, Arizona, California, Connecticut, Florida, Georgia, Idaho, Iowa, Louisiana, Minnesota, Montana, New Mexico, North Dakota, Pennsylvania, South Dakota, Texas, Utah, Virginia, and Wyoming.

One consideration when enacting this legislation is restitution to victims. Restitution is increasingly regarded as an essential component of fairness in dispositions for juvenile offenders. Offender accountability is heightened as restitution is incorporated into the disposition, especially if there was some type of property loss, damage, physical injury, or death. In reality, however, many states continue to

Focus on Delinquency

It happened in West Palm Beach, Florida. On Wednesday, May 16, 2001, a jury convicted Nathaniel Brazill, age 14, of second-degree murder in the shooting death of a teacher, 35-year-old Barry Grunow. Brazill was also convicted of aggravated assault for pointing a .25-caliber semiautomatic pistol at a math teacher as he fled.

Brazill had shot Grunow once between the eyes in the doorway of the teacher's Lake Worth Middle School classroom on May 26, 2000, after being sent home for throwing water balloons just before summer vacation. Brazill had returned to school with the weapon, which he used to kill Grunow. He said he wanted to talk to his girlfriend in Grunow's classroom and claimed that the gun went off unintentionally.

Brazill faced a sentence of up to 25 years in prison for the conviction. During the trial itself, he showed some emotion, crying after the prosecutor asked him what had happened to Grunow after the shooting. Except for frowning when the verdict was read, however, Brazill sat without emotion as the jury delivered its verdict. Bob Hatcher, the school principal, expressed relief over the verdicts, saying that the justice system worked. He said, "The jury found a verdict. I think it was a very fair and equitable trial."

What can school officials do to prevent such violence in the future? Should all schools have metal detectors through which students must pass? Should we make all schools in America similar to airport security? What do you think?

Source: Adapted from Amanda Riddle (2001, May 17), "Boy Who Shot Teacher Convicted of Second-Degree Murder," *Laredo Morning Times*, p. 10A (available at http://airwolf.lmtonline.com/news/archive/051701/pagea10.pdf).

debate how reparations will be imposed on either the youth, the youth's family, or both.

Concern for the victim is clearly an important element of the Balanced and Restorative Justice Model (BARJ), which has been adopted in many states. The NCJJ reported that in 2005, a total of 17 states had purpose clauses that included language consistent with the principles of BARJ (Griffin, Szymanski, and King, 2006). This philosophy and model of juvenile justice recognizes the importance of balancing attention to public safety, offender accountability to victims, and competency development for the juvenile offender.

SUMMARY

For youth who have been adjudicated delinquent, there are various dispositions available to juvenile court judges, ranging from nominal to custodial sanctions. Generally, the more-serious or repeat offenders are sanctioned with harsher penalties at the disposition hearing. Disposition options sometimes appear to be related to extralegal factors, such as gender, race, ethnicity, and/or socioeconomic status. The issue of disproportionate minority contact has received increased attention, and states have developed strategies to address the overrepresentation of minorities in the juvenile justice system.

Juvenile court judges consider both aggravating and mitigating circumstances in determining which dispositions are most appropriate to impose on youthful offenders. Aggravating factors include circumstances that make the offense more serious. Mitigating factors are those that decrease the seriousness of offense or decrease the culpability of the youth. Both types of factors were described.

Most states have adapted and use risk assessment measures. These measures attempt to forecast the risk a juvenile may present to the community if released or placed in a community-based therapeutic program. The greater the risk assessment, the greater the supervision required. One objective of risk assessment is to determine the type of supervision needed. Selective incapacitation is sometimes used to assign detention or incarceration for offenders who present a risk to the community.

Needs assessments are also determined. These are instruments that evaluate circumstances and needs and indicate which interventions or social services are appropriate for the youth. Risk and needs instruments are limited in one respect or another. Some juveniles may be incarcerated who should not be incarcerated, and some juveniles may receive nonincarcerative dispositions when incarceration is more appropriate. Offenders who are characterized as high risk for reoffending or as dangerous offenders but are actually not dangerous are called false positives. Those who are considered to be a low risk for reoffending or as nondangerous but who turn out to be dangerous are called false negatives.

Three general types of prediction have been identified. These are actuarial prediction, anamnestic prediction, and clinical prediction. Studies comparing the effectiveness of all prediction schemes show that they exhibit little differences in their overall effectiveness at predicting future behaviors successfully. However, actuarial prediction seems to be as accurate or more accurate than clinical prediction.

Risk instrumentation varies greatly among jurisdictions. However, risk instruments share common elements. Risk criteria usually include age, prior record of delinquent or status offending, number of prior commitments to juvenile facilities, escapes from those facilities, drug or chemical dependencies, alcohol abuse, family relationships and stability or instability, school adjustment problems and academic performance, and peer relationships. One major purpose of such instrumentation is classification. Classification enables authorities to place youth in programs that match treatments with needs and competencies for particular youth.

Predisposition reports are also prepared to assist the juvenile court judge in developing relevant and appropriate dispositions that balance concerns of public safety with the needs of the offender. These reports are similar to PSIs which are prepared for criminal offenders. Predisposition reports generally include a statement from the victim on the impact of the crime. Because juvenile probation officers often make dispositional recommendations based on the information provided in the reports, the documents assist judges in their decision making.

KEY TERMS

first-offender, 317
repeat offender, 317
Violent Juvenile Offender
    Programs (VJOPs), 318
aggravating
    circumstances, 320
flat time, 322
mitigating circumstance,
    322
risk prediction, 323
dangerousness, 323
risk, 323

predictors of
    dangerousness and
    risk, 324
risk/needs assessment
    instruments, 324
needs assessment, 324
selective incapacitation,
    325
false positives, 326
false negatives, 326
anamnestic prediction,
    327

actuarial prediction, 327
clinical prediction, 327
classification, 331
overrides, 343
predisposition reports,
    346
presentence investigation
    (PSI), 348
victim-impact
    statement, 353

QUESTIONS FOR REVIEW

1. How do first-offenders and repeat offenders differ? How does being a first-offender as opposed to a repeat offender make a difference in how dangerousness or risk is assessed?

2. What are aggravating circumstances? What are some types of aggravating circumstances? How might these circumstances affect judicial decision making in a juvenile disposition?

3. What are four mitigating circumstances? How do judges use mitigating circumstances to adjust the offender's punishment?

4. What are some major differences between risk assessment instruments and needs assessments instruments?

5. What is selective incapacitation? How is it used? What are false positives and false negatives? How do such designations occur?

6. What are three types of predictions? Which are more effective, and why?

7. What is a predisposition report? Who prepares this report? How are such reports used for determining a juvenile's disposition?

8. What is a victim-impact statement? How is it used to modify the severity of the disposition?

9. What are Violent Juvenile Offender Programs (VJOPs)? What are their functions?

10. What are some moral and ethical questions that have been raised about selective incapacitation? Is selective incapacitation successful? Why, or why not?

INTERNET CONNECTIONS

Bibliography on Gang Culture
http://www.streetgangs.com/bibliography/gangbib.html

Center on Juvenile and Criminal Justice
http://www.cjcj.org/

Center for the Prevention of School Violence
http://www.ncdjjdp.org/cpsv/

Help My Teen
http://www.helpmyteen.com/

Juvenile Law Center
http://www.jlc.org/

The National Center for Victims of Crime
http://www.ncvc.org/ncvc/

The National Council on Crime and Delinquency
http://www.nccd-crc.org/

National Center for Juvenile Justice
http://www.ncjj.org

National Juvenile Defender Center
http://www.njdc.info/

Youth Activism Project
http://www.youthactivism.com

10

Nominal Sanctions

Warnings, Diversion, and Alternative Dispute Resolution

Learning Objectives

AFTER READING THIS CHAPTER, THE STUDENT WILL BE ABLE TO:

- Summarize the philosophy and objectives of community-based corrections.
- Summarize delinquency prevention efforts and programs.
- Describe diversion and various diversion programs.
- Explain the goals and operation of day reporting centers.
- Summarize the effectiveness of community-based programs.
- Describe various disposition alternatives, including nominal dispositions.

(Courtesy of Dean John Champion)

Introduction

A youth writes on the walls in the junior high school locker room with a permanent marker. Another youth damages a neighbor's professionally landscaped flower garden. Are these cases worthy of a prosecution in a juvenile court?

This chapter will examine a broad range of dispositional options available to juvenile courts. These options include nominal sanctions, diversion, and Alternative Dispute Resolution (ADR). These types of sanctions or dispositions are applied in cases where juveniles pose the least risk to others or are considered to be low-risk first-offenders who are unlikely to recidivate.

The first part of the chapter defines nominal dispositions. Nominal dispositions are typically verbal warnings issued by judges in lieu of any formal adjudication for either status offending or delinquency.

The second part of the chapter discusses how many juveniles are diverted from the juvenile justice system through deferred prosecution and diversion. Various types of diversion programs will be defined and discussed. These programs attempt to constructively intervene in the lives of youth and hold them accountable for their actions without the formality of juvenile court processing. The use of teen courts, youth courts, or peer courts, for example, is increasing not only in the United States but internationally. In 2005, there were over 1,000 teen courts in the United States, and by 2007, there were approximately 1,250 (Schneider, 2007). Teen courts will be described in detail, including their respective strengths, weaknesses, and applications, and several specific teen courts will be illustrated to show how the youth court process functions.

The next section of this chapter describes day reporting centers. Located in one's community, day reporting centers offer an array of services and assistance to youth. The goals and functions of day reporting centers will be described, and several examples of day reporting centers will be provided, together with information on their success in treating and supervising juveniles involved in less-serious delinquent behavior.

The chapter concludes with an examination of ADR and restorative justice. These types of programs are known collectively as victim–offender mediation programs. These programs unite victims and youthful offenders for constructive purposes, and they offer youth the opportunity to face their victims and accept responsibility for their actions. The functions, uses, and operations of victim–offender mediation programs will be examined.

nominal dispositions

Pre-adjudicatory or adjudicatory disposition resulting in sanctions, such as warnings and/or probation.

Nominal Dispositions Defined

Nominal dispositions are verbal and/or written warnings issued to low-risk juvenile offenders, often first-offenders, for the purpose of alerting them to the seriousness of their acts and their potential for receiving harsher conditional sanctions if they reoffend. These sanctions are the least-punitive alternatives.

Nominal dispositions may be imposed by police officers in their encounters with juveniles. These verbal warnings or reprimands are often in the form of station-house adjustments, in which youth are taken into custody and released to their parents later, without any formal record of the incident.

Juvenile court judges are also encouraged to utilize the least restrictive sanctions after adjudicating juveniles as delinquents, status offenders, or children in need of supervision (CHINS). The use of incarceration as a sanction is within the judicial powers of juvenile courts, but state statutes and juvenile justice policy stipulate and encourage juvenile courts to identify and employ other options. As a result, secure confinement as a disposition has been used less frequently in recent years. There has been an increasing emphasis on allowing juveniles to remain at home in their communities, where a more therapeutic milieu exists for them to be rehabilitated. One such community-based option is the Delaware Bay Marine Institute (DBMI), a program that emphasizes sea-related activities and underwater skills, as discussed in Chapter 6. While the results of research on the DBMI were inconclusive, they illustrate that there are viable alternatives to incarcerating juveniles that may work as well as or better than simply placing them in secure residential facilities (Brandau, 1992).

For some juveniles, alternatives include doing little other than issuing certain verbal warnings or reprimands. For example, intake officers use nominal dispositions for juveniles if they determine that the youth referred merits only verbal warnings instead of more formal sanctions. If petitions are filed against juveniles, depending upon the circumstances, judges may find them to be delinquent in the adjudicatory process. However, these delinquent adjudications do not bind judges to implement conditional or custodial sanctions. Thus, judges may simply issue verbal warnings to

Diversion can involve participation in community-based programs where professionals work with youth.
(Courtesy of Dean John Champion)

adjudicated juveniles. These warnings are serious, however, especially after a finding that the juvenile is delinquent. Juveniles with prior records can face tougher dispositional options if they reoffend in the same juvenile court jurisdiction and reappear before the judge.

Diversion

The Juvenile Justice and Delinquency Prevention Act (JJDPA) of 1974 and its subsequent amendments were intended, in part, to deinstitutionalize status offenders and remove them from the jurisdiction of juvenile courts. Another provision of this Act was to ensure that adjudicated delinquent offenders receive the least-punitive sentencing option from juvenile court judges in relation to their adjudication offenses. In 1980, the National Advisory Committee for Juvenile Justice and Delinquency Prevention declared that juvenile court judges should select the least restrictive sentencing alternatives, given the nature of the offense; the age, interests, and needs of the juvenile offender; and the circumstances of the conduct. Thus, judicial actions are influenced, in part, by federal mandates or national recommendations.

diversion

Halting or suspension of legal proceedings against criminal defendants or youthful offenders after a referral to the justice system and possible referral of those persons to treatment or care programs administered by public or private agencies or organizations.

Diversion is not new. It is regarded as a form of deferred prosecution in which offenders, especially low-risk ones, are afforded an opportunity to prove that they are law-abiding persons. An early instance of diversion was created by Conrad Printzlien, New York's first chief probation officer. Printzlien was concerned that many youth were stigmatized by rapid prosecution and conviction, and he was determined to identify an alternative to unnecessary and unwarranted incarceration of juveniles. The result was the Brooklyn Plan, a deferred prosecution program that provided a way to distinguish situational offenders from more-serious chronic and persistent juvenile delinquents. Between 1936 and 1946, a total of 250 youth were handled in the Brooklyn Plan (U.S. District Court, Pretrial Services Agency, 2011). The program proved to be successful at decreasing recidivism among youth who were diverted and eventually was available in other cities.

A primary or intended consequence of diversion is to remove large numbers of relatively minor offenders from juvenile court processing as quickly as possible. However, other professionals caution that one unintended consequence of diversion is the development of wider, stronger, and different nets. This means, in simplest terms, that youth diverted from the formal juvenile justice system are captured in the nets of community-based agencies. Thus, if we view social control in its broadest terms, then more, as opposed to fewer, children will fall under some form of social control through diversionary programs.

Some advocates contend that diversion of offenders should be aimed at the client population that would otherwise have received formal dispositions if diversion had not occurred (Gavazzi et al., 2000). This client population consists of youth who have committed delinquent acts and not simply status offenses. However, critics suggest that status offenders may escalate to more-serious offenses if left untreated by the system. Therefore, intervention of some sort is thought to be necessary to prevent their involvement in more-serious offending. Status offenders, however, do not necessarily progress to more-serious offenses. Sometimes, their apparent involvement in more-serious offenses is a function of relabeling the same acts differently by police. On other occasions, status offenders may be upgraded to delinquents by juvenile court judges if they fail to obey valid court orders. If a status offender is ordered to attend school and does not, this action can provide judicial grounds for issuing a contempt of court citation, which can result in a formal delinquency proceeding. This particular use of juvenile court contempt power, especially against status offenders, is unpopular. Regardless of whether they are status offenders or have committed serious delinquent acts, youth who are diverted can engage in subsequent offending.

Benefits and Limitations of Diversion

Diversion has various benefits and functions. First, it decreases the caseload of juvenile court prosecutors by referring less-serious cases to probation departments. Of course, this also increases the supervisory responsibilities of probation departments, which must manage larger numbers of youth who were diverted in addition to juvenile probationers. A second function of diversion is that it seems to reduce recidivism in those jurisdictions where it has been used. A third intended consequence is to minimize juvenile institutionalization or placement in either secure or nonsecure residential facilities. A fourth function is that diversion is potentially useful as a long-range crime prevention measure. Finally, diversion can eliminate certain youth risks, such as suicide attempts that result from being confined in adult jails or lockups for short periods. The stress and anxiety generated from even short-term confinement for certain juveniles, including their propensity to commit suicide, has been described (Hayes, 2009). For some youth, diversion assists in avoiding the stresses of confinement or prosecution (Gallagher and Dobrin, 2007).

One of the consequences of diversion is that it may widen the net by including youth who otherwise would have received stationhouse adjustments by police or warnings from juvenile court judges. Much of this net-widening occurs through changes in police discretion and relabeling of juvenile behaviors as more serious. Another limitation is that some youth may develop perceptions that the juvenile justice system is lenient and will tolerate relatively minor lawbreaking.

One problem with utilizing diversion on a large scale is that not all status offenders or low-level delinquent offenders are suitable for diversion programs. Professionals cannot contend that all status offenders are alike or that all minor delinquent offenders share the same characteristics. For diversion programs to maximize their effectiveness, they target those offenders most amenable to having minimal contact with the juvenile justice system. Ideally, this necessitates the ability to identify certain youth who are at risk of becoming more-serious delinquent offenders or dangerous adult criminals. Clearly, it would be useful to identify particular factors that categorize certain youth as being at risk (Bernat, 2005). Thus, diversion could be selectively applied, depending upon whether specific youth possess more identifiable risk characteristics than others (Loukas, Suizzo, and Prelow, 2007).

Diversion Programs For Juveniles

Law Enforcement Strategies

Police have an important role in the prevention, intervention, and suppression of youth offending. As Lawrence (2007) contends, police are the most "visible" officials who respond to youth, and they play a significant role in influencing youth perspectives and attitudes (p. 204).

Recently, the police department and concerned citizen groups in Peoria, Illinois, established a Community Peace Conferencing program. Police are referring first-offenders who are involved in nonviolent behavior to a volunteer community program that focuses on restorative justice. By bringing together victims, offenders, and their families, youth have an opportunity to restore the harm that was done, demonstrate that they are accountable, and avoid formal prosecution (Griffin, 2010). These kinds of diversion initiatives are viewed as promising.

A recognized example of police work with youth is the Operation SHIELD in the Westminster Police Department in California, as discussed in Chapter 5 (Wyrick, 2000). In this program, patrol officers identify "at-risk youth" they encounter in the course of calls for service and then refer them to community programs and resources (Wyrick, 2000). The process begins with the Shield Resource Officer, who conducts a risk assessment and decides whether further action is appropriate and, if so, which agencies are suitable (Merlo and Sozer, 2009). This program demonstrates the important role of police officers in identifying youth who may be at risk and in preventing their victimization or delinquency.

Youth programs may involve learning skills such as home remodeling and handiwork.
(Courtesy of Dean John Champion)

Detention Alternatives in New York City

Another area in which diversion and the identification of alternatives occur is in detention. In 2006, New York City juvenile court officials were concerned about the lack of alternatives for youth other than traditional detention. At that time, detention costs exceeded $450 per day. In a collaborative effort with the Vera Institute, a risk assessment instrument was developed to determine which youth were in danger of not appearing for subsequent court proceedings. Youth were classified as low, medium, or high risk in terms of their likelihood to appear for further court dates. At the same time, professionals and interested individuals identified community-based alternatives to detention at three different levels of supervision that would provide the appropriate level of monitoring and treatment for youth (Fratello, Salsich, and Mogulescu, 2011). Preliminary analysis has found that by incorporating "risk assessment instruments" (RAIs) and identifying "alternatives to detention" for eligible youth at various risk levels, fewer youth have been incarcerated in detention, and recidivism has decreased (Fratello, Salsich, and Mogulescu, 2011, p. 4). This approach could serve as a model for other jurisdictions.

Balanced and Restorative Justice

The **Balanced and Restorative Justice (BARJ) model** emphasizes offender accountability, community protection, and competency development (Bazemore and Umbreit, 1995). In BARJ, the offender, the victim, and the community are involved in the process. It is anticipated that the participation of these diverse groups will aid in the successful reintegration of the youth and restore the community. Although there is variation from jurisdiction to jurisdiction in implementation, BARJ is often used for youth on probation or unofficial supervision (Merlo and Benekos, 2009). These kinds of programs have been utilized in Canada, Europe, Australia, New Zealand, and other countries for many years (Bazemore and Umbreit, 2001). Although the research on their effectiveness has been limited, Rodriguez (2005) found that youth in Arizona who were involved in BARJ had lower recidivism rates than youth in traditional supervision programs.

The Community Board Program

One innovation introduced by the Vermont juvenile courts is the **Reparative Probation Program**, which is a civil **mediation** mechanism. This program involves first- and second-time juvenile offenders who have been charged with minor offenses, often property offenses, where damage to or loss of property was sustained by one or more victims. The Community Board Program uses volunteers to meet with offenders and their victims as an alternative to a full juvenile court adjudicatory hearing (Karp, 2001). Mediation is conducted, and a mutually satisfactory solution is arranged by the **mediator**.

One of the positive aspects of this program is that victims can meet and interact with the offenders. As a result, victims may become involved and empowered. Their face-to-face encounters with youth who victimized them enable victims to relate details of the harm the youth caused. Some juveniles have also directly benefited from their confrontation experience. However, this type of mediation program does not

Balanced and Restorative Justice (BARJ) model

A juvenile justice system model that emphasizes accountability, public safety, and competency development.

Reparative Probation Program

Voluntary civil mediation mechanism involving minor offenders, where specially trained volunteers determine fair compensation to victims through a series of meetings.

mediation

A process whereby a third party intervenes between an offender and a victim to work out a noncriminal or civil resolution to a problem that might otherwise result in a delinquency adjudication or criminal conviction.

mediator

Third-party arbiter who resolves disputes between parties.

seem to work well with particularly young offenders. Older juveniles have higher maturity levels and are more responsive to mediation (Bannan, 2008).

Implications of Diversion Programs for Juveniles

As mentioned, one result of the JJPDA of 1974 was to deinstitutionalize status offenders and to attempt to remove them from the jurisdiction of juvenile courts. This has been done in some jurisdictions, but not in all of them. Thus, there is variation among jurisdictions about how juvenile offenders are processed and treated. In recent years, however, an increasing number of juvenile courts have imposed dispositions according to offender needs after a careful review of the youth using risk assessment instruments.

Overall, Mulvey and Iselin (2008) found that "juvenile justice professionals still make limited use of existing standardized instruments" and rely instead on "intuition" in responding to each case. In brief, using standardized risk assessment instruments seems to be contrary to the "principle of individualized justice" (Mulvey and Iselin, 2008, p. 38). Nonetheless, more sophisticated and reliable classification instruments for offenders are being devised. Additional information is needed about offender characteristics, their backgrounds, and specific circumstances for proper sanctions and treatments to be imposed by juvenile court judges. For diversion programs to be successful, they must target the most successful juvenile candidates, who most frequently are low-risk or first-offenders. These kinds of tools might be especially beneficial to intake officers and prosecutors who decide to use diversion for specific youth.

Some diversion programs, especially for youthful sex offenders, include some rather stringent conditions and may even involve participation in intervention projects designed to remedy certain manifested problems. Participants may receive individual, group, and family counseling and other therapies. Youth may also be exposed to psychophysiological assessments and various testing procedures (Bouhours and Daly, 2007).

Teen courts attempt to divert youth from the system. Juveniles may be asked to participate in classes on various issues.
(© Mikael Karlsson/Alamy)

CAREER SNAPSHOT

Name: Chanda Galloway Miller
Position: Coordinator, City of Holland Teen Court, Holland, Michigan

Colleges Attended: Hastings College and University of South Dakota

Degrees: B.A. in English Education and J.D.

(Courtesy of Dean John Champion)

Background

I did not set out to become an attorney. My goal was to teach English to middle-school students, and I did that. I have a heart for teens. They are in a vital stage of development and discovery, full of energy, and terribly vulnerable, unknown to themselves.

Twelve years after receiving my B.A., I entered law school. By then, my son was in elementary school. After law school, I began my legal career in private practice in South Dakota. After several years, we moved to Michigan, and I joined another private practice. While there, I heard of an opportunity to teach business law part-time at a local college. I applied and was selected. After a move to Iowa, I chaired a paralegal program at a community college. This was an excellent combination of teaching and law that I enjoyed enormously.

As my husband's career evolved, we began working internationally. Our first assignment was in Jakarta, Indonesia, and it was for five years. I joined an international law office and worked with attorneys to improve their English and their writing and case management skills. Our next assignment was in Beijing, for three years. I taught business law to university students. Then, we decided to return to the United States.

We settled in Michigan since our son was living here. I decided to change to a lifestyle of volunteering. I responded to an announcement in the newspaper for the position of Teen Court Coordinator, and I was fortunate to be offered the position.

Our Teen Court program is one of the oldest in the country, having started in 1991. It is also entirely operated by volunteers. The police and the prosecutor's office make referrals to the program. Since participation in the program is voluntary, one of my first responsibilities is to meet with the teen offender and his or her parents/guardians to review the process and obtain signatures on a consent form. Since we require the offenders to plead guilty and not use lawyers, they opt to give up some important rights.

One of the most interesting parts of the interview is talking with the teen about the offense committed. There are times when the youth's account is quite eye-opening for the parents and for me. I also review the court process to be certain that everyone is clear on what will happen, what the consequences may be, and to stress the confidentiality of the proceedings.

We conduct trials in a regular county courtroom. Sitting in on the trials and listening to the questions of the teen jurors is one of the best parts of this work. While a teen offender may be capable of misleading an adult or presenting dishonest answers to an adult's questions, this does not happen with other teens. The teen jurors seek information to know more about the offenders than just what they did wrong, inquiring about school, after-school activities, relationships with friends and family, and the impact their arrest has had not only on them but on their families. This is often another moment of considerable impact on the offenders, as they quite often have not really considered the effects of their action, especially on younger siblings.

Once the sentence is announced, I follow up with the offenders to provide them information on where they can apply to perform community service hours, always a part of our sentences, as well as other details. We are fortunate to be in a community with a number of not-for-profit organizations, making it easier for the students to locate placement.

It is wonderful to witness an offender seize this opportunity to clear his or her record, carry out the disposition in a timely manner, and move forward with a different attitude. We have had a number of participants who found locations for their community service where they enjoyed serving and continued volunteering there. When an offender make positive changes, such as becoming involved in after-school activities, it greatly increases the likelihood of success and makes all of us smile. The most difficult times are when an offender gets back into trouble immediately after going through our process. We offer a wonderful opportunity for teens to start fresh, and when they fail to do so, it is disappointing to all of us who are involved.

Advice to Students

There are no magic bullets when working with juveniles. Positive peer pressure can be significant. Youth courts throughout the country are built on that principle. Statistics are instructive, but they are no substitute for actually seeing a youth grow and change. Juveniles often make poor decisions but must be responsible for the consequences. After working in this field for a while, it is easy to become jaded. Try to view each offender individually. You can make a difference. Each time you reach a young person and help change his or her behavior pattern, you also reach everyone in that teen's sphere of influence. The ripple effect is amazing. There is no stereotype for juvenile offenders. Do not think of them in clichés.

Teen Courts

teen courts

Tribunals consisting of teenagers who judge other youth charged with minor offenses, much like regular juries in criminal courts, where juvenile prosecutors and defense counsel argue cases against specific juvenile offenders; juries decide sanction with judicial approval.

Increasing numbers of jurisdictions are using **teen courts** as an alternative to juvenile court for determining one's involvement in the act and the appropriate sanction. Teen courts are informal proceedings, where juries comprised of teenagers hear and decide minor cases. Judges may divert cases to these teen courts, where adults function only as presiding judges. The presiding judges are often judges or lawyers who perform such services voluntarily and in their spare time. First-offender cases, in which status offenses or misdemeanors have been committed, are sometimes handled with a variation of teen courts involving one's peers as judges.

The focus of teen courts is upon therapeutic jurisprudence, with a strong emphasis upon rehabilitation. One objective of such courts is to teach empathy to offenders. Victims are encouraged to take an active role in these courts (Peterson, 2005).

Teen courts are also known as youth courts, peer courts, and student courts (Preston and Roots, 2004). In1994, there were 78 active teen courts. By 2010, there were "1,050 youth-court programs operating in 49 states and the District of Columbia" (National Association of Youth Courts, 2011, p. 1). The 2004 resolution by the American Probation and Parole Association in support of youth courts is presented in Box 10.1.

States vary in terms of the eligibility requirements, age limits, and offenders that youth courts may consider. Most frequently, first-offenders and youth involved in minor delinquent acts or status offenses are included. More-serious offenses are usually

10-1 ▶

Resolution by American Probation and Parole Association in Support of Youth Courts

In 2004, the American Probation and Parole Association adopted the following resolution in support of youth courts:

Whereas, youth courts, also known as teen courts, peer courts, and student courts, are one of the fastest growing crime intervention and prevention programs in the nation.

Whereas, youth volunteers under the supervision of adult volunteers act as judges, jurors, clerks, bailiffs, and counsel for youth who are charged with minor delinquent and status offenses, problem behaviors or minor infractions of school rules, and who consent to participate in the program.

Whereas, youth courts engage the community in a partnership with the juvenile justice system, youth programs, schools, attorneys, judges, and police departments working together to form and expand diversionary programs responding to juvenile crime and problem behavior.

Whereas, youth courts increase the awareness of delinquency issues and problem behavior on a local level and mobilize community members, including youth, to take an active civil role in addressing the problem. Youth courts exemplify the practices of

empowering youth through involvement in developing community solutions to problems, teaching decision making and applying leadership skills.

Whereas, youth courts design effective program services and sentencing options that hold youth accountable, repair the harm to the victim and the community, and contribute to public safety.

Whereas, youth courts promote attitudes, activities, and behaviors that create and maintain safe and vital communities where crime and delinquency cannot flourish; and youth court practices provide a foundation for crime prevention and community justice initiatives, as well as embrace the principles of restorative justice.

Therefore, be it resolved, that the American Probation and Parole Association hereby recognizes the importance of youth courts to our communities and recommends that probation, parole, and community supervision agencies support and assist in the formation and expansion of diversionary programs, known as youth courts.

Source: Reprinted with permission from "Resolution in Support of Youth Courts," APPA Perspectives 28, p. 8 (2004).

referred at intake for formal processing and adjudicatory hearings. The accountability of participating youth is considerable, because youth must admit guilt before participating in teen courts (Butts and Buck, 2002). Furthermore, they must waive their confidentiality rights in most jurisdictions. An example of a teen court referral form is shown in Figure 10.1.

The Use of Teen Courts

The first cities to implement teen courts were Seattle, Washington, and Denver (Rasmussen, 2004). Subsequently, teen courts have been established in many other jurisdictions. Teen courts are an alternative to traditional juvenile court processing. They are designed to divert youth from the system who are involved in relatively minor offending. Youth who participate usually range in age from 10 to 16.

Teen court dispositions are related closely to community service as well as jury service (Karp, 2004). Thus, juveniles who are found guilty by teen courts may, in fact, serve on such juries in the future as one of their conditional sanctions (Rasmussen, 2004). Alternatively, they may be required to perform community service, such as working at the animal shelter, library, or nursing home; picking up trash in parks or ball fields; or assisting various community agencies.

Teen courts place a priority on educating youth about their responsibilities as individuals, family members, and citizens. As a part of one's diversion, conditional options, such as restitution, fines, or community service, may be imposed in those cases where property damage was incurred as the result of the juvenile's behavior (Chapman, 2005). Table 10.1 summarizes some of the data on teen courts based on a national survey conducted by Schneider (2007).

Teen Court Variations

Several variations of teen courts have been described (Butts and Buck, 2002). Four courtroom models of teen courts include (1) adult judge, (2) youth judge, (3) peer jury, and (4) tribunal. These variations are summarized in Table 10.2.

Adult Judge Model

The **adult judge model** of teen courts uses adult judges to preside over all actions. Generally, a youth acting as the prosecutor presents each case against a juvenile to a jury comprised of one's peers. A juvenile defense counsel offers mitigating evidence, if any, which the jury may consider. The jury is permitted to ask the youthful defendant any questions in an effort to determine why the offense was committed and any circumstances surrounding its occurrence. Subsequently, the jury deliberates and recommends the most appropriate disposition. The suitability of the recommended sanction, which is most often some form of community service and/or victim compensation or restitution, is decided by the judge. About half of all teen courts in the United States use the adult judge model.

Youth Judge Model

The **youth judge model** of teen courts utilizes a juvenile judge instead of an adult judge. As with the adult judge model, youth serve as prosecutors and defense counsel.

adult judge model

Version of teen court in which adult judges preside and youth perform the roles of prosecutor, defense counsel, and jury.

youth judge model

Youth court model in which a juvenile sits as the judge and other juveniles serve as prosecutors and defense counsel; very similar to the tribunal model, in which one or more youth perform the role of judge.

A|D|R

CENTER
Alternative Dispute Resolution Services and Training

TEEN COURT REFERRAL FORM

Teen/ Court is for first-time offenders only. Once we receive the referral, our office will verify that the student is a first-time offender. The student must also be enrolled and attending school full-time.

[Student has been cleared as a first-time offender by: _____ _____]

                                                         Last Name   Date

Referred by: _____   Referral Date: _____/_____/_____

Agency: _____   Phone #: _____

Student name: _____   DOB: _____/_____/_____ Age:_____

School: _____ Grade: _____   Race: _____ Sex: _____

Parent/Guardian: _____   Phone: (_____) _____-_____

Address: _____   Zip: _____

(Please circle type of crime)

Charge: _____ Victimless Crime—Person Crime—Property Crime

Date and time of incident: ____/____/_____ _____:_____

Explanation of charge:

_____

_____

_____

_____

_____

_____

Victim: _____ Parent: _____   Phone: _____

Address: _____   DOB: _____

Witness: _____   Phone: _____

Address: _____   DOB: _____

Please attach citation and other reports. Include any witness and/or victim statements.

Figure 10.1
Teen Court Referral Form
Source: Reprinted by permission of the ADR Center, Wilmington, North Carolina.

Table 10.1
TEEN COURT DATA IN THE UNITED STATES

Number of teen or youth courts in 2007	1,250
Location of courts	49 States and the District of Columbia
Peer jury model	Adult
Tribunal	Youth (1–3)
Number of youth accepted that begin process per year	Approximately 116,000
Success rate	Over 87% of youth complete the program
Estimated cost	Less than $500.00 per youth
Community service	Approximately 1.7 million hours performed by youth
Number of teen court volunteers	133,000, of which 88 percent are teens

Source: Compiled by authors based on data from J. Schneider (2007), *Youth Courts: An Empirical Update and Analysis of Future Organizational Needs.* Washington, DC: Hamilton Fish Institute on School and Community Violence, The George Washington University, pp. 16–18.

Table 10.2
TYPES OF TEEN COURTS

	Judge	Youth Attorneys	Jury/Role of Jury
Adult judge model	Adult	Yes	Recommend sentence
Youth judge model	Youth	Yes	Recommend sentence
Peer jury model	Adult	No	Question defendant, recommend sentence
Tribunal	Youth (1–3)	Yes	No jury present

A sentence is recommended by a peer jury, and the juvenile judge decides if it is appropriate. About a third of all teen courts use this model.

Peer Jury Model

In the **peer jury model**, an adult judge presides, while a juvenile jury hears the case against the youth. While both the adult judge and youth judge models use a peer jury, in this model no youth prosecutors or defense counsel are present. After hearing the case, the jury deliberates and makes a disposition, which the judge must approve.

Tribunal Model

In the **tribunal model**, one or more juveniles act as judges, while other youth are designated as prosecutors and defense counsel. The prosecution and defense present their

peer jury model
A peer jury is composed of other youth in the community who sit on the jury and decide the offender's punishment.

tribunal model
The tribunal model is similar to a peer jury model, in that one's peers serve as judges, defense counsel, and prosecutors and one's actions and determine punishments.

Focus on Delinquency

Police in Escondido, California, arrested a 17-year-old female for shoplifting $400 worth of clothing and jewelry from Macy's department store. The youth could have been referred to juvenile court to face theft charges and to be formally processed. This most likely would have resulted in formal adjudication, which would have given the girl a juvenile record. Instead, after reviewing the case, police, along with community service providers, volunteers, and teen peers, decided that the girl was a good candidate for peer court. She was given the opportunity to testify before a jury of five peers and a lawyer who served as judge.

The goal of peer court is to hold juveniles like this girl accountable for their delinquency, to teach them to engage in law abiding behavior, and to "get them back on track" while reducing crime and victimization. In addition, teen court reduces costs by avoiding the expense of juvenile court, and it provides a more productive response to young people by referring them to programs without their having to receive a formal sentence. In teen court, youth and their parents must agree to complete the peer jury sentence in 90 days, or the case is referred to juvenile court. In the Escondido teen court, 85 percent of the youth complete their sentences. The peer jury in this case sentenced the shoplifter to "20 hours of community service," to write letters of apology to Macy's and her parents, and to serve as a peer on three teen court hearings.

Source: Adapted from Morgan Cook (2011, August 22), "Escondido: Youth Court Gives Young Offenders Second Chance," *The North County Times* (available http://www.nctimes.com/news/local/escondido/escondido-youth-court-gives-young-offenders-second-chance/article_211136d3-0e62-5945-a216-2a84238a9c78.html?print=1).

case to the judges, who subsequently deliberate and return with a disposition. Again, the sanctions usually involve restitution or some form of victim compensation, community service, or combination of punishments, depending upon the circumstances.

The Success of Teen Courts

The growing popularity of teen courts as alternatives to formal juvenile court actions attests to their success in dealing with first-time, low-risk youthful offenders. Youth who function as judges, prosecutors, and defense counsel usually engage in training to perform these roles. In New York, for example, an average of 16 to 20 hours of training is required of youth court juvenile officials (Butts and Buck, 2002). In some courts, written tests are administered following one's training. These are intended to ensure that the participants understand fundamental legal principles.

Several national youth court guidelines have been articulated. These guidelines have been developed for (1) program planning and community mobilization, (2) program staffing and funding, (3) legal issues, (4) identified respondent population and referral process, (5) volunteer recruitment and sentencing options, (6) volunteer training, (7) youth court operations and case management, and (8) program evaluation.

Recidivism rates of teen courts have not been studied consistently throughout all jurisdictions. However, available information suggests that recidivism rates among youthful defendants who have gone through the teen court process are very low (less than 20 percent overall). Studies of teen courts indicate that youth emerge with a greater appreciation for and a better understanding of the law. They also appear to be more law-abiding when compared with youth adjudicated formally through juvenile courts. In light of this, a majority of states have adopted teen court models of one type or another (Chapman, 2005).

Some Examples of Teen Courts

Two examples of teen courts are the Anchorage Youth Court in Alaska and the Holland Teen Court in Michigan.

The Anchorage Youth Court

In Anchorage, Alaska, the **Anchorage Youth Court (AYC)** was established in 1989. Subsequently, 14 other youth courts, modeled after the AYC, have been established in Alaskan cities (AYC, 2005). The AYC targets first-offenders and uses volunteers from the community. The protocol of the AYC is outlined below.

> **Anchorage Youth Court (AYC)**
>
> Teen court established in Anchorage, Alaska, in 1989; cases include minor misdemeanor offenders; juries of one's peers decide punishments after youth admit guilt in advance of trial proceedings; sanctions include restitution and community service.

Intake and No-Contest Pleas. At the intake stage, a decision is made whether to recommend a youth for AYC. Low-risk first-time juvenile offenders may be offered the opportunity to enter no-contest pleas and attend AYC for sentencing. A no-contest plea means that the youth admits to the offense and avoids formal adjudication by a juvenile court judge. Youth volunteers serve as prosecutors, defense counsel, judges, clerks, bailiffs, and jurors for youth.

The Sentencing Options. The following sentencing options are available: (1) AYC classes, including anger management class, defensive driving class, property and theft crimes class, skills for life class, "Start Smart" and "Stay Smart" classes, victim-impact class, and weapons safety class; (2) an apology letter to the offender's family; (3) an apology letter to the victim; (4) community service; (5) diversity awareness; (6) drug/alcohol assessment; (7) an essay; (8) fire prevention program; (9) jail tour; (10) juvenile antishoplifting program, parent–adolescent mediation, restitution, and victim–offender mediation.

No-Contest Script. A no-contest script is presented to the defendant, the prosecutor, defense counsel, and the judges. The AYC no-contest script outlines the entire protocol for the AYC proceeding. The defendant is advised that one or more persons have been appointed to defend him or her. The charging document is read, outlining all charges against the offender as well as the teen's admissions to the alleged offenses. The defendant is asked whether the facts outlined in the charging document are true and enters a no-contest plea.

Prosecution and Defense Sentencing Recommendations. Both the prosecution and the defense have the opportunity to examine the case and make a sentencing recommendation to the AYC judges. These recommendations consider all factors from both the defense attorney's and the prosecutor's point of view, and both are provided with access to the list of sentencing options noted above.

Every youth processed by the AYC performs a certain number of hours of community service determined by the seriousness of the offense and the presence or absence of aggravating and mitigating circumstances. In addition, recommendations are used to select appropriate and meaningful sanctions that will demonstrate consequences and reinforce accountability.

Probation Officer's Recommendation and Victim-Impact Statement. A juvenile probation officer may prepare the equivalent of a predisposition report for any particular juvenile and make a recommendation. A probation officer's recommendation usually carries considerable weight. All of this information is considered by the judges.

Often, one or more victims is involved. The court notifies the victim(s) that the defendant has agreed to participate in the AYC (Figure 10.2). Information about the crime and damage or injuries to the victim(s) are solicited. Thus, victims have an opportunity to communicate in writing how the act committed by the youth affected them. The AYC can consider this information.

Oral Arguments to the AYC. Both the prosecution and the defense make oral arguments that reflect their written recommendations to the court.

Defendant's Statement to the AYC. Defendants are permitted to address the AYC judges on their own behalf. Youthful offenders may take this opportunity to accept responsibility for their crime(s), to show remorse, and perhaps, to argue for leniency.

Judicial Adjournment and Sentence Determination. AYC judges deliberate and eventually produce a sentencing document. The sentencing document is a unanimous decision by the judges, outlining the disposition and the reasons for it. The aggravating and mitigating factors considered by the judges are listed, along with a rationale for why these factors were considered to be important. The youth then consult with their attorneys and determine whether the sentence is accepted or whether they will file an appeal. In most cases, defendants agree to the AYC judicial sentencing terms.

Youth may be required to write letters of apology to victims in peer courts as a part of their sanction.
(Courtesy of Dean John Champion)

Anchorage Youth Court
PO Box 100359
Anchorage, AK 99510
Phone: (907) 274-5986 • Fax: (907) 272-0491
Email: info@anchorageyouthcourt.org

Dear (victim name),   August 31, 2011

APD Case # 11-__ was referred to McLaughlin Juvenile Intake regarding a case in which you were a victim. The juvenile defendant has agreed to attend Anchorage Youth Court for sentencing as a consequence of his/her crime.

The attached form is your opportunity to explain the effect of the crime to the Anchorage Youth Court judges who will sentence the defendant. You may fill out the form if you wish but are under no obligation to do so. If your property was damaged or you were injured and incurred medical bills as a result of this crime, please provide details on the form and attach any receipts. If full or partial restitution is ordered, you will be contacted when the money order is collected from the defendant.

Defendants usually appear in Anchorage Youth Court within a couple of weeks of the crime occurring. For the Anchorage Youth Court judges to consider your comments, we must receive the completed form by _____.
You may bring the completed form to our office at 838 W. 4th Avenue, mail it to us as P.O. Box 100359, or fax it to us at 272-0491.

Anchorage Youth Court is a non-profit 501(c)(3) educational organization which trains youth in grades 7-12 to represent and judge their peers in actual criminal cases. Members volunteer to serve as prosecuting and defense attorneys, judges, clerks, bailiffs and jurors for juvenile offenders who have committed misdemeanors and minor felonies. 89% of the defendants who complete the program do not commit another crime.

The sentencing options used at Anchorage Youth Court include community work service, a mandatory essay, educational classes about specific crimes, and restitution for property damage or medical bills for physical injury. Anchorage Youth Court holds the defendant himself/herself responsible for earning the money to pay for the Anchorage Youth Court service fee ($50), educational class fee(s) ($40-$125) and any restitution amount.

If you have any questions, please call me at 274-5986.

Sincerely,

_____

Denise Wike, AYC Legal Advisor

"Justice For Youth By Youth"

Figure 10.2
Anchorage Youth Court Letter and Victim-Impact Statement
Reprinted with permission from the State of Alaska Juvenile Court.

AYC

Anchorage Youth Court
PO Box 100359
Anchorage, AK. 99510
Phone: (907) 274-5986 • Fax: (907) 272-0491

Please return this form to Anchorage Youth Court by 3:00 p.m. (date)

Anchorage Police Department Case # 11-   AYC Case # 11-

1. How did the crime affect you and/or your family?

2. Did you or your family have any financial loss because of this crime?
    If so, describe any loss not covered by insurance and attach copies of receipts for repairing or replacing the damaged items, or your medical bills.

3. Please add any other comments you want the judges to hear.

_____   _____

Signature   Date

If you wish to be contacted after the sentence is complete, please provide a phone number: _____

"Justice for Youth by Youth"

Figure 10.2 *Continued*

The Success of the AYC. With many intervention programs, effectiveness is measured by recidivism. For the AYC, the recidivism rate is very low; only 11 percent of those processed return to juvenile court for a new offense. This means that there is nearly a 90 percent success rate and that most participants will not commit additional offenses. A majority of youth or teen courts in the United States have reported similar results, which attests to their growing popularity.

The Holland Teen Court

In 1991, several juvenile justice officials in Michigan examined alternative procedures to more formalized juvenile courts for processing less-serious juvenile offenders. They ultimately established the **Holland Teen Court (HTC)**, a successful project that has been expanded and emulated by other cities throughout Michigan and in other states. The goals of the HTC are (1) to interrupt developing patterns of criminal behavior, (2) to promote self-improvement, and (3) to educate peer jurors about the legal system and local authority processes. Judges are local attorneys and judges who volunteer to preside whenever a case is heard.

Acceptance into the HTC Program. Acceptance into the HTC is restricted to juvenile first-offenders between the ages of 10 and 17. Youth must admit their involvement in the alleged behavior, and they must agree to accept the sanction (Figures 10.3 and 10.4). Once they successfully complete the process, the charges against them are dismissed. Typical offenses considered for HTC resolution range from curfew violation and disorderly conduct to larceny under $100. Driving offenses are also included.

Peer Jury Composition. The peer jury consists of high-school students who receive instruction and then engage in practice sessions. The jury is trained to ask fair

> **Holland Teen Court (HTC)**
> Holland, Michigan, youth court program commenced in 1991 involving juveniles who have committed less-serious offenses; jurors consist of high-school students with general training in jury deliberations and sentencing matters; limitations on sentencing restricted to community service and restitution; very successful program with recidivism occurring in less than five percent of cases handled.

Holland Teen Court, Michigan, convenes to hear cases.
(Courtesy of Dean John Champion)

HOLLAND TEEN COURT
CONSENT FORM

JUVENILE NAME: _____

ADDRESS: _____

CHARGE: _____

HOLLAND TEEN COURT IS A VOLUNTARY PROGRAM THAT HAS BEEN EXPLAINED TO ME. I ADMIT THAT I AM GUILTY OF THE OFFENSE THAT I HAVE BEEN CHARGED WITH. I UNDERSTAND THAT I HAVE A RIGHT TO SEEK LEGAL COUNSEL. I UNDERSTAND THAT A JURY OF MY PEERS WILL HEAR MY CASE AND ASSIGN THE CONSEQUENCES THEY DEEM APPROPRIATE. THE CONSEQUENCES MAY INCLUDE, BUT ARE NOT LIMITED TO, COMMUNITY SERVICE, RESTITUTION, AN APOLOGY, COUNSELING, OR OTHER ALTERNATIVE OPPORTUNITIES PROGRAM. I UNDERSTAND THAT IF I FAIL TO APPEAR OR COMPLETE THE ASSIGNED CONSEQUENCES WITHIN A SPECIFIED TIME, MY CASE WILL BE REFERRED TO THE OTTAWA COUNTY PROBATE DEPARTMENT FOR CRIMINAL PROSECUTION. I UNDERSTAND THAT IF I SUCCESSFULLY COMPLETE THE CONSEQUENCES THAT THE TEEN COURT JURY ASSIGNS, THIS CHARGE WILL NOT BE HELD AGAINST ME IN ANY FUTURE PROCEEDINGS.

I AGREE TO THESE TERMS: _____   _____
                                                        NAME   DATE

PARENT/GUARDIAN CONSENT

THE HOLLAND TEEN COURT PROGRAM, AND THE CHARGE AGAINST MY CHILD, HAVE BEEN EXPLAINED TO ME. I UNDERSTAND THAT THIS IS A VOLUNTARY PROGRAM AND I HEREBY AUTHORIZE MY CHILD TO PARTICIPATE.

PARENT/GUARDIAN _____

Figure 10.3
Holland Teen Court Consent Form
Reprinted with permission of the Holland Teen Court.

questions and seek the truth relating to the offense(s). A strong focus is placed on the offender's feelings about the incident, his or her perspective regarding consequences for the illegal behavior, and the effect it has had on the offender's life and family and on the life of the victim. At the end of the session, the jury deliberates and determines the disposition to be imposed.

Sanctions. The following sanctions are typical choices for the HTC peer jury: (1) community service hours, (2) restitution, (3) an essay, or (4) an apology to the victim. As mentioned, the completion of all sanction requirements eventually results in a dismissal of all original allegations against a youth.

Success of the HTC. By 2008, the HTC had processed nearly 4,000 teens. Recidivism rates among these sentenced teens have been quite low (less than

---

REFUSAL TO PARTICIPATE

After being informed of my rights and the requirements of this program, I hereby refuse the services of this court, and ask that my case be referred back to the referring agency. I understand that by this act my case enters into the judicial system and may result in a court hearing.

Date: _____

_____
Signature of Juvenile

_____
Signature of Parent or Guardian

_____
Referring Officer

_____
Teen Court Coordinator/Staff

Figure 10.4
Refusal to Participate Form
Source: Reprinted with permission of the Holland Teen Court.

5 percent). Compared with the informal success standard of intervention programs for other types of offenders of 30 percent or less, the HTC is considered to be highly successful (HTC, 2008).

Day Reporting Centers

Goals and Functions of Day Reporting Centers

Day reporting centers were established first in England in 1974 to provide intensive supervision for offenders who would otherwise be incarcerated (Roy, 2004). Offenders in English day treatment centers typically lived at home while remaining under the supervision of a correctional administrator. Inmates would work or attend school, regularly participate in treatment programming, devote at least four hours a week to community service, and observe a strict curfew.

A variation on day treatment programs has been attempted in the United States for juvenile offenders. The first American day reporting centers were established in Connecticut and Massachusetts during the mid-1980s. During that period, there were 13 day treatment centers operating. By 2007, there were over 500 day treatment centers in 39 states (Office of Juvenile Justice and Delinquency Prevention, 2007).

Both male and female clients benefit from day treatment services. Since the mid-1970s, these programs have helped to expand the continuum of services available

> **day reporting centers**
> Established in England in 1974 to provide intensive supervision for low-risk offenders who lived at home; continued in various U.S. jurisdictions today to manage treatment programs, supervise fee collection, and handle other responsibilities, such as drug testing and counseling.

to at-risk and delinquent youth. These programs were developed through the collaborative efforts of educators, judges, and social service professionals and provide an effective alternative to out-of-home placements. Many day treatment programs are operated on a year-round basis, offering community-based, nonresidential services to at-risk and delinquent youth.

The centers provide a variety of treatments and services. Offenders report to these centers frequently, usually once or twice a day, and individual and group programs, classes, and supervision are available on site in most instances. For more-serious types of problems or illnesses, the center staff will refer clients to the appropriate community services, where they can receive specialized treatments. The types of services provided by most of these day reporting centers include the acquisition of job-seeking skills, drug-abuse education, group counseling, job placement services, academic instruction, vocational training, drug treatment, life skills training, individual counseling, transitional housing, and recreation and leisure activities (Henry and Kobus, 2007).

The goals of day treatment centers are to provide access to treatment and services, equip youth with relevant education and skills, reduce institutional overcrowding, protect the public, and build political support. Eligibility requirements stipulate that offenders are low-risk delinquents or criminals, with a good chance of succeeding in the community. Those with serious and violent prior records are usually excluded. However, in some jurisdictions, day reporting centers serve as intermediate sanctions for more delinquent offenders. Furthermore, some of these day treatment programs are offense-specific, such as day treatment for drug offenders.

Surveillance of day reporting center clients consists of on-site and off-site contacts. On-site contacts average 18 hours per week, where clients must be at these day reporting centers for treatment and special programming during the most intensive phases. Off-site surveillance includes visits to one's home, telephone contact, and unannounced visits to one's place of work or school.

Some Examples of Day Reporting Centers

The Moore County Day Reporting Center

The Moore County Day Reporting Center in North Carolina is a state-funded program that involves youth between 7 and 16 years of age who have been adjudicated delinquent. The juveniles arrive at the center every day after school hours to receive various services. In particular, this program targets youth who are nonviolent, who have a substance-abuse history, and who need to develop living skills (Dubowitz, Pitts, and Black, 2004).

Participation in the day reporting center is approved provided that clients meet the following eligibility requirements:

1. A Moore County resident.

2. Not charged with a serious or violent crime.

3. Have an approved residence.

4. Have access to a telephone.

5. Agree to abide by the conditions of the contract with the day reporting center.

6. Meet the requirements for intermediate punishment under the Structured Sentencing Act of 1994.

Youth who participate acquire valuable employment skills; participate in GED classes; undergo life skills training; participate in random drug testing; have access to a variety of mental health services, including group or individual counseling; participate in vocational rehabilitation programs; participate in health education courses; and undergo cognitive behavioral interventions. The cognitive behavioral interventions program is a 36-session program designed to change a person's thought processes to more law-abiding orientations. A number of youth have benefited from their participation in this day reporting program. The recidivism rate is less than 30 percent (Moore County Government, 2002).

The Englewood Evening Reporting Center

Some day reporting centers are operated during evening hours. This is true of the Englewood Evening Reporting Center, which operates between the hours of 4:00 P.M. and 8:00 P.M. weekdays in Englewood, Illinois, a Chicago suburb. The Englewood Center is an alternative site to serve juvenile offenders who would otherwise be held in the Juvenile Detention Center. The center was opened in 1995. Subsequently, the center has received a number of state awards for the services it provides to participating youth.

A part of the Cook County Circuit Court Juvenile Alternative Detention initiative, evening reporting centers such as the Englewood Center are "community-based facilities that operate through partnerships between sponsoring social service organizations and the court" (Office of the Chief Judge, 1998, para. 3). The juvenile court judge can order "nonviolent juvenile offenders awaiting disposition on a warrant or probation violation to report to the evening reporting center as an alternative to detention" (Office of the Chief Judge, 1998, para. 4). According to Chief Judge Donald P. O'Connell of the Cook County Court, youth are required to report to the center between the hours of 4:00 P.M. and 8:00 P.M. daily. At the center, they meet with professional staff, consisting of educational specialists, recreational specialists, and group workers, who "provide programs, activities, and workshops for a maximum of 25 youth. Transportation to and from the Englewood center and an evening meal are provided" (Office of the Chief Judge, 1998, para. 4) .

Chief Judge O'Connell has said that

[t]he purpose of the Circuit Court's support for establishing evening reporting centers is two-fold. First, we are helping at-risk kids avoid the possibility of being rearrested and sent to detention centers by getting them off the street and offering them positive, structured programming. We are able to do this through a low staff-to-client ratio of five to one, which ensures the personal attention that is simply not possible at the detention

center. The expectation is that stronger, safer neighborhoods are fostered by reducing the likelihood of delinquent activity and by providing various jobs to community residents (Office of the Chief Judge, 1998, para. 5).

The average cost per client at the Englewood center is $33 per day, which is significantly less than the $100 per day it would cost to hold the juvenile in detention facilities. This particular evening reporting center is in a community that has one of the highest rates of juvenile arrests and referrals to detention (Office of the Chief Judge, 1998, para. 7).

The Day Reporting Center for Juvenile Firearms Offenses

In McLean County, Illinois, a day reporting center is designed for juveniles who were in possession of firearms during the commission of delinquent acts. It is called the Day Reporting Center for Juvenile Firearms Offenses. The purpose of this program is to provide the juvenile court with meaningful sanctions for youth who were in possession of firearms. Three components of the program include (1) mandatory public service, (2) public health education addressing the risks of firearms and their possession, and (3) psychological evaluation with appropriate referrals.

Community service is a significant component of the program. Such service is designed to assist juveniles in assuming responsibility for themselves and for the community in which they live. Service to the local residents enables youth to form attachments and commitments that promote civility and safety within the community. Mandatory public health education is designed to instill in the juvenile participants a more complete understanding of the personal and public health risks associated with the unlawful use of firearms. A comprehensive psychological evaluation is required before a juvenile's acceptance into the program. All files are updated during the juvenile's participation. Referrals to psychological and/or counseling services are made where appropriate.

Each juvenile participates in the program for between 1 and 60 days. In addition to other services, juveniles receive tutoring, with an emphasis on those with a record of poor school performance. Time allocated for tutoring can also be used for the completion of homework. The main goal of this portion of the program is to teach the juvenile how to use his or her study time effectively. Group therapy, including presentations by professionals on positive peer relationships, drug education, handgun education, esteem building, and understanding of the juvenile court system, are also provided. Depending upon the youth's needs, individual therapy may be required as well. Basic life skills are incorporated in an instructional component of the program, which includes personal hygiene, meal planning, and preparation. The goal of this phase is to heighten juveniles' awareness of themselves and family members. The program is offered Mondays through Fridays, after normal school hours. Youth participants are expected to attend school and fulfill the obligations related to their courses.

There is strong parental input in this day reporting center. Parents are responsible for transporting their children to the center, and they are encouraged to become involved in all aspects of the program. Program officials maintain daily case notes on each juvenile, and they chart how well the youth is progressing toward attaining his or her goals. When the juvenile successfully completes the program, a full report of the juvenile is provided to the court.

The cost of maintaining each child in the day reporting program is $50 per day, compared with $92 per day if the juvenile were placed in secure detention in the McLean County Juvenile Detention Center. The recidivism rate of youth who have successfully completed the program is about 25 percent (McLean County Court Services, 2002).

The Predispositional Supervision Program

The Predispositional Supervision (PDS) Program in Geary County, Kansas, was established in 1996. The original purpose of this day reporting program was to reduce juvenile offending and recidivism. Local law enforcement officials in the county believed that the juvenile crime rate was directly related to substance abuse among youth. Therefore, early assessments and treatments of juveniles arrested for drug-related offenses were believed to be an effective means of decreasing offending.

The program is predispositional and is administered through the local community corrections office. Juvenile court judges in Geary County are provided with additional information about a youth's suitability for probation before disposition. Before the program was created, judges sometimes were unaware of a particular juvenile offender's needs and other problems, including behavioral/emotional problems.

Eligible offenders include adjudicated youth who have not yet received a disposition in their case. Before the dispositional hearing, the court can order the juvenile detained or released on bond. As a condition of the bond, the court can refer the juvenile to the PDS Program. Juvenile offenders must report to the community corrections day reporting center for an assessment. The day reporting staff conducts a needs assessment as well as a substance-abuse assessment. A plan is developed for each youth based on these results. A local professional supplies substance-abuse assessment and treatment.

The juvenile offender must report to the day reporting center from 8:30 A.M. to 5:00 P.M. daily. During this time, the juvenile participates in academic programs, job skills training, social skills training, anger management, conflict resolution, and community service for a maximum of 20 hours. All PDS-ordered youth meet in one classroom and are supervised by two staff members. The staff may utilize electronic monitoring for noncompliant youth. Curfews are generally ordered from 6:00 P.M. to 6:00 A.M., and clients are randomly monitored by the community corrections surveillance officers.

The maximum capacity is 30 clients, based on staff and space limitations. The average length of supervision varies between 30 and 60 days. Clients typically remain in the predispositional program four weeks.

The average cost of this experience is $155 per offender. The cost includes staffing, alcohol and drug evaluations, urinalyses, electronic monitoring, books, and software. The success of this program is reflected by the low, six percent rate of recidivism among its participants (Geary County Community Corrections, 2002).

Alternative Dispute Resolution

In most U.S. jurisdictions, youth are subject to **Alternative Dispute Resolution (ADR)**, or mediation, to resolve school problems (Bannan, 2008). The mediation process allows participants to resolve conflicts in a nonthreatening and nonpunitive atmosphere. Mediators are third-party individuals who help people in a dispute to express their points of view, identify their needs, clarify issues, explore solutions, and negotiate satisfactory agreements.

Mediation centers generally train students in different grade levels to serve as mediators so that they can intervene in school-based disputes among students. Several common components of these centers include (1) a conflict resolution curriculum that can be taught in either academic or residential settings, (2) a mediation program that trains residents and staff to help resolve conflicts among themselves, and (3) a reintegration component involving parents and residents developing terms of daily living for when the residents return home. By giving students a model for positive expression and conflict resolution, they hopefully can learn alternatives to violent and self-destructive behavior. Using these skills within the institutional setting, youth learn to interact successfully with their peers and adults.

Victim–offender mediation is an important and growing part of ADR. For juveniles who have committed property offenses, it is often beneficial for them to face their victims and learn how those victims have been affected by their losses. It is believed that these strategies increase offenders' accountability and that they are more inclined to accept responsibility for their actions (Bannan, 2008).

Some victim–offender mediation sessions may involve all parties, including family members, the child's attorney, social service agencies, and others associated with the case. The goal is to work toward an agreement and a restitution plan that everyone approves. This agreement is then submitted to the juvenile court judge for final authorization. The family-centered nature of the mediation process provides the social support youth need for long-term behavioral change associated with the mediation. No single victim–offender mediation model is applicable for all situations, however. Individual factors and circumstances must be considered to develop the best mediation plan (Bannan, 2008).

South Carolina has been operating juvenile arbitration programs since 1983, and the Lexington County Juvenile Arbitration Program is one example. The program is designed to "promote successful prevention and intervention strategies for at-risk juvenile offenders" (Alford, 1998, p. 28). Conditions of this program include the youth waiving his or her rights to legal representation and agreeing to permit impartial arbitrators to make a determination of guilt at the beginning of the hearing. Once the juvenile admits guilt, the hearing proceeds to a mutually satisfactory conclusion between the offender and the victim. If the juvenile does not admit guilt, then the arbitration proceedings are terminated, and the juvenile is referred to the juvenile court. Arbitrators are chosen from the community on the basis of their skill and expertise, and they complete approximately 20 hours of arbitration training before conducting sessions. During the period from 1995 to 1996, for instance, 370 juveniles were referred to the Lexington County Juvenile Arbitration Program, with a success rate of 94 percent. These sessions generated 4,666 hours of community service, and the restitution amount collected was $5,038. Comparable programs have been established in other jurisdictions, such as Cook County, Illinois, with similar successful results (Bannan, 2008).

SUMMARY

Half of all juveniles who enter the juvenile justice system annually are low-risk first-offenders. For many of these first-offenders, intake officers and judges use diversion to prevent these youth from experiencing the formal processes of juvenile courts. Several types of diversion programs were described. Not everyone qualifies for diversion, however, and intake staff and judges must exercise their best judgment in determining which offenders to refer to these programs.

Overall, diversion programs appear to be effective in reducing recidivism among low-risk youth or first-offenders. Adverse labeling is avoided, and youth acquire greater self-esteem and individual coping skills. They also have better school adjustment following their diversion experiences. Diversion programs can incorporate elements of rehabilitation, restitution, heightened accountability, and community service.

Teen courts are used increasingly as an alternative to formal juvenile court action. Teen courts, peer courts, or youth courts consist of youth who function as prosecutors, defense counsel, and juries for youth who have committed minor offenses. Originally established in Washington and Oregon, teen courts have proliferated. By late 2008, there were more than 1,300 teen courts operating in different U.S. jurisdictions. Teen courts are considered to be effective because one's peers, rather than adults, impose punishments. Punishments imposed by teen courts can involve community service and restitution. Teen court effectiveness in reducing recidivism among affected youth is impressive.

Another nominal option is day reporting centers, where day treatments for youthful clients are provided in their own neighborhoods. Youth participate in various programs and receive assistance through job placement services, individual counseling, life skills training, drug-abuse education, and drug treatment. The goals of day reporting centers are to assist youth in receiving the appropriate services in a structured environment, to reduce overcrowding, and to protect the public.

Juveniles may also participate in Alternative Dispute Resolution (ADR). ADR is a mediation program in which victims and youthful offenders can meet and resolve their conflicts. Parental and community involvement in ADR programs improve their effectiveness.

KEY TERMS

nominal dispositions, 360
diversion, 362
Balanced and Restorative
   Justice (BARJ) model,
   365
Reparative Probation
   Program, 365

mediation, 365
mediator, 365
teen courts, 368
adult judge model, 369
youth judge model, 369
peer jury model, 371
tribunal model, 371

Anchorage Youth Court
   (AYC), 373
Holland Teen Court
   (HTC), 377
day reporting centers, 379
Alternative Dispute
   Resolution (ADR), 384

QUESTIONS FOR REVIEW

1. How are nominal dispositions distinguished from conditional and custodial dispositions? What are some variations of nominal dispositions? How effective are they at reducing recidivism of disposed juveniles?

2. What is diversion? What are some of the eligibility requirements of prospective candidates for diversion?

3. What are some of the benefits and limitations of diversion?

4. How is diversion relevant to net-widening? How can judges be influenced to impose diversion in lieu of outright dismissals of cases that otherwise would not come before juvenile courts? Explain.

5. What is restorative justice? Who is involved? How are cases resolved?

6. What is meant by alternatives to juvenile detention? What are some options available?

7. What are teen courts? What types of juvenile offenders are the best types of clients for teen courts? How do teen courts function? What are the success rates of teen courts in reducing youth recidivism?

8. What are day reporting centers? What are some of their goals and functions?

9. What are two examples of day reporting centers? What are some of their characteristics, and which types of juveniles are served by them?

10. What is meant by ADR? Do you think it is an effective way of settling disputes between victims and youthful offenders? Why, or why not?

INTERNET CONNECTIONS

Childstats.gov: Forum on Child and Family Statistics
http://www.childstats.gov/index.asp

DrugSense
http://www.drugsense.org/

Gangs in the Schools

http://www.ericdigests.org/1995-1/gangs.htm

HandsNet

http://www.handsnet.org/

Idaho Youth Ranch

http://www.youthranch.org/

National Association of Youth Courts

http://www.youthcourt.net/

Office of Juvenile Justice and Delinquency Prevention

http://www.ojjdp.gov/

Office of Justice Programs

http://www.ojp.usdoj.gov/

PreventViolence.org: Strategies to Keep Youth Safe

http://www.preventviolence.org/

Stop the Drug War

http://www.stopthedrugwar.org

Teens, Crime, and the Community

http://www.ncpc.org/programs/tcc/

Youth Change: Your Problem-Kid Problem-Solver

http://www.youthchg.com

11

Juvenile Probation and Community-Based Corrections

Learning Objectives

AFTER READING THIS CHAPTER, THE STUDENT WILL BE ABLE TO:

- Describe the use of juvenile probation as an alternative to incarceration.
- Describe various juvenile probation programs.
- Describe the use of restitution programs.
- Understand Parental Liability for Youth Delinquency.
- Explain terms or conditions of probation.
- Define and understand recidivism.
- Understand Intermediate Sanctions for Juveniles.
- Explain intensive supervised probation.
- Understand the Balanced Approach and the use of victim-offender mediation in juvenile probation.
- Describe the use of house arrest and electronic monitoring.

(© Spencer Grant/Alamy)

Introduction

A 15-year-old black youth assaults two Latino youth and inflicts serious physical injuries as part of a racially motivated hate crime. A 12-year-old boy bludgeons his 17-month-old cousin to death for crying and interrupting his television cartoon show. Are either of these cases deserving of probation?

Probation is the most frequently used sanction by juvenile court judges. However, less than two-thirds of all youth adjudicated delinquent are placed on probation annually. The chapter opens with a definition of standard probation. This chapter will describe juvenile probation and a variety of other community-based programs.

All probation is conditional, although there are several common characteristics among most juvenile court jurisdictions that describe standard probation. These features will be described.

Additional requirements of probation orders include community service, restitution, home confinement, and electronic monitoring (EM). Youth also may be required to fulfill other conditions, including school attendance, vocational/educational training, or counseling. These various requirements will be discussed.

Intermediate punishments range between standard probation and secure confinement. Juvenile intensive supervised probation (JISP) is an intermediate punishment. The goals of intermediate punishment programs, which are community based, will be described. In addition, the eligibility requirements of several JISP programs will be featured, and the strengths and weaknesses of JISP programs will be discussed.

Juvenile probation officers (POs) are assigned different caseloads, depending upon their jurisdiction and the total number of juvenile offenders. Increasing numbers of juvenile probation departments are adopting the balanced approach, which seeks to ensure public safety, heighten offender accountability, and individualize the offender's needs. The relationship between juvenile POs and their clients will be explored.

Enabling legislation in most jurisdictions has established various community corrections agencies and services. Community corrections acts (CCAs) offer a wide variety of services to meet offender needs. Different types of community corrections initiatives, together with their purposes, goals, strengths, weaknesses, and effectiveness, will be highlighted.

Frequently, home confinement or house arrest is used concurrently with EM. These monitoring and supervisory methods have been effective in verifying an offender's activities and location. The functions, advantages, disadvantages, and usefulness of both EM and home confinement will be examined and discussed, and different types of EM programs will be identified and explained.

The chapter concludes with an examination of various conditions that accompany probation programs. These conditions are fines, victim compensation or restitution, victim–offender mediation, and community service. Each condition is imposed on a case-by-case basis, depending on the nature of the offense and the suitability for such sanctions and behavioral requirements. These conditions are intended to heighten offender accountability and ensure that the goals of juvenile justice are fulfilled. Evaluations of these sanctions will be made in terms of offender recidivism and other criteria.

Standard Probation for Juveniles

Standard Probation Defined

Standard probation is either a conditional or unconditional disposition that does not involve incarceration for a specified period following an adjudication of delinquency. Standard juvenile probation is a frequent disposition given by juvenile court judges. In fact, of all dispositional options available to juvenile court judges, standard probation is the most commonly used.

> **standard probation**
> Probationers conform to all terms of their probation program, but their contact with probation officers is minimal; often, their contact is by telephone or letter once or twice a month.

Probation exemplifies the philosophy of the early juvenile court. The first probation law was enacted in Massachusetts in 1878, although probation was practiced much earlier. John Augustus first developed probation in Boston in 1841. Even when the juvenile justice system became more punitive in the 1990s, probation was the dominant sanction (Merlo and Benekos, 2010).

In 2007, probation was the disposition imposed in approximately 56 percent of the cases (Livsey, 2010). This represents an actual decrease in the use of probation by juvenile court judges when compared to 1997. When compared to 1985, however, more youth were on probation in 2007. The kinds of cases that resulted in a youth being placed on probation have also changed. As Figure 11.1 shows, although most offenders who are placed on probation are property offenders, greater proportions of youth were placed on probation for person offenses, drug offenses, and public order offenses in 2007 than in 1985 (Livsey, 2010).

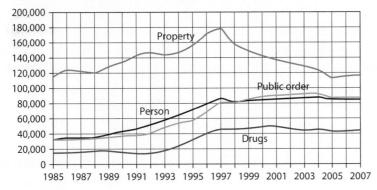

Adjudicated delinquency cases placed on probation, by offense, 1985–2007

Figure 11.1
Probation Dispositions Increased Between 1985 and 2007
Source: Charles M. Puzzanchera, Benjamin Adams, and Melissa Sickmund (2010).
Juvenile Court Statistics 2006–2007. Pittsburgh, PA: National Center for Juvenile Justice.

unconditional probation, unconditional standard probation

Form of conditional release without special restrictions or requirements placed on offender's behavior other than standard probation agreement terms; no formal controls operate to control or monitor the youth's behavior.

conditional probation

Program where the probationer is involved in some degree of local monitoring by probation officers or personnel affiliated with local probation departments.

special conditions of probation

Extra requirements written into a standard probation agreement, including possible vocational or educational training, counseling, drug or alcohol treatment, attendance at meetings, restitution, and community service.

There are several types of standard probation programs. Like their diversion program counterparts, probation programs for juveniles are either **unconditional probation** or **conditional probation**. **Unconditional standard probation**, another term for unconditional probation, basically involves freedom of movement for juveniles within their communities, perhaps accompanied by periodic reports by telephone or mail with a PO or the probation department. Because a PO's caseload is often large, with a hundred or more juvenile clients who must be managed, specialized individual attention is not a routine part of standard probation. The period of unsupervised probation varies among jurisdictions, depending on offense seriousness and other circumstances (Champion, 2008b).

Conditional probation programs may include optional conditions and program requirements, such as a certain number of hours of public or community service, restitution to victims, payment of fines, employment, and/or participation in specific vocational, educational, or therapeutic programs. It is crucial to any probation program that an effective classification system is utilized so that juvenile court judges can dispose of cases fairly and efficiently. It is standard practice for conditional probation programs to contain special conditions and provisions that address different youth needs. These special conditions are usually added by the juvenile court judge on the basis of information provided by juvenile POs.

The terms of standard probation are outlined in Figure 11.2 in a General Conditions of Supervision agreement. The probationer signs the form, thus consenting to the probation conditions. A witness also signs to attest to the probationer's signature. These terms may be accompanied by special conditions, known as **special conditions of probation**. The juvenile court judge and the PO use their discretion in deciding if these conditions would be beneficial to the youth. Thus, youth placed on standard probation may experience little outward change in their daily routines. Whenever special conditions of probation are attached, it usually suggests that the judge or PO has determined the youth should adhere to these additional terms for specific reasons. Some of these conditions include medical treatments for drug or alcohol dependencies, individual or group therapy or counseling, or participation in a driver's safety course. In some instances involving theft, burglary, or vandalism, restitution provisions may be included that require youth to repay victims for their financial losses. Some standard probation programs in the United States require little direct contact with the probation office. This reality may benefit POs, who often have large client caseloads. However, huge caseloads mean POs provide less individualized attention to youth, and some youth require more supervision than others while on standard probation.

Community service orders are increasingly used, although in some states, juvenile probation departments have found it difficult to find personnel to supervise youthful probationers. For instance, a North Dakota delinquent was ordered to perform 200 hours of community service. The community had about 500 residents, and the ordered work involved park maintenance and general cleanup duties. However, the youth did not perform this community service, because the probation department did not have

PROBATIONER: _____ **COUNTY**

GENERAL: The court may sentence the defendant to probation, which shall be subject to the following general conditions unless specifically deleted by the court. The probationer shall:

1. Pay supervision fees, fines, restitution or other fees ordered by the court.

2. Not use or possess controlled substances except pursuant to a medical prescription.

3. Submit to testing of breath or urine for controlled substance or alcohol use if the probationer has a history of substance abuse or if there is a reasonable suspicion that the probationer has illegally used controlled substances.

4. Participate in a substance abuse evaluation as directed by the supervising officer and follow the recommendations of the evaluator if there are reasonable grounds to believe there is a history of substance abuse.

5. Remain in the State of _____ until written permission to leave is granted by the Department of Probation or a county community corrections agency.

6. If physically able, find and maintain gainful full-time employment, approved schooling, or a full-time combination of both. Any waiver of this requirement must be based on a finding by the court stating the reasons for the waiver.

7. Change neither employment nor residence without prior permission from the Department of Probation or a county community corrections agency.

8. Permit the probation officer to visit the probationer or the probationer's work site or residence and to conduct a walk-through of the common areas and of the rooms in the residence occupied by or under the control of the probationer.

9. Consent to the search of person, vehicle or premises upon the request of a representative of the supervision officer if the supervising officer has reasonable grounds to believe that evidence of a violation will be found, and submit to fingerprinting or photographing, or both, when requested by the Department of Probation or a county community corrections agency for supervision purpose.

10. Obey all laws, municipal, county, state and federal.

11. Promptly and truthfully answer all reasonable inquiries by the Department of Corrections or a county community corrections agency.

12. Not possess weapons, firearms or dangerous animals.

13. Reports as required and abide by the direction of the supervising officer.

14. If under supervision for, or previously convicted of, a sex offense _____, and if recommended by the supervising officer, successfully complete a sex offender treatment program approved by the supervising officer and submit to polygraph examinations at the direction of the supervising officer.

15. Participate in a mental health evaluation as directed by the supervising officer and follow the recommendation of the evaluator.

16. If required to report as a sex offender under _____, report with the Department of State Police, a chief of police, a county sheriff or the supervising agency: (A) When supervision begins; (B) Within 10 days of a change in residence; and (C) Once each year within 10 days or the probationer's date of birth.

_____   _____
Probationer Signature   Date

_____   _____
Witness/Title   Date

Figure 11.2
General Conditions of Supervision

the money to pay a juvenile PO to monitor the youth for the full 200 hours. Despite these occasional limitations, probation program conditions typically address offender accountability. In a growing number of jurisdictions, drug courts are being established to deal more effectively with youthful substance abusers (Whiteacre, 2007).

Another related development is the use of report cards to keep communities involved and aware of how the juvenile justice system is working. In several states, juvenile probation departments have issued report cards to the community that explain what has been accomplished in the preceding year. From logging community service hours that youth have volunteered to publishing recidivism data, these report cards provide a level of accountability for courts and an opportunity for more cooperation and collaboration between probation staff and the community (Rubin, 2006). It is anticipated that such reports may be more frequent in the future.

Parental Responsibilities for a Juvenile's Delinquent Conduct

In some jurisdictions, parents of juveniles can be held financially liable for the actions of their delinquent children (Lee, 2008). For instance, D.D.H. was a Texas juvenile who committed burglary and larceny (*Matter of D.D.H.,* 2004). Following D.D.H.'s apprehension and adjudication, the court determined that the damages accruing to the victim amounted to $5,400, which included $4,500 to repair the property at the point where the burglary occurred as well as $900 for unrecovered stolen property resulting from the burglary. The juvenile court judge ordered D.D.H.'s parents to pay $5,000 in restitution to the victim for their son's delinquent acts as a special condition of the youth's probation orders. Although the parents appealed, a Texas appellate court upheld the juvenile court judge's restitution orders for the parents of the youth.

Juvenile Probationer Recidivism

Standard probation recidivism rate data are not uniformly maintained. Therefore, it is often difficult to forecast which juveniles will have the greatest likelihood of reoffending, regardless of their program.

The following steps have been recommended to reform juvenile probation in an effort to reduce recidivism:

1. *Research should drive policy.* Any and all new initiatives should include an evaluation component. Evidence-based programs should be expanded, especially programs that emphasize community involvement.

2. *Early intervention should be emphasized.* Interventions occurring earlier are more effective than those attempted in the offender's mid-teens.

3. *Paying just debts should receive priority.* Restitution and community service heighten offender accountability, and they can easily be integrated into the probation or parole program.

4. *Character building should be a part of probation programming.* Programs that include psychoeducational strategies are better at character building than those that are strictly punishment-centered.

5. *Violence prevention should be a priority in program development.* Juvenile probation must focus on efforts to suppress violent behavior. Programs that are educational in nature are more profitable compared with punishment-centered programs. These educational programs enable youth to learn how to cope more effectively with their environment. Such programs would include training in anger management, acquiring skills (social and emotional), improving moral reasoning, and instilling heightened self-esteem (Rosky, 2008).

Mission-Driven Probation Versus Outcome-Focused Probation

More effective juvenile probation appears to be both mission-driven and outcome-focused. Professional policies and practices in juvenile probation are outcome-focused.

For both individual offenders and entire juvenile PO caseloads, outcome-focused probation systematically measures the tangible results of its interventions, compares those results to its goals, and holds itself publicly accountable for any differences. Departments must measure more than just their failures (recidivism) and the sanctions they have imposed. Outcome measures provide evidence of the degree to which probation supervision goals have or have not been achieved, in essence measuring the department's performance in meeting system goals. Long-term measurement of outcomes indicates the degree to which probation supervision has impacted youthful offenders after their release in terms of changing their thinking, behaviors, and attitudes (Parker, 2005).

Mission-driven juvenile probation means that the work of probation must be directed at achieving clearly articulated and widely shared goals. It requires a commitment to a strategic plan or focus-group process that gives staff members an opportunity to define their values about the juvenile justice system—and about juvenile probation in particular—and to translate them into action and results. Such an effort will increase staff support and provide a basis for continuous feedback, evaluation, and improvement at the policy, program, and individual employee levels. Mission statements provide an organizational compass that points to an agreed-upon destination, and they are central to the operations and activities of any organization. What does juvenile probation stand for in the community? What is it attempting to accomplish? Ultimately, mission statements should be categorized into individual goals that are directed at protecting the public, holding the juvenile accountable for repairing harm caused to victims and the community, and engaging offenders in rehabilitative activities designed to address their most pressing problems and needs.

Restitution

Restitution is a frequent condition of probation. Programs that use restitution and enforce it seem to have lower recidivism rates. This is because offenders are required to repay victims for damages they inflict and take responsibility for their actions. Restitution requires a financial connection between what the youthful offenders did and how much it costs to compensate victims for their losses. Therefore, these tangible punishments are considered to be effective as delinquency deterrents (Taxman, 2005).

Juvenile Probation Camps

In the early 1980s, California experimented with several types of **juvenile probation camps** (Watson et al., 2003). These camps were county-operated and included physical activities, community contacts, and academic training. The camps were designed as dispositional alternatives to secure custody for youthful offenders. Eligibility requirements included first-offender status and nonviolent behaviors. Counselors worked with youth who were carefully screened before entering the program. By admitting small groups of youth, counselors maximized individualized attention for each youth.

Older juveniles who participated in these probation camps had lower rates of recidivism compared with younger youth. Overall, the camps were evaluated as successful in minimizing recidivism and enhancing the rehabilitation of participants. One reason for the lower rates of recidivism among youthful clients was the greater direct supervision by camp personnel. This circumstance is not unlike that found in communities where various methods of formal social control, including police and PO surveillance, are employed to supervise juvenile probationers and parolees. California maintains 67 probation camps and ranches, of which five are for female delinquents. Annually, about 3,800 males and females are placed in the probation camps (Nieto, 2008).

The Intensive Aftercare Program

Between 1988 and 1990, the **Intensive Aftercare Program (IAP)** was designed in Philadelphia to target serious youthful offenders (Altschuler and Armstrong, 2001). A sample of 46 youth committed to the Bensalem Youth Development Center was compared with a control group of 46 youth who received traditional aftercare probation services. While the IAP participants exhibited lower rates of recidivism compared with those subject to conventional aftercare probation, the differences were not significant. It was reported, however, that IAP officers believed their interventions with IAP youth were both rapid and positive. Thus, some officials believed that they were able to assist a few of the participants in avoiding subsequent rearrests. The successfulness of IAP in any particular jurisdiction often depends on the nature and quality of supervision received by clients (Meisel, 2001).

The Sexual Offender Treatment Program

Not all specialized programs for juvenile probationers are successful. For example, an assessment was made of the **Sexual Offender Treatment (SOT) Program** established by a juvenile probation department of a large midwestern U.S. metropolitan county in January 1988 (Lab, Shields, and Schondel, 1993). The program consisted of 20 peer-group meetings with psychosocioeducational intervention focus, supplemented by individual family counseling sessions with youth who had been adjudicated delinquent. Subsequently, an experimental program was conducted in which 46 youth referred to the SOT program were compared with a control group of 109 youth

CAREER SNAPSHOT

(Courtesy of Myra Ann Welborn-Weeks)

Name: Myra Ann Welborn-Weeks
Position: Program Coordinator, Wichita County Teen Court, Texas
Colleges Attended: Midwestern State University
Degrees: Bachelor of Applied Arts & Sciences; M.A. Public Administration

Background

It was never my intention to work with juveniles. I made the decision to go into the criminal justice field; however, my focus was to work with adults. Blame it on divine intervention or trends in the criminal justice system. In 1992, I began working with juvenile offenders and have been involved with juveniles to date.

My current position is Program Coordinator with the Wichita County Teen Court. This is a program designed to allow first-offender youth the opportunity to satisfy misdemeanors or minor offenses utilizing a peer judicial system. There are several examples of peer justice dating back to the early 1970s. However, one of the first documented teen court programs in the United States began in Grand Prairie, Texas, in the early 1980s. There are additional programs in Canada, Australia, and the United Kingdom.

I was aware that peer courts or teen courts were designed for first-offenders and that they did not involve juvenile probation. When the director of the existing teen court program resigned, I was afforded an unanticipated opportunity to become better acquainted with the teen court. After minimal research about teen courts, my attraction to the program was forged. This program was the epitome of early intervention. Youth with offenses in teen courts were receiving sentences more proactive than some serious felony offenders on probation. Teen courts, on average, have an 85 percent success rate. I was and still am "hooked" on teen courts as a proactive approach to intervention for youth who have committed a criminal offense.

The teen court model used in Texas is the adult judge model. In Texas, teen court trials are sentencing trials, so a plea of guilty or no contest is entered. The cases referred to teen court in Texas include status or children in need of supervision (CHINS) offenses as well as petty crimes. Sentences include community service, jury duty, and any other sanction that emphasizes restorative justice while educating the offender about the consequences associated with criminal behavior. Many courts also utilize sentencing options such as letters of apology, essays, workshops, counseling tools, and tours of participating agencies. Most often, youth are afforded from 30 to 90 days to complete the sanctions, at which time their offense is dismissed, leaving them with a clean slate. An adult volunteer with the Wichita County Teen Court and a victim of a tragic drunk driving accident has coined the phrase "erasable mistake." Youth are offered the chance to erase their criminal record and start fresh as they enter adulthood.

I am convinced that teen courts and peer justice are effective tools for working with youth. I have helped administer the Teen Court Association of Texas and the National Association of Youth Courts. Networking among coordinators is an effective way to develop new courts and enhance existing programs. Program development is an ongoing process, with input and idea sharing the driving forces for establishment and enhancement.

Advice to Students

It takes the entire community to nurture a child to adulthood. As a part of any community, be involved. Whether you chose to contribute as an educator, volunteer, parent, or citizen, youth need you. More than ever, we have absentee parents and overscheduled children. With technology enhancing lives, personal involvement decreases. Parents increasingly communicate in sound bites versus conversations. Kids learn to type rather than converse. As we discover ever-efficient ways to live our lives, the quantity of time spent with youth and children cannot become one more convenience. They need to hear and believe that adults are there for support and guidance. Parents are responsible for the development of their youth, but communities have a duty to facilitate the parents in every way possible.

I also want to emphasize the need to be patient with youth and specifically teens. Part of adolescence is trying on various personalities until finding one that fits. This may include hideous wardrobes and unbelievable forms of self-expression. Be confident that most teens will outgrow the offending behavior and, overnight, become the intelligent person that you thought would never appear.

Although it was never my intention to work with teens, it has been one of the most rewarding experiences of my life. I have experienced the gamut of emotions through my involvement with youth. I have helped young people choose a college and I have been present as young people were sentenced to life sentences without parole. It has never been easy, but as it has been said, nothing worthwhile is ever easy.

assigned to nonsexually specific interventions during the same period. Data sources included juvenile court and program records.

Essentially, youth handled by the SOT program fared no better than youth processed through normal, nonoffense-specific programming. Thus, these researchers concluded that simply knowing the symptoms and problems and designing specific interventions for those problems are not always entirely successful. Additional study is needed to identify appropriate treatment factors that might make a difference in reducing recidivism rates for sexual offending.

The Success of Standard Juvenile Probation

recidivism rate
Proportion of offenders who, when released from probation or parole, commit further crimes.

The success of standard juvenile probation as well as other probation and parole programs is measured according to the **recidivism rate** accompanying these program alternatives. Recidivism is measured in various ways, including new apprehensions or arrests, new adjudications, return to secure confinement, movement from standard probation to **intensive supervised probation (ISP)**, and violations of simple probation program conditions, such as drug or alcohol use and curfew violation (Clinkinbeard and Murray, 2008; Pires and Jenkins, 2007). **Recidivists** are offenders who commit new crimes or delinquent acts after having been previously convicted or adjudicated.

intensive supervised probation (ISP)
A method of supervising offenders more intensively compared with standard probation; usually involves more face-to-face contacts with clients, more frequent drug/alcohol checks, electronic monitoring, home confinement, and other restrictions; may also be known as IPS or intensive probation supervision.

Recidivism can be defined as a subsequent delinquency adjudication when a youth reoffends (Champion, 2008a). Historically, a recidivism rate of 30 percent has been established among researchers as the cutoff point between a successful probation program and an unsuccessful one. Programs with recidivism rates of approximately 30 percent or less are considered to be successful, while those programs with more than 30 percent recidivism are not viewed as particularly successful. No program presently has zero percent recidivism (Champion, 2008a).

Probation and Recidivism

For standard probation, which can refer to little direct regular supervision of offenders by POs, recidivism rates vary among the various state jurisdictions. Recidivism rates for these juveniles may range from 30 to 70 percent, depending upon the nature of their offenses and prior records. The following elements appear to be predictive of future criminal activity and reoffending by juveniles: (1) age at first adjudication, (2) a prior criminal record (a combined measure of the number and severity of priors), (3) the number of prior commitments to juvenile facilities, (4) drug/chemical abuse, (5) alcohol abuse, (6) family relationships (parental control), (7) school problems, and (8) peer relationships (Schaffner, 2006).

recidivists
Offenders who have committed previous offenses.

recidivism
New crime committed by an offender who has served time or was placed on probation for previous offense; tendency to repeat crimes.

At the beginning of the 20th century, when probation began to be used for juvenile supervision, Flexner and Baldwin (1914) issued a report entitled *Juvenile Courts and Probation*. Writing seven years following the establishment of the National Probation Association in 1907, Flexner and Baldwin described three important aspects of probation as it applied to juvenile offenders:

1. The period of probation should always be indeterminate, because judges cannot possibly fix the period of treatment in advance.

2. To be effective, probation work must be performed by full-time, professionally trained POs.

3. Probation is not a judicial function.

It is interesting to see how Flexner and Baldwin viewed the judiciary in establishing a specific term of probation and performing supervisory functions. They adhered to the belief that only professional POs should engage in such supervisory tasks and that the role of the judiciary should be minimal. The strong treatment orientation of probation is apparent as well, suggesting their belief that probation treatment programs should be tailored to fit the offender's needs. Furthermore, they underscored the authority originally assigned to POs and the leverage that POs could exert on their clients, including possible probation revocation if program infractions occurred.

States increasingly utilize probation rather than rely on sanctions like residential placement. As mentioned, California, for example, is reducing its reliance on juvenile correctional institutions, and counties are developing alternatives that incorporate probation with sanctions like community service and drug and alcohol treatment (Macallair, McCracken, and Teji, 2011). The decision to emphasize community-based alternatives may be based on economic considerations, closure of institutions, or research on their effectiveness. Based on California's and other states' historical and current use of probation, it is likely that its dominance will continue (Figure 11.3).

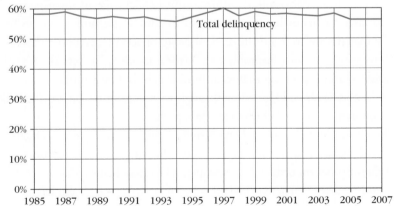

Probation remains the most likely sanction imposed by juvenile courts

Percentage of cases adjudicated delinquent, resulting in probation

Figure 11.3
Probation in the United States, 1985–2007
Source: Charles M. Puzzanchera, Benjamin Adams, and Melissa Sickmund (2010). Juvenile Court Statistics 2006–2007. Pittsburgh, PA: National Center for Juvenile Justice.

Focus on Delinquency

In Cherry Hill, New Jersey, two teens, ages 14 and 15, had a dispute over a girl and were exchanging text messages. The 14-year-old youth, along with two other teens, went to the home of the 15-year-old, confronted him about the messages, and challenged him to fight. The older youth went to kitchen, got a knife, and returned to the door, where he stabbed the other youth in the throat, puncturing the victim's voice box. The 15-year-old assailant denied self-defense and pleaded guilty to second-degree aggravated assault. The prosecution made the argument that the youth should receive two years of incarceration in a juvenile institution. The judge, Anthony Pugliese, sen-tenced the juvenile to three years of probation and 100 hours of community service. In addition, the judge prohibited contact between the two teens and ordered the juvenile offender to pay restitution and receive psychological evaluation. The victim recovered from his injury.

What sentence would you have imposed? Was probation sufficient? Was the victim's role a factor? What do you think?

Source: Adapted from Joe Green (2011, June 21), "Cherry Hill Teen Gets Probation in Non-Fatal Stabbing," Gloucester County Times (available at http://blog.nj.com/gloucestercounty_impact/print.html?entry=/2011/06/cherry_hill_teen_gets_probatio.html).

A successful probation program is one in which POs have an awareness of the juvenile offender's needs and weaknesses. One problem in some programs is that POs may have difficulty establishing rapport with their juvenile clients. A high degree of mistrust exists, in large part because the youth knows that information shared with the PO could be used against him or her in subsequent court proceedings. Similarly, POs encourage youth to share information about their activities and peers but are cognizant that this can have negative consequences for the youth.

Some POs have suggested an approach normally practiced by psychological counselors in developing rapport between themselves and their clients. For example, each PO should (1) thoroughly review the youth's case, including family and juvenile interviews and other background information; (2) "engage in introspection," and attempt to discover his or her own reactions to adolescents and responses to verbal exchanges; (3) attempt to "cultivate a relationship of acceptance rather than rejection and punitiveness;" (4) react favorably to a "critical incident," where the juvenile may make a mistake and expect reprimand or punishment but encounters acceptance and understanding instead; and (5) follow through with continued "support that bolsters juvenile confidence" in the PO (Sweet, 1985, p. 90).

When juveniles fail to comply with one or more terms of their standard proba-tion, they risk being held in contempt of court, because the juvenile court originally imposed their probation orders. For example, a PO may believe that a juvenile court judge should review a particular juvenile's behavior when he or she has not been in compliance with the terms of the judge's probation orders. A motion, such as the one shown in Figure 11.4, is filed for a judicial review of the juvenile to determine whether the allegations against the youth are true. Typically, POs ask for judicial review when information indicates that the youth has engaged in probation violations. The motion also contains a notice of a hearing, where these allegations may be made.

IN THE JUVENILE COURT
OF
DOUGHERTY COUNTY, GEORGIA

In The Interest of:

_____

Name _____   Race/Sex _____   DOB _____

File Number: _____

Referral Number/s: _____

_____

MOTION FOR JUDICIAL REVIEW

Now comes _____ and moves the Court to judicially review the probation

　　　　　　　　　Name

status of the above-mentioned juvenile.

Movant is of the opinion and belief that the juvenile and or parent are not cooperating with the juvenile's case manager and are not complying with the Court's Order of probation dated _____ in the following particulars:

1.   _____
2.   _____
3.   _____
4.   _____
5.   _____

This _____ day of _____, 20___.

　　　　　　　　　　　　　　　　　　　　_____

　　　　　　　　　　　　　　　　　　　　Signature of the Movant

NOTICE OF HEARING

The within and foregoing motion filed and said matter to come on for a review in the Juvenile Court of Dougherty County, Georgia, on _____ at _____ a.m./p.m., all interested parties should be present in Court to show cause, if any, why the conditions of probation have not been complied with, or why the conditions should not be enforced.

This _____ day of _____, 20_____.

shares files\probation\motion for judicial review

Figure 11.4
Motion for Judicial Review, Dougherty County, Georgia

Juveniles meet with probation officers in their offices on a regular basis.
(© Mikael Karlsson/Alamy)

If the allegations are supported, the judge will determine which steps should be taken to sanction the juvenile for noncompliance. Judges have an array of options, including intensifying one's supervision by POs, restitution, community service, fines, or participation in one or more counseling programs. Or, the judge can simply continue the youth's probation with a verbal reprimand or warning.

Some juveniles may not respond favorably to this experience. Chronic offenders, hard-core offenders, or psychologically disturbed juveniles may reject attempts by authorities to understand them or to assist them in any task (Cauffman, Steinberg, and Piquero, 2005). If youth are chemically dependent, their substance abuse may interfere with effective interventions. Where standard probation is not feasible, an **intensive supervision program (ISP)** may be required for certain offenders.

Intermediate Punishments for Juvenile Offenders

Understanding Intermediate Punishments

Intermediate punishments are community-based sanctions that range from **intensive probation supervision (IPS)** to nonsecure custodial programs. These programs include more intensive monitoring or management of juvenile behaviors through rigorous supervision. They may involve home confinement, EM, or both. Other

---

intensive supervision program, intensive probation supervision (IPS)

Offender supervision program with low officer-to-client ratio, close supervision, frequent drug and alcohol checks, and random visits at one's home or work; may include electronic monitoring and/or home confinement.

community-based services are included, where the goal is to maintain fairly close supervision over youthful offenders (Abrams, 2006). The successful ISP programs tend to be those that emphasize the sociostructural causes of delinquency and that use greater community participation and agency networking rather than focusing only on individual problems. Cognitive-behavioral interventions and participatory problem-solving activities are part of probation department programs designed to reduce offender recidivism and promote long-term law-abiding behaviors (Bernberg and Thorlindsson, 2007).

Intermediate punishment programs are operated in all states for both juvenile and adult offenders. They are sometimes referred to as **creative sentencing**, because they are somewhere between standard probationary dispositions and traditional incarceration sanctions that judges can impose. These alternatives to incarceration are regarded as positive interventions for a majority of youth who are brought to the attention of the juvenile justice system (Champion, 2008a).

The Goals of Intermediate Punishment Programs

There is considerable variation among intermediate punishment programs, but they do tend to exhibit similar goals or objectives. These include, but are not limited to:

1. Providing less-expensive sanctions compared with secure confinement.
2. Achieving lower rates of recidivism compared with standard probation.
3. Emphasizing reintegration into communities as the primary correctional goal.
4. Providing a greater range of community services and organizations in a cooperative effort to assist youthful offenders.
5. Minimizing the adverse influence of labeling that might stem from secure confinement.
6. Improving the personal, educational, and vocational skills of individual offenders, together with promoting acquisition of better self-concepts and greater acceptance of responsibility for one's actions.

Juvenile Intensive Supervised Probation

Intensive Supervision Programs, also known as **juvenile intensive supervised probation (JISP)**, have become increasingly popular for managing offender populations. Since the mid-1960s, these programs have been aimed primarily at supervising adult offenders closely, and in recent years, JISP programs have been designed for juvenile offenders as well. JISP can describe similar programs developed in different jurisdictions, regardless of whether the specific JISP designation is utilized by individual programs. A JISP disposition is a highly structured and conditional supervision program that serves as an alternative to incarceration and provides an acceptable level of public safety.

Juvenile court judges impose ISP for juveniles who are in need of greater supervision by POs. Because POs responsible for these youth must meet with and monitor

creative sentencing
Broad class of punishment alternatives to incarceration that are designed to fit particular crimes; may involve community service, restitution, fines, educational or vocational training programs, or other "good works" activity.

juvenile intensive supervised probation (JISP)
Program for youthful offenders, including home confinement, electronic monitoring, and other IPS methods.

them frequently, their caseloads are reduced substantially. Thus, JISP is more expensive than traditional standard probation. It is important to note that both the juvenile and the parents must sign the probation order, signifying their intent to comply with it. Just like standard probation, a violation of one or more of these intensive supervision conditions may result in a judicial review at the request of the PO.

Classification Criteria for Placement in ISP Programs

Juvenile court judges decide which juveniles to assign to various programs. This is part of the classification process. Historically, juvenile courts have preferred to utilize the expertise and knowledge of the judge and probation staff versus technology in determining dispositions. However, the level of accuracy associated with juvenile risk prediction instruments is steadily improving.

Classification is considered to be one of correction's greatest challenges (Clinkinbeard and Murray, 2008). Nevertheless, judges attempt to make secure or nonsecure confinement decisions based on the following elements: (1) judging the risk of continued criminal activity and the offender's need for services; (2) assisting probation and parole officers in developing better case plans and selecting appropriate casework strategies for a more effective case-management system; (3) enhancing planning, monitoring, evaluation, and accountability for a better management information system; and (4) allowing agencies to effectively and efficiently allocate their limited resources for a better workload deployment system.

Chronic recidivists and serious offenders are most likely to be placed in secure confinement. However, an increasing number of community-based programs are being designed to supervise such offenders closely and to offer needed services and treatments. It is helpful to review briefly some of the issues relating to the effectiveness of such interventions (Latessa, 2005). Depending upon the scores received by various juvenile clients when classified, they may or may not be assigned to ISP or to a community-based program. Theoretically, youthful offenders who are considered to be dangerous and violent are poor candidates for inclusion, because it is predicted that they might harm themselves or others. By contrast, those considered as not dangerous would be predicted to be good candidates for the program. However, assessment instrumentation does not always discriminate effectively.

Characteristics of JISP Programs

JISP programs for juveniles have been developed and are currently operating in most jurisdictions. Many of these JISP programs are operated on a county basis rather than on a statewide basis. Thus, it is difficult to find a state jurisdiction with a uniform policy and program information about JISPs that apply to all local agencies within that state.

Similar to their adult ISP program counterparts, JISP programs are designed for secure incarceration-bound youth and are considered to be alternatives to incarceration. JISP programs are different from other forms of standard probation in terms of the amount of officer–client contact during the course of the probationary period. For example, standard probation typically is considered to be no more than two face-to-face officer–client contacts per month. JISP programs might differ from standard probation according to the following face-to-face criteria: (1) two or three times per week versus once per month, (2) once per week versus twice per month, or (3) four times per week versus once per week.

Various services are included in JISP programs. Typically, POs act as brokers in identifying treatment options for offenders in different jurisdictions. These may include (1) mental health counseling; (2) drug and alcohol counseling; (3) academic achievement and aptitude testing; (4) vocational and employment training; (5) individual, group, and family counseling; (6) job search and placement programs; (7) alternative education programs; (8) foster grandparents programs; and (9) Big Brother/Big Sister programs. Even though not all JISP programs are identical, many share certain similarities. These include (1) recognition of the shortcomings of traditional responses to serious and/or chronic offenders (e.g., secure confinement or out-of-home placement), (2) severe resource constraints within jurisdictions that compel probation departments to adopt agency-wide classification and workload deployment systems for targeting a disproportionate share of resources for the most problematic juvenile offenders, (3) commitment to reduce the incidence of incarceration in juvenile secure confinement facilities and prevent overcrowding, (4) aggressive supervision and control as part of the get-tough movement, and (5) an interest in the rehabilitation of youthful offenders (Armstrong, 1991).

From reviewing the content of traditional ISPs, the following are basic characteristics of ISP programs:

1. Low client caseloads (i.e., 30 or fewer probationers).

2. High levels of offender accountability (e.g., victim restitution, community service, payment of fines, or partial defrayment of program expenses).

3. High levels of offender responsibility.

4. High levels of offender control (e.g., home confinement, EM, or frequent face-to-face visits by POs).

5. Frequent checks for arrests, drug and/or alcohol use, and employment/school attendance (e.g., drug/alcohol screening and coordination with police departments and juvenile facilities, teachers, family) (Fagan and Reinarman, 1991).

The Johnson County, Kansas, Juvenile Intensive Supervision Program

One example of a JISP program operated by a county is that of the Johnson County Department of Corrections in Kansas. Here, the court grants probation for a stipulated period of time, with the specific conditions of each probationer's supervision listed in the Probation Plan or Conditional Release Contract. Each client must abide by the written rules and regulations of the program, which will be reviewed by the Intensive Supervision Officer (ISO).

There are several levels in the ISP. Listed below are some of the minimum requirements of each:

Level I

1. Thirty days in length.
2. Three face-to-face contacts with the ISO per week.
3. Four random urinalyses/breath analyses per month as directed by the ISO.
4. Twenty hours of community service.
5. Curfew as directed.

Level II

1. Sixty days in length.
2. Two face-to-face contacts with the ISO per week.
3. Three random urinalyses/breath analyses per month as directed by the ISO.
4. Curfew as directed.

Level III

1. Sixty days in length.
2. One face-to-face contact with the ISO per week.
3. Two random urinalyses/breath analyses per month as directed by the ISO.
4. Curfew as directed.

Level IV

1. No specified minimum length.
2. One face-to-face contact with the ISO per week for the first 30 days.
3. One face-to-face contact every other week after a minimum of 30 days.
4. One random urinalysis/breath analysis per month as directed by the ISO.

The curfew is monitored on a random basis, and a face-to-face contact may include:

1. Visits to the probation office.
2. Visits to employment sites.
3. Home visits.
4. Meetings at other designated places.

In addition, the ISOs are required to have frequent contact with individuals who play a significant role in the life of the youth, such as family, friends, treatment providers, and sponsors.

Compliance with the previously stated requirements, and with any other requirements, allows the individual to progress through the ISP (Johnson County Department of Corrections, 2002).

Strengths and Weaknesses of JISP Programs

One major advantage of JISP programs is that they are substantially less expensive than the costs of incarcerating juvenile offenders. For instance, the Texas Youth Commission (2005) reports that juvenile incarceration represents the most expensive criminal justice option, averaging $124 as the daily expenditure per juvenile. Alternatively, juvenile probation programs manage youth at the rate of $10.50 per day. Various ISP programs in Texas average $30 per day per juvenile.

Another benefit is that JISP programs generally report lower rates of recidivism compared with standardized probation and other more conventional options. One reason is that JISP clients are more closely monitored and, thus, are given less opportunity to reoffend. Another reason is that prospective clients for JISP programs are more carefully screened. More-serious offenders are usually excluded, which may bolster the success rate of included clients (Gordon and Malmsjo, 2005).

There are also limitations or disadvantages of ISPs. After more than 25 years, there is still no standard definition of what constitutes an ISP (Corbett, 2000). The reality for most JISP programs is that local demands and needs vary among jurisdictions. Thus, the dominant themes of current JISP programs appear to be (1) front-end alternatives to secure confinement, (2) a combination of incarceration with some degree of community supervision (e.g., shock probation), and (3) community supervision following secure confinement.

In an experiment of intensive supervision probation in California, Hennigan et al. (2010) compared an experimental and a control group to determine differences. The experimental group was randomly assigned to intensive supervision probation, and the control group received regular probation supervision and services. Despite some initial success of the ISP youth, the researchers found that one frequent experience of intensive supervision probation is the increased likelihood of being apprehended for a technical violation. This is consistent with more intense monitoring of youth assigned to JISPs. The violation is often followed by a stay in the detention center. Over time, these institutional experiences have an adverse effect on the youth's future placement options and their perceptions of themselves. In addition, younger, lower-risk youth were more negatively affected than their older, higher-risk counterparts (Hennigan et al., 2010). These findings suggest that it is important to determine the appropriate age group and offense pattern when placing youth on intensive supervision probation. Also, alternative sanctions that are outside of institutional custody should be considered.

Termination of Probation Program

At some point, almost all juveniles placed on standard probation or JISP will complete their programs. Those who do not complete them will have other dispositions imposed, such as secure confinement or placement in an alternative setting (e.g., group home, boot camp, or wilderness experience). Judges are responsible for issuing orders terminating an offender's probation. Typically, POs provide relevant information for the judge's consideration. This includes a statement that the juvenile has completed all of the terms required by the original probation orders (Figure 11.5).

DOUGHERTY COUNTY JUVENILE COURT
Room 302
225 Pine Avenue
Albany, Georgia 31701

In the Interest of

Date of Birth: **Sex:**   **Race:**

<u>ORDER</u>

TERMINATION OF PROBATION

It appearing to the Court that the above-named juvenile, having been placed on probation under the supervision of the Court, has made satisfactory adjustment while on probation. It is further Ordered and Decreed that said child is hereby dismissed from probation and the Jurisdiction of this Court terminated.

ORDERED AND DECREED THIS

The _____ day of _____ 2004

_____
Judge/ Associate Judge
Dougherty County Juvenile Court

Figure 11.5
Termination of Probation, Dougherty County, Georgia

Based on the PO's recommendation to terminate probation, the juvenile court judge formally grants the request (Figure 11.5).

Case Supervision Planning

Caseload Assignments

caseloads
Number of cases that a probation or parole officer is assigned according to criteria of case assignment; caseloads vary among jurisdictions.

One strategy for assigning **caseloads** to POs employed in probation departments is to give smaller caseloads to improve officer–client interpersonal contact. Reduced caseloads for POs arguably intensify their supervision of, as well as the quality of their interaction with, offenders. Some studies have examined different levels of officer–client contact and have compared

---

Request for Termination

Date:

Child's Name:
Age:

Probation Officer:

Date of Probation:

Offense:

The above named juvenile is years of age has completed all conditions of probation as ordered by the Court. I am requesting to terminate from probation.

This juvenile is attending

This juvenile has paid a

This juvenile has completed

Probation Officer's Comments:

Figure 11.5
(Continued)

recidivism rates. PO caseload reductions were mandated by one of the recommendations of the Task Force on Corrections appointed by the President's Commission on Law Enforcement and the Administration of Justice in 1967 (Sturgeon, 2005).

Models of Case Supervision Planning

Case supervision planning may reflect alternative case assignment strategies presently used by different probation departments. The most popular model is the **conventional model**, which is the random assignment of probationers to POs on the basis of the PO's present caseload in relation to those of other POs. This is much like the **numbers game model**, in which the total number of probationers is divided by the total number of POs in a given department, and then each PO is allocated an equal share of the supervisory task. Thus, POs may supervise both dangerous and low-risk probationers.

Another model is the **conventional model with geographical considerations** which involves assigning probationers who live in a common geographic area to a designated PO. The intent is to reduce the PO's travel time between clients.

case supervision planning

A means whereby a probation or parole department makes assignments of probationers or parolees to probation or parole officers.

conventional model

Caseload assignment model in which probation or parole officers are assigned clients randomly.

numbers game model

Caseload assignment model for probation or parole officers in which total number of offender–client is divided by number of officers.

conventional model with geographical considerations

Similar to conventional model; caseload assignment model based on the travel time required for probation officers to meet with offender-clients regularly.

specialized caseloads model

Case assignment method based on probation officer's unique skills and knowledge relative to offender drug or alcohol problems; some probation officers are assigned particular clients with unique problems that require more than general expertise.

balanced approach

Probation orientation that simultaneously emphasizes community protection, offender accountability, individualization of treatments, and competency assessment and development.

In the **specialized caseloads model**, offender assignments are made on the basis of client risks and needs and on PO skills and interests in dealing with those offender risks and needs. Some POs may have specialized training and education in psychology or social work or in chemical dependency. Thus, if clients have psychological problems or alcohol or other drug dependencies, it is believed that POs with relevant expertise, skills, and education would be more effective in relating to them (Sturgeon, 2005).

Typically, POs deal with various kinds of offenders on their caseloads. Rather than specializing in working with one type of offender, they are more likely to counsel and supervise youth who were involved in both violent and property offenses as well as youth who were involved in drug and public order offenses. Figure 11.6 demonstrates the percentage of youth placed on probation for each of the four categories of delinquent offending in 1985 and 2007. These data illustrate the diverse types of offenders that can be found in probation caseloads today.

The Balanced Approach

Some of the problems of JISP have been attributable to different caseload assignment models or to other organizational structures and conflicting organizational goals that interfere with the performance of juvenile PO roles. One solution is the **balanced approach** (Seyko, 2001).

The balanced approach to juvenile probation is not an entirely punitive or rehabilitative formulation. Rather, it is a broad-based, constructive approach. It operates on the assumption that decision making must take into consideration the interests of all involved parties in the juvenile justice process, including offenders, victims, and the community. No participant should benefit at the expense of another party; instead, a balance should be attained. The balanced approach, therefore,

Offense profile of cases adjudicated delinquent, resulting in probation:		
Most serious offense	1985	2007
Person	17%	25%
Property	60%	35%
Drugs	8%	13%
Public order	16%	26%
Total	100%	100%
Cases resulting in formal probation	193,600	327,400
Note: Detail may not total 100% because of rounding		

Figure 11.6

Categories of Delinquency Adjudications that Resulted in Probation Dispositions, 1985 and 2007
Source: Charles M. Puzzanchera, Benjamin Adams, and Melissa Sickmund (2010). Juvenile Court Statistics 2006-2007. *Pittsburgh, PA: National Center for Juvenile Justice.*

simultaneously emphasizes community protection, offender accountability, and individualized competency assessment and development (Abatiello, 2005).

The balanced approach requires community leaders and juvenile justice system professionals to consider their juvenile codes and determine whether a balance exists between offender needs and community interests (Seyko, 2001). Punitive provisions of these codes should address the needs of both victims and juvenile offenders to the extent that restitution and victim compensation improve an offender's accountability and acceptance of responsibility. The fairness of the juvenile justice system should be assessed by key community leaders, and a mission statement should be drafted that has the support of diverse community organizations. Training programs can be created through coordination of chief POs in different jurisdictions, where offender needs may be targeted and addressed. All facets of the community and the juvenile justice process should be involved. The high level of community involvement will help to ensure a positive juvenile probation program that will maximize a youth's rehabilitative benefits (Ayers-Schlosser, 2005).

Some ISP programs may fail because they neglect to address problems suggested by the balanced approach. There are a number of reasons why case supervision planning can be unsuccessful:

1. *Purpose:* The purposes of case supervision planning have not been thought out carefully.

2. *Perceptual differences:* Offenders often change only when they find it necessary to change, not because professionals want them to change.

3. *Resistance:* Professionals do not always recognize that resistance to change is normal. Sometimes, POs prematurely shift emphasis to an enforcement orientation and rules of probation. Case planning starts to look more like the probation order whenever this occurs.

4. *Expectation:* Desired change is sought too quickly. Professionals sometimes expect too much from offenders or expect unrealistic changes to be made.

5. *Focus:* There is a tendency to focus on less serious problems to gain "success."

6. *Involvement:* Professionals may fail to involve offenders in the case-planning process.

7. *Stereotyping:* Case supervision planning is equated with treatment and rehabilitation. Thus, it is often rejected without an adequate consideration of its strengths.

8. *Getting too close:* Sometimes, POs are perceived as getting too close to offenders.

9. *Perceptions of accountability:* Nonspecific case plans may preclude criticism of professionals by supervisors.

10. *Use of resources:* There is tendency to exhaust community resources by referring involuntary offenders, those who are not ready to work on their problems.

11. *Measurement:* Probation successes or failures are not measured according to the designated case plan but, rather, according to arrests, convictions, or numbers of technical violations.

12. *Management:* There is a general lack of understanding or support for case supervision planning by management. POs are considered to be exclusively officers of the court, and judges do not expect offenders to change because of officer "treatments," only that someone shares the accountability whenever offenders commit new crimes or violate one or more of their probationary conditions.

13. *Training:* Staff members have not been adequately trained in the development, implementation, and evaluation of case plans. (Ellsworth, 1988, pp. 29–30)

The principles of JISP programs are sound. However, implementation problems, resource limitations, or organizational structure may hinder their success in various jurisdictions. Juvenile probation services should attempt to coordinate their programs and align their departmental performance objectives with those of community-based agencies that are a part of the referral network of services and treatments to maximize goal attainment. Consistent with the balanced approach to managing offenders, it has been recommended that for ISP programs to maximize their effectiveness, they should be individualized to a high degree so that a balance of punishment/deterrence and rehabilitation/community protection may be attained (Ayers-Schlosser, 2005). Public safety is one goal of any community-based program responsible for serious and violent juvenile offenders (Kennedy, 2005). At the same time, accountability to victims and the community must be considered. In the next section, some ISP programs that are viewed as community-based alternatives, in contrast with state operated or locally operated public programs, will be examined.

Community-Based Alternatives

Community Corrections Acts

Community-based corrections agencies and organizations have a long-standing tradition in juvenile justice and adult corrections. Originally, they attempted to alleviate prison and jail overcrowding by establishing community-based organizations that could accommodate some prison-bound offenders. However, corrections officials soon realized not only that the potential of such programs for offender rehabilitation and reintegration was great but that juveniles as well as adult offenders could benefit from them. Many states subsequently enacted **community corrections acts (CCAs)** aimed at funding local governments to create community facilities that could provide services and other resources to juveniles (Clear and Dammer, 2003).

The overall objective of community corrections agencies is to develop and deliver front-end solutions and alternative sanctions in lieu of state incarceration (Burrell, 2005). In 1984, the **American Correctional Association (ACA)** Task Force on Community Corrections Legislation recommended that CCAs should not target violent offenders. Rather, states should be selective about who meets their program requirements. It was suggested that (1) states should continue to house violent juvenile offenders in secure facilities, (2) judges and prosecutors should continue to explore various punishment options in lieu of incarceration, and (3) local communities should develop programs with additional funding from state appropriations

---

community corrections acts (CCAs)

Enabling legislation by individual states to fund local government units to provide community facilities, services, and resources to juveniles considered to be at risk of becoming delinquent or already delinquent and needing treatment/services.

American Correctional Association (ACA)

Established in 1870 to disseminate information about correctional programs and correctional training; designed to foster professionalism throughout correctional community.

(Huskey, 1984, p. 45). The ACA Task Force also identified the following elements as essential to the success of any CCA:

1. There should be restrictions on funding high-cost capital projects as well as conventional probation services.

2. Local communities should participate on a voluntary basis and may withdraw at any time.

3. Advisory boards should submit annual criminal justice plans to local governments.

4. There should be a logical formula in place for allocating community corrections funds.

5. Incarceration-bound juveniles should be targeted, rather than adding additional punishments for those who otherwise would remain in their communities (in short, avoid "net-widening").

6. Financial subsidies should be provided to local government and community-based corrections agencies.

7. Local advisory boards in each community should function to assess program needs and effectiveness, to propose improvements in the local juvenile justice system, and to educate the general public about the benefits of intermediate punishments.

8. A performance factor should be implemented to ensure that funds are used to achieve specific goals of the act.

Shawnee County Community Corrections

One example of a contemporary CCA is the Shawnee County, Kansas, community corrections program (Shawnee County Department of Community Corrections, 2002). During the period from 1996 to 1997, juvenile offender services were transferred from the Kansas Department of Corrections to the Kansas Juvenile Justice Authority (JJA). The JJA is the cabinet-level agency that has jurisdiction over youth as young as age 10 and can retain supervision until a youth reaches age 23 (Kansas JJJA, 2010). The JJA oversees prevention programs, community-based sanctions, and juvenile institutions.

One original purpose of the Kansas CCA was to divert prison-bound offenders from institutions to community-based intermediate sanction programs. In 2002, the Department of Community Corrections supervised chronic or violent offenders within the community. Effective community-based programming involves intensive supervision of these clients, together with solution-focused case-management services that assist offenders in becoming productive members of society. When Shawnee County Community Corrections was established, it was one of three units within the Shawnee County Department of Corrections. The Department of Corrections included the jail, the juvenile detention center, and community corrections. In 2000, community corrections became a separate department.

The juvenile community corrections program is a state and local partnership. It is designed to (1) promote public safety, (2) hold juvenile offenders accountable for their behavior, and (3) improve the ability of youth to live productively and responsibly in their communities (Shawnee County Department of Community Corrections, n.d.). In this respect, the juvenile program reflects the basic elements of the balanced approach.

The juvenile community corrections program strives to attain these stipulated goals in various ways. For example, the program promotes public safety by ensuring that manageable caseloads are maintained, allowing staff to closely supervise offenders in the community. For the goal of enforcing court-ordered sanctions, supervision plans are devised that meet the requirements of the court and provide structure. These are designed to improve the offender's ability to successfully complete the terms of his or her probation program. To restore losses to crime victims, payment of restitution by offenders is monitored, including the collection of court costs and supervision of community service work. Finally, the program assists offenders in changing their behavior. Offender participation in services provided by community corrections or community programs is enforced through close supervision to ensure compliance. Services include drug treatment, job search and maintenance skills, literacy enhancement, and life skills.

Several supervisory options are available, depending on the juvenile offender's needs. For example, a JISP program includes intensive monitoring and provides an intermediate sanction between standard probation and placement in a juvenile correctional facility for adjudicated juvenile offenders. The juvenile offender community case-management program consists of services provided for juvenile offenders who have been placed by the court in the care and custody of the JJA. The court may order out-of-home placement for certain juvenile offenders after all other reasonable efforts have been made to address the problems that caused their illegal behavior. Case-management services are provided to assist juveniles and their caregivers in finding resources that will meet their needs. Finally, the juvenile conditional release supervision program provides monitoring of juveniles who have been released from one of four JJA-operated juvenile correctional facilities and returned to the community. Community corrections officers monitor these juveniles so they comply with the conditions of their release. These officers also assist juveniles in accomplishing their aftercare plans.

The juvenile justice process in Shawnee County includes:

Arrest

1. Juvenile Detention Center (if danger to self or others during court process)
2. Adjudication (court determines if juvenile committed the offense; juvenile is adjudicated a delinquent offender)

Sentencing Alternatives

1. Place juvenile offender in parent's custody (to follow terms and conditions of the court, including making restitution).
2. Place juvenile offender on probation through court services for a fixed period (to follow terms and conditions of the court, including making restitution).
3. Place juvenile offender on ISP for a fixed period through community corrections (to follow terms and conditions of the court, including making restitution;

report to the ISO as required; submit to drug screens; use no alcohol or illegal drugs; follow mental health or drug treatment plan; perform community service work—20 hours; attend school; employment, if not enrolled in school; no firearms; other conditions as ordered by the court).

4. Place juvenile offender in custody of JJA (case management through community corrections) once reasonable efforts have been met for juveniles requiring more services (supervision plan may include similar items as ISP and may require placement out of the home).

5. Commit juvenile offender to a juvenile correctional facility (incarceration).

6. Conditional release supervision (follow conditional release requirements; similar requirements as outlined under ISP).

On any given day in Topeka and the Shawnee area, about 465 juvenile misdemeanors or felony offenders on probation are supervised by court services. Approximately 35 juvenile misdemeanors or felony offenders are on ISP, while 90 juvenile misdemeanors or felony offenders are on community case-management supervision. About 15 juvenile offenders are on conditional release and are supervised by community corrections, while 40 juvenile offenders are in a state juvenile correctional facility supervised by community corrections for reintegration planning. Overall, about 645 juveniles from Shawnee County are on some type of supervision for a criminal offense on any given day.

In the following sections, two intermediate punishments that are utilized for adult and juvenile offenders are examined. These include (1) EM and (2) home confinement.

Electronic Monitoring

Understanding EM

Electronic monitoring (EM), or **tagging**, is the use of electronic devices to verify that an offender is at a particular location during specified times. EM is also a system of home confinement aimed at monitoring, controlling, and modifying the behavior of offenders.

In EM, the offender wears an electronic bracelet/anklet or other electronic device in accordance with conditions set by the courts. The tagged person is monitored by computer 24 hours a day and is supervised by a private company or a combination of a company and the criminal justice authority, usually a probation department. The person must remain in the home under surveillance, unless authorized to leave for employment, school, participation in community treatment programs, or similar activities.

EM tends to be used for less-serious, nonviolent offenders who are identified by a risk formula. For juvenile offenders, EM enables them to remain in the community rather than in secure custody. In 2011, the American Bar Association passed a resolution endorsing the use of EM rather than detention for youth at government expense (American Bar Association, 2011).

electronic monitoring (EM)
Use of electronic devices that emit electronic signals; these devices, either anklets or wristlets, are worn by offenders, probationers, and parolees; the purpose is to monitor an offender's presence in a given area where the offender is required to remain or to verify offender whereabouts.

tagging
Being equipped with an electronic wristlet or anklet for the purpose of monitoring offender's whereabouts.

Usually, juveniles are ordered to be electronically monitored for a specified period. The period varies by jurisdiction, anywhere from 30 to 120 days. When a youth is placed on EM, he or she and the parent have to agree to the terms.

EM Origins

EM devices were first used in 1964 as an alternative to incarceration. Subsequently, EM was extended to include monitoring office work, employee testing for security clearances, and many other applications. Other countries also employ EM. For instance, England and Germany use EM for managing certain adult and youthful offenders.

Second Judicial District Judge Jack Love of New Mexico is credited with implementing a pilot EM project in 1983 for persons convicted of drunk driving and certain white-collar offenses, such as embezzlement (Houk, 1984). Subsequent to its use for probationers, the New Mexico State Supreme Court approved the program, because it required the voluntariness and consent of probationers as a condition of their probation programs. Judge Love directed certain probationers to wear anklets or bracelets that emitted electronic signals that could be intercepted by their POs, who conducted surveillance operations. After a short period of such judicial experimentation, other jurisdictions conducted their own experiments for offender monitoring with electronic devices. Eventually, electronic devices were being used for probationers and parolees and some inmates in jails and prisons.

How Much EM Is There in the United States?

Accurate statistical information about the extent and use of EM in the United States for either juveniles or adults is difficult to obtain. Most of this information is based on estimated rather than actual usage. Some of this information is derived from sales figures reported by firms that manufacture EM equipment. The number of electronically monitored clients fluctuates daily, and there are variations in length of time clients spend being monitored. However, the amount of time on EM averages about 12 to 15 weeks (Office of Juvenile Justice and Delinquency Prevention, 2007).

Surveys that seek accurate information about EM usage throughout the United States only obtain such information from about 25 percent of the jurisdictions canvassed (Seiter and West, 2003). After considering all of these limitations, however, virtually every report about EM shows that its frequency is increasing annually. For instance, in 1997, a report was issued showing that "31,236 probationers and parolees were being electronically monitored" (Schmidt, 1998, p. 11). In 1998, over 95,000 clients were being electronically monitored. By 2004, more than 150,000 persons were on EM and/or house arrest (Office of Juvenile Justice and Delinquency Prevention, 2007). Over 28,000 youth were involved in EM programs by 2007 (American Correctional Association, 2007).

electronic monitoring (EM) signaling devices

Apparatuses worn about the wrist or leg that are designed to monitor an offender's presence in a given area where the offender is required to remain.

Types of Signaling Devices

There are at least four types of **electronic monitoring (EM) signaling devices**. These include (1) continuous-signal devices, (2) a programmed contact devices, (3) cellular devices, and (4) continuous-signaling transmitters.

The first type, the continuous-signal device, consists of a miniature transmitter that is strapped to the probationer's wrist. The transmitter broadcasts an encoded signal that is received by a receiver-dialer in the offender's home. The signal is relayed to a central receiver over the telephone lines.

The second type of monitor is the programmed contact device, which is similar to the continuous-signal device. However, in this case, a central computer from the probation office is programmed to call the offender's home at random hours to verify the probationer's whereabouts. Offenders must answer their telephones and insert the wristlet transmitter into the telephone device. Their voices and signal emissions are verified by computer (Cadigan, 2001).

The third type of monitor is a cellular device. This is a transmitter worn by offenders and emits a radio signal that is received by a local area monitoring system. Up to 25 probationers can be monitored simultaneously with such a system.

The fourth type of monitor is the continuous-signaling transmitter that is worn by the offender. Like the continuous-signal device, this type also sends out continuous signals, but these may be intercepted by portable receiving units in the possession of POs. These are quite popular because POs may conduct drive-bys and verify whether offenders are at home during curfew hours.

These various wristlet or anklet transmitters are certainly not tamperproof. They are similar in plastic construction to the wristlet ID tags given patients at the time of hospital admissions. However, these electronic devices are somewhat sturdier. In addition, it is easy to determine whether the device has been tampered with (e.g., stretched, burned, or mutilated), because it is impossible to reattach without special equipment in the possession of the probation department. If tampering has occurred and probationers have attempted to defeat the intent of the device, they may be subject to probation revocation which may result in incarceration.

Types of Offenders on EM

The offenders placed on EM are selected because of their low likelihood of reoffending and the fact that their crimes are less serious, usually property offenses. Thus, a certain amount of "creaming", in which those most likely to succeed are selected. This is one reason why EM exhibits low recidivism rates among its participants in numerous jurisdictions.

In recent years, however, EM has been extended to include more violent juvenile offenders, such as violent juvenile parolees (Kubena, 2008). One reason may be that juvenile correctional facilities are overcrowded; another might be related to the assumption that closer supervision after release from an institution will preclude further offending. Because the public is concerned about community safety, greater use of EM equipment for such offenders enables professionals to verify the offender's location and exert appropriate surveillance and control.

When the alternative to EM is incarceration, most offenders—juveniles or adults—prefer EM to secure confinement. However, there are significant punitive dimensions of EM, including both physical and psychological. Probationers are required to be in a particular place at a designated time, and computer checks of whereabouts are frequent enough to cause stress for some clients. Being confined to the youth's house as a sanction is more serious than it sounds. Many electronically monitored clients point out that the EM program is in many ways equivalent to a jail sentence and that it is a punitive sanction (Gainey and Payne, 2003).

The SpeakerID Program

Some jurisdictions, such as the Dane County Sheriff's Office in Wisconsin, have implemented a **SpeakerID Program** (Listug, 1996). SpeakerID is a voice verification monitoring system allowing law enforcement and criminal justice agencies to monitor low-risk offenders under probation or house arrest. Implemented in October 1994, the SpeakerID program is an automated system that calls clients at their authorized locations at random times. When offenders answer their telephones, they are asked specific questions. Voice matches are verified perfectly. Thus, there is little likelihood that the offender can deceive the system with a previously recorded tape or some other device.

Prior to using SpeakerID, the Dane County Sheriff's Office used traditional ankle bracelets and wristlets. In 1996, there were between 30 and 35 offenders participating in this system. Because of the automated nature of the system, SpeakerID is cost-effective. Apart from initial start-up costs, the SpeakerID system costs about $3 per day per monitored offender. This compares favorably with jail and prison costs of $40 and $49 per prisoner per day, respectively, in Wisconsin.

Criticisms of EM

Some limitations of EM programs are that they are expensive to implement initially. The direct costs associated with their purchase or lease are seemingly prohibitive to local jurisdictions that are used to incarcerating juveniles and defraying their maintenance costs over an extended period. However, once a given jurisdiction has installed such equipment, it functions to reduce overall incarceration expenses that otherwise would have been incurred had these same youth been placed in secure confinement. The average cost of using this equipment in different probation and parole departments ranges from $5 to $25 per day, depending upon the intensity of the surveillance by POs. This is much less than the cost of maintaining a juvenile or adult under some type of residential custody per day.

In addition, EM programs require training on the part of the users. The costs and time associated with the training affect willingness of some jurisdictions to utilize the technology. EM is a delinquency deterrent for offenders. However, it is not foolproof. In spite of the fact that they may be easily tampered with, electronic wristlets and anklets only help to verify an offender's whereabouts. They do not provide television images of the activities probationers may be engaging in at the time.

EM has also been criticized as possibly violating the Fourth Amendment search-and-seizure provision, where electronic eavesdropping might be conducted within the home or bedroom. This argument seems to be without constitutional merit, because the primary function of such monitoring is to verify an offender's whereabouts.

SpeakerID Program

Electronic voice verification system used as a part of EM to verify the identity of the person called by the probation or parole agency.

In addition, it is considered to be voluntary to the extent that the offender could go to an institution in lieu of monitoring (Figure 11.7). Some sophisticated types of monitoring systems are equipped with closed-circuit television transmissions. However, even if such monitoring were so equipped, this additional feature would only intrude where offenders wished it to intrude, such as their living rooms or kitchens.

Despite these criticisms, the fact is that offenders may be inexpensively tracked through these monitoring systems and their whereabouts can be verified without face-to-face checks. For instance, a single juvenile PO may conduct drive-bys of client residences during evening hours and receive their transmitted signals with a portable unit. This silent means of detection is intended only to enforce one program element—namely, observance of curfews. Other checks, such as those conducted for illegal drug or alcohol use, must be verified directly, through proper testing and expert confirmation. EM is increasingly used in tandem with another sentencing option—home confinement.

In summary, proponents of EM report that it (1) assists offenders in avoiding the criminogenic atmosphere of prisons or jails and helps reintegrate them into their communities, (2) permits offenders to retain jobs and support families, (3) assists POs in their monitoring activities and has the potential for easing their caseload responsibilities, (4) gives judges and other officials considerable flexibility in sentencing offenders, (5) has the potential of reducing recidivism rates more than existing probationary alternatives, (6) is potentially useful for decreasing jail and prison populations, (7) is more cost-effective in relation to incarceration, and (8) allows for pretrial release monitoring as well as for special treatment cases, such as substance abusers, the mentally retarded, women who are pregnant, and juveniles.

Opponents of EM contend that (1) the potential exists for race, ethnic, or socioeconomic bias by requiring offenders to have telephones or to pay for expensive monitoring equipment and/or fees; (2) public safety may be compromised through the failure of these programs to guarantee that offenders will not endanger citizens by committing new offenses while free in the community; (3) the technology may be too coercive, and it may be unrealistic for officials to expect full offender compliance with such a stringent system; (4) lack of consistent information exists about the impact of EM on recidivism rates compared with other probationary alternatives; (5) persons frequently selected for participation are those who probably do not need to be monitored anyway; (6) technological problems exist, making EM somewhat unreliable; (7) it may result in net-widening by being prescribed for offenders who otherwise would receive less costly standard probation; (8) it raises right to privacy, civil liberties, and other constitutional issues, such as Fourth Amendment search and seizure concerns; (9) much of the public interprets this option as being lenient with offenders and perceives EM as a nonpunitive alternative; and (10) the costs of EM may be more than estimated. Typically, a supervision fee requirement also is imposed by jurisdictions (Figure 11.8). These fees are intended to offset the costs of EM and other ancillary expenses.

As identified above, issues regarding the use of EM continue to raise concerns, including the effectiveness of the technology for monitoring youth. For example, the

ELECTRONIC MONITOR CONDITIONS

Pursuant to the within and foregoing order, you have been conditionally released from secure detention on an electronic monitor pending a hearing, placement or as sanction. If you are to remain free of secure detention, you shall comply with the following terms and conditions of your release:

1. I realize that Secure Alert will monitor my compliance throughout my sentence.

2. I agree to remain at my residence at all times except for time allowed for school, work, medical treatment, or other types of evaluations or counseling as set forth in the curfew schedule. Furthermore, I understand that only my case manager can grant me a pass.

3. I understand that I will immediately notify my probation officer if I must leave my home because of an emergency. This notification does not necessarily constitute acceptance of the claimed emergency. Such determination will be made by the probation officer.

4. I know that my curfew restrictions will be enforced by the use of computer and satellite technology. I will wear a tamper proof, non-removable ankle bracelet 24 hours a day during the entire monitoring period.

5. I understand that I am responsible for keeping the batteries for the electronic monitor charged and attached to the ankle monitor device.

6. I understand that I will be held responsible for any damage, other than normal wear of the equipment. If I do not return the equipment, or do not return it in good working condition, or tamper with the equipment, I am subject to felony prosecution.

7. I agree that Glynn County Juvenile Court and Secure Alert are not liable for any damage incurred as the result of my wearing or tampering with the monitor device and that any damages associated with my wearing or tampering with the monitoring device are a result of my own negligence.

8. I understand that failure to comply with these terms constitutes violation of this electronic monitor agreement and may subject me to secure detention.

ACKNOWLEDGEMENT AND AGREEMENT

By my signature, I certify that I have read and understand the terms of conditional release as set forth above and I agree to abide by them

_____   _____
Youth signature   Date

_____   _____
Parent Signature   Date

_____   _____
Court Officer Signature   Date

_____   _____
Judge signature   Date

Figure 11.7
Electronic Monitor Conditions, Glynn County, Georgia

SUPERVISION FEE REQUIREMENT

As a Condition of Supervision, you are required to pay _____ a month to the Parole and Probation Division.

The _____ County Parole and Probation Division has an automated billing system. Our system automatically bills _____ on the first day of each month. Billing begins the first day of the month following the month of conviction. Example: If you were convicted on _____ the first billing would be September 1, _____ for the month of August.

Supervision fee payments are due by the 5th of each month.

At times other fees may be imposed such as Electronic Home Detention Fees, DUI Evaluation Fee, Polygraph Fees and Treatment Fees. Your Parole/Probation Officer will let you know if any of these fees apply to you. If so, you may make these payments at the above address.

PLEASE NOTE THE FOLLOWING:

1. Checks or Money Orders are to be make out _____ **County Parole and Probation Division** or **LCPP**. Do not make check or money order payable to a PO or Evaluator, otherwise your payment will be returned.

2. Our office does not take any payments for the Court such as fines and restitution. These need to be sent to:
    _____

3. **If you fail to pay your fees** you may be **ordered to do Work Crew, be returned to Court, or be directed to appear before a Hearing Officer.**

4. In order to leave the State on a temporary basis you are required to have a Travel Permit. **Travel Permits will not be issued unless supervision fees are current.**

5. In order to apply for **Early Termination** you will have to be **current on all fees.**

I have read or have had read to me the above information regarding fees, and I understand my obligation regarding fees.

_____   _____
Offender Signature   Date

_____   _____
Parent or Guardian Signature   Date

cc: white-offender yellow-file

Figure 11.8
Supervision Fee Requirement

traditional EM units generally send signals when barriers have been breached. Newer Global Positioning System (GPS) devices, however, permit almost 24/7 monitoring, with real-time updates and tracking that provides location history for the released juvenile offenders (Walker, 2011). The GPS technology uses tracking units that maintain surveillance by satellite-based navigation and are monitored by computer software that automatically reviews the data (Garmin Ltd., 2011). The GPS tracking devices are widely used across the United States to monitor various offenders, including sex offenders and other high-profile offenders. In Yakima County, Washington, juveniles who are released on GPS surveillance save taxpayers approximately $160 a day that it would cost to confine them in the Yakima County Juvenile Detention Center (Walker, 2011). The daily cost for GPS bracelets and monitoring is $5.50, and the real-time tracking helps ensure compliance. In Multnomah County, Oregon, GPS tracking has also been used with juvenile gang members (Hannah-Jones, 2010).

As with EM, concerns have been raised about the rights of youth being monitored with GPS devices. Since the system is 24/7, authorities know the whereabouts of youth all the time, and this could violate their Fourth Amendment search rights (Hannah-Jones, 2010). Because this technology continues to provide greater surveillance capabilities, a balance between public safety and personal rights will be significant. This was demonstrated in 2011, when the U.S. Supreme Court accepted a case involving police use of GPS tracking to monitor a suspect after the warrant had expired (Turley, 2011). The case, *Jones v. United States* (2011), underscores the potential for real-time/all time monitoring of an unlimited number of citizens.

Home Confinement or House Arrest

home confinement, home incarceration, house arrest

Program intended to house offenders in their own homes with or without electronic devices; reduces prison overcrowding and prisoner costs; intermediate punishment involving the use of offender residences for mandatory incarceration during evening hours, after a curfew, and on weekends.

The use of an offender's home as the principal place of confinement is not new. In biblical times, Saint Paul was sentenced in Rome to **house arrest** for two years, where he performed tent-maker services for others. **Home confinement** is a program of intermediate punishment involving the use of the offender's residence for mandatory incarceration during evening hours, after a curfew, and on weekends (Cadigan, 2001). In many jurisdictions, home confinement is used with EM.

Florida introduced the contemporary use of home confinement under the Correctional Reform Act of 1983, which provided that the home could be used as a form of intensive supervised custody in the community (Boone, 1996). At that time, corrections officials considered **home incarceration** to be an acceptable alternative to prisons or jails for certain low-risk offenders. Home confinement was seen as an inexpensive way of maintaining supervisory control over offenders who were judged not to be in need of costly incarceration. When Florida started to use home confinement in lieu of incarceration in institutions, prison costs averaged $30 per inmate per day, while home confinement required an expenditure of about $3 per offender per day. In the late 1990s, prison maintenance costs per prisoner were in excess of $75 per day in most jurisdictions, while home confinement costs had stabilized at about $5 per offender per day (Tonry, 1997). Today this program is intended primarily to restrict offender movement within the community together with specific sanctions, such as curfew, payment of fines, community service, and other requirements.

Functions and Goals of Home Confinement Programs

The functions and goals of home confinement programs include:

1. To continue the offender's punishment while permitting the offender to live in his or her dwelling under general or close supervision.
2. To enable offenders to perform jobs in their communities to support themselves and their families.
3. To reduce jail and prison overcrowding.
4. To maximize public safety by ensuring that only the most qualified clients enter home confinement programs and are properly supervised.
5. To reduce the costs of offender supervision.
6. To promote rehabilitation and reintegration by permitting offenders to live under appropriate supervision within their communities.

Relatively little is known about the extent to which home confinement is used as a sentencing alternative for juvenile offenders. Because probation is widely used as the sanction of choice except for the most chronic recidivists, home confinement is most often applied as an accompanying condition of EM. However, this disposition may be redundant, since curfew for juvenile offenders means home confinement anyway, especially during evening hours. As a day disposition, home confinement for juveniles would probably be counterproductive; juveniles are often required to attend school as a condition of probation. Again, because school hours are during the day, it would not be appropriate to deprive juveniles of school opportunities through some type of home confinement.

Home confinement is also useful for offenders who may be drug or alcohol dependent. POs can visit the homes of drug-dependent clients and perform instant checks to determine whether they recently used alcohol or drugs. While access to drugs or alcohol is relatively easy when a client is confined to his or her home, the threat of a random drug/alcohol test by a PO is often a sufficient deterrent. Needs assessments for certain offenders can determine which services they require, and they may be able to seek these services with probation department approval.

Advantages and Disadvantages of Home Confinement

Some of the advantages and disadvantages of home confinement were addressed at length as issues concerning home confinement when EM is also used. Briefly, the advantages to home confinement include (1) it is cost-effective, (2) it has social benefits, (3) it is responsive to local citizen and offender needs, (4) it is easily implemented, and (5) it is timely in view of jail and prison overcrowding. Some of the disadvantages of home confinement are (1) it may actually widen the net of social control, (2) it may be viewed by the public as not being a sufficiently severe sentence, (3) it focuses primarily upon offender surveillance, (4) it is intrusive and possibly unconstitutional, (5) race and class bias may enter into participant selection, and (6) it may compromise public safety.

Other ISP Program Conditions

Briefly reviewing judicial dispositional options, at one end of the sentencing spectrum, judges may adjudicate youth as delinquent, impose nominal sanctions, and take no further action other than to record the event. If the juvenile reappears before the same judge in the future, however, additional measures may be taken when the judge imposes a new disposition. Alternatively, the judge may divert juveniles to designated community agencies for special treatment. Juveniles with psychological problems, sex offenders, or those with drug and/or alcohol dependencies may be referred for special community treatments. At the other end of the spectrum of punishments are the more-serious, out-of-home sanctions, ranging from the placement of juveniles in nonsecure foster homes and camps or ranches or in secure facilities, such as detention centers, reform schools, and other residential facilities. The nonsecure placements are intended for youth who are involved in relatively minor offending and who are in need of a temporary placement where there is more supervision and treatment than in their own homes. The secure placements are usually reserved for the more-serious juvenile offenders.

In many jurisdictions, a PO assigned to a juvenile's case will conduct a home evaluation before judicial actions such as EM, home confinement, or other alternative sanctions are imposed. In most counties, POs conduct home evaluations and report the results of these evaluations to juvenile court judges, who then make a more informed decision about the most appropriate disposition to impose. As shown in Figure 11.9, a home evaluation or social history summary contains valuable information about the neighborhood, neighbors, gang presence (if any), family status, legal history of the family, proposed plan for the juvenile, and information that the investigating PO determines to be relevant.

Also helpful in juvenile court judge decision making are regular monthly reports filed by POs in different jurisdictions that outline the sociodemographic characteristics of youth under supervision, their numbers, number of terminations, transfers, commitments, court-ordered fines and their payment or nonpayment, and other factors. In some instances, psychological evaluations are also ordered. Juveniles may have been ordered to boot camps, to counseling, or to participation in youth clubs or other activities. Regular documentation of referrals and other relevant placement data enable judges to determine whether their dispositional orders are effective or in need of modification.

As mentioned, probation is the most commonly used sentencing option. Probation is either unconditional or conditional. This chapter has examined several conditional intermediate punishments, including IPS and community-based programs. A youth's assignment to any of these programs may or may not include conditions. Separately from the more intensive monitoring and supervision by POs, juveniles may be expected to comply with one or more conditions, including restitution, if financial loss was suffered by one or more victims in cases of vandalism, property damage, or physical injury. In addition, fines may be imposed, or the judge may

---

HOME EVALUATION REPORT

Sending State: _____   Receiving State: _____

Juvenile's Name: _____   DOB: _____

Placement Investigated:

Parent/Guardian:_____
Address: _____
Work Phone: _____   Home Phone #: _____

HOME NEIGHBORHOOD/PEERS: _____
_____
_____
_____

FAMILY STATUS (composition, interactions, at-risk family members, attitude):
_____
_____
_____

LEGAL HISTORY OF FAMILY (current charges, probation or parole status): _____
_____
_____

PROPOSED PLAN (school/employment, court ordered conditions):
_____
_____

OTHER COMMENTS: _____
_____
_____

Probation Officer: _____

Figure 11.9
Home Evaluation Report, Dougherty County, Georgia

specify some form of community service. These conditions may be an integral part of a juvenile's probation program. Violation of or failure to comply with one or more of these conditions may result in a probation revocation action. POs function as the link between juvenile offenders and the courts regarding compliance with these program conditions.

Restitution, Fines, Victim Compensation, and Victim–Offender Mediation

Restitution

restitution

Stipulation by court that offenders must compensate victims for their financial losses resulting from crime; compensation for psychological, physical, or financial loss by victim; may be imposed as a part of an incarcerative sentence.

Increasingly, **restitution** is a feature of probation programs. Several models of restitution include:

1. The financial/community service model, which stresses the offender's financial accountability and community service to pay for damages.

2. The victim/offender mediation model, which focuses on victim–offender reconciliation.

3. The victim/reparations model, in which juveniles compensate their victims directly for their offenses.

The potential significance of restitution, coupled with probation, is that it may reduce recidivism among juvenile offenders. Restitution orders impact juveniles directly, and having to repay someone for damages caused can result in youth awareness and sensitivity to the actual damages inflicted. This strategy may be rehabilitative for some offenders.

Fines and Victim Compensation

fines

Financial penalties imposed at the time of sentencing convicted offenders; most criminal statutes contain provisions for the imposition of monetary penalties as sentencing options.

Beyond reductions in recidivism, payment of **fines** and **victim compensation**, similar to restitution, also increase offender accountability. In context of the philosophical direction of juvenile courts, this condition is consistent with enhancing youth acceptance of responsibility for acts committed against others and the financial harm that youth may have caused. Some of these programs include restitution as a part of the program requirements. Restitution orders may be imposed by juvenile court judges with or without accompanying dispositions of secure confinement.

Victim–Offender Mediation

victim compensation

Financial restitution payable to victims by either the state or the convicted offenders.

victim–offender mediation

Third-party intervention mechanism whereby perpetrator and victim work out civil solution to otherwise criminal or delinquent action.

There is growing interest in programs for juvenile offenders that increase accountability, especially toward their victims. Since 1980, there has been greater awareness of and interest in **victim–offender mediation** as a means of resolving disputes between the juvenile perpetrator and his or her victim. Victim–offender mediation brings together victims, offenders, and other members of the community to hold offenders accountable not only for their crimes but for the harm they caused to victims (Sinclair, 2005). These programs provide an opportunity for crime victims and offenders to meet face-to-face to talk about the impact of the crime on their lives and to develop a plan for repairing the harm. Most of these programs work with juvenile offenders, although a growing number are involving adult offenders (Gregorie, 2005).

Also known as restorative justice or balanced and restorative justice, victim–offender mediation is prevalent in various countries. In 2004, there were over 1,500 programs in 22 countries (Lightfoot and Umbreit, 2004). In 2005, there were 700 victim–offender mediation programs in the United States alone. One unique feature of such programs is that they are dialogue-driven rather than settlement-driven. While not all victims are satisfied with the outcomes of such programs, most report that they are content to have had the opportunity to share their experiences with the offender. Many juveniles report being surprised at learning about the impact their actions had on the victims they confront.

Community Service

Associated with restitution orders is **community service**. Community service may be performed in different ways, ranging from cutting courthouse lawns and cleaning up public parks to painting homes for the elderly or repairing fences on private farms. Youth typically earn wages for this service, and these wages are usually donated to a victim compensation fund. The different types of community service activities are limited only by the imagination of the juvenile court and community leaders. Similar to restitution, community service orders are intended to increase offender accountability and individual responsibility (Sinclair, 2005).

community service
Any activity imposed on a probationer or parolee involving work in the youth's neighborhood or city; performed in part to repay victims and the city for injuries or damages caused by unlawful actions.

SUMMARY

Probation is a conditional, community-based sanction where probationers are supervised by juvenile POs for designated periods of time. It is the punishment most often imposed by juvenile court judges. Standard probation includes conditions such as reporting to POs in person at regular times and submitting written reports, obeying all laws, observing curfew, attending school, avoiding alcohol and drugs, not frequenting places where delinquent juveniles may be present or having any association with them, seeking counseling if directed by the court, not possessing firearms or any dangerous weapons, and participating in designated programs required by juvenile court judges. Probation is intended to be rehabilitative and reintegrative. Heightened accountability is also emphasized, including restitution requirements and community service. The success of any probation program is most often evaluated by recidivism rates. Risk and needs assessments are often used to determine individual offender needs and prescribe specific treatments to improve the youth's chances of remaining delinquency-free.

A broad class of intermediate punishments for juveniles has been identified. Intermediate sanctions include any dispositions that can be imposed between standard probation and secure confinement. Also known as creative sentencing, intermediate punishments have several goals, such as providing less costly sanctions compared with secure confinement; achieving lower recidivism rates compared with standard probation programs; providing a greater range of community services for juvenile clients; minimizing the adverse effects of labeling by reducing contact with the juvenile justice system; improving personal educational and vocational skills, which help to improve self-concept; and encouraging greater acceptance of responsibility.

JISP programs are also used and include EM, house arrest, and other interventions. Eligibility standards for entry into JISPs are strict. JISP effectiveness depends on factors that heighten offender accountability by increasing offender responsibility and promoting greater offender control through more frequent curfew checks, drug and alcohol testing, school visits, and employment checks.

Overall, JISPs are more expensive than standard probation programs. More successful JISPs emphasize a balanced approach, which is based on achieving three fundamental goals: (1) improving community protection through close offender surveillance and supervision, (2) using activities and engaging youth in programs that increase their accountability and awareness of the victim, and (3) individualizing treatments and services delivered to juveniles.

Several caseload assignment models were described, and each community has evolved different community-based programs based on the nature and types of juvenile offenders. The goals of many community-based programs are to promote public safety, hold youth accountable for their behavior, and improve their ability to live productively in the community by providing educational, vocational, and counseling services. The balanced approach is apparent in these programs.

EM programs are used to monitor offender whereabouts. Precise numbers of youth on EM are difficult to determine because of disparate techniques of record-keeping. The benefits, weaknesses, and strengths of EM were described. Home confinement or house arrest was also explained. The goals of home confinement are to enable offenders to remain in their communities and attend school or jobs at regular times, reduce the cost of offender supervision, promote rehabilitation and reintegration, reduce jail and prison overcrowding, and maximize public safety by using the home as a place of confinement where compliance can be strictly enforced.

Other JISP conditions were also described. These include restitution, fines, victim compensation, victim–offender mediation, and alternative dispute resolution. The success of these programs was discussed.

KEY TERMS

standard probation, 391
unconditional probation, 392
conditional probation, 392
unconditional standard probation, 392
special conditions of probation, 392
juvenile probation camps, 396
Intensive Aftercare Program (IAP), 396

Sexual Offender Treatment (SOT) Program, 396
recidivism rate, 398
intensive supervised probation, 398
recidivists, 398
recidivism, 398
intensive supervision program (ISP), 402
intensive probation supervision (IPS), 402
creative sentencing, 403

juvenile intensive supervised probation (JISP), 403
caseloads, 408
case supervision planning, 409
conventional model, 409
numbers game model, 410
conventional model with geographical considerations, 410

QUESTIONS FOR REVIEW

1. What is standard probation? What are some of its characteristics? What are some of the conditions of standard probation?

2. How does standard probation differ from probation with special conditions? What are some types of special conditions usually included in such probation orders?

3. What are juvenile probation camps? What is meant by intensive aftercare? Are such alternative sanctions effective at reducing recidivism? Why, or why not?

4. What are intermediate punishments? How do intermediate punishments differ from standard probation?

5. What are some goals of intermediate punishments? What are some of the criteria for placement in intensive supervised probation (ISP) programs?

6. What are four types of caseload models? Describe each.

7. What is case supervision planning? Is there an ideal caseload for probation/parole officers?

8. What is meant by the balanced approach? What are some of its important elements? Is it successful in dealing with delinquent offenders? Why, or why not?

9. What are home confinement and EM? Are home confinement and EM used together? Which type of juvenile clients are most appropriate for EM and/or home confinement? What are the goals and functions of these respective programs?

10. What is victim–offender mediation? Which juveniles are eligible for participating in such mediation? How successful are such programs in resolving disputes between juveniles and their victims?

INTERNET CONNECTIONS

Annie E. Casey Foundation
http://www.aecf.org/

Childhelp
http://www.childhelp.org/

CompassPoint Nonprofit Services
http://www.compasspoint.org/

Justice Technology Information Network
http://www.justnet.org/Pages/home.aspx

National Center for Youth Law
http://www.youthlaw.org/juvenile_justice/6/

Office for Victims of Crime
http://www.ojp.usdoj.gov/ovc/

Texas Juvenile Probation Commission
http://www.tjpc.state.tx.us/

Victim Offender Mediation Association
http://www.igc.org/voma

Wilderness Programs Etc.
http://www.wildernessprogramsetc.com

12

Juvenile Corrections

Custodial Sanctions and Aftercare

Learning Objectives

<small>AFTER READING THIS CHAPTER, THE STUDENT WILL BE ABLE TO:</small>

- Differentiate between short-term and long-term juvenile confinement facilities.
- Describe the purpose and operation of various juvenile correction facilities, including boot camps and ranches/camps.
- Characterize foster home placements and emancipation.
- Discuss the goals of juvenile corrections.
- Summarize the use of wilderness programs or projects.
- Summarize the purpose of shock probation.
- Explain boot camps or shock incarceration programs.
- Describe and discuss long-term and short-term secure placements for youth.
- Summarize how correctional treatment has changed and developed over the years.
- Understand disproportionate minority confinement and contact.
- Understand aftercare policy and aftercare revocation.
- Identify the issues, problems, and potential negative effects of juvenile institutionalization.
- Explain evidence based practice and its role in juvenile corrections.
- Understand the critical issues that juvenile corrections confronts.

(Renars Jurkovskis/Shutterstock.com)

Introduction

Just how effective is juvenile aftercare for controlling youth behavior after a period of incarceration? How well are juvenile residential facilities operated? Do they rehabilitate offenders? This chapter will examine juvenile corrections, particularly institutional corrections.

The first section describes various goals of juvenile corrections. These include deterrence, rehabilitation and reintegration, punishment and retribution, and isolation and control. Each goal will be described.

Next, residential placement alternatives will be described and discussed. The institutionalization of juvenile offenders may be in either nonsecure or secure facilities. Both types of facilities will be examined.

Nonsecure custody options include foster home placements, shelter care (group homes and halfway houses), as well as camps, ranches, experience programs, and wilderness projects. The goals of nonsecure programs will be examined, together with an evaluation of their effectiveness in rehabilitating and reintegrating youthful offenders. Several specific programs will be featured as examples of how various out-of-home placements function and how certain goals are achieved.

Secure confinement refers to residential facilities intended for youth who have been adjudicated delinquent for a serious person offense, drug offense, or repeated property offenses or who have been determined to be chronic offenders. Placement in a secure residential facility is the most severe sanction that the juvenile court judge can impose.

Some youth are placed in boot camps, which are military-like facilities with many rules and regulations. Boot camps will be described and defined, and their characteristics, primary goals and rationale, and a profile of boot camp clientele will be highlighted.

Juvenile aftercare is similar to parole in the adult system. Juvenile aftercare policies in various state jurisdictions will be identified, and criteria utilized in deciding which juveniles to place on aftercare will be described.

Next, juvenile probation and the revocation process will be examined. Three landmark U.S. Supreme Court adult probation and parole revocation cases will be identified, and a sampling of state cases involving probation and aftercare revocation actions will be described. A number of important issues upon which juvenile probation and parole revocation actions are based will be addressed as well.

Several important issues in juvenile corrections conclude this chapter. Should the private sector operate juvenile facilities, especially secure facilities? How should juvenile offenders be classified? Is there too much or too little use of secure confinement for juveniles? How can authorities distinguish clearly between those juveniles who might benefit from secure residential placement and those who do not deserve such a sanction? Another issue pertains to detaining juveniles, even for brief periods, in adult lockups or jails. Every year, attempts are made to avoid juvenile incarceration in adult facilities. Nonetheless, a certain proportion of those incarcerated in adult jails are juveniles. Finally, there is the issue of youth in adult prisons. These youth were transferred to adult court, convicted, and sentenced as adults. There are several reasons for the incarceration of youth in adult institutions. These issues will be examined in some detail.

Goals of Juvenile Corrections

The goals of juvenile corrections are (1) deterrence, (2) rehabilitation and reintegration, (3) punishment and retribution, and (4) isolation and control. These goals may at times appear to be in conflict. For instance, some jurisdictions stress delinquency prevention by keeping juveniles away from the juvenile justice system through diversions and warnings. However, other jurisdictions get tough with juveniles by providing more certain and stringent sanctions for their offenses. Professionals in the field agree that the ultimate measure of success for residential or institutional treatment programs is the assurance that youth exiting programs and facilities maintain positive gains and refrain from reoffending or engaging in other problem behaviors upon return to the community.

Deterrence

Significant deterrent elements of juvenile correctional programs include clearly stated rules and formal sanctions, behavior modeling and reinforcement, and a high degree of empathy and trust between the juvenile client and staff (Campbell and Gonzalez, 2007). Deterrence is based on the belief that the threat of incarceration in a secure

Juveniles can be held in both secure and nonsecure facilities.
(Courtesy of Mark C. Ide)

facility, even for a brief period, might prevent some juveniles from committing delinquent acts. And once in the institution, the individual experience is intended to specifically deter youth from engaging in future delinquent behavior. Therefore, if the threat itself does not prevent the delinquency, the reality of the sanctions youth experience should deter them from further delinquent behavior.

A natural intervention may also occur apart from any particular program designed to deter. As youth grow older, their rate of offending reaches a plateau and then begins to decline. Thus, many youth simply outgrow delinquency as they become mature.

Rehabilitation and Reintegration

Rehabilitation is the mainstay of juvenile corrections. The juvenile justice system assumes that youth are amenable to treatment and reform. As a result, rehabilitation exemplifies the philosophy of juvenile correctional programming, and various juvenile correctional programs stress internalizing responsibilities for one's actions while assisting youth in developing academic, social, and behavioral skills. Some programs attempt to diagnose and treat youth who are emotionally disturbed. Youth with drug and alcohol problems or anger management issues are also treated through a rehabilitative emphasis or approach.

Punishment and Retribution

One major impact of the get-tough policy adopted by many jurisdictions is that the juvenile justice system seems to be transferring more of its serious offenders to criminal courts, where they may conceivably receive harsher punishments (Wilson and Petersilia, 2002). This may be, in part, a reaction to allegations that juvenile courts are too lenient in their handling of offenders or that the options available to juvenile court judges are not sufficiently severe. As noted previously, the juvenile system is based on reform and rehabilitation, but changes to state statutes have, in some instances, altered the original language to reflect a more punitive stance. For those juveniles who are adjudicated delinquent for serious offenses and remain within the juvenile justice system for processing, secure confinement for longer periods is the most stringent response available. Nonetheless, juvenile court judges can impose a number of sanctions that may be deemed punitive.

Isolation and Control

Apprehension and incarceration of juvenile offenders, especially chronic recidivists, isolates them and limits their opportunities to reoffend (Gordon and Malmsjo, 2005). In principle, this philosophy is similar to selective incapacitation discussed in Chapter 9. Because the juvenile justice system recognizes the limitations of adolescent brain development and the fact that most youth will mature and stop engaging in delinquent behavior, the average length of juvenile incarceration in public facilities in the United States is less than 10 months (Office of Juvenile Justice and Delinquency Prevention, 2007). However, there is variation in the use and length of incarceration among states.

Current Juvenile Custodial Alternatives

The custodial options available to juvenile court judges are of two general types: (1) nonsecure and (2) secure. Nonsecure residential facilities are those that typically permit youth to have some movement within the community. Youth may be able to leave the program during the day, but they are compelled to observe the facility's rules, adhere to curfew regulations, avoid alcoholic beverages and drugs, and participate in specific programs that are tailored to their particular needs. These types of facilities include foster homes, shelter care (group homes and halfway houses), and camps, ranches, experience programs, and wilderness projects.

Secure custodial facilities are the juvenile counterparts to adult prisons or institutions. Such institutions are known by different names among the states. For example, secure, long-term confinement facilities might be designated as youth centers or youth facilities (Alaska, California, Colorado, District of Columbia, Illinois, Kansas, Maine, and Missouri), juvenile institutions (Arkansas), schools (California, Connecticut, and New Mexico), schools for boys (Delaware), training schools or centers (Florida, Indiana, Iowa, and Oregon), youth development centers (Georgia, Tennessee, and Nebraska), youth services centers (Idaho), and secure centers (New York). This listing is not comprehensive, but it illustrates the characterizations states use to refer to their long-term, secure confinement facilities.

Nonsecure Confinement

Nonsecure confinement involves placing certain youth in (1) foster homes; (2) shelter care (group homes and halfway houses); and (3) camps, ranches, experience programs, and wilderness projects.

Foster Homes

If the juvenile's parents are determined to be unable to properly care for the youth or the juvenile is abandoned or orphaned, **foster homes** can be used for temporary placement. Youth placed in foster homes are not necessarily law violators. They may be children in need of supervision (CHINS) or at-risk youth (Lee, 2008).

Foster home placement provides youth with a substitute family. A stable family environment is thought to be beneficial in cases where youth have no consistent adult supervision or are unmanageable or unruly in their own households. In 2007, an estimated 26,000 youth were under the supervision of foster homes in state-operated public placement programs (American Correctional Association, 2007). In addition to state-operated facilities, more than 510,000 youth were in the foster care system in 2009 (Adoption and Foster Care Analysis and Reporting System, 2010; The Pew Charitable Trusts, 2009).

Foster home placements are useful in cases where youth have been apprehended for status offenses or other minor infractions. A portion of youth placed in foster homes have mental, developmental, emotional, or disability issues (National Council on Disability, 2008). Most families who accept youth into their homes have been

foster homes
Homes that offer a temporary placement for youth in need of supervision or control; usually, families volunteer to act as foster parents and nurture and care for youth on a short-term basis.

investigated by state or local authorities in advance to determine whether they are able to be certified as foster parents. Socioeconomic factors and home stability are considered to be important for child placements (Loukas, Suizzo, and Prelow, 2007).

Foster parents may be relatives of the youth or adults who have no biological connection to the child. Couples or single parents can volunteer to be foster parents. Foster parents understand the complexities of children's lives when in their care, and they realize that most youth are placed with them for only a short period of time. Despite these positive features, foster homes are reserved for youth who are either status offenders or minor offenders and for whom remaining in their own home is not a viable option. Most foster parents are not trained as counselors, social workers, or psychologists. For youth who have committed minor offenses, however, a home environment, particularly a stable one, has certain therapeutic benefits (National Council on Disability, 2008).

The intent of foster home programs is not to furnish permanent housing for youth. Rather, foster homes are considered to be temporary. However, the length of time a youth is placed in foster care ranges. For example, the average length of stay in foster homes for youth in 2009 was 26 months. Approximately 19 percent waited from 1 to 5 months for permanent placement, 18 percent waited from 6 to 11 months, 13 percent waited from 12 to 17 months, and 11 percent waited for 5 years or longer (Adoption and Foster Care Analysis and Reporting System, 2010).

In terms of outcomes, the vast majority of children in foster care are returned to their parents. In 2009, approximately 50 percent were reunited with family or caretakers, 20 percent were adopted and placed with permanent families, 9 percent were under some type of guardianship, and 8 percent were adopted by relatives. In 2009, about 11 percent of youth in foster care were emancipated. **Emancipation** refers to the fact that they have reached the age of 18 and, in most states, are no longer required to live in foster care. The remaining foster care youth were either transferred to another agency or classified as runaways (Adoption and Foster Care Analysis and Reporting System, 2010).

emancipation

Youth previously placed in a foster home who are able to live independently after they reach a specified age. State statutes vary in the procedures to apply for legal emancipation and age requirements.

Shelter Care

Shelter care facilities are designed to hold children and youth in a home-like environment on a short-term basis. They are a temporary residence, and house parents and staff provide for children for as brief a period as a few hours or up to a few weeks. In 2006, there were approximately 175 shelter care facilities (Hockenberry, Sickmund, and Sladky, 2009). Shelter care facilities may be located in residential areas, and they look just like the other houses in the neighborhood. There are no signs, fences, or physical characteristics that differentiate these facilities. Shelter care differs from foster homes in that these facilities accommodate more children and in different age groups. However, like foster homes, shelter care is used primarily for children who are dependent or status offenders. Shelter care is not intended for violent or aggressive youth. Youth in shelter care are waiting to return home or for placement in a foster home or group home. In some cases, they are brought to shelter care on an emergency basis, because no relative or foster home is available for immediate placement. Shelter care facilities are short term placements for children and youth which may be for a few hours or a couple of weeks. By contrast, two longer term non-secure residential programs are also utilized for youth: (1) group homes and (2) halfway houses.

Group Homes. Juvenile court judges can also decide to place juveniles in **group homes**. Group home placement for youth is considered to be an intermediate alternative available to juvenile court judges. Group homes or halfway houses are community-based facilities that may be either publicly or privately administered (Spigel, 2008).

Usually, group homes have counselors or residents to act as parental figures for youth in groups of 10 to 20. Certain group homes, referred to as family group homes, are actually family operated. Thus, in a sense, they are an extension of foster homes for larger numbers of youth. In most group homes, nonsecure supervision of youth is the norm.

Group homes are popular as alternatives to incarceration, because they are able to offer residential community based placement, treatment, and supervision to youth (Abrams, 2006). In 2006, there were over 750 group homes according to the biannual census of residential facilities, and about 8,200 youth were in group homes (Hockenberry, Sickmund, and Sladky, 2009). In 2008, the census identified 661 group homes housing about 10 percent of all the juveniles in custody, or about 8,100 youth (Hockenberry, Sickmund, and Sladky, 2011).

Because most group homes are located in residential areas adjacent to other traditional family units, local residents may react negatively to their presence. Being in close proximity to a group home may cause some residents to feel unsafe and express fear that group home clients may pose risks or dangers to them or their children. However, statistics on group home residents do not support these fears. The number of youth accommodated by group homes is small, these youth are screened carefully for admission, and few, if any, zoning restrictions can be imposed to bar their presence in a community.

In Connecticut, for instance, state laws provide that any state or private agency must "notify town officials or residents before establishing a group home," and the types of clients the group home serves must be identified (Spigel, 2008, p. 1). However, Connecticut state law "prohibits local zoning regulations from treating group residences housing six or fewer youth with mental retardation, mental illness or physical disabilities, or substance abuse disorders in any way that differs from a single-family residence" (Spigel, 2008, p. 1). Thus, at least in Connecticut, group homes treating six or fewer youth with problems are not required to notify anyone of their location or to report their operation to town officials. Several lower federal appellate courts have ruled "that such notice requirements are discriminatory under the federal Fair Housing Act, because they treat people with mental or physical disabilities living in group homes differently from other people living in similar housing" (Spigel, 2008, p. 1). However, group homes cannot be clustered in any particular area. Local zoning authorities must be advised if a second or third group home is planned within 1,000 feet of an existing group home.

No model or ideal group home exists in the United States to be emulated by all jurisdictions, and what works well for youth in some communities may not work as effectively for youth in others. However, most successful group homes have strong

group homes
Community based facilities that provide youth with limited supervision and support; juveniles live in a home-like environment with other juveniles and participate in therapeutic programs and counseling; considered to be nonsecure residential facilities.

structural components, where all residents are obligated to participate in relevant program components, expectations are stipulated clearly, predictable consequences for rule violations are enforced, and regular monitoring by staff occurs. Thus, juveniles can live in a home-like environment and have contact and visits with their families.

Whether privately or publicly operated, group homes require juvenile residents to observe the rights of others, participate in various vocational or educational training programs, attend school, participate in therapy or receive prescribed medical treatment, and observe curfew. Urinalyses or other tests may be conducted randomly to check whether juveniles are taking drugs or consuming alcohol contrary to group home policy. If one or more program violations occur, group home officials may report these infractions to juvenile court judges, who retain dispositional control over the youth. Assignment to a group home is usually for a determinate period.

Group homes provide youth with the companionship of other juveniles and the guidance and supervision of staff familiar with the youth and his or her situation. Problem sharing often occurs through planned group discussions, in which the subjects vary from peer relations in school to suicide prevention. Staff members are available to assist youth in securing employment, addressing difficult school problems, arranging for tutorial services, and absorbing emotional burdens arising from difficult interpersonal relationships. In addition to the paid staff members in group homes, community volunteers may be utilized.

Each state has its own regulations for how group homes are established and operated. Training programs for group home staff vary, and few national standards are enforced relating to staff preparation and qualifications. Therefore, considerable variation exists among group homes relating to the quality of programs they can extend to the juveniles they serve (Corwin, 2005).

halfway houses

Non-secure residential facilities intended to provide an alternative to incarceration for offenders who reenter the community after confinement in an institution.

Halfway Houses. Halfway houses generally refer to community homes used by adult parolees recently released from prison. These halfway houses provide a temporary base of operations for parolees as they seek employment and readjust to life within their communities. Therefore, they are perceived as transitional residences halfway between incarceration and complete freedom. For many ex-inmates, exposure to unregulated community life is a traumatic transition from the rigidity of prison culture. The rules of halfway houses provide limited structure as well as opportunities to access the outside during the transitory stage.

parolees

Adult offenders who have served time in jail or prison but have been released to the community under supervision before serving the entire sentence imposed upon conviction.

For juveniles, halfway houses also operate as transitional residences. Thus, for juveniles who have served time in secure residential facilities because of delinquency adjudications, halfway houses frequently assist them in successful reentry in the community and in acquiring strategies for independent living. For example, the Virginia Department of Juvenile Justice operated two halfway houses for youth in 2011: (1) Abraxas House and (2) Hampton Place.

Abraxas House. Abraxas House is located in Staunton, Virginia. It is a structured transitional program for male juveniles ages 16 to 20 who have been released from juvenile correctional centers. The program emphasis is upon independent living skills, employment opportunities, educational services, and character development. Treatment services are also provided to assist adolescents with family issues, substance abuse issues, and sex offender issues on an as-needed basis.

Hampton Place. Hampton Place is located in Norfolk, Virginia. It is designed for male offenders from 17 to 20 years of age who have been committed there for direct care on a type of aftercare status. These residents are more closely supervised than youth in Abraxas House or Discovery House. Hampton Place residents are held accountable for their actions and assistance with community reentry and independent living is incorporated in the program (Virginia Department of Juvenile Justice, 2008).

Camps, Ranches, Experience Programs, and Wilderness Projects

Camps, ranches, and experience programs or **wilderness projects** are examples of programs typically located in unique settings. Although they primarily deal with less-serious offenders, these alternative nonsecure programs are also intended for youth who have been involved in repeated delinquent activities, and they are less costly than traditional institutional programs. Experience programs include various outdoor programs designed to improve a juvenile's self-worth, self-concept, pride, and trust in others. In 2006, a total of 115 programs were identified as ranches or wilderness camps for delinquent youth in the United States, and they were more likely to be operated by private agencies and organizations than the state or local government (Hockenberry, Sickmund, and Sladky, 2009). In 2008, the reported number of such facilities was 85 (Hockenberry, Sickmund, and Sladky, 2011).

> **wilderness projects**
> Experience programs that include various outdoor programs designed to improve a juvenile's self-worth, self-concept, pride, and trust in others.

Rawhide Boys Ranch. One example of an experience program is the Rawhide Boys Ranch (RBR), which is a faith-based residential care center in Wisconsin for at-risk teenage boys that began in 1960. It is based on a traditional family home model around which a cluster of youth homes is structured. Both public and private agencies can refer youth to the RBR. Juvenile courts are also a source of youth referrals, and families and relatives of youthful offenders can apply to have the RBR accept and assist youth who have had difficulties at home or in the community. The RBR can accommodate up to 60 boys at any given time, but there are strict screening requirements. Psychologically disturbed youth, or youth who suffer from severe mental illnesses, are typically referred to other places where better services for them exist.

Several living units are available, with each staffed by two to four resident instructors, a housekeeper, and a social worker. Additional social workers, work experience job trainers, family counselors, and instructors also assist the RBR youth. Youth are placed in the RBR program for an indeterminate period, depending upon their individual progress in achieving programming goals. Activities are focused upon family services, social services and case management, academic education, employment training, foster care services, and transitional services. These are the principal program components, although other assistance or support may be offered to youthful clients.

Program evaluations of the RBR have been conducted since 2003, and results indicate a 73 percent success rate among the RBR-discharged youth. That figure translates into a recidivism rate of 27 percent after a six-month follow-up period.

Thus, the RBR appears to achieve its goals of enabling youth to reenter society and live independent and law-abiding lives. To evaluate the recidivism and effectiveness of the RBR, the Youth Outcomes Questionnaire (YOQ), which measures numerous dimensions, including behaviors, moods, situations, and interpersonal relations, that commonly are found among troubled teens was utilized. The conclusion reached by Dr. Frank Cummings, a clinical psychologist who conducted the RBR evaluation, was that the RBR had produced sustained, positive outcomes in the lives of most court-referred youth following their discharge (RBR, 2008).

Secure Confinement

Official data indicate that delinquency and violent youthful offending peaked during the mid-1990s. The legislative response to such violence has been to get tough with juveniles. The get-tough movement generally equates with a number of changes that occurred in the 1990s, including revisions to state statutes lowering the age at which youth could be tried as adults and amendments regarding transfer or waiver procedures that made it easier to move youth into the adult court and, once there, to utilize adult sanctions at conviction. In the juvenile justice system, incarceration in a secure facility is the most stringent sanction that the judge can impose.

Confining juveniles in secure custody is generally an unpopular response to juvenile offending. In many jurisdictions, it is considered as a last resort. In Tennessee, for instance, juvenile corrections personnel will place juveniles on electronic monitoring and/or home confinement for 30, 60, or 90 days to determine if they can engage in law-abiding behavior. If they cannot remain law-abiding while on these programs, then secure confinement is ordered.

Secure confinement involves placing certain youth in (1) shock probation, (2) boot camps, and (3) industrial schools and other juvenile institutions.

Shock Probation

Shock probation or judicial release is an intermediate punishment where offenders initially are sent to a secure placement by the judge. After a period of time, usually between 90 and 180 days, the youth are released from secure confinement, reappear before the judge, and are ordered to serve the remainder of their disposition on probation. The actual term *shock probation* was first used by Ohio authorities in 1964. Shock probation is also known as **shock parole**. For adults, it technically involves probation after a release from jail or prison.

Sometimes, the term *shock probation* is used synonymously with *combination sentences* or *split sentences*. Other terms, such as *intermittent sentences*, *mixed sentences*, or *jail as a condition of probation*, are also used to refer to shock probation, although they have somewhat different meanings. **Combination sentences** or **split sentences** occur whenever judges sentence offenders to a term, a portion of which includes incarceration and a portion of which includes probation. **Mixed sentences** are utilized whenever offenders have been convicted of two or more offenses and judges sentence them to separate sentences for each convicted offense. **Intermittent sentences** can refer sentences that require offenders to be confined only on the

---

shock probation, shock parole

Intermediate punishment in which offenders are initially sentenced to terms of secure detention; after a period of time, usually between 90 and 180 days, they are removed from detention and sentenced to serve the remainder of their sentences on probation; the term *shock probation* was first used by Ohio authorities in 1964.

combination sentences, split sentences

Occur whenever judges sentence offenders to a term, a portion of which includes incarceration and a portion of which includes probation.

mixed sentences

Punishments imposed whenever offenders have been convicted of two or more offenses and judges sentence them to separate sentences for each convicted offense.

intermittent sentences

Occur whenever judges sentence offenders to terms such as weekend confinement only.

Boot camps involve youth in highly organized physical activities throughout the day.
(Courtesy of Dean John Champion)

weekend. **Jail as a condition of probation** is a sentence that prescribes a specified amount of jail incarceration prior to serving the remainder of the sentence on probation.

Technically, however, shock probation differs from all of these. Youth placed on shock probation do not know at the time of their dispositions that they are being considered for such a sanction. The judge informs them that they will be placed in a secure setting. Theoretically, the youth do not know that within three or four months, they will be released from incarceration, brought before the same judge, and placed on probation. This subsequent probationary disposition is contingent upon their good behavior during their incarceration. Thus, the premise is that they are "shocked" by their incarceration.

Shock probation is an unusual term, and it represents a unique policy. Recall that probation is a disposition in lieu of incarceration. Thus, this practice might more accurately be referred to as shock parole, because offenders previously incarcerated are resentenced to a supervised release program. The intent of shock probation is to encourage offenders to refrain from reoffending. In theory, the incarceration experience shocked them; and they are presumed to be more likely to comply with probation conditions and avoid engaging in delinquent or criminal behavior.

Boot Camps

Shock incarceration is best exemplified by juvenile **boot camps** (Parent, 2003). Also known as the **Army Model**, boot camp programs are highly structured, paramilitary, short-term correctional programs, lasting from 90 to 180 days, patterned after basic training for new military recruits. Juvenile offenders experience military organization,

jail as a condition of probation

Sentence in which a judge imposes some jail time to be served before probation commences; also known as shock probation.

shock incarceration, boot camps, Army Model

Boot camp programs are patterned after basic training for new military recruits; juvenile offenders are given a taste of hard military life, and such regimented activities and structure for up to 180 days are often sufficient to "shock" them into refraining from further delinquent behavior.

aggressive physical fitness programs, and strict discipline. Such regimented activities and structure for up to 180 days are intended to sufficiently shock youth into avoiding future delinquency or crime (Gover and MacKenzie, 2003). When successfully completed, boot camp participants may be released to community-based facilities for supervision.

Boot camps are perceived as a relatively recent correctional reform (Office of Juvenile Justice and Delinquency Prevention, 2007). Boot camp programs are operated for as short a time as 30 days or as long as 180 days. While boot camps were officially established in 1983, by the Georgia Department of Corrections Special Alternative Incarceration (SAI), the idea for boot camps originated in the late 1970s, also in Georgia (MacKenzie et al., 2001). By 2007, there were over 100 residential boot camps for adjudicated juveniles operating in 35 states (Office of Juvenile Justice and Delinquency Prevention, 2007). Established boot camp programs include the Regimented Inmate Discipline program in Mississippi, the **About Face** program in Louisiana, and the shock incarceration program in Georgia. These are paramilitary-type programs that emphasize strict military discipline and physical training.

About Face

Louisiana boot camp program which offers education, discipline, treatment and aftercare services for offenders.

The Rationale for Boot Camps. Boot camps have been established as an alternative to long-term traditional incarceration. Austin, Jones, and Bolyard (1993) outline a brief rationale for boot camps:

1. A number of youthful first-offenders now incarcerated will respond to a short but intensive period of confinement followed by a longer period of community supervision.

2. Youthful offenders will benefit from a military-type atmosphere that instills self-discipline and physical conditioning, which has been lacking in their lives.

3. The same youth need exposure to relevant educational training, vocational training, drug treatment, and general counseling services to develop more positive and law-abiding values and become better prepared to secure legitimate future employment.

4. The costs involved will be less than a traditional criminal justice sanction that imprisons the offender for a substantially longer period of time (Austin, Jones, and Bolyard, 1993, p. 1).

Boot Camp Goals. Boot camps have several goals. These include:

1. *To provide rehabilitation and reintegration:* Boot camps seek to improve one's sense of purpose, self-discipline, self-control, and self-confidence through physical conditioning, educational programs, and social skills training, all within a framework of military discipline.

2. *To inculcate discipline:* Boot camps are designed to improve one's discipline. Physical conditioning and structure are most frequently stressed in these programs. However, most boot camp programs also include educational elements

pertaining to literacy, academic and vocational education, intensive value clarification, and resocialization (Styve et al., 2000).

3. *To promote deterrence:* The sudden immersion into a military-like atmosphere is a frightening experience for participants. The rigorous approach to formal rules and authority is a challenging dimension of boot camp programs for youth, and it is intended to prevent their future offending.

4. *To ease jail/prison overcrowding:* Boot camps are believed to have an impact on jail and prison overcrowding. The short-term nature of confinement in boot camp programs with the participant's subsequent return to the community may help ease the overcrowding problem in correctional settings. It is believed that boot camp experiences are significant in creating more positive attitudes among participants (Gover and MacKenzie, 2003).

5. *To provide vocational and educational services:* An integral feature of most boot camp programs is the inclusion of some form of vocational and/or educational training. Educational training is also a key feature of the **Intensive Motivational Program of Alternative Correctional Treatment (IMPACT)** in Louisiana jurisdictions. As an alternative to traditional incarceration, boot camps can promote greater social and educational adjustment for clients reentering their communities (Office of Juvenile Justice and Delinquency Prevention, 2007).

Intensive Motivational Program of Alternative Correctional Treatment (IMPACT) Boot camp program operated in Louisiana; incorporates educational training with strict physical and behavioral requirements.

Profiling Boot Camp Participants. Who can participate in boot camps or shock incarceration programs? Youth may or may not be able to enter or withdraw from boot camps voluntarily. It depends on the particular program. Most boot camp participants are youthful offenders adjudicated delinquent for less-serious, nonviolent offenses who have not been previously incarcerated (Zachariah, 2002).

Representative Boot Camps. Two representative boot camps are the Camp Monterey Shock Incarceration Facility and the Georgia Special Alternative Program. These programs reflect the general nature of boot camps.

The Camp Monterey Shock Incarceration Facility. New York State has a major boot camp project, the Camp Monterey Shock Incarceration Facility. This program has the following features:

1. It accommodates 250 participants in a minimum-security institution.

2. It has 131 staff (83 custody positions).

3. Participants are screened and must meet statutory criteria; three-fourths of volunteers and one-third of applicants are rejected.

4. Participants form platoons and live in open dormitories.

5. Successful program completion leads to release to an intensive probation supervision program called "aftershock."

6. It includes physical training, drill, and eight hours daily of hard labor.

7. Offenders must participate in therapeutic community meetings, compulsory adult basic education courses, mandatory individual counseling, and mandatory recreation.

8. All participants must attend alcohol and substance abuse treatment.

9. Training in job-seeking skills and reentry planning is provided.

CAREER SNAPSHOT

(Courtesy of Raymond Robinson)

Name: Raymond Robinson
Position: Social Services Manager, Allegheny County Shuman Juvenile Detention Center, Pittsburgh, Pennsylvania

Colleges Attended: Indiana University of Pennsylvania

Degrees: B.A. in Criminology and M.A. in Criminology

Background

As a youth growing up on Pittsburgh's South Side, I often wondered what led youth to engage in delinquent behavior and why some progressed into more-serious offending. I would think to myself, "Why do we do the things we do?" With this in mind, I enrolled at Indiana University of Pennsylvania (IUP) to major in sociology. After graduating with a B.A. in Criminology, I worked as a counselor in a group home for adolescent boys, where I discovered my knack for working with youth.

After spending two years at the group home, I switched my focus and took a job in the mental health field working with youth in the home, community, and schools. This served as an eye-opener to me and helped me understand the connection between mental illness and acting-out behaviors among youth. I realized that youth with mental health disorders often act out similarly to delinquent youth, but the way in which they are handled often varies significantly! I eventually realized I preferred working with delinquent youth, and that led me to Shuman Juvenile Detention Center.

I started working at Shuman Center in 2001, as a caseworker in the Social Services Department. During that time, I earned my M.A. in Criminology from IUP. Soon after, I was promoted to Social Services Manger. I am currently responsible for developing resident programs and coordinating volunteers and community agencies. I work with my staff and other organizations to offer programs that foster the physical, social, and emotional development of youth. Whether it is instituting a yoga program to help youth deal with stress and stay active or creating a youth-run news broadcast for them to air their views on current events, I strive to make their stay in detention fruitful.

Shuman Center has been a leader in providing mental health screenings and services to detained youth. My earlier experiences in the mental health field have equipped me well, as I have had to establish relationships with various mental health agencies. I was also able to assist our staff in the management of youth with significant mental health needs through training and individual behavior plans. Detention centers throughout Pennsylvania also have enhanced their efforts to address the increasing number of youth identified with mental health needs.

Advice to Students

First, make sure the career you choose allows you to use your strengths. Often times our goals and wishes do not align with our strongest qualities. You may be successful at your chosen job, but you also may be selling yourself short by not using your full potential. Doing an internship in your field is a great way to see if a given job is a match for you.

Next, learn to be an effective communicator. Effective communication involves verbal and nonverbal communication. A slight change in tone, or relaxing the shoulders and opening your palms, can be the difference between diffusing a volatile situation, and having a youth violently act out. On other occasions, the best communication skill may be to say nothing. Many youth can often be best served by active listening. Showing youth that you have an interest in what they say, or just reaffirming what they are feeling, can often do more to help them than any intervention tool or behavioral technique.

Lastly, I encourage anyone looking to work with youth to always treat those in your care with dignity and respect. Far too often I have heard staff say that youth have to give respect to get respect. Taking that view does a disservice to the youth with whom we work. When you consider the backgrounds of the youth we work with and the experiences they have had with the juvenile justice system, I feel it is shortsighted for professionals to expect the youth we encounter to show us respect. Accordingly, I stress the importance of unconditional respect. It serves as a great personality trait to model to youth, and I feel it creates the best environment to foster new relationships. I have found that through positive relationships, youth are most receptive to what we as professionals have to offer. It is what they learn though those relationships that can lead them to make real changes in their life.

The Georgia Special Alternative Program. The Georgia Special Alternative Program involves two facilities and has the following features:

1. The program is for male offenders only.

2. Judges control the selection process, and SAI is a "condition of probation." If successful, boot camp graduates are released; judges do not ordinarily resentence them to probation.

3. The program includes physical training, military drills, and hard work. There are two exercise and drill periods daily, with eight hours of hard labor in between the two periods.

4. Participants perform limited community services.

5. There is little emphasis on counseling or treatment.

6. Youth receive drug abuse education and information about sexually transmitted diseases.

7. Participants are double-bunked in two 25-cell units at the Dodge facility. At the Burris facility, 100 inmates are single-bunked in four 25-cell units (MacKenzie, Shaw, and Gowdy, 1993).

Costs and Success of Boot Camps. The overwhelming majority of the evaluation research on boot camp programs indicates that they do not reduce recidivism (Duwe and Kerschner, 2008; Steiner and Giacomazzi, 2007). When the Office of Juvenile Justice and Delinquency Prevention (OJJDP) examined the recidivism rates at three specific boot camp program sites (Cleveland, Ohio; Denver, Colorado; and Mobile, Alabama) and compared the boot camp graduates' recidivism rates with those of youth who had been incarcerated in state or county institutions, no reduction in the recidivism rates of boot camp participants was found (Fritsch and Caeti, 2009).

Boot camps might be less costly to operate than traditional programs. For example, Duwe and Kerschner (2008) evaluated the Minnesota Challenge Incarceration Program and found that when the evaluation focused solely on the outcome of return to prison, no difference was found in the boot camp versus control group participants. However, if the reason for return (new crime versus a violation of supervised release conditions) was explored, boot camp graduates fared better. They also tended to remain in prison for those violations for a shorter period of time than the control group, and this cost less than the control group's incarceration.

When states use boot camps for offenders who would have been placed on regular probation, their costs can be increased. In brief, using boot camps in lieu of more-secure, long-term facilities may be cost-effective, but relying on boot camps when institutional placement is unnecessary only serves to widen the net and bring more offenders further into the system (Fritsch and Caeti, 2009). For those jurisdictions that rely on boot camps for youth who did not need the structure and discipline that they utilize, savings do not occur.

Industrial Schools and Other Juvenile Institutions

Historically, juvenile court judges determined that delinquent youth should be placed in reform schools. These were prison-like facilities with few amenities. Juveniles were assigned various menial tasks, and educational opportunities were limited. Some jurisdictions with reform schools offered different types of counseling and vocational and educational programs. However, for most of these youth, their prospects for learning useful skills and returning to the community as law-abiding young adults were bleak. If anything, youth emerged from these institutions as more hard-core offenders compared with when they entered. In fact, some of these youth went on to commit crimes as adults.

In the years since the first public juvenile correctional institution was opened in Massachusetts in the 1840s, there have been a number of changes in juvenile correctional facilities. Currently, various intervention programs for juveniles operate in virtually every community in the United States. These programs generally emphasize vocational training, acquisition of social and coping skills, education, substance abuse counseling, and mental health counseling. The success of these programs, coupled with the research that confining youth for long periods of time in institutions does not reduce their re-offending and, in fact, exacerbates it, has reinforced the emphasis on utilizing community-based programs rather than incarceration for youth (Mulvey, 2011).

Today, institutionalized juveniles in all states are held in facilities most commonly known as **industrial schools**, **training schools**, or **secure treatment facilities**. The use of the term *reform school* has been abandoned. In addition, no juvenile facility is called a prison, even though some secure juvenile facilities are prison-like in their construction and operation.

Industrial schools are not new. The term has been used for many years in different jurisdictions. In the 1950s, for instance, the Utah State Industrial School was the juvenile prison and also the place where most hard-core juvenile offenders were sent by juvenile court judges. In the 1960s, the Arizona State Industrial School was where Gerald Francis Gault (see Chapter 4) was incarcerated for allegedly making obscene telephone calls (*In re Gault,* 1967). Industrial schools, training schools, or secure treatment facilities in most states are operated either publicly or privately or through some kind of combination of public and private administration (OJJDP, 2007). Youth sent to these facilities are considered to be **commitment placements**, and they are held for longer terms compared with youth placed in detention.

Number and Types of Juveniles Held in Secure Facilities

The number of juveniles held in secure facilities varies (Figure 12.1). Given the rate of discharges and admissions, particularly in detention centers, the numbers are fluid from one day to the next. In 2006, there were 207 training schools or industrial schools in the United States, and 87 percent of them were public. Training schools comprise 32 percent of all state facilities (Hockenberry, Sickmund, and Sladky, 2009). When the census of youth in all state institutions in 2006 was conducted, there were

industrial schools, training schools, secure treatment facilities

Secure facilities where some juveniles are held for one year or longer; such institutions usually have different types of programming to aid in the rehabilitation and reintegration of youthful offenders, consisting of vocational and educational courses or programs, counseling for different types of youth needs, and other services; these facilities are largely self-contained like prisons, and they offer a limited range of medical and health services.

commitment placements

Judicially ordered confinement in a secure juvenile facility, usually for one year or longer.

On October 25, 2006, 44% of juvenile facilities were publicly operated; they held 69% of juvenile offenders

State	Juvenile facilities			Juvenile offenders			State	Juvenile facilities			Juvenile offenders		
	Total	Public	Private	Total	Public	Private		Total	Public	Private	Total	Public	Private
U.S. Total	2,658	1,166	1,483	92,093	63,502	28,426	Missouri	68	62	6	1,359	1,302	57
Alabama	67	13	54	1,822	806	1,016	Montana	18	7	9	227	147	52
Alaska	24	8	16	366	249	117	Nebraska	18	5	13	670	452	218
Arizona	48	17	27	1,765	1,383	292	Nevada	24	14	10	1,081	826	255
Arkansas	33	10	23	862	279	583	New Hamp-shire	8	2	6	194	103	91
California	248	119	129	14,855	13,209	1,646	New Jersey	53	43	10	1,579	1,467	112
Colorado	49	13	36	1,821	963	858	New Mexico	17	15	2	428	400	28
Connecticut	20	4	16	401	220	181	New York	184	46	138	3,834	1,971	1,863
Delaware	7	6	1	270	254	16	North Carolina	59	24	35	1,167	689	478
Dist. of Columbia	9	2	7	236	182	54	North Dakota	10	4	6	237	109	128
Florida	144	40	104	6,854	2,594	4,260	Ohio	95	66	29	4,352	3,983	369
Georgia	40	26	14	2,668	2,129	539	Oklahoma	48	16	31	960	675	260
Hawaii	7	3	4	134	117	17	Oregon	46	24	22	1,343	1,083	260
Idaho	22	14	8	542	489	53	Pennsylvania	151	31	120	5,316	1,312	4,004
Illinois	38	28	10	2,604	2,364	240	Rhode Island	17	1	16	297	165	132
Indiana	88	37	51	2,926	1,835	1,091	South Carolina	33	14	19	1,273	819	454
Iowa	74	15	59	1,173	361	812	South Dakota	23	7	14	514	195	297
Kansas	47	17	30	1,183	791	392	Tennessee	48	27	21	1,276	821	455
Kentucky	45	30	15	1,093	945	148	Texas	114	86	28	8,550	7,533	1,017
Louisiana	49	17	32	1,319	911	408	Utah	44	17	27	1,009	431	578
Maine	9	2	7	222	198	24	Vermont	4	1	3	54	26	28
Maryland	41	15	26	1,065	656	409	Virginia	64	60	4	2,191	2,132	59
Massachu-setts	60	19	41	1,269	448	821	Washington	36	29	7	1,485	1,420	65
Michigan	80	35	45	2,741	1,379	1,362	West Virginia	28	12	16	557	371	186
Minnesota	83	23	60	1,538	879	659	Wisconsin	73	21	52	1,511	895	616
Mississippi	20	17	3	447	400	47	Wyoming	23	2	21	453	134	319

Notes: "State" is the State where the facility is located. Offenders sent to out-of-State facilities are counted in the State where the facility is located, not the State where they committed the offense. Totals include 9 tribal facilities (holding 165 juvenile offenders) located in Arizona, Montana, Oklahoma, and South Dakota.

Figure 12.1
Number of Youth in Residential Placement and Number and Type of Facilities, by State, 2006
Source: Sarah Hockenberry, Melissa Sickmund, and Anthony Sladky (2009). Juvenile Residential Facility Census, 2006: Selected Findings. Washington, DC: Office of Juvenile Justice and Delinquency Prevention.

over 34,000 youth in custody in state facilities. However, this number refers to youth in state-operated detention centers, training schools, residential treatment programs, reception/diagnostic centers, and other facilities, including almost 500 state facilities in all (Hockenberry, Sickmund, and Sladky, 2009, p.3). There were also over 900 residential treatment programs in the United States in that year, but these tended to be operated by private agencies rather than the state (Hockenberry, Sickmund, and Sladky, 2009, p. 3).

Youth are committed either to short- or long-term detention or secure confinement, depending upon the particular stage of juvenile offender processing (Sabol, Minton, and Harrison, 2007). Prior to a formal adjudicatory hearing, juveniles may be detained in the custody of juvenile authorities. The judge must stipulate the reasons for the decision to detain the youth (Figure 12.2). These usually pertain to protecting others from the juvenile, protecting the juvenile from himself or herself while awaiting a formal adjudicatory hearing, fear that the youth will abscond before the hearing, or the absence of parents or legal guardians.

Typically, statistics on youth in placement include all youth under age 21 who are in either public or private secure facilities, who have been adjudicated delinquent by the juvenile court, who are in residential placement because of that offense, and who been assigned a bed by a given date. State use of residential placement varies considerably. For example, in 2007, South Dakota had a residential placement rate of 513 youth for every 100,000 youth in the state. By contrast, Vermont had a rate of 69 per 100,000 youth in the state (Sickmund, 2010). Furthermore, six states (California, Texas, Florida, Pennsylvania, Ohio, and New York) accounted for 46 percent of the youth in residential placement (Sickmund, 2010). It is not necesssarily true that most youth who are incarcerated in secure facilities are violent offenders. Youth can be committed for nonviolent property, drug, or public order offenses. The length of stay may vary according to one's offense or progress in the facility.

Persistent Problems of Nonsecure and Secure Confinement

There is tremendous variation among states in their use of residential facilities and policies, and there are a range of secure juvenile residential facilities in the United States that can be categorized based on size, location, whether they are public or private, and type of program. While institutions can emphasize custodial services for chronic or more-serious juvenile offenders, a range of programs and treatments, such as mental health services, is available, depending upon the diverse needs of the juveniles confined. Clarifying the mission and goals of corrections agencies helps staff to do a better job supervising youthful clientele. Institutional rules then tend to be framed in a more meaningful context, and incarcerated youth are able to cope more effectively with their confinement (Cauffman et al., 2007).

JUVENILE CORRECTIONS ■ CHAPTER TWELVE 449

ORDER FOR DETENTION

IN THE JUVENILE COURT OF GLYNN COUNTY, GEORGIA

IN THE MATTER OF: **CASE NO.:**
                               SEX:
                               DOB:
A CHILD   **AGE:**

WHEREAS a complaint has been made to the Court concerning the above-named child and the Court finding from information brought before it that it is necessary for the protection of said child and/or society that he or she be detained.

It is therefore ordered that said child be detained in the custody of the Court until further order of the Court or until released by a person duly authorized by the Court.

Said child is being detained pursuant to Official Code of Georgia Ann. 15-11-46 for the following reason(s):

   ( ) to protect the person or property of others or of the child;
   ( ) the child may abscond or be removed from the justification of the Court;
   ( ) because he has no parent, guardian or legal custodian or other person able
       to provide supervision and care for him and return him to the Court when
       required;
   ( ) an order for his detention or shelter care has been made by the Court
       pursuant to the Juvenile Proceedings Code.

It is further ordered that the place of detention shall be the _____
_____

ORDERED AND ADJUDGED, this the ____ day of _____, 2004.

_____

Figure 12.2
Order for Detention
Source: Juvenile Court of Glynn County, Georgia.

Architectural Improvements and Officer Training Reforms

In recent years, improvements have been made generally in the overall quality of juvenile secure confinement facilities throughout the United States. Evidence of improvement in juvenile corrections is demonstrated in the efforts in a number of jurisdictions to design and build more adequately equipped juvenile facilities that minimize overcrowding and provide meaningful programs for youth. Private interests also have assisted in providing modern designs and plant operations for secure juvenile facilities in states, such as California and Tennessee (Mendel, 2001).

With respect to training and professional development, little uniformity exists among states. Staff members are more aware of suicide prevention, safety, and victimization of youth today than in the past. Nonetheless, there have been a number of institutions where youth have been victimized by staff and other youth. These incidents have resulted in investigations, recommendations for change, and the elimination of some facilities.

Juvenile Detention Centers

The OJJDP promulgated specific guidelines for all juvenile detention facilities in the early 1980s. These guidelines were published as *Guidelines for the Development of Policies and Procedures for Juvenile Detention Facilities*. The OJJDP sought to establish national juvenile detention resource centers across the United States that would offer information, technical assistance, and training to juvenile detention professionals who wished to participate (King, 2005).

Detention centers are secure, short-term custodial facilities designed to hold youth. Most of them are public facilities, and they are also most frequently characterized as local institutions. In brief, these facilities are in or near the geographical area where the youth reside, and they are administered by local rather than state control. There were over 700 juvenile detention centers identified in 2006, and 36 percent of all youth in residential placement were held in detention centers (Hockenberry, Sickmund, and Sladky, 2009).

Because detention is the first secure institution that most youth encounter, suicide prevention is a critical component. Over 97 percent of the detention centers report that they administer some type of suicide screening at admission (Hockenberry, Sickmund, and Sladky, 2009). Detention centers also offer diagnostic programs, educational programs, counseling services, and recreational programs. In addition to academic classroom instruction, the educational dimension of such centers can assist in transmitting knowledge about communicable diseases, such as AIDS, and inform adolescents about the risks of alcohol, tobacco, and drugs. These centers can also help youth in managing their anger and provide them with opportunities to improve their general mental health (Cauffman et al., 2007).

In recent years, detention has increased for person, drug, and public order offenses (Figure 12.3), and more attention has been focused on the use of detention to hold youth awaiting court appearances. In 1992, the Annie E. Casey Foundation created the **Juvenile Detention Alternatives Initiative (JDAI)** to reduce the number of children who are detained unnecessarily, to decrease the number of youth who do not appear in court or who commit additional delinquent acts before their adjudication, to improve the environments where youth are confined, and to help guide public funds toward successful programs (Soler and Garry, 2009). Minority youth are overrepresented in detention facilities, and elimination

---

detention centers

Juvenile secure facilities used for serious and violent juveniles who are awaiting an adjudication hearing or placement in another facility.

Juvenile Detention Alternatives Initiative (JDAI)

Established in 1992 by the Annie E. Casey Foundation to improve the conditions of confinement for youth in detention, identify alternatives to detention, and address disproportionate minority confinement; over 80 U.S. detention centers participate.

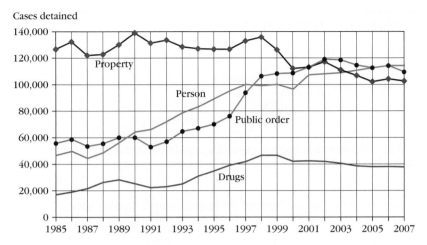

Cases detained

Figure 12.3

Cases Involving Detention Increased in Person, Drug, and Public Order Offenses, 1985 to 2007
Source: Charles M. Puzzanchera, Benjamin Adams, and Melissa Sickmund (2010). Juvenile Court Statistics 2006–2007. Pittsburgh, PA: National Center for Juvenile Justice.

of this practice is also included in the priorities. Currently, there are more than 80 JDAI locations in the United States; and the Foundation has been instrumental in helping them to assess their strategies and to create an equitable detention process (Soler and Garry, 2009).

Short- and Long-Term Facilities

Secure juvenile confinement facilities in the United States are either short-term or long-term. Short-term confinement facilities are designed to accommodate, on a temporary basis, those juveniles who are either waiting for juvenile court adjudication, subsequent residential placement, or transfer to criminal court. Whether a juvenile is held for a period of time in detention depends on the outcome of a **detention hearing**, where the appropriateness of the detention is determined (Figure 12.4).

Sometimes, youth are placed in detention because they are apprehended in another state as a runaway. Other youth may be violent and must be detained temporarily until more appropriate placements may be made. The designations "short term" and "long term" may range from a few days to about a year, respectively, although the average duration of **long-term detention** across all offender categories nationally is about six to seven months. The average short-term incarceration in public facilities for juveniles is about 30 days (OJJDP, 2007).

Some **short-term confinement** is preventive detention or pretrial detention, where juveniles are awaiting formal adjudicatory proceedings (Caudill and Hayslett-McCall, 2008). The U.S. Supreme Court upheld the constitutionality of pretrial or preventive detention of juveniles, especially dangerous ones, in the case of *Schall v. Martin* (1984). One objective of pretrial detention is to prevent certain dangerous juveniles from committing new pretrial delinquent acts (King, 2005). Juvenile court

detention hearing
Judicial proceeding held to determine whether it is appropriate to continue holding or detaining a juvenile prior to an adjudicatory hearing.

long-term detention
Period of incarceration of juvenile offenders in secure facilities that averages 180 days in the United States.

short-term confinement
Temporary placement in any incarcerative institution for adults or juveniles for a shorter period of time which typically ranges from 24 hours to about 30 days.

ORDER OF COMMITMENT

IN THE JUVENILE COURT OF GLYNN COUNTY, GEORGIA

In the interest of: **CASE NO.**

                                                     SEX:
                                                     DOB: **AGE:**

Petition(s) having been filed in this court and after hearing evidence in this court, this court has determined that the above-named child is subject to the jurisdiction and protection of this court as provided by law; and

After hearing evidence or upon the recommendation of the judge, no appeal having been timely filed, the court finds that the child committed the act(s) alleged in said petition(s), to wit:

_____

And that said child is hereby found to be in a state of: (place an "X" in appropriate space)

_____ delinquency and in need of treatment of rehabilitation.

_____ unruliness and in need of treatment, rehabilitation, or supervision. The court also finds that the child is not amenable to treatment or rehabilitation pursuant to O.C.G.A. §15-11-66(a)(1)(3).

The Court also finds that reasonable efforts have been made to prevent the unnecessary removal of the child from the child's home, and that removal is in the best interest of the child at this time.

It is further ordered that said child be and hereby is committed to the Department of Juvenile Justice, for care, supervision and planning as provided in O.C.G.A. §49-4A-8. The undersigned judge hereby recommends that the child be:

COMMITTED TO THE DEPARTMENT OF JUVENILE JUSTICE

The said Department of Juvenile Justice is authorized to provide such medical treatment, hospitalization and/or surgery as is considered necessary by competent medical authorities for said child.

It is further ordered that said child be released into the custody of _____
_____. Detained in the _____ pending placement by the Department of Juvenile Justice.

Considered, Ordered and Adjudged this the ____ day of _____, 2004.

_____
Juvenile Court of Glynn County

Figure 12.4
Order of Commitment
Source: Juvenile Court of Glynn County, Georgia.

judges conduct detention hearings to determine if preadjudicatory confinement is warranted.

Pros and Cons of Incarcerating Juveniles

There are proponents and opponents of juvenile secure confinement (Anderson and Rancer, 2007). Those favoring juvenile placement in secure facilities cite the disruption of one's lifestyle and separation from other delinquent youth as a positive dimension. For example, youth who have been involved with delinquent peers who engage in law-breaking activity might benefit from some separation, because these unfavorable associations would be interrupted or terminated (Taylor et al., 2008). Of course, juveniles can resume their delinquent behavior when released from incarceration. However, proponents contend that at least the existing pattern of interaction that initially contributed to the delinquency is temporarily interrupted (Dembo, Turner, and Jainchill, 2007).

Another argument in support of incarceration of juveniles is that long-term secure confinement is an appropriate response based on the actions of the youth. This is consistent with the contemporary punitive approach to juvenile sanctions. There is some evidence of a trend away from thinking about the best interests of youth and the utilization of strategies to make youth more accountable for their actions. This shift has prompted debate among juvenile justice scholars about the functions of juvenile courts and the ultimate aims of the sanctions they impose (King, 2005).

In some states, such as Texas, juvenile court judges have considerable control over juveniles and their secure confinement. For instance, in the case of *Matter of D.L.* (2006), D.L. was a juvenile charged with aggravated assault. The juvenile court judge ordered him to serve a six-year determinate sentence in a Texas Youth Commission secure facility. When the juvenile reached the age of majority in Texas and was short of the six-year determinate term, the trial court determined that D.L. be sent to an adult prison, where he should serve the remainder of his sentence. D.L. appealed, arguing that the Texas Youth Commission agent who asked that D.L. be transferred to a prison was testifying based on hearsay or reports from others about his prior record and institutional conduct. However, D.L.'s objections were overruled by a state appellate court, and he was remanded to a Texas prison for the remainder of his original sentence.

Opponents of long-term secure confinement of juveniles contend that there are possible adverse labeling effects from confinement with other delinquents and that youth may learn more criminal behavior as a result of this prolonged association with other offenders. Thus, juveniles might begin to label themselves juvenile delinquents and persist in reoffending when released from incarceration. Youth also may learn new delinquent techniques through their confinement with other offenders. Research indicates that most youth will cease to engage in delinquent behavior over time (Mulvey, 2011). Furthermore, longer confinement in juvenile institutions is not correlated with any decrease in offending (Stahlkopf, Males, and Macallair, 2010). By contrast, research indicates that these youth tend to reoffend more (Mulvey, 2011).

Most successful residential programs for juveniles have educational, vocational, and substance abuse treatment components. In recent years, organizations such as the American Correctional Association have promulgated standards for juvenile correctional facilities that provide educational and vocational goals for juvenile residents. Presently, educational programming is mandatory for all juvenile offenders, and educational programs in juvenile correctional facilities are required to follow the same laws and practices as their public school counterparts. These standards also are applicable to privately operated secure juvenile facilities (Kupchik, 2007).

Juvenile facilities may seek accreditation from various organizations, such as the Correctional Education Association (CEA). In October 2004, the Standards Commission of the CEA approved a set of standards for accrediting correctional educational programs in juvenile facilities, though the CEA actually began accrediting juvenile corrections educational programming in 1988. Both adult and juvenile institutions are now subject to CEA accreditation.

It may be appropriate to assess the rationale for placing youth in secure residential facilities. It is possible that incarceration as a punishment is the primary goal, without any tangible, long-range benefits, such as self-improvement or reduction in recidivism (Dembo, Turner, and Jainchill, 2007). However, when there is evidence that incarcerating juveniles for longer periods is related to their involvement in more-serious offenses, the long-term confinement of youth is clearly problematic (Mulvey, 2011). In addition, the fact that most youth stop offending and mature suggests that the system might consider doing less, rather than doing more, in terms of system involvement in the lives of youth.

Disproportionate Minority Confinement

Considerable attention has been directed in recent years toward the issue of **disproportionate minority confinement**, especially in juvenile facilities (Pope, Lovell, and Hsia, 2002). When Congress amended the Juvenile Justice and Delinquency Prevention Act (JJDPA) in 1988, a provision on disproportionate minority confinement was included. States participating in the funding program were required to develop strategies to reduce the proportion of minority youth in confinement if that percentage was greater than their percentage in the general population of the state (OJJDP, 2009b). In 2002, Congress mandated that states must go further and take steps to address **disproportionate minority contact** in the juvenile justice system. Rather than just focus on youth in confinement, the new requirements stipulated all parts of the juvenile justice system process. States that did not comply would lose part of their federal funding for programs (Soler and Garry, 2009). These amendments have helped to increase awareness of disproportionate minority representation in the juvenile justice system and to facilitate the implementation of successful initiatives to address the problem.

To study minority youth representation in residential placement, it is useful to first review arrest data. Arrest, detention, formal processing through the filing of a petition, an adjudicatory hearing, and a disposition hearing all are preceded by an

disproportionate minority confinement

Congress amended the Juvenile Justice and Delinquency Prevention Act in 1988 to require states receiving federal funds to determine if disproportionate minority confinement occurred in their jurisdictions; if a greater proportion of minority youth were confined in juvenile institutions than their share of the general population, states were to take steps to address the issue.

disproportionate minority contact

Congress amended disproportionate minority confinement portion of the Juvenile Justice and Delinquency Prevention Act in 2002 to include disproportionate minority contact; states that receive federal funds are required to determine if there are more minority youth at any stage of the juvenile justice process than there are in the general population and, if so, to implement strategies to address the problem.

arrest. Puzzanchera (2009) notes the disproportionate percentage of arrests represented by black youth. In 2008, black youth comprised 16 percent of the population ages 10 to 17. However, when all juvenile arrests for violent crimes in 2008 were examined, black youth represented 52 percent of all arrests. Thus, at the point of entry into the juvenile justice system, there were disproportionately larger numbers of minority youth compared with white juveniles.

It is beyond the scope of this book to explore the many reasons or explanations for such disproportionate representations of minorities in arrest data. One plausible explanation is that minority youth are often from the lower socioeconomic levels. Thus, they generally have more limited opportunities for success in school and other activities. In their analysis of juvenile arrest rates, Fite, Wynn, and Pardini (2009) evaluated two hypotheses to explain the differences. One hypothesis considered the consequences of exposure to early risk factors, and the other explored differential responses to youth with high risk factors. Overall, the data supported the role of early risk factors in contributing to higher arrest rates among black youth. In comparing white and black male youth, the authors found higher prevalence of conduct problems and low academic success with blacks. In addition, neighborhood conditions, delinquent peers, and problematic parent–child relationships also were more common with black than with white youth. These factors placed blacks at greater risk and contributed to higher arrest rates (Benekos, Merlo, and Puzzanchera, 2011).

Furthermore, there are disproportionate representations of black, Native-American, and Hispanic youth in juvenile corrections facilities (American Correctional Association, 2007). For example, in the census of residential placement, 767 black youth per 100,000 (based on youth ages 10 to 17 in the general population) were in residential placement, and 540 youth per 100,000 youth in placement were Native American (OJJDP Statistical Briefing Book, 2008). For Hispanics, there were 326 youth per 100,000 in residential placement, and for white youth, there were 170 youth per 100,000 in residential placement (OJJDP Statistical Briefing Book, 2008). This pattern persisted in almost all states in 2006. The overall minority population (black, Hispanic, Native Americans/Alaskan Natives, Asian/Pacific Islanders, and those identified as other race) represented only 39 percent of the juvenile population (age 10 and over) but 65 percent of those in residential placement. Minorities comprised 66 percent of all youth in residential placement in public facilities in 2006 (OJJDP Statistical Briefing Book, 2008). These data suggest that the issue of disproportionate minority confinement persists.

Various events transpire between a juvenile's arrest and subsequent disposition in juvenile court. Both legal and extralegal factors can influence decision making at each of the stages of the juvenile justice process. Ideally, only legal factors should be relevant to all decision making, but there is evidence that extralegal factors may operate as well. The pervasiveness of the disproportionality of minority confinement in the United States is underscored by the fact that minorities make up the majority of those confined in secure institutions in most states (Zhang, 2008).

Presently, the issue of race/ethnicity and differential juvenile justice processing is unresolved. There is considerable debate concerning whether minority youth are differentially involved in delinquent behavior or if the system selects and processes them differently. Although there is support for a model that incorporates both explanations, no clear consensus exists on the weight that should be assigned to the competing positions. Future research will move beyond determining which of these explanations is better and focus more on how to correct the problem (Piquero, 2008).

Juvenile Aftercare

Juvenile Aftercare Defined

aftercare

Describes a wide variety of programs and services available to juvenile offenders after a period of confinement; includes halfway houses, psychological counseling services, community-based correctional agencies, employment assistance, and medical treatment designed to aid in their reentry into the community.

Generally, **aftercare** (also known as parole) is a conditional, supervised release from incarceration granted to youth who have served a portion of their original sentences (Champion, 2008a). Aftercare for juveniles is similar to parole for adult offenders. Aftercare participants tend to have few job prospects, limited academic success, and insufficient family support systems. Often, they are returning to distressed neighborhoods (Griffin, 2010).

Aftercare, like parole, involves reentry, a critical phase in a juvenile offender's life. **Reentry** refers to the reintegration of a youth from residential placement to the community. Information suggests that youth in reentry are primarily male offenders 15 years of age or older and that they are more likely to have been released from secure public institutions (Snyder and Sickmund, 2006). Data on youth in the reentry phase of the juvenile justice system have shown that these youth benefit from extensive supervision and various support services when they reintegrate into the community (Snyder and Sickmund, 2006).

reentry

A comprehensive system of services and support used to facilitate successful adjustment to the community for youth leaving institutional confinement.

Purposes of Aftercare for Juveniles

The general purposes of aftercare are:

1. To reward youth for good behavior and progress during their confinement.
2. To alleviate overcrowding.
3. To reintegrate youth back into their communities and enhance their rehabilitation potential.
4. To deter youth from future offending by ensuring their continued supervision.

It is believed that the prospect of earning supervised release might induce greater compliance with institutional rules among incarcerated youth. In addition, aftercare is viewed as a continuation of the juvenile's sanction, because these programs are most often conditional in nature (e.g., observance of curfew, school attendance, staying out of trouble, participation in counseling programs, and vocational and educational training). Rather than an automatic release, aftercare should be based upon a well-defined mission, strategy, and a matching continuum of care, which might also include various enhancements. Considerable attention must also be given to community safety as well as offender rehabilitation (Parker, 2005).

A standard aftercare agreement places the offender under the supervision of the state youth corrections agency. Aftercare may specify one or more program conditions, such as mandatory attendance at vocational/educational programs or schools, therapy or counseling, community service, restitution orders, or fines and maintenance fees. Theoretically, aftercare planning starts as soon as the youth arrives in residential placement and continues until he or she has completed all the terms of the disposition.

Often, the public thinks that if the youth is free from custody, then the juvenile is completely unsupervised. This is not true. Both probation and aftercare are sanctions. The conditions specified under either probation or aftercare may be very limiting. Also, it is ordinarily the case that juvenile probation/parole officers have access to the premises where the youth is located. This intrusion is generally unrestricted; if youth are using drugs or in possession of illegal contraband, the aftercare officer may be able to detect it by surprise, through an unannounced visit. Youth may also be subject to random drug tests as a condition of their aftercare plan.

How Many Juveniles Are on Aftercare?

The number of youth who are on parole or aftercare may be decreasing. This is partly due to the fact that the number of youth in residential placement has been declining. In 2008, there were less than 81,000 youth in residential facilities, and this represented a significant drop from 2000, when over 108,000 youth were in residential placement (Sickmund, 2010). In 2009, the OJJDP estimated that there are 100,000 youth per year participating in reentry programs (OJJDP, 2009a). Although these youth are more likely to be released from public facilities, youth from private residential facilities also participate in reentry programs (Snyder and Sickmund, 2006).

Characteristics of Juvenile on Aftercare

Some jurisdictions, such as New York, have **juvenile offender laws**. These laws define 13-, 14-, 15-, and 16-year-olds as adults, under certain conditions, whenever they are charged with committing specified felonies. These youth may be tried as adults and convicted. When they are subsequently released from institutions, they are placed under adult parole supervision. Other jurisdictions do not have these juvenile offender laws but have waiver or transfer provisions for juvenile offenders.

As previously noted, selected studies of juvenile aftercare indicate that a majority are male youth and minority group members (OJJDP, 2007). Juveniles on aftercare share many of the same programs used to supervise youthful probationers. Intensive supervised probation programs are utilized for both probationers and parolees in many jurisdictions. Furthermore, juvenile aftercare officers often perform dual roles, because they supervise both juveniles on aftercare and probationers. An example of a juvenile aftercare agreement is shown in Figure 12.5.

juvenile offender laws
Statutes providing for automatic transfer of juveniles of certain ages to criminal courts for processing, provided they have been changed with specific felonies.

JUVENILE AFTERCARE AGREEMENT

WHEREAS, it appears to the Commissioner of Youth Services that

_____
(NAME)

❑ presently in custody at _____, and
❑ presently on aftercare, and

    WHEREAS, the said Commissioner, after careful consideration, believes that aftercare at this time is in the best interests of this said individual and the public.

    Now, THEREFORE, be it known that the Commissioner of Youth Services, under authority vested by law,   ❑ grants aftercare to,
                    ❑ continues aftercare for, _____
                                              (NAME)

and authorizes his/her release from the institution with the aftercare plan which has been approved. Upon being released he/she shall be and remain in legal custody and under the control of the Commissioner of Youth Services subject to the rules, regulations, and conditions of this aftercare as set forth on the reverse side of this agreement.

    Signed this _____ day of _____ 20_____.

COMMISSIONER OF YOUTH SERVICES
BY:

_____
(HEARING OFFICER)

❑ New Aftercare Agreement
❑ Restructured Aftercare Agreement

Figure 12.5
Juvenile Aftercare Agreement
Source: *Prepared by authors.*

Juvenile Aftercare Policy

The OJJDP has been involved in reentry programs for youth since the 1980s. The Second Chance Act of 2007, which became law in 2008, enabled the OJJDP to provide support to community-based agencies and organizations to assist youth in the reentry process through mentoring programs and services designed to aid in the transition between residential placement and the community (OJJDP, 2009a). Youth who are being released from residential placement typically require assistance in locating housing, community support networks, employment, and vocational or educational programs.

    In recognition of the difficulties that aftercare or youth in reentry were experiencing, a new program was started in Pennsylvania. Prior research found that youth in

Juvenile institutional programs can involve youth in vocational training programs working with animals.
(© Mikael Karlsson/Alamy)

the reentry process were no longer connected to their schools and did not have meaningful job prospects. The Reintegration Initiative focuses on what is being done to prepare youth to equip them with skills to find jobs. It involves a collaborative, multiagency effort of the state's two largest counties with funding from state and local agencies that work with placement agencies and private contractors to promote successful reintegration (Griffin, 2010). Working together, they have improved the academic and vocational programs for youth in residential placement and helped to provide them with the life skills training that they will need to survive in the community. In addition to teaching life skills and providing the vocational training, the agencies are working with prospective employers in communities who will hire these youth once they are released. Preliminary analysis suggests that these efforts are proving successful (Griffin, 2010).

To assess the effectiveness of one specific residential program, the OJJDP funded an evaluation of the Avon Park Youth Academy (APYA) in Florida and its reentry component, the STREET Smart Program (National Council on Crime and Delinquency, 2009). Youth committed by a juvenile court judge to the Florida Department of Juvenile Justice were placed in the APYA. Using a control group (youth who were in different residential programs and who were released under traditional aftercare programs) and the treatment group (APYA youth who were in the STREET Smart Program), the researchers found that Hispanic youth in the treatment group fared best in terms of employment and recidivism compared with youth in the control group during each of the three years of the study. Black youth in the treatment group also experienced some success when compared to the control group. However, the white youth in the APYA program were not as successful as the white youth in the control group. This study suggests that more research and evaluation of programs offered in residential placement facilities and in aftercare are essential to assess what works best in the long term for youth (National Council on Crime and Delinquency, 2009).

Between November 1987 and November 1988, Ashford and LeCroy (1993, p. 186) investigated state juvenile programs and provisions. They sent letters and surveyed all state juvenile jurisdictions, soliciting information on their juvenile aftercare policies. Their response rate was 94 percent, with responses from 47 of the 50 states. As a result of their survey, they developed a typology of juvenile parole that included eight different kinds of juvenile parole/aftercare used by states:

1. Determinate parole/aftercare (length of aftercare is linked closely with the period of commitment specified by the court; authorities cannot extend confinement period of juvenile beyond original commitment length prescribed by judge; juvenile can be released short of serving the full sentence).

2. Determinate aftercare set by administrative agency (aftercare release date is set immediately following youth's arrival at secure facility).

3. Presumptive minimum with limits on the extension of the supervision period for a fixed or determinate length of time (minimum confinement period is specified; youth must be placed on aftercare after that date unless there is a showing of bad conduct).

4. Presumptive minimum with limits on the extension of supervision for an indeterminate period (aftercare should terminate after fixed period of time; probation/parole officer has the discretion to extend aftercare period with justification for an indeterminate period; aftercare can be extended until youth reaches age of majority and leaves juvenile court jurisdiction).

5. Presumptive minimum with discretionary extension of supervision for an indeterminate period (same as point 4, except probation/parole officer has the discretion to extend aftercare of juvenile with no explicit upper age limit; lacks explicit standards limiting the extension of aftercare).

6. Indeterminate aftercare with a specified maximum and a discretionary minimum length of supervision (follows Model Juvenile Court Act of 1968, providing limits for confinement, but allows parole board authority to specify length of confinement and period of supervised release).

7. Indeterminate aftercare with legal minimum and maximum periods of supervision (board is vested with authority to place youth on aftercare at any time with minimum and maximum confinement periods).

8. Indeterminate or purely discretionary aftercare (length of aftercare is unspecified; may maintain youth on aftercare until youth reach the age of majority, then aftercare is discontinued; may release youth at any time during this period) (Ashford and LeCroy, 1993, pp. 187–191).

Ashford and LeCroy found that indeterminate or purely discretionary aftercare is the most popular type and determinate aftercare/parole is the least popular.

Deciding Who Should Be Placed on Aftercare

The decision to release particular juveniles from residential placement depends upon the jurisdiction. In some state jurisdictions, the dispositions imposed are indeterminate (Archwamety and Katsiyannis, 2000). In 32 states, early release decisions are at the discretion of the particular juvenile correction agency, whereas six states use boards exclusively and five other states depend upon the original sentencing judge's decision. Only a few states have determinate sentencing for youthful offenders; therefore, their early release is established by statute in much the same way as for adult offenders (Archwamety and Katsiyannis, 2000).

In New Jersey, for instance, a seven-member parole board appointed by the governor grants early release to both adult and juvenile offenders. In Utah, a Youth Parole Authority exists, which is a part-time board consisting of three citizens and four staff members from the Utah Division of Youth Corrections. Ideally, paroling authorities utilize objective decision-making criteria in determining which youth should be released short of serving their full terms. Thus, some critics have suggested that the primary early release criteria are related to one's former institutional behavior rather than to other factors, such as one's prospects for successful adaptation to community life, employment, and participation in educational or vocational programs (American Correctional Association, 2007).

Parole boards for both adults and juveniles are comprised of persons who make judgments about offenders on the basis of various factors. Predispositional reports prepared by juvenile probation officers, records of institutional behavior, a youth's appearance and demeanor during the aftercare hearing, and the presence of witnesses or victim statements may affect individual board members. Parole or aftercare decision making is an inexact science. When subjectivity intrudes into the decision-making process, a juvenile's rights are seemingly undermined. Thus, board decision-making profiles may exhibit evidence of early release disparities attributable to both legal and extralegal factors.

Recidivism and Aftercare or Parole Revocation

Recidivism refers to offenders who repeat or subsequently engage in further delinquent or criminal activity after they have been processed by the system. Definitions of recidivism vary. For example, recidivism might be a new arrest. Alternatively, it can refer to offenders who engage in the same offense repeatedly. Its definition could mean a second adjudication or a return to a placement where the youth previously had been held. Juvenile and adult programs strive to reduce recidivism, and programs frequently are evaluated based on their recidivism rates.

Parole revocation is the termination of one's parole program, usually for technical violations but sometimes for recidivism. When parole is revoked, there are several possible outcomes. One is that the offender will be returned to secure confinement. A less-harsh alternative is to move offenders to a different kind of program. For instance, if a juvenile is assigned to a halfway house as part of the aftercare program, the rules of the halfway house must be observed. If one or more rules are violated,

recidivism
New crime committed by an offender who has previously been adjudicated or convicted; prior act may have involved a disposition of probation or commitment to an institution.

parole revocation
Two-stage proceeding that may result in a parolee's reincarceration in jail or prison; the first stage is a preliminary hearing to determine whether the parolee violated any specific parole condition; the second stage is to determine whether parole should be terminated and the offender returned to an institution.

such as failing to observe curfew, failing drug or alcohol urinalyses, or committing new offenses, a report is filed with the court or the juvenile corrections authority for possible revocation. If it is decided that the juvenile's aftercare should be terminated, the result may be that the offender is placed under house arrest or home confinement, coupled with electronic monitoring. Thus, the juvenile would be required to wear an electronic wristlet or anklet and remain on the premises for specified periods. Other program conditions would be applied as well.

The fact is that one is not automatically returned to incarceration following a **parole or aftercare revocation hearing**. Usually, if a return to incarceration is not indicated, the alternatives available are limited only by the array of supervisory resources in the given jurisdiction. These options ordinarily involve more intensive supervision or monitoring of offenders. There may be other factors like severe overcrowding that may discourage revocation decisions to return youth to confinement.

The process of revocation for juveniles is not as straightforward as it is for adult offenders. The U.S. Supreme Court has not ruled thus far concerning how juvenile aftercare revocation should be handled. Furthermore, reliable statistical information about the extent of juvenile aftercare revocations is also lacking.

A probationer's or parolee's right to due process in any probation or parole revocation action was not really considered before 1967. Thus, technical violations, such as failing to submit monthly reports, violating curfew, filing a falsified report, or drinking alcoholic beverages, might result in a recommendation from one's probation/parole officer that the probation or parole program should be terminated.

parole or aftercare revocation hearing
Formal proceeding in which a parole board or designated authority decides whether the parole or aftercare program should be terminated or changed because of one or more program or rule infractions or the commission of a new offense.

Juvenile aftercare violations may result in a youth's apprehension, detention, and subsequent appearance before a juvenile court judge.
(Courtesy of Dean John Champion)

For adult parolees as well as for adult probationers, revocations are currently two-stage proceedings. The landmark cases that have directly affected parolees or probationers and their rights are *Mempa v. Rhay* (1967), *Morrissey v. Brewer* (1972), and *Gagnon v. Scarpelli* (1973). In these three cases, the U.S. Supreme Court justices established the due process rights of offenders who are either facing a deferred sentencing hearing, a parole revocation, or a probation revocation, respectively. Although the cases pertain to adult probationers and parolees, they are significant for juvenile probationers and youth on aftercare as well. Juvenile justice policies are often formulated or influenced on the basis of Supreme Court decisions about the rights of inmates, parolees, or probationers and the procedures involved in their progression through the criminal justice system. Thus, while these cases are not binding on juvenile court judges or juvenile paroling authorities, they provide a legal basis for actions in pertinent juvenile cases, if the juvenile justice system chooses to recognize them.

For juveniles, these three cases are important, because they provide juvenile courts and paroling authorities within juvenile corrections guidelines to follow. It is possible that the U.S. Supreme Court will eventually address probation and parole revocation issues pertaining to juvenile offenders.

Currently, probation and parole revocation proceedings for juveniles differ widely among jurisdictions. The philosophy of *parens patriae* is apparent in most juvenile cases. In some jurisdictions, explicit criteria exist for determining actions relating to juveniles on aftercare who violate program rules or commit new offenses. Statutory constraints also may regulate judicial or parole board decision making in these situations.

Examples of Probation and Aftercare Revocation for Juveniles

State statutes and decisions determine the types of situations and circumstances in which the probation or aftercare programs of juveniles can be revoked. These statutes and decisions provide some indication of what practices are prevalent in states as well as the basis for such revocation actions. However, as noted previously, these rulings pertain to adults rather than juveniles. They may inform juvenile court proceedings, but they are not required. Both juvenile courts and aftercare boards seek guidance from the U.S. Supreme Court or lower appellate courts in their own decision making pertaining to juvenile probation and aftercare.

Juvenile Probation and Aftercare Revocation Cases

Several cases involving revocations of juvenile probation and aftercare have been reported (see below). Probation revocation cases outnumber parole revocation cases by as much as 20 to 1. However, the same rationales used to revoke a probation program are also used to revoke an aftercare program. Thus, for all practical purposes, every jurisdiction can utilize similar criteria for both probation and parole revocation actions.

Some states offer boot camp programs for girls and boys.
(© dov makabaw/Alamy)

John L. v. Superior Court (2004)

John L. was a California juvenile who was adjudicated delinquent. During his probationary term, John L. committed new probation violations. The juvenile court conducted a **probation revocation hearing** and, on the basis of a preponderance of the evidence, extended John L.'s probationary term to the maximum term and intensified the nature of his probation supervision. John L. contested the court's decision, arguing that the beyond a reasonable doubt standard should be used. The appellate court disagreed and allowed the judge's ruling to stand. Under current California juvenile law, if a probation violation occurs, the violator could, at most, receive more restrictive placement within the original maximum term. In John L.'s case, the court held that the preponderance of evidence standard was sufficient to establish John L.'s involvement in the probation violations. Furthermore, new charges are treated like probation violations, and the judge may impose appropriate punishments within the limits of the original probationary term.

Can new probation violations result in more restrictive probation conditions and a longer probationary term within the maximum limits of one's original statutory probation requirements? Yes.

G.L.C. v. State (2005)

In Alabama, G.L.C. was on probation for a delinquent offense. However, G.L.C. violated his probation conditions and committed new offenses. Eventually, G.L.C. served three years of probation. By that time, G.L.C. had reached adulthood. The juvenile court judge sought to extend his probation and issued such an order. However, the order was overturned, because the judge no longer had jurisdiction over G.L.C. Jurisdiction had been transferred to the criminal court, due to G.L.C.'s new adult status. Since adult rules apply, G.L.C. could have either been incarcerated or placed on probation for the new offenses committed.

---

probation revocation hearing

Proceeding wherein it is determined whether to revoke an offender's probation program because of one or more violations.

Secure confinement for juveniles is not pleasant.
(Courtesy of Dean John Champion)

Can juveniles have their probationary terms extended by committing new offenses? Yes and no.

In re Jaime P. (2005)

In Illinois, a minor becomes an adult at age 21. Ordinarily, a juvenile court judge loses jurisdiction over the juvenile when the juvenile reaches this age. In the case of Jaime P., a Class X felony, murder, had been committed. Under other circumstances, terms of probation in Illinois for juveniles extend for a maximum of five years or until the juvenile reaches the age of majority. For Class X felonies, however, the term of probation may be extended beyond age 21. Jaime P. argued that his probation should be terminated when he reached age 21, but the court indicated that the five-year probationary rule did not apply in his case.

Can a juvenile's probation be terminated as the result of achieving adulthood? Yes and no.

In re M.O.R. (2004)

M.O.R. was a juvenile in the District of Columbia placed on probation after he admitted to his involvement in two counts of simple sexual assault. One of his probation conditions was that he participate in a sex offender counseling program. During his probation supervision, the probation officer reported M.O.R.'s progress; these reports were consistently favorable. Toward the end of M.O.R.'s probationary period, a review was conducted wherein the probation officer recommended that M.O.R.'s probation be allowed to terminate, because M.O.R. had responded positively to the counseling program. However, the judge refused based on a therapist's report that M.O.R.'s disorder could not be cured. On appeal, the appellate court reversed the juvenile court's decision, thus terminating M.O.R.'s probation program, because under

District of Columbia law, only the Director of Social Services is authorized to seek an extension of a probationary period. Any juvenile who is subject to an extension must receive proper notice and a hearing to determine that such an extension is warranted. The juvenile court has the authority to review and decide whether to continue a dispositional order if the recommendation by the director is to continue probation. However, if the Director of Social Services decides not to seek an extension of probation, the juvenile court may inquire into, but not review, the director's reasons. The decision to not seek an extension of probation is solely with the Director of Social Services, not the juvenile court.

Can a juvenile court judge order a continuation of sex offender therapy for a juvenile following a favorable recommendation for the termination of probation after a successful term of therapy? No.

State v. Steven B. (2004)

Steven B. was adjudicated delinquent in New Mexico but referred to a diversion program that required completion of school and other conditions. The actual disposition was deferred pending the successful completion of "Grade Court," an educational course of study. Steven B. subsequently violated a condition of the Grade Court, and the juvenile court judge placed him in weekend detention. Steven B. appealed, arguing that detention was excessive and not consistent with rehabilitation. Furthermore, no formal disposition had been entered yet. Thus, the detention was a violation of his due process rights. The appellate court upheld the judge's detention orders. The New Mexico juvenile code authorizes judges to detain children who are adjudicated but not yet disposed and who fail to comply with conditions of release. The juvenile court had the authority to order detention under this statutory provision.

Focus on Delinquency

A 16-year-old youth from River Hills, Wisconsin, used a machete to attack a younger youth in what was apparently an unprovoked assault. The 14-year-old victim required 20 stitches to his head and will have a scar from his wound. The teen who assaulted him turned 17 after the court hearings were scheduled. The youth, who was dressed as a "ninja" during the attack, admitted to the assault and was remorseful. He was charged with a felony of "substantial battery" but pleaded no contest to second-degree reckless injury. The Children's Court judge, Frederick Rosa, accepted the lesser charge because the youth was apologetic for his behavior and demonstrated that he would comply with the court. The use of a weapon and the seriousness of the assault were considerations in the case, but the judge determined that placing the youth in a secure facility was not necessary or warranted under the circumstances. The psychological assessment identified him as a low-risk and low-needs adolescent. The youth was sentenced to probation until he turns 18 and will receive close monitoring while continuing to live with his parents. The judge also ordered counseling for anger management and required the youth to write a letter of apology. The victim's family was in agreement with the disposition and did not want to see the youth incarcerated.

Should the "ninja" youth have been committed to secure confinement instead of probation? Should he have been placed in a halfway house initially? What do you think?

Source: Adapted from Dave Fidlin (2010, August 6), "Teen Gets Probation in 'Ninja' Attack," *Milwaukee Wisconsin Journal Sentinel* (available at http://www.jsonline.com/newswatch/100156394.html).

Can weekend detention be ordered by juvenile court judges for juveniles who violate diversion conditions prior to a formal disposition for delinquency? Yes.

In re Sheena K. (2004)

Sheena K. was a California juvenile who was placed on probation with the order to avoid associating with any persons who the probation officer determined were unsuitable. However, Sheena K. was not advised with whom she should avoid associating. Subsequently, she interacted with one or more persons who the probation officer did not approve of, and the officer sought Sheena K.'s probation program revocation. Sheena K. appealed, arguing that the condition imposed was unconstitutionally vague. The appellate court agreed and reversed Sheena K.'s probation revocation. The appellate court noted that although the condition prohibited the juvenile from associating with any person disapproved by the probation officer, the condition failed to include the requirement that the juvenile be informed of which persons were disapproved.

Can juveniles have their probation revoked for associating with persons disapproved by their probation officer without knowing who these disapproved persons are? No.

In re A.N.A. (2004)

A.N.A., a Texas juvenile probationer, violated one or more terms of his original probation orders. The judge placed A.N.A. on a 12-month probationary term according to A.N.A.'s original conditional disposition. Based on the probation violations, a modification order was entered to redispose A.N.A. to an additional probationary term. In the meantime, the 12-month probationary term for A.N.A. expired. Subsequently, the juvenile court judge imposed an additional 12-month probationary period on A.N.A., and A.N.A. appealed. The Texas appeals court upheld the 12-month probationary extension ordered by the juvenile court judge, because the order to modify A.N.A.'s probation had been entered before the expiration of A.N.A.'s original probationary term, and A.N.A. had violated the original probationary terms. (Compare this case with *G.L.C. v. State* (2005).)

Can a juvenile court judge extend the term of a youth's probation beyond an original period of probation pursuant to an adjudication of delinquency and a probation disposition? Yes.

In re Ruben D. (2001)

Ruben D., a juvenile, was committed to a residential school for a period of years. From time to time, the juvenile court judge would review Ruben D.'s institutional behavior and progress. On the basis of these reports, the judge decided to extend Ruben D.'s commitment to the institution for additional one-year periods. Following one such order, the juvenile parole board convened and acknowledged that Ruben D.'s original commitment order had expired. The parole board did not acknowledge the extension of the commitment order by the juvenile court judge. Ruben D. appealed, contending that he should be paroled because of the juvenile parole board's acknowledgement that his commitment term had expired. The appellate court upheld the juvenile court judge's authority to extend Ruben D.'s commitment by one-year periods until Ruben D. reached 21 years of age. The order that extended the commitment of Ruben D. was affirmed.

Can juvenile parole boards terminate a juvenile's commitment to an institution and grant parole despite a judge's order to continue the juvenile's commitment for a period of time until the juvenile is 21? No.

K.G. v. State (2000)

K.G., a female juvenile, was adjudicated delinquent and committed to a juvenile secure facility. Subsequently K.G. was placed on aftercare. The parole board implied that it would be a good idea for K.G. to participate in a particular program involving treatment for substance abuse, which was a problem K.G. had had before being committed. K.G. did not participate in the aftercare program, however, and the parole board sought to revoke her parole program. K.G. appealed, contending that no specific orders required her to participate in the aftercare program following the completion of the term of commitment. The appellate court reversed the parole board, holding that there was no showing that K.G. had been properly transferred to the aftercare program following the term of commitment. For a violation of an aftercare program to be upheld, a valid written order by the board must have been stipulated. Because no written orders had been violated, K.G. was reinstated into her aftercare program.

Can a juvenile have his or her aftercare revoked for violating an implied rather than written order requiring him or her to participate in a particular program following his or her release from commitment? No.

Selected Issues in Juvenile Corrections

An investigation of the number of youth in residential placement indicated that fewer youth were in placement in 2008 compared to 2000. In 2008, there were less than 81,000 youth in residential placements, and that was the lowest number since 1993 (Sickmund, 2010). Although the decrease in placement rates between 1997 and 2008 was 26 percent, the arrest rates for that same period of time declined by 33 percent (Sickmund, 2010). These data demonstrate that fewer youth are being arrested, but the decline in placement does not entirely reflect the decline in arrests (Figure 12.6). A number of explanations for this finding are possible. These include the increase in formal processing of youth in the system, the more punitive get-tough stance, and net-widening.

At the same time, there have been reports of abuse in juvenile correctional facilities by staff and other residents. In New York State, for example, following the 2006 death of Darryl Thompson, an emotionally disturbed 15-year-old youth, in the state's Tryon Residential Center, a two-year U.S. Department of Justice investigation found that in four state-run facilities, youth were subject to emotional abuse, excessive use of physical force, and extreme restraints. The Department of Justice had identified the New York juvenile justice system as regularly violating the constitutional

Between 1997 and 2008, the decline in placement rates (26%) was not as sharp as the decline in arrest rates (33%)

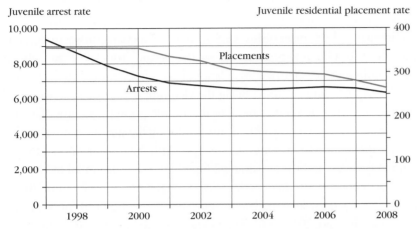

Figure 12.6

Comparison of the Decline in Arrest Rates with Residential Placement, 1997 and 2008

Source: Melissa Sickmund (2010). Juveniles in Residential Placement, 1997–2008. Washington, DC: Office of Juvenile Justice and Delinquency Prevention.

rights of youth and failing to provide adequate care to youth (Task Force on Transforming Juvenile Justice, 2009). In response, Governor David Paterson established the Task Force on Transforming Juvenile Justice to formulate recommendations for reforming the system and shifting the emphasis from punishment to a more rehabilitative model (Task Force on Transforming Juvenile Justice, 2009). The report included 20 recommendations for limiting the use of institutional placement and making facilities more therapeutic and supportive. Included in these recommendations, the Task Force favored a more balanced approach that "promotes public safety, holds youth accountable for their actions, and produces positive outcomes for young people and their families" (Task Force on Transforming Juvenile Justice, 2009, p. 11). The reform proposals provided direction for developing more community-based interventions, including services and support for reentry. The report underscored the importance of "ensuring system accountability" (Task Force on Transforming Juvenile Justice, 2009, p. 9).

In 2010, Governor Paterson announced a series of additional reforms to provide expanded oversight and to improve the conditions and operations of the four facilities that were targeted by the Department of Justice (Office of Children and Family Services, 2010). The reforms required enhanced policies and practices for use of restraint, for screening and assessment, for emergency responses and mental health care for youth, and for the addition of counselors and direct care staff (Office of Children and Family Services, 2010, para. 5). The Tryon Residential Center where Darryl Thompson died after he was restrained and held down by staff was scheduled to be closed (Karlin, 2010).

Sexual assault in confinement is another area that requires greater attention and concern. When the Prison Rape Elimination Act was signed into law in 2003, its provisions mandated data collection for youth and adult facilities. In accordance with the requirements, the Bureau of Justice Statistics conducted a survey of youth in 195 facilities, both public and private, during the period from 2008 to 2009 (Beck, Harrison, and Guerino, 2010). These data indicate that approximately 3,200 youth in custody (over 90 days) reported being the victim of one or more sexual assaults by either a staff member or another resident during the prior 12 months. This number represents about 12 percent of youth in custody during the survey time period. Of these 12 percent, the reported victimizations were primarily by staff members (over 10 percent) in the facilities, and the remaining 2.6 percent were categorized by the youth respondent as involving another resident (Beck, Harrison, and Guerino, 2010, p.1). According to these data, six states had victimization rates of 30 percent or more (Beck, Harrison, and Guerino, 2010, p. 5). These data are troubling and suggest that there may be a climate in certain institutions that tolerates or even condones youth victimization.

As discussed in Chapter 4, two judges in Luzerne County, Pennsylvania, received over $2 million dollars in kickbacks for sending kids to out-of-home placements. This extreme example highlighted concern about the rights and protection of children and youth, many of whom appeared in court without legal counsel (Juvenile Law Center, n.d.). After the kids for cash scandal, Governor Ed Rendell signed legislation to create the **Interbranch Commission on Juvenile Justice** (2010) which was charged with making recommendations to reform Pennsylvania's juvenile justice system to protect children and youth from future abuses.

These kinds of incidents are troubling for youth and society. They suggest that advocacy is an essential component of juvenile justice. In addition, there has to be ongoing monitoring of the due process protections of youth in court and the facilities where they are placed.

In 1985, the United Nations and National Council of Juvenile and Family Court Judges adopted policy statements about the juvenile justice system that bear directly on juvenile corrections (Office of the United Nations High Commissioner for Human Rights, 2005). The issues discussed in this final section may be better understood in the context of these statements. Several recommendations also have been made by Dwyer and McNally (1987, pp. 50–51):

1. Primary dispositions of juvenile courts should have a flexible range for restricting freedom, with the primary goal focused on the restoration to full liberty rather than on letting the punishment fit the crime; that no case dispositions should be of a mandatory nature but, rather, should be based on the discretion of the judge on predetermined dispositional guidelines.

2. Individualized treatment of juveniles should be continued, including the development of medical, psychiatric, and educational programs that range from least to most restrictive, according to individual need.

Interbranch Commission on Juvenile Justice

Appointed in Pennsylvania after the Luzerne County kids for cash scandal to investigate the juvenile justice system in the state and to assess its success in serving youth; made recommendations to improve the system's effectiveness and safeguard youth from any future abuse or mistreatment like that which occurred in Luzerne County.

3. While being held accountable, chronic, serious juvenile offenders should be retained within the jurisdiction of the juvenile court. As a resource, specialized programs and facilities need to be developed that focus on restorations rather than punishment.

4. Policymakers, reformers, and researchers should strive for a greater understanding as to the causes and most desired response to juvenile crime; that research should be broad-based rather than limited to management, control, and punishment strategies.

5. When the juvenile court judge believes that the juvenile under consideration is not amenable to the services of the court and based on the youth's present charges, past record in court, and his or her age and mental status, the judge may waive jurisdiction; that in all juvenile cases, the court of original jurisdiction be that of the juvenile court; that the discretion to waive be left to the juvenile court judge; that the proportionality of punishment be appropriate with these cases, but that the most high-risk offenders should be treated in small secure facilities.

Each of the issues discussed below is affected directly by these recommendations and policy statements. These issues include (1) the privatization of juvenile corrections; (2) the classification of juvenile offenders; (3) evidence-based practice; (4) juveniles held in adult jails or lockups; and (5) juveniles in adult prisons.

The Privatization of Juvenile Corrections

Juvenile residential placements have some of the same problems as adult correctional institutions. Overcrowding in residential facilities has been reported in a number of jurisdictions. For example, the 2006 census of juvenile residential facilities found that 31 percent of the facilities reported that the number of residents in custody resulted in their being either at capacity or over capacity (Hockenberry, Sickmund, and Sladky, 2009). The conditions of some of the facilities can best be characterized as deteriorating. With an emphasis on more punitive juvenile sentencing policies, youth in secure custody environments may need more advocates.

Privatization is one solution to overcrowding and to publicly operated facilities. **Privatization** refers to the establishment and operation of correctional services and institutions by nongovernmental interests, including private corporations and businesses (Armstrong, 2001). Private organizations and agencies have been involved in the delivery of services for youth since the beginning of the juvenile court. Private organizations operate shelter care facilities, detention centers, ranches and camps, training schools, and residential treatment centers (Sickmund, 2010). According to the census of juveniles in residential placement, private organizations dominate in group home placements (Sickmund, 2010).

Nonsecure and secure facilities are both publicly and privately operated. Florida is one of several states with various forms of private juvenile secure confinement. Historically, Florida has addressed youthful offending through incarceration,

privatization

Private agencies or corporations involved in the management and operations of correctional institutions.

including placement of serious offenders in reform or training schools (Rivers, Dembo, and Anwyl, 1998). The first private institution for male juvenile offenders opened in Florida in 1970. By 1972, four schools were operating in various jurisdictions throughout the state. Partly because of serious institutional overcrowding, Florida officials eventually decided to "shift their incarceration priorities to the development of less-secure, community-based facilities" (Pingree, 1984, p. 60). Florida's objectives are to (1) reduce the number of juveniles actually placed in secure confinement facilities and (2) provide juveniles with a broader base of community options that will be instrumental in helping them to acquire vocational training and education. Trained counselors work closely with Florida juvenile offenders to meet their psychological and social needs more effectively. The Florida model has served as an example for other jurisdictions.

When the private sector operates or administers juvenile facilities, they can be categorized as either "for profit" or "not for profit." A "for profit" designation refers to a corporation or organization that intends to make a profit on its involvement in juvenile corrections. By contrast, a "not for profit" corporation seeks to generate revenue to cover the costs associated with staff and overhead expenses but not to actually profit financially from its involvement in juvenile corrections. Most private correctional agencies or organizations that deliver services for juveniles are characterized as "not for profit" organizations.

Currently, juvenile correctional facilities comprise a large share of the private sector's business. According to the census data on residential facilities, 56 percent of all juvenile facilities are operated by the private sector (Sickmund, 2010, p. 3). However, there have been continuing debates about the effectiveness of private corrections (Kyle, 1998).

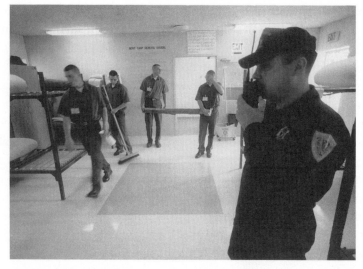

A small proportion of youth are actually confined in secure facilities.
(Courtesy of Mark C. Ide)

Privatization advocates report that these facilities can work cooperatively with the public sector in providing the best of both worlds for offenders. Private sector operations have the ability to recognize employees for excellent service performed and to implement new operational ideas more quickly compared with government organizations. However, these facilities may be more likely to experience rapid turnover in staff, because the benefits and salaries are not commensurate with those offered by public facilities. This instability in the staff can affect the institution or the care provided to youth.

In addition, private agencies and organizations are able to be more selective about which youth are admitted to their programs. Public facilities do not have this option. As a result, allegations of "creaming" have been made against private placement agencies or corporations. **Creaming** refers to the judicious selection of residents for programs where dangerous, violent, or chronic youth are excluded. Public facility advocates contend that such selectivity affects recidivism data and suggest that private facilities are viewed as more successful in preventing further offending when, in reality, they may select offenders for participation who are more likely to complete the program and refrain from reoffending.

creaming
Term used to refer to private agencies and organizations who selectively admit youth into their programs and facilities.

In summary, several important issues relating to the privatization of corrections for both adult and juvenile offenders have been outlined:

1. What standards will govern the operation of the institution?
2. Who will monitor the implementation of the standards?
3. Will the public still have access to the facility?
4. What recourse will members of the public have if they do not approve of how the institution is operated?
5. Who will be responsible for maintaining security and using force at the institution?
6. Who will have the responsibility for disciplinary procedures?
7. Will the company be able to refuse to accept certain offenders, such as those with AIDS?
8. What options will be available to the government if the corporation substantially raises its fees?
9. What safeguards will prevent a private contractor from making a low initial bid to obtain a contract and then raising the price after the government is no longer immediately able to reassume the task of operating the facility?
10. What safeguards will prevent private vendors, after gaining a foothold in the corrections field, from lobbying in support of philosophical changes for their greater profit? (Robbins, 1986, p. 29)

Classification of Juvenile Offenders

Classification of offenders is difficult because the state of the art in predictions of risk and dangerousness in such that little future behavior can be accurately forecasted (Lusignan and Marleau, 2007). This holds for juveniles as well as for adults. Fully

Suicide Screening	2000	2002	2006
Total juvenile offenders	110,284	102,388	92,093
Offenders in reporting facilities	104,956	100,110	79,477
Total offenders	100%	100%	100%
All youth screened	78%	81%	88%
Some youth screened	16%	12%	4%
No youth screened	6%	7%	8%

Figure 12.7
*Source: Sarah Hockenberry, Melissa Sickmund, and Anthony Sladky
(2009). Juvenile Residential Facility Census, 2006: Selected Findings.
Washington, DC: Office of Juvenile Justice and Delinquency
Prevention.*

effective classification schemes have not yet been developed and implemented for all types of juvenile offenders, although on the basis of descriptions of existing aggregates of offenders, we know that factors such as gender, age, nature of offense, seriousness of offense, and socioeconomic status may be more or less correlated (Loukas, Suizzo, and Prelow, 2007). Various types of classification instruments are utilized in juvenile justice.

Most frequently, juvenile residential facilities attempt to determine the risk of suicide (Figure 12.7). For example, data from the 2006 census on residential placement indicate that 34 percent of facilities use the Massachusetts Youth Screening Instrument (MAYSI) to assess the suicide risk of newly admitted youth (Hockenberry, Sickmund, and Sladky, 2009). Those institutions that do not use a specific risk assessment tool rely on professional or paraprofessional staff to conduct these screenings. Overall, 88 percent of the facilities reporting indicated that they use some type of screening process to evaluate suicide risk. These instruments and professionals or paraprofessionals help staff to identify youth who are at risk of suicide and to offer protection and services designed to help youth.

Flaws in classification schemes are made apparent when program failures are detected in large numbers (McGhee and Waterhouse, 2007). It has been suggested that risk assessment instruments could help inform judicial decisions in juvenile cases (Mulvey and Iselin, 2008). Rather than substitute risk assessment scores for the judge's discretion, these instruments could assist judges and professionals in determining the best approach to take and the youth's amenability to treatment. Judges could ask how the professional's recommended disposition concurs or deviates from that based on the risk assessment instrument. In that way, judges and staff would be able to retain their commitment to individualized justice and also ascertain which recommendations may be appropriate using the results of a more objective tool (Mulvey and Iselin, 2008).

Intake officers can make similar errors of classification when conducting initial screenings of juveniles. Overall, intake decisions seem to be based on intuition rather than on objective risk screening instruments (Mulvey and Iselin, 2008). Utilizing some type of screening device could assist intake staff not only in considering alternatives but also in reinforcing their own recommendations. The issue of false positives and false negatives is raised here, because some youth may be unfairly sanctioned for what authorities believe are valid predictive criteria of future dangerousness. Conversely, some youth avoid sanctions, because it is believed that they will not pose risks or commit serious offenses in the future. These assumptions sometimes are proven to be incorrect (Lusignan and Marleau, 2007).

Evidence-Based Practice

When determining which programs are most effective in juvenile justice, there has been an increasing emphasis on **evidence-based practice**. Rather than simply adopting a policy or strategy for dealing with youth based on tradition or opinion, evidence-based practice typically requires a theoretical foundation, a rigorous evaluation, and replication among different groups to assess program effectiveness. This is not always as easy as it appears. For more than a decade, evidence on which strategies have proven to be effective has been disseminated. However, only about five percent of youth who would be good candidates for these programs are in them (Greenwood, 2008). This is another issue that merits further attention. Specifically, how do we get states and local jurisdictions to adopt successful strategies?

> **evidence-based practice**
> Research conducted on programs that has a theoretical foundation and utilizes control and experimental groups to determine effectiveness; programs that have been proven to be successful after replication at various locations using a rigorous research design rather than using tradition or past practice.

More research has been conducted on programs in schools and in the community for youth and their families before placement in a residential facility than has been conducted on programs that work in residential placement. Overall, Greenwood (2008) found programs that emphasize specific skills areas, such as behavior management, "training in interpersonal skills, family counseling, group counseling, or individual counseling," have shown positive effects in youth in residential environments (p. 200). For youth who are in an institutional setting, cognitive-behavioral therapy, aggression replacement training, and family integrated transition are examples of programs that are relevant and successful (Greenwood, 2008, p. 200). However, for these strategies to be implemented, there has to be a system-wide commitment to them, uniform training of all participants, consistency in the delivery of the treatment, careful monitoring of practitioners who are working with youth, and a sophisticated evaluation process (Greenwood, 2008).

The Center for Juvenile Justice Reform at Georgetown University launched the Juvenile Justice System Improvement Project in 2011. Its goal is to work with the OJJDP to provide states with information on programs and strategies that are effective, to train professionals to implement them, and to assist professionals in various jurisdictions to evaluate these programs (Center for Juvenile Justice Reform, 2011). These collaborative approaches can improve current juvenile justice policy.

Greenwood (2008) contends that "[e]very year of delay in implementing evidence-based reforms consigns another cohort of juvenile offenders to a 50 percent higher than necessary recidivism rate" (p. 205). Absent such a commitment, juvenile offenders will be subjected to the same methods of the past and are likely to remain ill-equipped for the future.

Juveniles Held in Adult Jails or Lockups

Four of the most critical problems with placing juveniles in adult lockups or jails are that (1) youth are subject to potential assault from other inmates and staff, (2) these facilities were not intended for youth confinement and do not offer the programs and services most appropriate for youth, (3) youth are able to become more delinquent or criminal as a result of their incarceration with more-serious and chronic offenders, and (4) the reality of being confined in a jail can affect youth adversely. The latter problem leads to another that is even more serious—jail suicides. Juveniles can be especially suicide prone during the early stage of their incarceration in jails.

The JJDPA of 1974 has two provisions that address youth in adult institutions. It mandates "the removal of juveniles from adult jails and lockups" and it requires the "sight-and-sound separation of juveniles from adults in detention and correctional facilities" (The Mandates of the JJDPA, 1994, para. 1). The first part of this section of the law allows youth to be held for up to six hours awaiting transfer to a juvenile facility or release to a parent or guardian. When the Administrator of the OJJDP, the Honorable J. Robert Flores, testified before Senate Judiciary Committee in 2007, he reported significant progress in addressing these two issues. Specifically, he presented data illustrating that jail separation violations decreased by 98 percent from the time the JJDPA of 1974 was enacted until 2007 and that jail removal violations decreased by 95 percent (Flores, 2007). These data provide evidence that states have endeavored to comply with the requirements of the original legislation.

Currently, there are organized movements in some jurisdictions to mandate the complete removal of juveniles from adult jails, including even those youth being held for a short time. Civil rights suits as well as class action claims also have been filed by and on behalf of juveniles currently detained in adult facilities (Gallagher and Dobrin, 2007). In the Iowa case of *Hendrickson v. Griggs* (1987), a federal district judge, Donald E. O'Brien, ruled that the JJDPA could be used as the basis for a lawsuit seeking the permanent removal of juveniles from adult jails. Although there has been progress on this issue, more remains to be done to address the issue of youth in adult jails.

Juveniles in Adult Prisons

When youth are transferred to adult court for case processing, there is a possibility that if convicted, they will receive the same sentence that an adult would receive, including incarceration in prison. In *Graham v. Florida* (2010), the U.S. Supreme Court determined that life without parole sentences for juveniles who were tried as adults for nonhomicide offenses violated the Eighth Amendment prohibition against cruel and unusual punishment. However, the Supreme Court did not rule on life without parole sentences for youth who are tried as adults and convicted of homicide. Most juveniles are not convicted of homicide, and they do not receive a life sentence. Nonetheless, juveniles who were convicted in adult court can be sentenced to adult prison, where they are subject to the same conditions of confinement as adult offenders.

Juveniles sentenced to prison are more likely to experience **straight adult incarceration** than to be placed in a specific prison designed for youth (Fritsch and Caeti, 2009). In 2008, it was estimated that over 3,600 juveniles under the age of 18 were in state prisons (West and Sabol, 2009). Clearly, some of these youth were already considered to be adults by virtue of state statutes that terminated juvenile court jurisdiction at age 17. Nonetheless, the large majority of them were juveniles who had been transferred to adult court and then sanctioned as adults. In addition, the number of youth under age 18 in state prisons is disproportionately black and Hispanic (Merlo, 2000). Research also indicates that youth incarcerated with adults in prison are more likely to be victimized by other offenders when compared to youth in juvenile residential facilities, and they have a greater likelihood of reoffending after release (Austin, Johnson, and Gregoriou, 2000; Redding, 2010; Washington Coalition for the Just Treatment of Youth, 2009).

These data suggest that incarcerating youth in adult prisons is a significant issue and that juvenile institutions may be more appropriate for youthful offenders. Recent research on adolescent brain development, public opinion research, and legislative changes also signal a more treatment-oriented stance for the future. Taken together, it appears that this might be an ideal time to revisit the issue of incarcerating youth in adult prisons.

> **straight adult incarceration**
> Refers to youth in adult prisons where there is no special housing unit for them; instead, they are subject to regular incarceration and treated like other adult offenders.

SUMMARY

Each year, large numbers of youth are under correctional supervision in the United States. Juvenile corrections encompass all of the agencies, personnel, organizations, and institutions that supervise or hold youthful offenders. Juvenile probationers and those on aftercare as well as youth diverted from the system can be under the general supervisory control of one or more community corrections agencies. The goals of juvenile corrections include deterrence, rehabilitation and reintegration, punishment and retribution, and isolation and control. These goals were described and discussed.

Correctional facilities for juveniles include both secure and nonsecure settings. Nonsecure options include shelter care placement (halfway houses and group homes), foster home placement, and placement in camps, ranches, experience programs and wilderness experiences. These types of programs and facilities were described. These programs provide youth with skills and self-sufficiency and are intended to make them less dependent on adverse influences, such as other delinquent peers or adult offenders. Residential placement is intended for youth who need to be in a setting that offers treatment and more intensive supervision.

Boot camps are highly regimented, military-like facilities that use strict discipline, hard work, and physical training to provide unmanageable youth greater structure in their lives. Both male and female juveniles may be placed in boot camp programs. Youth who participate in boot camps are offenders who are carefully screened and scrutinized for inclusion. Boot camps and their operations were described.

Secure confinement for juveniles also includes industrial or schools or residential treatment programs and detention centers for both long-term and short-term confinement, respectively. Short-term detention of juveniles averages 30 days, while long-term confinement can be a year or longer. Judges determine if a youth should be held in detention or committed to the care and custody of a correctional agency.

Juvenile aftercare was examined. Juvenile aftercare is designed to alleviate industrial school overcrowding, permit youth to become reintegrated into their communities, develop opportunities for youth to apply the vocational skills and education they have attained in confinement, and deter youth from future offending by exercising regular supervision. Little, if any, U.S. Supreme Court case law exists concerning the conditions under which juvenile probation or parole can be revoked. Instead, juvenile court judges and parole boards have relied on the decisions of several key adult cases since the late 1960s. Several state-level cases involving probation and aftercare revocation proceedings for juveniles were examined.

Several juvenile corrections issues were discussed. These included the privatization of juvenile corrections, the classification of juveniles, evidence-based practice, holding juveniles in adult jails or lockups, and youth in adult prisons. Historically, the private sector has been engaged in juvenile corrections. However, the more recent trend is for private corporations to have a greater presence in the field of juvenile corrections. Various issues in this area were examined. A number of jurisdictions utilize classification techniques for juvenile offenders, and these instruments range from assisting professionals in determining suicide risk to helping judges select the appropriate disposition. Overall, evidence-based practice has been adopted by only a small number of jurisdictions. Research has identified a number of successful strategies for youth in residential placements.

Another issue is the removal of youth from adult jails, which has been in effect for approximately four decades. This initiative was described and explained. Progress in this area has been documented. The fifth issue concerns juveniles who have been transferred to adult court, convicted, and sentenced to incarceration in adult prisons. Youth in adult prisons have a greater risk of victimization from adult offenders and more opportunity to learn criminal behavior. Their recidivism rates also tend to be higher than those of youth retained under juvenile court jurisdiction and held in juvenile residential placement. With the recent research on adolescent brain development and public opinion, this might be an ideal time to reconsider the use of adult prisons for youth and to rely more on juvenile institutions.

KEY TERMS

foster homes, 435
emancipation, 436
group homes, 437
halfway houses, 438
parolees, 438
wilderness
    projects, 439
shock probation, 440
shock parole, 440
combination
    sentences, 440
split sentences, 440
mixed sentences, 440
intermittent sentences, 440
jail as a condition of
    probation, 441
shock incarceration, 441
boot camps, 441
Army Model, 441
About Face, 442

Intensive Motivational
    Program of Alternative
    Correctional Treatment
    (IMPACT), 443
industrial schools, 446
training schools, 446
secure treatment
    facilities, 446
commitment
    placements, 446
detention centers, 450
Juvenile Detention
    Alternatives Initiative
    (JDAI), 450
detention hearing, 451
long-term detention, 451
short-term
    confinement, 451
disproportionate minority
    confinement, 454

disproportionate minority
    contact, 454
aftercare, 456
reentry, 456
juvenile offender laws, 457
recidivism, 461
parole revocation, 461
parole or aftercare
    revocation
    hearing, 462
probation revocation
    hearing, 464
Interbranch Commission
    on Juvenile Justice, 470
privatization, 471
creaming, 473
evidence-based
    practice, 475
straight adult
    incarceration, 477

QUESTIONS FOR REVIEW

1. What are four goals of juvenile corrections? How effectively are these goals achieved?

2. What are foster homes? How do they differ from group homes?

3. What are halfway houses? What are their functions and goals?

4. What are wilderness experiences? What are their functions?

5. What is meant by shock probation? What are different types of shock probation? What are some major differences among them?

6. What is a boot camp? What are some specific goals and features of boot camps? Are boot camps effective? Why, or why not?

7. What are some major differences between short- and long-term secure juvenile facilities?

8. What is meant by juvenile aftercare? How much juvenile aftercare is there? Is juvenile aftercare successful? Why, or why not?

9. Which three adult probation and parole revocation cases have guided state juvenile probation and parole revocation decision making?

10. What are three examples of probation and parole revocation cases for juveniles?

INTERNET CONNECTIONS

BootCamps.com
http://www.bootcamps.com

Boot Camps Info
http://www.boot-camps-info.com

Building Blocks for Youth
http://www.cclp.org/building_blocks.php

California Prison Industry Authority
http://www.pia.ca.gov/

Center on Juvenile and Criminal Justice
http://www.cjcj.org/

Child Trends: Violent Crime Victimization
http://www.childtrendsdatabank.org/?q=node/75

Coalition for Juvenile Justice
http://www.juvjustice.org/

Families and Corrections Network
http://www.fcnetwork.org/

Federal Bureau of Prisons
http://www.bop.gov/

Juvenile Law Center
http://www.jlc.org/

Prison Activist Resource Center
http://www.prisonactivist.org/

Real Justice
http://www.realjustice.org/

Glossary

About Face Louisiana boot camp program which offers education, discipline, treatment and aftercare services for offenders.

Acceptance of responsibility Genuine admission or acknowledgment of wrongdoing; in federal presentence investigation reports, for example, convicted offenders may write an explanation and apology for the crime(s) they committed; a provision that may be considered in deciding whether leniency should be extended to offenders during the sentencing phase of their processing.

Act to Regulate the Treatment and Control of Dependent, Neglected, and Delinquent Children, Illinois Juvenile Court Act Passed by the Illinois legislature in 1899; established first juvenile court among states; also known as the Illinois Juvenile Court Act.

Actuarial justice The traditional orientation of juvenile justice, rehabilitation, and individualized treatment has been supplanted by the goal of efficient offender processing.

Actuarial prediction Projection of future behavior based on a class of offenders similar to those considered for parole; the traditional orientation of juvenile justice, rehabilitation, and individualized treatment has been supplanted by the goal of efficient offender processing.

Addams, Jane Established Hull House in Chicago in 1889; assisted wayward and homeless youth.

Adjudication Judgment or action on a petition filed with the juvenile court.

Adjudication hearing, adjudicatory hearing Formal proceeding involving a prosecuting attorney and a defense attorney in which evidence is presented and the juvenile's involvement is determined by the juvenile judge; about one-fifth of all jurisdictions permit jury trials for juveniles under certain circumstances.

Adult judge model Version of teen court in which adult judges preside and youth perform the roles of prosecutor, defense counsel, and jury.

Adversarial proceedings Opponent-driven court litigation in which one side opposes the other; prosecution seeks to convict or find defendants guilty, while defense counsel seeks to defend their clients and seek their acquittal.

Aftercare Describes a wide variety of programs and services available to juvenile offenders; includes halfway houses, psychological counseling services, community-based correctional agencies, employment assistance, and medical treatment designed to assist youth after their release from residential placement.

Aggravating circumstances Factors that may enhance the severity of one's sentence; these include brutality of act, whether serious bodily injury or death occurred to a victim during crime commission, and whether offender was on probation or parole when the crime was committed.

Alternative Dispute Resolution (ADR) Procedure in which a case is handled using an impartial arbiter and in which both parties agree to amicable settlement; criminal court is not used for resolving such matters; usually reserved for minor offenses; court-approved mediation programs in which civilians are selected from the community to help resolve minor delinquency, status offense, and abuse/neglect cases without formal judicial hearings.

American Correctional Association (ACA) Established in 1870 to disseminate information about correctional programs and correctional training; designed to foster professionalism throughout the correctional community.

Anamnestic prediction Projection of behavior according to past circumstances.

Anchorage Youth Court (AYC) Teen court established in Anchorage, Alaska, in 1989; cases include minor misdemeanor offenders; juries of one's peers decide punishments after youth admit guilt in advance of trial proceedings; sanctions include restitution and community service.

Anomie Condition of feelings of helplessness and normlessness.

Anomie theory Robert Merton's theory, influenced by Emile Durkheim, alleging that persons acquire desires for culturally approved goals to strive to achieve but adopt innovative, sometimes deviant means to achieve these goals (e.g., someone may desire a nice home but lack or reject the institutionalized means to achieve this goal, instead using bank robbery to obtain money to realize the culturally approved goal); implies normlessness.

Appeal to higher loyalties A technique of neutralization that suggests individuals have loyalties to groups or others; these loyalties are important and supercede any rules or laws that society imposes; offenders are engaging in acts to help their friends rather than to hurt someone else; their motives are altruistic.

Arraignment Following booking, a critical stage of the criminal justice process in which defendants are asked to enter a plea to criminal charges, a trial date is established, and a formal list of charges is provided.

Arrest Taking persons into custody and restraining them until they can be brought before court to answer the charges against them.

Atavism Positivist school of thought arguing that a biological condition renders a person incapable of living within the social constraints of a society; the idea that physical characteristics can distinguish criminals from the general population and are evolutionary throwbacks to animals or primitive people.

At-risk youth Any juveniles who are considered as more susceptible to the influence of gangs and delinquent peers; tend to be characterized as having learning disabilities, greater immaturity, lower socioeconomic status, and parental dysfunction as well as being otherwise disadvantaged by their socioeconomic and environmental circumstances.

Attachment The most important element of social control theory; refers to identification with parents, teachers, and peers as well as attention to their opinions and a sensitivity to their priorities; fosters conformity.

Automatic transfer laws Jurisdictional laws that provide for automatic waivers of juveniles to criminal court for processing; legislatively prescribed directive to transfer juveniles of specified ages to jurisdiction of criminal courts.

Bail Surety provided by defendants or others to guarantee their subsequent appearance in court to face criminal charges; available to anyone entitled to bail; denied when suspects are considered to be dangerous or likely to flee.

Balanced approach Probation orientation that simultaneously emphasizes community protection, offender accountability, individualization of treatments, and competency assessment and development.

Balanced and Restorative Justice (BARJ) A juvenile justice system model that emphasizes accountability, public safety, and competency development.

Banishment Sanction used to punish offenders by barring them from a specified number of miles from settlements or towns; often a capital punishment, because those banished could not obtain food or water to survive the isolation.

Barker balancing test Speedy trial standard in which delays are considered in terms of the reason or length and in accordance with time standards that have been established through an interpretation of the Sixth Amendment from the case of *Barker v. Wingo* (1972).

Beats Patrol areas assigned to police officers in neighborhoods.

Beccaria, Cesare (1738–1794) Developed classical school of criminology; considered to be "father of classical criminology"; wrote *Essays on Crimes and Punishments*; believed corporal punishment to be unjust and ineffective and that crime could be prevented by plain legal codes specifying prohibited behaviors and punishments; promoted "just deserts" philosophy; also endorsed a utilitarianism approach to criminal conduct and its punishment by suggesting that useful, purposeful, and reasonable punishments should be formulated and applied; also viewed criminal conduct as pleasurable to criminals, that they sought pleasure and avoided pain, and thus, that pain might function as a deterrent to criminal behavior.

Belief One element of social control theory; includes an understanding of respect for authority and the law; also refers to a recognition of the rights of others and adherence to a common value system.

Beyond a reasonable doubt Evidentiary standard used in criminal courts to establish guilt or innocence of criminal defendant and utilized in delinquency proceedings.

Big Brothers/Big Sisters of America (BBBSA) Federation of over 500 agencies to serve children and adolescents; adults relate on a one-to-one basis with youth to promote their self-esteem and self-sufficiency; utilizes volunteers who attempt to instill responsibility, excellence, and leadership among assisted youth.

Biological determinism View in criminology holding that criminal behavior has physiological basis; genes, foods and food additives, hormones, and inheritance are all believed to play a role in determining individual behavior; one's genetic makeup causes certain behaviors, such as criminality, to manifest.

Blended sentencing Any type of sentencing procedure in which either a criminal or a juvenile court judge can impose both juvenile and/or adult penalties.

Blueprints for Violence Prevention Evidence-based programs for delinquency prevention and intervention.

Bonding theory Key concept in a number of theoretical formulations; Emile Durkheim's notion that deviant behavior is controlled to the degree that group members feel morally bound to one another, are committed to common goals, and share a collective conscience; in social control theory, the elements of attachment, commitment, involvement, and belief; explanation of criminal behavior implying that criminality results from a loosening of bonds or attachments with society; builds on differential association theory; primarily designed to account for juvenile delinquency.

Boston Gun Project Police and probation officer partnership to target juveniles on probation for special supervision to reduce gun violence.

Bridewell Workhouse Sixteenth-century London jail (sometimes called gaol) established in 1557; known for providing cheap labor to business and mercantile interests; jailers and sheriffs profited from prisoner exploitation.

Bullying Prevention Program Targets bullies in elementary, middle, and high schools; vests school authorities with intervention powers to establish class rules for disciplining bullies and bullying behavior through student committees.

Career escalation Moving as a juvenile offender to progressively more-serious offenses as new offenses are committed; for example, committing new violent offenses after adjudications for property offenses is career escalation.

CASASTART Program Targets high-risk youth who are exposed to drugs and delinquent activity; decreases risk factors by greater community involvement.

Caseloads Number of cases that a probation or parole officer is assigned according to criteria of case assignment; caseloads vary among jurisdictions.

Case supervision planning Means whereby a probation or parole department makes assignments of probationers or parolees to probation officers or parole officers.

Certification Similar to waivers or transfers; in some jurisdictions, juveniles are certified or designated as adults for the purpose of pursuing a criminal prosecution against them.

Chancellors Civil servants who acted on behalf of the King of England during the Middle Ages; chancellors held court and settled property disputes, trespass cases, and minor property offenses as well as those involving thievery, vagrancy, and public drunkenness.

Chancery courts, Courts of equity Court of equity rooted in early English common law where civil disputes are resolved; also responsible for juvenile matters and adjudicating family matters, such as divorce; have jurisdiction over contract disputes, property boundary claims, and exchanges of goods disputes.

Child savers, child savers movement Organized effort during early 1800s in the United States, comprised primarily of upper- and middle-class interests who sought to provide assistance to wayward youth; assistance was often food and shelter, although social, educational, and religious values were introduced to children later in compulsory schooling.

Children in need of supervision (CHINS) Any children determined by the juvenile court and other agencies to be in need of care or supervision.

Children's tribunals Informal court mechanisms originating in Massachusetts to handle children charged with crimes apart from the system of criminal courts for adults.

Civil tribunals See children's tribunals.

Classical school Line of thought that assumes people are rational beings who choose between good and evil.

Classical theory A criminological perspective indicating that people have free will to choose either criminal or conventional behavior; people choose to commit crime for reasons of greed or personal need; crime can be controlled by criminal sanctions, which should be proportionate to the guilt of the perpetrator.

Classification Means used by institutions and probation/parole agencies to separate offenders according to offense seriousness, type of offense, and other criteria.

Cleared by arrest Term used by the Federal Bureau of Investigation in the *Uniform Crime Reports* to indicate that someone has been arrested for a reported crime; does not necessarily mean that the crime has been solved or that the actual criminals who committed the crime have been apprehended or convicted.

Clinical prediction Forecast of behavior based on professional and expert training and working directly with offenders.

Code of the street Norms and values of lower-class youth that emphasize violence and respect.

Combination sentences Occur whenever judges sentence offenders to a term, a portion of which includes incarceration and a portion of which includes probation.

Commitment One of the four elements of social control theory; refers to the individual's investment in conventional society as evidenced by efforts directed toward academic expectations and success, reputation, career, and society.

Commitment placements Judicially ordered confinement in a secure juvenile facility, usually for one year or longer.

Common law Authority based on court decrees and judgments that recognize, affirm, and enforce certain usages and customs of the people; laws determined by judges in accordance with their rulings.

Community corrections acts Enabling legislation by individual states to fund local government units to provide community facilities, services, and resources to juveniles who are considered to be at risk of becoming delinquent or who are already delinquent and need treatment/services.

Community policing Major police reform that broadens the police mission from a narrow focus on crime to a mandate that encourages police to explore creative solutions for a host of community concerns, including crime, fear of crime, disorder, and neighborhood decay; rests on the belief that only by working together will citizens and police be able to improve the quality of life in their communities, with the police acting not only as enforcers but also as advisors, facilitators, and supporters of new community-based, police-supervised initiatives.

Community prosecution Prosecutor's role extends beyond prosecuting criminal and delinquent cases; prosecutor forms partnerships with professionals in criminal justice and schools, faith-based groups, and other members of the community to prevent delinquency and crime, solve problems, and ensure public safety.

Community service Any activity imposed on a probationer or parolee involving work in the youth's neighborhood or city; performed in part to repay victims and the city for injuries or damages caused by unlawful actions.

Community Service Program, Inc. (CSP, Inc.) Established in Orange County, California; designed to instill self-confidence in youth, reduce parental and familial dysfunction, and establish self-reliance and esteem through family counseling therapy sessions.

Compulsory School Act Passed in 1899 by Colorado, this act targeted those youth who were habitually absent from school; encompassed youth who wandered the streets during school hours; originally designed to enforce truancy laws; erroneously regarded as the first juvenile court act, which was actually passed in Illinois in 1899.

Concentric zone hypothesis Series of rings originating from a city center, such as Chicago, and emanating outward, forming various zones characterized by different socioeconomic conditions; believed to contain areas of high delinquency and crime.

Concurrent jurisdiction Power to file charges against juveniles in either criminal courts or juvenile courts.

Condemnation of the condemners One of the five techniques that Gresham Sykes and David Matza explained; the actions or motives of the individuals who do not approve of the act are questionable; they arbitrarily single out the offender; rather than focusing on the offender, the system should focus on the actors condemning the behavior.

Conditional dispositions Results of a delinquency adjudication that obligate youth to comply with one or more conditions of a probation program, such as restitution, community service, work study, therapy, educational participation, or victim compensation.

Conditional probation Program in which a probationer is involved in some degree of local monitoring by probation officers or personnel affiliated with local probation departments.

Confidentiality privilege Right between the defendant and his or her attorney in which certain information cannot be disclosed to prosecutors or others because of the attorney–client relationship; for juveniles, records have been maintained under secure circumstances with access limited only to those in the criminal justice system who are involved in the case.

Conformity Robert Merton's mode of adaptation characterized by persons who accept institutionalized means to achieve culturally approved goals.

Consent decrees Formal agreements that involve children, their parents, and the juvenile court in which youth are placed under the court's supervision without an official finding of delinquency but with judicial approval.

Containment theory Explanation elaborated by Walter Reckless and others that positive self-image enables persons otherwise disposed toward criminal behavior to avoid criminal conduct and conform to societal values; every person is a part of an external structure and has a protective internal structure providing defense, protection, and/or insulation against one's peers, such as delinquents.

Contempt of court Citation by a judge against anyone in court who disrupts the proceedings or does anything to interfere with judicial decrees or pronouncements.

Conventional model Caseload assignment model in which probation or parole officers are assigned clients randomly.

Conventional model with geographical considerations Similar to conventional model; caseload assignment model based on the travel time required for probation or parole officers to meet with offender-clients regularly.

Convictions Judgments of a court, based on a jury or judicial verdict or on the guilty pleas of defendants, that the defendants are guilty of the offenses alleged.

Corporate gangs Juvenile gangs emulating organized crime; profit-motivated gangs that rely on illicit activities, such as drug trafficking, and violence to further their profits.

Courts of record Courts in which a written record is kept of court proceedings.

Court reporters Court officials who keep a written word-for-word and/or tape-recorded record of court proceedings.

Court unification Proposal that seeks to centralize and integrate the diverse functions of all courts of general, concurrent, and exclusive jurisdiction into a more simplified and uncomplicated scheme.

Creaming Term used to refer to private agencies and organizations who selectively admit youth into their programs and facilities.

Creative sentencing Broad class of punishments that provide alternatives to incarceration and are designed to fit particular crimes; may involve community service, restitution, fines, becoming involved in educational or vocational training programs, or becoming affiliated with other "good works" activity.

Crime control model Criminal justice model that emphasizes containment of dangerous offenders and societal protection; a way of controlling delinquency by incapacitating juvenile offenders through secure detention or through intensive supervision programs operated by community-based agencies.

Crime rate Statistic that presents the total number of crimes per 100,000 population.

Criminal-exclusive blend Form of sentencing by a criminal court judge in which either juvenile or adult sentences of incarceration, but not both, can be imposed.

Criminal-inclusive blend Form of sentencing by a criminal court judge in which both juvenile and adult sentences can be imposed simultaneously.

Criminal justice An interdisciplinary field studying the nature and operations of organizations providing justice services to society; consists of lawmaking bodies, including state legislatures and Congress, as well as local, state, and federal agencies that try to enforce the law.

Criminogenic environment Setting where juveniles may feel like criminals or may acquire the characteristics or labels of criminals; these settings include courtrooms, juvenile institutions, and adult institutions.

Cultural transmission theory Explanation emphasizing transmission of criminal behavior through socialization; views delinquency as socially learned behavior transmitted from one generation to the next in disorganized urban areas.

Curfew violators Youth who violate laws and ordinances of communities prohibiting them from being on the streets after certain evening hours, such as 10:00 P.M.; curfew itself is a delinquency prevention strategy.

Custodial dispositions Either nonsecure or secure options resulting from a delinquency adjudication; which involve placement in a group home, ranch, camp, or a juvenile custodial institution.

Dangerousness Defined differently in several jurisdictions; prior record of violent offenses; potential to commit future violent crimes if released; propensity to inflict injury; predicted risk of convicted offender or prison or jail inmate; likelihood of inflicting harm upon others.

D.A.R.E. (Drug Abuse Resistance Education) Intervention program sponsored and implemented by the Los Angeles Police Department; utilizes officers, familiar with drugs and drug laws, who visit schools in their precincts and speak to youth about how to say "no" to drugs; children are taught how to recognize illegal drugs and about different types of drugs and their adverse effects.

Day reporting centers Established in England in 1974 to provide intensive supervision for low-risk offenders who live in the community; continued in various U.S. jurisdictions today to manage treatment programs, supervise fee collection, and to meet other responsibilities, such as drug testing and counseling.

Deinstitutionalization Mandate that was part of the Juvenile Justice and Delinquency Prevention Act of 1974 requiring states to remove youth who had been placed in detention or other custodial institutions for their involvement in status offenses (e.g., running away, truancy, and curfew violations).

Deinstitutionalization of status offenses (DSO) Eliminating status offenses from the broad category of delinquent acts and removing juveniles from or precluding their confinement in juvenile correctional facilities; the process of removing status offenses from the jurisdiction of juvenile court so that status offenders cannot be subject to secure confinement.

Delinquency Act committed by an infant of not more than a specified age who has violated criminal laws or engages in disobedient, indecent, or immoral conduct and is in need of treatment, rehabilitation, or supervision; status acquired through an adjudicatory proceeding by juvenile court.

Demand waiver Requests by juveniles to have their cases transferred from juvenile courts to criminal courts.

Denial of injury One of the five forms of neutralization described by Gresham Sykes and David Matza; refers to offenders contending that their actions or behaviors did not really harm anyone and, therefore, they should not be blamed.

Denial of responsibility One of the five forms of neutralization described by Gresham Sykes and David Matza; individuals suggest that their behavior or actions are the result of forces beyond their control.

Denial of victim One of the five forms of neutralization described by Gresham Sykes and David Matza; refers to the offender suggesting that it is the victim's previous behavior that is really responsible for the current act; the offender suggests that the victim somehow "was asking for it."

Dependent and neglected children Youth considered by social services or the juvenile court to be in need of some type of intervention, supervision, or placement due to circumstances in their homes or families that are beyond their control.

Detention Confining youth for short terms in secure facilities, usually to await a juvenile court adjudicatory hearing or some other proceeding; some youth are placed in secure settings for short terms as a punishment for delinquent offending.

Detention centers Juvenile secure facilities used for serious and violent juveniles who are awaiting an adjudication hearing or placement in another facility.

Detention hearing Judicial proceeding held to determine whether it is appropriate to continue to hold or detain a juvenile prior to an adjudicatory hearing.

Determinism Concept holding that persons do not have a free will but, rather, are subject to the influence of various forces over which they have little or no control.

Differential association theory Edwin Sutherland's theory of deviance and criminality through associations with others who are deviant or criminal; includes dimensions of frequency, duration, priority, and intensity; persons become criminal or delinquent because of a preponderance of learned definitions favorable to violating the law over learned definitions unfavorable to it.

Differential reinforcement theory Explanation that combines elements of labeling theory and a psychological phenomenon known as conditioning; persons are rewarded for engaging in desirable behavior and punished for deviant conduct.

Direct file Prosecutorial waiver of jurisdiction to a criminal court; action taken against a juvenile who has committed a serious offense in which that juvenile's case is transferred to criminal court for the purpose of a criminal prosecution.

Discretionary powers Relating to the police role, police discretion is the ability of police officers to choose among a range of alternatives in dealing with a particular situation in a manner consistent with departmental policies and procedures; police have authority to use force to enforce the law if, in the officer's opinion, the situation demands it.

Discretionary waivers Transfer of juveniles to criminal courts by judges, at their discretion or in their judgment; also known as judicial waivers.

Dispose To decide the sanction to be imposed on a juvenile following an adjudication hearing.

Dispositions Sanctions resulting from a delinquency adjudication; may be nominal, conditional, or custodial.

Disproportionate minority confinement (DMC) Refers to the number and percentage of minority youth in correctional custodial institutions (e.g., detention centers, residential facilities, and reform schools); the rate of confinement for youth in these correctional environments exceeds their representation in the general youth population; in amendments to the Juvenile Justice and Delinquency Prevention Act of 1974, Congress directed the states to gather data and attempt to address this disproportionality.

Disproportionate minority contact In 2002, Congress amended the Juvenile Justice and Delinquency Prevention Act of 1974 to require states to gather data on minority youth who come to the attention of the juvenile justice system; and to determine if these contact data are commensurate with minority representation in the general youth population; rather than focusing only on youth in confinement, this reflects contacts with youth at all stage of juvenile justice processing.

Diversion Halting or suspension of legal proceedings against criminal defendants or youthful offenders after a referral to the justice system and possible referral of those persons to treatment or care programs administered by a public or private agencies or organizations.

Double jeopardy Subjecting persons to prosecution more than once in the same jurisdiction for the same offense, usually without new or vital evidence; prohibited by the Fifth Amendment.

Drift theory David Matza's term denoting a state of limbo in which youth move in and out of delinquency and in which their lifestyles embrace both conventional and deviant values.

Due process Basic constitutional right to a fair trial, presumption of innocence until guilt is proven beyond a reasonable doubt, the opportunity to be heard, to be aware of a matter that is pending, to make an informed choice whether to acquiesce or contest, and to provide the reasons for such a choice before a judicial official.

Due process model Treatment model based upon one's constitutional right to a fair trial, to have an opportunity to be heard, to be aware of matters that are pending, to a presumption of innocence until guilt has been established beyond a reasonable doubt, to make an informed choice whether to acquiesce or contest, and to provide the reasons for such a choice before a judicial officer.

Ectomorphs Body type described by William Sheldon; persons are thin, sensitive, and delicate.

Electronic monitoring (EM) Use of electronic devices that emit electronic signals; these devices, anklets, or wristlets are worn by offenders, probationers, and parolees; the purpose of such monitoring is to monitor an offender's presence in a given area where the offender is required to remain or to verify offender whereabouts.

Electronic monitoring (EM) signaling devices Apparatuses worn about the wrist or leg that are designed to monitor an offender's presence in a given area where the offender is required to remain.

Emancipation Youth previously placed in a foster home who are able to live independently after they reach a specified age. State statutes vary in the procedures to apply for legal emancipation and age requirements.

Endomorphs Body type described by William Sheldon; persons are fat, soft, plump, and jolly.

Evidence-based practice Research conducted on programs that has a theoretical foundation and utilizes control and experimental groups to determine effectiveness; programs that have been proven to be successful after replication at various locations using a rigorous research design rather than using tradition or past practice.

Evolving standards of decency Used to assess the progress of a maturing society in determining what is usual and cruel punishment in context of the Eighth Amendment.

Exculpatory evidence Information considered to be beneficial to defendants, tending to show their innocence.

Expungement orders, Sealing records of juveniles Deletion of one's arrest or court record from official sources; in most jurisdictions, juvenile delinquency records are expunged when one reaches the age of majority or adulthood or according to the legislative requirements stipulated in the particular jurisdiction.

Extralegal factors Characteristics influencing intake decisions, such as juvenile offender attitudes, school grades and standing, gender, race, ethnicity, socioeconomic status, and age.

False negatives Offenders predicted not to be dangerous who turn out to be dangerous.

False positives Offenders predicted to be dangerous who turn out not to be dangerous.

Family model Established under the Juvenile Law of 1948; exists in all jurisdictions and hears any matters pertaining to juvenile delinquency, child abuse and neglect, and child custody matters; both status offenders and delinquents appear before Family Court judges; similar to juvenile court judges; Family Court judges have considerable discretionary authority; decide cases within the *parens patriae* context.

Felonies Crimes punishable by imprisonment in prison for a term of one or more years; major crimes; any index offense.

Fetal alcohol spectrum disorders Refers to a range of effects in an individual whose mother drank alcohol during pregnancy; includes physical, learning, or mental effects, which can be long term.

Fetal alcohol syndrome Consequences that alcohol has on the developing fetus.

Fines Financial penalties imposed at the time of sentencing convicted offenders; most criminal statutes contain provisions for the imposition of monetary penalties as sentencing options.

First-offender Criminals who have no previous criminal records; these persons may have committed crimes, but they have only been caught for the instant offense; first-time offender.

Flat time Frequently known as hard time; the actual amount of time one must serve while incarcerated.

Foster homes Homes that offer a temporary placement for youth in need of supervision or control; usually, families volunteer to act as foster parents and nurture and care for youth on a short-term basis.

Gangs Groups who form an allegiance for a common purpose and engage in unlawful or criminal activity; any group gathered together on a continuing basis to engage in or commit antisocial behavior.

Gemeinschaft Term created by Ferdinand Tonnies, a social theorist, to describe small, traditional communities where informal sanctions were used to punish those who violated community laws.

Gesellschaft Term created by Ferdinand Tonnies, a social theorist, to describe more formalized, larger communities and cities that relied on written documents and laws to regulate social conduct.

Get-tough movement View toward criminals and delinquents favoring maximum penalties and punishments for crimes or delinquent acts; any action toward toughening or strengthening sentencing provisions or dispositions involving adults or juveniles.

Graffiti Removal Initiative Program Community program designed as a condition of probation in cases of vandalism in which youth must remove graffiti from public buildings or houses; used in conjunction with other program conditions.

G.R.E.A.T. (Gang Resistance Education and Training) Established in Phoenix, Arizona; police officers visit schools and help youth understand how to cope with peer pressure to commit delinquent acts; topics of educational programs include victim rights, drugs and neighborhoods, conflict resolution, and need fulfillment.

Group homes Community based facilities that provide youth with limited supervision and support; juveniles live in a home-like environment with other juveniles and participate in therapeutic programs and counseling; considered to be nonsecure residential facilities.

Guardians ad litem Special authorities or guardians appointed by the court in which particular litigation is pending to represent a child or youth in court.

Habeas corpus Writ meaning "produce the body"; used by prisoners to challenge the nature and length of their confinement.

Halfway houses Nonsecure residential facilities intended to provide an alternative to incarceration for offenders who reenter the community after confinement in an instution.

Hands-off doctrine Policy practiced by the federal courts in which official court policy was not to intervene in matters relating to juvenile issues; belief that juvenile justice are in the best position to make decisions about welfare of juveniles.

Hard time Also known as flat time; actual amount of secure confinement juveniles must serve as the result of a custodial disposition from a juvenile court judge.

Hedonism Jeremy Bentham's term indicating that people avoid pain and pursue pleasure.

Hidden delinquency Infractions reported by surveys of high-school youth; considered to be "hidden," because it most often is undetected by police officers; disclosed delinquency through self-report surveys.

Holland Teen Court (HTC) Holland, Michigan, youth court program commenced in 1991 involving juveniles who have committed less-serious offenses; jurors consist of high-school students with general training in jury deliberations and sentencing matters; sentencing is restricted to community service and restitution; very successful program with recidivism occurring in less than five percent of cases handled.

Home confinement, Home incarceration, House arrest Program intended to house offenders in their own homes with or without electronic devices; reduces prison overcrowding and prisoner costs; intermediate punishment involving the use of offender residences for mandatory incarceration during evening hours after a curfew and on weekends.

Hospital of Saint Michael Custodial institution established at request of the Pope in Rome in 1704; provided for unruly youth and others who violated the law; youth were assigned tasks, including semiskilled and skilled labor, which enabled them to get jobs when released.

Houses of refuge Juvenile institutions, the first of which was established in 1825 as a means of separating juveniles from the adult correctional process.

Incident Specific criminal act involving one crime and one or more victims.

Inculpatory evidence Information considered as adverse to defendants or tending to show their guilt.

Indentured servants, indentured servant system Voluntary slave pattern; persons without money for the passage from England entered into a contract with merchants or businessmen, usually for seven years wherein merchants would pay for their voyage to the American colonies in exchange for their labor.

Index offenses, Index crimes Specific felonies used by the Federal Bureau of Investigation in the *Uniform Crime Reports* to chart crime trends; eight index offenses are listed (aggravated assault, larceny, burglary, vehicular theft, arson, robbery, forcible rape, and murder).

Industrial schools, Training schools, Secure treatment facilities Secure facilities where some juveniles are held for one year or longer; such institutions usually have different types of programming to aid in the rehabilitation and reintegration of youthful offenders, consisting of vocational and educational courses or programs, counseling for different types of youth needs, and other services; these facilities are largely self-contained like prisons, and they offer a limited range of medical and health services.

Innovation Robert Merton's mode of adaptation in which persons reject institutionalized means to achieve culturally approved goals; instead, they engage in illegal acts, considered to be innovative, to achieve their goals.

Intake Critical phase in which a determination is made by a juvenile probation officer or other official whether to release juveniles to their parent's custody, detain juveniles in formal detention facilities for a later court appearance, or release them to parents pending a later court appearance.

Intake hearings, intake screenings Proceedings in which a juvenile official, such as juvenile probation officer, conducts an interview with a youth charged with a delinquent or status offense and his/her parents or guardian to determine the best strategy for dealing with the behavior that resulted in the referral to court.

Intake officer Juvenile probation officer or other court representative who conducts screenings and preliminary interviews with alleged juvenile offenders and their families.

Intensive Aftercare Program (IAP) Philadelphia-based intervention for serious youthful offenders involving intensive counseling and training for acquiring self-help skills; recidivism of participants was greatly reduced during the study period of 1980 to 1990.

Intensive Motivational Program of Alternative Correctional Treatment (IMPACT) Boot camp program operated in Louisiana; incorporates educational training with strict physical and behavioral requirements.

Intensive supervised probation (ISP) Controlled probation overseen by probation officer; involves close monitoring of offender activities by various means; also known as intensive probation supervision (IPS).

Intensive supervision program, Intensive probation supervision (IPS) Offender supervision program with the following characteristics: (1) low officer-to-client ratio (i.e., 30 or fewer probationers), (2) high levels of offender accountability (e.g., victim restitution, community service, payment of fines, partial defrayment of program expenses), (3) high levels of offender responsibility, (4) high levels of offender control (home confinement, electronic monitoring, frequent face-to-face visits by probation or parole officers), and (5) frequent checks for arrests, drug and/or alcohol use, and employment/school attendance (drug/alcohol screening and coordination with police departments and juvenile halls, teachers, and family).

Interbranch Commission on Juvenile Justice Appointed in Pennsylvania after the Luzerne County kids for cash scandal to investigate the juvenile justice system in the state and to assess its success in serving youth; made recommendations to improve the system's effectiveness and safeguard youth from any future abuse or mistreatment like that which occurred in Luzerne County.

Intermediate punishments Sanctions existing somewhere between incarceration and probation on a continuum of criminal penalties; may include home incarceration and electronic monitoring.

Intermittent sentences Occur whenever judges sentence offenders to terms such as weekend confinement only.

Interstitial area In concentric zone hypothesis, the area nearest the center of a city undergoing change, such as urban renewal; characterized by high rates of crime.

Involvement One element of social control theory; refers to the work, sports, school, and recreational activities that necessitate large blocks of time and indicate that a person is engaged with these pursuits and the community.

Jail as a condition of probation Sentence where judge imposes some jail time to be served before probation commences; also known as shock probation.

Jail removal initiative Action sponsored by the Office of Juvenile Justice and Delinquency Prevention and called for in the Juvenile Justice and Delinquency Prevention Act of 1974 to dissuade law enforcement officers from taking juveniles to jail.

Jails City- or county-operated and -financed facilities to contain those offenders who are serving short sentences; jails also house more-serious prisoners from state or federal prisons through contracts to alleviate overcrowding; jails also house pretrial detainees, witnesses, juveniles, vagrants, and others.

Judicial waivers Decision by juvenile judge to waive juvenile to the jurisdiction of criminal court.

Judicious nonintervention Use of minimal intervention in a youth's behavior and environment to effect changes in behavior.

Jurisdiction Power of a court to hear and determine a particular type of case; territory within which a court may exercise authority, such as a city, county, or state.

Just deserts/justice model Stresses offender accountability as a means to punish youthful offenders; uses victim compensation plans, restitution, and community services as ways of making offenders pay for their offenses; philosophy that emphasizes punishment as a primary objective of sentencing, fixed sentences, abolition of parole, and abandonment of the rehabilitative ideal; rehabilitation is functional to the extent that offenders join rehabilitative programs voluntarily.

Juvenile-contiguous blend Sentence by a juvenile court judge in which the judge can impose a disposition beyond the normal jurisdictional range for juvenile offenders; for example, a judge may impose a 30-year term on a 14-year-old offender, but the juvenile is entitled to a hearing when he or she reaches the age of majority to determine whether the remainder of the sentence shall be served.

Juvenile courts Formal proceeding with jurisdiction over juveniles, juvenile delinquents, status offenders, dependent or neglected children, children in need of supervision, or infants.

Juvenile court records Formal or informal statements concerning an adjudication hearing or court referral or actions involving a juvenile; a written document of a juvenile's prior delinquency or status offending.

Juvenile delinquency Violation of the law by a person before his or her 18th birthday; any illegal behavior committed by someone within a given age range punishable by juvenile court jurisdiction; whatever the juvenile court believes should be brought within its jurisdiction; violation of any state or local law or ordinance by anyone who has not yet achieved the age of their majority.

Juvenile delinquent, Delinquent child Anyone, who, under the age of majority has committed one or more acts that would be crimes if adults committed them.

Juvenile Detention Alternatives Initiative (JDAI) Annie E. Casey Foundation established this program in 1992 to improve the conditions of confinement for youth in detention, identify alternatives to detention, and address disproportionate minority confinement; over 80 U.S. detention centers participate.

Juvenile-exclusive blend Type of sentence in which a juvenile court judge can impose either adult or juvenile incarceration, but not both, as a disposition and sentence.

Juvenile-inclusive blend Form of sentencing in which a juvenile court judge can impose both adult and juvenile incarceration simultaneously.

Juvenile intensive supervised probation (JISP) Program for youthful offenders, including home confinement, electronic monitoring, and other intensive supervised probation methods.

Juvenile Justice and Delinquency Prevention Act (JJDPA) of 1974 Legislation recommending various alternatives to incarcerating youth, including deinstitutionalization of status offending, removal of youth from secure confinement, and other rehabilitative treatments.

Juvenile justice system Stages through which juveniles are processed, sanctioned, and treated after arrests for juvenile delinquency.

Juvenile Mentoring Program (JUMP) Federally funded program administered by the Office of Juvenile Justice and Delinquency Prevention; promotes bonding between an adult and a juvenile relating on a one-to-one basis over time; designed to improve school performance and decrease gang participation and delinquency.

Juvenile offender laws Statutes providing for automatic transfer of juveniles of certain ages to criminal courts for processing, provided they have been changed with specific felonies.

Juvenile offenders Children or youth who have violated laws or engaged in behaviors that are known as statute offenses.

Juvenile probation camps California county-operated camps for delinquent youth placed on probation; established in the early 1980s; these camps include physical activities, community contacts, and academic training.

Labeling Process whereby persons acquire self-definitions that are deviant or criminal; process occurs through labels applied to them by others.

Labeling theory Explanation of deviant conduct attributed to Edwin Lemert whereby persons acquire self-definitions that are deviant or criminal; persons perceive themselves as deviant or criminal through labels applied to them by others; the more that people are involved in the criminal justice system, the more they acquire self-definitions consistent with the criminal label.

Law enforcement agencies, law enforcement Any organization with the purpose of enforcing criminal laws; the activities of various public and private agencies at local, state, and federal levels that are designed to insure compliance with formal rules of society that regulate social conduct.

Legal factors Variables influencing the intake decision relating to the factual information about delinquent acts; include crime seriousness, type of crime committed, prior record of delinquency adjudications, and evidence of inculpatory or exculpatory nature.

Legislative waiver Legislative mandate also known as automatic waiver that requires certain youth to have their cases tried in criminal courts because of specific offenses that have been committed or alleged.

Life without parole Penalty imposed as maximum punishment for youth convicted as adults in states; provides for permanent incarceration of offenders in prisons, typically without parole eligibility.

Litigation explosion Rapid escalation of case filings before appellate courts, often based upon a landmark case extending rights to particular segments of the population, such as jail or prison inmates or juveniles.

Lockups Small rooms or cells designed for confining arrested adults and/or juveniles for short periods, such as 24 hours or less.

Lombroso, Cesare (1835–1909) His school of thought linked criminal behavior with abnormal, unusual physical characteristics.

Long-term detention Period of incarceration of juvenile offenders in secure facilities that averages 180 days in the United States.

Looking-glass self Concept originated by Charles Horton Cooley in which persons learn appropriate ways of behaving by paying attention to how others view and react to them.

Lower class focal concerns Walter Miller used this term to refer to those aspects of the subculture that are important; these aspects require attention by members of the subculture.

Mandatory waiver Automatic transfer of certain juveniles on the criminal court usually on the basis of (1) their age and (2) the seriousness of their offense; for example, a 17-year-old in Illinois who allegedly committed homicide would be subject to mandatory transfer to criminal court for the purpose of a criminal prosecution.

Mediation A process whereby a third party intervenes between an offender and a victim to work out a noncriminal or civil resolution to a problem that might otherwise result in a delinquency adjudication or criminal conviction.

Mediator Third-party arbiter who resolves disputes between parties.

Medical model Also known as the treatment model; considers criminal behavior as an illness to be treated; delinquency is also a disease subject to treatment.

Mesomorphs Body type described by William Sheldon; persons are strong, muscular, aggressive, and tough.

Miranda **warning** Statement given to suspects by police officers advising suspects of their legal rights to counsel, to refuse to answer questions, to avoid self-incrimination, and other privileges.

Misdemeanor Crime punishable by confinement in city or county jail for a period of less than one year; a lesser offense.

Mitigating circumstances Factors that lessen the severity of the crime and/or sentence; these include young age, cooperation with police in apprehending other offenders, and lack of intent to inflict injury.

Mixed sentences Punishments imposed whenever offenders have been convicted of two or more offenses and judges sentence them to separate sentences for each convicted offense.

Model Program Guide (MPG) A database of evidence-based programs that provides a continuum of strategies for delinquency prevention and intervention.

Modes of adaptation Ways that persons who occupy a particular social position adjust to cultural goals; the institutionalized means to reach those goals.

Monitoring the Future Survey Study of 3,000 high-school students annually by Institute for Social Research at University of Michigan; attempts to discover hidden delinquency not ordinarily disclosed by published public reports.

Multisystemic Therapy (MST) A Blueprints for Violence Prevention program that provides intensive family- and community-based treatment for managing delinquents with serious antisocial behavior.

National Crime Victimization Survey (NCVS) Published in cooperation with the U.S. Bureau of the Census, a random survey of 60,000 households, including 127,000 persons 12 years of age or older; includes 50,000 businesses; measures crime committed against specific victims interviewed and not necessarily reported to law enforcement officers.

National Juvenile Court Data Archive Compendium of national statistical information and databases about juvenile delinquency available through the National Center for Juvenile Justice, under the sponsorship of the Office of Juvenile Justice and Delinquency Prevention; involves acquisition of court dispositional records and publishing periodic reports of juvenile offenses and adjudicatory outcomes from different jurisdictions.

National Youth Gang Survey (NYGS) Conducted annually since 1995; purpose of the survey is to identify and describe critical gang components and characteristics and to track gang activities.

National Youth Survey Study of large numbers of youth annually or at other intervals to assess extent of delinquency among high-school students.

Needs assessment Instruments to identify social, psychological, and mental health needs of the youth.

Net-widening Bringing juveniles into the juvenile justice system who would not otherwise be involved in delinquent activity; applies to many status offenders; also known as widening the net.

Neutralization theory Holds that delinquents experience guilt when involved in delinquent activities and that they respect leaders of the legitimate social order; their delinquency is episodic rather than chronic, and they adhere to conventional values while "drifting" into periods of illegal behavior; to drift, the delinquent must first neutralize legal and moral values.

New York House of Refuge Established in New York City in 1825 by the Society for the Prevention of Pauperism; school managed largely status offenders; compulsory education was provided; strict, prison-like regimen was considered to be detrimental to youthful clientele.

Nolle prosequi Decision by prosecution to decline to pursue criminal case against defendant.

Nominal dispositions Pre-adjudicatory or adjudicatory disposition resulting in minor sanctions, such as warnings and/or probation.

Noninterventionist model Philosophy of juvenile delinquent treatment meaning the absence of any direct intervention with certain juveniles who have been taken into custody.

Nonsecure custody, nonsecure confinement Custodial disposition in which a juvenile is placed in a group home, foster care, or other nonsecure residential setting where he or she is permitted to leave with permission of parents, guardians, or supervisors.

Numbers game model Caseload assignment model for probation or parole officers in which total number of offender-clients is divided by number of officers.

Nurse–Family Partnership (NFP) A Blueprints for Violence Prevention program that provides intensive home visitation by trained nurses during prenatal and early childhood years.

Office of Juvenile Justice and Delinquency Prevention (OJJDP) Agency established by Congress under the Juvenile Justice and Delinquency Prevention Act of 1974; designed to remove status offenders from the jurisdiction of juvenile courts and dispose of their cases less formally.

Once an adult/always an adult provision Legislation stipulating that once a juvenile has been transferred to criminal court to be prosecuted as an adult, then regardless of the criminal court outcome, the juvenile can never be subject to the jurisdiction of juvenile courts in the future; in short, the juvenile, once transferred, will always be treated as an adult if future crimes are committed, even if the youth is still not of adult age.

Operation SHIELD (Strategic Home Intervention and Early Leadership Development) Police program in Orange County,

California, to identify at-risk children and youth and refer them to appropriate social service agencies for early intervention services.

Operation TIDE A composite of federal, state, and local law enforcement officers dedicated to reducing violence attributable to guns and gangs.

Overrides Actions by an authority in an institution or agency that overrules a score or assessment made of a client or inmate; raw scores or assessments or recommendations can be overruled; the function of override is to upgrade or downgrade the seriousness of offense status, thus changing the level of custody at which one is maintained in secure confinement; may also affect the type and nature of community programming for particular offenders.

Parens patriae Literally "parent of the country"; refers to doctrine in which the state oversees the welfare of youth; originally established by the King of England and administered through chancellors.

Parolee Adult offender who has served time in jail or prison but has been released to the community under supervision before serving the entire sentence imposed upon conviction.

Parole revocation Two-stage proceeding that may result in a parolee's reincarceration in jail or prison; the first stage is a preliminary hearing to determine whether the parolee violated any specific parole condition; the second stage is to determine whether parole should be terminated and the offender returned to an institution.

Parole or aftercare revocation hearing Formal proceeding in which a parole board or designated authority decides whether a parolee's parole or aftercare program should be terminated or changed because of one or more program infractions or the commission of a new offense.

PATHS Program Promoting Alternative Thinking Strategies Program; aimed to promote emotional and social competencies and to reduce aggression and related emotional and behavioral problems among elementary-school children.

Pathways Developmental sequences over the course of one's adolescence that are associated with serious, chronic, and violent offenders.

Peer jury model A peer jury is composed of other youth in the community, who sit on the jury and decide the offender's punishment.

Perry Preschool Program Provides high-level, early childhood education to disadvantaged children to improve their later school life and performance.

Petition Official document filed in juvenile courts on juvenile's behalf, specifying reasons for the youth's court appearance; document asserts that juveniles fall within the categories of dependent or neglected, status offender, or delinquent; the reasons for such assertions are usually provided.

Pittsburgh Youth Study (PYS) Longitudinal investigation of 1,517 inner-city boys between 1986 and 1996; studied factors involved in what caused delinquency among some youth and why others did not become delinquent.

Placed Judicial disposition in which a juvenile is placed in the care and custody of a group or foster home or other type of out-of-home facility or program; may also include secure confinement in an industrial school or comparable facility.

Placement One of the several dispositions available to juvenile court judges following formal or informal proceedings involving juveniles for whom either delinquent or status offenses have been alleged; adjudication proceedings yield a court decision about whether facts alleged in petition are true; if so, a disposition is imposed that may be placement in a foster or group home, wilderness experience, camp, ranch, or secure institution.

Plea bargaining Preconviction agreement between the defendant and the state whereby the defendant pleads guilty with the expectation of either a reduction in the charges, a promise of sentencing leniency, or some other government concession short of the maximum penalties that could be imposed under the law.

Police discretion Range of behavioral choices available to police officers within the limits of their power; selective enforcement of the law.

Poor Laws Regulations in England in the Middle Ages designed to punish debtors by imprisoning them until they could pay their debts; essentially, imprisonment was for life or until someone could pay the debts for them.

Positive school of criminology School of criminological thought emphasizing analysis of criminal behaviors through empirical indicators, such as physical features, compared with biochemical explanations; postulates that human behavior is a product of social, biological, psychological, or economic forces; also known as the Italian School.

Positivism Branch of social science that uses the scientific method of the natural sciences and suggests that human behavior is a product of social, biological, psychological, or economic factors.

Predictors of dangerousness and risk Assessment devices that attempt to forecast one's potential for violence or risk to others; any factors that are used in such instruments.

Predisposition reports Documents prepared by juvenile probation officer for juvenile judge; purpose of report is to furnish the judge with background about juveniles to make a more informed sentencing decision; similar to the presentence investigation report.

Preponderance of the evidence Standard used in civil courts to determine defendant or plaintiff liability and in which the result does not involve incarceration.

Presentence investigation (PSI) Inquiry conducted about a convicted defendant at the request of the judge; purpose of inquiry is to determine worthiness of defendant for probation or sentencing leniency.

Presumptive waiver Requirement that shifts the burden to juveniles for defending against their transfer to criminal court by showing they are capable of being rehabilitated.

Pretrial detention Holding delinquent or criminal suspects in incarcerative facilities pending their forthcoming adjudicatory hearing or trial.

Preventive detention, preventive pretrial detention Authority to detain suspects before trial without bail when suspects are likely to flee from the jurisdiction or pose serious risks to others.

Primary deviation Part of the labeling process whenever youth engage in occasional pranks and not especially serious violations of the law.

Privatization Private agencies or corporations involved in the management and operations of correctional institutions.

Proactive units Police units assigned to monitor and patrol high-delinquency areas in an effort to deter youth from engaging in illegal conduct.

Probable cause Reasonable belief that a crime has been committed and that the person accused of the crime committed it.

Probation Sentence not involving confinement that imposes conditions and retains authority in sentencing court to modify conditions of sentence or resentence offender for probation violations.

Probation revocation hearing Proceeding wherein it is determined whether to revoke an offender's probation program because of one or more violations.

Project New Pride One of the most popular probation programs, established in Denver, Colorado, in 1973; a blend of education, counseling, employment, and cultural education directed at those more-serious offenders between the ages of 14 and 17; juveniles eligible for the New Pride program must have at least two prior convictions for serious misdemeanors and/or felonies; goals include (1) reintegrating participants into their communities through school participation or employment and (2) reducing recidivism rates among offenders.

Project Safe Neighborhoods An initiative undertaken in many communities to reduce gun violence by banning possession of firearms by those with criminal records.

Prosecution and the courts Organizations that pursue cases against juvenile offenders and determine whether they are guilty or innocent of the offenses alleged.

Prosecutors Court officials who commence civil and criminal proceedings against defendants; represent state or government interest, prosecuting defendants on behalf of state or government.

Psychoanalytic theory Sigmund Freud's theory of personality formation through the id, ego, and superego at various stages of childhood; maintains that early life experiences influence adult behavior.

Psychological theories Explanations linking criminal behavior with mental states or conditions, antisocial personality traits, and early psychological moral development.

Radical nonintervention Similar to a "do-nothing" policy of delinquency nonintervention.

Reactive units Police youth squad units that respond to calls for service when suspicious youth activities of delinquency are reported.

Reality therapy model Equivalent of shock probation in which short incarcerative sentences are believed to provide "shock" value for juvenile offenders and scare them from reoffending behaviors.

Rebellion Mode of adaptation suggested by Robert Merton in which persons reject institutional means to achieve culturally approved goals and create their own goals and means to use and seek.

Recidivism New crime committed by an offender who has previously been adjudicated or convicted; prior act may have involved a disposition of probation of commitment to an institution.

Recidivism rate Proportion of offenders who, when released from probation or parole, commit further crimes.

Recidivists Offenders who have committed previous offenses.

Reentry A comprehensive system of services and support used to facilitate successful adjustment to the community for youth leaving institutional confinement.

Reeve Chief law enforcement officer of English counties, known as shires.

Referrals Any action which involves bringing a youth to juvenile court by a law enforcement officer, interested citizen, family member, or school official; usually based upon law violations, delinquency, or unruly conduct.

Reform schools Different types of vocational institutions designed to both punish and rehabilitate youthful offenders; operated much like prisons as total institutions.

Regimented Inmate Discipline Program (RID) Oklahoma Department of Corrections program operated in Lexington, Oklahoma, for juveniles; program stresses military-type discipline and accountability; facilities are secure and privately operated.

Rehabilitation model Concept of youth management similar to medical model in which juvenile delinquents are believed to be suffering from social and psychological handicaps; provides experiences to build self-concept; experiences stress educational and social remedies.

Relabeling Redefinition of juvenile behaviors as more or less serious than previously defined; example would be police officers who relabel or redefine certain juvenile behaviors, such as curfew violation, as loitering for purposes of committing a felony, such as burglary or robbery; relabeling is associated with political jurisdictions that have deinstitutionalized status offenders or divested juvenile courts of their authority over specific types of juvenile offenders; as a result, police officers lose power, or their discretionary authority, to warn such juveniles or take them into custody; new law may mandate removing such juveniles to community social services rather than to jails; in retaliation, some officers may relabel status behaviors as criminal ones to preserve their discretionary authority over juveniles.

Reparative Probation Program A voluntary civil mediation program involving minor offenders in which specially trained volunteers determine fair compensation to victims through a series of meetings.

Repeat offender Any juvenile or adult with a prior record of delinquency or criminality.

Restitution Stipulation by court that offenders must compensate victims for their financial losses resulting from crime; compensation for psychological, physical, or financial loss by victim; may be imposed as a part of an incarcerative sentence.

Restorative justice Mediation between victims and offenders whereby offenders accept responsibility for their actions and agree to reimburse victims for their losses; may involve community service and other penalties agreeable to both parties in a form of arbitration with a neutral third party acting as arbiter.

Restorative policing Police-based family group conferencing with participants including police, victims, youth, and their families to discuss the harm caused by the youth and to create an agreement to repair the harm; similar to restorative justice.

Retreatism Mode of adaptation suggested by Robert Merton in which persons reject culturally approved goals and institutionalized means and do little or nothing to achieve; homeless persons, bag ladies, vagrants, and others sometimes fit the retreatist profile.

Reverse waiver Motion to transfer juvenile's case from criminal court to juvenile court following a legislative or automatic waiver action.

Reverse waiver hearings, reverse waiver actions Formal proceedings to contest automatic transfer of juveniles to jurisdiction of criminal courts; used in jurisdictions with direct file or automatic transfer laws.

Risk Potential likelihood for someone to engage in further delinquency or criminality.

Risk prediction Assessment of some expected future behavior of a person, including criminal acts, arrests, or convictions.

Risk/needs assessment instruments Predictive devices intended to forecast offender propensity to commit new offenses or recidivate.

Ritualism Mode of adaptation suggested by Robert Merton in which persons reject culturally approved goals but work toward lesser goals through institutionalized means.

Runaways Juveniles who leave their home for long-term periods without parental consent or supervision.

SARA Proactive policing approach that uses Scanning, Analyzing, Responding, and Assessing to guide problem solving.

Scared Straight Juvenile delinquency prevention program that sought to frighten samples of delinquent youth by having them confront inmates in a Rahway, New Jersey, prison; inmates would yell at and belittle them, calling them names, cursing, and yelling; inmates would tell them about sexual assaults and other prison unpleasantries in an attempt to get them to refrain from reoffending.

Scavenger gangs Groups formed primarily as a means of socializing and for mutual protection.

Screening Procedure used by intake and prosecution to define which cases have prosecutive merit and which do not; some screening bureaus are made up of police and lawyers with trial experience. Decision to divert cases from the court to other agencies and organizations or to proceed with formal proceeding.

Sealing records of juveniles See expungement orders.

Secondary deviation Part of labeling theory that suggests violations of the law become a part of one's normal behavior rather than just occasional pranks.

Secure custody, secure confinement Incarceration of juvenile offender in a facility that restricts movement in community; similar to adult penal facility involving total incarceration.

Secure treatment facility Facility that confines youth who have failed in less-intensive programs; emphasis is on therapeutic interventions and close monitoring.

Selective incapacitation Incarcerating individuals who show a high likelihood of repeating their previous offenses; based on forecasts of potential for recidivism; includes, but not limited to, dangerousness.

Self-report, self-report information Surveys of youth (or adults) based upon disclosures these persons might make about the types of offenses they have committed and how frequently they have committed them; considered to be more accurate than official estimates.

Sexual Offender Treatment (SOT) Program Treatment program for juvenile offenders adjudicated delinquent on sex charges; includes psychosocioeducational interventions, therapies, and counseling.

Shires Early English counties.

Shock incarceration, Boot camps Also known as the Army Model, boot camp programs are patterned after basic training for new military recruits; juvenile offenders are given a taste of hard military life, and such regimented activities and structure for up to 180 days are often sufficient to "shock" them into refraining from further delinquent behavior.

Shock probation Intermediate punishment in which offenders are initially sentenced to terms of secure detention; after a period of time, usually between 90 and 180 days, they are removed from detention and sentenced to serve the remainder of their sentences on probation; the term *shock probation* was first used by Ohio authorities in 1964.

Short-term confinement Temporary placement in any incarcerative institution for adults or juveniles for a shorter period of time which typically ranges from 24 hours to about 30 days.

Situationally based discretion Confronting suspicious behavior or crime in the streets on the basis of immediate situational factors, time of night, presence of weapons, and numbers of offenders; requires extensive personal judgments by police officers.

Social control theory Explanation of criminal behavior that focuses upon control mechanisms, techniques, and strategies for regulating human behavior, leading to conformity or obedience to society's rules posits that deviance results when social controls are weakened or break down, so that individuals are not motivated to conform to them.

Social learning theory Applied to criminal behavior, theory stressing the importance of learning through modeling others who are criminal; criminal behavior is a function of copying or learning criminal conduct from others.

Society for the Prevention of Pauperism Philanthropic society that established first reformatory in New York in 1825, the New York House of Refuge.

Sociobiology Scientific study of causal relationship between genetic structure and social behavior.

Socioeconomic status (SES) Station or level of economic attainment one enjoys through work; acquisition of wealth; the divisions between various levels of society according to material goods acquired.

Sourcebook of Criminal Justice Statistics Compendium of statistical information about juvenile and adult offenders; includes court facts, statistics, and trends as well as probation and parole figures and considerable additional information; published annually by the Hindelang Criminal Justice Research Center at the

University of Albany, SUNY; funded by grants from the U.S. Department of Justice, Bureau of Justice Statistics.

SpeakerID Program Electronic voice verification system used as a part of electronic monitoring to verify the identity of the person called by the probation or parole agency.

Special conditions of probation Extra requirements written into a standard probation agreement, including possible vocational or educational training, counseling, drug or alcohol treatment, attendance at meetings, restitution, and community service.

Specialized caseloads model Case assignment method based on the unique skills and knowledge of probation/parole officers (POs) relative to offender drug or alcohol problems; some POs are assigned particular clients with unique problems that require more than general PO expertise.

Split sentences See combination sentences.

Standard probation Probationers conform to all terms of their probation program, but their contact with probation officers is minimal; often, their contact is by telephone or letter once or twice a month.

Standard of proof Norms used by courts to determine validity of claims or allegations of wrongdoing against offenders; civil standards of proof are (1) clear and convincing evidence and (2) preponderance of evidence, while criminal standard is beyond a reasonable doubt.

Stationhouse adjustments Decisions made by police officers about certain juveniles taken into custody and brought to police stations for processing and investigation; adjustments often result in verbal reprimands and release to custody of parents.

Status offenders Anyone committing a status offense, including runaway behavior, truancy, curfew violation, and loitering.

Status offenses Violations of statute or ordinance by a minor that, if committed by adult, would not be considered as either a felony or a misdemeanor; any acts committed by juveniles which would (1) bring them to the attention of juvenile courts and (2) not be crimes if committed by adults.

Statute of limitations Maximum time period within which a prosecution can be brought against a defendant for a particular offense; many criminal statutes have three- or six-year statute of limitations periods; there is no statute of limitations on homicide charges.

Statutory exclusion Legislative provisions that automatically exclude certain juveniles and offenses from the jurisdiction of the juvenile courts; offenses include murder, rape, and armed robbery.

Stigmas, stigmatization Social process whereby offenders are perceived as having undesirable characteristics as the result of incarceration or court appearances; criminal or delinquent labels are assigned those who are processed through the criminal and juvenile justice systems.

Straight adult incarceration Refers to youth in adult prisons where there is no special housing unit for them; instead, they are subject to regular incarceration and treated like other adult offenders.

Strain theory A criminological theory positing that a gap between culturally approved goals and legitimate means of achieving them causes frustration, which leads to criminal behavior.

Subculture of delinquency A culture within a culture where the use of violence in certain social situations is commonplace and normative; Marvin Wolfgang and Franco Ferracuti devised this concept to depict a set of norms apart from mainstream conventional society in which the theme of violence is pervasive and dominant; learned through socialization with others as an alternative lifestyle.

Support Our Students (SOS) program After-school intervention providing learning opportunities to children in high-crime areas.

Sustained petitions A finding that the facts alleged in a petition are true; a finding that the juvenile committed the offenses alleged, which resulted in an adjudication.

Sweat shops Exploitative businesses and industries that employed child labor and demanded long work hours for low pay.

Tagging Being equipped with an electronic wristlet or anklet for the purpose of monitoring offender whereabouts.

Taken into custody A decision made by a police officer that a youth should be held temporarily.

Teen courts Tribunals consisting of teenagers who judge other youth charged with minor offenses, much like regular juries in criminal courts, in which juvenile prosecutors and defense counsel argue cases against specific juvenile offenders; juries decide sanction with judicial approval.

Territorial gangs Groups of youth organized to defend a fixed amount of territory, such as several city blocks.

Theory A set of propositions from which a large number of new observations can be deduced; an integrated body of definitions, assumptions, and propositions related in such a way to explain and predict relations between two or more variables.

Totality of circumstances Sometimes used as the standard whereby offender guilt is determined or search and seizure warrants may be obtained; officers consider the entire set of circumstances in their decision to proceed with questioning a youth and allowing him/her to waive the right to counsel.

Traditional model Juvenile court proceedings characterized by less-formal adjudications, greater use of detention.

Training schools Traditionally referred to as "reform schools"; usually state-managed institutions designed to educate and rehabilitate youth.

Transfer hearings Proceedings to determine whether juveniles should be certified as adults for purposes of being subjected to jurisdiction of adult criminal courts where more severe penalties may be imposed.

Transfers Proceedings in which juveniles are remanded to the jurisdiction of criminal courts; also known as certifications and waivers.

Transportation Early British practice of sending undesirables, misfits, and convicted offenders to remote territories and islands controlled by England.

Treatment model See medical model.

TRIAD model A policing model used in schools, which includes enforcement, teaching, and counseling roles for officers.

Tribunal model Similar to a peer jury model, in that one's peers serve as judges, defense counsel, and prosecutors and one's actions and determine punishments.

Truancy courts Special courts that convene to determine strategies to utilize for youth who absent themselves from school.

Truants Juveniles who are habitually absent from school without excuse.

Unconditional probation, unconditional standard probation Form of conditional release without special restrictions or requirements placed on offender's behavior other than standard probation agreement terms; no formal controls operate to control or monitor probationer's behavior.

Uniform Crime Reports (UCR) Official source of crime information published annually by Federal Bureau of Investigation; accepts information from reporting law enforcement agencies about criminal arrests; classifies crimes according to various index criteria; tabulates information about offender age, gender, race, and other attributes.

Victim compensation Financial restitution payable to victims by either the state or convicted offenders.

Victim-impact statement Appendage to a predisposition or presentence investigation report that addresses the effect of the defendant's actions against victims or anyone harmed by the crime or delinquent act; usually compiled by the victim.

Victimization Basic measure of the occurrence of a crime; a specific criminal act affecting a specific victim.

Victim–offender mediation Third-party intervention mechanism whereby perpetrator and victim work out civil solution to otherwise criminal or delinquent action.

Violent Juvenile Offender Programs (VJOPs) Procedures designed to provide positive interventions and treatments; reintegrative programs, including transitional residential programs for those youth who have been subject to long-term detention; provides for social networking, provision of educational opportunities for youth, social learning, and goal-oriented behavioral skills.

VisionQuest Carefully regulated, intensive supervision program designed to improve the social and psychological experiences of juveniles; reintegrative program to improve one's educational and social skills; wilderness program.

Waiver hearing Formal juvenile court processes usually requested by prosecutor to transfer juvenile charged with various offenses to a criminal or adult court for prosecution.

Waiver motion Formal request by prosecutor to juvenile court judge asking to transfer juvenile's case from juvenile court to criminal court.

Waivers See transfers.

Wilderness projects Experience programs that include various outdoor programs designed to improve a juvenile's self-worth, self-concept, pride, and trust in others.

With prejudice To dismiss charges, but those same charges cannot be brought again later against the defendant.

Without prejudice To dismiss charges, but those same charges can be brought again later against the defendant.

Workhouses Early penal facilities designed to use prison labor for profit by private interests; operated in shires in mid-sixteenth century and later.

XYY **theory** Explanation of criminal behavior suggesting that some criminals are born with an extra *Y* chromosome, characterized as the "aggressive" chromosome compared with the passive *X* chromosome; an extra *Y* chromosome produces greater agitation, greater aggressiveness, and criminal propensities.

Youth judge model Youth court model in which juveniles perform the role of judges and other juveniles serve as prosecutors and defense counsel; very similar to the tribunal model, in which one or more youth perform.

Youth Services Bureaus (YSBs) Various types of diversion programs operated in the United States for delinquency-prone youth.

Youth squads Teams of police officers in police departments whose responsibility is to focus on prevention as well as particular delinquency problems.

Youth-to-Victim Restitution Project Program operated by the juvenile court in Lincoln, Nebraska; based on the principle that youth must repay whatever damages they have inflicted on victims; enforcement of restitution orders decreased recidivism among delinquent offenders.

Zone of transition The area that is both nearest the city center and undergoing rapid social change; believed to contain high rates of crime and delinquency.

Bibliography

Abatiello, Jennifer D. (2005). "Juvenile Competency and Culpability: What the Public Deserves." Unpublished paper presented at the annual meeting of the Academy of Criminal Justice Sciences, Chicago, IL (March).

Abbott-Chapman, J., Carey Denholm, and Colin Wyld (2007). "Pre-Service Professionals' Constructs of Adolescent Risk-Taking and Approaches to Risk Management." *Journal of Sociology* 11:241–261.

Abrams, Laura S. (2006). "From Corrections to Community: Youth Offenders' Perceptions of the Challenges of Transition." *Journal of Offender Rehabilitation* 44:31–53.

ACT 4 Juvenile Justice (n.d.). *Juvenile Status Offenses.* Retrieved on November 16, 2011, from http://www.act4jj.org/media/factsheets/factsheet_17.pdf.

Adams, Benjamin and Sean Addie (2010). *Delinquency Cases Waived to Criminal Court, 2007.* Washington, DC: Office of Juvenile Justice and Delinquency Prevention.

Adams, Kenneth (2003). "The Effectiveness of Juvenile Curfews on Crime Prevention." *The Annals of the American Academy of Political and Social Science* 587:136–159.

Addams, Jane (1912). *Twenty Years at Hull House with Autobiographical Notes.* New York, NY: The MacMillan Company.

Administrative Office of Pennsylvania Courts (2009). *Supreme Court to Take Luzerne County Case; Rarely Used King's Bench Powers to be Used.* Retrieved on October 1, 2010, from http://www.pacourts.us.

Administrative Office of the Courts (2011). *Screenings and Assessments Used in the Juvenile Justice System: Evaluating Risks and Needs of Youth in the Juvenile Justice System.* Retrieved on December 3, 2011, from http://www.courts.ca.gov/cfcc-delinquency.htm.

Adoption and Foster Care Analysis and Reporting System (2008). *Adoption and Foster Care Analysis and Reporting System Report.* Washington, DC: Adoption and Foster Care Analysis and Reporting System.

Adoption and Foster Care Analysis and Reporting System (2010). *Adoption and Foster Care Statistics. Report #17.* Retrieved on April 9, 2011, from http://www.acf.hhs.gov/programs/cb/stats_research/afcars/tar/report17.htm.

Agnew, Robert, Shelley Keith Matthews, Jacob Bucher, Adria N. Welcher, and Corey Keyes (2008). "Socioeconomic Status, Economic Problems, and Delinquency." *Youth & Society* 40(2):159–181.

Aisenberg, Eugene, Penelope K. Trickett, Ferol E. Mennen, William Saltzman, and Luis H. Zayas (2007). "Maternal Depression and Adolescent Behavior Problems: An Examination of Mediation Among Immigrant Latino Mothers and Their Adolescent Children Exposed to Community Violence." *Journal of Interpersonal Violence* 22:1227–1349.

Alford, Susan (1998). "The Effectiveness of Juvenile Arbitration in South Carolina." *APPA Perspectives* 22:28–34.

Altschuler, David M. and Troy L. Armstrong (2001). "Reintegrating High-Risk Juvenile Offenders into Communities: Experiences and Prospects." *Corrections Management Quarterly* 5:72–88.

American Bar Association (2011). *American Bar Association Urges Use of Electronic Monitoring for Juvenile Offenders.* Resolution 104 D. Adopted by the House of Delegates. Retrieved on April 28, 2011, from http://www.abanow.org/2011/01/104d/.

American Correctional Association (2007). *2007 Directory.* College Park, MD: American Correctional Association.

Anchorage Youth Court (2005). "Youth Courts Strive for Sustainability." *Gavel* 16:1–4.

Anderson, Carolyn M. and Andrew S. Rancer (2007). "The Relationship Between Argumentativeness, Verbal Aggressiveness, and Communication Satisfaction in Incarcerated Male Youth." *The Prison Journal* 87:328–343.

Anderson, Elijah (1999). *Code of the Street: Decency, Violence, and the Moral Life of the Inner City.* New York, NY: W.W. Norton & Co.

Anleu, Sharyn L. Roach (2010). *Law and Social Change,* 2nd ed. Thousand Oaks, CA: Sage Publications.

Apel, Robert J., Shawn Bushway, Robert Brame, Amelia Haviland, Daniel Nagin, and Raymond Paternoster (2007). "Unpacking the Relationship Between Adolescent Employment and Antisocial Behavior: A Matched Samples Comparison." *Criminology* 45:67–97.

APPA Perspectives (2004). "APPA Resolves Support for Youth Courts." *APPA Perspectives* 28:8.

Applegate, Brandon K., Robin King Davis, and Francis T. Cullen (2009). "Reconsidering Child Saving: The Extent and Correlates of Public Support for Excluding Youths from the Juvenile Court." *Crime and Delinquency* 55:51–77.

Archwamety, Teara and Antonis Katsiyannis (2000). "Academic Remediation, Parole Violations, and Recidivism Rates

Among Delinquent Youths." *Remedial and Special Education* 21:161–170.

Armour, Stacy and Dana L. Haynie (2007). "Adolescent Sexual Debut and Later Delinquency." *Journal of Youth and Adolescence* 36:141–152.

Armstrong, Edward G. (2008). "Critiques of Drug Courts: Rhetoric and Reality." Unpublished paper presented at the annual meeting of the Academy of Criminal Justice Sciences, Cincinnati, OH (March).

Armstrong, Gaylene (2001). *Private vs. Public Operation of Juvenile Correctional Facilities*. New York, NY: LFB Scholarly Publishing.

Armstrong, Troy L. (1991). *Intensive Interventions with High-Risk Youths: Promising Approaches in Juvenile Probation and Parole*. Monsey, NY: Criminal Justice Press.

Arya, Neelum (2011). *State Trends: Legislative Changes from 2005 to 2010 Removing Youth from the Adult Criminal Justice System*. Washington, DC: Campaign for Youth Justice.

Ashford, Jose B. and Craig Winston LeCroy (1993). "Juvenile Parole Policy in the United States: Determinate Versus Indeterminate Models." *Justice Quarterly* 10:179–195.

Austin, Andrew (2003). "Does Forced Sexual Contact Have Criminogenic Effects? An Empirical Test of Derailment Theory." *Journal of Aggression, Maltreatment, and Trauma* 8:41–66.

Austin, James, Kelly D. Johnson, and Maria Gregoriou (2000). *Juveniles in Adult Prisons and Jails: A National Assessment*. Washington, DC: Bureau of Justice Assistance.

Austin, James, Michael Jones, and Melissa Bolyard (1993). *The Growing Use of Jail Boot Camps*. Washington, DC: U.S. Department of Justice, Office of Justice Programs.

Ayers-Schlosser, Lee (2005). "2004 Juvenile Justice Summit: The Oregon Update." Unpublished paper presented at the annual meeting of the Academy of Criminal Justice Sciences, Chicago, IL (March).

Backstrom, James G. and Gary L. Walker (2006). "The Role of the Prosecutor in Juvenile Justice: Advocacy in the Courtroom and Leadership in the Community." *William Mitchell Law Review* 33:963–988.

Baltimore County, Maryland (2010). *School Resource Officer (SRO) Program*. Retrieved on October 22, 2010, from http://www.baltimorecountymd.gov/Agencies/police/community/sro.html.

Bannan, Rosemary (2008). "Tracking Resilience and Recidivism Mediation of Cook County Youth, 1999–2007." Unpublished paper presented at the annual meeting of the

Academy of Criminal Justice Sciences, Cincinnati, OH (March).

Barfeind, James (2008). *Predisposition Report Writing*. Missoula, MT: University of Montana.

Barnes, Allan R. (2005). "Weed and Seed Initiative: An Evaluation Using a Pre/Post Community Survey Approach." Unpublished paper presented at the annual meeting of the Academy of Criminal Justice Sciences, Chicago, IL (March).

Baron, Stephen W. (2007). "Street Youth, Gender, Financial Strain, and Crime: Exploring Broidy and Agnew's Extension to General Strain Theory." *Deviant Behavior* 28:273–302.

Baron, Stephen W. and David R. Forde (2007). "Street Youth Crime: A Test of Control Balance Theory." *Justice Quarterly* 24:335–350.

Bayley, David H. and Christine Nixon (2010). *The Changing Environment for Policing, 1985–2008*. Washington, DC: National Institute of Justice and Harvard Kennedy School of Government.

Bazemore, Gordon, Jeanne B. Stinchcomb, and Leslie A. Leip (2004). "Scared Smart or Bored Straight: Testing Deterrence Logic in an Evaluation of Police-Led Truancy Intervention." *Justice Quarterly* 21(2):269–299.

Bazemore, Gordon and Mark S. Umbreit (1995). "Rethinking the Sanctioning Function in Juvenile Court: Retributive or Restorative Responses to Youth Crime." *Crime & Delinquency* 41(3):296–316.

Bazemore, Gordon and Mark S. Umbreit (2001). *A Comparison of Four Restorative Conferencing Models*. Washington, DC: U.S. Department of Justice, Office of Justice Programs, Office of Juvenile Justice and Delinquency Prevention.

Beaver, Kevin M., Matt Delisi, and Michael G. Vaughn (2008). "The Intersection of Genes and Neuropsychological Deficits in the Prediction of Adolescent Delinquency and Self-Control." Unpublished paper presented at the annual meeting of the Academy of Criminal Justice Sciences, Cincinnati, OH (March).

Beaver, Kevin M., John Paul Wright, and Matt Delisi (2007). "Self-Control as an Executive Function: Reformulating Gottfredson's and Hirshi's Parental Socialization Thesis." *Criminal Justice and Behavior* 34:1345–1361.

Beccaria, Cesare Bonesana (1764). *On Crimes and Punishments*. Indianapolis, IN: Bobbs-Merrill, 1963; reprinted edition.

Beck, Allen J., Paige M. Harrison, and Paul Guerino (2010). *Sexual Victimization in Juvenile Facilities Reported by Youth, 2008–09*. Washington, DC: U.S. Department of Justice, Bureau of Justice Statistics.

Becker, Howard S. (1963). *Outsiders: Studies in the Sociology of Deviance*. New York, NY: Free Press.

Belshaw, Scott H. and Dean Lanham (2008). "OC Pepper Spray and the Juvenile Justice System in Texas: A Review of the Recent Changes and Policy Recommendations." Unpublished paper presented at the annual meeting of the Academy of Criminal Justice Sciences, Cincinnati, OH (March).

Bender, Valerie, Melanie King, and Patricia Torbet (2006). *Advancing Accountability: Moving Toward Victim Restoration*. Pittsburgh, PA: National Center for Juvenile Justice.

Benekos, Peter J. (2010). "School Safety and Youth Policy: Lessons from Zero Tolerance." Paper presented at the Second International Symposium on Children at Risk and in Need of Protection, Ankara, Turkey (April).

Benekos, Peter J. and Alida V. Merlo (2005). "Juvenile Offenders and the Death Penalty: How Far Have the Standards of Decency Evolved?" *Youth Violence and Juvenile Justice* 3(4):316–333

Benekos, Peter J. and Alida V. Merlo (2007). "Police and Juveniles: Redux." Paper presented at the Seventh Annual Conference of the European Society of Criminology, Bologna, Italy.

Benekos, Peter J. and Alida V. Merlo (Eds.) (2009). *Controversies in Juvenile Justice and Delinquency,* 2nd ed. Cincinnati, OH: Anderson/LexisNexis.

Benekos, Peter J., Alida V. Merlo, and Charles M. Puzzanchera (2011). "Youth, Race, and Serious Crime: Examining Trends and Critiquing Policy." *International Journal of Police Science Management* 13:1–17.

Bentham, Jeremy (1790). *An Introduction to the Principles of Morals and Legislation*. New York, NY: Hafner, 1948; reprinted edition.

Bernat, Frances P. (2005). "Evaluating Schools at Hope: Alternative Paradigm to Kids at Risk." Unpublished paper presented at the annual meeting of the Academy of Criminal Justice Sciences, Chicago, IL (March).

Bernberg, Jong G. and Thorolfur Thorlindsson (2007). "Community Structure and Adolescent Delinquency in Iceland: A Contextual Analysis." *Criminology* 45:415–444.

Bilchik, Shay (1996). *State Responses to Serious and Violent Juvenile Crime*. Pittsburgh, PA: National Center for Juvenile Justice.

Billings, F. James, Tanya Taylor, James Burns, Deb L. Corey, Sena Garven, and James M. Wood (2007). "Can Reinforcement Induce Children to Falsely Incriminate Themselves?" *Law and Human Behavior* 31:125–139.

Bishop, Donna M. (2009). "Race, Delinquency and Discrimination: Minorities in the Juvenile Justice System." In: Peter J. Benekos and Alida V. Merlo (Eds.), *Controversies in Juvenile Justice and Delinquency,* 2nd ed. (pp. 223–252). Cincinnati, OH: Anderson/LexisNexis.

Bishop, Donna M. (2010). "Juvenile Law Reform: Ensuring the Right to Counsel." *Criminology & Public Policy* 9:321–325.

Bishop, Donna M., Charles E. Frazier, Lonn Lanza-Kaduce, and Lawrence Winner (1996). "The Transfer of Juveniles to Criminal Court: Does It Make a Difference?" *Crime & Delinquency* 2(2):171–191.

Bjerk, David (2007). "Measuring the Relationship Between Youth Criminal Participation and Household Economic Resources." *Journal of Quantitative Criminology* 23:1573–1579.

Blevins, Kristie R. (2005). "The Correctional Orientation of 'Child Savers': The Level, Sources, and Impact of Support for Juvenile Correctional Workers." Unpublished paper presented at the annual meeting of the Academy of Criminal Justice Sciences, Chicago, IL (March).

Boone, Harry N., Jr. (1996). "Electronic Home Confinement: Judicial and Legislative Perspectives." *APPA Perspectives* 20:18–25.

Botchkovar, Ekaterina V., Charles R. Tittle, and Olena Antonaccio (2009). "General Strain Theory: Additional Evidence Using Cross-Cultural Data." *Criminology* 47(1):131–176.

Bouhours, Brigitte and Kathleen Daly (2007). "Youth Sex Offenders in Court: An Analysis of Judicial Sentencing Remarks." *Punishment and Society* 9:371–394.

Bowman, Cathy (2005). "Involvement of Probation and Parole in Project Safe Neighborhoods." Unpublished paper presented at the annual meeting of the American Probation and Parole Association, New York, NY (July).

Bowman, Marvella A., Hazel M. Prelow, and Scott R. Weaver (2007). "Parenting Behaviors, Association with Deviant Peers, and Delinquency in African American Adolescents." *Journal of Youth and Adolescence* 36:517–527.

Boyd, Rebecca J. and David L. Myers (2005). "Impact of Risk and Protective Factors for Alcohol Use Among a Rural Youth Sample." Unpublished paper presented at the annual meeting of the Academy of Criminal Justice Sciences, Chicago, IL (March).

Bradley, Tracey (2005). "Holistic Representation: Identifying Success." Unpublished paper presented at the annual training institute of the American Probation and Parole Association, New York, NY (July).

Bradsher, Keith (2000, January 14). "Boy Who Killed Gets 7 Years; Judge Says Law is Too Harsh." *New York Times*. Retrieved on November 11, 2010, from http://www.nytimes.com/2000/01/14/us/boy-who-killed-gets-7-years-judge-says-law-is-too-harsh.html?ref=nathaniel_abraham.

Brandau, Timothy J. (1992). *An Alternative to Incarceration for Juvenile Delinquents: The Delaware Bay Marine Institute*. Ann Arbor, MI: University Microfilms International.

Bratina, Michele P. (2008). "ADHD and School-Related Behavioral Problems: A Futile Mix?" Unpublished paper presented at the annual meeting of the Academy of Criminal Justice Sciences, Cincinnati, OH (March).

Brewer, Steven L. (2008). "In the Yard: Bullying in School and Prison Systems." Unpublished paper presented at the annual meeting of the Academy of Criminal Justice Sciences, Cincinnati, OH (March).

Brookbanks, Warren (2002). "Public Policy, Moral Panics, and the Lure of Anticipatory Containment." *Psychiatry, Psychology, and the Law* 9:127–135.

Brown, Ben (2006). "Understanding and Assessing School Police Officers: A Conceptual and Methodological Comment." *Journal of Criminal Justice* 34(6):591–604.

Brown, Joe M. (2005). "The Future of Juvenile Justice: Does Determinate Sentencing in Juvenile Court Serve the Same Purpose as Certification to Criminal Court?" Unpublished paper presented at the annual meeting of the Academy of Criminal Justice Sciences, Chicago, IL (March).

Browning, Katharine and Rolf Loeber (1999). *Highlights of Findings from the Pittsburgh Youth Study*. Washington, DC: Office of Juvenile Justice and Delinquency Prevention Programs.

Buckler, Kevin G., Marc Swatt, and Patti R. Salinas (2008). "Public Support of Capital Punishment: Assessing the Importance of Core Values and Racial Sentiment." Unpublished paper presented at the annual meeting of the Academy of Criminal Justice Sciences, Cincinnati, OH (March).

Buffington-Vollum, Jackqueline, John F. Edens, and Andrea Keilen (2008). "Institutional Violence Among Capital Inmates: The Impact of Changing Death Row." Unpublished paper presented at the annual meeting of the Academy of Criminal Justice Sciences, Cincinnati, OH (March).

Bureau of Justice Statistics (2008). *Annual Reports*. Washington, DC: U.S. Department of Justice, Bureau of Justice Statistics.

Burek, Melissa W., John Liederbach, Craig Winston, and Mitch Chamlin (2008). "Minority Juvenile Arrests: Mitigated or Instigated by Policing Practices?" Unpublished paper presented at the annual meeting of the Academy of Criminal Justice Sciences, Cincinnati, OH (March).

Burfeind, James W. and Dawn Jeglum Bartusch (2011). *Juvenile Delinquency: An Integrated Approach,* 2nd ed. Boston, MA: Jones and Bartlett.

Burgess, Robert and Ronald Akers (1966). "Differential Association–Reinforcement Theory of Criminal Behavior." *Social Problems* 14:128–147.

Burillo, Kristen (2010). "Less Capable Brain, Less Capable Teen?" Mercyhurst Civic Institute, Erie, PA *The Civic Column* 2(2):1–8.

Burke, Alison (2008). "Gender Specific Delinquency Prevention: The Unique Needs of Girls." Unpublished paper presented at the annual meeting of the Academy of Criminal Justice Sciences, Cincinnati, OH (March).

Burrell, William D. (2005). "Leaders for the Future: Two Views of Leadership Development." Unpublished paper presented at the annual meeting of the American Probation and Parole Association, New York, NY (July).

Busseri, Michael A., Teena Willoughby, and Heather Chalmers (2007). "A Rationale and Method for Examining Reasons for Linkages Among Adolescent Risk Behaviors." *Journal of Youth and Adolescence* 36:279–289.

Butts, Jeffrey A. (1996a). *Offenders in Juvenile Court*. Washington, DC: Office of Juvenile Justice and Delinquency Prevention.

Butts, Jeffrey A. (1996b). "Speedy Trial in Juvenile Court." *American Journal of Criminal Law* 23:515–561.

Butts, Jeffrey A. and Janeen Buck (2002). *The Sudden Popularity of Teen Courts*. Washington, DC: Urban Institute.

Butts, Jeffrey A. and Gregory J. Halemba (1996). *Waiting for Justice: Moving Young Offenders Through the Juvenile Court Process*. Pittsburgh, PA: National Center for Juvenile Justice.

Butts, Jeffrey A., Howard N. Snyder, Terrence A. Finnegan, Anne L. Aughenbagh, and Rowen S. Poole (1996). *Juvenile Court Statistics 1993: Statistics Report*. Washington, DC: Office of Juvenile Justice and Delinquency Prevention.

Bynum, Tim (2005). "Evaluating Project Safe Neighborhoods in the Eastern District of Michigan." Unpublished paper presented at the annual meeting of the Academy of Criminal Justice Sciences, Chicago, IL (March).

Cadigan, Timothy P. (2001). "PACTS." *Federal Probation* 65:25–30.

Caeti, Tory J., Craig Hemmens, and Velmer Burton (1996). "Juvenile Right to Counsel: A National Comparison of

State Legal Codes." *American Journal of Criminal Law* 23(3):611–632.

California Youth Authority (2008). *Predictions of Risk.* Sacramento, CA: California Youth Authority.

Campbell, Jacob and Brian Gonzalez (2007). *Juveniles Involved in the Juvenile Justice System.* Spokane, WA: Eastern Washington University, School of Social Work.

Carrington, Peter J. and Jennifer L. Schulenberg (2004). *Prior Police Contacts and Police Discretion with Apprehended Youth.* Ottawa, ON: Canadian Centre for Justice Statistics.

Cary, Pauline L. (2005). "ADHD and Juvenile Delinquency: A Review of the Literature." Unpublished paper presented at the annual meeting of the Academy of Criminal Justice Sciences, Chicago, IL (March).

Case, Stephen (2007). "Questioning the 'Evidence' of Risk that Underpins Evidence-Led Youth Justice." *Youth Justice* 7:91–105.

Caudill, Jonathan and Karen Hayslet-McCall (2008). "Short-Term Stay at the Gray Door Hotel: Assessment of Juvenile Pre-Trial Detention on Future Recidivism." Unpublished paper presented at the annual meeting of the Academy of Criminal Justice Sciences, Cincinnati, OH (March).

Cauffman, Elizabeth, Laurence Steinberg, and Alex R. Piquero (2005). "Psychological, Neuropsychological, and Physiological Correlates of Serious Antisocial Behavior in Adolescence: The Role of Self-Control." *Criminology* 43:133–176.

Cauffman, Elizabeth, Frances J. Lexcen, Asha Goldweber, Elizabeth P. Shulman, and Thomas Grisso (2007). "Gender Differences in Mental Health Symptoms Among Delinquent and Community Youth." *Youth Violence and Juvenile Justice* 5:297–307.

Center for Juvenile Justice Reform (2011). *Juvenile Justice System Improvement Project.* Washington, DC: Georgetown University. Retrieved on April 24, 2011, from htttp://cjjr.georgetown.edu/jjsip/jjsip.html.

Champion, Dean J. (1994). *Measuring Offender Risk: A Criminal Justice Sourcebook.* Westport, CT: Greenwood Press.

Champion, Dean J. (2005). *Probation, Parole, and Community Corrections,* 5th ed. Upper Saddle River, NJ: Prentice Hall.

Champion, Dean J. (2008a). *Probation, Parole, and Community Corrections,* 6th ed. Upper Saddle River, NJ: Prentice Hall.

Champion, Dean J. (2008b). "Sentencing Differentials According to Private vs. Court-Appointed Counsel." Unpublished paper presented at the annual meeting of the Academy of Criminal Justice Sciences, Cincinnati, OH (March).

Champion, Dean J. (2009). *Leading U.S. Supreme Court Cases: Briefs and Key Terms.* Upper Saddle River, NJ: Pearson/Prentice Hall.

Champion, Dean J. and G. Larry Mays (1991). *Juvenile Transfer Hearings: Some Trends and Implications for Juvenile Justice.* New York, NY: Praeger.

Chapman, Yvonne K. (2005). "Teen Courts and Restorative Justice." Unpublished paper presented at the annual meeting of the Academy of Criminal Justice Sciences, Chicago, IL (March).

Chapple, Constance L. (2005). "Self-Control, Peer Relations, and Delinquency." *Justice Quarterly* 22:89–106.

Chapple, Constance L. and Katherine A. Johnson (2007). "Gender Differences in Impulsivity." *Youth Violence and Family Justice* 5:221–234.

Chen, Xiaojen, Lisa Thrane, and Les B. Whitbeck (2007). "Onset of Conduct Disorder, Use of Delinquent Subsistence Strategies, and Street Victimization Among Homeless and Runaway Adolescents in the Midwest." *Journal of Interpersonal Violence* 22:1156–1183.

Chesney-Lind, Meda and Katherine Irwin (2006). "Still the 'Best Place to Conquer Girls': Girls in the Juvenile Justice System." In: Alida V. Merlo and Joycelyn M. Pollock (Eds.), *Women, Law and Social Control,* 2nd ed. (pp. 271–291). Boston, MA: Allyn and Bacon.

Chesney-Lind, Meda and Randall G. Shelden (2004). *Girls, Juvenile Delinquency, and Juvenile Justice,* 3rd ed. Belmont, CA: Wadsworth/Thompson Learning.

Chiang, Shu-Chuan, Shaw-Ji Chen, Hsiao-Ju Sun, Hung-Yu Chan, and Wei J. Chen (2007). "Heroin Use Among Youths Incarcerated for Illicit Drug Use: Psychosocial Environment, Substance Use History, Psychiatric Comorbidity, and Route of Administration." *American Journal of Addictions* 15:233–241.

Choi, Yoonsun (2007). "Academic Achievement and Problem Behaviors Among Asian Pacific Islander American Adolescents." *Journal of Youth and Adolescence* 36:403–415.

Choi, Alfred and Wing T. Lo (2002). *Fighting Youth Crime: Success and Failure of Two Little Dragons.* Singapore: Times Academic Press.

Clear, Todd R. and Harry R. Dammer (2003). *The Offender in the Community,* 2nd ed. Belmont, CA: Wadsworth/Thomson Learning.

Clinkinbeard, Samantha and Colleen Murray (2008). "Treatment Belonging and Support as Predictors of Future-Oriented Planning Among Incarcerated Offenders." Unpublished paper presented at the annual meeting of the Academy of Criminal Justice Sciences, Cincinnati, OH (March).

CNN Wire Staff (2011). *Philly Mayor: "No Excuses" for Flash Mob Attacks*. Retrieved on November 28, 2011, from http://articles.cnn.com/2011-08-09/justice/pennsylvania.curfew_1_flash-mob-curfew-mayor-michael-nutter?_s=PM:CRIME.

Coalition for Juvenile Justice (2007). *History and Current Strategy*. Washington, DC: Coalition for Juvenile Justice.

Cohen, Albert K. (1955). *Delinquent Boys*. New York, NY: Free Press.

Congressional Research Service (2007). *Juvenile Justice: Legislative History and Current Legislative Issues*. Washington, DC: Congressional Research Service.

Conley, Darlene J. (1994). "Adding Color to a Black and White Picture: Using Qualitative Data to Explain Racial Disproportionality in the Juvenile Justice System." *Journal of Research in Crime and Delinquency* 31:135–148.

Cook County Court (2002). *The Englewood Evening Reporting Center*. Chicago, IL: Cook County Court.

Cooley, Charles Horton (1902). *Human Nature and the Social Order*. New York, NY: Scribner's.

Copes, Heith and J. Patrick Williams (2007). "Techniques of Alienation: Deviant Behavior, Moral Commitment, and Subcultural Identity." *Deviant Behavior* 28:247–272.

Corbett, Ronald P. (2000). "Juvenile Probation on the Eve of the Next Millennium." *APPA Perspectives* 24:22–30.

Corwin, Joe-Anne (2005). "Juvenile Correctional Education Standards Approved." *Corrections Today* 67:83.

Cox, Steven M., Jennifer M. Allen, Robert D. Hanser, and John J. Conrad (2008). *Juvenile Justice: A Guide to Theory, Policy, and Practice*, 6th ed. Thousand Oaks, CA: Sage Publications.

Crawford, Kim (2007, September 20). "Grant to 'Supercharge' Local Efforts to Fight Guns, Gangs." *The Flit Journal First Edition*. Retrieved on November 28, 2011, from http://www.psnworks.org/.

Crawley, William R., Joel Ritsema, and Doug McKenzie (2005). "Exploring the Experience of Collective Identity and Conflict in Schooling." Unpublished paper presented at the annual meeting of the Academy of Criminal Justice Sciences, Chicago, IL (March).

Crooks, Claire V., Katreena L. Scott, David L. Wolfe, Debbie Chiodo, and Steve Killip (2007). "Understanding the Link Between Childhood Maltreatment and Violent Delinquency: What Do Schools Have to Add?" *Child Maltreatment* 12:269–280.

Cullen, Francis T., John Paul Wright, Shayna Brown, Melissa M. Moon, Michael B. Blankenship, and Brandon K. Applegate (1998). "Public Support for Early Intervention Programs: Implications for a Progressive Policy Agenda." *Crime and Delinquency* 44(2):187–204.

Cullen, Frank T. (2006). "It's Time to Reaffirm Rehabilitation." *Criminology & Public Policy* 5(4):665–672.

Dahlgren, Daniel C. (2005). "Emotional Sociology and Juvenile Delinquency: The Value of Interpreting Emotional Subculture of Gangs." Unpublished paper presented at the annual meeting of the Academy of Criminal Justice Sciences, Chicago, IL (March).

Daigle, Leah E., Francis T. Cullen, and John Paul Wright (2007). "Gender Differences in the Predictors of Juvenile Delinquency: Assessing the Generality-Specificity Debate." *Youth Violence and Juvenile Justice* 5:254–286.

D'Angelo, Jill M. and Michael P. Brown (2005). "Missouri Juvenile Justice Reform Act: Comparison of Case Outcomes from 1994 and 2000." Unpublished paper presented at the annual meeting of the Academy of Criminal Justice Sciences, Chicago, IL (March).

Dario, Lisa and David Holleran (2008). "A Re-Examination of Christian Fundamentalism and Support for the Death Penalty." Unpublished paper presented at the annual meeting of the Academy of Criminal Justice Sciences, Cincinnati, OH (March).

Davidson-Methot, David G. (2004). "Calibrating the Compass: Using Quality Improvement Data for Outcome Evaluation, Cost Control, and Creating Quality Organizational Cultures." *Residential Treatment for Children and Youth* 21:45–68.

Death Penalty Information Center (2010). *Juveniles and the Death Penalty*. Retrieved on November 26, 2011, from http://www.deathpenaltyinfo.org/juveniles-and-death-penalty.

Decker, Scott H. (2005). "Evaluating Project Safe Neighborhoods in the Eastern District of Missouri." Unpublished paper presented at the annual meeting of the Academy of Criminal Justice Sciences, Chicago, IL (March).

Dedel, Kelly (2006). *Juvenile Runaways*. Washington, DC: U.S. Department of Justice, Office of Community Oriented Policing Services.

Dembo, Richard, Charles W. Turner, and Nancy Jainchill (2007). "An Assessment of Criminal Thinking Among Incarcerated Youths in Three States." *Criminal Justice and Behavior* 34:1157–1167.

Dembo, Richard, Jennifer Wareham, and Norman G. Poythress (2006). "Introduction: AIW Special Issue." *Journal of Offender Rehabilitation* 43(4):1–6.

Dembo, Richard, Marina Shemwell, Julie Guida, James Schmiedler, Kimberly Pacheco, and William Seeberger (2000a). "A Longitudinal Study of the Impact of a Family Empowerment Intervention on Juvenile Offender Psychosocial Functioning: An Expanded Assessment." *Journal of Child and Adolescent Substance Abuse* 10:1–7.

Dembo, Richard, Gabriella Ramirez-Garnica, Matthew Rollie, James Schmielder, Stephen Livingston, and Amy Hartfield (2000b). "Youth Recidivism Twelve Months After a Family Empowerment Intervention." *Journal of Offender Rehabilitation* 31:29–65.

DiIulio, John J. (1995, November). "The Coming of the Super-Predator." *Weekly Standard* 27:23–28.

Dinkes, Rachel, Jana Kemp, and Katrina Baum (2009). *Indicators of School Crime and Safety 2009* (NCES 2010–012/NCJ 228478). Washington, DC: National Center for Education Statistics, Institute of Education Sciences, U.S. Department of Education, and U.S. Department of Justice, Bureau of Justice Statistics, Office of Justice Programs.

Dubowitz, Howard, Stephen C. Pitts, and Maureen M. Black (2004). "Measurement of Three Major Subtypes of Child Neglect." *Child Maltreatment* 9:344–356.

Duran, Robert (2005). "Manufacturing Gang Fears: A Critique of the Police Suppression Industry." Unpublished paper presented at the annual meeting of the Academy of Criminal Justice Sciences, Chicago, IL (March).

Dussich, John P.J. and Chi Maekoya (2007). "Physical Child Harm and Bullying-Related Behaviors: A Comparative Study in Japan, South Africa, and the United States." *International Journal of Offender Therapy and Comparative Criminology* 51:495–509.

Duwe, Grant and Deborah Kerschner (2008). "Removing a Nail from the Boot Camp Coffin: An Outcome Evaluation of Minnesota's Challenge Incarceration Program." *Crime and Delinquency* 54(4):614–643.

Dwyer, Diane C. and Roger B. McNally (1987). "Juvenile Justice: Reform, Retain, and Reaffirm." *Federal Probation* 51:47–51.

Edmondson, W.A. Drew (2003). *Execution Date Set for Hain.* Retrieved on September 29, 2010, from http://www.oag .state.ok.us/oagweb.nsf/srch/0A951D018C14AA1C86257 2B4006F5F7D?OpenDocument.

Egley, Arlen, Jr., James C. Howell, and John P. Moore (2010). *Highlights of the 2008 National Youth Gang Survey.* Washington, DC: Office of Juvenile Justice and Delinquency Prevention.

Eitle, David, Lisa Stolzenberg, and Stewart D'Alessio (2005). "Police Organizational Factors, the Racial Composition of the Police, and the Probability of Arrest." *Justice Quarterly* 22:30–56.

Ellsworth, Thomas (1988). "Case Supervision Planning: The Forgotten Component of Intensive Probation Supervision." *Federal Probation* 52:28–33.

Ellsworth, Thomas, Michelle T. Kinsella, and Kimberlee Massin (1992). "Prosecuting Juveniles: *Parens Patriae* and Due Process in the 1990's." *Justice Professional* 7:53–67.

Ellwanger, Steven J. (2007). "Strain, Attribution, and Traffic Delinquency Among Young Drivers: Measuring and Testing General Strain Theory in the Context of Driving." *Crime and Delinquency* 53:523–551.

Emeka, Traqina Q. and Jon R. Sorensen (2009). "Female Juvenile Risk: Is There a Need for Gendered Assessment Instruments?" *Youth Violence and Juvenile Justice* 7(4):413–330.

Empey, Lamar T. and Jerome Rabow (1961). "The Provo Experiment in Delinquency Rehabilitation." *American Sociological Review* 26:679–695.

Erez, Edna and Kathy Laster (1999). "Neutralizing Victim Reform." *Crime and Delinquency* 45:530–553.

Esbensen, Finn-Aage, Bradley Brick, Chris Melde, Karin Tusinski, and Terrance J. Taylor (2008). "The Role of Race and Ethnicity in Gang Membership." In: Frank van Gemert, Dana Peterson, and Inger-Lise Lien (Eds.), *Youth Gangs, Migration, and Ethnicity.* Devon, UK: Willan Publishing Company.

Estell, David B., Thomas W. Farmer, and Beverly D. Cairns (2007). "Bullies and Victims in Rural African-American Youth: Behavioral Characteristics and Social Network Placement." *Aggressive Behavior* 33:145–159.

Estell, David B., Thomas W. Farmer, Matthew J. Irvin, Jana H. Thompson, Bryan C. Hutchins, and Erin M. McDonough (2007). "Patterns of Middle School Adjustment and Ninth Grade Adaptation of Rural African-American Youth: Grades and Substance Use." *Journal of Youth and Adolescence* 36:477–487.

Fagan, Jeffrey A. (1990). "Treatment and Reintegration of Violent Juvenile Offenders: Experimental Results." *Justice Quarterly* 7:233–263.

Fagan, Jeffrey A. and Craig Reinarman (1991). "The Social Context of Intensive Supervision: Organizational and Ecological Influences on Community Treatment." In: Troy L. Armstrong (Ed.), *Intensive Interventions with High-Risk*

Youths: Promising Approaches in Juvenile Probation and Parole (pp. 341–394). Monsey, NY: Criminal Justice Press.

Fagan, Jeffrey and Valerie West (2005). "The Decline of the Juvenile Death Penalty: Scientific Evidence of Evolving Norms." *The Journal of Criminal Law & Criminology* 95(2):427–497.

Farina-Henry, Samuel and Kelly Vaughan (2010). *Graham v. Florida* (08-7412); *Sullivan v. Florida* (08-7621). Cornell University Law School, Legal Information Institute. Retrieved on October 1, 2010, from http://topics.law.cornell.edu/supct/cert/08-7412.

Farrington, David P. and Maria M. Ttofi (2010). *School-Based Programs to Reduce Bullying and Victimization*. Washington, DC: U.S. Department of Justice, National Institute of Justice.

Fast, Diane K. and Julianne L. Conry (2009). "Fetal Alcohol Spectrum Disorders and the Criminal Justice System." *Developmental Disabilities Research Review* 15(3):250–257.

Feiring, Candice, Shari Miller-Johnson, and Charles M. Cleland (2007). "Potential Pathways from Stigmatization and Internalizing Symptoms to Delinquency in Sexually Abused Youth." *Child Maltreatment* 12:220–232.

Feld, Barry C. (1993). "Juvenile (In)Justice and the Criminal Court Alternative." *Crime & Delinquency* 39(4):403–424.

Feld, Barry C. (1998). "Abolish the Juvenile Court: Youthfulness, Criminal Responsibility, and Sentencing Policy." *Journal of Criminal Law & Criminology* 88:68–136.

Feld, Barry C. (1999). *Bad Kids: Race and the Transformation of the Juvenile Court*. New York, NY: Oxford University Press.

Feld, Barry C. (2007). "Final Results from Investigation of Blended Sentencing in Ohio and Vermont." Unpublished paper presented at the annual meeting of the American Society of Criminology, Atlanta, GA (November).

Feld, Barry C. and Shelly Schaefer (2010a). "The Right to Counsel in Juvenile Court: Law Reform to Deliver Legal Services and Reduce Justice by Geography." *Criminology & Public Policy* 9(2):327–356.

Feld, Barry C. and Shelly Schaefer (2010b). "The Right to Counsel in Juvenile Court: The Conundrum of Attorneys as an Aggravating Factor at Disposition." *Justice Quarterly* 27(5):713–741.

Ferzan, Ibrahim Halil (2008). "Comparison of Juvenile Justice System and Delinquency in the United States and Turkey." Unpublished paper presented at the annual meeting of the Academy of Criminal Justice Sciences, Cincinnati, OH (March).

Fite, Paula J., Porche Wynn, and Dustin A. Pardini (2009). Explaining Discrepancies in Arrest Rates Between Black and White Male Juveniles. *Journal of Consulting and Clinical Psychology* 77:916–927.

Flesch, Lisa M. (2004). "Juvenile Crime and Why Waiver Is Not the Answer." *Family Court Review* 42(3):583–596.

Flexner, Bernard and Roger N. Baldwin (1914). *Juvenile Courts and Probation*. New York, NY: Harcourt.

Flores, J. Robert (2007). *Testimony Before the U.S. Senate Committee on the Judiciary on reauthorization of the Juvenile Justice and Delinquency Prevention Act, December 5*. Retrieved on April 15, 2011, from http://www.ojjdp.gov/about/florestestimony120507.html.

Foley, Roger P. (2008). *Disposition and Post-Disposition: Predisposition Reports*. Retrieved on November 26, 2011, from http://www.rpfoley.com/lawyer-attorney-1530476.html.

Fratello, Jennifer, Annie Salsich, and Sara Mogulescu (2011). *Juvenile Detention Reform in New York City: Measuring Risk Through Research*. New York, NY: Vera Institute of Justice.

Free Press (2007). *Operation Proves How Team Work Beats Crime*. Retrieved on November 16, 2011, from http://www.psnworks.org/.

Freivalds, Peter (1996). *Balanced and Restorative Justice Project (BARJ)*. Washington, DC: Office of Juvenile Justice and Delinquency Prevention.

Friday, Paul C. and Xin Ren (2006). *Delinquency and Juvenile Justice Systems in the Non-Western World*. Monsey, NY: Criminal Justice Press.

Frisher, Martin, Llana Chrome, John Macleod, Roger Bloor, and Matthew Hickman (2007). *Predictive Factors for Illicit Drug Use Among Young People*. London: Home Office Research, Development and Statistics Directorate.

Fritsch, Eric and Tory Caeti (2009). "Youth Behind Bars: Doing Justice or Doing Harm?" In: Peter J. Benekos and Alida V. Merlo (Eds.), *Controversies in Juvenile Justice and Delinquency*, 2nd ed. (pp. 203–222). Cincinnati, OH: Anderson/LexisNexis.

Gainey, Randy R. and Brian K. Payne (2003). "Changing Attitudes Toward House Arrest with Electronic Monitoring." *International Journal of Offender Therapy and Comparative Criminology* 47:196–209.

Gallagher, Catherine A. and Adam Dobrin (2007). "Risk of Suicide in Juvenile Justice Facilities: The Problem of Rate Calculations in High-Turnover Populations." *Criminal Justice and Behavior* 34:1362–1376.

Gamble, Thomas J. and Amy C. Eisert (2009). "Delinquency Theory: Examining Delinquency and Aggression Through a Biopsychosocial Approach." In: Peter J. Benekos and Alida V. Merlo (Eds.), *Controversies in Juvenile Justice and Delinquency,* 2nd ed. (pp. 53–84). Cincinnati, OH: Anderson/LexisNexis.

Garmin Ltd. (2011). *What Is GPS?* Retrieved on November 27, 2011, from http://www8.garmin.com/aboutGPS/.

Gavazzi, Stephen M., Deborah Wasserman, Charles Partridge, and Sarah Sheridan (2000). "The Growing Up FAST Diversion Program." *Aggression and Violent Behavior* 5:159–175.

Geary County Community Corrections (2002). *Pre-Dispositional Supervision Program.* Geary County, KS: Geary County Community Corrections.

Gelber, Seymour (1990). "The Juvenile Justice System: Vision for the Future." *Juvenile and Family Court Journal* 41:15–18.

Geller, Bill and Lisa Belsky (2009). *A Policymaker's Guide to Building Our Way Out of Crime: The Transformative Power of Police-Community Developer Partnerships.* Washington, DC: U.S. Department of Justice, Office of Community Oriented Policing Services.

George, Rani and George Thomas (2008). "Ethnic Identity and Self-Esteem as Protective Factors from Violence Risk Among Minority Youth." Unpublished paper presented at the annual meeting of the Academy of Criminal Justice Sciences, Cincinnati, OH (March).

Giblin, Matthew J. (2002). "Using Police Officers to Enhance the Supervision of Juvenile Probationers: An Evaluation of the Anchorage CAN Program." *Crime & Delinquency* 48(1):116–137.

Glaze, Lauren E. (2010). *Correctional Populations in the United States, 2009.* Washington, DC: U.S. Department of Justice, Bureau of Justice Statistics.

Glueck, Sheldon and Eleanor Glueck (1950). *Unraveling Juvenile Delinquency.* New York, NY: Commonwealth Fund.

Goffman, Erving (1961). *Asylums.* Garden City, NY: Anchor Press.

Gomez, Fernando and Juan Jose Ganuza (2002). "Civil and Criminal Sanctions Against Blackmail: An Economic Analysis." *International Review of Law and Economics* 21:475–498.

Gordon, Jill A. and Paige Malmsjo (2005). "The Impact of Offender Characteristics on Recidivism: An Evaluation of Barrett Juvenile Correctional Center." Unpublished paper

presented at the annual meeting of the Academy of Criminal Justice Sciences, Chicago, IL (March).

Gover, Angela R. and Doris Layton MacKenzie (2003). "Child Maltreatment and Adjustment in Juvenile Correctional Institutions." *Criminal Justice and Behavior* 30:374–396.

Grant, Lorna Elaine (2008). "The Recent Development of Jamaican Gangs in Schools." Unpublished paper presented at the annual meeting of the Academy of Criminal Justice Sciences, Cincinnati, OH (March).

Graves, Kelly N. (2007). "Not Always Sugar and Spice: Expanding Theoretical and Functional Explanations for Why Females Aggress." *Aggression and Violent Behavior: A Review Journal* 12:131–140.

Greenleaf, Richard G. (2005). "A Survey of Gang and Non-Gang Members Regarding Their Attitudes Toward the Police, Community, and Crime: A Chicago Study." Unpublished paper presented at the annual meeting of the Academy of Criminal Justice Sciences, Chicago, IL (March).

Greenwood, Peter (2008). "Prevention and Intervention Programs for Juvenile Offenders." *The Future of Children* 18:185–210.

Gregorie, Trudy (2005). "Victims' Rights and Issues: Educating Judicial and Court Personnel." Unpublished paper presented at the annual training institute of the American Probation and Parole Association, New York, NY (July).

Griffin, Patrick (2008). *National Overviews. State Juvenile Justice Profiles.* Pittsburgh, PA: National Center for Juvenile Justice.

Griffin, Patrick (2010). *Models for Change: Innovations in Practice.* Pittsburgh, PA: National Center for Juvenile Justice.

Griffin, Patrick, Linda Szymanski, and Melanie King (2006). *National Overviews. State Juvenile Justice Profiles.* Pittsburgh, PA: National Center for Juvenile Justice.

Grisso, Thomas (1998). *Forensic Evaluation of Juveniles.* Sarasota, FL: Professional Resource Press.

Grisso, Thomas and Richard Barnum (2000). *Massachusetts Youth Screening Instrument, Second Version (MAYSI-2): User's Manual and Technical Report.* Boston, MA: Massachusetts Department of Youth Services.

Hagan, Frank E. (2011). *Introduction to Criminology: Theories, Methods, and Criminal Behavior.* Thousand Oaks, LA: Sage Publications, Inc.

Hannah-Jones, Nikole (2010, October 4). "Multnomah County Turns to GPS Tracking to Fight Gang Violence." *The Oregonian.* Retrieved on November 27, 2011, from http://www.oregonlive.com/portland/index.ssf/2010/10/multnomah_county_turns_to_gps.html.

Haraway, Daniel Scott (2008). "The Juvenile Waiver: The Perfect Solution for Serious Juvenile Offenders?" Unpublished paper presented at the annual meeting of the Academy of Criminal Justice Sciences, Cincinnati, OH (March).

Hart, Likisha (2005). "Learning Disabilities and Juvenile Delinquency: Examining the Correlation Between Labeling and Delinquent Behavior." Unpublished paper presented at the annual meeting of the Academy of Criminal Justice Sciences, Chicago, IL (March).

Hayes, Lindsay M. (2009). *Characteristics of Juvenile Suicide in Confinement.* Washington, DC: Office of Juvenile Justice and Delinquency Prevention.

Haynie, Dana L., Darrell Steffensmeier, and Kerryn E. Bell (2007). "Gender and Serious Violence: Untangling the Role of Friendship Sex Composition and Peer Violence." *Youth Violence and Juvenile Justice* 5:235–253.

Haynie, Dana L., Peggy C. Giordano, Wendy D. Manning, and Monica A. Longmore (2005). "Adolescent Romantic Relationships and Delinquency Involvement." *Criminology* 43:177–210.

Henderson, Thomas A., Cornelius M. Kerwin, Neal Miller, Randall Guynes, Hildy Saizow, Robert C. Griesser, and Carl Baar (1984). *The Significance of Judicial Structure: The Effect of Unification on Trial Court Operations.* Washington, DC: U.S. Government Printing Office.

Hennigan, Karen, Kathy Kolnick, Tian Siva Tian, Cheryl Maxon, and John Poplawski (2010). *Five Year Outcomes of a Randomized Trial of a Community Based Multi-Agency Intensive Supervision Juvenile Probation Program.* Washington, DC: U.S. Department of Justice, National Criminal Justice Reference Service.

Henry, David B. and Kimberly Kobus (2007). "Early Adolescent Social Networks and Substance Use." *The Journal of Early Adolescence* 27:346–362.

Hensley, Christopher, Suzanne E. Tallichet, and Stephen D. Singer (2005). "Exploring the Possible Link Between Childhood and Adolescent Bestiality and Interpersonal Violence." Unpublished paper presented at the annual meeting of the Academy of Criminal Justice Sciences, Chicago, IL (March).

Herman, Susan and Cressida Wasserman (2001). "A Role for Victims in Offender Reentry." *Crime and Delinquency* 47:428–445.

Hill, Malcolm, Moira Walker, Kristin Moodie, Brendan Wallace, Jon Bannister, Furzana Khan, Gill McIvor, and Andrew

Kendrick (2007). "More Haste, Less Speed? An Evaluation of Fast Track Policies to Tackle Persistent Youth Offending in Scotland." *Youth Justice* 7:121–137.

Hinduja, Sameer, Justin W. Patchin, and Trevor Lippman (2008). "Cyberbullying Among Middle Schoolers: Focusing in on the Causes and Consequences." Unpublished paper presented at the annual meeting of the Academy of Criminal Justice Sciences, Cincinnati, OH (March).

Hirschi, Travis (1969). *Causes of Delinquency.* Berkeley, CA: University of California Press.

Hockenberry, Sarah, Melissa Sickmund, and Anthony Sladky (2009). *Juvenile Residential Facility Census, 2006: Selected Findings.* Washington, DC: Office of Juvenile Justice and Delinquency Prevention.

Hockenberry, Sarah, Melissa Sickmund, and Anthony Sladky (2011). *Juvenile Residential Facility Census, 2008: Selected Findings.* Washington, DC: Office of Juvenile Justice and Delinquency Prevention.

Holland Teen Court (2008). *The Holland Teen Court.* Holland, MI: Holland Teen Court.

Holsinger, Alex M. and Edward J. Latessa (1999). "An Empirical Evaluation of a Sanction Continuum: Pathways Through the Juvenile Justice System." *Journal of Criminal Justice* 27:155–172.

Hooton, Earnest A. (1939). *Crime and the Man.* Cambridge, MA: Harvard University Press.

Houk, Julie M. (1984). "Electronic Monitoring of Probationers: A Step Toward Big Brother?" *Golden Gate University Law Review* 14:431–446.

Huff, C. Ronald (1989). "Youth Gangs and Public Policy." *Crime and Delinquency* 35(4):524–537.

Huskey, Bobbie L. (1984). "Community Corrections Acts." *Corrections Today* 46:45.

In re Gault, 387 U.S. 1 (1967) at 4, 78–79.

In re Winship, 397 U.S. 358 (1970) at 360, 368.

Ingram, Jason R., Justin W. Patchin, Beth M. Huebner, John M. McCluskey, and Timothy S. Bynum (2005). "Family Environment, Peers, and Delinquency: A Path Analysis." Unpublished paper presented at the annual meeting of the Academy of Criminal Justice Sciences, Chicago, IL (March).

Ingram, Jefferson (2008). "The Future of Death Penalty Litigation: The End of the Road with *Baez v. Rees.*" Unpublished paper presented at the annual meeting of the Academy of Criminal Justice Sciences, Cincinnati, OH (March).

Interbranch Commission on Juvenile Justice (2010). *Report to the General Assembly, Governor Edward G. Rendell and the*

Supreme Court of Pennsylvania. Philadelphia, PA: Administrative Office of Pennsylvania Courts.

Iowa City Police Department (2011). *Juvenile Procedures*. Section OPS-19. Retrieved on November 26, 2011, from http://www.icgov.org/site/CMSv2/File/police/generalOrders/genorder38.pdf.

Janoski, Dave and Michael R. Sisak (2011, February 19). "Defense, Prosecution Declare Victory in Ciavarella Conviction." *The Scranton Times Tribune*. Retrieved on November 26, 2011, from http://thetimes-tribune.com/news/defense-prosecution-declare-victory-in-ciavarella-conviction-1.1107461#axzz1Giy0s42X.

Jarjoura, Roger G., Megan LaMade, Mark Livingston, Michael Roberts, Matthew Abney, and Jessie Skinner (2008). "An Assessment of the Punitive Nature of Juvenile Court Dispositions." Unpublished paper presented at the annual meeting of the Academy of Criminal Justice Sciences, Cincinnati, OH (March).

Johnson County Department of Corrections (2002). *Juvenile ISP Conditions & Guidelines*. Johnson County, KS: Johnson County Department of Corrections.

Johnson, Kay (2005). "Trauma and Substance Abuse Treatment for Women Offenders." Unpublished paper presented at the annual meeting of the American Probation and Parole Association, New York, NY (July).

Jones, Judith B. (2004). *Access to Counsel*. Washington, DC: Office of Juvenile Justice and Delinquency Prevention.

Juvenile Law Center (n.d.). *Luzerne County "Kids for Cash" Juvenile Court Scandal*. Retrieved on February 26, 2011, from http://www.jlc.org/luzerne/.

Juveniles Who Have Sexually Offended (2001). Retrieved on December 3, 2011, from http://www.ncjrs.gov/html/ojjdp/report_juvsex_offend/sum.html.

Kansas Juvenile Justice Authority (2010). *Strategic Plan FY 2011–2012*. Retrieved on December 3, 2011, from http://www.jja.ks.gov/documents/Public/Public_StrategicPlan2010.pdf.

Karlin, Rick (2010, October 21). "Last Days of Tryon End in Silence." *Times Union Online*. Retrieved on April 15, 2011, from http://www.timesunion.com/default/article/Last-days-of-Tryon-end-in-silence-716103.php.

Karp, David R. (2001). "Harm and Repair: Observing Restorative Justice in Vermont." *Justice Quarterly* 18:727–757.

Karp, David R. (2004). "Teen Courts." *APPA Perspectives* 28:18–20.

Katz, Charles M., Vincent J. Webb, and Scott H. Decker (2005). "Using the Arrestee Drug Abuse Monitoring (ADAM) Program to Further Understand the Relationship Between Drug Use and Gang Membership." *Justice Quarterly* 22:58–88.

Kelly, Katharine (2005). "Auto Theft and Youth Culture: A Nexus of Masculinities, Femininities, and Car Culture." Unpublished paper presented at the annual meeting of the Academy of Criminal Justice Sciences, Chicago, IL (March).

Kempf-Leonard, Kimberly (2010). "Does Having an Attorney Provide a Better Outcome?" *Criminology & Public Policy* 9:357–363.

Kempf-Leonard, Kimberly and Pernilla Johansson (2007). "Gender and Runaways: Risk Factors, Delinquency, and Juvenile Justice Experiences." *Youth Violence and Juvenile Justice* 5:308–327.

Kennedy, David M., Anthony A. Braga, Anne M. Piehl, and Elin J. Waring (2001). *Reducing Gun Violence: The Boston Gun Project's Operation Ceasefire*. Washington, DC: U.S. Department of Justice, National Institute of Justice.

Kennedy, Sharon (2005). "Increasing the Effectiveness of Probation and Parole Through Research." Unpublished paper presented at the annual training institute of the American Probation and Parole Association, New York, NY (July).

Kent v. United States, 383 U.S. 541 (1966) at 561.

Khalili, Ahmad (2008). "Neighborhood Quality of Life and Delinquency: A Contextual Explanation of Juvenile Delinquency." Unpublished paper presented at the annual meeting of the Academy of Criminal Justice Sciences, Cincinnati, OH (March).

Kidd, Sean A. (2007). "Youth Homelessness and Social Stigma." *Journal of Youth and Adolescence* 36:291–299.

King, Tammy (2005). "Juvenile Detention: A Descriptive Study of Rule Infractions." Unpublished paper presented at the annual meeting of the Academy of Criminal Justice Sciences, Chicago, IL (March).

King, Tammy, Kelly Melvin, and Jennifer Biederman (2008). "Juvenile Detention Facilities: Challenges and Changes." Unpublished paper presented at the annual meeting of the Academy of Criminal Justice Sciences, Cincinnati, OH (March).

Kitsuse, John I. (1962). "Societal Reaction to Deviant Behavior: Problems of Theory and Method." *Social Problems* 9:247–256.

Klein, Malcolm W., Susan L. Rosenzweig, and Ronald Bates (1975). "The Ambiguous Juvenile Arrest." *Criminology* 24:185–194.

Knoll, Crystal and Melissa Sickmund (2010). *Delinquency Cases in Juvenile Court, 2007*. Washington, DC: Office of Juvenile justice and Delinquency Prevention.

Kohlberg, Lawrence (1981). *The Philosophy of Moral Development*. New York, NY: Harper and Row.

Konty, Mark (2005). "Microanomie: The Cognitive Foundations of the Relationship Between Anomie and Deviance." *Criminology* 43:107–132.

Kretschmer, Ernest (1936). *Physique and Character*. London: Kegan, Paul, Trench, and Trubner.

Kuanliang, Attapol (2008). "A Comparison of Institutional Violent Misconduct Between Juvenile and Adult Prisoners." Unpublished paper presented at the annual meeting of the Academy of Criminal Justice Sciences, Cincinnati, OH (March).

Kubena, Jiletta (2008). "Juvenile Offender Reentry: An Examination of the Issues." Unpublished paper presented at the annual meeting of the Academy of Criminal Justice Sciences, Cincinnati, OH (March).

Kuntsche, Emmanuel, Ronald Knibbe, Rutger Engels, and Gerhard Gmel (2007). "Drinking Motives as Mediators of the Link Between Alcohol Expectancies and Alcohol Use Among Adolescents." *Journal of Studies on Alcohol and Drugs* 68:76–85.

Kupchik, Aaron (2007). "The Correctional Experiences of Youth in Adult and Juvenile Prisons." *Justice Quarterly* 24:247–270.

Kurlychek, Megan C. and Brian D. Johnson (2010). "Juvenility and Punishment: Sentencing Juveniles in Adult Criminal Court." *Criminology* 48(3):725–758.

Kwak, Dae-Hoon and Seok-Jin Jeong (2008). "Juvenile Justice Decision Making in a Midwestern State: Does Type of Court Matter?" Unpublished paper presented at the annual meeting of the Academy of Criminal Justice Sciences, Cincinnati, OH (March).

Kyle, Jim (1998). "The Privatization Debate Continues." *Corrections Today* 60:88–158.

Lab, Steven P., Glenn Shields, and Connie Schondel (1993). "Research Note: An Evaluation of Juvenile Sexual Offender Treatment." *Crime and Delinquency* 39:543–553.

LaMade, Megan (2008). "Juvenile Courts: Who Receives Punishment?" Unpublished paper presented at the annual meeting of the Academy of Criminal Justice Sciences, Cincinnati, OH (March).

Lane, Jodi, Susan Turner, Terry Fain, and Amber Sehgal (2005). "Evaluating an Experimental Intensive Juvenile Probation Program: Supervision and Official Outcomes." *Crime & Delinquency* 51(1):26–52.

Lansford, Jennifer E., Shari Miller-Johnson, Lisa J. Berlin, Kenneth A. Dodge, John E. Bates, and Gregory S. Pettit (2007). "Early Physical Abuse and Later Violent Delinquency: A Prospective Longitudinal Study." *Child Maltreatment* 12:233–245.

LaSean, Glenda (2008). "Juvenile Interrogation Techniques: A Law Enforcement Perspective." Unpublished paper presented at the annual meeting of the Academy of Criminal Justice Sciences, Cincinnati, OH (March).

Latessa, Edward J. (2005). "Increasing the Effectiveness of Probation and Parole Through Research." Unpublished paper presented at the annual training institute of the American Probation and Parole Association, New York, NY (July).

LaTorre, Diana Tecco (2008). "A Closer Look at Child Abuse Laws." Unpublished paper presented at the annual meeting of the Academy of Criminal Justice Sciences, Cincinnati, OH (March).

Lawrence, Richard A. (1984). "The Role of Legal Counsel in Juveniles' Understanding of Their Rights." *Juvenile and Family Court Journal* 34:49–58.

Lawrence, Richard A. (2006). *School Crime and Juvenile Justice*, 2nd ed. New York, NY: Oxford University Press.

Lawrence, Richard A. (2009). "Violence and Schools: The Problem, Prevention, and Policies." In: Peter J. Benekos and Alida V. Merlo (Eds.), *Controversies in Juvenile Justice and Delinquency*, 2nd ed. (pp. 107–130). Cincinnati, OH: Anderson/LexisNexis.

Lee, Byung Hyun (2008). "The Impact of Parental Supervision and Control on Delinquent Behaviors." Unpublished paper presented at the annual meeting of the Academy of Criminal Justice Sciences, Cincinnati, OH (March).

Lee, Vivien and Peter N.S. Hoaken (2007). "Cognition, Emotion, and Neurobiological Development: Mediating the Relation Between Maltreatment and Aggression." *Child Maltreatment* 12:281–298.

Leiber, Michael J. (1995). "Toward Clarification of the Concept of 'Minority' Status and Decision Making in Juvenile Court Proceedings." *Journal of Crime and Justice* 18:79–108.

Lemert, Edwin M. (1951). *Social Pathology*. New York, NY: McGraw-Hill.

Lemert, Edwin M. (1967a). *Human Deviance, Social Problems, and Social Control*. Englewood Cliffs, NJ: Prentice-Hall.

Lemert, Edwin M. (1967b). "The Juvenile Court—Quests and Realities." In: *Task Force Report: Juvenile Delinquency and Youth Crime* (pp. 91–106). Washington, DC: President's Commission on Law Enforcement and the Administration of Justice.

Lemmon, John H., Thomas L. Austin, and Alan Feldberg (2005). "Developing an Index of Child Maltreatment Severity Based on Survey Data of Child and Youth Services Professionals." Unpublished paper presented at the annual meeting of the Academy of Criminal Justice Sciences, Chicago, IL (March).

Lemmon, John H. and P.J. Verrecchia (2009). "A World of Risk: Victimized Children in the Juvenile Justice System—An Ecological Explanation, A Holistic Solution." In: Peter J. Benekos and Alida V. Merlo (Eds.), *Controversies in Juvenile Justice and Delinquency*, 2nd ed. (pp. 131–171). Cincinnati, OH: Anderson/LexisNexis.

Levick, Marsha and Neha Desai (2007). "Still Waiting: The Elusive Quest to Ensure Juveniles a Constitutional Right to Counsel at All Stages of the Juvenile Court Process." *Rutgers Law Review* 60(1):175–205.

Lewis, Terri, Rebecca Leeb, Jonathan Kotch, Jamie Smith, Richard Thompson, Maureen M. Black, Melissa Pelaez-Merrick, Ernestine Briggs, and Tamera Coyne-Beasley (2007). "Maltreatment History and Weapon Carrying Among Early Adolescents." *Child Maltreatment* 12:259–267.

Lexington Herald Leader (2003, December 9). "Governor Commutes Stanford's Sentence." *Lexington Herald Leader*, p. B3.

Liberman, Akiva, Stephen W. Raudenbush, and Robert J. Sampson (2005). "Neighborhood Context, Gang Presence, and Gang Involvement." Unpublished paper presented at the annual meeting of the Academy of Criminal Justice Sciences, Chicago, IL (March).

Lightfoot, Elizabeth and Mark Umbreit (2004). "An Analysis of State Statutory Provisions for Victim–Offender Mediation." *Criminal Justice Policy Review* 15:5–25.

Lipsky, Michael (2010). *Street-Level Bureaucracy: Dilemmas of the Individual in Public Service, 30th Anniversary Expanded Edition.* New York, NY: Russell Sage Foundation.

Listug, David (1996). "Wisconsin Sheriff's Office Saves Money and Resources." *American Jails* 10:85–86.

Livsey, Sarah (2010). *Juvenile Delinquency Probation Caseload, 2007.* Washington, DC: Office of Juvenile Justice and Delinquency Prevention.

Loeber, Rolf, David P. Farrington, and David Petechuk (2003). *Child Delinquency: Early Intervention and Prevention.* Washington, DC: Office of Juvenile Justice and Delinquency Prevention.

Lord, George F., Shanhe Jiang, and Sarah Hurley (2005). "Parental Efficacy and Delinquent Behavior: Longitudinal Analysis of At-Risk Adolescents in Treatment." Unpublished paper presented at the annual meeting of the Academy of Criminal Justice Sciences, Chicago, IL (March).

Loukas, Alexandra, Marie-Anne Suizzo, and Hazel M. Prelow (2007). "Examining Resource and Protective Factors in the Adjustment of Latino Youth in Low Income Families: What Role Does Material Acculturation Play?" *Journal of Youth and Adolescence* 36:489–501.

Lusignan, Richard and Jacques D. Marleau (2007). "Risk Assessment and Offender–Victim Relationship in Juvenile Offenders." *International Journal of Offender Therapy and Comparative Criminology* 51:433–443.

Lynch, Mary Ellen, Claire D. Coles, Tammy Corley, and Arthur Falek (2003). "Examining Delinquency in Adolescents Differentially Prenatally Exposed to Alcohol: The Role of Proximal and Distal Risk Factors." *Journal of Studies on Alcohol* 64(5):678–686.

Macallair, Daniel, Catherine McCracken, and Selena Teji (2011). *The Impact of Realignment on County Juvenile Justice Practice: Will Closing State Youth Correctional Facilities Increase Adult Criminal Court Filings?* San Francisco, CA: Center on Juvenile and Criminal Justice.

Mack, Kristin Y., Michael J. Leiber, Richard A. Featherstone, and Maria A. Monserud (2007). "Reassessing the Family-Delinquency Association: Do Family Type, Family Processes, and Economic Factors Make a Difference?" *Journal of Criminal Justice* 35:51–67.

MacKenzie, Doris Layton, James W. Shaw, and Voncile B. Gowdy (1993). *An Evaluation of Shock Incarceration in Louisiana.* Washington, DC: U.S. Department of Justice, Office of Justice Programs.

MacKenzie, Doris Layton, Angela R. Grover, Gaylene Styve Armstrong, and Ojmarrh Mitchell (2001). *A National Study Comparing the Environments of Boot Camps with Traditional Facilities for Juvenile Offenders.* Washington, DC: U.S. Department of Justice.

Majd, Katayoon and Patricia Puritz (2009). "The Cost of Justice: How Low-Income Youth Continue to Pay the Price of Failing Indigent Defense Systems." *Georgetown Journal on Poverty Law & Policy* 16:543–583.

Maloney, Dennis M., Dennis Romig, and Troy Armstrong (1988). "Juvenile Probation: The Balanced Approach." *Juvenile and Family Court Journal* 39:1–63.

Marchese, Marc C. (1992). "Clinical Versus Actuarial Prediction: A Review of the Literature." *Perceptual and Motor Skills* 75(2):583–594.

Marriott, Sinead. (2007). "Applying a Psychodynamic Treatment Model to Support an Adolescent Sentenced for Murder to Confront and Manage Feelings of Shame and Remorse." *Journal of Forensic Psychiatry and Psychology* 18:248–260.

Martin, Richard, Hal Turk, Leonardo Norman, and Ralph Ioimo (2008). "Alabama Youth Gang Survey." Unpublished paper presented at the annual meeting of the Academy of Criminal Justice Sciences, Cincinnati, OH (March).

Maruna, Shadd, Amanda Matravers, and Anna King (2004). "Disowning Our Shadow: A Psychoanalytic Approach to Understanding Punitive Public Attitudes." *Deviant Behavior* 25:277–299.

Massachusetts Statistical Analysis Center (2001). *Implementation of the Juvenile Justice Reform Act.* Boston, MA: Massachusetts Statistical Analysis Center.

Matrix Research and Consultancy (2007). *Evaluation of Drug Intervention Programs.* London: Home Office Online Report, Home Office Research and Development and Statistics Directorate.

Mattingly, Marion (2011). Word from Washington. *Juvenile Justice Update* 17(1):1, 13–15.

Matza, David (1964). *Delinquency and Drift.* New York, NY: Wiley.

Mauro, David M. (2005). "Total Gang Awareness." Unpublished paper presented at the annual training institute of the American Probation and Parole Association, New York, NY (July).

Maxson, Cheryl and Malcolm Klein (1995). "Investigating Gang Structures." *Journal of Gang Research* 3(1):33–42.

McAra, Lesley and Susan McVie (2010). "Youth Crime and Justice: Key Messages from the Edinburgh Study of Youth Transitions and Crime." *Criminology and Criminal Justice* 10(2):179–209.

McCartan, Lisa M. and Elaine Gunnison (2007). "Examining the Origins and Influence of Low Self-Control." *Journal of Crime and Justice* 30:35–62.

McCold, Paul and Benjamin Wachtel (1998). *Restorative Policing Experiment: The Bethlehem Police Family Group Conferencing Project.* Bethlehem, PA: Real Justice.

McDevitt, Jack (2005). "Evaluating Project Safe Neighborhoods in the District of Massachusetts." Unpublished paper presented at the annual meeting of the Academy of Criminal Justice Sciences, Chicago, IL (March).

McGarrell, Edmund F. (2005). "Comprehensive Examination of the Project Safe Neighborhoods Initiative." Unpublished paper presented at the annual meeting of the Academy of Criminal Justice Sciences, Chicago, IL (March).

McGarrell, Edmund F. and Natalie Kroovand-Hipple (2007). "Family Group Conferencing and Re-Offending Among First-Time Juvenile Offenders." *Justice Quarterly* 24:221–246.

McGarrell, Edmund F., Natalie Kroovand-Hipple, Nicholas Corsaro, Timothy S. Bynum, Heather Perez, Carol A. Zimmermann, and Melissa Garmo (2009). *Project Safe Neighborhoods—A National Program to Reduce Gun Crime: Final Project Report.* Washington, DC: U.S. Department of Justice, National Institute of Justice.

McGhee, Janice and Lorraine Waterhouse (2007). "Classification in Youth Justice and Child Welfare: In Search of 'The Child.'" *Youth Justice* 7:107–120.

McGuire, Joseph T. and Matthew M. Botvinick (2010). "Prefontal Cortex, Cognitive Control, and the Registration of Decision Costs." *Proceedings of the National Academy of Sciences of the United States of America* 107(17):7922–7926.

McKeesport CASASTART (2008). *The CASASTART Program.* McKeesport, PA: The CASASTART Program.

McKeiver v. Pennsylvania, 403 U.S. 528 (1971) at 551.

McLean County Court Services (2002). *Day Reporting Center for Juveniles Possessing Firearms.* McLean County, IL: McLean County Court Services.

McMorris, Barbara J., Sheryl A. Hemphill, John W. Toumbourou, Richard F. Catalano, and George C. Patton (2007). "Prevalence of Substance Use and Delinquent Behavior in Adolescents from Victoria, Australia and Washington State, United States." *Health Education and Behavior* 34:634–650.

McNamara, Robert Hartman (2008a). "The Issues Surrounding Juvenile Curfews." Unpublished paper presented at the annual meeting of the Academy of Criminal Justice Sciences, Cincinnati, OH (March).

McNamara, Robert Hartmann (2008b). *The Lost Population: Status Offenders in America.* Durham, NC: Carolina Academic Press.

McNeill, Fergus and Susan Batchelor (2004). *Persistent Offending by Young People: Developing Practice. (Issues in Community and Criminal Justice: Monograph 3.)* London: Napo.

McSherry, Joseph (2008). "Characteristics and Outcomes of Transferred Youth to Criminal Court." Unpublished paper presented at the annual meeting of the Academy of Criminal Justice Sciences, Cincinnati, OH (March).

Mears, Daniel P., Carter Hay, Marc Gertz, and Christina Mancini (2007). "Public Opinion and the Foundation of the Juvenile Court." *Criminology* 45:223–257.

Meisel, Joshua S. (2001). "Relationships and Juvenile Offenders: The Effects of Intensive Aftercare Supervision." *The Prison Journal* 81:206–245.

Mellins, Claude A., Curtis Dolezal, Elizabeth Brackis-Cott, Ouzama Nicholson, Patricia Warne, and Heino F.L. Meyer-Bahlburg (2007). "Predicting the Onset of Sexual and Drug Risk Behaviors in HIV-Negative Youths with HIV-Positive Mothers: The Role of Contextual, Self-Regulation, and Social-Intervention Factors." *Journal of Youth and Adolescence* 36:265–278.

Mendel, Richard A. (2001). *Less Cost, More Safety: Guiding Lights for Reform in Juvenile Justice.* Washington, DC: American Youth Policy Forum.

Merlo, Alida V. (2000). "Juvenile Justice at the Crossroads". *Justice Quarterly* 17(4):639–661.

Merlo, Alida V. and Peter J. Benekos (2000). *What's Wrong with the Criminal Justice System: Ideology, Politics, and the Media.* Cincinnati, OH: Anderson Publishing Company.

Merlo, Alida V. and Pete J. Benekos (2009). "Reflections on Youth and Juvenile Justice." In: Peter J. Benekos and Alida V. Merlo (Eds.), *Controversies in Juvenile Justice and Delinquency,* 2nd ed. (pp. 1–25). Cincinnati, OH: Anderson/LexisNexis.

Merlo, Alida V. and Peter J. Benekos (2010). "Is Punitive Juvenile Justice Policy Declining in the United States?: A Critique of Emergent Initiatives." *Youth Justice* 10(1):1–22.

Merlo, Alida V. and M. Alper Sozer (2009). "Police, Youth, and Crime Prevention: Examining the Best Practices." In: Sener Uludag, Cemil Dogutas, Osman Dolu, and Hasan Buker (Eds.), *Children in Conflict With the Law: Multidisciplinary Cooperation in Solving Problems and Best Practices* (pp. 139–162). Ankara, Turkey: Turkish National Police and Turkish National Police Academy.

Mersky, Joshua P. and Arthur J. Reynolds (2007). "Child Maltreatment and Violent Delinquency: Disentangling Main Effects and Subgroup Effects." *Child Maltreatment* 12:246–258.

Mertens, Jennifer (2006). "Kids with Guns: How Agencies Have Made Strides to Get Guns Out of the Hands of Juveniles." *Law Enforcement Technology* 33(10):14–20.

Merton, Robert K. (1957). *Social Theory and Social Structure.* New York, NY: Free Press.

Metts, Michelle (2005). "Involvement of Probation and Parole in Project Safe Neighborhoods." Unpublished paper presented at the annual meeting of the American Probation and Parole Association, New York, NY (July).

Michigan Judicial Institute (2010). *Juvenile Justice Benchbook: Delinquency & Criminal Proceedings, rev. ed.* Retrieved on November 16, 2001, from http://courts.michigan.gov/mji/resources/jjbook/jjbench.htm.

Miller, Joel and Jeffrey Lin (2007). "Applying a Generic Juvenile Risk Assessment Instrument to a Local Context: Some Practical and Theoretical Lessons." *Crime and Delinquency* 53:552–580.

Miller, J. Mitchell, Holly Ventura Miller, and J.C. Barnes (2007). "The Effect of Demeanor on Drug Court Admission." *Criminal Justice Policy Review* 18:246–259.

Miller, Kirk (2007). "Traversing the Spatial Divide: Gender, Place, and Delinquency." *Feminist Criminology* 2:202–222.

Miller, Walter (1958). "Lower Class Culture as a Generating Milieu of Gang Delinquency." *Journal of Social Issues* 14(3):5–19.

Minton, Todd (2010). *Jail Inmates at Midyear 2009, Statistical Tables.* Washington, DC: U.S. Department of Justice, Bureau of Justice Statistics.

Moore County Government (2002). *Moore County Day Reporting Center.* Moore County, NC: Moore County Government.

Morris, Sherill and Camille Gibson (2008). "Impact of Victimization and Trauma on Female Assaultive Behavior." Unpublished paper presented at the annual meeting of the Academy of Criminal Justice Sciences, Cincinnati, OH (March).

Moseley, Ivyann (2005). "Exposure to Violence and Its Relation to Problem-Solving Strategies." Unpublished paper presented at the annual meeting of the Academy of Criminal Justice Sciences, Chicago, IL (March).

Mueller, David and Lisa Hutchison-Wallace (2005). "Verbal Abuse, Self-Esteem, and Peer Victimization." Unpublished paper presented at the annual meeting of the Academy of Criminal Justice Sciences, Chicago, IL (March).

Mulvey, Edward P. (2011). *Highlights to Pathways to Desistance: A Longitudinal Study of Serious Adolescent Offenders.* Washington, DC: Office of Juvenile Justice and Delinquency Prevention.

Mulvey, Edward P. and Anne-Marie R. Iselin (2008). "Improving Professional Judgements of Risk and Amenability in Juvenile Justice." *The Future of Children* 18:35–51.

Murrell, Pamela R. (2005). "Advocating for Children in the Juvenile Justice System." Unpublished paper presented at the annual meeting of the Academy of Criminal Justice Sciences, Chicago, IL (March).

Musser, Denise Casamento (2001). "Public Access to Juvenile Records." *Corrections Today* 63:112–113.

Myers, Bryan (2004). "Victim Impact Statements and Mock Jury Sentencing: The Impact of Dehumanizing Language on a Death Qualified Sample." *American Journal of Forensic Psychology* 22:39–55.

Nagin, Daniel S., Alex R. Piquero, Elizabeth Scott, and Laurence Steinberg (2006). "Public Preferences for Rehabilitation Versus Incarceration of Juvenile Offenders: Evidence from a Contingent Valuation Survey." *Criminology & Public Policy* 5(4):627–652.

National Advisory Committee on Criminal Justice Standards and Goals (1976). *Juvenile Justice and Delinquency Prevention: Report of the Task Force on Juvenile Justice and Delinquency Prevention.* Washington, DC: U.S. Government Printing Office.

National Association of Youth Courts (2011). *Facts and Stats.* Retrieved on December 3, 2011, from http://www.youthcourt.net/?page_id=24.

National Center for Juvenile Justice (2010). *OJJDP Statistical Briefing Book.* Retrieved on March 9, 2011, from http://ojjdp.ncjrs.gov/ojstatbb/court/.

National Center for Juvenile Justice (n.d.) *State Juvenile Justice Profiles.* Retrieved on November 28, 2011, from http://www.ncjj.org/Research_Resources/State_Profiles.aspx.

National Center for Victims of Crime (2011). *Victim Impact Statements.* Retrieved on November 26, 2011, from http://www.ncvc.org/ncvc/main.aspx?dbName=DocumentViewer&DocumentID=32515.

National Council on Crime and Delinquency (2009). *In Search of Evidence Based Practice in Juvenile Corrections: An Evaluation of Florida's Avon Youth Park Academy and STREET Smart Program.* Washington, DC: U.S. Department of Justice.

National Council on Disability (2008). *Youth with Disabilities in the Foster Care System: Barriers to Success and Proposed Policy Solutions.* Washington, DC: National Council on Disability.

National Gang Center (2010). *Best Practices to Address Community Gang Problems: OJJDP's Comprehensive Gang Model,* 2nd ed. Washington, DC: Office of Juvenile Justice and Delinquency Prevention.

National Gang Center (n.d.). *National Youth Gang Survey Analysis.* Retrieved on November 26, 2011, from http://www.nationalgangcenter.gov/Survey-Analysis/Measuring-the-Extent-of-Gang-Problems#homicidesnumber.

National Gang Intelligence Center (2009). *National Gang Threat Assessment.* Washington, DC: U.S. Department of Justice.

New Mexico Juvenile Justice Division (2002). *Decision Tree for Juvenile Decision Making.* Santa Fe, NM: New Mexico Juvenile Justice Division.

Nieto, Marcus (2008). *County Probation Camps and Ranches for Juvenile Offenders.* Sacramento, CA: California Research Bureau.

Norris, Michael, Sarah Twill, and Chigon Kim (2008). "9/11 and Juvenile Court Net-Widening." Unpublished paper presented at the annual meeting of the Academy of Criminal Justice Sciences, Cincinnati, OH (March).

North Carolina Department of Juvenile Justice and Delinquency Prevention (2008). *Support Our Students (SOS).* Raleigh, NC: North Carolina Department of Juvenile Justice and Delinquency Prevention.

Office of Children and Family Services (2010). *Governor Paterson Announces Settlement with USDOJ to Continue Efforts to Transform the Juvenile Justice System.* Retrieved on February 28, 2011, from http://www.ocfs.state.ny.us/main/rehab/Jul%2014%202010_%20Paterson%20Press%20Release%20DOJ%20Juvenile%20Justice.asp.

Office of Juvenile Justice and Delinquency Prevention (2007). *Juvenile Offenders and Victims: National Report.* Washington, DC: Office of Juvenile Justice and Delinquency Prevention.

Office of Juvenile Justice and Delinquency Prevention (2008). *Female Delinquents: Patterns and Trends.* Washington, DC: U.S. Government Printing Office.

Office of Juvenile Justice and Delinquency Prevention (2009a). "Department of Justice Sets High Priority on Reentry Programs for Ex-Offenders". *OJJDP News at a Glance* (November/December). Retrieved on April 16, 2011, from http://www.ncjrs.gov/html/ojjdp/news_at_glance/228602/pfv.html.

Office of Juvenile Justice and Delinquency Prevention (2009b). *Disproportionate Minority Contact.* Washington, D.C.: Office of Juvenile Justice and Delinquency Prevention.

Office of Juvenile Justice and Delinquency Prevention (n.d.). *OJJDP Model Programs Guide.* Retrieved on November 26, 2011, from http://www.ojjdp.ncjrs.gov/mpg/.

Office of Juvenile Justice and Delinquency Prevention Deinstitutionalization of Status Offenders Best Practices Database (n.d.). *Status Offense Statistics.* Retrieved on November 26, 2011, from http://www2.dsgonline.com/dso2/dso_about_status_offense_statistics.aspx.

Office of the Chief Judge, Circuit Court of Cook County (1998, November 23). *Chief Judge O'Connell Brings Award Winning Evening Reporting Center for Juveniles to Englewood.* Retrieved on December 3, 2011, from http://www.cookcountycourt.org/publications/press-releases/1998/nov23a98.html.

Office of the United Nations High Commissioner for Human Rights (2005). *United Nations Standard Minimum Rules for the Administration of Juvenile Justice.* Retrieved on November 27, 2011, from http://www2.ohchr.org/english/law/beijingrules.htm.

OJJDP Statistical Briefing Book (2008). *Census of Juveniles in Residential Placement.* Retrieved on April 15, 2011, from http://ojjdp.ncjrs.gov/ojstabb/corrections/qa08203.asp?qaDate=2006.

Ousey, Graham C. and Pamela Wilcox (2007). "The Interaction of Antisocial Personality and Life-Course Predictors of Delinquent Behavior." *Criminology* 45:313–343.

Owens-Sabir, Mahasin C. (2007). *The Effects of Race and Family Attachment on Self-Esteem, Self-Control, and Delinquency.* New York, NY: LFB Scholarly Publishing.

Parent, Dale (2003). *Correctional Boot Camps: Lessons from a Decade of Research.* Washington, DC: U.S. National Institute of Justice.

Parker, Chauncey G. (2005). "Expanding the Role of Probation and Parole in Public Safety Partnerships." Unpublished paper presented at the annual training institute of the American Probation and Parole Association, New York, NY (July).

Peterson, B. Michelle, Martin D. Ruck, and Christopher J. Koegl (2001). "Youth Court Dispositions: Perceptions of Canadian Juvenile Offenders." *International Journal of Offender Therapy and Comparative Criminology* 45:593–605.

Peterson, Scott (2005). *The Growth of Teen Courts in the United States.* Washington, DC: Office of Juvenile Justice and Delinquency Prevention.

Petrosino, Anthony, Carolyn Turpin-Petrosino, and Sarah Guckenberg (2010). *Formal System Processing of Juveniles: Effects on Delinquency.* Campbell Systematic Reviews. Oslo, Norway: The Campbell Collaboration.

Pingree, David H. (1984). "Florida Youth Services." *Corrections Today* 46:60–62.

Piquero, Alex R. (2008). "Disproportionate Minority Contact" *The Future of Children* 18:59–80.

Piquero, Alex R., Francis T. Cullen, James D. Unnever, Nicole L. Piquero, and Jill A. Gordon (2010). "Never Too Late: Public Optimism About Juvenile Rehabilitation". *Punishment & Society* 12:187–207.

Pires, Paulo and Jennifer M. Jenkins (2007). "A Growth Curve of the Joint Influences of Parenting Affect, Child Characteristics and Deviant Peers on Adolescent Illicit Drug Use." *Journal of Youth and Adolescence* 36:169–183.

Platt, Anthony N. (1969). *The Child Savers: The Invention of Delinquency.* Chicago, IL: University of Chicago Press.

Pope, Carl E., Rick Lovell, and Heidi Hsia (2002). *Disproportionate Minority Confinement: A Review of the Research Literature from 1989 Through 2001.* Washington, DC: U.S. Department of Justice, Bureau of Justice Statistics.

Porterfield, Austin L. (1943). "Delinquency and Its Outcome in Court and College." *American Journal of Sociology* 49:199–208.

Preston, Frederick W. and Roger I. Roots (2004). Introduction: Law and Its Unintended Consequences. *American Behavioral Scientist* 47:1371–1375.

Proctor, Amy and Janet Mullings (2008). "Youth Maltreatment and Gang Membership Among Youth Incarcerated in Texas." Unpublished paper presented at the annual meeting of the Academy of Criminal Justice Sciences, Cincinnati, OH (March).

Project Safe Neighborhoods (2005). "Project Safe Neighborhood." Unpublished paper presented at the annual meeting of the Academy of Criminal Justice Sciences, Chicago, IL (March).

Puzzanchera, Charles M. (2009). *Juvenile Arrests 2008.* Washington, DC: U.S. Department of Justice, Office of Juvenile Justice and Delinquency Prevention.

Puzzanchera, Charles M. and Benjamin Adams (2010). *National Disproportionate Minority Contact Databook.* Developed by the National Center for Juvenile Justice for the Office of Juvenile Justice and Delinquency Prevention. Retrieved on November 26, 2011, from http://ojjdp.ncjrs.gov/ojstatbb/dmcdb/.

Puzzanchera, Charles M., Benjamin Adams, and Melissa Sickmund (2010). *Juvenile Court Statistics 2006–2007.* Pittsburgh, PA: National Center for Juvenile Justice.

Puzzanchera, Charles M., Benjamin Adams, and Melissa Sickmund (2011). *Juvenile Court Statistics 2008.* Pittsburgh, PA: National Center for Juvenile Justice.

Rasmussen, Andrew (2004). "Teen Court Referral, Sentencing, and Subsequent Recidivism: Two Proportional Hazards Models and a Little Speculation." *Crime and Delinquency* 50:615–635.

Rawhide Boys Ranch (2008). *Rawhide*. New London, WI: Rawhide Boys Ranch.

Reckless, Walter (1967). *The Crime Problem*. New York, NY: Appleton-Century-Crofts.

Reconnecting Homeless Youth Act of 2008 (2008). Public Law No. 110-378. Retrieved on October 16, 2010, from http://www.govtrack.us/congress/bill.xpd?bill=s110-2982.

Redding, Richard E. (2010). *Juvenile Transfer Laws: An Effective Deterrent to Delinquency?* Washington, DC: Office of Juvenile Justice and Delinquency Prevention.

Reddington, Frances P. (2005). "The Status of Juvenile Justice in Chicago." Unpublished paper presented at the annual meeting of the Academy of Criminal Justice Sciences, Chicago, IL (March).

Rehling, William R. (2005). "Adult Consultation for Minors in Custody During Interrogation." Unpublished paper presented at the annual meeting of the Academy of Criminal Justice Sciences, Chicago, IL (March).

Rhoades, Philip W. and Kristina M. Zambrano (2005). "Leading Practice to Theory: Data Driven Strategic Delinquency Prevention Planning Goes Regional." Unpublished paper presented at the annual meeting of the Academy of Criminal Justice Sciences, Chicago, IL (March).

Rivers, Anthony L. (2005). "Appropriateness of Juvenile Transfer to Adult Court." Unpublished paper presented at the annual meeting of the Academy of Criminal Justice Sciences, Chicago, IL (March).

Rivers, James E., Richard Dembo, and Robert S. Anwyl (1998). "The Hillsborough County, Florida Juvenile Assessment Center." *The Prison Journal* 78:439–450.

Robbins, Ira (1986). "Privatization of Corrections: Defining the Issues." *Federal Probation* 50:24–30.

Rockhill, Anna, Beth L. Green, and Carrie Furrer (2007). "Is the Adoption and Safe Families Act Influencing Child Welfare Outcomes for Families with Substance Abuse Issues?" *Child Maltreatment* 12:7–19.

Rodriguez, Nancy (2005). "Restorative Justice, Communities, and Delinquency: Whom Do We Reintegrate?" *Criminology & Public Policy* 4:103–130.

Rosky, Jeffrey W. (2008). "Examining Resiliency Within the Contexts of Self-Control Theory and Life Course Analysis." Unpublished paper presented at the annual meeting of the Academy of Criminal Justice Sciences, Cincinnati, OH (March).

Ross, Caitlin (2011). "Exploring Policy Changes for Juvenile Justice". Unpublished paper presented at the annual meeting of the Academy of Criminal Justice Sciences, Toronto, Canada (March).

Ross, James (2008). "Impact of Court Personnel Interpersonal Dynamics on Delinquency and Status Offense Petitions." Unpublished paper presented at the annual meeting of the Academy of Criminal Justice Sciences, Cincinnati, OH (March).

Roy, Sudipto (2004). "Factors Related to Success and Recidivism in a Day Reporting Center." *Criminal Justice Studies* 17:3–17.

Runaway and Homeless Youth Act (1974). Title III of the Juvenile Justice and Delinquency Prevention Act of 1974. Title 42, U.S. Code: Section 5601 note.

Rubin, H. Ted (2006). "Juvenile Justice Systems are Issuing Accountability Report Cards to their Communities." In: Carol R. Flango, Chuck Campbell, and Neal Kauder (Eds.), *Future Trends in State Courts 2006* (pp. 93–94). Williamsburg, VA: National Center for State Courts.

Sabol, William J., Todd D. Minton, and Paige M. Harrison (2007). *Prison and Jail Inmates at Midyear 2006*. Washington, DC: U.S. Department of Justice, Bureau of Justice Statistics.

Salinas, Patti Ross (2008). "Juvenile Justice Alternative Education Programs in Texas." Unpublished paper presented at the annual meeting of the Academy of Criminal Justice Sciences, Cincinnati, OH (March).

Salzinger, Suzanne, Margaret Rosario, and Richard S. Feldman (2007). "Physical Child Abuse and Adolescent Violent Delinquency: The Mediating and Moderating Roles of Personal Relationships." *Child Maltreatment* 12:208–219.

Sampson, Rana (2009). *Bullying in Schools*. Washington, DC: U.S. Department of Justice, Office of Community Oriented Policing Services.

Sanford v. Kentucky, 109 S.Ct. 2969 (1989) at 2980.

Santana, Edwin L. (2005). "Total Gang Awareness." Unpublished paper presented at the annual training institute of the American Probation and Parole Association, New York, NY (July).

Sawicki, Donna Rau, Beatrix Schaeffer, and Jeanie Thies (1999). "Predicting Successful Outcomes for Serious and Chronic Juveniles in Residential Placement." *Juvenile and Family Court Journal* 50:21–31.

Schaefer-McDaniel, Nicole (2007). "'They Be Doing Illegal Things': Early Adolescents Talk About Their Inner-City Neighborhoods." *Journal of Adolescent Research* 22:413–436.

Schaffner, Laurie (2005). "Gender Responsive Programs for Girls: Theory into Practice." Unpublished paper presented at the annual meeting of the Academy of Criminal Justice Sciences, Chicago, IL (March).

Schaffner, Laurie (2006). *Girls in Trouble with the Law.* New Brunswick, NJ: Rutgers University Press.

Schexnayder, Vena M. (2008). "Solutions to School Violence." Unpublished paper presented at the annual meeting of the Academy of Criminal Justice Sciences, Cincinnati, OH (March).

Schmidt, Annesley K. (1998). "Electronic Monitoring: What Does the Literature Tell Us?" *Federal Probation* 62:10–19.

Schneider, Jeffrey (2007). *Youth Courts: An Empirical Update and Analysis of Future Organizational Needs.* Washington, DC: Hamilton Fish Institute on School and Community Violence, The George Washington University.

Schur, Edwin (1973). *Radical Nonintervention: Rethinking the Delinquency Problem.* Englewood Cliffs, NJ: Prentice Hall.

Schwalbe, Craig S. (2008). "A Meta-Analysis of Juvenile Justice Risk Assessment Instruments: Predictive Validity by Gender." *Criminal Justice and Behavior* 35(11):1367–1381.

Schwartz, Ira M. (1989). *(In)justice for Juveniles: Rethinking the Best Interests of the Child.* Lexington, MA: D.C. Heath and Company.

Scott, Elizabeth S. and Laurence Steinberg (2008). "Adolescent Development and the Regulation of Youth Crime." *Future of Children* 18(2):15–33.

Sedlak, Andrea J., David Finkelhor, and Heather Hammer (2005). *National Estimates of Children Missing Voluntarily or for Benign Reasons.* Washington, DC: Office of Juvenile Justice and Delinquency Prevention.

Seigel, Larry J. and Brandon C. Welsh (2009). *Juvenile Delinquency: Theory, Practice, and Law,* 10th ed. Belmont, CA: Wadsworth/Cengage.

Seiter, Richard P. and Angela D. West (2003). "Supervision Styles in Probation and Parole: An Analysis of Activities." *Journal of Offender Rehabilitation* 38:57–75.

Sellin, Thorsten (1930). "The House of Correction for Boys in the Hospice of Saint Michael in Rome." *Journal of the American Institute of Criminal Law and Criminology* 20(4):533–553.

Seyko, Ronald J. (2001). "Balanced Approach and Restorative Justice Efforts in Allegheny County, Pennsylvania." *The Prison Journal* 81:187–205.

Shafer, Joseph A., David L. Carter, and Andra Katz-Bannister (2004). "Studying Traffic Stop Encounters." *Journal of Criminal Justice* 32:159–170.

Shaw, Clifford R. and Henry D. McKay (1972). *Juvenile Delinquency and Urban Areas,* rev. ed. Chicago, IL: University of Chicago Press.

Shawnee County Department of Community Corrections (2002). *Shawnee County Community Corrections.* Topeka, KS: Shawnee County Department of Community Corrections.

Shawnee County Department of Community Corrections (n.d.). *History and Purpose.* Retrieved December 3, 2011, from http://www.snco.us/ccor/default.asp#history_and_purpose.

Sheldon, William H. (1949). *The Varieties of Delinquent Youth.* New York, NY: Harper.

Shepherd, Robert E., Jr. (1999). "The Juvenile Court at 100 Years: A Look Back." *Juvenile Justice,* VI(2):13–21.

Shine, James and Dwight Price (1992). "Prosecutors and Juvenile Justice: New Roles and Perspectives." In: Ira M. Schwartz (Ed.), *Juvenile Justice and Public Policy: Toward a National Agenda* (pp. 101–133). New York, NY: Lexington Books.

Short, James F., Jr. and F. Ivan Nye (1958). "Extent of Unrecorded Juvenile Delinquency: Tentative Conclusions." *Journal of Criminal Law and Police Science* 49:296–302.

Sickmund, Melissa (2010). *Juveniles in Residential Placement, 1997–2008.* Washington, DC: Office of Juvenile Justice and Delinquency Prevention.

Sinclair, Jim (2005). "Victim's Rights and Issues: Educating Judicial and Court Personnel." Unpublished paper presented at the annual training institute of the American Probation and Parole Association, New York, NY (July).

Sisak, Michael R. and Patrick Sweet (2011, September 23). "'Boss' Conahan Sentenced to 17½ Years." *The Citizens' Voice.* Retrieved on December 3, 2011, from http://citizensvoice.com/boss-conahan-sentenced-to-17-years-1.1207996#axzz1bXtwmYIs.

Slater, Dashka (2004). "Killing Their Young." *Legal Affairs.* Retrieved on November 26, 2011, from http://www.legalaffairs.org/issues/September-October-2004/story_slater_sepoct04.msp.

Slater, Michael D., Andrew F. Hayes, and Vallerie L. Ford (2007). "Examining the Moderating and Mediating Roles of News

Exposure and Attention on Adolescent Judgments of Alcohol-Related Risks." *Communication Research* 34:355–381.

Slesnick, Natasha, Jillian L. Prestopnik, Robert J. Meyers, and Michael Glassman (2007). "Treatment Outcome for Street-Living, Homeless Youth." *Addictive Behaviors* 32:1237–1251.

Snyder, Howard N. (2001). "Epidemiology of Official Offending." In: Rolf Loeber and David P. Farrington (Eds.), *Child Delinquents: Development, Intervention, and Service Needs* (pp. 25–46). Thousand Oaks, CA: Sage Publications.

Snyder, Howard N. and Melissa Sickmund (1999). *Juvenile Offenders and Victims: 1999 National Report.* Pittsburgh, PA: National Center for Juvenile Justice.

Snyder, Howard N. and Melissa Sickmund (2006). *Juvenile Offenders and Victims: 2006 National Report.* Pittsburgh, PA: National Center for Juvenile Justice.

Snyder, Howard N., Melissa Sickmund, and Eileen Poe-Yamagata (2000). *Juvenile Transfers to Criminal Court in the 1990's: Lessons Learned from Four Studies.* Washington, DC: Office of Juvenile Justice and Delinquency Prevention.

Soler, Mark and Lisa M. Garry (2009). *Reducing Disproportionate Minority Contact: Preparation at the Local Level.* Washington, DC: Office of Juvenile Justice and Delinquency Prevention.

Song, Juyoung and Sheila Royo (2008). "An Empirical Test of General Strain Theory: Explaining Delinquency Among Korean Youth." Unpublished paper presented at the annual meeting of the Academy of Criminal Justice Sciences, Cincinnati, OH (March).

Souhami, Anna (2007). *Transforming Youth Justice: Occupational Identity and Cultural Change.* Cullompton, UK: Willan.

Spano, Richard, Craig Rivera, and John Bolland (2006). "The Impact of Timing of Exposure to Violence on Violent Behavior in a High Poverty Sample of Inner City African American Youth." *Journal of Youth and Adolescence* 35:681–692.

Spencer, Renée (2007). "'It's Not What I Expected': A Qualitative Study of Youth Mentoring Relationship Failures." *Journal of Adolescent Research* 22:331–354.

Spigel, Saul (2008). *Group Home Notice Requirements.* Hartford, CT: Department of Children and Families.

Springer, Nicollette and Autumn M. Frei (2008). "Propositional Integration of Anomie and Conflict Theories: A Multilevel Examination of School Delinquency." Unpublished paper presented at the annual meeting of the Academy of Criminal Justice Sciences, Cincinnati, OH (March).

Stahlkopf, Christina, Mike Males, and Daniel Macallair (2010). "Testing Incapacitation Theory: Youth Crime and Incarceration in California." *Crime and Delinquency* 56(2): 253–268.

Steinberg, Laurence (2009). "Should the Science of Adolescent Brain Development Inform Public Policy?" *American Psychologist* 64(8):739–750.

Steiner, Benjamin and Andrew L. Giacomazzi (2007). "Juvenile Waiver, Boot Camp, and Recidivism in a Northwestern State." *The Prison Journal* 87:227–240.

Stewart, Eric A. and Ronald L. Simons (2009). *The Code of the Street and African-American Adolescent Violence.* Washington, DC: National Institute of Justice.

Stinchcomb, Jeanne B., Gordon Bazemore, and Nancy Riestenberg (2006). "Beyond Zero Tolerance: Restoring Justice in Secondary Schools." *Youth Violence and Juvenile Justice* 4(2):123–147.

Streib, Victor L. (1987). *The Death Penalty for Juveniles.* Bloomington, IN: Indiana University Press.

Streib, Victor L. (2003). "Standing Between the Child and the Executioner: The Special Role of Defense Counsel in Juvenile Death Penalty Cases." *American Journal of Criminal Law* 31(1):67–115.

Sturgeon, Bill (2005). "Case Management of Youthful Offenders in the Community." Unpublished paper presented at the annual training institute of the American Probation and Parole Association, New York, NY (July).

Styve, Gaylene J., Doris Layton MacKenzie, Angela R. Grover, and Ojmarrh Mitchell (2000). "Perceived Conditions of Confinement: A National Evaluation of Juvenile Boot Camps and Traditional Facilities." *Law and Human Behavior* 24:297–308.

Sullivan, Christopher J., Bonita M. Veysey, Zachary K. Hamilton, and Michele Grillo (2007). "Reducing Out-of-Community Placement and Recidivism: Diversion of Delinquent Youth with Mental Health and Substance Use Problems from the Justice System." *International Journal of Offender Therapy and Comparative Criminology* 51:555–577.

Sullivan, Christopher J., Norin Dollard, Brian Sellers, and John Mayo (2010). "Rebalancing Response to School-Based Offenses: A Civil Citation Program." *Youth Violence and Juvenile Justice* 8(4):279–294.

Sullivan, Terri N., Albert D. Farrell, Wendy Kliewer, Monique Vulin-Reynolds, and Robert F. Valois (2007). "Exposure to Violence in Early Adolescence: The Impact of Self-Restraint, Witnessing Violence, and Victimization on

Aggression and Drug Use." *The Journal of Early Adolescence* 27:296–323.

Sungi, Simeon P. (2008). "Preventing Juvenile Delinquency: A Fundamental Human Rights Perspective." Unpublished paper presented at the annual meeting of the Academy of Criminal Justice Sciences, Cincinnati, OH (March).

Sutherland, Edwin H. (1939). *Principles of Criminology*. Philadelphia, PA: Lippincott.

Sutherland, Edwin H. (1951). "Critique of Sheldon's Varieties of Delinquent Youth." *American Sociological Review* 16:10–13.

Swain, Randall C., Kimberly L. Henry, and Nicholas E. Baez (2004). "Risk-Taking, Attitudes Toward Aggression, and Aggressive Behavior Among Rural Middle School Youth." *Violence and Victims* 19:157–170.

Swanson, Cheryl G. (2005). "Incorporating Restorative Justice into the School Resource Officer Model." Unpublished paper presented at the annual meeting of the Academy of Criminal Justice Sciences, Chicago, IL (March).

Sweet, Joseph (1985). "Probation as Therapy." *Corrections Today* 47:89–90.

Sykes, Gresham M. and David Matza (1957). "Techniques of Neutralization: A Theory of Delinquency." *American Sociological Review* 22(6):664–670.

Szymanski, Linda A. (2002). *Juvenile Delinquents' Right to a Jury Trial. NCJJ Snapshot* 7(9). Pittsburgh, PA: National Center for Juvenile Justice.

Szymanski, Linda A. (2007). *Upper and Lower Age of Delinquency Jurisdiction (2007 Update). NCJJ Snapshot 12(10)*, Pittsburgh, PA: National Center for Juvenile Justice.

Szymanski, Linda A. (2008a). *Confidentiality of Juvenile Delinquency Hearings (2008 Update). NCJJ Snapshot* 13(5). Pittsburgh, PA: National Center for Juvenile Justice.

Szymanski, Linda A. (2008b). *Juvenile Delinquent's Right to Counsel and Waiver of That Right (2008 Update). NCJJ Snapshot* 13(8). Pittsburgh, PA: National Center for Juvenile Justice.

Szymanski, Linda A. (2008c). *Juvenile Delinquents' Right to a Jury Trial (2007 Update). NCJJ Snapshot,* 13(2). Pittsburgh, PA: National Center for Juvenile Justice.

Szymanski, Linda A. (2010a). *Can Juvenile Delinquents be Fingerprinted? NCJJ Snapshot* 15(3). Pittsburgh, PA: National Center for Juvenile Justice.

Szymanski, Linda A. (2010b). *Are There Some Juvenile Court Records That Cannot Be Sealed? NCJJ Snapshot* 15(4). Pittsburgh, PA: National Center for Juvenile Justice.

Szymanski, Linda A. (2010c). *Can Sealed Juvenile Court Records Ever Be Unsealed or Inspected? NCJJ Snapshot* 15(5). Pittsburgh, PA: National Center for Juvenile Justice.

Task Force on Transforming Juvenile Justice (2009). *Charting a New Course: A Blueprint for Transforming Juvenile Justice in New York State*. New York, NY: Vera Institute of Justice.

Taxman, Faye (2005). "Tools of the Trade: Incorporating Science into Practice." Unpublished paper presented at the annual meeting of the American Probation and Parole Association, New York, NY (July).

Taylor, Terrance J., Adrienne Freng, Finn-Aage Esbensen, and Dana Peterson (2008). "Youth Gang Membership and Serious Violent Victimization: The Importance of Lifestyles/ Routine Activities." Unpublished paper presented at the annual meeting of the Academy of Criminal Justice Sciences, Cincinnati, OH (March).

Texas Youth Commission (2005). *Certification Rates in Texas, 1990–1999*. Austin, TX: Texas Youth Commission Department of Research and Planning.

The Disaster Center (2011). *United States Crime Rates 1960– 2010*. Retrieved on October 20, 2011, from http://www. disastercenter.com/crime/uscrime.htm.

The Mandates of the Juvenile Justice and Delinquency Prevention Act (1994). Washington, DC: Office of Juvenile Justice and Delinquency Prevention.

The Pew Charitable Trusts (2009). *Progress on Court Reforms: Implementation of Recommendations from the Pew Commission on Children in Foster Care*. Retrieved on April 9, 2011, from http://www.pewtrustsorg/Reports/Foster_care_ reform/KAW-Courts-Assessment-October2009. pdf?n=5828.

Thompson v. Oklahoma, 108 S.Ct. 2687 (1988) at 2700.

Thurman, Quint C. and Jihong Zhao (2004). *Contemporary Policing: Controversies, Challenges, and Solutions*. Los Angeles, CA: Roxbury.

Title 18, U.S. Code: Section 5031, 2009.

Titterington, Victoria B. and Volker Grundies (2007). "An Exploratory Analysis of German and U.S. Youthful Homicide Offending." *Homicide Studies* 11:189–212.

Tonry, Michael (1997). *Intermediate Sanctions in Sentencing Guidelines*. Washington, DC: U.S. National Institute of Justice.

Tontodonato, Pamela and Frank E. Hagan (2009). "What Causes Delinquency? Classical and Sociological Theories of Crime." In: Peter J. Benekos and Alida V. Merlo (Eds.), *Controversies in Juvenile Justice and Delinquency,* 2nd ed. (pp. 27–51). Cincinnati, OH: Anderson/LexisNexis.

Torbet, Patricia and Linda Szymanski (1998). *State Legislative Responses to Violent Juvenile Crime: 1996–1997 Update*. Washington, DC: U.S. Department of Justice, Office of Juvenile Justice Delinquency Prevention.

Torbet, Patricia and Douglas Thomas (2005). *Advancing Competency Development: A White Paper for Pennsylvania*. Pittsburgh, PA: National Center for Juvenile Justice.

Torbet, Patricia, Richard Gable, Hunter Hurst, and Imogene Montgomery (1996). *State Responses to Serious and Violent Juvenile Crime*. Washington, DC: Office of Juvenile Justice and Delinquency Prevention.

Toth, Reid C. (2005). "Limiting Discretion at Intake: An Analysis of Intake Data from North Carolina Juvenile Courts." Unpublished paper presented at the annual meeting of the Academy of Criminal Justice Sciences, Chicago, IL (March).

Trester, Harold B. (1981). *Supervision of the Offender*. Englewood Cliffs, NJ: Prentice Hall.

Trojanowicz, Robert and Bonnie Bucqueroux (1990). *Community Policing: A Contemporary Perspective*. Cincinnati, OH: Anderson.

Trulson, Chad R. and Darin Haerle (2008). "The Final Chance for Change: Recidivism Among a Cohort of the Most Serious State Delinquents." Unpublished paper presented at the annual meeting of the Academy of Criminal Justice Sciences, Cincinnati, OH (March).

Trulson, Chad R., James W. Marquart, and Janet Mullings (2005). "Towards an Understanding of Juvenile Persistence in the Transition to Young Adulthood." Unpublished paper presented at the annual meeting of the Academy of Criminal Justice Sciences, Chicago, IL (March).

Tubman, Jonatha G., Andres G. Gil, and Eric F. Wagner (2004). "Co-Occurring Substance Abuse and Delinquent Behavior During Early Adolescence: Emerging Relations and Implications for Intervention Strategies." *Criminal Justice and Behavior* 3:463–488.

Turley, Jonathan (2011, November 11). "Supreme Court's GPS Case Asks: How Much Privacy Do We Expect?" *The Washington Post*. Retrieved on November 27, 2011, from http://www.washingtonpost.com/opinions/supreme-courts-gps-case-asks-how-much-privacy-do-we-expect/2011/11/10/gIQAN0RzCN_story.html.

Turner, Michael G., Jennifer L. Hartman, and Donna M. Bishop (2007). "The Effects of Prenatal Problems, Family Functioning, and Neighborhood Disadvantage in Predicting Life-Course-Persistent Offending." *Criminal Justice and Behavior* 34:1241–1261.

Uchida, Craig D., Shellie Solomon, Charles M. Katz, and Cynthia E. Pappas (2006). *School-Based Partnerships: A Problem-Solving Strategy*. Washington, DC: U.S. Department of Justice, Office of Community Oriented Policing Services.

Urban, Lynn S. (2005). "The Effect of a Curfew Check Program on Juvenile Opportunities for Delinquent Activity." Unpublished paper presented at the annual meeting of the Academy of Criminal Justice Sciences, Chicago, IL (March).

U.S. Department of Justice, Federal Bureau of Investigation (2009). *Uniform Crime Report, 2008*. Washington, DC: Government Printing Office.

U.S. Department of Justice, Federal Bureau of Investigation (2010). *Uniform Crime Report, 2009*. Washington, DC: Government Printing Office.

U.S. Department of Justice, Federal Bureau of Investigation (2011). *Uniform Crime Report, 2010*. Washington, DC: Government Printing Office.

U.S. District Court, Pretrial Services Agency (2011). *Diversion Programs*. Retrieved on November 27, 2011, from http://www.miept.uscourts.gov/pages/diversion_program.cfm.

U.S. General Accounting Office (1995a). *Juvenile Justice: Minimal Gender Bias Occurred in Processing Noncriminal Juveniles*. Washington, DC: U.S. General Accounting Office.

U.S. General Accounting Office (1995b). *Juvenile Justice: Representation Rates Varied as Did Counsel's Impact on Court Outcomes*. Washington, DC: U.S. General Accounting Office.

Valdez, Avelardo (2007). *Mexican American Girls and Gang Violence: Beyond Risk*. New York, NY: Palgrave Macmillan.

van Wijk, Anton Ph., Bas R.F. Mali, Ruud A.R. Bullens, and Robert R. Vermeiren (2007). "Criminal Profiles of Violent Juvenile Sex and Violent Juvenile Non-Sex Offenders: An Explorative Longitudinal Study." *Journal of Interpersonal Violence* 22:1340–1355.

Virginia Department of Juvenile Justice (2008). *Halfway Houses*. Richmond, VA: Department of Juvenile Justice.

Vivian, John P., Jennifer N. Grimes, and Stella Vasquez (2007). "Assaults in Juvenile Correctional Facilities: An Exploratory Study." *Journal of Crime and Justice* 30:17–34.

Walker, Heather (2011, October 21). "GPS Tracking Yakima's Youngest Criminals." *KIMATV.com*. Retrieved on November 27, 2011, from http://www.kimatv.com/news/local/132360343.html.

Wallace, Scyatta A. and Cynthia B. Fisher (2007). "Substance Use Attitudes Among Black Adolescents: The Role of Parent, Peer, and Cultural Factors." *Journal of Youth and Adolescence* 36:441–451.

Wallace, Lisa, Kevin Minor, and James Wells (2005). "Defining the Differential in Differential Oppression Theory: Exploring the Role of Social Learning." Unpublished paper presented at the annual meeting of the Academy of Criminal Justice Sciences, Chicago, IL (March).

Wallenius, Marjut, Raija-Leena Punamaki, and Arja Rimpela (2007). "Digital Game Playing and Direct and Indirect Aggression in Early Adolescence." *Journal of Youth and Adolescence* 36:325–336.

Walls, Melissa L., Constance L. Chapple, and Kurt D. Johnson (2007). "Strain, Emotion, and Suicide Among American Indian Youth." *Deviant Behavior* 28:219–246.

Washington Coalition for the Just Treatment of Youth (2009). *A Reexamination of Youth Involvement in the Adult Criminal Justice System in Washington: Implications of New Findings about Juvenile Recidivism and Adolescent Brain Development.* Retrieved on February 20, 2011, from http://www.columbialegal.org/files/JLWOP_cls.pdf.

Watson, Donnie W., Lorrie Bisesi, Susie Tanamly, and Noemi Mai (2003). "Comprehensive Residential Education, Arts, and Substance Abuse Treatment." *Youth Violence and Juvenile Justice* 1:388–401.

Watts-Farmer, Kalori Niesha (2008). "What Is the Effect of the Juvenile Waiver on the Juvenile Justice System?" Unpublished paper presented at the annual meeting of the Academy of Criminal Justice Sciences, Cincinnati, OH (March).

Weisel, Deborah Lamm (2004, Updated 2009). *Graffiti.* Washington, DC: U.S. Department of Justice, Office of Community-Oriented Policing Services.

West, Angela D. (2005). "Smoke and Mirrors: Measuring Gang Activity with School and Police Data." Unpublished paper presented at the annual meeting of the Academy of Criminal Justice Sciences, Chicago, IL (March).

West, Heather C. and William J. Sabol (2009). *Prison Inmates at Midyear 2008—Statistical Tables.* Washington, DC: U.S. Department of Justice, Bureau of Justice Statistics.

White, Elvira M. (2008). "The Ethical and Theoretical Orientation of a State Sentencing Commission When Drafting Juvenile Law Recommendations." Unpublished paper presented at the annual meeting of the Academy of Criminal Justice Sciences, Cincinnati, OH (March).

White, Michael D., James J. Fyfe, Suzanne P. Campbell, and John S. Goldkamp (2001). "The School-Police Partnership: Identifying At-Risk Youth Through a Truant Recovery Program." *Evaluation Review* 25(5):507–532.

Whiteacre, Kevin W. (2007). "Strange Bedfellows: The Tensions of Coerced Treatment." *Criminal Justice Policy Review* 18:260–273.

Whitehead, Michele (2008). "Juvenile Justice: Delinquency and the Formation of Public Policy." Unpublished paper presented at the annual meeting of the Academy of Criminal Justice Sciences, Cincinnati, OH (March).

Wicks-Nelson, Rita and Allen C. Israel (2005). *Behavior Disorders of Childhood,* 6th ed. Upper Saddle River, NJ: Prentice Hall.

Wilkerson, Dawn (2005). "Organizational Structuring within Juvenile Justice: Why Reform Is Needed." Unpublished paper presented at the annual meeting of the Academy of Criminal Justice Sciences, Chicago, IL (March).

Williams, Frank P. and Marilyn McShane (2009). "Youth, Drugs, and Delinquency". In: Peter J. Benekos and Alida V. Merlo (Eds.), *Controversies in Juvenile Justice and Delinquency,* 2nd ed. (pp. 85–106). Cincinnati, OH: Anderson/LexisNexis.

Wilson, E.O. (1975). *Sociobiology: The New Synthesis.* Cambridge, MA: Harvard University Press.

Wilson, James Q. and Richard J. Herrnstein (1985). *Crime and Human Nature.* New York, NY: Simon and Schuster.

Wilson, James Q. and Joan Petersilia (2002). *Crime: Public Policies for Crime Control.* Oakland, CA: Institute for Contemporary Studies Press.

Wilson, John J. (2001). *1998 National Youth Gang Survey.* Washington, DC: Office of Juvenile Justice and Delinquency Prevention.

Wolf, Robert V. (2010). *Community Prosecution and Serious Crime: A Guide for Prosecutors.* Washington, DC: Bureau of Justice Assistance.

Wolfgang, Marvin and Franco Ferracuti (1967). *The Subculture of Violence.* London: Tavistock.

Wolfgang, Marvin, Robert M. Figlio, and Thorsten Sellin (1972). *Delinquency in a Birth Cohort.* Chicago, IL: University of Chicago Press.

Worling, James R. (1995). "Adolescent Sex Offenders Against Females: Differences Based on the Age of Their Victims." *International Journal of Offender Therapy and Comparative Criminology* 39:276–293.

Worrall, John L. and Larry K. Gaines (2006). "Effect of Police–Probation Partnerships on Juvenile Arrests." *Journal of Criminal Justice* 34(6):579–589.

Wyrick, Phelan A. (2000). *Law Enforcement Referral of At-Risk Youth: The SHIELD Program.* Washington, DC: Office of Juvenile Justice and Delinquency Prevention.

Xiaoying, Dong (2005). "A Study of Young Offenders Who Desist from Re-Offending." Unpublished paper presented at the annual meeting of the Academy of Criminal Justice Sciences, Chicago, IL (March).

Yeager, Clay R., John A. Herb, and John H. Lemmon (1989). *The Impact of Court Unification on Juvenile Probation Systems in Pennsylvania.* Shippensburg, PA: Center for Juvenile Justice Training and Research, Shippensburg University.

Young, Malcolm C. and Jenni Gainsborough (2000). *Prosecuting Juveniles in Adult Court: An Assessment of Trends and Consequences.* Washington, DC: The Sentencing Project.

Zachariah, John K. (2002). *An Overview of Boot Camp Goals, Components, and Results.* Washington, DC: Koch Crime Institute.

Zahn, Margaret A., Susan Brumbaugh, Darrell Steffensmeier, Barry C. Feld, Merry Morash, Meda Chesney-Lind, Jody Miller, Allison Ann Payne, Denise C. Gottfredson, and Candace Kruttschnitt (2008). *Violence by Teenage Girls: Trends and Context.* Washington, DC: Office of Juvenile Justice and Delinquency Prevention.

Zhang, Yu (2008). "The Effect of Race, Gender, and Family Background on Juvenile Transfer Decisions." Unpublished paper presented at the annual meeting of the Academy of Criminal Justice Sciences, Cincinnati, OH (March).

Zimmermann, Carol A. and Edmund F. McGarrell (2005). "The Effects of Family Group Conferencing and Family Bonding on Delinquency Desistance." Unpublished paper presented at the annual meeting of the Academy of Criminal Justice Sciences, Chicago, IL (March).

Case Index

Name Index

A

Abatiello, Jennifer D., 31, 114, 411
Abbott-Chapman, J., 30, 67
Abrams, Laura S., 403, 437
Adams, Benjamin, 24–25, 31–32, 177, 213–214, 218, 220, 227, 231–233, 249, 258–259, 273–275, 279, 282, 319, 391, 399, 410, 451
Adams, Kenneth, 14
Addams, Jane, 48
Addie, Sean, 279, 282
Administrative Office of Pennsylvania Courts, 152
Administrative Office of the Courts, 216
Adoption and Foster Care Analysis and Reporting System, 435–436
Agnew, Robert, 94, 101–102
Aisenberg, Eugene, 249
Akers, Ronald, 106
Alford, Susan, 384
Altschuler, David M., 396
American Bar Association, 415
American Correctional Association, 416, 435, 455, 461
Anchorage Youth Court (AYC), 373
Anderson, Carolyn M., 453
Anderson, Elijah, 97
Anleu, Sharyn L. Roach, 304
Ann, Myra, 397
Anwyl, Robert S., 472
Apel, Robert J., 88, 90, 94
APPA Perspectives, 368
Applegate, Brandon K., 7
Arcene, James, 155
Archwamety, Teara, 461
Armour, Stacy, 11, 20
Armstrong, Edward G., 189
Armstrong, Gaylene, 471
Armstrong, Troy L., 297, 396, 405
Arya, Neelum, 21
Ashford, Jose B., 460
Austin, Andrew, 198
Austin, James, 442, 477
Ayers-Schlosser, Lee, 411–412

B

Backstrom, James G., 28
Baez, Nicholas E., 92
Baldwin, Roger N., 398–399
Baltimore County, Maryland, 203
Bannan, Rosemary, 366, 384–385

Barfeind, James, 353
Barnes, Allan R., 68
Barnes, J.C., 189
Barnum, Richard, 216
Baron, Stephen W., 101, 222
Bartusch, Dawn Jeglum, 190
Batchelor, Susan, 283
Bates, Ronald, 192
Baum, Katrina, 65
Bayley, David H., 177
Bazemore, Gordon, 120, 203, 365
Beaver, Kevin M., 82, 101, 231
Beccaria, Cesare, 83–84
Beck, Allen J., 470
Becker, Howard S., 99
Bell, Kerryn E., 69
Belshaw, Scott H., 69
Belsky, Lisa, 177
Bender, Valerie, 118
Benekos, Peter J., 6, 8, 64, 120, 143, 148, 167, 202, 206, 230, 252, 365, 391, 444, 455
Bentham, Jeremy, 84–85
Bernat, Frances P., 363
Bernberg, Jong G., 403
Biederman, Jennifer, 300
Bilchik, Shay, 234, 307
Billings, F. James, 132
Bishop, Donna M., 29, 87, 232–234, 261, 284
Bjerk, David, 14
Black, Maureen M., 380
Blackmore, Rebecca, 232
Blackshere, Justice, 138
Blevins, Kristie R., 45, 53
Bolland, John, 272
Bolyard, Melissa, 442
Boone, Harry N., Jr., 422
Botvinick, Matthew M., 167
Bouhours, Brigitte, 111, 120, 321, 366
Bowman, Cathy, 70
Bowman, Marvella A., 67, 90, 103, 108, 316
Boyd, Rebecca J., 111–112
Bradley, Tracey, 320
Bradsher, Keith, 305
Brandau, Timothy J., 236, 361
Bratina, Michele P., 65
Brewer, Steven L., 66
Brighton, Jacob, 138
Brookbanks, Warren, 21

Subject Index